MASTER OF THE RING

The Extraordinary Life of Jem Mace Father of Boxing and the First Worldwide Sports Star

Graham Gordon

Published by Milo Books in 2007

ISBN 978 1 903854 69 3

Typeset in Bembo by Avon DataSet Ltd,
Bidford on Avon, Warwickshire

Printed and bound in Great Britain by
Cox and Wyman, Reading

MILO BOOKS
The Old Weighbridge
Station Road
Wrea Green
Lancs
PR4 2PH

FOR MY FATHER

CONTENTS

Prologue   vii

PART 1: THE INNOVATOR (1831–1861)

1.   A Broken Violin   3
2.   Black Jack Davey and the Schoolmaster's Daughter   14
3.   Vitriol and Gunpowder   27
4.   Last Request of a Noble Lord   37
5.   Selina   44
6.   The Ringmaster   59

PART 2: CHAMPION OF ENGLAND (1861–9)

7.   The Fighting Stevedore   77
8.   Sawdust, Tinsel and Riot   95
9.   The Girl from the Riding School   111
10.   The 'Cowardly Englishman' and the Knockout Tour   128
11.   The Liverpool Olympics   140
12.   Self-Made Toff and Working-Class Hero   148
13.   Arrested in a Bedroom   164
14.   A Naked Lady from New Orleans   179
15.   The Myth of the Queensberry Rules   188

PART 3: CHAMPION OF AMERICA (1870–7)

16.   From Broadway to Bourbon Street   203
17.   Assassins of the Lower East Side   223
18.   Coast to Coast   241
19.   The Music Professor's Wife   257
20.   The Bonanza King   269

PART 4: THE GLOBETROTTER (1877–83)

21.   The Master of Science   283
22.   A Belt of Virgin Gold   299
23.   The Terror and the Strong Boy   309
24.   Trans-American Tabloid   323
25.   Fiasco at Madison Square Garden   333

PART 5: THE BOXING REVOLUTIONARY (1884–92)

26.   Thwarted Divorce   351
27.   The Boxing Revolution Begins   379
28.   Young Enough to be His Granddaughter   397
29.   The End of a Revolution   402

PART 6: THE LEGACY (1892–1910)

30.   Sons of Jem   417
31.   The Acclamation of an American Legend   428
32.   The Coronation Tournament   435
33.   Not a Penny to his Name   448
34.   Mace and Race   459
35.   Old Man from Fun City   474

      Epilogue   485
      Acknowledgments   490
      Appendix   491
      Sources   498
      Index   502

Prologue

IN THE SUMMER of 2004, the Olympic Stadium in Athens played host to perhaps the most spectacular opening ceremony ever seen at a Games. To the booming countdown of an amplified heartbeat, fireworks lit the evening sky. The culmination was a single flaming arrow – the symbolic Olympic flame – 'launched' from a giant video screen into a reflecting pool. Fire erupted in the middle of the stadium, creating a burning image of the rising Olympic rings, representing the five continents of the world. Over the following fortnight, nearly four billion people would watch on television as over 10,500 athletes from 201 countries competed for medals in twenty-eight different sports.

One hundred and forty nine years earlier, at a remote and secret location in rural Suffolk, England, only a few score men watched furtively – scouting for the disruptive appearance of the police – as a twenty-four-year-old itinerant fiddler made his effective debut as a full-time bareknuckle fighter. His name was Jem Mace.

The connection between these two events, separated by a century and a half, is this. When Mace first appeared, organised sport comprised essentially only prizefighting – which was illegal – the corrupt world of professional running and 'the sport of kings', horseracing. And it centred on only two countries, Britain and the USA. By the time of Mace's death in 1910, and thanks to him above anyone else, sport had become, throughout the English-speaking world, not only a lawful pastime but a spectacle and an act of theatre, something which could be watched, seated in comfort, by both men and women in electrically lit arenas. The Olympic Games, which were revived in Britain in the city of Liverpool in 1863, had been organised by others, but Mace, Champion of England at the time, had given them his enthusiastic support. The Games later resumed as an international event at Athens in 1896 – and the rest is history.

Mace was, in his heyday, the most famous sportsman in the world. Yet in an era when the epitome of Englishness was held to be C.B. Fry, the public school and Oxford-educated team games captain, Mace, who was born in a smithy, never went to school and was believed to be a Romany, was looked down on as having what is commonly called 'a streak' in him. His personal life was, in the Victorian and Edwardian eras, scandalous. He married three times (twice bigamously), took two mistresses, both of whom were in their late teens at the time, seduced the most famous actress of the day, fathered fourteen children by five different women and had numerous amorous encounters with barmaids and showgirls in London, New York, New Orleans, San Francisco and Paris.

Given both his celebrity and his notoriety, why did his name, one very familiar to the readers of the British, American and Australian newspapers of his day, drop out of recognition for so long? Only in 2002 was a proper memorial erected over what had been his unmarked grave. Why is he not hailed as a hero of English sport and a pioneer of sport the world over? Why was he rightly named the Father of Boxing only to be footnoted in history books? Certainly by the 1960s, Mace's status as the Father of Boxing had been airbrushed out by Hollywood. As an Englishman, he did not fit the need for an all-American father for the ultimate American sport, boxing. Biopics such as *The Great John L.* and *Gentleman Jim* had long since installed Irish-Americans John L. Sullivan and Jim Corbett in the fistic pantheon.

But it was not Sullivan who transformed the outlawed sport of prizefighting. Sullivan proclaimed his allegiance to the Queensberry Rules but proceeded to flout them at every turn to suit his own purposes. Nor was it Corbett who, although a scientific boxer of the highest class, freely admitted that the changes which had elevated the sport were due to Mace. As for the Marquess of Queensberry himself, the ignoble lord was a bloodthirsty adherent of the unreformed prize ring who merely lent his name to a set of rules drawn up for amateur boxing. These rules were completely inadequate for professional boxing, a fact pointed out consistently by Mace throughout the long series of exhibitions which he gave, above all in Australia. Eventually, Mace's partnership with the renegade aristocrat the Earl of Lonsdale saw the Queensberry Rules revised, with specific numbers of rounds stipulated and with a clear points system (itself derived from Mace's personal boxing style) established.

Mace was in fact the first World Champion and, as such, he stands at the head of a lineage which would later include greats like Jack Dempsey, Joe Louis, Muhammad Ali and Mike Tyson. A brilliant stylist and master of feinting and footwork, he heralded the classic boxers of the 20th century, men such as Billy Conn, Archie Moore and Willie Pep. Echoes of his style persist into the 21st century in many leading boxers. Mace was not only an elegant boxer, however, but also an ultra-powerful puncher. The first man to target the junction of upper and lower jaw and to find that target with shots of immense force, his barefisted despatch of Bob Brettle and Joe Goss, both of whom he left insensible for several minutes, were the effective template for the epic knockouts of the 20th century – delivered by much heavier men aided by padded gloves – Rocky Marciano's volcanic *volte face* against Jersey Joe Walcott, Ray Robinson's obliteration of Gene Fullmer and Muhammad Ali's uncoiled-spring despatch of George Foreman.

Jem Mace brought to fruition a golden generation of Australian boxing which, in the persons of Peter Jackson, Bob Fitzsimmons, Jim Hall, Young Griffo, Billy Murphy and others, took the world by storm in the last decade of the 19th century. Soon America's cleverest young boxers, future champions such as Kid McCoy and Philadelphia Jack O'Brien, began to base their style on his. As a trainer, Mace's star pupil was Larry Foley, whose gym in Sydney was the effective forerunner of the great American gyms of Stillman's and the Kronk, just as Foley himself was the first of the master trainers, a line extending through Charlie Goldman to Eddie Futch and Emanuel Steward. In a sport notorious for the racism of Sullivan and Corbett, Mace also championed and befriended great black boxers such as Peter Jackson and Sam Langford.

But Mace's influence went beyond boxing. He was a superb all-round athlete. Competing in the London Prize Ring, he needed to be an excellent wrestler whose sleight of hand and foot could overthrow much taller and heavier men. A splendid runner, he competed as a pedestrian and could run half a mile in barely over two minutes. He was a skilled fencer, who saw a clear parallel between the left jab and the thrusting movements of foil and epee and between left and right hooks and the roundhouse hits delivered with a sabre. And it was through him that fencing's points system paved the way for a similar scoring system in boxing. Mace's love of all individual sports led to him putting on shows containing boxing, wrestling, running, cycling and gymnastics, in both Britain and the USA, thus boosting the other sports by their being presented together with what was then the major sport of boxing.

But Mace was more than a boxer and an athlete. A gifted violinist who once aspired to a career in music, he was attracted to the world of the circus from an early age. He made himself into a performance artist who could spar with boxing gloves, play fiddle or give demonstrations of 'Greco-Roman statues', displaying his muscular physique for feminine admirers. Mace not only was the proprietor of his own circus but also worked for several of the leading companies of the day. His main business manager was England's leading equestrian director, a man who worked with all the major circuses. And it was the marriage of the seemingly incompatible worlds of prizefighting and show business which gave birth to gloved boxing as the first modern spectator sport. Characteristically, Mace's shows included instrumental music, brass bands, singing, Highland dancers, and comedians.

In an age when few people ventured beyond their own village or town, Mace travelled the world. Taking advantage of the railway boom and the advent of the steamship, he journeyed the length and breadth of the British Isles, crisscrossed America by transcontinental railroad, ventured into the Australian outback and included Canada, New Zealand and South Africa on his global itinerary. An Englishman by birth and upbringing, he lived in both America and Australia for a number of years. He was a hero in New Orleans and San Francisco and hoped to settle in New York until falling foul of a minority of politically motivated Irish-American hoodlums. The peak of his career came in Australia, where he was perhaps the first sports star in an emerging nation and where his popularity was pervasive. Even the outlaw Ned Kelly, hostile to most things English, met Mace and came to respect him.

Mace's nearly eighty years of life were ones in which England was, save only for five years, blissfully free from war – and it seemed as if sport had sublimated the bellicose urge. What's more, he emerged as a kind of Victorian anti-hero, representing the worlds of the prize ring and the circus, both considered sinful by middle-class evangelists – including, ironically, his own son – but loved by both the aristocracy and the working classes.

At home equally in the rugged world of the ring and the magical world of showbusiness, Jem Mace was, by his conviviality and sense of comradeship, a man amongst men. By his magnetic personality, good looks, unbounded confidence, driving ambition and playful humour, he also drew women to him. Despite his appetite for wenching, he had a genuine empathy for women which set him apart from macho stereotypes.

Mace was entirely deprived of education, as were the vast majority of boys of his class in the rural England into which he was born. Throughout his life there was a contrast, often frustrating to him, between his keen intelligence and his semi-literacy. Equally, his capacity for imaginative business enterprises contrasted with his carelessness over money and the compulsive gambling which was his downfall. The last few years of his life were spent in near poverty and his final collapse came on a disused pit heap in Jarrow. Nevertheless, his influence not only on boxing but on sport and society would continue unabated even as his name receded into an undeserved obscurity.

Mace's ring nickname, 'The Gypsy', may or may not have had any kind of foundation in fact and he would, despite his lifelong friendship with the Romany community, always insist on his purely Anglo-Saxon ethnicity. But it came to have a talismanic significance. Mace lived more in a day than most people did in a month and more in a year than many did in half a lifetime. A pimpernel whose exact path through life remains elusive even to this day, his charisma was compelling and his influence has endured.

PART ONE

THE INNOVATOR

(1831–1861)

1

A Broken Violin

IT WOULD BE a son – and 'no ordinary son' at that. With those words, the gypsy fortune teller assured the pregnant young woman opposite her that her unborn child was to be a boy. Ann Mace was pleased but curious. She pressed for more details. The gypsy smiled and shook her head.

Like a many a superstitious country girl, Ann had sought out the services of a Romany palm-reader to disclose what her future held. She was six months with child and anxious about the outcome. As she left the gypsy camp with a friend, a bulldog barked and the women turned to witness two men squaring up for a fight. Music from the nearby caravans stopped and a crowd began to gather. At the front stood a beautiful woman, watching the fighters intently. Whether the quarrel was over her or over a game of cards, it was impossible to tell. Ann returned to her village and reflected on the prediction. For the rest of her pregnancy, she wondered if there was some connection between the gypsy woman's words and the fight she had witnessed, but her husband William dismissed it as coincidence.

Ann's previous son, born three years earlier and christened James, had shuddered violently when the holy water was sprinkled on his tiny body at baptism. By that night he was shivering uncontrollably and the next day he was dead. So when her new baby arrived – on 8 April 1831 – she had a right to feel apprehensive. But this child was a lusty boy. He yelled heartily as the christening rite was performed on a spring day at Saint Mary the Virgin, and again as his name was written into the parish register at Beeston-next-Mileham. He, too, was named James; everyone would call him Jem.

Beeston was a small village, deep in the heart of rural Norfolk, and William and Ann Mace were working-class country folk. William (Bill), who was in his mid-twenties, came from nearby Fransham and worked as a blacksmith, as did his three brothers, Tom, James and Barney. Ann, whose maiden name was Rudd, was a year younger than her husband and was Beeston-born. She was already the mother of three surviving children, the oldest of whom was also called William. He had been born out of wedlock and was baptised with the surname Mace Rudd. Two months later, his parents married and he was, from then on, simply a Mace. He was nearly eight years older than Jem.

Bill and Ann lived in Street Lane in a tenanted cottage owned by the aristocratic Windham family of Felbrigge Hall in Norwich. They were members of the Church of England but less religious than most country people, attending church irregularly. Like most rural working-class English boys in the reign of William IV, Jem received no education. His parents were semi-literate, and from childhood Jem was called upon to help his father at his itinerant forge, and life on the road precluded schooling. It was assumed that, like his father and uncles before him, he would become a blacksmith. He did very heavy work for a young boy and gradually built up powerful upper-body muscles.

From an early age, there was something different about Jem Mace. Unlike his male relatives on the Rudd side, and unlike his brother Billy, he was small – but lean and very nimble. Where the others were stolid, he was quick-thinking and eager to learn about life. Where their pastime was to drink ale, his was to wander off on his own into the woods, to observe wildlife and listen to birdsong. His favourite relative was his uncle Barney, who at nineteen had broken with family tradition and married a fifteen-year-old gypsy, Lurena Baker. He had fallen in love after meeting her at a fair in the county town of Norwich and Barney and Lurena then returned to live near Beeston in a Romany clan camp on the road to the small town of Swaffham. Jem was fascinated by Romany life. He loved the exotic atmosphere, flamboyant clothes and tales of travel far and wide – but, above all, he adored the music and dancing, in particular the sound of the gypsy fiddle.

Barney and Lurena had a son named Leopoldius, born on 13 January 1839. By now, with Queen Victoria's reign having begun two years earlier, the Civil Registration of Births, Marriages and Deaths Act had made it compulsory to notify the state. 'Pooley', as he would always be called, was nearly eight years younger than Mace and would look up to him as to a brother. Jem did not get on well with his own brother, Billy, and began to feel that Pooley was his true kith and kin. They would become close and lifelong friends. The rivalry between Jem and Billy was heightened by the fact that they were the two surviving sons of the family. Jem would be far closer to his sisters Hannah and Eliza, who were older than he, and Anne and Amelia, who were younger.

From his boyhood, there were rumours that Jem Mace was of gypsy origin. When he first became a pugilist, he was nicknamed 'The Swaffham Gypsy', shortened to 'The Gypsy' after he began his full-time career as a prize-fighter. Mace resented this, and in his autobiography, *Fifty Years A Fighter*, spoke of 'the assertion, oft-times repeated, that I have gypsy blood in my veins'. He asserted that 'this statement is completely untrue', attributing the notion to the fact that Pooley, by then his constant companion in circuses and boxing booths, was half-Romany.

But Mace received the nickname around the time of his first recorded fights, when he was eighteen and Pooley only nine, and therefore too young to be present. There are good reasons why anyone should, in the nineteenth century, have denied the slightest hint of Romany origin, even if he knew it was true. Until 1780, only half a century before Mace's birth, there had been laws on the statute book rendering any person liable for imprisonment for the mere fact of being a gypsy. And as late as 1654, gypsies had been hanged at Bury St Edmunds in Suffolk under the sixteenth century laws which had expelled Romanies from England on pain of death. After these laws were repealed, Romanies moved back to England from the Scandinavian countries to which they had been deported. But anti-gypsyism was still rampant. For every English person who, like the Norfolk novelist George Borrow, romanticised the nomadic lifestyle of the travellers, there were many more who feared and detested Romany folk.

The counties on the east coast of England, particularly rural ones such as Norfolk, were favoured by Roma men, some of whom married out or fathered children by English girls. They worked principally as travelling smiths, horse and cattle dealers and itinerant musicians. William Mace Senior roamed through Norfolk and Suffolk as a travelling smith, playing fiddle at various fairs. This was at about the time when, due to the construction of macadamised roads, travel in England generally became quicker and easier.

In regard to music, if nothing else, Mace would take after his father, who was also dark-haired, brown-eyed and of a darker complexion than most, despite his Anglo-Saxon features. Mace's life would be characterised by wanderlust and, in this way, he conformed to the gypsy stereotype. Both as a teenager and an old man he was constantly in the company of Romanies, but in no sense was he a full ethnic gypsy, or even a half-Romany. Nevertheless, while there is no evidence that he was a quarter Roma (through his father's side), it remains a distinct possibility.

Mace was a natural athlete. He could run fast and for hours, and could easily out-wrestle other boys. At his uncle Barney's, he learned how to ride. He felt an instinctive kinship with horses and soon showed that he had the makings of a firm but fair horseman, riding at full gallop and gracefully guiding his steed over lofty jumps.

His parents increased their income by taking in lodgers. One was an old sailor who didn't have long to live, and Jem listened, fascinated, to the ancient mariner's tales of voyages round the world. On his tenth birthday, the old man gave him his violin as a present. He was jubilant and closely guarded his prize possession. The sailor told him he had bought it in Cremona, the Italian city which specialised in the manufacture of high-quality musical instruments. Mace took his violin to uncle Barney's and was taught the basics of fiddle-playing by the gypsy musicians. He learned fast and before long used to take the violin into the woods and mimic the sounds of the birds on the strings of his instrument.

The worlds of music and nature seemed far preferable to Mace than the daily grind in the forge. One day he injured his fingers with a hammer. Suddenly his inner rage that he had no say in his own future – except to work, like his father, at the anvil – erupted. Scared that he had damaged his violin skill in the accident, he hurled the hammer to the floor and told his father that he would never become a blacksmith. His father cursed and slapped him. Throughout his eleventh year there would be various similar incidents, until his father gave up in despair. While Bill finally left his son alone, his older brother did not. Billy taunted him about his love of music and fondness for gypsy company.

Mace was repeatedly cuffed, out of sight of his mother, to whom he never complained, and his lack of a sense of family became ingrained at an early age. Inwardly he swore that he would get even with Billy as soon as he was old enough to confront him.

An obvious outlet for Mace's suppressed anger was fights on the village green at Beeston. At that time football was scarcely known in Norfolk, but fighting between the lads of the village was as commonplace as ball games became in later decades. His strength, from his enforced stint at the forge, and his will to win made him a fighter from the start and by the time he was fourteen he had thrashed a score of other lads his own age, as he later recalled.

> Everybody learned to use his fists in those days; rich and poor, gentle and simple. Fighting was the one thing talked about. Every little village possessed its 'champion', and these used to meet one another, usually on Sunday, and fight to the finish with naked fists. I remember there was an old barn about a mile out from Beeston, to which the 'fancy men' of the surrounding villages used to come to settle who was best. The battles I have seen in that barn! Why, some of them would not have discredited the regular ring.

Another motivation, as he became an adolescent, was to win one of the prettier local girls – who favoured the strongest fighting lads. The family cottage stood next to a nonconformist chapel and opposite The Ploughshare Inn. To his intense annoyance, Sunday morning lie-ins, after a visit to the gypsy camp the previous evening, were frequently disturbed by the preacher shouting out sermons at the top of his voice. But there was more to it than just that. It seemed to Mace, young as he was, that the preacher was against all expressions of life, energy and daring. He heard him denounce music, dancing, card-playing, gambling, even lying (as he liked to do) on the ground, staring at the 'blue dome' of the sky instead of working or worshipping. Above all, the preacher railed against 'hellish and damnable lust'.

These sermons left Mace with a lifelong indifference to religion in general and a strong dislike of fundamentalism in particular. On the other hand, he gazed with fascination at The Ploughshare yard. He didn't dream of being old enough to drink there, as Billy did, and wondered why it was apparently necessary to dull your brain with liquor before you could enjoy yourself. But in the yard of The Ploughshare, bare-knuckle fights took place – not as a result of quarrels, but for the hell of it. The combatants were roared on by a drunken throng. What intrigued him was the way, even if only some-times, that the smaller man could get the better of a hefty opponent by dodging out of the way of his punches and landing a couple of his own while the big man was off-balance. He determined to do likewise against Billy as soon as he was old enough.

The 'knockout blow' had, of course, not been invented. So the two combatants simply hammered each other till one cried 'enough', or fell insensible by reason of the succession of blows rained on him by his opponent.

Some of the fiercest fights I have ever seen, outside the Prize Ring, were fought by young fellows of seventeen, or thereabouts, for the possession of the lasses. A village lad, in those days, stood little chance of getting a sweetheart that was worth having unless he was able to use his fists. The prettiest girls went to the hardest hitters. This was regarded so much as a matter of course, by both the girls and the boys, that I have repeatedly seen one of the former stand patiently by while two of the latter fought for her, and then, when the contest was finished, walk off quietly with the victor.

These impromptu matches were called 'love fights', and usually took place outside The Ploughshare and directly opposite the Mace cottage, giving young Jem a grandstand view from his bedroom window. The village stocks were also close by, and someone was usually in them on a Saturday night. 'The prisoner also got a good view,' recalled Mace, 'for the crowd, always sympathetic and good-natured, used to keep a clear space for him to see the "fun", besides supplying him with beer and 'bacca.' Gameness and hard-hitting were well regarded, but the highest praise was reserved for a 'good lad', by which was meant a clever fighter, whose guile and trickery could vanquish greater brawn.

Before Mace was fourteen, Bill realised that it was useless to try and make a blacksmith out of him – though the lad's ability on the violin indicated that he had skill in his hands. When Bill learned that a cabinet maker named Fox was looking for young apprentices, he packed Jem off. This meant leaving home and walking twenty miles to Wells-next-the-Sea. None of this bothered Mace in the slightest and off he set, his violin stowed in a kitbag.

It turned out that Fox was a publican of the Green Dragon as well as a cabinet maker. Although he taught Mace the basics of cabinet making, he'd been in the habit of using his apprentices as cheap labour. Wells was not far from the great neo-Palladian aristocratic estate of Holkham Hall, from which logs would be carted down into Fox's yard to be sawn for timber. For a while Mace got out of this chore. His boss, noting his skill with the violin, arranged for him to play for customers. Mace was happy to do this at first. Coins were freely thrown into his violin case in appreciation of his ability to play the popular tunes of the day – not to mention his own composition, 'The Cuckoo Song', improvised as he walked through the woods. Between the ages of ten and twelve, he had mastered his instrument. Now, between fourteen and fifteen, he was being paid to play in public.

In the eighteen months he spent at Wells, Mace became increasingly aware that his earnings from fiddle-playing were far less than Fox's increased takings at the bar. Many extra customers were attracted to the Green Dragon by its star violinist. His resentment came to a head one day when Fox ordered him to join in with sawing up trees sent down from Holkham Hall for logging. In an incident similar to that at his father's forge, he soon flung down his saw and stood defiantly, hands on hips. For a moment, Mace thought Fox was going to hit him and half hoped he would, so that he could strike back at his taskmaster. But Fox, obese and wary of the sturdy teenager, instead ordered him to stay in his room. This was enough to convince Mace to return home. He slipped out of the pub and spent the rest of the day and the whole of the short summer night hiding out on the sand dunes. At dawn he began to walk back to Beeston. His father fully accepted that Fox was no true cabinet maker and that Jem was right not to become an underpaid sawyer, but he wrongly assumed that the whole episode would persuade Jem to settle down at the smithy.

He did try, but the only happy note for him was the presence of his youngest sister, six-year-old Amelia, for whom he had great affection. He decided to have no more to do with such a dismal life and, between his fifteenth and sixteenth birthdays, left home for good – without a word to his parents. He rose before daybreak and, slamming the door behind him, strode off into the world. For some time he supported himself as an itinerant violinist, playing outside pubs and at fairgrounds, but he could always find a home with Barney and Lurena.

Barney's occupation as a farrier meant that he was in demand wherever horses were, and he and Lurena reverted to the travelling lifestyle of her forebears. During Mace's years on the road there were two further additions to Barney's family of three; one of these, Augustus (Gus), became a friend of Mace's in future years. Mace often slept in their caravans in such places as Creake and Heacham, on or near the Norfolk coast by The Wash. His connection with a well-known, part-Romany family meant that he was usually sure of a bed for the night as he ventured further afield in Norfolk and Suffolk.

Before long he became known throughout East Anglia as a gifted violinist and was hired to play at Romany weddings. Soon the horse dealers at the markets became aware that Mace was also an excellent rider and he was employed both to break in horses and to show them off. His equestrian skills brought him into conflict with the gypsy youths who previously had the field to themselves. They challenged him to fist fights. He was happy to take them on and, more often than not, give them a hiding.

One day a publican bet that none of his customers could punch through the inch-thick wooden panel of a door. Several tried and failed, succeeding only in damaging the panel and their hands. But Mace won the bet, driving his fist clean through the wood. Realising his unusual hitting power, especially for a lad in his mid-teens, he made money at travelling boxing booths, where local lads were challenged to take on experienced bruisers. He learned how to fight, both with bare knuckles and with gloves, and took part in numerous pub fights, fought for bets in skittle alleys.

He was a good-looking lad, lean and muscular. That, combined with his musical and equestrian skills, attracted the attention of girls his own age. He was a confident talker, a joker and a polite listener. He was also an inveterate wanderer. For some two-and-a-half years he roamed throughout East Anglia; indeed there were few towns or villages in Norfolk and Suffolk which he did not visit. At times, however, he would seek solitude in woodland or on isolated beaches, relaxing and daydreaming. Mace enjoyed the travelling life but was not content, as he felt that there was no real prospect of a career for him.

Around the time of his eighteenth birthday, he paid a visit to the bustling fishing port and burgeoning seaside resort of Great Yarmouth. He stayed with one of his many cousins, a couple by the name of Jackman, who ran a pub called the Gallon Can. Mace used this as a base for his violin playing, but went busking around the town's many pubs where easy pickings were to be had for an accomplished musician. But outside one seafront pub an incident occurred which was to change the course of his life.

Mace had been playing outside to appreciative crowds for several hours when three burly fishermen emerged from the pub, clearly fighting drunk. The leader took one look at the young musician and strolled over to him. Completely unprovoked, he raised his fist and, with one blow, smashed the fiddle in half, to the raucous laughter of his two mates. Mace was aghast but soon an intense fury welled up within him. He demanded, and got, a duel with the first fisherman. It took him fifteen minutes before he beat the man helpless, to the cheers of a hastily gathered crowd who were completely on his side. Then he demanded that each of the other two should battle him in turn. It took twice as long to knock out the second fellow but he finally fell back on the cobblestones and was lucky not to injure his head seriously. The third now made a run for it but was swiftly caught up by Mace – although he managed to get away when Mace slipped almost as he was about to seize him.

By this time the other two fishermen had slunk off to the jeers of the crowd. Mace, however, was greeted with great applause and coins were showered into his violin case to help him buy a new instrument. His speed of movement was commented on by members of the crowd, to whom Mace disclosed that he was already a paid pedestrian. Pedestrianism was the name then given to track sprinting, a popular working-class sport in which, as with horseracing, men competed with each other for cash prizes. It was also a focus for heavy gambling. Mace mentioned that he had already won cups for winning sprint events, but he did not reveal that he had also won a substantial sum of money by wagering on a race which he knew full well was fixed.

As the crowd dispersed, Mace noted that women in particular seemed fascinated, doubtless by the way the hands which would coax such delightful melodies from a taut stringed instrument had suddenly been transformed into instruments of ruthless vengeance. Unfortunately for him, all of the ladies were accompanied. The most dramatic point of this momentous evening came at the end, when a local toff gave him a sovereign. He added the words, 'You should become a prize-fighter, young lad.'

That night Mace lay awake, thinking matters over. He was dismayed by the wanton destruction of his prize possession. He was appalled by the brute hatred for artistry which the fishermen had shown. But he was elated by his own ability to dish out punishment to them. By morning he had decided: he would indeed become a prize-fighter. He did not yet want to give up his life as a musician but he was eager to increase his earnings as a part-time bare-knuckle fighter, or pugilist. The problem was that the entire sport of pugilism was run from London and Mace had no contacts in the metropolis. He stuck to his ambition to become a prize-fighter as soon as a chance offered itself but, in the meantime, he would continue making a living as a musician.

Mace teamed up with a circus showman by the name of Bunny Blythe and went on a tour of the Lincolnshire Fens. His dual role was to perform as a violinist and see off any trouble-makers. In mid-century England, circuses were by far the leading form of popular entertainment. The arrival of a travelling circus, with its acrobats, equestrians, fiddlers and clowns, was eagerly awaited in every small town throughout the land. Sometimes, however, gangs of young hooligans – whose target would be the many gypsy or foreign people in the tents – would attack the circus and try to drive it away. Mace's expertise with his fists came in handy.

His involvement with circuses would continue throughout his life. The bustle and clatter of the circus held a strong appeal, as did the nomadic way of life. In the world of the circus, Mace's skill as a violinist earned him the nickname of 'The lad with the golden arm'.

But those who had witnessed his ruthless yet instinctively skilful demolition of the three thugs who had broken his cherished violin would have considered that it suited him down to the ground.

2

Black Jack Davey and the Schoolmaster's Daughter

A SUNDAY MORNING and Jem Mace had just been paid. He never worried about money and never tried to save. Instead, he strode right over Mousehill Heath to join the gypsies, ready for a ball. In nearby Norwich the solid citizens were hurrying to get ready for church. The scene in the gypsy camp could not have been more different. This was the day they set aside for music, singing and dancing. It began at dawn, would not stop until the sun sank, and made an indelible impression on the young fighter.

> My, what a day that was, to be sure! The gipsies were all in their best attire; the men in velveteen coats and knee-breeches, with white silk stockings, and shoes adorned with big past buckles; the girls and young women in silks of all the colours of the rainbow, and wearing an abundance of jewellery that flashed and sparkled n the sunshine. All day long we danced and sang, and then sang and danced again, until the sun sank to rest, and the big round harvest moon came out above the scattered pine-trees, flooding all the purple heath with white radiance.

Aged eighteen, Mace was already a hero to the travellers whose caravans stretched out amid the purple heather. No matter that he had just beaten one of their own, Farden Smith. Here was a fellow who lived up to their ideal of a man: both a fighter and a musician. He was at once handed a fiddle and asked to play, but preferred to use his own new violin. Seeing a gypsy girl giving him the eye, he sent her back to his lodgings in Timberhill Street to bring it. When she returned, he played for hours, to wild appreciation. In the evening, other musicians took over and he danced with the lass more and more. Mace was entranced by her long dark hair, sparkling brown eyes and the glimpses of her bare legs under her swirling purple skirt. As night fell under a harvest moon they strolled hand-in-hand deep into the pine woods and made love.

One of the songs Mace played on Mousehill Heath was 'Black Jack Davey', sometimes called 'Gypsy Davey' or 'The Gypsy Laddie'. It was a melody already known for more than a century throughout rural England, and told the story of a dark-eyed gypsy rambler who had seduced a blonde country lass into leaving her rich husband to lead a roving life with him – exchanging a world of comfort, security and boredom for a life of hardship, uncertainty and excitement. The phrase 'blackjack' signified various things: a game of cards; a gypsy man's black leather waistcoat; or a sweet much loved by women, made of treacle and spice with a hint of chocolate. Mace is also a type of spice and there were those who thought the story and its title particularly suited the fighter. He was, after all, a rover and a ladies' man.

It was at about this time that Mace began privately to question his origins and his previous certainty that his ancestors were Anglo-Saxon country tradesmen. An illiterate youth, he could rely only on what he'd been told – he was incapable of checking the parish records, even if he had wished to spend his time on such a dull task. And the records could not exclude the possibility that one of the Mace women, or even one of the Rudd girls, had, a generation or two past, yielded to the advances of a gypsy and then been left to pass off the resulting child as her husband's. Before long, Mace discounted the story, preferring to believe in his own remarkable personality as the secret of his success with women. And of his own unshakeable confidence as the key to his exceptional skill as a musician, dancer, and, in time to come, master boxer. Mace would never shake off the pugilistic nickname of 'The Gypsy'. It was something he resented, friendly as he was to the Romany community. He felt it was inappropriate, an attempt to take him down a peg. When he left Norfolk, he would leave 'Black Jack Davey' off the set list whenever he played violin in public.*

---

*The song had already crossed the Atlantic and would resurface over a century later on the flipside of a rockabilly record by Warren Smith – before being reworked first by Bob Dylan and then by The White Stripes. Thus a song popularised in East Anglia by Jem Mace would end up at the heart of American rock 'n' roll.

Mace hadn't forgotten the words he'd heard from the toff at Great Yarmouth. He began his prize-fighting career in the spring of 1849, promoting himself by saying he was prepared to take on all comers for either £5 or £10 a time. His first pugilistic encounter was with Sydney Smith at Wisbech, Cambridgeshire, and after a two-hour scrap, he won. His second fight ended when he knocked out Charles Pinfold in four rounds, before a crowd of 500 people. His third fight was against the hulking Farden Smith, in Norwich.

He was known as the King of the Gypsies, and was a regular giant, standing 6ft 2in in his stocking feet, and broad in proportion. Like my fight with Pinfold, this was brought off on Norwich Hill. Or rather, I should say, that it was attempted to be brought off, for we made the grand mistake of choosing market-day, and the crowds were so tremendous, and the obstruction they caused so great, that the police swooped down upon us after we had fought four or five rounds, and we had to take to our heels to escape being arrested.

This was what had brought them to Mousehill Heath on that Sunday. Mace was expecting to resume but Smith had clearly had enough. He conceded the fight at once and handed his opponent the money. Unsurprisingly, Jem was in the mood to celebrate. For six years, between the ages of eighteen and twenty-four, he was a semi-professional prize-fighter. These fights, dangerous and gruelling, were fought under the rules of the London Prize Ring (often abbreviated to LPR), which had been drawn up in 1838. They differed from modern boxing in three main ways. First, bouts were fights to the finish with no fixed number of rounds; a round ended when one man was knocked down or dropped to his knees after a blow to take a rest. The fight was over when one man was unable or unwilling to stand in the middle of the ring and toe the line. Second, they were a mixture of boxing and stand-up wrestling. Third, they were fought with bare knuckles.

Prize fights attracted large crowds. Gambling on the result, both by the contestants and spectators, was a central feature. Contemporary paintings depict men stripped to the waist, wearing a belt and sometimes a coloured sash above knee breeches, stockings and, to grip the open turf, studded boots.

Unlike many other fighters, Mace was careful to drink in moderation. His favourite was a glass of port with an egg beaten up in it, a good mixture for keeping his head clear. But he found it far harder to resist the temptation of gambling. As fights took him further afield into other counties, much of the talk was about horseracing. Jem was fascinated by the atmosphere at racecourses and started to visit Newmarket regularly – and a lifelong habit of high-stakes gambling on horses began.

Although Mace gained a sense of pride and self-fulfilment from his semi-professional pugilistic excursions, he was in his element in the quite different world of the travelling musicians, with whom he was still working. The troupe travelled the length and breadth of Norfolk, one of England's largest counties. The atmosphere was one of abandoned fun and enjoyment. This was an antidote to the dullness of everyday life and the strictness of the Church. Liquor flowed and, as the musicians heightened the tempo, lads and girls took to the dancefloor, captivated by the tunes and fast rhythms. Besides his skills as a musician, he was an excellent dancer, far exceeding most other men in his natural grace of movement.

About this time, Mace began courting sixteen-year-old Mary Ann Barton, a pretty, dark-haired girl who, like him, lived in Norwich, albeit in suburban Thorpe, not in the rough Timberhill quarter. There was strong mutual attraction and before too long Mary became pregnant. She was worried that Mace might leave her; musicians had a reputation for such behaviour. Mary, who was an intelligent girl, came from a strict home which had taken its values from her schoolmaster father, Thomas Barton. Born in Ireland of Scottish descent, he had come to England in his youth. Like all middle-class girls in mid-Victorian Britain, Mary was worried about what was then the disgrace of being an unmarried mother.

She knew little or nothing of her Jem's prize-fighting activities. But she did know that many young men earned money by working in boxing booths, which were legal because they were always time-limited and because gloves were used. Before he and Mary became lovers, Mace was already earning money sparring in the booths at Norwich market.

One day Nat Langham – Middleweight Champion of England –

visited Norwich on a scouting mission. He had begun his working life as a framework knitter in Leicestershire before making his way to London as a young man, determined on a career as a pugilist, and intended to become a matchmaker. He'd heard on the prize-fight grapevine that Norfolk was fast becoming a cradle of talented bare-knuckle scrappers and, taking advantage of the extension of the Eastern Counties Railway line, he set off by train from London on a business trip to Norwich. Hearing news of two promising young fighters who were out of town, he moved on to where he was told they were. The two were Jem Mace and Bunny Blythe, and Langham watched them fight each other in the booth at Lincoln Fair.

He watched Mace in action and liked what he saw, noting that he stood only about 5ft 9 in tall and seemed to weigh no more than ten stone (140lb). This didn't deter Mace from boldly taking on taller and heavier men. As well as that, Mace's approach was not in the usual style of an untrained country boy. He seemed to be a natural born boxer, cool, cunning and agile. Langham made his decision: he offered Mace a job fighting in his travelling boxing booth at £2 a week with all expenses paid.

Langham's booth was the finest of its kind in England. The youths who boxed there, with gloves, were only one notch below the professional prize-fighters of London. Although they were kept in the provinces for the time being, they could make what was big money for those days, compared to the pittance they would earn in their regular jobs. Sometimes they took on an unknown who was up for a scrap with 'one of Langham's lads' but on special occasions they would have a plum bout with another up-and-coming semi-pro or a veteran working for a last payday. Above all there was the prospect of getting on the London circuit. This was, of course, Jem's dream.

Within a week of shaking hands on a deal with Langham, Mace had been taken by his new boss to Horncastle Fair in Lincolnshire. It was there that he took on local hero Tom Brewer, using gloves. Brewer was older, taller and heavier and had a face described by Mace as being 'as hard as a marble mantelpiece'. But youth and class told and, after nearly two hours, Mace was the winner.

A week after Jem's nineteenth birthday, he took on the veteran Jack Pratt, just beyond Norwich. Confident that he could see off old Jack, and too busy enjoying himself with his music and with girls, he had not prepared properly for the fight. He knew the fight would be with bare knuckles, but, though he'd done that before, he didn't fully realise the potential danger and injured first one fist and then the other, against Pratt's head. Even though his hands swelled like balloons, he had the guts to go on for a full three hours but in time could do little more than slap his opponent. Mace's seconds threw in the sponge.

Langham exploded with rage. His affected lisp, in imitation of the toffs whose patronage he courted, abruptly left him. His temper was worsened by Mace's admission that he'd done no proper training and, above all, hadn't pickled his fists. Langham told him that he would only fight in the booths for the rest of the year. 'Next time you're in for a real fight with the raw 'uns, you pickle 'em both,' he said. Then he snarled, 'and if you don't, you'll get the sack!'

He turned on his heel and strode off. Mace knew his future was on the line and began soaking his hands every night in mixtures of horse radish, whisky or even hedgehog fat before letting it dry while he slept. It did little for his love life but among the consolations was the thought that his alternative musical career would be less likely to be jeopardised by broken hands. Early next year he took on Pratt again and made short work of him.

Mace didn't let Mary down. He was keen to marry above himself from a social point of view and felt embarrassed when Mary discovered that he was illiterate. For the first time in his life he wondered where he could get some much-needed education. On 21 July 1851, James Mace, aged twenty, married seventeen-year-old Mary Ann Barton at the parish church of Thorpe Hamlet, just outside Norwich. He gave his occupation as a 'dealer', to disguise the amount of money he was making from prize-fighting. George Perowne, the best man, was experienced in the Prize Ring as a second and, before long, Mace told his new bride the full extent of his pugilistic activities.

During the first part of their married life, they lived in Norwich, at Silver Road, but if Mace had been hoping that Mary would help him learn to read and write, he was soon disappointed. Although she had signed her name in the parish register at Thorpe, while he could only make his mark, this was a practised one-off designed to impress him. In fact, Mary was barely literate herself. Her father believed there was no point in a girl being taught anything other than cooking and sewing. Their first son, James Mace junior, was born on 10 March 1852 at Beeston. Mace's mother had expressed a wish to meet his bride, and while visiting the village, Mary went into labour and gave birth in his parents' house.

For several years, Mace's fighting career did not develop as fast as he wanted; his boss had accepted one last challenge for his middleweight crown and was therefore concentrating on his own career. Langham's opponent was the leading contender Tom Sayers, born in Brighton, Sussex, and a bricklayer by trade before moving to London. He was a skilful boxer with an extremely strong punch for a man who was far smaller and lighter than most. Langham versus Sayers, at Lakenheath, Suffolk, in 1853, was one of the fiercest fights in the history of the LPR. It was won by Langham – but at a cost. Sayers, although nearly blinded by his blows, left Langham with serious injuries and although he pulled through it was initially feared he might not survive. After this brush with death, Langham wisely decided to retire from the ring and became a publican in London. Proving himself an astute businessman, he established a virtual monopoly of the fight game in west London. It would be several years before he turned his attention to Mace's career.

By this time Mary had given birth to their second child. Alfred, named after Mary's brother, was born on 13 January 1854 in the family home at The Paddock in the rural Pockthorpe district of Norwich. As a result of his family commitments, Mace was now having to give more and more time to prize-fighting. His reputation was continuing to grow and three intended opponents called off fights with him – preferring to pay up than face him in the ring. Not only was he a powerful puncher but he had an unusual style which was very difficult to counter.

Jem Mace's fighting style was based on the fact that he could move far more quickly than most of his opponents. His natural agility, honed by a pedestrian's knack of acceleration, saw to that. Indeed, he often seemed like a dancer facing men in lead boots. While ignorant onlookers shouted, 'Coward!' – much to Mace's amusement – those in the know and ready to gamble knew they were onto a good thing. Second, he perfected the left jab, fired straight from the shoulder, in order to keep his opponents indefinitely at bay, while at the same time enraging them as his fist thudded time and time again into their faces. Langham had been the first master of the jab and would often win 'first blood' as his razor-sharp punches cut open foes' brows and eyelids. So devastating a weapon had Nat's jab been that it was nicknamed 'Langham's pickaxe' by followers of the LPR. And what his boss innovated, Mace took to an even higher level. Third, Mace was a master of the feint, seemingly about to throw a punch with one hand and then delivering a cross with the other. Mace's tactics wore his opponents down and they chased him in vain. Even when he seemed to be cornered he was so good at narrowly dodging punches that he was one of the very few pugilists who showed almost no sign on his face of what he did for a living. This was in complete contrast to the typical prize-fighter look: permanently swollen eyes, scars, broken noses and cauliflower ears. Excellent as his defence was, Mace hit with real punching power. He would wait patiently for his opponents to tire before moving in and unleashing a series of right-handers which would dump them on the turf.

In the early years of his marriage, Mace was often away from home. He used his winnings to set up his own boxing booth, travelling widely in the east of England, taking on and beating challengers with the gloves. He would earn extra money at fairgrounds and race meetings by playing the violin, which he did left-handed, although he was ambidextrous as a boxer. A pet bulldog always accompanied him.

It was in 1855, at the age of twenty-four, that Mace took the decision to become a full-time pugilist. In doing so, he had much to gain. Prize money for a championship bout could be up to £100. His opportunities for travel would extend throughout the south of England. But he also had much to lose. Prize-fighting was illegal in every county of the land. It had been that way since 1750, just a few decades after its emergence as a sporting pursuit. This was not due to any act of Parliament but because the sport's original leading patron, the Duke of Cumberland, had turned against it. The Duke, a son of George III, had the nickname 'Butcher Cumberland' and was one of the most bloodthirsty generals in British history. But when Cumberland lost money as a result of a losing bet on the champion, Jack Broughton, he closed down Broughton's Amphitheatre in

London out of spite. Other authorities throughout the land tamely followed suit and prize-fighting became an underground sport. Its famous contests would thenceforth take place outside remote towns and small villages. Ironically, pugilism flourished as a result of the patronage of the next monarch, George IV, who was already the Regent during the madness of his father, King George III. Both in the Regency era and his own reign, George IV continued his enthusiasm for the bare-knuckle game. So too did many of his aristocratic friends. For the better part of twenty years, the police scarcely dared to interfere with prize fights.

All this took place before Jem Mace was born, but he knew the history of his sport well. As veteran pugilists reminisced, so Mace took mental note of everything he heard. During his own lifetime, prize-fighting had become a working-class attraction. It was that very fact which enraged the industrial employers. They knew that if a fight took place in their localities, men would take the day off in droves to see it, making the journey by train. To avoid protests from the churches, fights were never held on Sundays, the one day all working men were allowed to be off work, so Mondays and Tuesdays were always the days chosen.

Prize-fighting's biggest enemies were the evangelists. They were shocked by the bloodshed and even more shocked by the ironic language which working men used to describe their excursions: 'Holy Monday' and 'Saint Tuesday'. Although the pugilists were fighting of their own free will, nonconformist preachers classed the Prize Ring along with the bear pit and badger run. Even worse, in their eyes, was the fact that the fight attracted drunken rowdies and all-too-sober pickpockets. Few women attended, and most of those who did were prostitutes. One of the prize ring's foremost opponents was the reforming Member of Parliament John Bright. The son of a Lancashire textile manufacturer and a devout Quaker, Bright held the key interest in the *Morning Star* and was connected to the Dial, whose self-declared mission was to 'purify the daily Press' by excluding not only reports of criminal cases but 'so-called sporting news'. Adjectives such as 'brutal', 'barbarous', 'disgusting' and 'horrid' were regularly applied to prize-fighting in the columns of both publications, which campaigned for more pro-active policing.

Mace thus became an outlaw, going about his business risking serious injury, and even death, with the ever-present possibility of police disruption. Although arrests were infrequent, they did occur. Punishment was not usually severe for fighting itself, but if an opponent was to lose his life, charges of manslaughter would result and a long prison sentence would be imposed. Mace took the risk. Confident in his own skills, he was well aware of the hypocrisy of the police. They would often allow a window of opportunity of about an hour before they moved in to stop a bout. If a mill was arranged, as it frequently was, at the boundary of three counties, a commanding officer would often sit on horseback watching the bout with interest – unless and until his opposite number in the neighbouring county confirmed by a map that it was under the first officer's jurisdiction.

But the chances of 'getting away with it' were increasing in the railway age. Prize-fighting's wealthy backers had started to charter 'railway specials'. These would carry the fighters, their seconds and the spectators at far higher speeds than galloping police horses. These spectators would be wealthy enthusiasts of prize-fighting, the 'Fancy', as they were called, men from whom the word 'fan' is derived. They thought nothing of paying up to £4 a head for a ticket and, if need be, even more to charter one of the steamboats which plied the Thames and were another means of defying the magistrates.

In other ways too, Mace was entering the Prize Ring at an opportune time. For a start, the nation was at war against Tsarist Russia, on Russian soil in the Crimea. As had happened half a century before, during the Napoleonic Wars, the belligerent mood of the nation chimed with the mindset of pugilism. Although Mace was, as a man on the bohemian margins of society, unmoved by flag-waving, he benefited from the public mood, as did all fighters. Such episodes as the Charge of the Light Brigade, albeit a failure, were extensively covered in *The Times*, which dwelt at length on qualities of 'British pluck'. And, after all, argued the upper-class supporters of the LPR, the Corinthians, as they liked to call themselves, where were these qualities best exemplified if not in the Prize Ring? Suddenly, the middle-class magistrates were on the back foot. Alarmed by the Hyde Park Riots in the middle of the war, when working men demonstrated violently against the ban on Sunday concerts in the park, they were suddenly far less eager to send policemen out to disrupt prize fights. It was an attitude which would last for several years after the end of the Crimean War in 1856.

The year in which Mace began his full-time career also saw the Corinthian toffs take over the recently formed Pugilistic Benevolent Association (PBA). Although they made no attempt to organise all aspects of bare-knuckle fighting, they decided to have a new Champion's Belt made by London's majestic jewellers, Hancock's of Bond Street. They stipulated that this new belt must be competed for at least once a year, within six months of signing the Articles of Agreement between the Champion and his challenger – usually for stakes of no less than £200 a side. It was the responsibility of the fighter to find wealthy backers who would raise the stakes on his behalf in order to defray the cost of arranging a prize fight.

On the eve of battle, the Belt had to be delivered to the Committee of the PBA. But if the Champion remained undefeated for three years, he would have the right to keep the Belt. They thus gave powerful financial and emotional incentive to all young prize-fighters, Mace included, and delivered a potent sporting symbol, one which would be the forerunner of such others as football's FA and World Cups, and tennis's Wimbledon Plate.

What the Prize Ring desperately needed was a champion worthy of such a trophy. For too long the heavyweight titleholders – men such as Bendigo, Ben Caunt and the 'Tipton Slasher' – had been, at best, brave but completely unskilled thumpers and, at worst, a bunch of drunken clowns who couldn't be relied on to keep the Belt safe. But, within a couple of years, Tom Sayers, undefeated at middleweight except by Langham, had moved up a division and, while still scarcely above the middleweight limit, had become Heavyweight Champion. Sayers' success was a great incentive to Mace. It convinced him that he need not limit himself to the middleweight division. If a man was good enough, as Sayers obviously was, he was big enough. Mace was five years younger than Sayers and believed that, with time on his side, he could eventually overthrow the new champion whose deeds were already the talk of London.

Because pugilism was an illegal activity, Mace could never openly be described as a prize-fighter. On official documents he was always referred to as a 'musician' (sometimes specifically as a 'violinist') or occasionally as a 'horse dealer' or simply 'dealer', as on his marriage certificate. Nevertheless, he was keen to move up in the world. Mary might barely be able to read and write but she had social and cultural awareness. The Norwich in which she had grown up was a different city to the one Mace knew when he made his home there in his late teens. The city, once the third largest in England, still teemed with activity. But whereas she'd grown up in suburban Thorpe, just outside the city boundary at the time, he moved right into the heart of the medieval city when he first arrived at the age of eighteen. Its walls enclosed a larger area than any other in Europe, a sign of its former status.

Mace's home before he married had been in the notorious Timberhill district, long a haven for prostitutes. He kept clear of their solicitations but frequented the Cattle Market district after dark. Here were hundreds of pubs and hordes of street vendors and busking musicians – and girls who were not harlots but free with their sexual favours. Close by, Norwich Castle was the place where public executions were carried out. Mary shuddered at the thought and took care to avoid the area on hanging days. The dubious record crowd for a public hanging in England was held, for a time, by Norwich with an estimated crowd of 50,000 turning out on one occasion. These included thousands who made the journey from the surrounding countryside, thus swelling the throng to beyond the entire population of the city itself. As for Mace, he'd watched a couple of executions out of curiosity but had no time for the voyeurism of the mob. He knew full well that many of the hangman's victims were more outlaws than vicious criminals. They were from the wrong side of the tracks, vagabonds and gypsies in many cases.

Once they were married, Mary opened her husband's eyes to a different world. As they strolled together down the fashionable Gentleman's Walk, near the ancient cathedral, or by the side of the gently flowing River Wensum, she suggested visits to the Theatre Royal to see a play. Mace agreed and was delighted by the drama. Before long, the famous opera singer Jenny Lind, the so-called 'Swedish Nightingale', performed in the city. The couple attended and he was fascinated by the music. From then on, theatre visits would be an integral part of his life.

* * *

Jem Mace's first fight as a full professional took place on 2 October 1855 at Mildenhall in Suffolk. His opponent was Bob 'Slasher' Slack and, as his nickname implied, Slack was not noted for his scientific approach. As he towered above Mace, the 'Slasher' must have thought he was in for an easy afternoon's work. The reverse was the case. Evading Slack's rushes with ease, Mace bloodied the taller man's face with his left jab, then moved in with fierce right hands and ended with a two-fisted barrage. It was all over within twenty minutes. Slack was prostrate on the turf unable to get to his feet unaided within thirty seconds, as the rules of the LPR demanded.

Mace, as a novice professional, had fought Slack for a purse of a mere fiver. But Langham had already established a connection with the celebrated London prize-fighting chronicle *Fistiana*, which duly dispatched a reporter to Mildenhall. The power of the press was shown by the fact that Mace's name became known in London in a matter of days. Langham knew he was on to a good thing but deliberately kept his protégé out of the limelight for some time. He did not want Mace's Norwich backer, the wealthy publican Thomas Cubitt, to establish a foothold in London. After Cubitt's attempts to set up more fights had fallen through, Langham summoned Mace to town. Jem saw his chance and took it. By now Mary was pregnant with their third child and he knew an opportunity to make a fortune for himself and his family had arrived. He had no hesitation in leaving for London.

He was an outlaw in the eyes of every magistrate in the land but he rode the train from Norwich to Shoreditch as a prince of the Prize Ring. 'Black Jack Davey' had come to town.

3

Vitriol and Gunpowder

THE OLD HAYMARKET ran direct towards Leicester Square and was the hub of Victorian London nightlife. From dusk till dawn, Chinese lanterns lit the surrounding streets and the district swarmed with revellers. They packed out the pubs until three in the morning. Even then, the alehouses, none of which were subject to restrictions, would stay open till daybreak if there were still customers to serve. The Old Haymarket was, in effect, a traffic-free zone, with drivers stopping their coach and horses at either end to let passengers out. The street itself thronged with acrobats, fire-eaters and buskers playing violin, cornet and accordion. The barrage of noise was heightened by barrel organs and German bands. After a meal outside an oyster bar, men and women, sporting the latest fashions, moved into 'song and supper rooms', where they stayed for hours. For those with darker desires, there were gambling dens and opium smoking cellars. Above all, there were countless brothels where prostitutes, both street-walkers and high-class courtesans, entertained their customers.

Danger also stalked the streets around the Old Haymarket. The Metropolitan Police Force had been in existence for over a quarter of a century but this was one district which its 'peelers' preferred to avoid. All kinds of villainy flourished. Pickpockets thrived, but far worse was the robbery with violence. This was carried to extremes by thugs who bludgeoned their victims or even garrotted them. A rough and ready drunk sprawled legless in the gutter was easily parted from his wallet, though there was usually little in it. The main targets were aristocrats, who were detested anyway and whose suit pockets were often stuffed with banknotes. These young toffs wanted to carouse but they wanted to do so in safety – and Nat Langham was just the man to provide such a service.

In addition to his thriving pub, the Cambrian Stores in Leicester

Square, Jem Mace's boss had established an exclusive gentlemen's sporting club in St Martin's Lane. It was named the Rum-pum-pas, and once a week members dined in a large upper room within a boxing ring. Their lavish meal would be topped off with champagne or brandy, before the ring was cleared and boxing exhibitions began. Mace joined the ranks of the novice professionals who sparred together to the applause of the watching young aristocrats, all of whom were Prize Ring enthusiasts. If they were up for it, the toffs could challenge the new boys. On his debut at the club, Mace got the better of both Lord Drumlanrig and three older professionals, ending up with £7 in his pocket after a collection.

At the Rum-pum-pas, Langham learned of the dangers young gentlemen faced on their nights out in the Old Haymarket. He immediately formed a corps of bodyguards, all of whom were professional pugs, and hired them out to the toffs. A couple of instant hidings handed out to would-be robbers were sufficient to spread the word. From then on, gentlemen could stroll unharassed with a couple of bodyguards keeping an eye open for trouble and their lips sealed about the misdemeanours of the toffs. In return, the bodyguards could count on generous tips to add to Langham's wages. Mace soon joined the ranks and was intrigued by what he saw.

On his nights off, Mace, who was, to all intents and purposes, a single man again, left his room at Langham's pub, The Cambrian Stores off Leicester Square, and headed into the West End. One of his favourite ports of call was the Cyder Cellars in Maiden Lane. This was frequented by wealthy older men and their often younger wives and girlfriends. It was the custom, especially as the liquor flowed, for men in the audience to be asked on stage to do a turn. They usually tried a song, but when Mace was first called, he strode up and borrowed a violin from a member of the house band. At once the Cellars hushed and he performed his own 'Cuckoo Song', the one he'd composed as a boy in the Norfolk woods. When he'd finished, applause broke out, and he launched into a medley of current hit songs. He was called on for an encore but, to the surprise of the audience, disappeared backstage, telling them he would soon return.

It was women Mace now had in mind. He returned to perform an act known as 'Grecian Statues', which he'd first developed with Bunny

Blythe's Circus. Grecian Statues was starting to become popular in the country circuses, but before his performance, had rarely been seen in the capital. It consisted of athletes, wearing little more than a loincloth, flexing their muscles and striking poses like ancient Greek warriors preparing for battle. At the close of his act came the unmistakable sound of female sighing, and later, as he returned from the dressing room in his evening suit, many a woman's eye was trained on him. To his dismay, all were accompanied and so he hurried on to the Old Haymarket.

On his future evenings out, Mace often headed there straight away. Although no one knew his name, all the thugs knew he was 'one of Langham's guards'. Even had they wished to attack him mob-handed, they knew better, for Langham would have sent in teams of his own bully-boys to exact a fearsome revenge.

At that time, dance halls were known as 'casinos', and Mace began to visit both of the main casinos in the West End: the Argyll Rooms in Windmill Street and the Holborn Casino. The Argyll Rooms had been closed by the magistrates in 1852, bowing to evangelical pressure, only to re-open the following year. The religionists detested dancing and regarded it as sinful in its own right, let alone what it 'would most certainly lead to'. Mace would cast a quick eye over the girls dancing with each other and dressed in fine ball gowns with long velvet gloves, lace necklaces and high-heeled bootees. He lost no time inviting them onto the dancefloor and delighted them with his own exceptional skill as a dancer. Immaculately dressed, well-mannered, charming and full of playful humour, he could have passed for a young aristocrat but for his Norfolk accent. Even so, this was far removed from Cockney talk and only emphasised the fact that he was 'different'. When asked about his occupation, he answered that he was a musician, omitting any mention of the outlawed Prize Ring. He never left either of the casinos without a pretty girl on his arm. It would not be long before they would arrive at one of the Oxford Street bordellos which, to supplement their earnings from prostitutes' rooms, would also be rented out to young couples.

The reason Mace could afford a year as a bodyguard and man about town was that Langham wanted to keep him out of the public eye, so that he could bet on him at long odds when his London Prize

Ring debut was announced. It was to be against Bill Thorpe, on 17 February 1857. The stakes were £50 and betting on the outcome was expected to be many times more. Thus, for three full months, Langham ordered Mace into strict training. The man he chose as Mace's trainer was Billy Clark. Clark was regarded as the toughest taskmaster in the business. A former prize-fighter, he had fought numerous battles as the 'Belfast Chicken', the 'chicken' metaphor indicating a fighter who had begun his career at an early age. Clark was barely fifteen when he first stepped through the ropes. Born in Ireland but brought to England as a child, he fought out of Manchester. He was a rugged battler and a veteran of countless mills, but had to give up his career early because of a succession of injuries to his hands. As a trainer he made it his business to devise what he considered the best method of protecting knuckles from the effects of striking opponents' heads.

Although Clark was only three years older than Mace, he looked a dozen years his senior and the two had little in common. Clark was a blunt, outspoken Lancastrian who mistrusted Mace and made negative remarks about his love for the latest fashions and his gambling. Clark was an authoritarian. To Mace, he was a sergeant major who, he suspected, despised him as a dandy and an upstart. But if there was no love lost, Clark was well aware of Mace's boxing skills and thus that his potential value to Langham was immense. Mace, for his part, recognised someone whose spartan training methods would give him an edge over his rivals.

Clark's regime was to wake Mace at dawn for a quick warm bath and light breakfast. The pair would then run five miles out and five miles back, with Mace clad in two sweaters and a balaclava. In due course the distance was increased until they jogged twenty miles a day. Clark monitored Mace's weight and, if it was not what the trainer considered right, thought nothing of ordering him to run uphill pushing a loaded cart. All meals were light and alcohol was forbidden.

Every evening, Clark made sure that Mace pickled his fists in a mixture of copperas (green vitriol), whisky and gunpowder. As a result of the hardening process, his hands turned pitch black. Clark even went so far as to smear some of this concoction over Mace's forehead, nose and cheeks to protect against dreaded facial cuts. 'He was very anxious to treat my face and ribs in like fashion,' said Mace, 'but against this one thing I protested successfully, for I was as vain as a girl of my torso. The result was that I presented a curious contrast when I at length entered the ring, my face and hands being well-nigh as black as a negro's, the whole skin of my body was in sheen and colour like to old ivory.'

From a monetary point of view, Mace needed no reminder of his obligations to his family. Already, on 4 March 1856, the child Mary had conceived before her husband's departure for London, was born: a daughter, named Adelaide after one of Mary's sisters. Like her brother Alfred, she was a healthy baby, more robust than her older brother James.

Mace entered the ring against Thorpe an intimidating sight, the vitriolic mixture applied to his face having hardened into a mask. It was not long before Thorpe had more to fear than Mace's appearance. Roared on by a rabid crowd on desolate Canvey Island in Essex, where the bout had been moved at the last minute, Mace outclassed his experienced opponent, thrashing him round all four corners of the ring before pole-axing him with a one-two to the brow and nose. Despite Thorpe's bravery, he was rendered helpless within half an hour. Mace was acknowledged as a 'coming man' and, with close to £3,000 successfully wagered on him at good odds, his aristocratic backers were delighted.

Just as Mace relied on Langham and his toffs for financial backing, so he depended on the sporting press to promote his reputation. The periodical *Bell's Life in London* had a virtual monopoly of sporting coverage in mid-Victorian England. While it dealt extensively with horseracing and, slightly less, with cricket and pedestrianism, the chief focus of its voluminous columns was the Prize Ring. *Bell's Life* had been built up, over a period of thirty years, by its respected and fair-minded editor, Vincent George Dowling, who also published the pugilistic annual *Fistiana*. After Dowling's death in 1852, his son Frank, a barrister-at-law, took over. A man of a different stripe, he had all the education his father had paid for but little of the old man's reputation for fairness.

Frank Dowling was puffed up with self-importance and his temper was as notorious as Langham's. Invariably clad in a black cloak, burgundy coat and trousers with blue stripes, he sported a wide-brimmed bowler hat and his mutton chop whiskers framed a haughty face with an eagle-eyed stare behind the monocle clinging to his craggy brow. It gave him a look of permanent disapproval over anything which did not live up to the high standards of pugilistic excellence which, he seemed to believe, he alone was capable of judging. The editor of *Bell's Life* was the one man who could publish LPR challenges and often acted as stakeholder for both fighters. Seeing that he was also either the referee or the person who chose the referee in all-important bouts, Dowling's power was enormous. In addition, he personally wrote a report on all mills involving novice fighters, and his verdict could make or break a young fighter.

Mace seemed to get off to a good start with Dowling. After watching him dispose of Thorpe, Dowling wrote, 'Mace is one of the best boxers (I) have seen for many a long day. He is a quick and rapid fighter and hits with judgment, precision and remarkable force . . . when he is in danger he has the ability to get out of it in clever style.' Dowling summed up by saying that 'it will require an opponent of first-class ability to beat him', but sowed a seed of doubt by preceding this with 'if his pluck (is) in any way equal to his other qualifications'.

Only a month after the Thorpe fight, tragic news from Norwich arrived. His first-born, James Mace Junior, had died after the sudden onset of meningitis on March 20, only ten days after his fifth birthday. Mary had been at his bedside throughout his brief illness at the family home in Bull Close Road. His death was both deeply distressing and a grim reminder of the high incidence of child mortality in mid-Victorian Britain. Mace returned to Norwich for the funeral and remained for some time before he was obliged to go back to London.

Mary told him that she wished, for obvious reasons, to leave Bull Close Road as soon as possible. Having seen how pugilists profitably combined their occupation with that of publican, Mace came up with the idea of putting his name down for a public house – and Mary readily agreed. With Jem away in London, she did the negotiations: she was also a better business person than her husband and he felt that it might help to take her mind off her loss. Shortly after his return to London, he was pleased to be told that she was pregnant again.

The next bout which Langham arranged was against Mike Madden, a fighter of Irish descent noted less for skill than for durability – he had won one of the longest fights on record. The stakes were £50 a side. Mace versus Madden, in October 1857, was notable only for the fact that it was called off at the last moment, followed by crowd disorder verging on a riot. Langham was considerably at fault in triggering this off. When Frank Dowling appointed Dan Dismore as the referee, Langham vehemently objected. Dismore was a rival publican with whom Langham had quarrelled. He believed Dismore was intent on poaching Mace from him – and, indeed, Dismore had been one of the first to befriend Jem on his arrival in London.

At this point another well-known referee, Captain Barclay, volunteered to take Dismore's place, to Langham's all too obvious satisfaction and to the fury of Madden's supporters. The flames were fuelled by ethnic tensions: Dismore was also of Irish descent and Madden's supporters were almost entirely Irish immigrants. From their point of view, the English toffs were violating their own treasured rulebook to put down the despised so-called 'Paddies'. Within moments, a score of fights broke out between the rival sets of supporters which were only stopped by a prompt announcement that Mace was to pay forfeit, that there would be a rematch within six months – plus a white lie that there was news of the police arriving. Both sets of supporters ran off as fast as they could.

There was at first only a bald statement in *Bell's Life* about a disagreement over the referee and an adjournment. In an adjudication the next day, the paper asserted that Mace had made his mark on the Articles of Agreement, that he knew that Langham had accepted Dismore and that he had refused to fight without good reason. There was a clear imputation of cowardice, and Mace was obliged to pay Madden forfeit.

In August 1857, Mace returned to Norwich. Mary had learned of a vacancy at the White Swan, in Swan Lane, and the brewery was delighted to have the most famous young man in Norwich as its tenant. The sporting public were soon crowding the place out and the profits came in very handy when, on 13 February 1858, Mary gave birth to another boy. It was common to call a child by the name of a deceased sibling, especially in the case of a first-born son who had been named after his father, so the child was also given the name James.

* * *

Under the accepted procedures of the LPR, no one knew for certain, until the scheduled day itself, the precise location of a fight. A rendezvous would be mutually agreed between the two fighters, their seconds and backers, at one of several London railway stations. A time was set to muster and, once assembled, the whole party, including spectators with pre-paid tickets, simply printed 'there and back', boarded their chartered train. It would take them well beyond London to a place the police would find difficult to reach. The two favourites were the Kent marshes and the Essex beaches. The field of battle would be a last-minute choice, depending on ground conditions and the co-operation of the few residents to be found in such remote areas. The entire operation had to start before dawn, to get a head start on the police, and the slightest delay increased the risks. Tension was high and tempers frayed easily.

If Mace was largely an innocent bystander in the aborted encounter with Madden, he was entirely to blame for what happened when they were next scheduled to meet. The date was set for May 10 1858, the rendezvous 6 a.m. at London Bridge Station.

The night before, Mace and Clark stayed at a pub on Holborn Hill. Clark went to his room early but Mace lingered at the bar, not to drink but because a barmaid had been giving him the eye. He lost no time in asking the full-breasted and tightly-bodiced girl when she was due to finish work, went to his bedroom and waited for her. So great was Jem's desire that he forgot to lock the door and, unfortunately, Clark returned, intent on giving him one last word of pugilistic advice. When he saw what was going on, he ordered the sobbing girl to get dressed and go back to her room before confronting Mace. It was an unwritten rule of the LPR that a man should refrain from sex, even with his wife, in the days before a fight. Clark told Mace what he thought of him and the young fighter lost his temper and struck Clark. The trainer, who knew he would come off worst, stormed out of the pub.

Mace returned to the bar but his erstwhile lover had remained in her room. For only the second time in his life, the first being a youthful binge at the age of sixteen, he got drunk, before staggering to his room. By the time he woke up, the hour for the pre-fight rendezvous had long since passed. In any case, he was in no condition to fight. He got out of the pub, where, fortunately for him, his identity was unknown, but, dismayed and hungover, resumed his drinking bout. After a long pub crawl, he disappeared and was found by friends later in the afternoon, sleeping it off at a cricket ground in south London. Clark absolved himself of blame by telling Langham first. Langham was a man of the world who, in other circumstances, might have laughed off the whole episode. He certainly was not going to drop his most profitable asset because of a youthful, if monumental, act of folly. After a ferocious bawling out, Mace was ordered back to Norwich until the hue and cry had died down.

Mace soon learned, though, that it would be impossible to return to Norwich. Frank Dowling, already hostile to him because of the initial aborted fight, jumped to the conclusion that once again he had been too scared to show up. Asserting that Mace had 'funked it' after hearing the stationmaster describing the death in the ring of Madden's previous opponent, Jack Jones, he described Mace in the columns of *Bell's Life* as 'the most unmitigated coward and imposter that ever laid claim to the title of a fighter' and sneered that there was 'no chance of Mace ever again appearing in the fistic arena'. In Norwich, news that Mace, the hero of the city, had behaved – according to *Bell's Life* – as an 'arrant cur' who had been 'trembling all over' and who had fled from the rendezvous like a 'stricken deer', had an explosive effect. Most people retained a naive gullibility about media exaggeration and falsehood. Many had lost large sums of money betting on Mace and it was not surprising that Dowling's words acted like a match to a barrel of gunpowder. A mob torched Mace's home and attempted to burn it to the ground. Prompt police action prevented the destruction of the White Swan but Mary and the three children had to seek refuge elsewhere. The memory of being driven out of a house of liquor and gambling, with flames blazing like the fires of hell, would haunt the memory of four-year-old Alfred.

At this stage, Mace had only a handful of friends left in his home county. Of these, the most stalwart was his cousin Pooley, now aged nineteen. Pooley, who knew all about the barmaid, told Mary that her husband was no coward but had got drunk after a quarrel with Clark over tactics. After the arson attack, takings at the White Swan fell dramatically and by the beginning of the next year the pub was closed. No one then could have ever imagined that, in future years, a plaque would be unveiled near the spot, proudly asserting that Jem Mace had been the landlord between 1858 and 1859.

4

Last Request of a Noble Lord

IN FUTURE YEARS, Jem Mace would refer to them as 'the blackest days of my life'. These were the weeks when he went to work on an all-day basis, rising at dawn and returning at sundown to his lonely London room. He had neither the cash nor the heart to escape from that room on his one day off, and could scarcely bear to pick up his beloved violin and coax notes from it. For the first time since his adolescence, he was without feminine company; and for the first time since he slammed the door of his parents' house behind him and strode out into the world on his own, he began to doubt himself, at least as far as his career in his chosen profession was concerned. He wept alone as he remembered the life he'd lived in the fairs and circuses of his native Norfolk – where Mary and the children remained. But Mace was never down for long, either in the ring or outside it. Artist and musician though he undoubtedly was, he was also a fighter and he resolved to wait out the time of his disgrace. 'I knew in my heart,' he later wrote, 'that I was no coward, as people were saying, but just a silly, hot-headed young man, who had gone and got drunk when he should have been attending to business, and now bitterly regretted his folly.'

Nat Langham imposed an indefinite ban on Mace, and he was barred from the Rum-pum-pas, where the best money was to be made from sparring, both with other aspiring professionals and the young Corinthians of the Fancy. Eventually he was allowed into another of Langham's establishments, in the same street, St Martin's Lane, but a world away from the toffs' sporting club. The Mitre, a working-class pub with a boxing saloon in the back. Here Jem would be lucky to receive a shilling for an hour in the ring. After paying for his keep he had no cash left – and no alternative – but to sit in his room at the Mitre and reflect, which was exactly what Langham intended.

Then out of the blue came a lucky break: to the surprise of

Langham, one of the toffs whom he usually saw at the Rum-pum-pas came to the Mitre. Viscount Drumlanrig was otherwise known as Archibald William Douglas, the Marquess of Queensberry. Not yet forty, he preferred to be known by the title he used before he succeeded his father as Marquess. The Douglas family, originally Scottish barons, had become one of the greatest aristocratic dynasties in the land. They were also afflicted by what some termed 'the Douglas curse' and were notorious for madness, sexual scandal and sudden and violent death.

Drumlanrig did not at first recognize Mace from the Rum-pum-pas, and asked him to enter the ring for a few timed rounds. Although athletic and an excellent boxer, he stood no chance against a professional over a dozen years younger than he was and, before long, his white shirt was spattered with blood. Even so, he impressed Mace with the fierceness of his body punching and by refusing to flinch when jabs found their mark. The aristocrat asked Mace his name, and then immediately remembered him – and that he was under a cloud.

Langham, watching, was taken aback when Drumlanrig asked why Mace had been 'banned'. He attempted a reply but Drumlanrig cut him short. Punishment, he remarked, was one thing; persecution another.

'Whom,' asked Drumlanrig, addressing Mace, 'would you like to fight?'

'Bob Brettle,' replied Mace.

Mace was a natural middleweight, and with Langham retired and Sayers installed as heavyweight champion, the new middleweight titleholder was Brettle, from Birmingham.

'Well,' said Drumlanrig, turning to Langham, 'match him against Brettle, or any other man his weight. You won't regret it, I promise you. If you don't care to do it for Mace's sake, do it for mine. It is the last favour I shall ever ask of you.'

Without further explanation of his last remark, he left.

A few days later, on 6 August 1858, Viscount Drumlanrig, the Marquess of Queensberry, went rabbit shooting with some of his aristocratic chums. He disappeared unnoticed and was found dead with his shotgun by his side. His demise was put down as accidental death but the whole sporting community knew he had killed himself.

Drumlanrig had built up vast debts gambling at cards, which was doubtless why he was frequenting the lowly Mitre and not his usual sporting clubs. His words to Langham had, indeed, been his last request.

Langham was in a quandary. He genuinely believed that Mace's punishment for the Madden fiasco should last longer but felt sure Drumlanrig would have mentioned to other members of the Fancy that Mace should be given an early chance to redeem himself. And he knew that it would not do for a man in his position to be seen as defying the Establishment.

From his earliest days in the ring, Langham had courted the aristocracy. With his first winnings from fights in his native Leicestershire, he had moved to Cambridge and opened a pub. When a couple of aristrocratic university students dropped in at The Ram, he seized his chance and offered boxing lessons. An intelligent and astute businessman, he was soon making big money. Not only that, but, when he later moved to London, he was recognised, as he fully intended, by the same men he had taught at Cambridge and who now formed the natural clientele of the Rum-pum-pas. So eager was Langham to be considered an honorary aristocrat that he styled his dark hair in waves just like them, and his high forehead and deep-set eyes accentuated the false impression that he was not a man of humble origin. All things considered, Langham felt bound to honour the last request of a noble lord.

There was, however, Frank Dowling to consider. Mace would have to challenge Brettle for the middleweight championship and the challenge had to be published in the columns of *Bell's Life*. Nat got round the problem by means of a crafty ruse: he took Brettle into his confidence, not a great risk because he was one of the steadiest and best liked men in the fight game. Accordingly, it was communicated to Dowling that 'an unknown from the provinces' had challenged Brettle and that his backer would be George Brown. Dowling believed Brown to be an independent agent but he was, in fact, a sidekick of Langham. Dowling fell for the ruse and published the details. The mill would be at £100 a side and would take place near the mouth of the River Medway, with trains departing from London on September 21.

On the day, Langham was nowhere to be seen, but when Dowling clapped eyes on Mace in the company of Brown his lip curled with disdain and he insulted him for the entire railway journey. His obvious intent was to rile and provoke the young man.

'Mace, do you really mean to say you have actually put in an appearance?' he sneered.

Mace was furious but knew that if he struck Dowling, his career really would be over. Dowling's words – that Mace would never fight again – would become self-fulfilling. He stared down Dowling and kept a lid on his temper by biting his lip so hard that it bled, while inside his head he repeated the mantra, 'You bastard! I'll show you today – I'm no coward, goddam you!'

Dowling's tactics continued at the chosen site for the mill, a spot near the mouth of the 'Little River', as the Medway, a tributary of the Thames, was known in the fight game. The tranquility of the scene, with its shield of oak and elm trees, was rudely shattered when Dowling pointed out Mace in theatrical style. The editor's language was far removed from his prose style when he turned to Brown and barked out in a stentorian voice, 'What, George, do you mean to say you've brought out that damn cur without a chain?' Predictably, there was a storm of booing from Brettle's supporters, while Mace's blood boiled at the ultimate insult of comparison to a mongrel dog.

What followed stunned Mace's supporters, none of whom knew what had happened on the train and few of whom had heard Dowling's insult. Expecting him to deal with Brettle in the careful, scientific way in which he had demolished Slack and Thorpe, they were open-mouthed as he lashed out at Brettle in two-fisted style. His temper, for what would be the first and last time in the ring, got the better of him. He held no grudge against Brettle but his suppressed rage simply erupted against his only permissible target. Soon the entire crowd was rocking as Mace made no attempt to spar for an opening. He launched into a fierce attack and drew first blood by splitting Brettle's ear. The experienced Brummie hit back hard, briefly dropping Mace to the turf, but he rose at once and smashed open Brettle's cheek with a fierce right. Rarely had the Fancy seen a scrap quite like this, with caution thrown to the wind and powerful blows traded at high speed. The heavy betting only encouraged the crowd to further fits of exhortation.

The bout ended as dramatically as it had begun: Brettle led with a left and hurled a right which landed on the point of Mace's chin. Mace went down as if he had been poleaxed and remained motionless on the turf for just over thirty seconds, despite his seconds' efforts to revive him, something which the LPR rules still permitted. Stunned as he was, it was notable that he had not lost consciousness. Mace at least had succeeded, in most people's eyes, in proving that he was no coward.

Frank Dowling would not relent. He cast suspicion on the fact that the fight lasted only a few minutes and he asserted, in print, that Mace could have carried on and should 'stick to teaching boxing and forsake the Prize Ring' – for which his 'lack of courage' made him unsuitable. Bob Brettle was appalled by this, even though it worked to his advantage. When they spoke out of earshot of their backers, he suggested to Mace that he might be best advised to make a new start outside London. Brettle offered to help by taking him to Birmingham, where he was kingpin. He was preparing for retirement in a couple of years and was already setting himself up as a matchmaker. Mace took him up on the offer without a moment's hesitation and went to live at Brettle's pub, The White Lion, in Digbeth.

The few months he spent in Birmingham, where he worked as a bouncer, were, in some ways, a relief. Though his earning capacity was still limited, he had the satisfaction of knowing that he was no longer dependent on Langham. In comparison to Langham, Brettle was a hero; in comparison to Dowling, he was a saint. True, Birmingham was at the time a rough city, but Mace was accustomed to the sight of poverty. He had lived in London's East End and knew the wretched conditions of the slums. He noted that, for every born and bred Brummie, there was at least one other person who had come to the city from Scotland, Ireland and, in particular, Wales to answer the demand for labour in the hardware factories. These people craved entertainment in their brief hours of leisure and there seemed to be little around to provide it. It was a thought he would keep in the back of his head for the time being.

In January 1859, Brettle matched him against Birmingham's Posh Price. The Black Country towns, and in particular Birmingham, were by now the cradle of pugilism in England, just as Bristol and, of course, London had once previously been. Many of the country's leading mid-century pugilists hailed from the area and Price, whose nickname 'Posh' signified that he was half gypsy, was hoping to join them. His clash with Mace was scheduled to take place on Aldershot Common, far to the south in Hampshire. This was partly because the environs of Birmingham were just outside the 100-mile limit, which was the accepted radius of the London Prize Ring. In addition, Midlands magistrates had become intensely hostile to pugilism. They had now a more valid reason than the old gripes about disrupting the working day and shocking the evangelicals. Birmingham and, even more so, Nottingham were notorious for criminal gangs who had fastened onto prize-fighting. This was due to high stakes betting on the outcome of fights. Not only were half-drunken fight enthusiasts a perfect target for pickpockets, as of old, but the Midlands gangs had taken to betting heavily on the outcome of fights. If it seemed that a fight was not going the way they had bet, they had been known to invade the ring and bring it to a halt. This was one of the reasons, as well as arranging benefits for veteran fighters, why the Pugilistic Benevolent Association had been formed: to provide a corps of ring-keepers to keep the hooligan elements out.

Mace, throughout his life, and even more so than most other prize-fighters, detested the underclass who infested the sport in the 1850s and 1860s. He had nothing but contempt for men who resorted to head-butting and kicking anyone who got in their way and whose favourite targets typically included well-spoken and even elderly men. The phrase he used to describe them was 'human vermin'.

Mace versus Price proved relatively free of crowd disorder. Now cool-headed again, Mace stalked Price and waited for the bigger man to lunge and miss – then he stepped in, as he had done against all his opponents before the Madden fiasco. His boxing skills, agility and tactics seemed even better than before and, using his left jab in characteristic style, he handed Price a merciless whipping. After a mere quarter of an hour, Price, brave though he was, could take no more and Mace walked away with the entire £50 purse.

His reputation, however, was not yet restored. Dowling would never again write that Mace was a no-show slacker, or even insinuate, as he'd done before the mob torched the White Swan, that its landlord had bet on himself to lose. But he dismissed Mace's victory over Price as being gained over an inferior opponent whom no one had any reason to fear. In his worst-ever verbal assault, Dowling described him as 'the most chicken hearted man ever to pull off a shirt'. Such character assassination reinforced a growing belief that Mace had taken a dive against Brettle. It was well-known in pugilistic circles that Mace was a compulsive gambler and rumours began to spread that he had taken money from some of Brettle's backers to pay off debts incurred at Newmarket racecourse. This was unfounded. It was true that Mace was guilty of sharp practice in his bets on fixed foot traces in the notoriously corrupt world of pedestrianism. It was not true that he took part in fixed fights – not out of any abstract sense of morality, but because his pride and ambition wouldn't allow it. Mace was obliged to conclude that basing himself in Birmingham could never be the answer to his problems with the Press.

He parted company with Brettle on good terms. As for the city itself, he had a feeling that he would return and, though he longed to live it up again in London, Birmingham would always have a place in his affections. His return to the capital meant a return to the East End and cheap lodgings in Shoreditch, but by now Mace had had more than enough of aspiring swells such as Langham and pseudo-toffs like Dowling. Yes, he owed much to the late Lord Drumlanrig, who was a gentleman as well as an aristocrat, but the fight game belonged to the urban working class, the immigrants and the ethnic minorities. It was dear to the hearts of all those who knew poverty from the cradle to the grave, and for whom discrimination was a fact of life: the Cockneys, Irish, Jews and expatriate black Americans. And after all, by virtue of his ring nickname if nothing else, were these not the folk to whom he himself belonged?

In the columns of *Bell's Life*, he was described for the first time in print as 'The Gypsy', and Dowling's 'arrant cur' comment, likening him to a mongrel dog, stank of racism. The East End signified solidarity in numbers for the underdogs of the world and its collective passion for boxing inspired those with the strength, the skill and, above all, the desire to hit back, to defy what feeble souls felt was inescapable fate and to do so in the only arena in which they could – the London Prize Ring.

5

Selina

SHOREDITCH WAS THE very heart of the East End. 'The Ditch' began at London Wall and sprawled over a square mile or so before funnelling out into Hoxton to the north. To the east it merged with Bethnal Green and, closer to the river, the great Jewish ghetto of Whitechapel; and, in dockland itself, Wapping, with Stepney beyond. The core of the Ditch was Brick Lane and Sclater Street, the latter being the terminus of the Eastern Counties Railway and a frequent rendezvous for prize-fight excursions.

Shoreditch market day, on Sundays, was held in Hare Street. Here the liveliness of the district was on display, a colossal relief from the daily grind for its unskilled labourers. The smell of roasting chestnuts mingled with that of winkles in vinegar. Pigeon races were staged and songbirds could be bought and sold – goldfinches, thrushes, starlings and larks. Street preachers came to thunder against 'the vices of this place' – thousands of deserted mothers left to support themselves and forced into prostitution. The preachers were largely ignored, as were their polar opposites, the hawkers of pornographic photographs.

Taprooms, as the pubs were locally called, were filled to the brim and the talk was often of prize-fighting. Where would the next mill take place? Down the river in the Kentish Marshes or on the Essex beaches? Maybe most men could afford to attend only once in their life, but they could hear all about it and see the paintings of the champions on the walls of their 'local'. Some would speculate from what street, if not in the Ditch then in Whitechapel or Stepney, the next prize-fighter might arise to challenge 'them Brummies' and make the East End working man once again the top of the pugilistic ladder.

Back in Shoreditch, Mace supported himself by pedestrianism, which was still a sport for professionals and hadn't yet mutated into track and field athletics. He had always been an excellent middle-distance runner and good sprinter. Pedestrianism might be a shady sport, replete with match-fixing and rigged betting, but it was relatively free of police disruption, and top peds such as Bill 'The Crow-catcher' Lang, Bob Fuller and Siah Albison could make money which, if not big in prize-fight terms, enabled them to make a good living. Although he was just short of top class, Mace could win enough cups to get by while his pugilistic career was on hold. What's more, he began to travel to the North of England for the first time, to watch pedestrian races. He observed how the Northern workers were better paid than their London counterparts and noted that pedestrian races were run on a Saturday afternoon, a key day of working-class freedom, as the passage of the Factory Acts had increasingly reduced the number of hours men had to work. He took part himself in the Sheffield Handicap, and his trainer, Alf Milner, claimed Mace had run the half mile in two minutes.

Jem had been bitterly frustrated by his inability to answer back to Dowling. The editor of *Bell's Life* lived by the pen, while Mace remained illiterate. He had based his earlier hopes for formal education on the belief that Mary could teach him, only to be staggered by the revelation of her own semi-literacy. Now, in his late twenties, his frustration – that he could not match his thoughts with written words – was deepened by the festering rage that he could not even attempt the briefest of letters to put his own case in print. He made up his mind to use his savings to take lessons in reading and writing. There was no shortage of people in the East End who supplemented their earnings by teaching illiterate adults. Many were foreign immigrants, notably from Prussia, which had enjoyed compulsory public education for half a century. A German baker called Brabach numbered several pugilists among his pupils. Mace, in later years, was very reluctant to speak about his early illiteracy, most likely because of lifelong feelings of bitterness against Dowling over the barbs he had to endure without a chance to reply. He never made it clear who taught him to read and write, whether it was Brabach or, more likely, Fred Abrahams.

Abrahams was Jewish, born in Whitechapel. He and his wife made a living from the stage but were frequently out of work due to the seasonal nature of their profession. He was fascinated by pugilism and got to know Mace, eventually becoming his business manager. In future years, Mace's penmanship was surprisingly clumsy for a man who had always liked to sketch pictures in rare idle moments. His formal letters would mostly be dictated but all who knew him agreed that the graphic language was his and his alone. In that sense, he would write as he spoke: with fluency and flair. His reading of *Bell's Life* would be laborious and he would sometimes become impatient and get one of the women in his life to speed-read it to him. But he would never again be at a loss to learn what exactly Dowling and other scribes were saying about him, nor be without means of countering their propaganda.

Little by little, he began to see that he had been too reliant on Langham for patronage. The Cambrian Stores might have become the most famous of sporting public houses but it was by no means the only one – the London Prize Ring centred around a chain of such establishments in the West End. While *Bell's Life* might publish challenges, it was in the pubs that the gauntlet was thrown down, that bets were laid and stakes collected. Here, the flow of conversation was the lifeblood of pugilism and recognised as such. The slang term used in the LPR world for a house run by a sporting publican was a 'drum'. It signified a tight cylinder safe from police interference and also a place where support for this or that prize-fighter could be passionately talked over, shouted out and, in general, 'drummed up'.

The chain of drums included Langham's Cambrian Stores, for sure, but stretched from Chelsea to The Strand. All the drums were run by former prize-fighters, those with sufficient intelligence, gift of the gab and business smarts to ensure their commercial success. The principal drums in the West End were Alex Reid's Lowndes Arms in the King's Road, Alex Keene's Three Tuns in Soho, Johnny Broome's The Rising Sun in Air Street, Piccadilly, Dan Dismore's place in Holborn, Watkins' in Villiers Street, Charing Cross, and the house of the brilliant ex-lightweight champion Owen Swift, in the Old Haymarket.

Mace made himself a regular in every one of these. He repaired his earlier disagreement with Dismore, for which Langham had been chiefly responsible, and became fast friends with most of the other landlords. Many resented Langham and were surprised to find how open, friendly and relaxed Jem was when he was away from his former mentor. The drums would indeed be the places where his reputation

– both as a fighter and a man – was built up. The drums were also frequented by men who would never quite make the grade as pugilists but who knew the fight game inside out. Many made a living as seconds. They kept in their man's corner, plied him with bottles of water to swig between rounds, pointed out weaknesses in an opponent which he might not see at close range, and offered loud vocal encouragement and moral and tactical support. Many were also amateur surgeons well able to lance a facial swelling or staunch blood. Among the most notable were Jack Macdonald, Jemmy Welsh, Johnny Broome, Bob Fuller the pedestrian, Jack Hicks and the half-Romany Bos Tyler. Mace went gambling at the races with Hicks but it was Tyler who would become his favourite second.

The East End had a rival chain of drums, poorer but bustling with life and passion for prize-fighting. These were not the sort of places where one of the swells was likely to be seen, but what they lacked in hefty individual stakes was compensated for by the sheer number of small contributions. The East End drums were popular with minority communities such as the Irish and the Jews; indeed green, the colour of Irish nationalism, was also that of the sashes East End fighters wore. Two of the leading East End drums were the house of ex-champion Jem Ward, the Black Diamond in Wapping, and Lipman's King of Prussia in Whitechapel. But the biggest of all was the Blue Anchor in Anchor Street, Bethnal Green.

The host at the Blue Anchor was 'Big Bill' Richardson, who had been born in the heart of old London, at Aldgate. He had worked as a navvy before becoming a prize-fighter and later a sporting publican. Close-cropped and grizzled, Richardson lacked the reflexes and agility to be a top pugilist but his aggression was legendary and his strength phenomenal. Had he been born later, he would certainly have become a champion weightlifter. He gave demonstrations in the bar parlour of his own pub and thought nothing of lifting two 112lb (51kg each) weights above his head in one hand and the same with the other, thus powering a total of 448lb (204kg). These totals would not be matched by Olympic weightlifters snatching bars until the very closing years of the 20th century. His prowess was so renowned that the phrase 'as strong as a bull or as old Bill Richardson' was well-known in London for half a century.

But Richardson was far from being a mere strongman. With minimal education, and dependent on his wife for book-keeping, he had by innate commercial savvy built the Anchor into the most thriving alehouse in the East End. Much of his business centred on pugilism, and his position in the East End was the equivalent of Langham's in the West. Although he loathed the criminal underclass, he had strong political views about the grinding poverty endured by the working class and would, in due course, became a pioneer of soup kitchens. Richardson had witnessed every single one of the mills for both the heavyweight and middleweight championships since he was a lad. His knowledge of prize-fighting was unequalled and his judgment respected even by such as Dowling, who kept well clear of him if he could. His command of language was extremely vivid and, in his later years, many young boxing reporters quoted him at length – with swear words omitted.

Right from Mace's LPR debut against Slack at Mildenhall, Richardson had stated that the Norfolk prodigy was the cleverest boxer and the fiercest hitter he'd seen in twenty years. But he believed that Mace had made a mistake in tying himself to Langham, whose perceived tendency to kiss up to toffs was anathema to Richardson. Although Richardson did not actively seek to succeed Brettle as Mace's backer-in-chief when he returned to London, it would be only a matter of time before Mace, who lived not far from the great drum of the Blue Anchor, would seek him out, and as the 1850s ended, their partnership was sealed.

By now, Mace's connections with Norfolk were virtually over. On 3 January 1860, his father, William, died suddenly at Beeston from a brain haemorrhage, at the age of fifty-six. Mace did not go to the funeral, for he resented the years his father had spent trying to bully him into becoming a blacksmith, thus sacrificing his chance of an education, and he had never been close to his mother.*

---

* There is no further trace of Ann Rudd Mace, who may have remarried or reverted to her maiden name. Her elder son, William (Billy) Mace, lived until he was nearly eighty and in due course reverted to his original surname of Rudd.

He also still felt an intense anger against the bullying he had suffered from his brother Billy, at a time when he'd been too small to stand up to him. Beefy Billy, by now married and thirty-six years old, had become the landlord of the Bell Inn at Beeston, a job for which he had qualifications of a sort since he had spent many an hour boozing behind its doors. Had Mace set eyes on his older brother, the urge to punish him would have been difficult to resist. In the circumstances, it was best to avoid a confrontation.

Had he made the journey to Norfolk, Mace would also have been able to visit Mary and the children in Norwich. But despite his affection for the youngsters, he was by no means eager for the company of his wife. They had seen little of each other for a couple of years and, though Mary still loved him, his feelings had cooled. His change of heart was linked to an affair, of which Mary was unaware, with a London girl he had been dating for several months and had developed strong feelings for.

The new girl in his life was seventeen-year-old Selina Hart. Born on 12 July 1842, at Back Church Lane, Whitechapel, she was eleven years younger than Jem and eight years Mary's junior. Selina was Jewish and lived with her widowed mother, Frances, at 7 James Place, in the household of her sister and brother-in-law, Julia and Simon Phillips (also Jewish). Selina made parasols in a nearby workshop. Mace often visited Whitechapel, probably in connection with learning reading, writing and arithmetic. Richardson had spoken of setting him up in a drum of his own, but one in which Richardson would have a controlling financial interest. While Jem had got away with illiteracy in the relatively tranquil White Swan, it would be different in a bustling East End pub where cash takings had to be perfectly reckoned and where labels on spirit bottles had to be read at a glance.

Mace was intrigued by Whitechapel. For all its poverty, it was one of the most cosmopolitan quarters in London. Jews were predominant but there were also many Irish, not to mention Germans, at that time economic migrants from an underdeveloped land. And there were gypsy tinkers and a tiny minority of blacks from the West Indies. Whitechapel teemed with life and the contrast with rural Norfolk could not have been greater. It was noted for its 'dancing saloons', where any rough band comprising fiddle, cornet and clarinet struck up the dashing strains of the polka in smoke-filled rooms with sanded floors lit by jets of gas. On Saturday nights, Cable Street was thronged with young revellers, as was Ratcliffe Highway. There was no shortage of prostitutes, notably outside the notorious music hall in Wellclose Square, but Mace shrugged his shoulders and walked on whenever he was approached. He had never needed to pay for sex and didn't intend to start now.

He met Selina at the Redowa, off Ratcliffe Highway, and, given his preference for lithe and dark women, was immediately taken by the petite, brown-eyed, olive-skinned girl clad in a moonlight satin dress. She was dancing with a girlfriend who was dressed in similar style but in white muslin trimmed with scarlet flowers. Both wore shiny fishnet stockings. Pausing long enough to discern that Selina was the more attractive, Jem noted with a smile that the pair had declined the approaches of two ruddy young Germans, probably from the local sugar bakery. He didn't hesitate. Politely asking the friend if she would kindly excuse him, he took Selina by the waist and she followed his dashing lead as they waltzed around the dance floor.

Selina was entranced from the start by the confident young man in his late twenties. She was impressed to learn that he was a musician, but supported himself primarily by foot races at pedestrian grounds. At first she took him as being a fellow Jew – more, as she later told him, on account of his suave manner and sobriety than his physical appearance.

Soon afterwards, he disclosed that he was in danger in Whitechapel because gamblers were prone to attack pedestrians against whom they had bet. He had seen for himself that, in the St George section in particular, knives and bludgeons were regularly wielded and that Leman Street police station was hard-pressed to contain the violence. Mace had not yet achieved instant recognition for who he was, but if someone was to spot him, he would be, as an up-and-coming pugilist, a choice target for a gang of roughs.

He began to take Selina to the West End. Their favourite club was Caldwell's in Dean Street, Soho. There, for eightpence admission, young men and women could enjoy four hours of dancing every night. Caldwell's had a better reputation than the Argyll or the Holborn Casino and even a select committee of the House of

Commons investigating public houses had failed to find any reason why it should be closed down – a failure that had greatly disappointed the evangelicals. After an evening at Caldwell's, they did what many young couples did who lived either with parents or in lodgings: rented a room for the night at one of the bordellos off Oxford Street and consummated their passion.

★ ★ ★

The first opponent Richardson and Mace selected, at the start of the new decade, was cleverly chosen. Bob Travers, real name Charlie Jones, was a twenty-three-year-old fugitive slave from Virginia, USA, known simply as 'The Black'. He was highly regarded in the middleweight division and had beaten Mike Madden. By the conventions of the LPR, if Mace beat Travers it would be the equivalent of him having beaten Madden in one of their two aborted bouts.

When Mace and Travers clashed on the Essex beaches in 1860, for £100 a side, the mill spanned two separate days. On February 20, Mace, ring rusty after a layoff of more than a year, got off to a bad start. Travers landed heavy punches and cut him badly, although the wound was staunched. After that they traded hard blows, but only twenty minutes into the fight, the police arrived and told everyone to clear off. They resumed the next day on desolate, windswept Canvey Island. Soon Travers began to tire, while Mace remained fresh and as elusive as ever. Travers was noted for his courage and stood up to fierce body punching for nearly an hour and a half. Mace mentally prepared himself to go on for longer but, after a total of 63 rounds over the two fights, Travers had had enough. He fell without being hit, the only way he could bring the fight to a close without suffering serious injury. Although he was thus obliged, by LPR rules, to pay Mace forfeit, Mace publically described Travers as 'perhaps the bravest man I ever fought'.

Two months later, a fight took place which would go down as the most momentous in the history of the Prize Ring. Tom Sayers, Champion of England, had been challenged by John C. Heenan, who claimed the American title after the retirement of the previous holder, John Morrissey. Their eagerly awaited and heavily publicised contest took place at Farnborough in Hampshire on 17 April 1860. Officially, only the English title was at stake, but by common consent it was the first-ever fight for the Heavyweight Championship of the World – or at least the three continents where pugilism was established: Europe (i.e. England and Ireland), North America and the British colonies in Australia.

Interest in pugilism in the US had surged immensely in the wake of the huge influx of Irish immigrants fleeing the Great Famine of 1845-9. Most of the top fighters were, like Morrissey and Heenan, Irish-Americans. Sayers, in Mace's eyes, was a source of admiration, not only for his skill and pluck but his sportsmanship and, above all, the way he had shown that a top-class middleweight could outfight most heavyweights in a division where anyone could compete, regardless of weight. Nevertheless, he had set his sights on a clash with Sayers in due course.

On the day of Heenan versus Sayers, Mace was among the 12,000 spectators who made their way to Farnborough. It seemed as if the old epic days of pugilism had been revived. Writers such as Charles Dickens and William Thackeray were at ringside, together with the Prime Minister, Lord Palmerston, various members of Parliament, a couple of lords of the realm and even an Anglican bishop. Heenan was a skilled mechanic from Troy in New York State who had been working as a panel beater in Benecia, California. 'The Benecia Boy', although no scientific boxer, was a splendid athlete and excellent wrestler who, at 6ft 2½in, towered over Sayers and tipped the scale at 195lb, almost fourteen stone. The English champion conceded no less than six inches in height, 40lb in weight and seven years in age to his American challenger.

After two hours, twenty minutes of fascinating and fluctuating struggle, during which Sayers' remorseless jabbing had virtually blinded Heenan in one eye, the great fight was cut short due, first, to the arrival of the police, and second, to the invasion of the ring by English hooligans who feared an imminent Heenan victory. The referee lost control, and in the confusion, the ropes were cut and the match had to be called a draw. As a result, neither Sayers nor Heenan, despite their heroic struggle, had the right to call himself World Champion.

Heenan versus Sayers transcended boxing. Relations between

Britain and the US had been deteriorating for some time due to intense commercial competition. Back home, the American press roused the public and rooted for Heenan, while doubting that he would ever get a fair shake out of the English. In Britain, too, the contest was seen as symbolic of the rivalry between the old imperial power and the dynamic trans-Atlantic republic. Even Queen Victoria had asked to be kept informed.

Nevertheless, Mace was not the only one to leave Farnborough in dismay. He was furious at the way in which the yobs, or 'roughs' and 'blackguards' as they were then called, had forced a classic fight to be abandoned because they feared they would lose their bet. Certain gangs of hooligans, especially the infamous Nottingham Lambs and others from Birmingham and London, were regular prize-fight attenders and bet large sums on the outcomes. They would often force contests to be abandoned if things weren't going their way. They also besieged the railway specials and robbed those on board. Mace foresaw that, epic as the Sayers–Heenan match had been, the manner of its ending would cause immense problems for the LPR. Its enemies would have a field day exploiting the disorders and be immensely boosted in their attempts to have prize-fighting stamped out.

At this time came a dramatic development in Mace's personal life: Selina told him she was pregnant and, hoping for marriage, was stunned to hear he had a wife and three children in Norwich. He would have gladly divorced Mary, if he could have done, to wed Selina but although divorce had – by the Matrimonial Causes Act passed only three years before – been opened up to all classes of society, Mary was an innocent party and Mace had no grounds on which to seek a legal termination of his marriage.

Selina's appeal went beyond sensual attraction. She seemed to Mace to be emotionally sweeter than Mary, she was certainly more adventurous and, despite her working-class background, was literate and more intelligent. Mary had settled into domesticity all too easily, as it seemed to her errant husband, and appeared stodgy in comparison with the vivacious Selina. Selina's spirits revived when he showed no inclination to dump her. As to his wretched wife (as Selina considered her), if the woman stayed in Norwich then Selina could be his mistress in London. Yes, her family would be shocked at them living openly together, but would probably change their attitude for the sake of the baby. If Mary found out, then, so Selina supposed, she could divorce her husband and leave him free to marry.

But Selina had not realised that the new legislation was weighted in favour of men. Adultery, by itself, was sufficient for a man to dispose of his wife, but was not enough for a woman to escape from her husband. A wife had to prove an additional offence, such as cruelty. As the year went on, the situation remained the same. Selina was so young and slight that she managed to hide the physical signs of her pregnancy from her mother and sister for some time. But eventually Jem was forced into a choice which he would have preferred to avoid.

Bill Richardson, who, at the time, knew nothing of Mace's liaison, told him that he would help to set him up in a drum of his own in Shoreditch. A vacancy had been noted at the pub formerly run by the champion at seven stone, Joe Hoyles. Richardson had good reasons of his own for doing this: Mace would be no rival because Richardson would have the major share in the property and because it would be too far from the Blue Anchor to be in direct competition. What Bill figured was that the lustre of Mace's name, as the most promising young fighter in the land, would attract great business to the pub – from which Richardson would benefit. But he did not want Mace to move in on his own. He was well aware of his carelessness with money and gambling. The best way to curb this was to remind him of his family responsibilities by installing his wife and children at the pub. What's more, Richardson had heard that Mary Mace had a better head for business. Her husband would therefore be the star attraction and she the business manager.

Jem was under pressure from not only Richardson but Mary herself. She'd had enough of being a pugilistic widow, stuck in Norwich, and was anxious to be reunited with her husband and to bring the children to London. She was smart enough to know that aspiring pugilists usually acquired their own London drum and expected Mace to be no different, especially as he had told her himself, in days gone by, that this was his ambition.

When the crunch came, Mace put his career before love. During an intense emotional encounter, he told Selina that, to his everlasting regret, their relationship must finish. Selina, still only eighteen, was heartbroken, but her family took a pragmatic view: a baby was due and it had to be supported. The Phillipses knew a lawyer, a man who bought kosher meat at Simon's butcher's shop. He told them that new legislation made provision to sustain an unmarried mother if the father of her child would not, or could not, stand by her. Unlike most people at the time, Phillips could afford to hire a lawyer, and a letter was sent to Mace threatening him with a paternity suit if he did not agree to provide for the unborn child. Mace put his cards on the table to Richardson, who decided to act fast. He had already lined up a re-match with Brettle for Brettle's middleweight title. The purse on offer would be £400 – a large slice of which would be at the mercy of Phillips' lawyer if, as was probable, he found out about it. But if the bout was delayed, the Phillipses, who still seemed to believe that Mace was a mere pedestrian, would settle for far less.

In August 1860, his daughter was born. Her birth was not registered which, especially in London and in cases of illegitimacy, was not uncommon at a time when there were no penalties for defying the law. The baby was named Frances, after her grandmother. A Deed of Settlement was prepared for signature, whereby Selina would accept the lump sum of £15, payable immediately, on condition that she waived her right to sue Mace for maintenance in the future. The Deed was signed and witnessed, on Mace's behalf, by Jack Hicks. As Richardson saw it, Mace had been bailed out in the nick of time – paying off Selina with a pittance a month before he stood to earn over twenty times that amount for one fight. Not only that but, with the news that Sayers had retired following the mill with Heenan, Richardson was convinced that Mace would be Champion of England in a matter of months, with all the potential to draw custom to the Shoreditch pub which that entailed. Under the code of the LPR, if Mace could defeat Brettle, the one man who had ever beaten him, then he would have a 'clean record' and thus be in an excellent position to challenge for the heavyweight title.

The whole episode showed Mace in a highly unfavourable light. An oblivious Mary had been two-timed; Selina, a young and emotionally vulnerable woman, had been betrayed, and her child would have to exist on far less than could reasonably have been expected if Mace's true earning potential had been known to her. In his own mind, however, he sought to convince himself that he'd had no other choice than to break with Selina. He had not wanted to, and his feelings for her remained strong, but he knew that he would never see her again – and never set eyes on his daughter. His resentment turned against Mary, and when she later rejoined him, it soon became clear that they were a couple in name only.

Like Mace's previous battle with Travers, his second bout with Brettle was fought over two successive days. This was as a result of police disruption, which had revived in intensity after Heenan–Sayers. On September 19, the pair were halted at Wallingford in Oxfordshire after only a dozen minutes and ordered to clear off. Once again the Essex beaches, although wide open to sandstorms, even in autumn, seemed the safest spot to avoid the constabulary. On Foulness Island battle resumed, but to the widespread astonishment of most onlookers, Mace swept aside the title-holder in a mere seven minutes. While it superficially resembled their first clash in that Mace attacked from the start, catching Brettle off guard, the difference this time was Mace's cold ferocity rather than the wild temper which had sprung from Dowling's insults. He had nothing against Brettle personally; indeed he liked Bob, who had gone out of his way to help him in time of need. But, like all fighters, he had to shut out sentiment.

No one could recall such speed of hand as Mace rained in blows from every angle. It seemed to Richardson that he was stepping far beyond the bounds of conventional pugilism. Those who watched his feet, as well as his hands, saw moves of astonishing grace and fluidity. His 'pretty dancing', as Mace himself called it, was the foundation for his devastating punching on that day. Brettle, an experienced and crafty boxer, was unable to prevent Mace from cutting off the ring and manoeuvring him against the ropes. Finally, he measured Brettle with a left jab and sent over a beautifully timed right hand which had every ounce of his weight behind it. It exploded on Brettle's jaw and sent the Birmingham warrior down in a crumpled heap. He lay unconscious for almost a minute, the victim of a true knockout.

Mace had the satisfaction of watching Frank Dowling take down notes at high speed. While he said nothing at the time, he had already revised his opinion of Mace as a fighter and would pen a report to that effect. As Mace thought over the course of the fight the following day, he recalled the precise point of impact of his fist against Brettle's jaw and fully noted the destructive impact it had had. Most of this was lost on the small crowd but what they all knew was that, almost two years to the day from the debacle at Medway Island, Mace had wiped the slate clean.

Shortly after taking the middleweight crown, Jem went into a photographic studio for a full-length portrait, stripped to the waist and clad in prize-fighting breeches, stockings and leather boots. It captured him at a key moment, as he stood on the cusp of fistic greatness. Aged twenty-nine, he looks about five years younger, with a full head of dark, wavy hair, long on top but trimmed short behind the ears. His skin is pale and his complexion gives no hint of Romany origin. His full lips are firmly set and he has a strong, almost bulldog, jaw. The expression in his eyes is cold, hard, proud and uncompromising.

From a pugilistic point of view, the most striking thing is his guard, which is held in a relaxed way, his leading left fist at waist level, right carried just below the line of the chest. The contrast between this portrait and drawings of prize-fighters from the pre-photographic age – who were usually depicted with both fists held head-high – is unmistakeable and emphasises that while stand-up wrestling was at the heart of their game, for Mace it was only an accessory. He was a good wrestler, to be sure, but he aimed for destruction with his fists, using throws only in an emergency or as a surprise manoeuvre.

Mace was only the second pugilist to enter the photographic studio, the first being Tom Sayers, Champion of England. Here, for the first time, were working-class men caught not as nameless faces in the crowd but as heroic individuals in their own right. There was no specific belt awarded to the holders of the middleweight championship but Mace's associates wished to acknowledge that the new titleholder was, in their view, a fighter of rare and exceptional talent and a remarkable man, and they subscribed a special belt to be awarded in his honour. The inscription on it read, 'Presented to James Mace. In the year 1860 by his backers and friends as a small token of respect. For his manly and straightforward conduct in and out of the ring.' Had Selina's family been aware of this ceremony, those words would doubtless have rung hollow: his adventures with his lover had been marked by deviousness from first to last. What the devotees of the LPR meant by manliness and straightforwardness was, of course, something quite different. Mace's masculinity was signified, inside the ring, by his bravery and the unprecedented power of his punching. Outside the ring he earned the accolade by conviviality and comradeship, such as he had fully demonstrated in the sporting drums of London.

Word spread quick in the East End, among pugilism's vast constituency of working men, that there was soon to be a new tenant at a taproom in Holywell Lane, just west of Sclater Street Station in Shoreditch. On 13 December 1860, Jem Mace took over at the Old King John.

6

The Ringmaster

HE TOO HAD been born in Norfolk – at Ber Street, Norwich, to be exact. He had also fallen in love with travelling fairs when he first saw them as a lad. He, just as much, was a man of exceptional athleticism and agility, and equally he was a lover of horses, able to win their affection and master them. There the resemblance ended. If people sometimes asked questions about Jem Mace's ethnicity, that of William Darby was in no doubt. His father came from a British colony in the New World and was of African descent. It's not clear whether John Darby was a house slave on an American or a West Indian plantation, but he finished his days as a butler in the household of a rich Norfolk family. There he met William's mother, Mary Stamps. Thus young William knew the world of the wealthy in his early childhood, the world of silver salvers and wine cellars, quite different from the humble cottage where Mace was brought up and the spit-and-sawdust alehouses which his brother frequented.

But sawdust would figure largely in William Darby's life. Orphaned in his teens, he began in the circus with William Batty and became a notable acrobat in Batty's troupe. Three years before Mace was born, he was the star of the show at the Norwich Parthenon, where he appeared on playbills as 'Young Darby'. As time passed, he added equestrianism to his skills, then became a tightrope walker. By the mid-1830s, and after a series of sensational performances at the Royal Amphitheatre in Liverpool, his horsemanship was acclaimed when he was described as 'the loftiest jumper in England'. It would be only a matter of time before he would want his own show. Indeed, it was probably only the absence of black entrepreneurs, and the misplaced but understandable concern that he might be accepted only as a performer, not a businessman, that made him wait so long. In 1841, aged forty-five, he set up his own circus and boldly called it the Circus

Royal. At the same time, he gave himself the moniker by which he is known in circus history, the Hispanic-sounding Pablo Fanque. Six years later, Fanque made his London debut. Significantly, it was at Astley's Amphitheatre, where the eccentric English cavalryman Philip Astley had founded the modern circus in 1767. The *Illustrated London News* paid a lavish tribute to Fanque's immense skill as a horse rider, which he fully demonstrated with his superb black mare, Beda. This praise was his effective coronation as the king of the sawdust ring and, for a dozen years and more, his reign continued.

Fanque realised that the North of England had now become the country's most fruitful hunting ground for the new entertainment industry which he led. The highest wages in the land were those paid, as a result of the Industrial Revolution, to the people who worked in the North – the textile workers of Lancashire and Yorkshire in particular. These people craved entertainment and had it served up to them by the bucketload through Fanque's circus. Summer and winter, except only in the harshest snowed-under weeks around the turn of the year, his wagons would arrive in every one of the cotton and woollen mill towns, where customers came in droves to sit under the big top. He made Manchester his base but toured every sizeable town and city between Liverpool to the west and Hull in the east.*

By 1861, Fanque was in dire need of a boost. His position was under threat from other circuses, notably Ginnett's in England, Howe and Cushing's, who operated in England and America, and Charles Hengler, who was based in England and toured France, Prussia and Russia. Successful as Fanque remained, he realised that he relied unduly on clowns and equestrians. In the winter of 1861, sitting in his plush office in chilly Stockport and clad in tweed suit and overcoat, he mulled over his invitation to Mace to tour with the Circus Royal. Luring Mace from the Prize Ring, albeit temporarily, would take a lot

---

* One of the Circus Royal's playbills from Rochdale survived into the twentieth century and was picked up by John Lennon at an antique shop. His imagination fired, he wrote the whimsical song 'Being for the Benefit of Mr. Kite' (which referenced the name of Pablo Fanque) and it featured on the Beatles' landmark Sgt Pepper album. Thus Fanque, one of the key figures in the history of the circus, would be acknowledged by Lennon, one of the key figures in the development of rock.

of money. However, Fanque had followed the career of his fellow townsman with keen interest and was well aware of Mace's love of circus life and his earlier touring with Bunny Blythe. He also knew that he was an accomplished violinist and did Grecian Statues routines. But the biggest draw that Mace could provide would, of course, be his boxing skill, which he could demonstrate indoors, with gloves and without fear of police interference. All that would be needed was a sparring partner – and it so happened that Fanque knew Mace's cousin, Leopoldius 'Pooley' Mace.

Pooley's parents, Barnabas and Lurena, were a prolific and imaginative couple. Of their eleven other children, only two, Walter and Herbert, were conventionally named. The others boasted such exotic monikers as Leonora, Madonna, Zeblira and Robina among the girls and Augustus, Tiras, Bosevannah, Trafalgar and Montrossor among the lads. Lurena reinvented herself as 'Lavinia' once the family eventually moved from the caravan trail to the Norwich suburbs, and their unconventionality ran deep. Tirey became an itinerant musician, while Gus set himself up as a photographer, a novel occupation at the time.

But the only offspring who would take his place in sporting history was the eldest, Leopoldius. As the new decade began, Pooley turned twenty-one. He enjoyed his jobs in Norfolk, where he alternated between horse-breaking and being a circus hand. Pooley was 6ft, broad-shouldered and powerful, and hoped to make a name for himself in his home county as a prize-fighter, and in due course he did so, making a successful debut near Kings Lynn in September 1862. Swarthy and swaggering, he was used to having his way with local girls and didn't intend to marry before he was thirty. He longed for the excitement of London and was soon given the chance, for Mace needed a right-hand man. Principally this was because he wished to bring about a pugilistic innovation – namely, to have a regular sparring partner, something unusual at the time. Pooley was suited to the role. Although he lacked his cousin's skill and killer instinct, he was a good fighter in his own right. He knew Mace's style inside out, so by boxing with Pooley, Jem became more accustomed to aiming his punches accurately at taller men. Pooley joined the training team – Billy Clark would soon depart for America, where he continued in the fight game for the rest of his long life, and John Miller, an erstwhile pedestrian who had been in Mace's corner when he fought Slasher Slack, took Clark's place.

Mace found training with Pooley far more fun. The pair would jog side by side, day after day and mile after mile, cracking jokes about their Norfolk youth as they sped on. Pooley introduced a skipping rope to their training sessions. He was a wizard with the rope and with it Mace increased his already considerable agility. Pooley could also stand as Mace's umpire, a role frequently necessary in the days when referees kept out of the ring and breaches of the rules, especially during wrestling, were not as easy to spot as in modern boxing. As dedicated as Pooley was in all matters related to the fight game, he was a different man away from the training ground. Like his cousin, he enjoyed horse race meetings, gambling and wenching.

Pooley's laid-back temperament contrasted with Mace's more fiery nature and he was something of a jester and prankster, an easy-going man of the world whose quips did much to defuse the tension which surrounded the approach of a title fight, exacerbated always by the need to 'dodge the coppers'. He became Mace's closest friend, a soulmate, someone whose devotion to his twenty-nine-year-old cousin was absolute. The presence of the dark-skinned, black-moustached Pooley at ringside led to the misconception that the two were brothers and further cemented the myth of Jem's gypsy origins.

As Pooley arrived on the London scene, so Mary and the three children were installed at the Old King John. Mary needed no persuasion. She was eager to move to London, not only to be with her husband but to live in the great city. In this metropolis Mace would, she hoped, become one of many famous men and not the centre of attention he'd been in Norwich. What's more, Alfred, Adelaide and young James would receive a better education. Although schooling was not yet compulsory, the capital had many schools, run by the Church. Mace decided that his three youngsters would not go to a nonconformist school but an Anglican one. Alfred, at six, was already old enough to start.

As the new host at the Old King John, he showed the same style he'd demonstrated at the White Swan and which would be his hallmark. The tap room was rough and ready, as was any other in

Shoreditch, but trouble was almost unknown – after all, the middle-weight champion of England was the landlord. But it went beyond that, for Mace had the charisma, confidence and humour to stop any aggression in its tracks. He continued to enjoy a couple of drinks, but limited his intake, and was never drunk. In all-male company in the small, crowded bar, Mace cursed heartily but his command of the English language was fluent and imaginative and he never resorted to mindless, repetitive swearing.

What made him years ahead of his time was his willingness to welcome accompanied women into the tiny upstairs lounge. Initially this came as something of a surprise to both sexes but Mace, as well as having a passionate desire for young and attractive women, had a genuine affection for and empathy with all good-natured members of what bourgeois Victorian males dubbed 'the fair sex'. Throughout his life he loathed the use of foul language or crude sexual innuendo in front of women. If any man broke this unwritten rule at the Old King John he would be ejected by the boss himself, an experience unlikely to be forgotten in a hurry. Mace's strictness in these matters contrasted with his carelessness at the till. Though he had a good head for the big picture in matters of business, the routine of totting up and book-keeping bored him. His barmen were, of course, quick to notice this and one or two of them pocketed part of the plentiful takings for themselves.

* * *

Early in 1861, Mace was the central figure in a remarkable scene at Bloomsbury Street. The manager of a book shop had been ejected by four officers of the Society for the Suppression of Vice, who condemned his books as heretical. They seized the premises, preventing further sale. The manager appealed to Mace for help and he led a group of prize-fighters to the shop. When the manager was refused entry to his own shop, they threw out three of the officers. The fourth was armed with a cutlass and threatened Mace with it. Mace pointed to his own chest and quietly said, 'Just strike here.' Then he stood and stared. The man lost his nerve. Mace disarmed him and led him out of the shop, which was thus restored to its rightful occupant.

The incident encapsulated Mace's audacity, cold nerve and sheer force of personality. The Society for the Suppression of Vice were doubtless the kind of people who condemned the Prize Ring and eventually helped to stamp it out.

In January 1861, Bill Richardson arranged a week-long benefit for the Coventry weavers, who were in great distress due to an economic downturn. The Pugilistic Benevolent Association, of which he was the chief ring-keeper, mustered most of its finest talents at Westminster Baths. The Baths were sold out nightly for exhibitions of sparring, where the wearing of skintight gloves meant the police had no grounds to interfere, even if they had dared to disrupt an event where pugilistic services were freely given and where the proceeds went to charity. Tom Sayers topped the bill, while Mace, as middleweight champion, came second. He eagerly sought out Sayers and, although it was hardly the time and place to issue a challenge, made his intentions known after they shook hands. His admiration for the 'Little Wonder' from Brighton was entirely genuine. The previous year he had been among the first to buy a memorial bust of England's national hero, sold in bulk in honour of his performance against Heenan at Farnborough. Its true purpose was to provide Sayers with an annuity for the rest of his life, something his backers felt he was entitled to, but on condition that he never risked injury by fighting again. If the public was surprised to hear of his retirement, Mace was dismayed. For all his high regard for Sayers, Mace believed he could defeat him. Brave, hard-hitting and crafty though Sayers was, Mace was convinced that his superior boxing skill and ring generalship would prevail – and he was five years younger. He also believed that he could talk Sayers out of retirement and persuade him to return to the Prize Ring one last time.

Sayers' successor as champion was the bulky but ponderous Sam Hurst, whose skill was minimal but whose hitting power had seen off his rival for the vacant throne, Tom Paddock, cracking two of Paddock's ribs in the process. The Fancy, however, had stayed away. Hurst represented a return to the crude levels of the 1840s and 1850s, whereas Sayers was numbered among the legendary champions of yesteryear. Mace had already signed articles to meet Hurst but, though he craved the championship, he would have far preferred to win it from Sayers himself rather than by default. Mace put all these points to

Sayers and assured him that his backers would put up enough money to provide a huge purse. Sayers listened but deferred the issue by telling Mace that he must first defeat Hurst. Then he added, without committing himself, that he 'would see about it'. Within a week, a letter arrived at the Old King John, signed by Pablo Fanque, that would open a new chapter in his life. Fanque offered Mace a guaranteed salary of no less than £70 a week for a six-week tour. He jumped at the chance and took Pooley with him as his sparring partner.

The match between Mace and Hurst was not due for eight months. Hurst was recovering from a broken ankle suffered when he slipped on some ice-covered steps, and he was perfectly amenable to a delay. Sam Hurst was, in fact, a very poor boxer who would never have got anywhere in prize-fighting but for the fact that it still included stand-up wrestling. An excellent wrestler, he had previously been Champion of Lancashire, a county where wrestling was more popular than any other. For this reason, Hurst couldn't be taken lightly. A colossus, he stood 6ft 2in tall and weighed seventeen stone. But Sam was of low intelligence and regularly the target of practical jokes. His nickname, 'The Stalybridge Infant', bore this out. Nevertheless, a throw from the gargantuan Cheshireman carried the danger of a fractured skull.

Mace had to leave the Old King John to fulfil his engagement with Fanque, and with a fight looming, the last thing he wanted was to get out of condition standing behind the beer pumps. The pub had to be left in good hands as the takings often exceeded £100 a night – the nineteen-year-old Cockney barman, Tommy Hutton, would take care of the till and act as bouncer, but the real manager of the Shoreditch pub, while her husband was away, would be Mary, who was organised, numerate and kept a strict eye on the till. Already Jem's favourite sister, Amelia, now twenty-one, was in residence and gave invaluable assistance in improving the Old King John's appearance. A cousin of Jem's, Matilda Mace, aged twenty, was also staying, as was Mary's younger sister, Martha Barton, who was sixteen.

The workload was too great for all of Mary's children to be looked after in the Holywell Lane alehouse. Alfred was away at school for much of the day but four-year-old Adelaide was cared for by another of Jem's sisters, Anne, who lived with her bricklayer husband Charlie Perry in the High Street in Acton, then on the western fringe of London. As for three-year-old James, arrangements were made for him to be minded by Emma Smithdale, one of a married couple of woollen workers from Norwich who were friends of the Maces. They had moved as a result of the decline of the East Anglian wool trade and lived at St David's Cottages in Lewisham.

Mace would be the star turn of the Circus Royal and he and Pooley would be safe from police interference, not only because gloves would be worn but because these would be time-limited exhibitions with little risk of bloodshed. Many men in the crowds that flocked to see him had, at least once, travelled to stand up at a bare-knuckle fight, but could now view the action seated in comfort in their home town. The women were even more fascinated. No self-respecting female could ever be seen in the vicinity of a prize-fight, but now they could watch this most masculine of activities in comfort, in numbers and unharassed. Both Jem and Pooley won many admirers.

The six-week tour suited Mace down to the ground. First, the money was beyond his wildest dreams. Even when fighting Brettle for the middleweight title, he had won only £300 and was risking, as in any prize fight, serious injury. Now he would earn almost half as much again for a mild exchange of pulled punches. Secondly, he would enter the sawdust ring and demonstrate that, in his eyes, pure boxing was a skill, almost an art and not the 'sheer brutality' of the 'ruffians of the ring', as the anti-prize-fight lobby insisted. Finally, the razzmatazz and tinsel of circus life appealed to him greatly, as did the constant travelling.

While touring with Fanque, Mace passed through Hurst's home town of Stalybridge in Cheshire. Large crowds of Northerners assembled to see the middleweight who had the nerve – as they saw it – to challenge 'Big Sam'. Betting was already running in favour of Hurst, and Mace deliberately put on an inept show against his taller cousin so that the odds against him would lengthen further. To his delight, they duly did and it was at that time that he placed a substantial bet on himself to win. Once the circus tour was over, the cousins returned to Norfolk and went into strict training near the big red barn at Swaffham where Jem, as a boy, first watched men settle disputes with bare knuckles. As the date of the clash drew nearer and the odds on Hurst shortened, a few made clear their dissent from the majority opinion: predictably, Richardson, since he was Mace's chief backer and, in any case, had championed his skills from the first day he saw him fight, but now Frank Dowling too, of all people. Dowling had been stunned by Mace's performances against Travers and in the return with Brettle. He publicly rescinded his criticism of Mace's courage and stated that his only reservation was whether the fight would be allowed to come off.

So intense was the hostility of the law enforcement authorities, in the wake of the virtual riot at Farnborough, that it was believed that the police might make pre-emptive arrests. However, even though the toffs were now reluctant to risk their personal safety, the aristocratic Press still wrote in favour of bare-knuckling. In an influential piece, the *Saturday Review* praised what it called 'the manly, true British bulldog spirit' exemplified by the prize-ring and which was, it averred, the foundation of the British Empire. In a subtler piece of argument, the paper took to task the constant comments of the anti-pugilism lobby that fights should be banned partly because of the danger of serious injury, but even more so because spectators were voyeurs, revelling in the prospect of witnessing such happenings at ringside. The publication contrasted the LPR with tightrope walking – which had become all the rage. The leading tightrope walker was former trapeze artist Jean Francois Grave, whose stage name was Blondin. Two years earlier, he had succeeded in crossing Niagara Falls on a tightrope bridge suspended 100 feet above the rapids. Now the Frenchman was in London, drawing sell-out crowds to Crystal Palace to watch him walk the high wire blindfold and pushing another man in a wheelbarrow. He scorned safety nets and his astounding balance and sheer nerve were unparalleled, but some of his imitators had fallen to their deaths. As the *Saturday Review* argued, there were doubtless, among those flocking to Crystal Palace, some who did so in the hope of gloating over his bloody demise. In short, Blondin's chosen profession was more dangerous than Mace's and attracted more depraved voyeurs, yet no one was saying it should be banned.

Some thought the article might help to restrain the magistrates and police, but those who organised the Hurst–Mace mill for the title were taking no chances. The plans of battle were drawn up by Richardson and Mace with almost military precision. Harry Brunton, the sporting publican who backed Hurst, was made fully aware of them. Mace's intelligence and organising ability stood out like a beacon in the arrangements for the fight, in which he played a dominant role, for he was determined that there would be no repetition of the gross violence which had tainted the Heenan–Sayers encounter the year before. He took a number of measures against hooligans. First, he doubled the number of ring-keepers, most of whom were fighters and whose job was to guard the outer ring, itself made double the usual strength by means of interlaced cord and stout supporting stakes. Second, other former bareknuckle battlers were deputed to watch out for roughs in London and stop them getting on the railway specials, tearing up their tickets if necessary. As for the tickets themselves, he made sure that they were only printed vouchers with no information of which railway station to assemble at or the time of rendezvous. The genuine members of the Fancy knew only that they had to go to selected sporting pubs, whence they would be driven to Fenchurch Street station at daybreak. Finally, Mace employed various cronies to spread false rumours that Paddington would be the place of departure, not Fenchurch Street. Using these tactics, he succeeded both in keeping out the roughs and outwitting the police. Ironically, Paddington saw a pitched battle between coppers and criminals while Mace, Hurst, their entourage and the respectable spectators set off in peace and quiet by chartered train from Fenchurch Street at dawn.

Mace, Richardson and the small group who helped them put these plans into practice had a further trick up their sleeves. As they arrived at Southend, the general assumption was that the fight would take place in Essex; in fact, a flotilla of steam tugs had been chartered which would take them across the Thames to land on the Kentish side. Here everyone disembarked on an island, curtained off by tall reeds, in the mouth of the Medway. There wasn't a soul in sight as they pitched the ring on a perfect summer morning. It was 9am on 18 June 1861, at Medway Island, when Mace, the challenger, and Sam Hurst, the champion, contested the heavyweight title of England.

Despite the hour, the sky was cloudless and the sun strong. The two fighters presented an almost amusing contrast as they came up to the

mark. Mace was as lean and fit as a trained greyhound but the giant
Hurst, who towered over him and outweighed him by 75lb, presented
an awesome sight.

> I can see him now as he stood there, the sunlight gleaming on
> his great muscles that bulged from his swarthy skin like bosses
> of beaten bronze. His broad, deep chest was covered with thick,
> matted hair, so that it more nearly resembled that of a gorilla
> than aught that was human. There was, however, nothing else
> apelike about him, his carriage and figure being, so far as
> proportion went, models fit for a sculptor. His immense arms,
> brown and sinewy, were gnarled like the branches of an oak
> tree, and his fists, black with prolonged pickling, were as big as
> cannon-balls and as rough and hard as two lumps of slag from
> a furnace.

Mace later admitted to misgivings as he eyed his fearsome
opponent, yet at the same time was 'all agog to be at him', his nerves
stretched to the edge of hysteria. He knew full well that his opponent
would be mighty dangerous in the opening minutes. At all costs he had
to stop the gigantic wrestler from grappling with him, for he ran the
risk of serious injury, not only from a throw itself but from the fact that
Hurst was entitled, under the rules of the LPR, to hurl his full weight
on top of his falling foe. Mace had already told his seconds, Bos Tyler
and George Woodey, to smear oil on his entire upper body so that
Hurst's hands would lose their grip.

From the beginning, Jem danced out of reach as Hurst rushed him.
In the second round, due more to clumsiness than intent, one of
Hurst's spiked, outsize boots came down hard on Mace's foot. For
minutes the pain was intense but he managed to keep out of the way.
As Hurst continued with his bull-like rushes and wild swings, Mace
jabbed him relentlessly in the face. In the fourth round, Hurst's body
became a swollen mass of bruises as hammer blows struck home time
and again. Hurst was both brave and enraged but his sole tactic was to
keep rushing in. Each time he did, Mace calmly stepped aside and
clouted his eyes, and by the end of the sixth round, Hurst was nearly
blind and the blood was streaming down his face. He began to stagger,
and the spectators, all of them hardened to bloodshed, shouted, 'For
God's sake, stop it!' But the referee had no such power and Hurst's

seconds, Jerry Noon and Jem Hodgkiss, hesitated to throw in the sponge. Hurst himself growled that he wouldn't give up. Befuddled and desperate, he still believed he could succeed in seizing Mace and dashing him to the ground. Suddenly, Mace himself moved into close range and there was a collective gasp from the crowd as he somehow shifted his weight and dumped his gigantic opponent on the turf. It destroyed Hurst psychologically. At last, he had come to grips with the maddening will of the wisp who had tormented him – only to be humiliated at his own game.

As Hurst staggered to his corner, Noon and Hodgkiss told him in no uncertain terms to give up. Bob Brettle went into the ring and pleaded with the 'Infant' to stop at once. But Hurst, defiant as ever, merely muttered 'No!' and pushed him away. In the next round, Mace, certain of victory, altered his tactics to finish matters off. He sped in and blasted Hurst in the face with left and right hands so ferocious that Hurst's blood streamed down Mace's own chest and even spattered his face like crimson tattoos. By the eighth, Jem was in a quandary. He had no wish to permanently injure his brave foe, but by the rules of the LPR the bout could not be stopped while Hurst remained willing to continue. Deaf to the entreaties of his seconds and Brettle, he was staggering about the ring, trying to locate his opponent.

> I did not know what to do, for the poor fellow was now quite blind and kept tottering aimlessly around the ring. 'Look where he's going to, Jerry!' I called out to Jerry Noon, who was helping to second him. The giant heard my voice, and made a rush in the direction whence he supposed it to come from, his huge arms whirling like flails, his sightless and battered face working convulsively.

Having cunningly lured his opponent in, he now fired a left jab like a piston rod between the on-rushing Hurst's eyes. Mace felt sure he had given him the coup de grace. Hurst sank to the turf. But for all his pitiful lack of skill, his courage was as great as his strength, and he rose within a few seconds. Mace lowered his fists, reluctant to hit a man who was by now helpless. 'Give up, Sam,' he said in a quiet but determined voice. Still Hurst refused to surrender the crown of his own free will. Mace then threw in a combination of punches to the jaw and body which finally stretched Hurst's massive bulk on the grass. After thirty seconds, 'Time' was called, and Mace was duly hailed as the new champion, with his predecessor stretched unconscious on the turf. He had an anxious wait for a couple of minutes longer before Noon and Hodgkiss succeeded in reviving Hurst. To the relief of all, principally Mace himself, Hurst had survived the fifty-minute onslaught which culminated in his knockout. He had been exposed as a dinosaur who, relying purely on brute strength and pluck, should never have made a career for himself in the prize-ring, let alone have held, albeit only for a matter of months, the Championship of England.

Jem Mace stood revealed as a supreme boxer-puncher, the first in a lineage of such figures which would begin in this, the Dark Age of fighting, and would extend into the as yet undefined world of boxing with gloves. As soon as he received a thumbs-up from Noon, Mace went straight to Hurst's corner and praised his bravery. Satisfied that Sam was coherent, albeit badly injured, he raised his arms aloft to acknowledge the cheers of the crowd, then made a victory speech. What he had to say and how he said it went far beyond the few mumbled comments which typified the pugs of his day. Mace's speech was a tour de force of audacity, self-confidence and tongue-in-cheek wit.

> Gentlemen, there lies Sam Hurst, one of the gamest men that ever stepped into the ring. You have seen how bravely he fought today, and I want you to show your appreciation for him in a practical way. Gold will do if you haven't got silver, and I don't mind accepting banknotes if it so happens you haven't a sovereign handy. But mind, gents, no coppers please. I want you all to give. Those who have backed me will, I am sure, toe the scratch without being asked twice, while you who have backed Hurst ought to give also, for if you have lost your money, it has not been the fault of your man, who has fought for you pluckily and well.

Mace's showmanship was amply rewarded. As he strolled round the ring, men elbowed each other aside to get close to the hero of the hour. Some showered coins into the top hat he held out; others pressed notes into his palm, eager, as he knew they would be, both to show their wealth and to shake his hand. Holding up his arm in acknowledgement, he made for Hurst's corner, gave the proceeds to Noon and waited till he had counted it out. The total was no less than £35 – seven times as much as Jem had scrapped for when he first entered the prize-ring.

No sooner had they counted it than police appeared on the horizon. Everyone had to escape fast, by prepared boats which had been moored in the Medway. Hurst, who was unable to walk, let alone run, was lifted by half a dozen men, placed in a spare cart and trundled to the river's edge in the nick of time. Mace sat back in another boat while Pooley took the oars. They sped away up the river, met up with Hurst and his backers and made for the special train which was ready to take them back to the capital. By the time Hurst was brought back to his lodgings in London, however, he was still only semi-conscious. To have called a doctor would have run the risk of criminal charges against all participants, including Hurst himself. Jem sat among Big Sam's friends and they waited all night at his bedside until it was clear that he was out of danger.

In due course, Hurst was his old self, but he heeded his pals' advice to end his prize-fighting career and Mace threw a ceremonial party at the Old King John. The pub was packed with both workers and wealthy men, together with their ladies. The toffs footed the bill for the whole evening and champagne flowed until the early hours. Before closing, Mace organised another a whipround for Hurst, who was still suffering from the effects of a dislocated jaw. He cheered up considerably as Mace counted him out a further £15. As for Mace, he was richer by £400 from the purse alone – but several times more from having backed himself at good odds against the titleholder and favourite. More important still, he had realised his ambition to be crowned Heavyweight Champion of England.

One witness to the contest was the sporting journalist Henry Downton Miles, then a reporter for *Bell's Life*. Miles would, in later years, publish *Pugilistica*, a massive history of the Prize Ring, spanning a century and a half. 'Volumes could not prove more demonstratively the value of skill in the art of boxing as turning the scale against mere weight and strength than this one-sided contest of Mace and Hurst,' he would write. 'The mere facing of such a giant and exchanging shots at close quarters involves a confidence and coolness that shows no small amount of personal courage. As to Mace's attack and defence, they were in every respect indicative of the master . . . This battle elevated to the Championship of England one of the most finished boxers who had ever gained the title.'

Mace was presented with the Champion's Belt, which incorporated the one he had been awarded the previous year when he became the champion of the so-called 'hidden weights'. This spectacular piece of jewellery was twelve inches in diameter and thirty-eight in circumference, leather-backed and made of sterling silver panels. Of these, three depicted mythical figures, two classical and one contemporary; one depicted a pugilist in fighting attitude; another a lion couchant; and yet another was inscribed with Mace's name and the date of his becoming Champion of England.★

In defeating Hurst, Mace had achieved many things. Though Hurst was a decent man, he had stood surrogate for all those who had ever tried to put Mace down, to slight him or to cast doubt on his reliability – from his late, unlamented father to the still powerful if now contrite Dowling. Among the Fancy, only the most aged could recollect anyone comparable to the new champion. More than sixty years before, a few classic boxers had, for a brief period, raised pugilism beyond the level of the marathon bloodbath. Men like Richard Humphreys and Daniel Mendoza met each other in clashes which were marked by skill and cunning rather than brute force. There had also been men of great agility and punching power, such as Jem Belcher, but none could recall a fighter who combined skill, guile, mobility and calculated fierceness as Mace did. The way in which he outwitted Hurst and ultimately destroyed him caused those few onlookers who were Biblically minded to speak of 'David and Goliath'. Toffs who had visited Spain

---

★ In the subsequent century and a half, this historic belt would have sundry owners, most notably the celebrated American boxing historian Nat Fleischer, of the Madison Square Garden Boxing Hall of Fame in New York City. In 2005, the belt, part of the Stanley Weston collection, was sold for $58,000 through Geppi's Memorabilia Road Show of Timonium, Maryland. It was the lead item in the largest ever collection of boxing memorabilia auctioned at any one time, and it identified Mace as an icon in the history of sport.

compared Mace to a matador, bravely side-stepping an enraged bull before lancing it. Back in Norfolk, they would speak of him as an 'ox-dropper' – a slaughterman who stunned cattle with accurate stave blows before dispatching them. But for Mace himself, his triumph was the practical application of his principles of boxing as science, of sport as art. From his boyhood, he had loved the circus as much as he loved the boxing ring and, as he became Champion of England, his performance was akin to that of a circus ringmaster cracking the whip to ensure the obedience of an animal and to hold the audience spellbound.

PART TWO

CHAMPION OF ENGLAND

(1861–9)

7

The Fighting Stevedore

MARY KNEW. IT was four in the morning when he came home. She pretended to sleep as he entered their room but he made no attempt to rouse her. She lay awake as he slept, deeply, on the far side of the bed. It had never been like this before. In the old days he would always have woken her. In their twenties, it was a longed-for hour of passion, after the children's voices had at last fallen still. But now, on the day after his thirtieth birthday, which he'd spent hundreds of miles from home, Mary knew that her marriage would never be the same. She had, of course, been aware of his appetite for women – she had never deceived herself as to his fidelity while he was in London and she remained in Norwich. This hadn't troubled her . . . or at least not that much. She knew that women would always seek him out and that he could never resist the lure of a petticoat. Jem never tried to hide it from her; that was his nature. Still, by a thousand touches and glances, little gifts and surprise vacations, he had also shown her that he knew the difference between love and raw desire.

Not long afterwards, Mary overheard, amid gales of raucous male laughter in the Old King John, some crude wordplay regarding the events of 8 April 1861, the day when her husband had promised faithfully to return from his trip north and spend his birthday with his family in their London home. And had failed to do so, without even attempting an excuse. He had, as Mary knew, gone north to raise stake money for his battle with Sam Hurst. He had spent the night in Newcastle, at a pub in Clayton Street. The Cock Inn was an outpost of pugilism and its landlord, John Young, was one of the new breed of sporting publicans. Far removed from London as his alehouse was, Young could be relied upon to drum up cash from his fellow Geordies in the name of a good scrap. Mace had taken the train north and, en route, met up with George Woodey. Woodey was not only one of his seconds but a self-styled gentleman who came from Norwich and who had stayed loyal to Mace during the dark days after the Madden fiasco. Woodey was, at the time, also one of Mace's main backers. He knew the Newcastle area well and Mace took little persuading to enhance his own cause by putting in a personal appearance.

Jem took an instant liking to Newcastle, with its earthy, friendly and outgoing people. Soon what began as a duty turned into a brief holiday. His delight was soon increased by an unusual feature of the Cock Inn. Whereas many pubs employed a barmaid and some a couple, Young's hostelry deployed no less than four, all in their early twenties. At the Old King John, Mary had taken care that the only female bar staff were relatives. It was not long before Mace's roving eye detected four inviting glances and, in the early hours, with the customers gone, and Young and his wife asleep and Woodey snoring away in his own room, he made his way along the corridor where the girls were sleeping two to a room. News travelled fast on the pugilistic grapevine and it wasn't long before stories of Mace's prodigious wenching found their way back to Shoreditch.

Mary confided in her sister Martha, who, at sixteen, was already wise in the ways of the world. Martha had seen for herself how women competed for Jem and had overheard girls talking about sharing him. Mary should, Martha thought, give careful consideration to her situation, which was, at that time, one in which men held all the cards and a woman had only her youth and beauty to offer. As a friend as well as a sister, she refrained from adding any comment on the toll that four pregnancies had taken on Mary's figure. Sure, many a man lived in cosy domesticity with a wife who was still a good-looking woman as well as a mother of several young children. But Mace was not 'many a man'. Whatever the truth about his antics in Newcastle, his late return to London and his indifferent attitude towards her told Mary that there was, or had been, someone in his life who was more of a threat to her than an army of barmaids. In time she would learn the name of the woman whose existence would blight her life.

In contrast, Jem Mace, Heavyweight Champion of England, had learned the name of his foremost rival even before the crowd dispersed at Medway Island. Gasps of surprise were heard as a tall young man vaulted into the ring and confronted him. In the manner of a medieval jouster throwing down the gauntlet, he drew a sparring glove from his breast pocket and flung it at Mace's feet.

'Jem Mace,' he cried, 'I am Tom King and I hereby challenge you to fight me for the championship belt you have just won. My backers have their money ready, and I am willing to meet you anywhere and at any time you please, the sooner the better.'

'Very well,' said Mace. 'I will fight you.'

They shook hands, while the company crowded round and cheered.

Unlike Hurst, Tom King was a perfectly proportioned athlete. Twenty-five years of age, 6ft 2½in tall and thirteen stone, he came from the ancient heartland of the bareknuckle code, London's East End. Born at Silver Street in Stepney, King had sailed the seas as a lad before working in the docks at Wapping, soon becoming an assistant stevedore. His musculature was developed by the heavy work and his desire to escape was intensified by the stench of the Peruvian guano which his team unloaded to be carted off for fertiliser.

While he still remained single, King lodged with an old widow named Winburne off the Commercial Road. 'Old Ma' Winburne, as neighbours called her, was a tough old bird and, having never had a son, came to regard Tom in a maternal light. He was a quiet, intelligent young man who read books and had little interest in alcohol. It thus came as an immense surprise one day when King was seen in a dockside punch-up with a big, lazy blackguard who frequently disrupted work, getting away with it because no one could match him in a fight, and who one day insulted the stevedore who bossed King's gang. King gave the bully a piece of his mind. Relishing the chance to beat up someone he thought was a milktoast, the lout took off his coat and threatened to shut King's mouth. King showed no fear and hit back hard. Everyone downed tools and a ring of men formed, not only dockers and stevedores but freight checkers and even a couple of policemen, who did not tend to intervene in a fair fight. In the typical style of a roughhouse bully, his adversary swung wild punches, but King, as if born a boxer, simply stepped aside and calmly jabbed him in the face. When the bully refused to give up, King went after him with both fists and pummelled him into the concrete, bruised and bleeding. He had raised his fists only to defend himself and was cheered by every man on the dockside.

Tales of the incident spread through the East End and reached the ears of Jem Ward in his drum on the Ratcliff Highway. The former champion of England was now in his late fifties but was still a powerful man. Suspecting that he had unearthed a future star, Ward sent for King and put on the gloves with him in the back room of his alehouse. After a couple of months' tuition in the finer points, Ward deemed King ready for the ring and advertised in *Bell's Life* that he had a twenty-five-year-old 'unknown' who was ready to take on any man at £50 a side. King's rise was meteoric. Where Mace had taken six years to arrive at the summit of the LPR, King was challenging him barely six months after vaulting the prize-ring ropes for the first time. He had caused a sensation by demolishing Tom Truckle, an ex-Royal Navy sailor who had been heavily backed by his own officers at Portsmouth and who many tipped as a future champion. But Mace had not yet seen King fight and was waiting for the chance to do so before deciding how serious a challenger the 'Stepney Stevedore' would prove to be.

Meanwhile, Mace stepped up his involvement with the world of the circus, where he was now in great demand. Within a week of his defeat of Hurst, Howes and Cushing offered him a short-term contract. He did nineteen gigs in six weeks, ranging from Southport in Lancashire through Liverpool and Manchester and finishing in Bristol. Three weeks later, he was on the road with Fanque once more, with fortnightly stopovers in Lancashire, Yorkshire and Derbyshire.

Like all enthusiasts of pedestrianism, Jem also greeted the arrival in England of the American long-distance runner 'Deerfoot' with keen interest. Deerfoot, an American Indian of the Seneca tribe, was originally called Hut-go-so-no-deh but anglicised his name to Lewis Bennett. Having defeated all competition in the US, he came to England, the heartland of pedestrianism, in September 1861. He lost his first race before he had acclimatised, but from then on he remained invincible in a series of matches. Deerfoot's defeat of British record holder Jack White in a four-mile race outside Manchester, which Mace travelled to watch, led to him being proclaimed in some quarters as 'World Champion'. This was the very concept first used in pugilism when Heenan and Sayers clashed the year before. Mace now claimed that he himself was the outstanding performer in the ring in exactly the same way as 'Deerfoot' was on the track.

In October, after finishing his well-paid stint with Fanque, Mace went down to Farnborough to watch Tom King in action against Tommy Broome, younger brother of Johnny, and another outstanding prospect. Mace surprised those who knew him by producing pen and paper and making a few rough notes. It had been thought that he was still illiterate but when he was asked who'd taught him to read and write, he just smiled and gave no answer. His notes were brief because it was soon clear that King was in a different class to Broome, who lasted only twenty minutes. King's hand speed was phenomenal and he'd been well schooled by Ward. Although his technique was solid rather than brilliant, he had a considerable advantage over Mace in weight and height. Mace went into strict training the next day, over three months before the fight was scheduled to take place.

That December, Jem's name was mentioned during the proceedings of a scandalous court case. A young Norfolk aristocrat, Lord William Frederick Windham, was brought before a Commission of Lunatic Inquiry at Gray's Inn. His uncle wanted him disinherited on grounds of insanity and claimed that 'Mad Windham' used to make a nuisance of himself on the Eastern Counties railways. He had ended up by marrying a notorious London courtesan. But, in court, Windham appeared perfectly lucid. Amongst other things, he testified that Mace's ancestors had been, at Beeston, tenants of his own forebears for more than a hundred years. The case against him was found not proven. Jem was delighted about this because, as he saw it, it gave the lie to assertions that the Maces were gypsies.

In the New Year, he intensified his training. John Miller, a fine long-distance runner who Mace found easy company, helped him develop his already exceptional stamina as they clocked up the mileage deemed necessary for the champion to reach peak fitness. Never before had roadwork been so emphasised in a fighter's training and it was Mace who, in this way, was the first to demonstrate the concept of the boxer as all-round athlete.

On the morning of 28 January 1862, a ferocious wind lashed the whole south-eastern corner of England. With the temperature hovering just above zero and rain falling without let-up, the conditions for Tom King's challenge to Jem Mace for the Championship of England were as foul as could be imagined. In some ways they may have been a blessing in disguise. There had been rumours of hooligans crashing the railway specials and alarmed chief constables threatened to have both Mace and King arrested. In the event, the muster at London Bridge was orderly. Mace, King and the paying spectators were quickly entrained and the locomotive briskly hauled the carriages off to their destination. Back in the East End, local rivalry was intense. Mace, by now an adopted Londoner, was the hero of Shoreditch, while King carried the flag for his native Stepney. In their respective pubs, Richardson and Ward had drummed up stake money, the first for Mace and the second for King.

An hour down the line, they arrived at Godstone in Surrey. The area was wooded, inaccessible and dead quiet. Mace, in keeping with his aspiration to be a fashion leader, had grown his hair longer and it was pomaded dark to blend with his new, immaculately waxed moustache. His stance bore a hint of a crouch, with feet planted so as to enable him to shift his weight easily from one foot to another. His eyes had, as noted by those at ringside, a piercing gleam which radiated supreme self-confidence. King stood upright, carrying his guard relatively low, as did the champion. He was a tall, pale-skinned man as lean as a whippet, with short, dark hair, a lantern jaw, prematurely sunken cheeks and cold, staring, vigilant blue eyes. Both he and Mace began to shiver from the moment they took off their shirts and faced the driving rain, and they rubbed their torsos vigorously to restore circulation. When impatient spectators began to catcall, King cut them short with a mock invitation to take his place. While the rain-drenched crowd shouted for action, Mace's chief second, Jack Hicks, was on his hands and knees, testing the going underfoot. He knew his man would be disadvantaged by conditions that slowed speed of movement.

* * *

From the square-off, it was obvious that here Mace faced an opponent who would test him to the limit. King's reach was far longer than the champion's and, after some preliminary sparring, he began to jab to the face as Ward had taught him. Mace deliberately abandoned his usual tactics, adapting spontaneously to the atrocious conditions. He knew he would have to fight King at close quarters and that he would have to take punishment he normally would have avoided. His jab-and-get-away tactics, often so destructive against taller men, would be nullified in these circumstances, so he opted to attack his challenger's body rather than his head, even punching King's arms to drain his energy and weaken his wrestling action. Mace believed that wrestling was a weak point in King's armoury. And if he was thrown himself, the danger of serious injury would be lessened by the quagmire underfoot.

Rocked by a right cross to his cheekbone, King almost got a headlock on Mace but was left dumbfounded as he somehow slipped out of his grasp. This incredible sleight of hand and foot carried more than a hint of the circus about it and made neutral spectators laugh and cheer and won them over to his side. King felt a fool, but he was nothing if not determined. He kept his temper and used his long reach to jab downwards onto Mace's face, drawing 'first blood' by cutting his lip, and then blackening his left eye. Mace was not deterred from continuing his non-stop body barrage and targeted the 'mark', or solar plexus, the highly vulnerable epigastric nerve centre. But King's hands were far faster than those of any man Mace had encountered and the usually elusive champion needed time to adjust to it. In the meantime, he was taking punishment.

By the twenty-second round, Mace's left eye was entirely closed and his mouth swollen and distorted. He seemed headed for defeat, and betting in the crowd swung towards King. Some wondered about the wisdom of Mace's tactics and others, perhaps influenced by Dowling's propaganda in earlier years, felt sure that the Norfolk man would be exposed as a 'Flash Harry' when he was at last obliged to take punishment instead of meting it out. Moments of farce punctuated the drama as each man in turn lost his footing and rose with his arms caked in mud. But, while the rain was incessant, the fight continued to fluctuate. Mace was slowly but surely reading King's punches and, in the style which had made him famous, was dodging them at the last split-second. But, in the twenty-seventh, attempting to close in, under the taller man's guard, to seize and throw him, he slipped slightly. King reacted immediately and unleashed a tremendous uppercut, which knocked Mace down. He fell on the back of his head but the impact was cushioned by the treacle consistency of the soil. As Mace rose, well within the thirty-second time limit, his right eye was puffed and swollen. Many thought he was done for.

King inadvertently helped Mace out of this crisis by striking him a glancing blow which effectively lanced the lump which was threatening his vision. With the swelling gone from his right eye, Mace began to turn the tide. The first sign was King gasping for breath as Mace's body punching wore him down. As he slowed, Mace was able to put his gameplan fully into effect and nimbly back-heeled King to the ground. King's fall was only one of many as round after round terminated with Mace hurling him into the mud. Undaunted, King got up, smiled defiantly and resumed.

The turning point came in the thirty-third round. King copied Mace's early tactics and shifted his attack to the body, landing a swinging sledgehammer of a punch under Mace's left armpit. He felt as though his ribcage had caved in.

'Oh Jack,' whispered the champion, as chief second Hicks led him to his corner, 'I am in pain.'

Cleverly, Hicks turned Mace's thoughts away from his agony.

'In pain?' he said. 'Of course you're in pain. But what about Tom? You don't suppose he feels exactly comfortable, do you?'

Mace realised both the effect of his own body punching and also King's fading stamina, and his pain subsided. Fortunately for him, King's punch had left his ribs undamaged.

As King slowed down, so Mace stepped up a gear. Soon his mastery was there for all to see and he peppered the challenger's face with left jabs, punctuated by right-hand body shots. The devastating impact of these blows was vividly described by Mace himself many years later – 'The broad red blotches, each one the size of a baby's head, mottled Tom's white skin like the crimson blobs on a child's toy rocking horse.'

By the forty-third, King was reduced to amateurish rushing, born out of sheer exhaustion. His jaw began to drop and, as soon as it did, Mace hurled a fierce right. It missed the chin but landed full on his opponent's throat. Then, with immense cunning, Mace seized King as he began to fall. Preventing him from crashing backwards of his own momentum, he got what wrestlers called a 'crook' on him, pivoting King half around and dashing him face forwards to the ground. King was rendered unconscious by the fall and remained inert for several minutes, not hearing the call of 'Time' or the referee's acclamation of Mace's victory. Then he scrambled to his feet and shook hands with the champion.

The mill at Godstone had been a clash of titans. While it did not go down in the annals of pugilism as one of the classic encounters, it was, in view of the conditions, an epic. King was revealed as a formidable fighter, brave, bold, clever and athletic. That he could hold the ring with so wily a competitor as Mace, and that he could do so with less than two hours' previous experience in the LPR, bore witness to his innate ability and fighting heart. As for Mace, he had been badly disadvantaged by the abominable conditions. He had looked far older than his thirty years in the first half of this fight, yet he had found immense reserves of courage and fought with great tactical cunning in order to retain the Champion's Belt. No one had seen Mace take punishment like this before and few had believed that he could do so. For all his fluid boxing skill, Mace was proud of his wrestling ability, which did not rely on brute force but on nimbleness. 'The superiority of Mace as a scientific pugilist alone enabled him to contend with and finally defeat his brave, powerful and, in size and physique, formidable antagonist,' summed up H.D. Miles in *Pugilistica*. Though this first clash between Mace and King harked back to the crudest and most primitive days of prize-fighting, with the two protagonists grappling in the mud, it had more than one distinctly modern aspect: Mace's conditioning was excellent, his stamina a testament to the endless hours of roadwork he had put in, side by side with Miller, Pooley or both.

* * *

While Mace and King had experienced an hour of hell in the name of 'the noble art of self-defence' or 'the manly art', as the Fancy variously called bareknuckle fighting, the mill workers of Lancashire were enduring a winter of the most grievous distress in living memory. The immediate cause of the cotton recession was the out-break, in 1861, of the American Civil War. Until then, the importation of raw cotton from the United States had been uninterrupted. The raw cotton picked by black slaves on the plantations of the Old South was shipped to Liverpool and then moved by train to the Lancashire mill towns, whose damp climate was ideal for weaving garments. The slave-owning states had formed themselves into a Confederacy to uphold their declared right to maintain the 'peculiar institution' of slavery – on which, as they saw it, their prosperity depended. And they were prepared to defy President Abraham Lincoln's Army of the Union so as to preserve States' Rights. While the British Government, under Lord Palmerston, remained neutral, the Confederacy, bitterly disappointed, sought to test this by embargoing all shipments of raw cotton to England. Thus, by the winter of 1861–2, a quarter of a million Lancashire weavers were laid off from the cotton mills and forced onto parish relief. They existed just above the poverty line. Barely able to afford bread, they certainly had no money for circuses.

The likes of Pablo Fanque were hit very hard by this, and takings of his Circus Royal in such towns as Bolton and Blackburn, Rochdale and Oldham, were decimated. Fanque's business crisis occurred at a time when, in his mid-sixties, his energy was declining. He spent much time in the tranquility of his second home in rural Norfolk, rueing his concentration on Lancashire towns. When he died ten years later, he was destitute.

There were many rivals for Fanque's crown. By the 1850s, over 100 different circus firms operated in Britain, their numbers swollen by the expansion of the national railway network the previous decade. Fanque's repertoire of equestrians, acrobats, clowns and jugglers was also being challenged by a younger generation of entrepreneurs who added to his formula – this was increasingly the age of the trapeze artist, tightrope walker and, later, lion tamer. After Fanque's ruin following his concentration on one part of the country, no one else would make the same mistake again.

Frederick Ginnett had noted Fanque's great moment of success when he introduced Jem Mace as a circus attraction. The son of a Frenchman who had been brought to England as a prisoner during the Napoleonic Wars, Ginnett showed much of the flair for circus which characterised his father's homeland. He sought Mace out within a few weeks of the King clash at Godstone. What's more, he went far beyond

Fanque's offer of the previous year. Convinced that Mace as a boxer-violinist-statuarist would be a unique drawing card for both male and female spectators, he offered him a share of the takings, together with all-expenses-paid accommodation at first-class hotels, instead of a guaranteed salary. And he offered not a six-week stint in the North West but a six-month nationwide grand tour. Ginnett told Mace that he could expect to earn £50 a week for 26 weeks – a total of £1,300. All Mace had to do, apart from the occasional violin solo – which would be a labour of love – was put in a few rounds sparring with padded gloves. As Ginnett realised, the presence of a renowned prize-fighter, not on the run from the police in some rainswept backwater but within a mile or so from a working-class family home, would be an enormous attraction, heightened by the frisson that, like all pugilists, Mace was, by definition, an outlaw. As for Pooley, he would be welcome in a minor role. But Ginnett intended to have Tom King as well as Jem Mace on the bill. The idea was to draw in the crowds with a sanitised version of Godstone. He left it to Mace to persuade King.

When Mace first arrived at Old Ma Winburne's, she was reluctant to let him in. King's bruises had only just healed, she said, whereupon he showed her the marks King's blows had left on him. She relented. King was not at first pleased to see Mace because he was biding his time with the intention of issuing a challenge for a rematch. The Fancy were almost unanimous in agreeing that this was King's due. He did not wish to be deflected from his preparations by joining a circus, but when he was told about the money he was likely to earn, had a rapid change of heart.

The six months that Mace and King spent touring with Ginnett's Circus were probably the most carefree of Mace's life. He had no responsibilities whatever, since the entire organisation was looked after by Ginnett, and saw almost the whole of England, including many places previously unknown to him. The exhibitions of sparring drew enormous crowds and he was also able to play fiddle again in public from time to time, to appreciative audiences. Mace and King stayed at the best hotels and lived like lords. What's more, Mace preferred Ginnett's Circus to the Circus Royal. Ginnett had not only offered him far better terms than Fanque had been able to, but he did not have to contend with Fanque's Christian zeal and attempts to get him to church.

At the beginning of the tour, Mace sensed some lingering resentment on King's part and, after being confronted, King told him frankly that he was sure he hadn't done himself justice at Godstone and that he couldn't rest until he had a second chance. He told Mace that his own seconds had urged him to force the pace in the early rounds, whereas if left to his own plan, he would have preferred to conserve his energy for the long haul.

'Do you believe you can beat me, Tom?' asked Mace.

King looked him straight in the eye and answered, 'Yes.'

Mace at once shook hands on a rematch and told King that it would happen before the year was out – but added, in no uncertain terms, that the result would be the same.

After this gentleman's agreement had cleared the air, England's two leading active pugilists became friends, though they had little in common. Both liked to drink, in moderation, but while Mace would cast a longing eye over pretty girls working in the circus, King kept busy writing long letters to his girlfriend in London, whom he would marry in a couple of years. He never showed any disapproval of Mace's lifestyle – how he chose to behave was his own business – but the contrast between them was most marked when it came to horse-racing. King studied form, carefully selecting nags to bet on, and if he thought there was nothing on, kept his wallet in his pocket. Mace, flush with money like never before and careering round the provinces with time on his hands, let rip. He lost a tenner at Aintree, blew fifty at Doncaster and kissed goodbye to a couple of hundred at Newmarket.

Back in London, Nat Langham, who had been ill for a while, regained his former vigour. He had put up some of the stakes for King's challenge and had actually travelled to Godstone as a member of King's party, but after Mace's triumph, he made a fresh approach to his former protégé. He was, it became clear, eager to become his chief backer once again. Mace was reluctant to return to Langham's camp. He resented the way Langham had disciplined him after the Madden fiasco and was well aware that it was due to Bob Brettle and, above all, Bill Richardson, that he'd got the chance to revive his career.

As for Richardson, he was far from pleased at the turn of events. It had been Big Bill who had helped set Mace up in the Old King John, which was a second investment for him, even though the Blue Anchor continued to be a thriving drum. Now Mace was rarely present at his own pub, which was being run by Mary, with the assistance of Tommy Hutton. Since Mace had been away with the circus, takings had declined – after all, the presence of the Champion of England had been a magnet for customers. Richardson had little use for what he considered the frivolity of the circus and when Mace returned to London, he told him what he thought in blunt language. He made no threat about withdrawing his backing but told Mace to cut short his tour with Ginnett and get back to work at what was, after all, their joint investment. After a blazing row, Big Bill strode out.

By the time Ginnett's grand tour finally ended, articles were due to be signed if the King rematch was to come off before the end of the year, as Mace had promised. Neither man was in any doubt that a full three months of training would be needed for them to reach peak fitness for a clash which was bound to test both of them to the limit. But Nat Langham made it clear to King that he wouldn't back him, sneering that he had no chance against Mace. When Jem Ward tried and failed to raise the stake money, Richardson succeeded in so doing.

Richardson had long harboured a loathing of Langham, who he regarded as an upstart from the sticks, a man motivated purely by greed and who he once referred to as a 'whoremaster', implying that Langham was not above furnishing prostitutes to the young swells who frequented the Rum-pum-pas. That gentleman's club was, after all, only a stone's throw from the Alhambra in Leicester Square, in whose forecourt working girls plied for custom among the unaccompanied men who visited the notorious music hall.

Despite the poisonous atmosphere surrounding it, the match went ahead with Richardson resolutely backing King. Mace, who had honoured his contract with Ginnett, had little option other than to rely on Langham, whatever his bitterness towards his old boss and even though he privately sympathised with Richardson's point of view – which was shared by Ward and King. The fact that the match did go ahead surprised many. Rumours of corruption had begun to spread throughout London. These were taken up by certain sections of the press who were hostile to the Prize Ring anyway and who now clamoured to have the fight stopped. Thus, on the day scheduled for the mill, 28 November 1862, the South Western Railway Company, which had agreed to provide a special train, backed out at the last moment. Frantic negotiations with the Eastern Counties Railway Company produced a fresh rendezvous, to the immense relief of King, who had been training hard in Woodford. Mace had seemed more blasé about the difficulties and those who were always prepared to jump to conclusions about him pointed out that he had trained at Newmarket, hard by the great racecourse. Of course, they said, he's been gambling. Of course, they said, he's not been preparing properly. Of course, they said, he did not hold the title dear. While the first part was actually true, the second and third were definitely not. Yes, he was the one, not King, with something to lose. Yes, he was smitten with circus life. But no, when it came to the crunch, his immense pride in his fistic abilities was paramount. He relished the challenge and didn't intend to let the Stepney Stevedore take his crown.

On the eve of the match, the drums both in the West End and in the East were packed out. With drink flowing all night long, tongues were loosened and word got out to the roughs that there would be a rendezvous at Fenchurch Street Station at 4 a.m. Jem and Pooley decided to take a horse and cab and get there a full hour in advance but, as they arrived, they could already see a few well-known black-guards lurking in the gaslit gloom. Before too long, a hooligan mob a couple of hundreds strong seized the forecourt. Their targets were the swells, dressed in finery with their wallets stuffed with betting cash. A few younger members of the Fancy had succeeded in fighting their way through to the platform but many more were forced back. Scarcely had the toffs descended from their cabs than they were beaten, kicked and robbed. Throughout the whole disgraceful episode, the officers of the Metropolitan Police Force stood by with arms folded. The mob knew they could act with impunity because the constables were under instructions from their officers to do nothing to help promote pugilism.

Mace approached the Officer Commanding, a Chief Inspector, and argued that while prize-fighting was, of course, illegal, it was the Inspector's clear duty to prevent robbery with violence, one of the most serious offences on the statute book. To enable otherwise law-abiding people to attend a fight did not constitute promoting it. And while the Chief Inspector had no right to arrest the participants at Fenchurch Street, he could fulfil his obligations by telegraphing all police forces in neighbouring territories the exact time of departure from London. Unable to answer Mace's logic, the policeman grew more and more embarrassed and walked off without a word. When the ring keepers and stewards of the Pugilistic Benevolent Association arrived they too were attacked by the roughs. Bob Travers was robbed of his gold watch and chain, even though he was using knuckledusters to defend himself, but what finally saved the day was the arrival of Big Bill Richardson. To avoid possible police charges against himself, Richardson waited till a group of young hotheads tried to attack him – then he calmly produced the butt end of a broken billiard cue and struck out with it. The effect was immediate and the mob dispersed, convinced by the only language they understood.

'I consider the authorities were principally to blame,' Mace later commented. 'That we were going to do something that was nominally illegal . . . was perfectly true. But I did not think then, and I do not consider now, that the police were justified in allowing us to be mobbed well-nigh to death by a collection of the most dangerous ruffians in London. They might have found some other way of punishing us after committing the offence, and prevented the rabble from cracking our skulls in advance.'

A couple of hours later, the fighters and their entourages were on the Essex coast at Thames Haven, waiting for a couple of steamers, chartered overnight, to take them across the river and up the Medway. But, in the impromptu manner which had come to typify the LPR, King was taken by the sight of a stretch of a pristine lawn behind a sturdy oak barn. He suggested they fight it out there and, without hesitation, Mace agreed. This was 'just the place for a mill'. Had the opponents of pugilism heard those words, they would have conflated them with the violence which had occurred at Fenchurch Street. To them, a bruiser was a bruiser, a savage who revelled in brutality and whose day was incomplete without a punch-up. The Corinthians, however, knew different. Both Mace and King had, as lads, needed to know how to defend themselves, the former against anti-gypsy thugs, the latter against dockland bullies. Now Mace, the itinerant musician, and King, who was a devoted gardener and flower-grower, were inspired by the idea of doing battle in one of nature's amphitheatres.

Mace–King 2 did not last as long as their first clash. Complete after thirty-eight minutes, it was largely one-sided. Given the fine conditions – a mild day in late autumn – the betting at Thames Haven strongly favoured the champion. Indeed Johnny Gideon, the leading bookmaker of the time, was covering himself by offering 20 to 1 on. For a few minutes, an upset looked on the cards as King bluffed Mace by forcing the pace again despite having expressed regret for having done so at Godstone. He'd also been practising his wrestling and hip-tossed Mace, who fell upside-down on the top of his head, but was unhurt. In response to shouts of 'Are you all right, Jem?', Mace cynically responded, 'I'm fine. Don't fret! You'll see some more rounds for your money.' Indeed they did, with Mace back to his best, jabbing and moving in what, in future years, would become the classic style. Time and time again, his left thudded into King's face.

After thirty-one rounds, King's eyes were nearly closed and his face had swollen to almost double its normal size. As he reeled and staggered from the onslaught, Gideon's stentorian voice seemed to sum up the imminent outcome. 'A hundred to one on Mace!', he bellowed. But Mace suddenly lost his footing on a piece of bloodstained turf. A trifle overconfident, as he stood poised on the brink of victory, he was marginally slower than usual in regaining his balance. In that fraction of a second, King risked his own knuckles by delivering a roundhouse shot with all the ferocity born of utter desperation. It detonated on the side of Mace's jaw. Mace fell poleaxed. His seconds hauled him to his corner and, as they believed, revived him. But Mace, though he toed the line once more – to all appearances ready to continue the fight – was concussed and in deadly danger. King was quick to notice what Mace's seconds couldn't or wouldn't. Speaking in a low voice, he said, 'Chuck it in, Jem, you're done for.' Mace shook his head feebly, whereupon King gently pushed his semi-conscious opponent to the ground, half holding him so that the fall wouldn't be too heavy. Mace slowly lost consciousness. King had taken the title.

All night long, Mace lay awake in pain at the Old King John, nursed by his sister Amelia who, fearing that his jaw was broken, wanted to call a doctor, but by the morning the pain had eased. In his *Pugilistica*, H.D. Miles later would pay tribute to both contestants: 'There can be little question of the fact that King's decisive victory was more immediately due to the tremendous hit to which Mace had laid himself open by his over-eagerness to plant what he considered the coup de grace on his gallant adversary. His skill in administering as well as avoiding punishment had given him an apparent best but he had not reduced the courage and confidence nor exhausted the strength of his dangerous antagonist.'

As time went by, Mace would reflect on his shock defeat at Thames Haven and link it in his mind with his own dispatch of Brettle in their second fight. For the moment, all he knew was the anguish of being on the brink of victory, only to have it torn away. Desperately eager to secure a rematch, he waited only till the tell-tale swellings on his lower jaw had subsided before rising at dawn, taking a horse-drawn omnibus from Shoreditch to the West End and making his way to the offices of *Bell's Life*.

While the printers were hard at work on the issue which would carry Dowling's report on King–Mace 2, he waited for the editor's arrival. Although Dowling's attitude had changed radically from a couple of years earlier, Mace wasn't sure how the 'Bible of Pugilism' would react to the idea of a third match between himself and King. It might be ruled that another challenger would have to be accommodated first, but Mace had brought the first instalment of his stake money with him and intended to make his challenge without delay.

When Dowling arrived, he displayed all the pompous relish in the power of the Press which was his to exercise – but none of the hostility which had earlier characterised his attitude. 'Very well, Mace,' he intoned. 'I will see to it that your challenge is published.' Then he added, significantly, 'King will have to meet you again or surrender the Belt.' Suddenly Dowling gestured for Mace to enter the composing room ahead of him, where the printers were hard at work on a report of the fight at Thames Haven. It was one which would emphasise Mace's early mastery, rather than his shock defeat. Clearly the irascible editor was about to make a public apology, albeit delivered in his own ironic and indirect manner.

'Gentlemen!' he barked. Getting instant quiet, he lowered his voice. 'Allow me to introduce you to . . . "The Coward"!'

That ironic quip, muttered under his breath, was as close to an apology as he would ever utter. The printers erupted. Cheers broke out, trays of type were hurled into the air and one man after the other queued to shake Mace by the hand. It was clear how much, in previous years, these skilled craftsmen had resented being obliged to print, on pain of dismissal, what they rightly believed to be a tissue of lies about him.

Four years earlier, Mace had to restrain himself from attacking Dowling at Medway Banks. Now he found himself shaking hands with the all-powerful editor and sharing a bottle of champagne with him. The turnaround was as total as could be imagined but he had done it on his own terms. By the skill and bravery which he had shown against Travers and Hurst, in the rematch with Brettle and in both victory and defeat against King, he had demonstrated his quality both as an athlete and as a man. He might temporarily have had to yield the glittering Champion's Belt but the lustre of his reputation was fully restored.

8

Sawdust, Tinsel and Riot

IT WAS THE hit song of the summer and its creator milked the applause for all he was worth. He strutted across the music hall stage in the garb of a Champagne Charlie – a rich and fashionable gentleman – bemoaning his lovelorn comeuppance. The audience, working-class every man and woman of them, laughed as he paused knowingly between the verses of the very lyric they had been humming along with him:

> Once I was happy but now I'm forlorn
> Like an old coat that's tattered and torn
> Left in this world to fret and to mourn
> Betrayed by a maid in her teens.
> The girl that I love she was handsome
> I tried all I knew her to please.
> But I couldn't please her one quarter so well
> As the man on the flying trapeze.

George Leybourne, writer and performer of 'The Man on the Flying Trapeze', was no toff; he was a Cockney mechanic who became a comedian and doubled as a songwriter. But the hero of the flying trapeze was no mere figment of his imagination, unlike the anonymous 'swell' who had been his unsuccessful rival for the affections of the beautiful eighteen-year-old girl. The man in question was a Frenchman, one Jules Leotard, born in Toulouse and the star aerealist of the Cirque Franconi. He was not yet twenty when he first starred at London's Alhambra and he would top the bill both there and in Cremorne Gardens throughout the 1860s. Leotard died at twenty-eight of a mysterious disease but his surname resurfaced in the late twentieth century as an exercise outfit beloved by Jane Fonda's aerobics disciples.

Leotard and Leybourne were two of the three great stars who emerged from the circus world in the early 1860s. The other was Blondin. Leotard's forte was the athleticism and bravado with which he swung between five trapezes, turning somersaults between each one. Blondin's was a sense of balance so fine-tuned that it made even the most nimble seem elephantine in comparison, not to mention a cold nerve which enabled him to perform feats on the high wire which led some spectators to cringe and avert their eyes even as others craned their necks skywards. Blondin was, like Leotard, French. While England had reinvented the modern circus, it was France and later Russia – and ultimately America – whence its most dazzling stars came. Indeed it was in the US, at the Canadian border by Niagara Falls, that Blondin had first made his name at the age of thirty-five, walking across the half a kilometer gorge on a rope just 3in in diameter. One false step would have sent him to death in the rapids below.

Blondin crossed Niagara many times more, each traverse more dangerous than the last: blindfolded, pushing a wheelbarrow, on stilts or even carrying his manager piggyback. Finally, he carried a stove, sat down, and fried himself an omelette halfway across. He had begun training for his epic adventures at the age of six in his father's Cirque Franconi at Lyon, and by 1861 was wowing sell-out crowds at the Crystal Palace for the then astounding sum of £1,200 for 12 performances. Charles Dickens, sensing voyeurism, lamented 'half of London is eager for some dreadful accident'.

Across town, in Leicester Square, Blondin's fellow countryman Leotard was packing the Alhambra. Erected in 1854, it was a Moorish-style building with minarets and a sumptuous fountain under the central dome and took its name from the great edifice at Granada in Spain. It was soon converted into a music hall, later a ballet hall and finally a theatre. What the circus represented for mid-Victorian Britain was sin – sin as denounced by the bourgeoisie and the fundamentalists and as delighted in by rakes, writers, artists and the fun-loving sections of the working class. The concept of 'sin' embraced sex appeal and sensuality, risk-taking, spectacle and a devil-may-care attitude to life. This was what Blondin and Leotard embodied and it was sympathetically parodied by Leybourne. As for Dickens, when not lamenting Blondin's antics at the Crystal Palace, he was off to Paris with his

American writer friend Wilkie Collins to celebrate *filles de joie* in Montmartre.

This then was the world which Mace entered when, in 1862, he acquired his own circus – and these were the performers who inspired him. The circus world was also first cousin to the dramatic stage, which had intrigued him since his visit to the Theatre Royal in Norwich. If it was the success and vast earning potential of Blondin and Leotard which opened Mace's eyes to the status of top circus stars, it was the self-styled 'Lord' George Sanger who clinched his decision to become an impresario. Sanger had been born in Berkshire four years before Mace and was a man of uncertain ethnicity. What was quite certain was that the sensational performances of the recently formed Sanger's Circus in Liverpool in 1855 had put Lord George in pole position to succeed Fanque as the king of the British circus. Not yet thirty, and destined to become a millionaire, Sanger had introduced the first Indian lions to the circus. In those days, long before zoos, these were a great exotic attraction. Sanger and his wife, the voluptuous dancer, Pauline De Vere, set the pace in the circus world. While Pauline became an exotic fashion icon in sequins and tinsel, Lord George swaggered round the sawdust ring in a shiny top hat and fur-lined coat, a diamond tie pin gleaming at his throat as he barked orders to his troupe and brandished his ringmaster's whip.

As Mace moved deeper into this world, so he began to change his appearance. His style partly derived from that affected by those toffs who, like him, were in their early thirties, but stemmed far more from Sanger. As first seen at Godstone, his hair was grown longer and pomaded dark, while he sported an immaculately waxed moustache. Now he wore a top hat of the chimney pot style, polished and gleaming like a mirror. Over his black suit, his diamond tie pin, silk waistcoat and gold watch and chain, he sported a fully buttoned-up frockcoat adorned with a large, flowing cravat. His boots were wafer thin and made of patent leather. Thus clad, he strolled around Newmarket, home of the Cambridgeshire and the Cesarewitch races, Epsom Downs, where rich and poor mingled on Derby Day, and Ascot, where the Gold Cup was contested before the cream of London society. There were few young women who didn't notice him. The daughters of the aristocracy would regret that, as a prize-fighter, he was off-limits but, for the others, even as he risked his money on extravagant bets, he was regarded as the potential catch of the season. Or, as some remarked, a future Sanger who had yet to meet his own Pauline de Vere.

He first announced his intention of setting himself up in his own circus in 22 June 1862, taking out a flamboyant ad on the front page of the showbusiness weekly *The Era*. Further ads resulted in the assembly of a group of musicians as the Jem Mace Brass Band. Clowns and acrobats followed and the Jem Mace Circus opened its doors at Brighton on August 17. Travelling with his eponymous circus for the rest of the year made it clear to Mace that he should quit the Old King John, for which he no longer had any time. True, he'd enjoyed many a convivial night there and would miss the camaraderie and repartee, but not half as much as he would miss the roaring, bustling life of the circus, rolling by night train from gig to gig, always on the move and always ready for a fresh dawn in a new town. He told Richardson of his intention and this went down well with Big Bill, who wanted Mace out. The drum at Holywell Lane had become the key to the East End chain and Mace no longer belonged to the East End. Though he was still a hero, Langham's presence by his side at the second King fight had marred the day. Langham's all too evident dismay when King won, and his all too obvious haste to get out of Thames Haven, had caused the East End men to boo and jeer him. Now Big Bill would buy Mace out, their temporary quarrel would be patched up and the Old King John would be added to Richardson's burgeoning empire in Shoreditch.

For a while Mace and King hung around together. As the fight score between them remained at one each, there was mutual respect and a measure of genuine friendship. Like Mace, King was an intelligent man and although his interests didn't stretch to music, their conversation would cover not only the Prize Ring but horseracing, circus life and the swells with their rival political allegiances. Sometimes Tom Sayers tagged along when they went for a drink. He was not a brainy man – indeed, he was at a loss as to how to employ his time now that he'd quit the ring. He had no head for business and had failed disastrously in a sawdust and tinsel adventure with Howe and Cushing's Circus. Still, he was a good bloke, as likeable as they came – when sober. For a time, while Mace took a few weeks off from his own circus, the three went drinking at the White Swan in the Commercial Road. On a whim, one evening, Sayers asked his mates to take the train down to Brighton with him and stay overnight at a hotel. Brighton was his hometown and he was sometimes nostalgic for it, and was always up for a full night's boozing in the taverns along the shore. Mace took him up on it like a shot, but would leave the taverns to Sayers. What interested Mace about Brighton was its reputation for naughtiness. It was already a seaside resort, a frequent port of call for circuses and theatre companies. Showgirls abounded and his pulse quickened at the thought.

Tom King declined. Never a boozer, he was engaged to be married and didn't want to put himself in the way of feminine temptation. Obviously he couldn't tell the other two that, so he cried off with an excuse about having to finish some work he was doing to refurbish Old Ma Winburne's house. This was the humble little abode where King still lived even though he was Champion of England. Mace riposted that he would go down to King's lodgings and get his suitcase. He would come back with it and then King would have to go with them. King laughed and bet him a couple of bottles of champagne that he wouldn't manage it. Thinking he was onto a winner, Jem strode down to London Street and knocked on the door. Old Ma Winburne leaned out of an upstairs window demanding to know who was there. Jem told her that he had been sent by Tom King to get his suitcase and she was to pack a few things in it for a business trip to Brighton. But the old lady refused, saying that she would never give anything of Tom King's to anyone but Tom himself. Mindful that the Champion's Belt reposed in Tom's room, she would not let Mace into the house and she harangued him from the window. Jem pleaded, joked and even bluffed her that he would force the door but the sturdy old Cockney woman was adamant.

'Don't try to fool me with that rubbish!' she shouted and let the sash window down with a bang. Jem had to return to the pub, admit defeat and pay up for the 'fizz'.

Then out of the blue came the shock news of King's retirement. Without a word to anyone, he had, in December 1862, made his way to the offices of *Bell's Life* and formally returned the Champion's Belt to the safekeeping of Dowling. Mace was stunned – not only was Tom a mere twenty-seven years of age, but he had never even discussed the possibility of quitting the ring. True, Mace had not brought up the possibility of another fight, but he'd been sure that, after a couple of months of enjoying his champion status, King would grant him the return for which he had already received Dowling's blessing. Now that was not going to happen unless King could be persuaded to reverse his decision.

Mace called on him at his lodgings and asked King for his reasons. Knowing that he was shortly to be married, he wondered if he'd allowed himself to be influenced by his future bride. King laughed and said that was not the case. As far as he was concerned, the prize-ring was a short-term investment which he intended to use to set himself up as a bookmaker. Mace argued that he could perfectly well combine the two, if he so wished, but King dug his heels in. Mace changed his tactics and made a public challenge using the stage of the Holborn Empire, then a music hall, as his platform. Producing £100 from his wallet, a sign of the ease with which Mace acquired money and the carelessness with which he regarded it, he offered the cash publicly to King if he would accept the fight. This was not stake money, it was a personal inducement, but still King refused.

Some time after, the pair met by chance outside Tattersall's, the bookmakers. Mace lost his temper and cuffed King about the face. King, of course, hit back and thus the very mill which everyone in the fight game, except King himself, wanted to see began – not in some far-off deserted beach in Essex, or soggy Kentish marshland, but on the streets of London. Barely thirty people witnessed Mace's rash action, which had put them both in danger of arrest. Fortunately, the police constable who first arrived on the scene decided only to disperse the gathering crowd.

'Now then, you chaps,' said the constable, 'just stop that and clear, or I'll fight the pair of you myself.'

Not surprisingly, both fighters burst out laughing, to the further ire of the constable, who indignantly informed them that he was the champion boxer of his division.

'Well allow me to inform you,' replied King, 'that *I'm* the champion of *England*.'

'And allow me to inform you,' retorted the now furious bobby, 'that you are a liar. Tom King is the champion of England. I know him well, and you're not a bit like him. Why, you might as well try and stuff into me that your blackguardly pal here is Jem Mace! Be off, the pair of you, or I'll have you locked up, and then you can tell the beak in the morning what your real names are. I warrant they are well enough known at Bow Street.'

As the grinning pugilists walked off, the bobby followed a few yards behind, still muttering.

'Tom King, indeed. Jem Mace, huh. The cheek of it! A couple of lazy loafers. I don't suppose either of 'em can box for nuts.'

Mace and King rarely met again. Over the years, there were a few encounters at the races. Mace was not one to carry a grudge and, when they did meet, they spoke good-naturedly. As for King, he did indeed become a bookmaker, amassed a small fortune and went to live in domestic tranquility in rural Hampshire, where he spent much of his time cultivating his garden.

Mace was obliged, by the rules of the LPR, to wait out the time beyond which King's right to the Belt would lapse. Meanwhile, he remained the 'People's Champion' and his status was implicitly acknowledged at the Criterion Hall in Leicester Square. Before a large crowd, including almost all the sporting celebrities of the day, he received a standing ovation as he stood before a table bearing not only the trophies he had won in the prize-ring but some of his pedestrian medals. The orchestra struck up 'See the Conquering Hero Comes' and he was presented with an elegantly chased special gold cup weighing over six pounds and valued at 500 guineas. It was the gift of a benefactor whose surname bore an extraordinary resonance for Mace and Pooley, who was also present. The name was Windham, the latest scion of the family who resided at Felbrigge Hall in Norwich and on whose estate in Beeston Mace had been born. The 'mad lord' had been vindicated at Gray's Inn and was pleased to share a platform with Mace, another of polite society's villains but also a popular hero of the hour.

This public adulation did not satisfy Mace. Frustrated by King's refusal to re-enter the ring, he knew the title and Belt would not be his again, by the rules of the LPR, until he had received a challenge and disposed of it. There was no shortage of up-and-coming fighters but, by common consent, they were not in King's class, let alone in Mace's. To take his mind off being thwarted in his attempt to recover the title, Jem launched a two-month tour with his circus. Before touring the north of England, he made his first ever visit abroad. In a tour set up by his future business manager Harry Montague, Mace was reported in Paris, together with his company which now included such charming young French women as the lovely-sounding Mesdemoiselles Rosalinde, Louise, Blanche and Violette.

By this time, the imposing John Heenan had returned to England from the US. Supremely indifferent to warfare, as were most pugilists, including Mace, he was glad to be out of his native land at a time when it was convulsed by the American Civil War. A working-class Northerner with Irish parents, Heenan supported the Union against the landowning southern Confederacy but that was as far as it went. He far preferred to spend his time in the drums of London's West End.

One day Heenan was propping up the bar at Owen Swift's in the Haymarket and chatting amiably with his old foe Sayers when Mace walked in – and saw the one man who was certainly once good enough to enter the ring with him and dispute the Championship of England, and another over whom a victory would make him the Champion of the World. He strode over to Heenan, who was four years his junior and, at twenty-eight, still in peak condition.

'Not another retired man?' he said sarcastically.

When Heenan hesitated to reply, Mace dared him to issue a challenge. Heenan refused, whereupon the pugnacious Sayers exclaimed, 'If you won't fight Mace, I will.' Those words were music to Mace's ears. From the moment he entered the London Prize Ring, he'd set his sights on Sayers, but lost his chance to challenge him in the aftermath of Sayers's epic clash for the world title. It was generally accepted in the bareknuckle world that, despite Tom King's shock victory at Thames Haven, Mace was the best man then active. But many still argued that Sayers had been even better.

Mace's pride was hurt by that judgment. He was convinced that his superior agility and boxing brain would lead him to victory against the 'Little Wonder', as Sayers was known. He immediately reached into his wallet, took out a fiver and plonked it onto the counter to bind the match. Sayers, bored with life outside the ring, at once covered the sum but to Jem's dismay a group of Sayers' minders took him to one side. Fingers were wagged and, a few minutes later, he returned shamefaced and asked for his fiver back. Mace's anger was doubled by the suspicion that Sayers' so-called chums were more interested in securing money to bet on a different mill than in preserving Sayers' health. As Mace contemptuously tossed the note onto the counter, he looked Sayers hard in the eye and told him that it was about time that he got his pride back.

'Take your bloody money,' he snapped, 'if you've not got the pluck to face me.'

With that parting shot he strode out of Swift's house, deeply suspicious that Heenan had other business in town than merely swapping ring reminiscences in the Haymarket.

Exasperated by the turn of events since King's sudden retirement, Mace was tempted to return full-time to the circus, but was stopped in his tracks by a challenge. Not, as he had hoped, from Heenan or Sayers, but one Joe Goss. Goss's backers had not lost sight of the fact that Mace, though dethroned as heavyweight champion, was still the middleweight title-holder. This was Goss's fighting weight at the time. Given that the Champion's Belt could not be at stake, Goss's backers knew that he was not an attractive foe to Mace, though it would not be easy for him to ignore a challenge in view of his remarks about money and pride in Swift's House – soon common knowledge. Goss's backers, a group of wealthy businessmen from Birmingham, came up with a novel idea. They already had £400 upfront. If Mace could find backers to put up another £600, the fight would take place winner-takes-all. This was an unusual arrangement but one which would net the victor the unprecedented purse of £1,000.

Joe Goss, a half-gypsy from Wolverhampton, was twenty-five and a man of unprepossessing appearance. His brawny arms seemed too big for his body, while his legs were bulky and bandy. His lips seemed fixed in an odd half-smirk. In fact, he was a cheerful man of low intelligence who had little pure boxing skill. What he lacked in finesse, he made up for with his ability as a wrestler and, above all, in durability. Twice he'd fought mills of over three hours and, on one occasion, one of only ten minutes less. He was a known 'hard knock' with a phenomenal ability to withstand punishment and emerge victorious. Goss had found it difficult to hold down a job before entering the Prize Ring at nineteen. So high was his pain threshold that his father had turned him in to the police on one occasion in an attempt to preserve him from potential injury in a fight. This only made Goss more determined to make money the only way he knew how – with his fists. Though he was not in the same class as King, he was vastly more experienced.

At one time, the clash looked unlikely to come off. First there was a matter of finding the stakes, but Big Bill Richardson, now reaping huge takings at both the Blue Anchor and the Old King John, had not deserted Mace. At a stroke, he deposited a cheque for £330 in support of Mace. This was more than matched by Goss's backers.

In order to outlast the durable Goss, Mace placed particular emphasis on roadwork. He regularly ran many miles a day in training, accompanied by several noted pedestrians. This demanding schedule was a quantum leap beyond the old prizefighters and their relatively limited 'training for wind' (i.e. stamina). What's more, it typified Mace's belief in the links between all individual sports. He had been a promising runner before deciding to concentrate on the prize ring, and the way in which he married pedestrianism with bareknuckle fighting would help pave the way for the far more athletic performers in the future sport of gloved boxing.

More serious was the close call at the weigh-in. Despite his apparently adequate regimen, Mace had not had to face the iron discipline of Billy Clark. Both he and his chief trainer, John Miller, were stunned to find, forty-eight hours before the weigh-in, that he was 4lb too heavy for the middleweight limit, then fixed at 10st 10lb. In those days, with no Turkish baths to sweat weight off, Miller worked on two fronts to get him into shape: first he ordered him to fast for two whole days, before improvising a makeshift sauna, where Mace sat in a room heated by two fires for hours on end, in the height of summer, wearing a pair of shorts and covered in thick woollen blankets. A desperate situation clearly required desperate measures, as Mace stood to lose both £500 and the one title which remained his. Still, he could reflect, as he sat sweating it out, that it had taken Goss nearly two hours to finish off Posh Price, whom he had disposed of in twenty minutes. If only he could make the weight limit, his task ought not to be too difficult.

At the weigh-in, at the Greyhound in Waterloo Road, Mace tipped the scale at 10st 9lb 14¾oz: £1,000 was, at least potentially, saved by little more than an ounce. Mace's clash with Goss was one which held little fistic interest for him, despite the unprecedented purse. Nevertheless, 1 September 1863 turned out to be possibly the most extraordinary bout in his entire ring career. What gave the mill its spark was its regional rivalry. Mace was an adopted Londoner but Goss was regarded as the champion of the Midlands, the area which had been producing a series of top ring battlers for a generation and which resented the supremacy, not only in sporting matters, of the capital. Possibly over 1,000 men took the train from Birmingham to cheer Goss on. This made the potential for crowd trouble far greater and the task of disguising the railway rendezvous all but impossible. Even on the day of the weigh-in, twenty-four hours in advance, a crowd of Brummie roughs rushed the toll gate at Waterloo Bridge and crossed without paying.

During the night, bars were wrecked and landlords were threatened with beatings until they divulged that Paddington was the muster point. By 2 a.m., a mob of 5,000 had seized the station concourse and were fighting among themselves, broad Brummie shouts jarring with Cockney twang. Thieves were out in force as well, and nearly all were brandishing bludgeons or heavy sticks. This time the police did not stand by as they had done at Fenchurch Street – they absented themselves totally, washing their hands of both illegality and criminality. The thieves and thugs acted with total impunity on Paddington Forecourt, seizing cabs by the wheels and overturning them. Horses reared up in terror, disgorging their loads onto the street, before bolting, trailing empty cabs rattling and rocking dangerously behind them. In the mayhem, thugs head-butted and kicked their victims and made off with money and valuables.

Two hours of rioting had not abated by the time Mace arrived before dawn. Recalling the incident many years later, he would brilliantly compare the scenes with the hooliganism that had attended his second fight with King. So much worse were the scenes in central London on that day that he would describe the Fenchurch Street disturbances as being 'like a zephyr to a blizzard' in comparison with those now witnessed at Paddington. Although a score of burly ring-keepers, all former bare-knuckle fighters, guarded the station gates, Mace and his travelling entourage had to fight their way through a mob of about 400 blackguards in order to reach them.

> Obviously there was but one way, if we did not want to be left behind, and that was to fight our way through. We waited a little while for reinforcements, and then, to the number of about twenty, we dashed into the thick of it. I simply used my fists, and I should think I bowled over a dozen or more of the roughs. Others, however, thinking, I suppose, that the occasion warranted it, used knuckle-dusters, life-preservers, and loaded canes.
>
> Old Bill Richardson was our leader, and he was a host in himself. He carried his favourite weapon, a billiard cue sawn in halves, with which he did terrible execution. He told me afterwards, in confidence, that he was afraid he had killed one or two of the thugs. I should not have been surprised, for there were fewer uglier customers in all London than old Bill when his temper was once roused.

It took them twenty minutes to fight their way through to the platform, where they found Goss and his crowd, similarly dishevelled from the melee.

> We could gaze now from comparative safety over the surging human sea outside, and a terrible sight it was to behold . . . I can see in my mind's eye the vast panorama of upturned faces, brutalized by vice and every vile passion, wanly lit by the big lamps outside the station. The roaring never wholly ceased . . . the mob made one of its periodical attempts to rush the gates, thereby coming into conflict with our guards. There must have been a score of broken heads amongst London's roughs that day, for the defenders of the gates laid about them unmercifully with the loaded heads of their whalebone whips, so that in one of the last and most determined of the rushes I saw at least a dozen would-be stormers knocked bleeding and senseless to the ground in the space of as many seconds.

However, even on board the pugilists found that half a dozen drunken ruffians had succeeded in boarding the train and were annoying respectable spectators in another carriage by bellowing puerile and obscene songs. The matter was dealt with by Big Bill in his own inimitable style: he waited till the journey got underway, then strode up to the hooligans and said if they did not behave themselves, he would throw each one in turn out the window when the locomotive was at full speed. There was no further trouble. As the sun rose, the railway special glided through the woods and stubble of Oxfordshire, stopping to pick up a contingent of Oxford undergraduates, who tipped off the pugilists that the county constabulary were under strict orders to prevent a fight taking place on their territory. As a result it was decided that the train would not stop until it had reached Wootton Bassett in Wiltshire. Then Mace and Goss were held up while an old farmer demanded, and got, a sovereign bribe to allow his meadow to be used. But after five minutes of cautious sparring, a detachment of police arrived on horseback from Swindon. For once the chief inspector was a fair-minded man. He would, he said, if it were left to him, have allowed the fight – and even watched it himself. As Mace and Goss had committed a criminal offence by actually starting a prize fight, he might well have arrested them, but he could not bring himself to; indeed, he arranged for the principals and spectators to walk under police escort the four miles to Swindon where their train had first stopped. They were then seen off out of Wiltshire.

By this time, the railway officials had lost patience, maintaining that they had fulfilled their contractual obligation. The whole party was obliged to return to Paddington, a round trip of 166 miles, with nothing gained except that they were still free men. At least the ruffians had long since dispersed and so cabs were easily chartered to move on to Fenchurch Street. There had been no time to arrange a railway special and this led to the fighters, their backers and the spectators boarding the scheduled train to Purfleet in Essex, close to the then desolate shoreline. This prompted the unfounded but widespread suspicion that Mace and Richardson had conspired with railway officials to stage a charade and take a cut from the profits made from a sudden flood of requests for return tickets to Purfleet. The suspicions of chicanery and profiteering would be taken up by the anti-prize-fight lobby, which already had more campaigning ammunition following the riotous assembly at Paddington. It was true that 2,000 extra people boarded the 1:30 p.m. to Purfleet, an excursion which would normally have seen a dozen or so on board, but many of these were roughs who typically didn't stop at the ticket office but simply got on. Half a dozen who had ensconced themselves in the luxurious first-class carriage reserved for Jem Mace were summarily taken by the scruff of the neck by Pooley and Tyler and dumped out on the platform.

When the party reached Purfleet, it was obvious that there were still far too many roughs around for the fight to be attempted without risk of riot. With no time to charter a steamer special, on the spur of the moment members of the Fancy paid local cocklers a guinea a time to take them across the Thames to Plumstead, a marshland near the Kentish shore. With these tiny boats loaded to double the normal capacity, the prize-fight party survived a perilous journey against tidal waters, pitching and rolling across the waves. It was a minor miracle that no one perished. Not till 3 p.m., a full eleven hours after the initial muster at Paddington were Mace and Goss able to do battle at Plumstead for the middleweight championship of England.

Mace began with even more than his customary caution, seeking both to size up Goss's style and to avoid any impatient charge from the young Midlander after his long, vexatious wait and tiresome trip. But in defiance of his seconds' advice, Goss retreated, and was soon pinned on the ropes. Mace jabbed him hard to the mouth, and as Goss tried to counter, blocked the shot with his right and fired a fierce left to the brow which drew first blood. Seeming to be well on top in the opening rounds, Mace was caught off guard by a heavy blow to the right eye which soon began to swell badly. This caused great excitement among the Brummies who, anticipating a turnaround, shouted out, 'The young 'un wins!'

This was the spur for Goss to advance boldly. Mace, who always watched his opponents' eyes like the experienced poker player he was, spotted a look of exultation as the young buck closed in. Feigning that he was hurt, Mace backpedalled and lured Goss to where his supporters were most densely congregated. With him momentarily distracted, half turning his head towards the shouts of encouragement in his ear, Mace ducked sideways under his guard, sprang upright and, as Goss wheeled back to face him, delivered a roundhouse right high to the side of the jaw and put Goss down.

In the sixth, Mace struck home hard with both hands. He was about to follow up when Goss dropped to one knee. This was an accepted way to end a round, when one fighter was getting the worst of it and sought a breather, but Goss had gone down without being directly struck. Showing more cunning than Mace had credited him with, he tried to lure Jem into a foul, namely striking a fallen man, but it was Goss who had infringed the rules, albeit craftily. He had timed his move to fall into the limbo between a legitimate drop and a fall without being struck, which could have led to Mace's disqualification. Mace was following through fast on a lower trajectory and had to check himself quickly to avoid striking a technically fallen opponent.

Goss's tactics convinced Mace that the Midlander had little to offer in the way of science, that he would rely on obvious tricks and his power to soak up punishment. Mace had gone into the fight with no pre-conceived strategy. If neither he nor his seconds had watched an opponent in action, then he would wait and see, and when he had his foe sized up, he would improvise. Goss was clearly far more menacing as a wrestler than as a boxer. His blows carried little weight but two fierce throws shook up Mace. Back in his corner, the champion decided to make Goss tire himself out. He began to dance around the ring, his shuffle perplexing Goss as it had others. The crowd reaction varied from initial disbelief and even catcalls from the uninitiated, to gleeful applause when Mace proceeded to leave his foe looking foolish as he tried, and failed, to get to grips with him.

Predictably, an infuriated Goss began swinging wildly. This suited Jem: either he dodged the punch or he parried it, almost contemptuously, with his forearm, or he countered with a stiff jab. The 'Young 'Un' had never faced anything like this before and the more he lost his cool, the more Mace played him up, laughing in his face at his clumsiness. As Goss slowed, Mace began his delayed attack. In the twelfth, he gashed his challenger's cheek to the bone with a left smash and hurled a ferocious right to the nose. The contrast in their appearance was extreme: Goss's mouth was distorted, his eyebrow split, his cheeks streaming blood and his nose ludicrously swollen; Mace was unmarked save for a slight puffiness around one eye. Despite the hiding, Goss stuck to his task, seeming to hope that endurance might somehow see him through.

The rest of the bout saw Mace calmly stalking Goss, moving in with a flurry of punches, then resuming his panther-like tread. But Goss would not surrender: he was a brave man indeed and one who was easier to hit than to hurt. In the seventeenth, Mace trapped Goss on the ropes and caught him hard on the temple. Then he drove a shot to the throat which made Goss look like his eyes had started from their sockets. Somehow Goss got out of the trap and began to fight back – to the clear surprise of Mace – but he denied Goss space by working the angles and his next attack was ruthless. A barrage of blows to the brows brought blood streaming from Goss's eyes, his features lacerated by the impact of corkscrew shots. Mace rationed these deadly blows because of the danger of damage to his own fists and waited for Goss's arms to drop, then he marshalled him against the ropes. Sizing up the target, he delivered a punch of unprecedented ferocity to the precise point where the upper jaw separates from the lower. For the first time in their lives, experienced spectators saw a man spin like a top, then stagger to the ground with vacant eyes and pitch forward senseless on his face. Goss's upper body lay motionless while his legs twitched convulsively.

The loser, he was not badly hurt but it was fully five minutes before he came to. He had contributed only his marvellous bravery to the mill, while a multitude of things about Jem Mace – his dancing style, his deadly accurate jabbing, the calculation of his strategy and his ability not only to respond to the crowd's mood but to influence it directly – were beginning to take boxing out of the stultifying confines of the old Prize Ring, as did his devastating, unanswerable finish.

9

The Girl from the Riding School

HIS SISTER KNEW the full story. She was the only woman he would ever really confide in and he told her what she had long suspected – that, in addition to his various occasional 'wenches', there had been a woman who had completely displaced Mary in his affections. A woman who, nevertheless, he had given up while she was carrying his child. He had stared blankly, waiting for recrimination, but Amelia offered none. She knew her brother was a special kind of man. She had sensed something of it as a child when she heard him slam the door of their parents' home as a lad of fifteen and stride out into the world with only his violin. There were eight years between them and she had always looked up to him. For all his fame and fortune in the all-male world of the ring, he was, as Amelia knew, an artist at heart. Yes, he remained a champion in a world where previously butchers and coal heavers had held the crown, yet he was a musician and as such had found his way back to the world of the circus. And there was no way in the world that Mary, her earnest sister-in-law, would ever cut it in the sawdust and tinsel world.

Amelia had only one question, and she tensed as she asked it, holding back tears and hoping the answer would be the one she dearly wished: yes, he said, before she had even finished the sentence, firmly and truthfully, he had made provision for the child. Mace's relationship with Selina Hart would not be their secret for long, but it was one which he knew Amelia would never be the one to reveal. Nor would Martha Barton, Mary's sister and confidante, who knew how few were the days which Mace was now spending at the Old King John – where Bill Richardson had been happy for them to continue living – and how heavy was the workload that Mary faced. Martha had heard something on the grapevine but never mentioned it to Mary; after all, the three Mace children were the paramount concern. And as Martha knew, their father enjoyed the time, albeit limited, which he had with his children: not just kidding around in boxing gloves with Alfred, as his oldest surviving son entered his tenth year; not just fooling about with James Junior, by now five and in school but full of energy and mischief as soon as he got home, but with Adelaide too. Seven years old and no tomboy, her father had sent her for piano lessons and he did little sketches for her, a wild blob of colours which he said were circus animals.

When Mary finally found out, it was from Jack Hicks's wife. Mace's chief second had blabbed one night when he was drunk but kept the bit about the witness statement quiet. He was too fly to let that out, even in his cups, so what Mary discovered was the name of the woman who was no longer her rival but who, emotionally speaking, had robbed her of her husband, of the man she'd known and loved since they were teenagers in Norwich a dozen years before. No, it was not a surprise; no, she hadn't been so dumb as to think that his adventures were only one-night stands; but yes, it was still a wound, a deep one, and something which could not be glossed over for the sake of the children.

Had she been on her own, Mary might have been obliged to put up with all the absences, the indifference and the stunning news that he'd fathered a child. But by the summer of 1863, she was only alone, in the emotional sense, when she was in her own home at Holywell Lane. The new man in her life was John Richard Roberts, born and bred in London and a tailor by trade, thirty-one years old and as ordinary and unremarkable as his name. From Mary's point of view, that was half his attraction – she knew fame, and she'd seen and heard enough of it: the nights when half the East End, or so it seemed, had poured into their small abode; the nights when the drunken toasts had gone on till the early hours while she tried to sleep upstairs or to pacify the bewildered children; the nights when the toffs and their ladies, those women who would hardly give her a second glance, invaded her house and home; the nights when the fight crowd gathered for an evening of drink and gluttony and wild wagers. And in particular, the night when an oaf from Bradford had invaded her kitchen and proceeded to carve and roast a whole lamb's carcass before taking it out into the bar and proceeding to consume it. To win some stupid bet and, as he thought, to impress the landlord.

Dick Roberts wanted no part of that world. He was a quiet man, studying to become an optician. He detested pugilism and would never have dreamed of taking a railway special to the Kentish Marshes. He had never raised his fist in anger, had little interest in drink and didn't waste his money on wagers. Most of the women he'd met had dismissed him as a bore. Yet he was, in the summer of 1863, if not yet in possession of the Champion of England's woman, at least on the brink of it. He held back not from scruple but from the fear that he might be visited by Mace himself and reduced to pulp within seconds.

Roberts need not have worried. By this time Mace had ceased to care what Mary might do when she ventured out of Shoreditch on some pretext or other. He did not know but, even if he had, he would not have cared less that Roberts was in love with his wife and that his love for her touched her heart in a way it had not been touched for years. When Mary told him she knew about Selina and wanted them to part, she was careful to make no mention of Dick Roberts. Mace did not speak about what they had once meant to each other and made no effort to dissuade her. His only question was about the children. Their proper place was in London, in school, not on the road with their father's circus, and Mace, who had never had a formal education, was determined that his offspring would not lack for it – Alfred had already been noted by his teachers as an intelligent boy. Although he would not be able to see them regularly, he insisted that they see him when he was back in town. He would provide Mary with money to feed, clothe, house and school them. Mary agreed. It was the best deal she could expect, or that any woman who was the wife of a wealthy man but whose marriage had failed could expect at that time.

When the Matrimonial Causes Act of 1857 was first brought in, it was denounced by opponents as 'an adulterer's charter'. In their view, it would be an easy way for a man to dispose of a wife he no longer wanted, especially if he had found another woman. The act did allow women to petition for divorce as well, but there was a double standard: a man could cast off his wife provided there was proof of her adultery and, if there was no hint of her having been unfaithful, he could take his leave and, two years later, get a divorce on the grounds of desertion. His sole real obligation was to maintain their children, provided, that is, that she remained alone. But if there was the slightest hint of her being 'with another man', then the husband's duty to provide for his children was abrogated. Given the gross inequality of earnings in mid-century Britain, a woman with divorce on her mind had to watch her step with the utmost care. However, if a woman chose to file for divorce from her husband, she had to prove not only adultery but 'aggravated adultery'. In other words, his adultery had to be aggravated by an additional form of misconduct. His wife now had to prove either that her husband had been cruel, or that he was insane, or that he had been convicted in court of a sexual offence. Unless she could do this, she could not divorce him.

The implications for the Maces were made obvious when they consulted their respective lawyers. Of all the possible grounds for divorce against a man, most were inapplicable to Jem, but there was one possible cause which some of Mary's women friends thought she might consider: cruelty. This was considered at that time to be a purely physical matter; the notion of emotional cruelty was barely even a concept. On the other hand, a prize-fighter, a man whose job involved inflicting physical hurt without compunction, might well be considered in a court of law, by virtue of his illegal occupation alone, to be a potential wife beater. Mary dismissed the suggestion with contempt. Mace had never struck her or even threatened to. He abhorred the very thought of a man lifting his hand against a woman and had made his feelings plain: any man, be he pugilist, bar customer or circus performer who had ever bragged of so doing became an instant outcast as far as he was concerned.

Until the details of the separation were finalised, Mary and the children continued to live at the Old King John. She then wanted out and moved the children into rented accommodation a mile and a half away in Hoxton. Though far from genteel, it was a cut above Shoreditch in terms of social class. The rent would be paid from Mace's account, together with full provision for the three children. Thus, in September 1863, Jem and Mary Mace formally separated. Despite his considerable fame, it was not reported in the newspapers of the day, which rarely publicised such matters. Mary was saddened but relieved, while her former husband looked forward to a life of untrammelled freedom on tour with the circus. He knew that Mary would, whenever he was at leisure in London, hand over the children to either Amelia or Martha, who would return them to their home after they'd spent time with their father. Thinking no more of it, he turned his footsteps to the heartland of the circus, in the North of England.

* * *

Hannah Boorn reached her sixteenth birthday on 31 August 1863. She was already a fully mature young woman, both physically and mentally, and lacked only the experience of being in love to realise her emotional potential. Hannah's sophistication stemmed from her background in the circus. Her father, Benjamin, had been born at Buckland, near Dover, and had learned to ride horses at an early age and later to break them in. He came to London as a lad, met and married Hannah's mother when they were teenagers and earned his living for a while as a door-to-door salesman. That was his occupation when Hannah was born in 1847 at Hewitt's Field Grove in Hackney. Hannah's mother was the daughter of a news vendor and had learned to read and write at a time when it was still rare for working-class girls to do so. Boorn had the rudiments of education and his children would all be fully literate and numerate. They were familiar with newspapers because their grandfather sold them and indeed Fannie, the eldest daughter, married William Jacey, a printer and compositor.

In time the ambitious Boorn set himself up as an equestrian director. A brilliant horseman, he found employment with several of the leading circuses of the day and taught all of his six children to ride at an early age. They followed him into circus employment as they entered their teens. Boorn's skills brought him to the attention of Charles Hengler, who was of German descent and frequently toured his circus in Prussia. By 1860 he was venturing further afield and Hengler's Circus received an invitation to perform in Russia. The Boorns' youngest four children, including Hannah, made the trip with their parents and visited both the imperial capital, St Petersburg, and the ancient capital, Moscow. Hannah's youngest brother, Alfred, was born in Russia when she was thirteen and already a circus equestrienne, though she resumed her studies for a further year when the family returned to London and she went to work at her father's riding school. There he made money giving lessons to city folk who wished to ride as a hobby, and trained equestrians of both sexes for the circus.

Hannah was the most accomplished of the Boorn youngsters and was an extremely pretty girl, with big brown eyes, dark skin and long dark locks which she combed vigorously as she studied herself in a tiny pink hand mirror. Her figure was full and firm and, at least while performing as a circus equestrienne, she could display her legs, something which, during the Victorian age, was taboo. Her limbs were long and her thighs sturdy but feminine. Trained to the saddle for a dozen years, she was quick to learn the bareback style which was increasingly in vogue in the circus.

It was towards the close of 1863 when Mace first cast eyes on her. She was standing bare-legged in ballerina pose on her black mare, being carried at a fast trot around the perimeter of the sawdust ring. He sensed that she knew immediately who he was. She had dismounted and was whispering to other girls while trying to catch his eye; as soon as his penetrating gaze met hers, she flushed slightly and lowered her eyelids. At first he noted only what every other man in the circus noted: that Hannah was a very attractive and vivacious girl. But when her father came to collect her, Jem felt sure he recognised Ben from somewhere on the sawdust circuit. If he was not mistaken, he was not only a man of means but one who was in high demand with circus troupes and probably looking to set himself up on his own, or to amalgamate with another circus. And at forty-two, he was only ten years older than Mace and still looking forward to making a fortune. Hannah seemed to know who her admirer was and her father certainly did, as he was acquainted with the prize-fight world. He lost little time in introducing them.

Mace detected at once that she was not just another of the many girls who had crossed his path. She was amazingly confident for sixteen, and soon he was the one who was listening fascinated as Hannah recounted tales of life in Russia which, under the young Tsar Alexander II, was modernising rapidly. Alexander II had succeeded to the throne in the middle of the Crimean War and been appalled by Russia's backwardness, military and otherwise, which led to defeat at the hands of Britain and France on her own soil. This had led him to accept Western influence in popular culture and to embrace the circus on a level with the dramatic stage. Her stories of the splendours of St Petersburg were so vivid that Mace felt the itch to visit the city himself. And, of course, not alone but with the lovely young lady who beguiled him with these narratives.

Hannah had told her mother that, within seconds of spying Jem Mace, she had the instinctive feeling that she would become his wife. It seemed obvious to both of them that there was no other woman in his life – he was always in male company or on his own. Hannah and her mother knew nothing of the prize-ring but, when Mace thought about it, it was perfectly possible that Boorn might know that he was still a married man, albeit separated from his wife. Jem deployed Pooley to find out what Boorn knew about the LPR but it turned out that his knowledge extended only to pugilistic matters. He had, to Mace's relief, picked up nothing on the grapevine about the private lives of fighters.

Although Hannah didn't speak with a strong Cockney accent, Mace detected that she was a Londoner. He asked her to write her name in his address book and she complied with a flowing signature. What a contrast to the schoolmaster's daughter who had pulled the wool over his eyes on their wedding day in Thorpe – and what a contast to the values implanted in Mary's head by, as Jem saw it, that old fool of a Scottish schoolmaster father. Here, in the world of the circus, was a modern young woman who was equipped to be the wife of the entrepreneur he was on the cusp of becoming. In love as they soon were, Mace would need to approach the subject of marriage with care. Many men in his situation, legally separated from a wife but not divorced, would not even have considered it, but he cared nothing for the strictures of the Church. He'd always detested the talk of preachers and what he saw as their cant about 'the sanctity of marriage' and 'living in sin', the phrase they used to describe an unwed couple who lived together as man and wife. Mace cared nothing for the law either, except if he could manipulate it to serve his purposes. He had stood beyond the law since, at the age of eighteen, he had first raised his fists in a bareknuckle fight. If he needed to commit bigamy in order to go through a marriage ceremony with Hannah, then he would do so. And he would, it seemed, have to do so. Boorn might consider the business partnership which Mace was offering to be a splendid prospect, but he didn't intend to give a virtual dowry for his daughter without the security of a wedding ring. Similarly, Hannah's mother had impressed on her that she was not to yield to Mace's advances until their vows had been publicly made. Of course, as Mace saw it, he could lie to Hannah about his marital status but, if she then found him out, she might never believe him over anything else again. Not knowing that his dilemma was soon to be resolved, he withdrew himself temporarily from her tempting presence and decided to spend Christmas in Manchester, while she and her family went home to London.

As the circus began to vie with the Prize Ring for Mace's attention, and following the break-up of his marriage, he began to base himself in Manchester, establishing an interest in a pub in the city centre in Boundary Street, off Oxford Road. This provided him with a domicile and a regular income. Jem was well known in the city due to his earlier tour with Fanque and Manchester was thus a good place from which to operate his own circus. There was another reason why he decided on a move there – it had become the capital of pedestrianism. Although the city was growing at an incredible rate, there were far more open spaces within its boundaries than in London. Unlike the Prize Ring, professional running was not illegal, despite evangelical hostility to the heavy gambling which it attracted. In the decades before the advent of Association football, pedestrianism was England's premium legal sport and Manchester was its hub.

Between 1850 and 1865, four great cinder tracks were laid in the city, each attached to a well-known public house: the Snipe Inn at Ancoats, Belle Vue House, Copenhagen Grounds by the Shears Inn at Newton Heath, and the City Grounds in the heart of the city centre. Three of these had a circuit of at least a quarter of a mile and each could accommodate thousands of spectators. Mace intended to create a rival track at Boundary Street which would go one further, in size and capacity, than the others. But to his anger, he was upstaged by the dynamic, albeit mentally unstable, entrepreneur George Martin, the self-styled 'wizard of pedestrianism', who bought up sixteen acres of land on the main road to Oldham. Martin's Royal Oak Grounds, together with the Copenhagen Grounds and the City Grounds, were the venues for the great series of mile races in the early 1860s featuring such top athletes as Siah Albison, Bill Lang, Teddy Mills and Bill

Richards, during which the world record was smashed several times. Mace was present at some of these and he noticed, with annoyance, the way in which Martin had established connections with influential local politicians who were chatting amiably with him. He took due note against the time when a similar opportunity might arise elsewhere.

Having seen Heenan hanging round the West End drums earlier in the year, it was no surprise when Mace learnt that he had been matched in a major prize fight. Clearly that was why Heenan had come to England. He had seemed uninterested in Mace's offer to take him on in the ring and it was now clear why: his backers were wealthy Americans and they were prepared to put up no less than £1,000 in stake money for him – to fight Tom King. In fact, Heenan had originally left America with the intention of challenging Mace for the English Championship Belt but Mace's defeat by King, and King's subsequent retirement, had altered the equation. King had returned the Belt to Dowling's office and there it remained. While Heenan and his buddies might try to promote the fight as being for the World Championship, neither Dowling nor the Committee of the PBA would agree to that. Thus any mention of the Belt was kept out of the Articles of Agreement. These were subtleties which would be lost on the American fight public, which had to rely purely on its own media for coverage. If Heenan won, he could return to the States and promote himself as the first undisputed World Champion; if King won, he would be richer by £2,000 on winner-takes-all. This mighty purse was what tempted King out of retirement. At first disbelieving that he would succeed in finding the unprecedented stake money, King was persuaded by various backers, notably the businessman Charlie Bush.

As for Mace, he regarded the upcoming bout with contempt. He sneered as he read about the spurious claim of a world title being contested and was reassured by Dowling's non-recognition and that of the PBA. But he was angry when he learned that, in contrast to his own fights with King, the police intended to let the mill take place with no hint of interference – in fact they would even occupy the forecourt at London Bridge station with a force of several hundred men to protect ticket-holders from being attacked by hooligans. He heard of the diligence of one Superintendent Bradford and concluded, whether accurately or not, that Bradford must have been bribed. Still, curiosity got the better of Mace and he decided to go down to London to watch the mill. Preoccupied with other matters, he had been off the fight scene for a few months and had not turned up at the payment of the stakes for his victory over Goss, leaving Bill Richardson to collect on his behalf. *Bell's Life* had been quick to condemn him for his absence, declaring it 'an unheard of slight to The Fancy'.

King and Heenan fought on 8 December 1863 at Wadhurst in Sussex, just over the Kent boundary from the genteel suburban town of Tunbridge Wells. Tom Sayers, Heenan's opponent from the world title clash in 1860, was now in his old foe's corner. The bout lasted only thirty-five minutes. The American, clearly ring-rusty, relied almost wholly on the wrestling tactics which had served him well against Sayers, but King was much taller than Sayers and could use his height for leverage. He also blasted the American with a barrage of body shots, thus forcing him to release his neck holds. One of Heenan's fierce throws did leave King on the turf groaning in pain but Jerry Noon's distracting trickery – he falsely claimed that the Englishman had been kicked – enabled King's other second, Bos Tyler, to revive him and bring him up to the scratch as the thirty-second limit was nearly up. King, shocked by how close he'd come to a fluke defeat, then delivered an almighty beating, jabbing Heenan to the point of blindness and eventually causing him to collapse, puking blood from the battering to his belly. Heenan would return to the States angry, and rightly so, that he'd been cheated out of a victory to which, under LPR rules, he was entitled. King would return to his rose garden an even richer man. Despite his disdain for the spurious world title claims of both combatants, Mace could only applaud Heenan's bravery in standing up to King to the point where he was in danger of his life. Even so, his gesture of taking the hat round for the plucky American cunningly served to remind the spectators of what he considered the true pecking order.

George Courthorpe, the owner of the land at Wadhurst, was furious about his tenant's agreement with the prize-fight party. He took the two fighters and their seconds to Lewes Crown Court and King, Heenan and Sayers were bound over not to engage in a further fight. It was a hollow victory for the authorities, since Sayers was already retired, King had returned for one mill only and Heenan was going back to the States for good. Mace was also summonsed and charged with aiding and abetting, but with his whole career at stake, he argued that he'd been a mere spectator. To his immense but coolly concealed relief, the magistrate ordered Courthorpe to drop charges against him.

The fistic implications of the fight were obvious to all knowledgeable observers. First, King had triumphed by superior boxing skill, reflecting not only what Jem Ward had taught him but what he'd learned in combat against Mace. Second, the clash threw light on the respective merits of not only King and Heenan but Mace and Sayers. King might be far cleverer than Heenan (with the American admittedly disadvantaged by a three-year layoff) but against Mace at Godstone, he'd lost when the conditions were all in his favour, and at Thames Haven he'd been a lucky winner after taking a beating for much of the fight. As for Sayers, his epic clash at Farnborough had seen him unable to defeat Heenan.

Bell's Life did not publish rankings for prize-fighters. Had it done so, and on a consistent basis, the order might well have seen Sayers and Heenan vying for third place, with King second and Mace first. When he considered the result, Mace became more confident than ever in his own ability to defeat Sayers, whose name still carried great weight with the public. He knew that Sayers was unhappy in his retirement and that he could not flourish in any other environment except the Prize Ring. Even Sayers' attempts to become a second had been shown up. At Wadhurst, his naivety, in contrast to Noon and Tyler, had been obvious. Mace was sure that if he could only get Sayers away from his cronies in London, he could coax him into a fight. Once in the ring, Mace would make his supremacy clear.

Meanwhile, Mace had received a letter out of the blue from his sister Amelia with important news: she had heard from Martha Barton that Mary was not living alone but had, in fact, been living for some time with Dick Roberts in the rooms which he rented in Gopsall Street, Hoxton. The children were being adequately looked after, but Martha did not like the arrangement. Mary putting her mark on a Deed of Separation was one thing; living openly with Roberts was another. Mary's marriage had ended in failure but this was far from an ideal arrangement for Alfred, Adelaide and James Junior. Mace saw his chance at once – there was no question of Mary being merely a lodger. Roberts was a single man in his early thirties, not some old dodderer, and Mace went back to London to consult his lawyer. Surely he had a cast-iron case for divorce? Yes, responded the lawyer. Under the Matrimonial Causes Act, there seemed to be a *prima facie* case of simple adultery. Right, said Mace, I might be a wealthy man, and I've maintained my children, no doubt about that, but I'm damned if I'm going to carry on doing so if another man is posing as their stepfather. Keep up the payments for now, cautioned the solicitor, adding that it might be only a matter of weeks for the case to reach court.

But hard evidence would be needed, so a private investigator was hired to spy on Roberts's house. He made a sworn statement that Mary went there and stayed the night. Accordingly, on 11 December 1863, a petition in the name of James Mace was filed with the Court of Divorce seeking a divorce from his wife Mary Ann Mace on the grounds of her adultery with John Richard Roberts. What's more, Mace, as usual in need of ready money because of his constant gambling, demanded that Roberts pay him no less than £500 in damages. A barrister was instructed and the matter seemed all sewn up: by spring he would be free of Mary, who would have to decide for herself whether she wanted to continue with this nobody or whether she wanted the maintenance payments for her children. Above all, he would be free to do what he pleased and he eagerly anticipated lying with Hannah in his arms.

But there were delays. Mary was slow in answering his charge and Roberts even slower. Mace did not know what Mary was up to – and he was in for a rude awakening. Eventually she returned to her own lawyer's office. Whatever the legal eagle's private view of her assertion that 'Mr. Roberts is just a friend', he was obliged to take Mary's word if he was also taking her money. But she had more, much more, to add, which interested her solicitor greatly, for it promised the opportunity to further his career by winning a high-profile case against one of the most famous men in the land. What Mary now had was a witness statement in the name of one Mary Marshall, who testified that, four years earlier, when she was living near Selina Hart, she used to see Jem

Mace spend the night there when Selina was home alone – with her mother and the Phillipses away visiting other relatives. This could make a key difference to the outcome of the case if the judge were to decide that Mary had committed adultery with Roberts but only because Jem had driven her to it by cheating with Selina. Mace was informed by his own lawyer not merely that Mary had denied adultery with Roberts, but that she had evidence of his adultery with Selina.

It would not be an open-and-shut case and Mace took a decision of which his lawyer knew nothing: he told Hannah about Mary and Selina and that he'd been seeking a divorce, but that Mary was trying to block it. Hannah soon stifled her tears. She was not going to let some middle-aged woman – as she viewed Mary – spoil her wedding plans. And, as far as Selina was concerned, this was all before her time. So Mace once had a mistress? In the circus world, such arrangements were commonplace. What's more, Hannah revealed her awareness of the new divorce law. Mace might have cheated on Mary, she said, but that wasn't sufficient to disqualify his petition or to let Mary off the hook about this fellow Roberts. However, as Hannah was only too well aware, there was one other person who must be considered: her own father. He would be shocked and might withhold his consent to the marriage, as he was entitled to do, in view of Hannah's age; girls under twenty-one needed paternal consent to marry. Boorn might have laughed about such a set of circumstances if they concerned other people, but not if his darling daughter was at the centre of the scenario. And it would be very difficult, as Hannah now told Mace, to keep a divorce case from her parents – it would be in the papers, the very papers which her brother-in-law printed and her grandfather sold. Mace could obtain his divorce but at the cost of alienating Hannah's parents and her entire family.

Between them, the lovers decided on an alternative scenario: Mace would ask Ben for Hannah's hand in marriage and Hannah would tell her mother that nothing would be dearer to her heart. The wedding would then go ahead while they were awaiting Mace's divorce. It would be a bigamous marriage, of course, albeit, as they saw it, only for a matter of months. Hannah's family would discover the truth in due course but by then it would be a *fait accompli*. The marriage had to take place well away from London, so Mary did not get word of it; her precise motives in resisting divorce were not clear, although she felt that she didn't deserve the blame for the break-up of her marriage. But apart from the matter of responsibility, she had little to gain. The children were being provided for, as matters stood, and as she could not prove any other matrimonial offence against Mace, she could not cross-petition for divorce herself. Thus she would not be free to marry Roberts.

Mace and Hannah duly went about arranging their marriage, with Boorn still in the dark about giving his consent to a bigamous union. If he was surprised that no banns were read out, but that a licence was obtained instead, he said nothing. On 17 February 1864, Hannah Boorn, who falsely added a year to her age to make herself seventeen, walked down the aisle to meet thirty-two-year-old Jem Mace at the altar of the Anglican Church of St John's in Manchester. Mace chose to describe himself as a musician, one of his several occupations. As he prepared to sign the parish register, he lied that he was a bachelor. The newlyweds lived in Manchester, at Boundary Street, and Hannah adjusted easily to life in a pub. She was happy simply to be with Jem and had reason to believe that it would only be a few months before he would be formally divorced. She would, of course, have wished to have married in the usual way but, in her eyes, bigamy was at worst a regrettable necessity and certainly not, as Church-based morality dictated, a source of shame. What mattered was that she was in love and that Mary would become history in a matter of months.

From Mace's point of view, he had beside him a beautiful young woman, brought up to circus life, open-minded and sensual, well-travelled and used to meeting interesting people. Thanks to Amelia he had the ammunition to shoot down Mary when the case came to court. Boorn might be startled when he discovered the full truth, but at least he would recognise Mace's determination to make Hannah his wife, and their prospective joint enterprise in the circus would not be jeopardised. But if Mary were to learn about Hannah, then Mace's case would be compromised.

On March 1, Mace – after a fortnight's adulterous romp with his teenage 'bride' – presented himself at his lawyer's office, heard the charges that he'd committed adultery with Miss Hart at her home and 'at diverse low places in Middlesex', took the Bible in one hand and brazenly lied that he'd ever had Selina's knickers off anywhere on earth. Faced with charges and denials, the judge who was listed to try the case decided that he would do so on oral evidence alone. Meanwhile, he struck out Mace's claim for damages against Roberts.

On 30 June 1864, the case of Mace v Mace and Roberts was heard at the Court of Justice and Matrimonial Causes in Westminster, before a judge whose legal title of Mr Justice Ordinary in fact cloaked the identity of Sir James Plaisted Wilde. It was the fifth and last case heard on that day. Three previous petitions had been successful: two from husbands alleging adultery had resulted in decrees nisi; one by a wife alleging both adultery and cruelty had the same outcome. Mace was confident as his turn came but, unlike the Prize Ring, the court of justice depended not on his ability to 'carry the referee with me in my fists', as he would later put it, but on the argumentation of counsel and on the law as interpreted by the judge. His counsel, Mr Beesley, went through the facts of the case in so far as they favoured Mace. The emphasis was obviously on the Deed of Separation having been executed at Mary's wish, only to be followed by her observed co-habitation with Roberts. Mr Beesley added that Mace had been maintaining his three surviving children and that his wife did not dispute that.

The judge enquired as to Mr Mace's occupation. For once there could be no subterfuge. The name 'James Mace' was by now one of the most famous in the land. It might be possible to trick some old vicar in Manchester but not a London judge. Any man who belonged to 'polite society', in other words the upper class and the high bourgeoisie, would know the names of the top pugilists in the land, whatever he might think about bareknuckle fighting. The judge merely nodded as Mr Beesley uttered the words 'prize-fighter'.

Mary's counsel, Mr Horne Paine, delivered the Answer. Staring around the courtroom, as if denying any one to contradict him, he intoned that Mrs Mace was not guilty of adulterous intercourse. However, Mace had himself been involved in just such a liaison. Mr Horne Paine spoke slowly as he added the words 'a few years ago'. Then he sought the judge's permission to introduce a further witness. Mace bit his lip and clenched his fists in suppressed fury as Jack Hicks took the stand. He revealed the details of the Deed of Settlement he had witnessed four years earlier, whereby Mace paid Selina Hart to waive any future claim for his maintenance of their child. Selina herself, the classical 'woman scorned', had spoken not a word to bring down the man who had once loved her and who still held a place in her heart. Instead, he had been betrayed by a man who had paid lip-service to the much touted 'manly code' of the Prize Ring, only to sell out his comrade when the price was right.

The judge was not deceived into thinking that Mary's relationship with Roberts was platonic, but it was clear that Mace and Selina Hart had been sexually involved well before Roberts came into the picture. In the opinion of his lordship, Mace's affair with Selina had very probably 'conduced' to his wife's liaison with Roberts. Thus there was no reason for making this case an exception to the general rule, that a petitioner who had been guilty of adultery was not entitled to come to court for a dissolution of his marriage on account of the respondent's adultery. He finished with the words 'accordingly I dismiss this petition', adding only that Mace must pay his wife's costs of £105. Whether the judge had acted strictly in accordance with his interpretation of the Matrimonial Causes Act and with precedent case law would never be known. Many people conjectured that the outcome might have been different had Mace not been, as a pugilist, an outlaw by definition.

Mace had thus been thwarted in his wish to get rid of Mary Ann Barton for ever. He couldn't have cared less that his wife was sleeping with another man. He'd played by 'their rules', the rules of a society to which he felt he'd never belonged. What did the aptly named Mr Justice Ordinary know about risking your life in the Prize Ring? Of standing in the biting cold and pouring rain and trading blows for an hour or more with a determined and ruthless opponent? What did Mr Justice Ordinary know of life on the road, of entertainment, of music not played in some genteel concert hall but before an exuberant crowd of working-class families, released from the drudgery of their mill town servitude? What did that fat bloated old fool sitting on his arse pontificating about legal niceties know about youth and life and the pleasures of the flesh?

The details of the case were reported in five paragraphs of *The Times*, including the words 'the well-known prizefighter Jem Mace'.

They would be read by Hannah's relatives. From their point of view, the most important thing was that Hannah's name did not appear in print. This woman, Mary Mace or Mary Roberts, whatever she chose to call herself, knew nothing of Hannah's existence and even if she found out, there was nothing she could do about it. Mace's divorce case did not become generally known. Whereas in the twenty-first century a famous sportsman and entertainer would expect the merest rumours about his personal life to become instant tabloid fodder, in the mid-nineteenth century, with no compulsory schooling, the majority of the population remained illiterate. The newspapers of the educated did refer briefly to divorce cases but there was, at that time, no mass market for scandalous gossip.

Mary had achieved nothing by her formal 'Answer and Countercharge', not even the prevention of Mace from remarrying, albeit bigamously. She had failed to clear her own name and was not free to remarry. She had the children, of course, but she had had them anyway. It remained to be seen how her new life would be with Roberts. Mace's ambiguous marital status would become well-known in the world of the London Prize Ring. Few men there would pay it the slightest heed. But, as for the circus-goers who heard rumours of the truth about 'the girl from the riding school', it merely served to add to Mace's roguish reputation.

Three years earlier, in 1861, Queen Victoria's German-born husband, Albert of Saxe-Coburg-Gotha, the Prince Consort, had died. The monarch, whose love for him had been extraordinary, given that theirs was of course an arranged dynastic marriage, had been grief-stricken by his death. As the years passed, she still remained a virtual recluse at Windsor, and public affection for her, which had been great during the days of her youth, began to fade. The downbeat atmosphere surrounding the monarchy did not chime with the general mood. The wish for release from the strictures of middle-class morality was strong and no man incarnated the mood of unbridled hedonism and defiance of the bourgeoisie more than Jem Mace. Indeed, Edward, Prince of Wales, the heir to the throne and a rakish young man in his mid-twenties, would spy Mace at a theatre, address him as 'Jem' and warmly shake his hand.

10

The 'Cowardly Englishman' and the Knockout Tour

ON A CLEAR autumn day, the Wicklow Mountains appeared to the south as the ship steamed into Dublin Bay. Mace was in a reflective mood as he spied them in the distance. He was struck by their beauty and by the contrast with the flat plain of Norfolk and Suffolk, the landscape of his youth. Gregarious man of action as he was, there were still times when he preferred to be alone with his thoughts. The emerald headland of Howth seemed to him to be the gateway to a beautiful land, and the journey to it had appealed to his innate sense of adventure.

And yet Mace was, from a strictly professional point of view, deeply reluctant, even angry, to have to make this journey. When he received his first American challenge, he accepted it without hesitation. He had assumed, quite naturally, that the clash would take place in one of the usual locations. When Heenan had challenged Sayers, they met in Hampshire; when Heenan had confronted King, it had been in Kent. But this new Irish-American was a man of a very different stripe to the 'Benicia Boy'. Joseph Coburn was born in 1835, within a month of Heenan, but unlike him was not a native-born American. Coburn came from Middletown in County Armagh. Living in close proximity to the Ulster Presbyterian loyalists of predominantly Scottish extraction, the Northern Catholics felt their Irish identity in a particularly intense way. For a Northerner such as Coburn, the mere fact of the Act of Union in 1800, by itself, meant that Ireland was under alien rule. And he had personally experienced the Great Famine of 1845–9, during which well over a million Irish men, women and children starved to death and for whose effects all Roman Catholic Irish held England responsible. Although he did not join the Fenian Brotherhood, he almost certainly was a sympathiser. The Fenian

Brotherhood had been set up in the US by Irish immigrants and was dedicated to the overthrow of British rule in Ireland, using violent methods if necessary.

Whereas many Irish immigrants to the US aspired only to unskilled labour, Coburn was a skilled monumental stonemason by trade. Taking up bareknuckle boxing, he disdained the all-action style of his fellow Irish-born American pugilists, John Morrisey and Yankee Sullivan (James Ambrose). Instinctively, he boxed in the scientific manner which, 3,000 miles away, Nat Langham had used and then passed on to Mace. As well as genuine boxing skill, Coburn possessed immense durability, remaining undefeated in a three-and-a-half-hour battle for the middleweight championship of America. Coburn was, like Mace, a man no more than 5ft 9½in tall who relied on speed, footwork and tactical cunning. Like Tom King he had two fast hands but he lacked King's fighting heart. He had put on the gloves to spar with Heenan before the Benicia Boy first departed for England and had been content to evade Heenan's powerful hitting without in any way forcing the pace, even for purposes of an exhibition.

For a full five years, Coburn was out of the ring, having invested his savings from stonemasonry in a saloon on Grand Street in New York City. But when Heenan refused his challenge for the Heavyweight Championship of America, Coburn claimed the right to contest it for himself. With Heenan away in England, Coburn took on Mike McCoole, another Irish-American, in Maryland in May 1863. Although Coburn had shown no interest in the American Civil War then raging, his defeat of McCoole, who hailed from St Louis, Missouri, was taken as symbolic of the cataclysmic conflict between Northern Yankees and Southern Confederates. Coburn and McCoole had nothing in common except Irish ethnicity. McCoole, a Mississippi riverboat deckhand, was tall, suntanned, burly, boozy and crude. Coburn was wiry and pale-skinned with wavy hair already half receded. His sharp features wore a sardonic sneer. After an hour and ten minutes, Coburn's sidestep and left jab had outwitted McCoole and so battered his features that his seconds threw in the sponge.

Acclaimed as heavyweight champion of America, Coburn waited for the result of the Heenan–King fight. When King won, he sent over a challenge but this time King's retirement remained permanent, whereupon Coburn challenged Mace to come to America and fight him. Mace received Coburn's challenge in January 1864, when he was immersed in personal matters. That, combined with Coburn being unknown in England, caused him to decline, but as the year unfolded and the issues in Mace's private life were resolved, he could ignore Coburn no longer. The retirement of King and then of Heenan, which soon followed, left him standing alone among the four fighters who had dominated pugilism for half a decade. Alone except, of course, for Tom Sayers.

Sayers' presence as one of Heenan's seconds at the Wadhurst mill had convinced Mace how much his rival missed the Prize Ring. Early in the year, he had invited Sayers to Manchester and the two had sparred with the gloves on. It seemed Sayers was more than ready to return and to afford Mace the opportunity to demonstrate whether or not he was, as the contemporary phrase had it, 'the cleverest man of his day'. But as soon as Sayers returned to London, his cronies prevailed on him not to risk his annuity in a one-off fight with Jem. The exasperated Mace accepted Coburn's challenge when the American finally offered to come to England. The stakes were large, £500 a side, and both Coburn and Mace went on separate sparring tours as a promotional stunt. Then Coburn appeared to throw a spanner into the works: he and his backers suddenly insisted that the match must take place in Ireland. Coburn was adamant. He would 'not face Mace with an English crowd at his back'. He cited the treatment handed out to Heenan at Farnborough. The entire US press believed that Heenan would have won if English hooligans had not invaded the ring. What's more, said Coburn, Heenan had been a victim of injustice at Wadhurst when Noon's diversionary tactics had prevented what would have been the American's victory, albeit by a lucky throw.

Coburn had touched on matters which the anti-prize-fight lobby was eager to keep close to the surface. True, there had been no hooliganism at Wadhurst, unlike Farnborough, but, besides Noon's chicanery, there were widespread, albeit unfounded, rumours of corruption. It had been alleged in the London media that Heenan's inept performance was easily explained: he'd been doped by his chief second, Jack MacDonald, who was being paid for the purpose. MacDonald countered with an allegation that Heenan had sold the fight. However absurd these rumours, they caused a sensation and helped to sell *The Sportsman*, a rival to *Bell's Life*. All this was grist to the mill to the alliance of industrialists, reformers and evangelicals who loathed prize-fighting and wanted to see it stamped out. Now they had bribery and corruption to add to the sins for which the 'ruffians of the ring' were responsible, in addition to riotous assembly and, of course, 'unspeakable brutality'. With such bad publicity, the chances of the match between Mace and Coburn coming off in England were diminishing.

Mace's usual backers did not want to go to Ireland, but to a lavish spender and gambler such as he was, a purse of £1,000 was a very attractive one. And when he learned that *Bell's Life* intended to send reporters to Ireland to cover the bout, he became convinced. To his anger, the Committee of the Pugilistic Benevolent Association had refused to recognise his bout with Goss as being for the Heavyweight Championship, but it was in the offices of *Bell's Life* where the Champion's Belt still remained. With King having abdicated and Heenan as pretender to the throne, he would go to Ireland, dispose of Coburn and call on Dowling to return the trophy which, he felt, symbolised his supremacy. As Coburn was the new Champion of America, Mace would, if he defeated him, become Champion of the World. Mace succeeded in convincing one of the less well-known sporting publicans, Harry Brunton, to back him, and took ship from Liverpool.

Mace trained hard in Ireland. With him was his now customary trainer, the pedestrian John Miller. The Irish were, by tradition, a fighting race but pedestrianism was new to them. Mace and Miller decided to exploit this to their financial advantage. They bet on Mace to lose in a foot race against an Irish novice and Mace eased up so as to allow the jubilant lad to win. Mace duly cleaned up at the bookies. Rumours began to circulate that this was a betting coup and the Royal Irish Constabulary were asked to look into it. Ireland's police were, however, far more concerned with stopping the upcoming prize-fight. They began to shadow Mace, Brunton, Miller and most of Mace's entourage wherever they went. Furthermore, both fighters were denounced throughout every parish in Ireland where it was thought possible that the mill might come off. Mace, used to the hostility of nonconformist preachers back home in England, now found that the Roman Catholic clergy of Ireland were just as ill-disposed towards him. Phrases like 'brutal and disgusting exhibition' were uttered and parishioners were warned that their souls were in mortal danger if they went to witness it. Fearing that no one would turn up, the leading Irish railway company curtly refused to lay on a special train. Nevertheless, Mace intended to go through with it.

When his party met with Coburn and his backers at Woodruff's Hotel in Pierstown on 3 October 1864, the day before the scheduled fight, he agreed to travel by open train to a proposed battlefield at a spot known to the Irish as Kilmartin and to the English as Gould's Cross, nearly 100 miles from Dublin near the town of Thurles in County Tipperary. In and around Dublin itself, Mace had been warmly welcomed as an apolitical sportsman, but out in the countryside things would be different. The Western counties, including Tipperary, had been the ones to suffer most grievously in the Famine. It was there that anti-English feeling was fiercest and where the influence of the Catholic Church was at its height. Coburn might be, as a pugilist, a bad example but he was at least an Irishman, a native son, whereas Mace was soon being characterised as a symbol of English oppression. Still, despite warnings from Brunton, Mace was prepared to go to Tipperary.

But he was certainly not prepared to go along with Coburn's next manoeuvre. Mace assumed that Coburn would accept the representative of *Bell's Life* as referee. Dowling had not travelled but had sent over a young reporter named Smith. Coburn refused to accept Smith and argued that Dowling had not seen fair play for Heenan at Wadhurst and that he could thus not rely on Smith. Miller then suggested Edwin James, a journalist on the *New York Clipper* who had travelled with Coburn's party, as a compromise candidate, but James, who was looking distinctly apprehensive, refused. This prompted Coburn to propose the name of James Bowler, an Irishman, as the official. Mace would not have that. Bowler had no known pugilistic credentials and there were rumours that he was Coburn's brother-in-law. By this time tempers were fraying all around and the meeting broke up without agreement, with Coburn insisting that he would be at the chosen place at the chosen time on the following day.

That evening, disillusioned by the turn of events, Brunton walked

A rare photograph of the young Jem Mace, fresh in London from Norwich, sometime around 1857. His unmarked face attests to both his youth and his defensive skills.

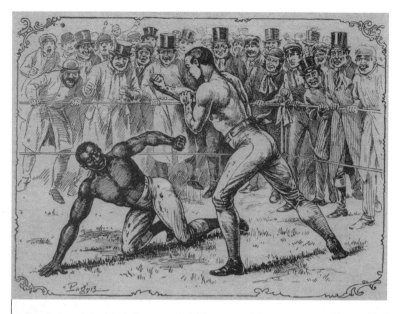

Mace battered the black American Bob Travers to defeat in 1860, and later called him 'one of the gamest fighters I ever stood up to.' This depiction is from the magazine *Famous Fights*.

The self-styled 'Lord' George Sanger, master showman and king of the British circus world, who inspired Mace's decision to acquire a travelling troupe of his own.

The taskmaster: middle-weight champion Nat Langham discovered Mace, took him into his travelling booth – and disciplined him after a youthful act of folly.

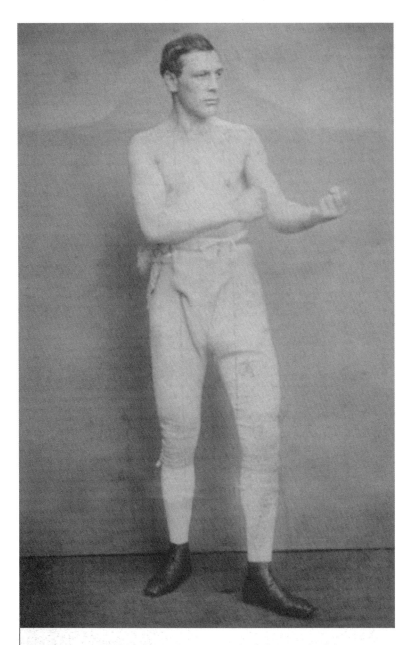

The thirty-year-old Mace in 1861, posing in the fighting garb of the prize ring. Having recently crushed Sam Hurst, he was now Heavyweight Champion of England.

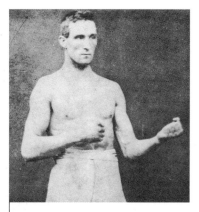

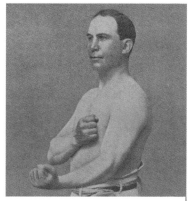

East End stevedore Tom King lost to Mace in 43 brutal rounds, only to take his title with a lucky blow in their rematch. He quickly retired from the ring, though the two later clashed in a street fight.

Cheerful, brawny Joe Goss made up for his lack of boxing skill with great strength as a wrestler and all-round durability.

Right: Mace rests his hands on his hips and still avoids Joe Goss's blows on the way to a victory hailed as 'the grandest bit of fighting ever seen'. They fought on a strip of marshland in Kent.

Resting His Hands on His Hips.

Mace (**below**) displayed his physique for audiences in so-called Grecian Statues routines, popular during the Victorian era. Performers flexed their muscles and struck poses like ancient warriors preparing for battle. His real business was in the ring, however, as a contemporary depiction of Mace challenging the winner of the fight between Tom Sayers (**left**) and American John Heenan (right) for the 'world' title shows. In the event, he fought neither.

The beguiling American actress Adah Isaacs Menken conquered Mace's heart with 'the peerless beauty of her radiant womanhood'. Her admirers included writers, fighters and royalty. She died in Paris at the age of 33.

An Englishman in New York: Mace became a Broadway stage star and, always a smart dresser, quickly adopted American fashions.

Fight matchmaker Harry Hill was one of the most influential men in the American ring and his Manhattan club became something of a base for Mace.

American titleholder Tom Allen lost to Mace in 1870 in a bout to decide the first ever Heavyweight Champion of the World.

Elegant but deadly. From left to right: Billy Edwards, who fought for the world lightweight title, Pooley Mace, Jem's cousin and sparring partner, and Mace himself, then world champion. The photo was taken in San Francisco 1872.

out on Mace and boarded a steamer to Holyhead to catch the overnight train to London. This left Jem in a plight. Even in Ireland, even without his stakeholder, he was bound by the rules of the LPR. If he didn't turn up at the appointed time and place he was bound to pay Coburn forfeit. If he did show, he would expect either to be the victim of crowd intimidation or to lose the putative World Championship by Bowler finding some opportunity, during the course of the mill, to disqualify him without good reason. Coburn and the rest of the American party duly went to Gould's Cross and proceeded to pitch a ring while surrounded by 100 armed police, apparently awaiting the arrival of Mace and thus the commission of an arrestable offence – a breach of the peace. When Mace failed to turn up, Coburn threw his glove into the empty ring and then brazenly announced himself as World Heavyweight Champion. That done, he and his cronies returned to Dublin claiming the purse of £1,000.

Mace had resolved his dilemma by voluntarily going to the police a few hours before he was due in the ring. He could claim he had been arrested and thus was not liable for forfeit to Coburn. Exactly as he anticipated, he was obliged to spend several hours in custody before the police, who failed to proceed with the charge of conspiring to fix a foot race, eventually released him due to lack of evidence. It was therefore not physically possible for him to be at the fight venue at the right time. To Mace's anger, however, Coburn claimed £100 in expenses, which he was entitled to do under the Articles of Agreement. Mace left Miller to hand the money over. Coburn was not satisfied with that and his backers claimed the entire purse. The stakes had been deposited with the youthful representative of *Bell's Life*, Smith, who, assuming that Mace had been arrested, and not wishing to act without Dowling's authority, returned with the stakes to London. The party of English 'sports' who had descended on Ireland for the fight spent one last evening in the bars and brothels of Dublin before returning by ship via Holyhead.

Following this fiasco, Mace was due to return via Liverpool the following day but, before he did so, a remarkable incident occurred in Dublin. Mace, Miller and a few others went for a few drinks in Temple Bar – then, as now, Dublin's liveliest quarter. During the course of a long evening it became known that copies of a printed sheet ballad were selling well. The ditty was entitled 'The Cowardly Englishman' and it mocked Mace as being afraid to take on a 'son of Erin'. It had obviously been prepared well in advance by Coburn's party, both in pursuance of a claim for the purse and to humiliate Mace. With Mace unable to defend himself publicly against such an accusation, the ballad gained rapid credence. It chimed with the image that the hostile powers, notably the Church, wished to propagate.

One man who had heard the ditty sung and who believed it implicitly, burst into the bar where Mace was drinking. Taunting him, he offered him out to fight on the street. Ever since he began to earn a living in the ring, Mace had made it a rule never to raise his fists against anyone other than a fellow prize-fighter. From the day when, as a lad, he punished the bullies who broke his violin in Great Yarmouth, the only other street fight he engaged in was the brief set-to against King outside Tattersalls. It was as simple as this: an ordinary man ran the risk of being killed against a professional fighter. It was a rule he would break only a couple of times in his life and then only when compelled to defend himself. But his challenger was a different proposition. It soon emerged that he was Bartholomew 'Bartley' Gorman, a bareknuckle fighter and a member of the Irish travelling community, and popularly known as 'King of the Gypsies'. Gorman was a powerful man and an experienced pugilist, whose fights took place largely at gypsy camps and fairs and so went unrecorded. As an Irishman, he saw Mace as a symbol of hated English rule, and, as a gypsy, he believed that Mace, whom he supposed to be a fellow Romany, had let the side down.

What followed was perhaps the strangest fight in Mace's career. He and Gorman, jackets off and shirt sleeves rolled up, faced each other on the streets of Temple Bar. Mace, despite being Champion of England, was at a disadvantage. The cobblestones inhibited his usual grace of movement while at the same time threatening Gorman with a skull fracture if Mace knocked him down. Within minutes a crowd of men, predictably, had emptied out of the taverns and gathered in Essex Street to cheer on Gorman, who had at first believed the story of 'The Cowardly Englishman' and expected to meet a 'Fancy Dan', someone with a few tricks of the trade up his sleeve but no fighting heart. As they began to trade blows, suddenly the cry went up: 'Police!' The crowd dissolved and both men took to their heels. But whereas Gorman, who knew the narrow streets like the back of his hand, got away, Mace did not and he spent the night in the cells of the Dublin Bridewell. On finding that he had a ticket on him for a boat return to Liverpool the following day, the Royal Irish Constabulary dropped charges of breach of the peace, did not announce Mace's arrest and contented themselves with confirming that he had indeed boarded ship.

Mace's scrap with Gorman had been the brightest moment of his unhappy sojourn in Ireland. Unlike Coburn, for whom Mace retained a lifelong dislike, the unsung Gorman had battled with nothing at stake but personal pride – and Dubliners had seen for themselves that this Englishman was no coward.*

As soon as he was home, Mace addressed the urgent matter of the return of his stake money. He wrote a letter to Dowling and posted it to the offices of *Bell's Life*. This was, after all, the first time since the Madden fiasco that a fight in which he was scheduled to take part had not come off. In his letter, he put the blame fairly and squarely where he believed it lay and emphasised that he had not let his supporters down: 'I have, for the sake of my backers, taken every pains in training' . . . 'I was never more fit or better in my life . . . I am greatly disappointed at not being permitted to meet Coburn' but (Coburn) 'placed an insurmountable obstacle against our fighting . . . I have reason to suppose that Coburn was not even training, that he entered this engagement with no intention of fighting'. Mace ended boldly, 'I consider myself entitled to the stakes.' The tenor of the letter impressed Dowling and he did not delay in returning the money. Mace announced that he would pay it back at Newmarket races and he was true to his word, although most backers declined to accept it.

The fiasco in Ireland had left a sour taste. According to the

---

* Gorman, from then on, held Mace in the highest esteem. His verdict on the Champion of England would, in the Gorman family, be handed down from father to son. Neither Mace nor Gorman could remotely have anticipated that Bartley's lineal descendant and namesake would, over 100 years later, claim the Championship of England. And that the title would be an unofficial one – with bareknuckle fighting not merely the sport of outlaws but in a world where boxing with gloves had totally displaced it.

Committee of the PBA, Mace was technically only the middleweight champion, the Championship proper being in abeyance following Tom King's retirement and the non-emergence of a genuine English challenger at heavyweight. Yet had Coburn been willing to confront him, and assuming that Mace would have prevailed, he would have been acclaimed by the Fancy as the first undisputed Champion of the World. For a couple of years, Mace lost interest in the Prize Ring – but he most certainly did not lose interest in the art of boxing. He simply combined it with the circus.

Gorman's impromptu challenge made Mace think: there was no shortage of men, known tough customers in their towns, who would be only too delighted to take him on. He remembered that mentality from his days as a youngster in Langham's boxing booth. What if he could somehow combine such challenges with his circus act? He had made money by sparring for Ginnett with King, but there was no King left, no one of near-equal status to himself. But there were dozens of Gormans: men who had the raw strength and pluck to enter the ring with him but not enough science to put on a sparring exhibition. Now that was the beauty of it, he reflected. And just as he had once offered money, albeit in vain, to King from the stage of the Holborn Empire, he would now offer money to 'any man in the house' who could simply stand up to him in the ring for a given period.

The sole requirement would be for men to come forward who had the courage – or foolhardiness – to enter a roped square with the foremost fighter of his time. The police could no more interfere than they could halt a sparring exhibition. Boxing gloves would be worn and thus the risk of bloodshed greatly diminished, but, unlike in an exhibition of sparring, there would be a clear winner: either Mace or his opponent. Unlike the London Prize Ring, it would not be a fight to the finish and therefore it would be legal, with a timekeeper and a bell signalling the duration of the fight. Mace did not ponder the formula long. He decided to set the time limit at ten minutes – long enough to grip the attention of an urban audience but short enough to offer hope to a challenger that he might somehow hold out. The number of rounds, he decided, would be three of three minutes, with two half-minute intervals for a challenger to clear his head and regain his wind. The prize, for any man who lasted, would be £5.

Mace was greatly assisted in the promotion of 'fistic tourneys' by his newly appointed business manager, then referred to as a factotum, Harry Montague. He had first met Harry while touring with Ginnett in 1861. Montague was Ginnett's equestrian director and later was secretary of Myers Great American Hippodrome and Circus and 'agent in advance' for other circuses. He doubled as a sporting publican and he and Mace became close friends. Montague's eye for detail complemented Mace's vision but Harry was in the vanguard of modern techniques of publicity. Already, he had acted as Mace's 'agent in advance' in Ireland and it would be through the marriage of boxing and the circus that the new world of sport as spectacle would spring.

When Mace's Circus announced that its proprietor, the self-styled 'Champion Pugilist of the World', would take on all comers in any town where the big top tent was pitched for the night, many, not only in the entertainment world but in his former home, the LPR, predicted commercial disaster. Some thought that few ordinary men would dare to enter the same roped square as Jem Mace. Others reckoned he would need longer than three rounds to dispose of any strong young man with a modicum of pluck and an ounce of know-how. After all, prize-fighting habitually lasted half an hour, an hour and even up to two hours. And Mace himself had relied on his pickaxe left jab to cut opponents up before moving in for the kill. In going for 'knockouts', he was putting his fists under enormous stress. One way or another, he apparently had backed a loser.

But Mace was proved right. His assessment of the psychology of the working-class male was far more accurate than his critics'. Wherever Mace's Circus travelled – and it journeyed the length and breadth of the land – men would wait in line, if need be, to take on the 'People's Champion'. Fired sometimes by bravado and sometimes by whisky, they clambered through the ropes. It was the chance to be famous for ten minutes – to brag to your mates that you had stood face-to-face with the world's greatest boxer. Hell, you simply had to stay there and fight it out and, if you succeeded, you would be rewarded with a sum many times more than the average weekly wage. If you didn't, you had still proved your nerve and, to use a key phrase from those days, 'manliness'. And you had done so in front of a crowd of cheering men, all on your side, not to mention the chance of impressing the girls who would be in the audience. And that fellow up there on stage, the man with the now receding hairline, high forehead and small moustache, well he looked more like the musician he was said to be than a bruiser.

The sceptics had also underestimated the new power at Mace's disposal. The gloves would not be skintight gloves designed just to blunt the cutting edge of bare knuckles, but padded 'mufflers' weighing several ounces. As Jem was well aware, when his own gloves had become soaked with sweat they weighed heavier still. He thus had at his disposal, if need be, a virtual cosh. And, like all pugilists, he had sufficient knowledge of human anatomy to know against which precise points his blows would be most telling, and far more capacity than most to land those blows with perfect timing and accuracy.

Night after night, in town after town, Mace put on his 'knockout show'. The term 'knockout', which was new to the English language, meant simply that a man was 'knocked out of time'. And here was yet another innovation: his 'time' would not be the thirty seconds stipulated in the rules of the LPR, in which a man must get to his feet after being knocked to the ground and come up to scratch. It would be ten seconds, and ten only. It was thus easier for Mace to dispose of an opponent than in the Prize Ring.

The fact that a circus fight with Mace could be so quickly, even mercifully, curtailed baffled those who detested the 'brutality' of the Prize Ring. It would not, however, be long before they seized on the term 'knockout' and ignorantly insisted that it must always entail a long period of unconsciousness. The only danger of Mace losing his money was if he faced, as he occasionally did, a 'dodger' who went down at the slightest impact to take a valuable breather for several seconds. Mace's response to such opponents was to deliver an uppercut from hip height. It usually did the trick.

Mace realised that the crowd, while expecting that he would win, hoped that the unknown challenger would put up a show. He therefore carried the challenger, at least until the middle of the second round and sometimes longer. He used every trick he had to make a no-hoper look game before finishing him off with a shot between the eyes, behind the ear, over the heart or full on the jugular vein. If an opponent was overly aggressive or swearing loudly, he would be crumpled up in agony by a blow to the 'mark', or the third button of the Victorian gentleman's waistcoat; in anatomical terms, the epigastric nerve centre or solar plexus. When this happened, cheers often rose from the audience as if greeting the demise of a pantomime villain.

The most significant blow struck by Mace on the knockout tour was delivered at Bolton, where he was challenged by an iron foundry-man. The man was big, brawny and aggressive – and in that no different from countless other hopefuls – but he also turned out to be agile, quick and durable. The crowd were agog as Mace hit him so hard that he burst a new boxing glove, and they were on the edge of their seats when the clock showed less than thirty seconds before the foundryman could claim his winnings. Mace finally aimed for the solar plexus, and rendered his almost successful challenger briefly uncon-scious. Showing his customary mastery of crowd psychology, Mace compensated the swiftly recovered man with a sovereign 'to drink your health and mine'. The man and his mates responded to Mace with the old English song 'For He's a Jolly Good Fellow'.

At Bolton, Mace had recalled, in a flash, how he'd finished off Brettle at Foulness Island and Goss at Plumstead Marshes. Then he had risked his naked fists against their jawbones. Now his hand was shielded by leather and his punch was delivered with the force of a cosh. The nameless foundryman was on the receiving end in the moment of the birth of the knockout. Thus Mace laid down the template for the great future knockouts of boxing history.

11

The Liverpool Olympics

THE FIRST OLYMPIAD of the Modern Era took place in Liverpool in 1862, the brainchild of thirty-three-year-old Charles Melly. Born in Liverpool, he was already one of the city's wealthiest citizens, having made a fortune as a cotton merchant. He, his wife and three young children were attended by eight servants at their mansion, Riversley, situated in verdant splendour at Aigburth, then outside the city boundary. Melly had founded the Liverpool Athletic Club fewer than six months before, but his confidence was as boundless as his love for the classical culture of Ancient Greece. 'I believe this Athletic Club will only be the beginning of a movement which will soon become general . . . throughout the kingdom,' he prophesied – and he was proved right. The Liverpool Olympic Festival, as Melly styled it, lasted as an annual event for only five years, but during that time, enthusiasm for track and field athletics spread from Liverpool throughout the North. A Northern-based National Olympian Society was formed, while in 1866 the Amateur Athletic Club in London held its first annual championships, capitalising on Melly's idea but anxious to keep control of athletics in the metropolis.

By the use of such terms as 'athletics' and 'olympian', the emerging sport of track and field was deliberately distancing itself from the notoriously corrupt world of professional pedestrianism. Athletics was to be a purely amateur sport. Although athletics was dominated by the British, it was the Frenchman Pierre de Coubertin who successfully campaigned for the revival of the ancient Athenian Games in Athens itself in 1896. De Coubertin's festival, Les Jeux Olympiques (Olympic Games), was an international event but its origins lay in the Liverpool Olympic Festival which preceded it thirty-four years earlier, the year before De Coubertin's birth.

Unlike Melly, the son of an immigrant Swiss entrepreneur who became agent to the Viceroy of India, Jem Mace had been denied any education, let alone a classical one. Although he and Melly were close contemporaries, Mace was earning a living as an itinerant fiddler and horse breaker while Melly was still at his desk at Rugby School absorbing Latin lessons. Nevertheless, each would become interested in the sport to which the other belonged. Melly had long enjoyed sparring with boxing gloves while Mace was fascinated by the celebration of athletic prowess which the Liverpool Olympic Festival represented. As a professional pedestrian, Mace was precluded from entering the events in Liverpool but he was a regular spectator at the Liverpool Olympics. Typically, he regularly gambled on the events, which included the 100 yards, 300 yards, mile, four-mile walk, high jump, long jump, pole leap and throwing the disc. These events (or their metric equivalents) would eventually be competed for at Athens and the successor Olympics. Other future Olympic sports such as gymnastics, fencing and Greco-Roman wrestling were also competed for in Liverpool and there was even an Olympian Parade of the athletes before competition began. 'The proceedings will, in point of interest and display, be such as have never been seen before in Liverpool,' predicted the *Liverpool Mercury*.

With Mace, Champion of England, being pointed out among the crowd, Melly swiftly became aware of his presence. They were introduced by Melly's friend, John Hulley, another educated man, lover of the classics and enthusiast for the ideals of amateur sport. Hulley lived even further outside the city than Melly, inhabiting a mansion at Rainhill in Lancashire. Where Melly was a speechmaker and visionary, the more down-to-earth Hulley was his invaluable assistant, a man who loved administrative details and the specifics of organization. Hulley was the Secretary of the Liverpool Athletic Club while Melly was President. Mace was by this time well familiar with the London toffs whose acquaintance he'd made as a bodyguard, in Langham's service, in the mid-1850s. But the swells he knew were members of the Fancy, most of them Tories and with little interest in the advancement of the poor. Talking to Melly and Hulley, he noted an immediate difference. These two scions of Midland public schools did not affect the typical drawl and 'dontchaknow' of London toff speech. More importantly, Melly was a radical. Perturbed by the appalling poverty in the slum areas of Liverpool, he contributed to the provision of schools and hospitals and had funded the opening of a public playground. He believed that sport should be open to all classes and his watchword was the old Latin tag *Mens Sana in Corpore Sano* – 'a healthy mind in a healthy body'. He spoke of 'men whose gymnasium is, as it were, the world', such as 'sailors and open air labourers'.

Mace was highly impressed with the organisers of the Liverpool Olympic Festival, with the feast of athletics which they provided and, above all, the crowd of 12-15,000 they attracted despite being held on the city outskirts at Mount Vernon. The site, a parade ground, belonged to the Army, who promptly sold it off, so the next year, 1864, Melly and Hulley renamed their club the Athletic Society of Great Britain, called the annual event the Grand Olympic Festival and moved to within the perimeter of the Zoological Gardens. Even bigger crowds attended and, on the opening Saturday, Mace saw a stream of carriages, horse-drawn buses and a human tide on foot moving out of the city and up London Road and Brunswick Road. He had not seen anything like this even on his regular visits to the Grand National at neighbouring Aintree. The crowd was boisterous rather than unruly, the police contented themselves with a monitoring role and the bookies thrived.

Boxing was included but Mace had, for the time, to hide a smile at the clumsy efforts of the contestants. Nevertheless, the enthusiasm of the Liverpool populace for sport and entertainment made a lasting impression on him. What's more, his enthusiastic presence at these events was in itself a boost to Olympic revivalism. Here was the country's leading professional sportsman openly endorsing the Olympic ideal.

By 1865, Mace had taken a pub in Leeds, where his friend, Harry Montague, lived. Montague was far better educated than the average sporting publican and operated various business ventures from the Ship Inn in Briggate. Mace's pub was in Cross Cemetery Street and he gave boxing lessons there to wealthy local men who could afford his fees. As in Manchester, and as on tour with his own and other circuses, the magistrates did not intervene. Even the Knockout Tour had gone unmolested. It wasn't merely the wearing of gloves and the time limit but the fact that there were no stakes to be competed for and no side bets that made it legally very difficult to designate such events as prize fights.

The LPR itself was by now in a state of rapid decline. This was symbolised by the fate of a previous great. After he'd been warned not to risk his annuity by fighting Mace, Tom Sayers, already a heavy drinker, descended into alcoholism and his wife left him. Mace had little sympathy. He had liked Sayers, while well aware of his modest intelligence, and had respected him greatly as a fighter, but by now the contest he had dreamed of, against Sayers, could never take place. What's more, Sayers' notorious drunkenness was grist to the mill of the anti-prize-fight lobby. In the columns of newspapers they referred to Sayers as an 'awful example' and claimed his state was typical of pugilists. In fact, as Mace retorted, it was not. There had been several others who had taken to drink as soon as their ring career ended and died in their thirties or forties – but there were just as many, if not more, who remained sober and healthy and lived well into their seventies or eighties, well beyond the lifetime of the average working man.

By early 1865, Sayers was diagnosed with diabetes and tuberculosis, the former being alcohol-induced. For several months, in the spring, his symptoms were in remission and, at a loss as to how to occupy himself, he travelled north out of curiosity regarding the success of Mace and Montague's drums. This led to a pathetic incident which Jem witnessed, to his regret. Sayers had been boozing all day and became truculent when advised to return home on the last train for London. Even though he was drunk, and had to walk with the aid of a stick, few men dared to take him on. Mace was sent for, whereupon Sayers gave vent to a torrent of abuse. Over the hearth of the pub hung portraits of himself, Mace, King and Heenan, the four outstanding fighters of the era. Sayers staggered over to them and pointed with his walking stick to the likeness of Heenan.

'He's a good man,' he slurred.

Then he touched his own portrait.

'He's a good man.'

Finally he went to the painting of Mace.

'But this,' he hissed, 'is a bloody duffer!'

With that, he drove the point of his stick through the face of

Mace's portrait. Mace and Montague restrained him and, despite his curses of protest, saw him safely onto the London train.

Yet Mace's admiration for Sayers' fighting qualities never diminished. 'I should like to say that he was, when in his prime, one of the gamest and fastest fighters who ever put up a hand,' he wrote years later. 'He was, though, most deceptive in appearance, his arms being no thicker than a girl's. Yet his hitting powers were terrific and his small, sharp knuckles gashed like the edge of a razor.'

On 7 August 1865, Hannah gave birth to the couple's first child, in Leeds. She was named Amelia Martha, in honour firstly of her father's beloved sister and secondly of Martha Barton, his 'sister in law', who kept open the link to his three older children still living in the Roberts household in Hoxton and being partly maintained by Mace.

By this time, with Mace inactive in the Prize Ring for two years, two aspiring young pugilists were matched for the title, with the approval of the Pugilistic Benevolent Association: Andrew Marsden and Joe Wormald. According to the PBA, the winner of their mill would be entitled to the Belt. Wormald won and duly claimed the Belt. To Mace, this was nonsense. He had never stated that he had retired; he had not fought simply because of the dearth of good opposition. He at once challenged Wormald, and articles were signed for a fight scheduled for the end of September 1865. Mace regarded Wormald with such disdain that he did not bother to go into strict training. He preferred to enjoy himself at Doncaster races and, on meeting some of his friends there for the St Leger, only a week before the scheduled bout, told them to bet on him, while also remarking that the fight might well not come off at all.

Mace's instinct that a reluctant Wormald might seek an opportunity to back out was confirmed a couple of days later when he cried off with a doctor's note. He had allegedly worked out excessively with some dumbbells, straining the muscles of his lower forearm! Mace picked up £120 in forfeit money, but to head off the PBA, who seemed determined that they alone were competent to recognise who was champion, he issued an immediate challenge: he was ready to face any man, British or American, within twelve months, the stakes to be deposited at Montague's pub. In designating the Ship Inn at Leeds, Mace was distancing himself from the classical Prize Ring. But he could, and did, respond by stating that it was the London media who were campaigning against bareknuckle boxing. Other fighters remained wary of offending the PBA and it would not be until the next year that his challenge was taken up.

★ ★ ★

On 15 November 1865, an event took place which should have served as a memorial to the London Prize Ring but in fact tarnished its declining reputation still further. The funeral was held of Tom Sayers, who a week earlier had died of consumption at his home in Camden Town. Jem Mace intended to travel south and join various other pugilistic notables. *Bell's Life* remarked on the talk caused by his absence and strongly implied that he had slighted Sayers' memory. But Mace was, at the time, in Liverpool, preoccupied with an important development in the history of glove boxing.

A crowd of many thousands followed Sayers' hearse from the house and at first all went well. Sayers was only thirty-nine and the principal mourners were his father and his two young children. There was also his devoted dog, a huge mastiff to whom he had given the name 'Lion'. It rode alone in an open carriage behind the hearse, sitting bolt upright and scarcely twitching a muscle. But as the cortege edged to the gates of Highgate Cemetery, a drunken rabble of alleged 'fight enthusiasts' disrupted the solemn occasion. They were refused entry to the cemetery where, by the express wish of Sayers' father, the coffin was to be interred in the presence only of family and friends, including pugilists. The mob then attacked the police – most of them were beaten back but others got through and began vandalising headstones. Only after they had done considerable damage were the police able to evict them and allow the funeral to finish.

When he heard what had happened, Mace's loathing for the low-lifes reached a new depth of intensity. The devoted Lion crouched disconsolately at his master's graveside and Mace could only but compare the demeanour of a dumb animal (who died within days and whose image was carved into Sayers' monumental gravestone) with the appalling crowd trouble that preceded it. It made him ponder the need to somehow remove pugilism from its ambience of heavy drinking, hooligan mobs and underclass blackguards.

He returned to Liverpool, where he had been appointed Instructor in Boxing at the newly opened Myrtle Street Gymnasium. The prime movers in this enterprise were once again Melly and Hulley. Melly personally defrayed most of the £10,000 costs of construction and Hulley, by now Chairman of the National Olympian Society, was the Gymnasiarch. This term was borrowed from Ancient Greece and signified the principal official in charge of the training of athletes. 'Gymnasium' itself, then a word familiar only to classical scholars such as Melly and Hulley, came from the same source. The pair's intentions were to provide the opportunity for physical exercise and training not to aristocrats or paid professionals but to 'ordinary persons'. This could not include the labouring classes, whose leisure time was limited and whose wages were too low to enable them to pay even modest fees, but in Liverpool, as in other prosperous provincial cities, there was a growing class of young, relatively well-off skilled tradesmen and clerical workers. These men did not do physically demanding tasks in their daily routine but were keen to learn sporting skills, and due to gradual legislation establishing Saturday as a work-free day, they had the time in which to acquire them. Not only that but many had expressed an interest in participating in indoor sport and evening training, both of which, with gas lighting, were now practical even in the winter.

The lavish opening ceremony saw Mace introduced alongside his fellow instructors in athletics, wrestling and fencing. The ceremony was conducted by Edward Henry Stanley, better known as Lord Stanley, a leading Tory MP who had already held Cabinet office and would do so again the following year during the Prime Ministership of his father, the 14th Earl of Derby, to whose title he was to succeed in 1869. The Stanleys were one of the great aristocratic families and their sumptuous estate, Knowsley Hall, lay just to the north of Liverpool. The patronage of such aristocrats, in conjunction with the fundraising of the wealthy philanthropist Melly, was conferring a new social status on the sport which Mace had been selected to represent. But it was not prize-fighting which Stanley, Melly and Hulley desired to promote but pure boxing, i.e. 'the noble art of self-defence', with gloves, separated from wrestling and participated in by amateurs.

Jem Mace's appointment at Myrtle Street signified a change of emphasis. The swells such as he had known when he first went to London were avid members of the Fancy. These men, of the same generation as himself, had been alienated from the bareknuckle code by the hooliganism which had befouled it ever since Heenan v Sayers, but had not lost their love of what they called 'sparring'. When Mace first arrived at the gymnasium to begin tuition, he heard hostile shouting from the Baptist Chapel next door. He laughed at their comments about 'the wages of sin', for he considered himself well rewarded. Mace's transition to Myrtle Street was a surprising development for the former outlaw, the so-called gypsy and the devil-may-care circus showman. He was not the kind who would easily be content with anything resembling a 'regular job'. But, as he reflected on his journey from the East End via Manchester and Leeds to the remarkable city of Liverpool, he determined to turn the opportunity first provided by the Liverpool Olympics to his personal advantage.

12

Self-made Toff and Working Class Hero

HE HAD BEEN to this place with Hannah many times and, before her, with Selina. He had frequented the beautiful pleasure gardens in Chelsea ever since arriving in London as a young man of twenty-five and there was no spot in the entire capital he loved as much. Now, ten years on, as he took the familiar threepenny steamer ride from Hungerford Bridge to Cadogan Pier, a plan formed in his mind. He wished to consider it objectively and not to be distracted by feminine company. That was why he was alone – and, to avoid the endless congratulations, handshakes and autograph hunters, he was slightly but sufficiently disguised.

He got off the boat and made his way to the riverside entrance of the Cremorne Gardens, paid his shilling admission at the gate and walked through the place from end to end. So often he'd delighted in the Gardens but now he was looking at them as the model for a venture he had in mind. The Gardens, formerly the estate of Lord Cremorne, had been put out to commercial lease the year before Victoria became Queen. They had already been a great attraction for over twenty years, but it was not until Edward Tyrrell Smith became lessee and proprietor, in 1861, that they hit the heights of their immense popularity and became the talk of the town. On special occasions, such as Derby Night, they drew crowds of 15,000.

Tyrrell Smith was one of London's foremost impresarios. He had begun as a publican in Holborn, where he attracted custom by employing buxom barmaids in bloomers, then he took over Astley's Amphitheatre, the birthplace of the English circus, the Alhambra in Leicester Square and, finally, obtained the lease of Cremorne. Among the most spectacular of the acts there was Natator, the Man-Frog, who remained underwater for minutes on end in a 6ft-deep goldfish bowl, visible through plateglass, standing on his head, eating a sponge cake or smoking a pipe. Jem saw huge crowds of children fascinated with Natator's antics but found it boring, whereas the tightrope walk across the Thames by 'the female Blondin', Madame Genevieve, was compelling. Madame Genevieve was, in fact, the petite but courageous Selina Young, the granddaughter of James Bishop, a famous showman. A few years before, Mace and Selina Young had had a brief but lively acquaintance.

On this occasion, he did not allow his thoughts to wander to Selina Young, Selina Hart or to his lovely young wife, Hannah. He strolled in the warm afternoon sunshine past young parents with half a dozen excited children in tow, a grandmother helping to keep the youngsters fed and watered. He briefly bypassed old men dozing on the benches under the elm trees, grateful for an hour or two of fresh air away from the smoke-filled stench of the city. He was among the crowds who watched a balloon ascent, the gondola filled with cigar-chomping swells laughing and joking as they swirled away over the river towards Surrey. He smiled at the children fascinated by puppet shows at the Marionette Theatre and appreciated as much as anyone the horses doing dressage routines.

As dusk approached, in the hours before the midnight bell rang to clear the gardens, Cremorne became a fairyland with the lawns shimmering emerald green. Summer breezes wafted in from the river and gave respite from the heat previously afforded only by glasses of lemonade and soda or by trespass in the fountains. After waiting only for a brief but eruptive display of fireworks, the families cleared the Gardens and waited for a horse-drawn omnibus to take them back to the wretched dwellings from which many had temporarily been liberated. By now a crowd of young revellers, men and girls, had arrived. Jem walked with them along the promenades lit by flickering gas lamps and looked on as they made their way up to the so-called Crystal Platform, where the brightly uniformed band played waltzes, polkas and galops. The dancers comprised about 1,000 souls, not all of whom came as partners. There were also prostitutes, who came in pairs, danced together and waited to be approached by men. Provided they did not solicit openly, they were safe from arrest by the watching police constables.

Cremorne Gardens had its bitter enemies. Chief among them was

Canon John Cromwell, the principal of St Mark's Divinity Training College, which loomed almost opposite the entrance. His allies included both the Chelsea Vestry and the Chelsea Baptist Chapel and they denounced Cremorne in their sermons as a place of sin, campaigning with fanatical persistence to have it closed down. During Tyrrell Smith's proprietorship they would fail, but the danger of proximity to religious zealots was not lost on Mace. He completed his evening at the centre of the twelve-acre grounds, close by the American Bowling Green. Here, in the Cremorne Hotel itself, he pondered as he sipped a glass of choice Cremorne sherry. Next door, but separate, were the grounds of Ashburnham House. It was also under Tyrrell Smith's management. Although Smith was not greatly interested in sport, he had hired the hall once or twice for horse trotting contests, for non-competitive exhibitions of Greco-Roman wrestling, and to Madame Pereira, the elegant French gymnast.

Mace had, of course, based himself on various role models during his rise to fame and fortune. Langham had been his Prize Ring mentor but his own achievements had far surpassed Langham's. In the circus, he'd learned from Pablo Fanque, Fred Ginnett and George Sanger. He sought to emulate the three of them, and though he had not succeeded, he had no intention of playing second fiddle to the ubiquitous Tyrrell Smith.

It was not only Tyrrell Smith's dominance that made Mace determined to avoid London when risking the prime business venture of his life. The leases were far dearer in the capital than in the provincial cities and it was in the provinces that he would seek to give his answer to Cremorne Gardens. What's more, as he well knew from the circus, wages were higher in the north and disposable income for entertainment on Saturday afternoons or weekday evenings greater. But where? Much as he liked the people of Newcastle, it was too remote, and though the two great textile cities of Manchester and Leeds were prosperous, they were also, he felt, dull, and consumed by the nonconformist work ethic. While there was some rebellion in Manchester there was little in Leeds; still, he considered Leeds, if only because it was the home of his good friend Montague, who would be a very useful man to have around. In some ways, Mace was admirably suited to succeed in business, but while he was adventurous, bold, had vision and was streetwise, he was no administrator. He had become literate relatively late in life and was careless over money. His pleasure came from taking risks, not accounting for coppers. Montague, a broad-minded man with a similar outlook but a shrewd business brain, was just the person to deal with the bookkeeping, leases and press publicity. But, whether Harry liked it or not, the northern Cremorne would not be in Leeds or Manchester. It would be in Liverpool.

Liverpool was then the acknowledged second city of England. Its population had risen at an astonishing rate since the start of the century and was approaching half a million. It was easily reached by rail from London, Manchester or the Lancashire cotton towns – the Railway Age had begun there the year before Mace was born, when the first track was laid, between Liverpool and Manchester. Liverpool was also the world's greatest port, benefiting from the American trade in raw cotton and the transatlantic passenger liners of the Cunard Company, which departed from New York or Halifax or the St Lawrence Estuary. Liverpool was now a cosmopolitan city with a considerable ethnic minority population, notably Irish, Germans, Scandinavians and Eastern European Jews, a mix that had acted as a curb on the puritanical tendencies which had taken hold in Manchester and Leeds and were even threatening Tyrrell Smith's amusement empire in London. As well as this, Liverpool's demography was unusual. As 'Cottonopolis' (a nickname later applied to Manchester too), it had more wealthy men than any city outside London. They lived in luxury in the Georgian mansions just to the south of the city centre and stretching out towards the independent township of Toxteth Park.

Another independent township, though it was cheek by jowl with Liverpool, was West Derby, with its sub-district of Everton high on the hill dramatically overlooking the Mersey and the long line of docks clustered along its northern bank. Crouched parallel with the docks lay Scotland Road – or 'Ireland Road' as some nicknamed it – and the warren of streets which led off it and housed, in conditions of abject poverty, the dock labourers, mostly Irish immigrants, whose casualised labour and subsistence wages allowed them little time for leisure. The skilled working classes and newly emerging lower middle class in East Liverpool were at pains to distance themselves from the Liverpool

Irish. The latter, predominantly Roman Catholics and living in the north of the city, sustained a level of alcohol consumption which was the highest in England, while the inhabitants of the east had other recreational outlets. There was already an appetite for sport and entertainment, as the annual Olympic Festival had shown, sited after the first couple of years in West Derby, where ground rents were even lower than in Liverpool proper.

Such were Mace's considerations as he sat in Cremorne Gardens. While watching the Liverpool Olympics, he had noticed an expanse of waste ground to the east. Intrigued, he began wandering across the green fields and vaulted over a hedge covered with hawthorn blossom and wild roses. He had come across a tumbledown alehouse – one which, nevertheless, attracted a steady stream of customers. He asked its name off one of the locals, a 'Dicky Sam', as working-class non-Irish Liverpudlians were then called, and was told that it was the Strawberry Tavern. Mace smiled, as he had not noticed a single strawberry growing wild, although there was no shortage of gooseberry bushes. He made his way inside, where he was not recognised, ordered a glass of port and took in the scene.

The reason for its popularity quickly became obvious. Lying just beyond what were then the Liverpool city limits, people could go to the still rural Strawberry without hindrance from the police. In the parlour, old men, reeking of tobacco, were swilling grog and, as they told him, could do so till midnight, which, in nearby Liverpool, was not allowed. Bagatelle was being played and money staked on the outcome. This alone might have caused a revocation of a licence in the city. And in the secluded alcoves, laid out so that any couple could have one to themselves, whisky was being served to kissing and fondling youths and girls. It was enough to cause a Baptist minister heart failure on the spot – but it was most definitely good for business.

Mace was determined to acquire the lease of this piece of waste ground, popularly known as Strawberry Bank or the Strawberry Grounds. It would require a sizeable chunk of his capital and more to develop the place into a provincial Cremorne Gardens, but he was never one to resist a gamble. If he failed, he would be bankrupt, but if he succeeded, a fortune awaited. He at once sent Montague to negotiate for a lease. In surprisingly quick time, the lease was assigned in Mace's name and a team of gardeners set to work clearing the wilderness. Not surprisingly the locals were at first enraged, fearing that their exclusive rural idyll would disappear, but they were soon assuaged by news that the Tavern would remain, even though the Strawberry Hotel was being erected nearby. As for the frolicking of the local young couples, that would now take place not in the alehouse alcoves but outside in the tree-shrouded arbours of landscaped gardens, lit by gas lamps. An esplanade stretched round the perimeter of these newly named Strawberry Gardens and visitors could take their ease at continental-style tables to which waiters would bring tea and the local delicacy, shrimps, at a shilling a time.

The area was fenced off, with a main entrance in Hygeia Street. There was a small admission charge but the custom attracted brought about hefty profits – more than enough to provide a small band to play polkas for lively dancing and to end the evening with slow and smoochy quadrilles. As at Cremorne, the customers were a mixture of skilled artisans and their girlfriends, or wealthier young men looking to pick up local girls. As to the former regulars, they were allowed in on the nod by the gatekeeper and left in peace in the Tavern, where they were even indulged by the provision of a skittle alley. Mace, Hannah and Amelia lived at the hotel and sometimes the infant watched with excitement, along with the young crowd in the gardens, as a firework display from the neighbouring zoo, an event in which Mace had a financial interest, illuminated the night sky with such events as The Siege of Algiers and The Eruption of Mount Vesuvius.

In April 1866, an advertisement appeared in *Sporting Life* for the Strawberry Hotel and Grounds, West Derby Road, near Liverpool, proprietor Jem Mace. It announced that there would be recreational facilities such as 'a bowling green, race grounds, croquet rounds, quoits, skittle courts etc'. The 'etc.' included, of course, a gymnasium and boxing ring.

Strawberry Gardens was no Cremorne Gardens – this was, after all, a provincial city, albeit an unusually proud and lively one – but it had one attraction which Cremorne could never boast: the proprietor himself, still only thirty-five and as boundlessly energetic as ever. Within days of opening, the Gardens had become Liverpool's leading attraction. The people of East Liverpool, Everton and West Derby

Village spent evening after summer evening there. Saturdays brought folk from the Lancashire industrial towns of Prescot, St Helens, Wigan and Preston; from the shipyards of Birkenhead, a ferryboat ride away on the other side of the Mersey, and from the ancient city of Chester. The takings averaged £300 a day, of which a third was clear profit. The star of the show was Mace himself – sometimes he gave exhibitions of sparring with Pooley and other pugilists, or violin performances, or demonstrations of one more of his manifold skills.

Mace had been interested in fencing since as long as he could remember and, while in London he used his prize-fighting money to attend Angelo's Fencing Academy in St James Street, run, for about a century, by a dynasty of fencers of Italian origin. Many famous English swordsmen deplored the spread of French- and Italian-style fencing, with its lightweight weapons, at the expense of the swashbuckling old English broadsword style. Mace did not agree. To him, the English style was as obsolete as the 'Tipton Slasher' and Sam Hurst in pugilism. He soon became adept, impressing his tutors with his agility, quick reflexes and ability to second-guess an opponent's intentions and to take evasive action.

By the 1860s he had become a masterly fencer, skilled with all three main weapons. He liked the foil for its flexibility and the epee for its power, but also enjoyed using the sabre – with which hits to the head were allowed – and the more he did so, the more the limitations of the bareknuckle code became clear to him. A prize-fighter had nothing but his fists to deploy, but when he used gloves, as in sparring exhibitions, his hands were protected. To Mace's mind, there was a clear parallel between this and the bulkier knuckle guards of the sabre fencer. What's more, he could, with a sabre, generate power by the use of round-arm hits. A punch to the head with bare fists carried the risk of broken knuckles, whereas with padded gloves he could strike with impunity against hard but vulnerable parts of an opponent's body, such as the jaw and the temples.

Mace was well aware of the history of his chosen sports. Fencing had begun as a sanitised form of duelling but the use of metal head foils, swordtip buttons and torso protectors greatly reduced the risk of serious injury. He began to think that, given the strength of the anti-prize-fight lobby, something similar might be needed in pugilism if it were not to be hounded out of existence. What's more, fencing was strictly time-limited. A decision was rendered by 'points', scored when a buttoned sword point hit the head or torso of an opponent. The aim was to strike your opponent more than he struck you – the first to fifteen was the winner. The tempo of a fencing bout was brisk and gripping to watch but too complex to carry mass appeal.

Determined to keep on the right side of the law in Liverpool, Mace stressed the mandated use of gloves in all exhibitions at the Strawberry Gardens and emphasized the comparisons between boxing – or sparring, as he sometimes called it – and fencing, a legal sport and one which, he was quick to realise, was stereotyped in the minds of magistrates and the constabulary as a gentlemanly, as well as manly, enterprise. He began publicly to advocate the use of gloves. He had an additional motivation and had already expressed it while at the Myrtle Street Gymnasium. Throughout his career in the Prize Ring, he feared that the jarring impact on his wrists as he struck his opponents would result in injuries which could curtail his alternative career as a violinist. However, his emphasis on ten-second knockouts and on the use of gloves was met only with incomprehension within the fight game.

The Liverpool public was not much interested in such niceties – they were up for 'a bit of fun'. If there would be no blood, then there would certainly be thunder, and the presence of women would reduce the potential for beer-swilling and brawling. The Strawberry Hotel was 'open all hours'. It did a roaring trade, with many men coming in on the hope of shaking hands with the Champion of England. Women also came to cast an admiring glance at him or, out of curiosity, to see Hannah and Amelia. The Mayor of Liverpool and his councillors were delighted at the custom brought into the city, since many visitors spent time shopping before making their way up to the Strawberry Grounds. Two people who reacted very differently were Melly and Hulley. They felt upstaged by their former boxing instructor, who had now chosen to give lessons at his own place instead. Worse, the 1866 Olympic Festival had to be moved well out of Liverpool to the seaside resort of Llandudno in Wales because it was feared that that it would suffer in comparison with the Strawberry Grounds.

* * *

Barely six weeks after the opening of the Strawberry Gardens, Jem Mace returned to the Prize Ring to meet a new challenge from an old opponent. Joe Goss, now based in Northampton, had lost at middleweight to Mace three years earlier and now decided to take him on at heavyweight. Mace had been out of the ring for two-and-a-half years but Goss had only fought once during that time and was the better part of a stone heavier, while Mace's weight had scarcely varied.

From the start, their fight aroused suspicions in the sporting press. After his trip to Ireland, Mace had said that he would not fight again, and although it was early days, the Strawberry Gardens appeared to be paying rich dividends. Mace had rapidly become a popular hero in the city for putting on 'one hell of a show' and, preoccupied with his new venture, his period of training was relatively brief. Assuming he defeated Goss in a mill not confined by weight, he would be officially reconfirmed as Champion by the PBA. But, in the eyes of the fight-loving public, he had been such ever since Tom King retired. What really set red flags waving was that Nat Langham re-emerged as promoter: his arrangements were made under a cloak of great secrecy but it transpired that he had sold nearly £1,000-worth of tickets and that Mace and Goss had agreed to divide the spoils evenly.

Their clash, at Meopham in Kent, south of Gravesend and west of Rochester, turned out to be one of the most bizarre encounters in LPR history. On 24 May 1866, they faced each other for just over an hour, but never got further than one round. They simply circled, occasionally shadowboxing, but without a single blow being struck in anger. Mace, in utter contrast to his usual dancing style, stood his ground, while Goss, once noted as a rusher, consistently back-pedalled. After the referee had several times urged action, he washed his hands of this 'fight that never was', took the only course open to him and declared it a draw.

It was fortunate for both men that Langham's hyper-secretive preparations had led to the almost total absence of roughs. As it was, the farce was punctuated by constant jeers and catcalls. A draw meant that all bets were off. No one lost out on that score and both noncombatants deputed assistants to repay backers there and then. The matter didn't end there. *Bell's Life* reverted to its old hostile attitude towards Mace but this time included Goss in its strictures. *Sporting Life*, newly launched and a rival to the old Dowling monopoly, but without any history of personal animosity towards Mace, was just as vehement, and worse was to follow. The celebrated satirical magazine *Punch* published a devastating four-line verse by poet and wit Sir Frank Burnand:

> *Jem Mace and Joe Goss in their last little brush*
> *Displayed a most delicate grace*
> *For Mace merely Goss-sipped over claret and punch*
> *And Goss only made a Grim Mace*

Both were asked by *Bell's Life* to give a written explanation. Goss, illiterate like his circle of friends, was unable to do so, but an angry Mace, concerned about his reputation and the possible commercial damage of bad publicity, delivered his response. Although written in Montague's hand, it was, as Montague later made clear, dictated word for word by Mace. He pleaded injury as the cause of his own static performance, stating that he had been unable to train for three weeks because of a badly sprained ankle that neither his trainer nor his doctor had been able to treat, except for the wearing of an elastic stocking. He allowed the match to proceed not because of personal greed but in order not to let down his backers. Suddenly he gave vent to a powerful burst of indignation against *Bell's Life*, something which he had felt intensely for many years, despite Dowling's public retraction of his former charge of cowardice. He wrote:

> I have the full satisfaction of knowing that I've held the Belt for five years against all comers great and small; I have taken more money from your office than any man who ever entered the ring; and that my conscience tells me that, in my last encounter, I did that which was right, although to my own loss, in saving the money of my backers and friends. For me to have forced the fight would have been sheer madness.

Many years later, Mace's version of events would differ somewhat. He stuck to his original story but maintained that he had jarred his ankle only a few days before the fight and so could not have been as badly affected as he made out at the time. He also offered, for the first time, an explanation of Goss' inactivity – one which strains credulity. He said that, while returning to London in the train, Goss had rolled up his shirt sleeve and rubbed off some pink paint from his forearm to expose flesh which was bruised black and blue. This had, according to the 'Wolverhampton Wonder', occurred two days before when he had strained his muscles while lifting dumbbells. Goss's alleged mishap was exactly the same as that apparently sustained by Wormald the previous year when he cried off, albeit with a doctor's note, much to Mace's scorn. The odds against both fighters suffering muscle strains almost simultaneously would be great but Mace definitely had been injured, having stumbled during a long-distance run with the pedestrians Dick Brighton and Joe Thomas. Both confirmed this at the scene of the mill to Bill Richardson, but Richardson had already asked Mace to remove his boots and socks to see for himself. The ankle was not merely bruised but badly swollen.

While Mace's genuine injury was covered by his boots, it is scarcely credible that Goss's bruises could have avoided detection by Mace and/or his seconds during their time in the ring. Goss was no coward but had clearly been advised by his own seconds to play a waiting game and not allow Mace to counter-punch him. When Mace stood his ground, Goss, caught by surprise, had no alternative plan. He simply backed off all the more and the result, with Mace unable to move fluently, was a stalemate. Customarily in the Prize Ring, fighters fought on even if their arms were badly injured, but Goss came up with a cock-and-bull yarn which wouldn't have deceived Old Ma Winburne, let alone Mace.

There were good reasons, however, for Mace to cover up for Goss. Had he expressed any scepticism publicly, Goss would have been blackballed by the PBA, and as he was, at that time, Mace's only credible opponent, Mace might well have been denied the opportunity to fight again in the foreseeable future. Still, to clear the air as quickly as possible they would have to fight again. Mace urged Goss to challenge him but to allow him sufficient time for his ankle to heal. Goss issued just such a challenge, adding that he would fight at any weight, and for up to £500 a side – more than double what had been staked at Meopham. Both fighters were condemned by both *Bell's Life* and the Pugilistic Benevolent Association, the latter reviving the old, unjustified accusation of cowardice against Mace.

Mace, although annoyed by Goss's time limit, accepted the challenge and summoned him to Kelley's Bar in Liverpool to discuss details. When Goss arrived, he found the tables had been turned. Mace made two important stipulations in the Articles, both of which were to impact on the history of boxing. First, he demanded that instead of the 24ft ring then in vogue, the mill would take place in a 16ft ring. This would give Goss far less chance to backpedal and, conversely, would place less strain on Mace's healing foot because the distance covered during the fight would be far less. Second, Mace insisted that all four seconds should get out of the ring as soon as both fighters had come to the scratch. This was not the custom in the LPR. Seconds were at liberty to remain within the ropes, which gave more opportunity for sharp practice, the most notorious example of which had been Jerry Noon at Wadhurst – and Mace believed Goss would employ Noon in the upcoming fight. Goss argued against these conditions but Mace's force of personality decided the issue. The date was set for 6 August 1866.

Mace immediately resumed training, knowing that his reputation was on the line. In London and elsewhere there had been scepticism over the Meopham episode. Only in Liverpool was public opinion wholly in his favour. In July, Mace took a short break. Having never acted as a second before, he decided to give it a try at a contest near Croxall, a village conveniently close to the intersection of the boundaries of Staffordshire and Derbyshire. The combatants, Peter Morris and George Holden, were little known but Goss acted as the other second. News leaked out that the champion and his foremost rival were there and the police swooped and arrested them both, together with the two pugilists. They were charged with conspiring to bring about a breach of the peace but Mace's many wealthy friends in Liverpool secured the release of all four on six months' bail. Needless to say, the imminent mill for the title was not disclosed.

In his autobiography, Mace incorrectly states the fight's location as Walsall and claims that he served a jail sentence straight after. According to him, his ankle benefited from the enforced rest. In fact his case was not heard until January 1867 and his recovery occurred in less colourful circumstances: he took a course of sea baths in the staid Welsh seaside resort of Llandudno. On returning to Liverpool, he found his status as a local hero had doubled. Liverpudlians had a reputation for backing anyone they considered unjustly treated by authority. Gratifying though this was, it was impractical for Mace to train at the Strawberry Grounds, where he was besieged by well-wishers, so he trained ten miles north of the city. Invigorated by the easing of his ankle pain, his preparation was more thorough than it had ever been. Assisted by a team of pedestrians and pugilists, he ran for mile after mile, day after day, across Formby Sands and further toned his shoulders and arms by rowing in the nearby river Alt. He sparred intensively and unleashed the full weight of his blows on the punching bag. He confided to Pooley that he had never felt better in all his life, his only concern being that a warrant for his arrest had been issued in London. When he had previously been accosted at Croxall by the arresting officer, Mace, who knew the law in so far as it applied to his own profession, had demanded to see the warrant and had to back down when it was produced. But now he was supremely confident as he took the overnight train to London.

The rendezvous for the contest was not at any railway station. In a further sign of growing hostility to the Prize Ring, every single railway company had declined Langham's offer to hire a special train, so the spectators travelled by chartered river steamer. This at least led to the virtual exclusion of the rough element, who could not afford tickets priced at three guineas. Although the muster was at Hungerford Bridge, Mace decided to board at St Paul's Pier, where he believed there would be fewer, if any, police. He and Montague, who was continuing to look after his finances, booked into a small, upmarket hotel close to St Paul's Cathedral. They were both dressed as toffs, and for diguise Mace wore a monocle. The contrast with Goss, who was lurking in an East End alehouse kitted out like a costermonger, could not have been greater. Having successfully avoided recognition by half a dozen policemen on his way to the riverside, Jem nearly missed the steamer; the captain did not recognise him and, fearing that he and Montague might be off-duty coppers, told the helmsman not to stop. Fortunately, Montague possessed a foghorn voice and roared out Mace's identity. The steamer, packed with spectators, slowed down but the captain still refused to land and told them both to jump for it. Montague only just made it but Mace leaped on board with his usual athleticism, his blackened fists immediately leading to his enthusiastic recognition.

Eight o'clock chimed from a distant clock near Purfleet in Essex when Mace and Goss toed the line for the third time, near what would later become the Dartford Crossing. The fickleness of the Fancy was shown by the shouts of 'Give the bastard no rest, Joe!' Mace had once been a favourite with them, but whereas Goss was perceived as a country bumpkin whom they could patronise, Mace's emergence as an entrepreneur in the disconcertingly democratic North caused resentment. At ringside, Richardson, who had had his ups and downs with Mace but was now once again on his side, scrutinised Goss's stance. Banking on his exceptional reach, he seemed determined to keep Mace at bay, with his head held well back and chin tucked in. Turning his gaze to his man's corner, Richardson sensed that Mace, stung by the storm of criticism after the last fight and drumming his feet impatiently, would not fight his usual cautious opener. He was only too right.

Mace sprang out. He ducked under Goss's guard and delivered a slashing uppercut which tore open the Midlander's mouth, producing 'first blood'. Then Mace delivered a right cross which gashed Goss's right eyebrow to the bone and caused the blood to spurt out from the wound. Mace's next blow ripped Goss's face from cheek to chin and, sensing the shock that his onslaught had caused, he seized Goss and hip-tossed him to the turf. If Goss had even considered backpedalling, it was out of the question in the smaller ring which, with all four seconds banished, they alone inhabited. In fact, he stood his ground bravely and tried to fight back, but Mace cut off the ring in expert fashion. Determined to blot out the slightest doubt either as to his honesty or superiority, Mace went after his man with unprecedented ferocity. Goss gallantly stood up to him as long as he could and tried to counter-attack, but Mace contemptuously dodged his punches.

After twenty-nine minutes, Goss was helpless. He had only survived so long by going to ground when struck. He did this a score of times and rested for nearly the full thirty seconds before rising to face renewed assault. Finally, he was driven to his knees, then began to stagger drunkenly about the ring. It was obvious that he was concussed and, rather than inflict lethal injury, Mace simply avoided his helpless opponent until he stumbled to the floor by his own momentum and was counted out. Goss was a dreadful sight, with his face a mass of bruises, his lips grotesquely distorted, his nose three times its normal size and his forehead an open wound.

At ringside, young reporters from *Sporting Life* asked Richardson for his opinion of Mace's display. 'It was the grandest bit of fighting ever seen!' replied the man who had witnessed every major fight since the revised Rules of the London Prize Ring had been issued nearly thirty years earlier. Mace's achievement on that August day in 1866 was to reduce Goss, an experienced, strong, mobile and brave fighter to the same level of pitiful helplessness as the dinosaur Hurst five years earlier. He had revealed himself as the supreme boxer-puncher, ducking and weaving so that Goss's blows connected only with air, then unleashing shots of such power and accuracy that seasoned observers gasped openly. His insistence on a 16ft ring, his mastery of it, and the fact that no second stood between him and his target, speeded up the unfolding drama so that spectators were gripped as never before, while his final series of punches seemed almost simultaneous, so great was his hand speed. Only once had he resorted to a wrestling throw and in every respect he had seemed to belong on a different planet to those, even the best of them, who had appeared in the Prize Ring before him. The birth of gloved boxing was nearer than any onlooker would have guessed. As the counterfoils for the steamer return were whipped by a fierce wind into the muddy waters of the Thames, few could have anticipated that it was not only one of the greatest fights in the history of the LPR, but also the last. Mace returned promptly to Liverpool, and a civic reception.

As his train pulled into Lime Street Station, he was met by a crowd of working men who carried him shoulder-high into the street outside. Opposite, on the plateau of St George's Hall, Harvey Lonsdale Elmes' magnificent neo-classical edifice, cheered an estimated 10,000 people. For once in his life, policemen were working on his behalf, marshalling the crowds. As the proprietor of the Strawberry Grounds and the newly reconfirmed Champion of England, he had brought prestige to a grateful city. He took pride of place in a carriage-and-four and was driven around Liverpool city centre in its plush seats, preceded by a brass band, as spectators rushed to wave to him through the windows of the vehicle.

That night Mace was guest of honour at a banquet held in the city's elegant Georgian Town Hall. Over 100 guests attended, civic dignitaries included. Six dozen bottles of champagne were uncorked and the contents poured into a massive silver bowl. The evening ended with many inebriated, but not Mace. Relaxed and affable, he acknowledged the choruses of 'For he's a jolly good fellow!' He had good reason to be content. He was at the height of his fame and fortune and, in addition to the money he'd made from the Prize Ring and the Strawberry Gardens, the circus was flourishing. His gambling was relatively controlled – despite spending a lot of time away from home, particularly at the races – and he even tried his own hand as a bookmaker. Then there were the racehorses which he owned and which, wearing his colours, were already widely backed by the many who combined a love of the turf with a love of the ring. The cheers that rang out in the heart of Liverpool were music to the ears of the son of a Norfolk smith, the itinerant fiddler and so-called gypsy who dressed like a self-made dandy but who had become a working-class hero.

13

Arrested in a Bedroom

IT HAD ONCE been a quiet village three miles from the West End, but by now Chelsea was a densely populated suburb extending between Brompton Road and the Thames, west of Sloane Street and extending down the stretch of river known as Battersea Reach. Beyond the Chelsea Embankment lay what was then Cheyne Walk, picturesque and relatively tranquil. The area was a bohemian enclave, the abode of artists and writers. Dickens had lived there, as had Algernon Swinburne and Dante Gabriel Rossetti. In Cheyne Row, Thomas Carlyle, the famous historian, was still in residence. But to its newest resident, one of the main attractions of Cheyne Walk was undoubtedly its proximity to Cremorne Gardens.

Jem had grown fond of Liverpool but it was not London – and Hannah, a Londoner, longed to return home. While the Strawberry Gardens would remain his main investment, Mace didn't need to be there much. He would return to the metropolis late in 1866 – where he was shortly presented with the Ilustrated Sporting News Belt – and would live in an area both stylish and private. The family's new house was at Milman Row. Hannah was expecting a second child and with servants to attend to all domestic duties for the first time, she was free to devote herself to her husband, Amelia and, in time, the new arrival – if she chose to follow the norm for a Victorian middle-class woman. But early in January 1867, Mace's sister Amelia conveyed some startling news: Mary Ann Mace, or Roberts as she was usually known, had died suddenly at the home she shared with her common-law husband at George's Place, Essex Street, Hoxton, of acute appendicitis. She was thirty-three years old.

Jem was stunned at the news. His former bitterness evaporated and there were, of course, his three children to be taken care of. In such circumstances, it was expected that the children would be looked after by female relatives but Mace's circumstances were not the usual ones. Hannah was his wife, their union arguably now legitimate as a result of Mary's demise, and he wished to be reunited with his children. It would cause him no financial problem and Hannah agreed to the idea. When they moved to Milman Row, Alfred, Adelaide and James were respectively thirteen, ten and nine years old, and all were still at school. They had been greatly distressed by the sudden loss of their mother but seemed to have little wish to stay with Dick Roberts, even if he had been ready and willing to look after them – which he did not seem to be.

Adelaide was a straightforward child. Mace arranged for her to resume singing and piano lessons but was disappointed to learn that, although conscientious, she had little affinity for music. James was no scholar but he was athletic. He seemed impressed with his father's celebrity status and was pleased to see a boxing ring being constructed in the house. He wanted to learn the 'noble art', seeing it as a path to his own future fame, and Mace promised to teach him. By far the one who had the most difficulty in adjusting was Alfred. Although he did not seem to pine unduly long for his mother, he was slow to form a bond with the father he had rarely seen in nearly four years. A tall and sturdy boy, he was dark-eyed and dark-skinned. It wasn't long before Mace bought him a pair of gloves and began to teach him the rudiments of boxing. Alfred learned well and quite enjoyed what he learnt but far preferred to spend hours cooped up with a book. He was a serious lad, with no interest in music and, although it was clear that Mary hadn't brainwashed the children against their father, there was a definite barrier between father and son – not made any easier by the fact that Alfred didn't take to Hannah.

James soon showed that he had more natural aptitude for boxing than his elder brother, and when he asked if he could also learn to fence, his father was only too happy to oblige. On June 15 the Mace family was completed when another daughter, Hannah Ada, was born, to be known as Ada to distinguish her from her mother. What the neighbours thought of this new family is unclear. While his wife described him as a musician, it quickly became known that he was a circus proprietor who played the violin with his own company. Pooley's visits were certainly remarked on by neighbours. South

Chelsea was not used to visitors who looked distinctly Romany, and in due course it became known that Mace was the most famous prize-fighter in the land. Most of the Chelsea literati were too busy with their own business to pay much heed and were broad-minded men who were not shocked by Mace's outlaw status.

One neighbour was Charles Foster Talgutt, who sought Mace out and asked to spar with him. Talgutt was robust and enthusiastic but not particularly skilful and Jem had to exercise considerable care so as not to injure him. Talgutt, or C.F., was already well known in South Chelsea as an eccentric who stood out even in a district used to un-conventional behaviour. Although a landscape architect by profession, and a very gifted one, he clung to the misguided belief that he was a Renaissance man. Despite a complete lack of talent, he insisted on competing with the best-known men of his day in their various specialities. C.F. wrote poems and painted watercolours, sending the latter to some of the leading artists of the age who quietly laughed at his amateurish efforts. Undeterred or unaware, he wrote a novel and sent the manuscript to his friend, Charles Dickens, the acknowledged master of the form. Dickens, who had now retired to his country home at Gad's Hill in Kent, had to be blunt to prevent C.F. from making a fool of himself by seeking publication.

Before going on to eventual professional success as the designer of West London's system of drainage and sewerage, Talgutt was distracted by failed affairs with several leading actresses. He propounded unusual views on sex, which one day, after a couple of rounds of gentle sparring, he sought to expound to Mace. Talgutt believed that a man should strive to avoid ejaculating during intercourse – and not because it was the only absolute form of contraception available. Nor was it some proto-Tantric technique for extending mutual pleasure. The fact was that he was convinced that even one ejaculation was injurious to male health. Mace listened tolerantly but when he repeated the anecdote to Pooley, the pair couldn't restrain a fit of laughter. Mace's ability to satisfy his female partners was in sharp contrast to the gross sexual ignorance of many Victorian Englishmen. Whereas discussion of sexual matters was taboo in most Victorian circles, it was far from being the case in the Romany world or that of the circus. Certainly Mace had no intention of heeding Talgutt's quack nostrums, as his eventual paternity of probably fifteen children by six different women would testify.

Despite his line of work, Mace was never a violent man. Partly this was a by-product of his ability to drink in moderation, but mostly it stemmed from his disdain for what he called 'cowardly' behaviour and 'blackguardism', namely displays of cheap machismo and bullying. A prize-fighter, in his view, had a particular duty to exercise restraint in view of his ability to inflict serious injury on someone not trained in self-defence. Once, when doing the rounds of the West End drums with Pooley, who could also hold his liquor, racial abuse was shouted at his cousin by two burly, boozed-up seafarers. Jem rebuked them and warned them several times, but the pair, neither of whom recognised the Maces, would not stop and began to stalk them. Suddenly the culprits found themselves hurled into a back alley and a few punches from Pooley were sufficient to shut one thug's mouth while Jem silenced the other with a single blow. The cousins quietly went on their way.

* * *

Inspector George Silverton sat at his desk in Scotland Yard knitting his brows as he surveyed the contents of his little black book. In it he saw inscribed the names of men regarded as pugilistic heroes – but not by him. They might be known familiarly by the diminutives of their forenames – Joe, Tom and Ned – or even by nicknames such as 'The Wolverhampton Wonder' and 'The Irish Giant', but to him they were common criminals. Their names appeared in his book with surnames first, together with their physical descriptions, details of their arrests for breach of the peace and information on their whereabouts. 'Goss, Joseph' was a prominent entry; 'Allen, Thomas' was another, and 'O'Baldwin, Edward' was figuring more and more. But always the name over which Inspector Silverton's pen hovered was 'Mace, James'. To capture him and see him convicted was the Inspector's greatest wish.

Silverton was as ambitious as he was dedicated, rising rapidly from constable to inspector by the age of thirty-five. This made him only one year younger than his quarry, Mace – the 'so-called champion', as

Silverton described him. While Mace lived in luxury at Milman Row, Silverton lived in a modest house in Little Vine Street. It was sufficient for his wife and two children, though, and only a short walk from his place of work. At Scotland Yard, he was recognised as an expert on the London Prize Ring thanks to his youth in Gillingham. With Rochester and Chatham, it comprised the three towns which lay to the east of the River Medway's mouth; to the West lay the Kentish marshes which Silverton had roamed as a boy. His expertise was based not on a fascination with the fights that took place there but on a puritanical dislike of the Fancy, to whose obliteration he was committed.

Before joining the Metropolitan Police, Silverton was stationed at Newmarket in Cambridgeshire. It was there that he had spied on Sayers while the 'Little Wonder' was preparing for his mill with Heenan in 1860. Orders had been given from Scotland Yard to the Cambridgeshire Constabulary that Sayers should be allowed to carry out his training unhindered with full details noted, in order to bring a charge of conspiracy to breach the peace. Only when Sayers attempted to take the train to London was he to be arrested. Sergeant Silverton had considered this a great mistake. The London Prize Ring was, he argued, hand in glove with the horseracing community and some trickery was likely to be used to get Sayers to London and then to Farnborough. He seethed as he watched Sayers stroll down Newmarket High Street undisguised, mobbed by well-wishers. He repeated to his superiors that Sayers should be arrested without delay but they did not comply and, to Silverton's particular disgust, Sayers got away – on a Sunday of all days – in a horse box, disguised as one of a number of stable hands who were taking their racehorses by railway to a meeting near London. Silverton had been proved right, and he was transferred to Scotland Yard. After reaching his thirtieth birthday, he was promoted to Inspector and tasked with the curtailment of the LPR.

There were times when Silverton noted with satisfaction that the pugilists seemed to be contributing to their own downfall. Sometimes this was due to fixed fights, sometimes known as 'crosses', which were a clear fraud on the public. Bob Brettle had taken part in one against a man named Jack Rooke on a New Year's Eve. Brettle and Rooke merely sparred for an hour or so before the police arrived and cleared them off. Next, after a night's drinking, they briefly resumed at another location, having telegraphed their intentions to the police. Three months later, they fleeced the spectators again, having sold railway tickets in large numbers only to circle each other for nearly two hours without striking a blow. This farce had taken place before Silverton's promotion but it had begun the process of souring the prize-fighting public.

The anti-prize-fight lobby was immeasurably strengthened by the growth of hooliganism. At a bout between Ned O'Baldwin and Andrew Marsden, a notorious Midlands gang facetiously named the 'Nottingham Lambs' stoned O'Baldwin because he had clearly got the better of the man on whom they had placed their bets. Although Marsden was unconscious, O'Baldwin and the referee were forced to flee. With no declared winner, all bets were off and the Lambs had saved their money, even though O'Baldwin was later handed the stakes. As a result of this atrocious episode, *Bell's Life* refused to allow its staff to officiate at prize-fights and began to concentrate on reporting other sports, notably cricket, in its columns.

In the 1860s, the reputation of pugilism was tarnished by rampant hooliganism, motivated by gambling rather than gang rivalries. Still, as Silverton considered the situation, prize-fighting might be dying but it was, unfortunately, not yet dead. He and his officers would act with zeal but there were factors beyond their control. Fights could be staged outside the 100-mile radius provided for by the rules of the LPR, in areas where magistrates had a reputation for leniency. The Inspector had been thwarted in this way when Mace and Goss finally surrendered to their bail at Derbyshire Quarter Sessions in January 1867. They pleaded guilty and were sentenced, together with Holden and Morris, to one month's imprisonment. Mace served his sentence in the grim bastion of Derby Gaol but, to Silverton's fury, the prison governor, a retired military officer, treated him as a V.I.P. prisoner and placed him in a cell from which he could watch a travelling fair pitched nearby.

Goss and Tom Allen were not arrested at all when they fought a non-title bout in early March 1867. Allen, who hailed from that great cradle of fighters, Birmingham, was, at twenty-six, regarded as 'a coming man' and a potential threat to Mace, but due to continual police harassment the Goss–Allen mill had to be fought in three rings at three different times, in Gloucestershire, and ended in an inconclusive draw which denied Allen the chance to meet Mace. Still, as Silverton noted with satisfaction, Goss and Allen had decided that they couldn't continue their 'careers'. In July 1867, they emigrated to the USA to pursue their clash in a country where prize-fighters enjoyed far more latitude within the law. While the Inspector would have preferred their prosecution and imprisonment, he could at least cross their names off his list.

Even the gloomy, grim-faced Inspector was seen smirking at the next farce. O'Baldwin had been matched with Joe Wormald and a special train was chartered. Three hundred spectators travelled on it at exorbitant prices but the Irishman missed the train. When the ring was pitched, Wormald was expected to enter it alone and, under LPR rules, claim the purse for himself, but he failed to do so, probably fearing the reaction of O'Baldwin's supporters at ringside. It was rumoured that the police had telegraphed their colleagues that the big Irishman had been seen boarding a passenger train and his arrival at the place of battle was imminent. When the police arrived before O'Baldwin, the spectators fled and so did Wormald. As for the hapless O'Baldwin, he was denied the return of his stake money, to which, under the rules, he was entitled.

Much depended on the strictness or otherwise of local magistrates. Before Goss left for America, he had been arrested en route to a fight with O'Baldwin but had escaped with a warning. At Portsmouth in Hampshire, on the other hand, when a minor fight ended with the death of one participant, charges of manslaughter were brought against not only his opponent but also an Army captain and an instructor at the Portsmouth military gymnasium. Far more to Silverton's liking was an Act of Parliament which banned the chartering of railway and river steamer specials for purposes of assisting in bringing off a prize-fight. This was in 1867, a year which was to prove momentous in the history of boxing. That same year another source of revenue for the railways was cut off, namely the chartering of special trains for the purposes of watching public executions. No law needed to be passed in respect of the railway companies themselves; quite simply, Parliament, to the regret of Silverton, who believed that public hangings taught criminals a salutary lesson, legislated the end of the open gallows.

Mace had observed the above events with mixed feelings, infuriated by those who compared public executions with prize-fights as examples of obsolete barbarism. He had nothing but contempt for the mob who revelled in the hanging of a defenceless man, whatever his crimes. In his mind, there was no comparison between such an event and a prize-fight. Combat between pugilists was for him 'the noble and manly art of self-defence', a fight between equals of exemplary bravery, willingly entered into and between whose participants there was a bond of genuine comradeship.

Equally Mace made no attempt to hide his disgust at the hooliganism and corruption which, throughout the 1860s, had surrounded the Prize Ring. Many years later, in his autobiography, he would write,

> the reasons for this death knell of what was once the favourite sport of all classes of Englishmen are not far to seek . . . fights 'on the cross' were frequent and this, together with the disgraceful rowdyism . . . served to alienate the good old race of sports-loving noblemen and gentlemen who were once its chief supporters. Their places were taken largely by sporting publicans, some of whom were very good fellows indeed but some of whom, on the other hand, were not. Trickery among the latter was rampant. They would get up a match, sell perhaps two or three hundred tickets for a 'special excursion' to see it at from two to four guineas apiece, and in the end, after all, there would be no fight, the unwary speculators being, of course, diddled out of their money.

Thus, for what he believed would be the next successful defence of his title, Mace decided to take arrangements into his own hands.

His opponent was to be Ned O'Baldwin, who had issued a challenge. The so-called 'Irish Giant' had been born at Lismore in County Waterford, but as a boy his family had emigrated to England and he'd grown up in Birmingham. Gigantic he certainly was, standing almost 6ft 5in. Ned was a fighter rather than a boxer but he was both agile and brave. Not only would Mace be conceding over eight inches in height and three stone in weight, but he was nine years older. O'Baldwin had proved his mettle by beating Marsden before he had to run for his life from the Nottingham hooligans. This had caused Mace to stand up for O'Baldwin then, and he did so again after O'Baldwin's no-show against Wormald. Mace's own career had nearly been ruined by the Madden fiasco, and O'Baldwin had far more justification for missing the rendezvous than he had nine years before. As a result, Mace unhesitatingly accepted O'Baldwin's challenge, and articles were signed for £200 a side and the Belt, the fight being scheduled for 15 October 1867. O'Baldwin, who wrote his surname as Baldwin for purposes of the mill, was reassured that no money would be given up unless fairly won in an active fight.

Nevertheless, from the moment both fighters went into training, it was obvious that there was unprecedented police surveillance. Baldwin, who was preparing with Mace's one-time second, the treacherous Jack Hicks, had been obliged to move his quarters twice, from Surbiton to Walton-on-Thames and then to Epsom. Ironically, Hicks' reputation put Mace more at ease, as he regarded Hicks as the one man cunning enough to avoid the police at all costs. As for Jem himself, with Miller having emigrated to America he had now made Pooley his chief trainer and promoted Pooley's younger brother, Gus, aged twenty-two, to deputy. The Mace cousins found themselves harried from pillar to post and it wasn't long before a tipoff from a sympathetic police constable alerted them to the fact that Inspector George Silverton was on the case.

With Liverpool out of the question due to pressure from well-meaning but irritating supporters, Mace's disrupted training took in no less than six different places – Hammersmith, Margate, Yarmouth, Hindhead, Newmarket and Woodford – but with every move they made, the police seemed to be one jump ahead. There was no traitor in the camp, it was simply that Silverton had trained his plainclothes officers in the art of tailing a suspect while remaining unseen, one of the first recorded instances of something which would later become standard practice worldwide. Even while running at the desolate Devil's Punchbowl, a large natural amphitheatre near Hindhead, Mace noticed a policeman lurking in the heather. Clearly Silverton was busy preparing a dossier on conspiracy. The harassment reached its height in Newmarket as the date of the fight drew near, and it was obvious that the Inspector was attempting to forestall any repeat of the ploy Sayers had used seven years before. His final sessions were based at a well-known sporting pub, the Bald Faced Stag, at Woodford, but it was now Mace who was as much at bay as any hunted animal.

On the eve of battle, the three Maces, together with principal second Bos Tyler, decided to move separately, and with Jem disguised, to Herne Hill, then on the south-eastern outskirts of London. They arrived at the local station-master's house, handy for boarding the early morning passenger train from Ludgate Hill Station to Dover via Chatham, one of the key Medway Towns. Even more important, they would be staying in the house of a known enthusiast of the fight game, who concealed his trips to Prize Ring mills under the cover of railway business.

The decision to go to Herne Hill had been taken in conjunction with the publican Jack Coney. With Mace now distancing himself from Langham and with Bill Richardson under constant police surveillance, someone less high profile was needed to co-ordinate events down the line. What happened next would throw up the unproven suspicion that Coney was acting as a paid police informer. The station-master had provided a furnished bed-sitting-room on the first floor for Mace's use, while Bos, Pooley and Gus had rooms upstairs. The station-master's wife cooked Jem's favourite meal, steak and kidney pudding, and he went to bed at eight in the evening. The night before a fight would be one of the rare occasions when Mace would be asleep before midnight. With Tyler in his own room, Pooley and Gus decided on a game of cards but at eleven o'clock the homely atmosphere was brought to an abrupt end.

A policeman knocked at the front door and, when it was opened, a dozen other coppers burst in, with Inspector Silverton marching in front. They went straight to the special apartment where Mace was still asleep, enveloped in bedclothes.

'What do you want?' Pooley enquired in a calm voice.

'I want Jem Mace,' said Silverton, 'and there he is over there.'

As the fighter awoke, rubbing his eyes, he heard Gus demand to see Silverton's warrant — and the Inspector's sneering reply that he didn't need one. His speed of reaction after being awoken from a deep sleep was astonishing. Clad only in a night shirt, he jumped to his feet, dashed out the lamp with one hand and then picked up a heavy oak chair which stood at his bedside, holding it menacingly above his head. The raging sense of injustice and of utter defiance of authority which lay at the core of his personality, and which, outside the ring, was sublimated by music and sexual passion, was now harshly exposed. He threatened Silverton and his officers in a tone so fierce as to stun even his two cousins before giving vent to language some of which Gus had never heard him use before.

'You want Jem Mace, you cunt, do you? Get out, you fuckin' bastard or I'll break every fuckin' jaw in the room!'

While one of the blue-uniformed policemen struck a light, Silverton ordered 'seize him!' As several officers rushed at Mace, he hurled the chair at head height, narrowly missing Silverton. The object crashed into the washbowl and mirror, shattering the glass into a score of pieces and loosening the bowl from its stand. By now Gus assumed a fighting stance but Pooley, who had visions of the three of them being hanged at Newgate Prison on a murder rap, did not. He would vividly remember for the rest of his life Mace's blazing eyes as he swore at Silverton and threw the heavy oak chair. In those moments the hurt Mace felt over his past tribulations resurfaced. Silverton represented all those who had ever tried to humiliate him – Coburn, Dowling, Fox the cabinet-maker, his detested brother and, above all, his late unlamented father. When the police rushed him again, he lashed out with his fists. Fortunately for the officers, he did not make contact and was seized by his shirt, but somehow he slipped out of this and, buck-naked, made for the open window. At this point, English humour, as represented by the joker Pooley, saved the situation. He indicated to Jem the absurdity of trying to escape without clothes, and as his cousin at last calmed down, handed him his garments. As soon as Jem was dressed, all three were formally arrested. Tyler, who had stayed in his room upstairs throughout the commotion, remained at liberty – a fact which some thought significant – while Jem, Pooley and Gus were handcuffed, placed under police escort and driven through the deserted streets at midnight to Marlborough Street police station, where they were formally charged. Jem demanded bail but the duty inspector refused it and locked them in cells for the night.

After delivering the trio into custody, Silverton and more of his men went to Ludgate Hill Station and observed riotous scenes, which indicated how careless Coney, Mace's deputy, had been regarding the supposed secrecy of arrangements. Silverton refused to order his men to stop the ruffians attacking ticketholders on the grounds that to intervene would, in his view, be abetting an illegal activity.

The following day, October 15, Baldwin waited on time for the railway special to arrive, only to receive news by telegram that Mace had been arrested. He took to his heels but some of the frustrated would-be spectators repaired straight to Marlborough Street Magistrates Court. There followed the case of Regina versus Mace, Mace and Mace: James Mace, 36, described as a boxing instructor, Leopold Mace, 27, a horse dealer, and Augustus Mace, 22, a photographer, were charged with conspiring to cause a breach of the peace, namely by making arrangements to participate in an illegal prize-fight. While the three remained in the dock, Silverton went into the witness box, lovingly grasped the Holy Bible and swore to tell the truth, the whole truth and nothing but the truth. He described his visits to Herne Hill and Ludgate Hill stations and gave an account of what happened there. He testified that James Mace had not replied directly to the charge but that he had boasted that he could find forty gentlemen, each one of whom could find a sum of £500 to bail him out. He added that Mace had bragged that, before the week was out, he would fight as planned despite all the magistrates in the country. Silverton concluded his evidence by asserting that James Mace had threatened to kill him at the first chance he got.

After all the accused had pleaded guilty, Mr Lewis, their counsel, stressed that the arrest had been carried out without a warrant. But the magistrate ruled that his task was only to consider the evidence before him and that conspiracy had been admitted. By distorting the evidence in order to allege that Mace had cold-bloodedly uttered a threat to murder him after being charged at Marlborough Street, Silverton had overlooked the possibility of bringing a charge of attempting to cause grievous bodily harm by hurling furniture at the arresting officers. The magistrate seemed uninterested in anything other than preventing the fight from going ahead at a later date. Addressing the Maces, he pontificated on the evils of prize-fighting and threatened Jem with twelve months' imprisonment. He then seemed to back down, probably unnerved by the appearance of members of the aristocracy in the public galleries. There was the storng possibility of Jem becoming the central figure in a cause celebre and, accordingly, the magistrate merely bound him over to keep the peace in the sum of £1,000: £500 from himself and £250 from two persons who would stand surety for him.

Mr Lewis then pleaded that Mace's financial situation was such that he could not pay the sum. He had, claimed Mr Lewis, no regular income beyond what he earned as a humble boxing instructor. While this was technically accurate, it was of course intended to obscure the wealth he had derived from the proprietorship of the Strawberry Gardens and his circus. Still, Lewis seemed to know more than people in the public galleries. The magistrate countered by commenting on the fact that hundreds of tickets for the fight had been sold at between £2 and £4 a head, money which he knew would not be refunded and much of which would undoubtedly find its way into Mace's account. At this stage, Lewis made the startling claim that his client had already 'been through' bankruptcy proceedings. Mace had, it was true, overreached himself during the previous year. His bookmaking business, to which he was ill-suited, was in difficulties despite Montague's best efforts, and his racehorses had proved costly failures. Mace's profligacy was catching up with him. His gambling debts, both on failed bets and from unsuccessful coups at cards, amounted to far more than the figure of his bail. But his counsel's clever use of words merely hinted at imminent bankruptcy, which was an outcome Montague had mentioned but only as a means of bringing Mace to his senses before his capital was decimated.

Sir Thomas Henry, the magistrate, seemed unconvinced by Lewis' arguments but had no wish to be seen as the man who made a martyr out of a popular hero by sentencing him to a long period in jail. Sir Thomas was convinced that Mace would be bailed out by the Corinthians; the important thing was, as he saw it, not punishment but prevention. He therefore offered to reduce the bail by half and the surety to one of £300 or even £150, on condition that Mace would not fight again in England and Wales during the next two years. As to Pooley and Gus, he would require £100 each and two sureties each for £50. After a brief conference between Mr Lewis and the defendants, money was brought forward and Mace's two cousins were immediately discharged, on condition that they agreed not to assist in the promotion of a prize-fight during the time stipulated. There was dead silence in the court when the magistrate addressed Mace.

'How do I know whether you will fight or not, even if I release you on bail? You have not pledged yourself.'

'Yes, I do,' mumbled Mace. 'I can't afford to pay, so I can't fight.'

'What is that you say?'

'I won't fight now under these circumstances.'

Later in the day, Coney brought forward the required amount and he was discharged.

As for O'Baldwin, who had not been brought to court, he claimed the purse for the aborted fight on the grounds that he had fulfilled his part of the contract. Not surprisingly this was refused, whereupon O'Baldwin, formerly a victim and now the villain, went to the office of *Bell's Life* and threatened to bludgeon the stakeholder if money was not handed over to him. This disgraceful incident soured the connection between the editor and the sport which he had once championed. Still, there was more to the situation than just that. The factors that had led to the decay of the Prize Ring – corruption, hooliganism and the implacable hostility of the evangelical lobby – were severe enough, but Silverton's persecution of Mace was the final straw. The arrest and successful prosecution of the champion sent shockwaves through the pugilistic community.

Within months, the exodus of leading British fighters to America would be almost complete. From the heavyweights, both Wormald and O'Baldwin would cross the Atlantic. Brettle, who had re-emerged as middleweight champion, did likewise, as did two brilliant young lightweights, both at the very start of their careers and considered, Mace alone apart, the two best pound-for-pound boxers in the country. One was Arthur Chambers, aged twenty, from Salford in Lancashire, a former Royal Navy sailor; the other was twenty-three-year-old Billy Edwards, another Birmingham man. Edwards was a friend of Pooley and knew Jem. These departures inevitably increased the pressure on Mace to follow suit. Even after his two-year ban expired, there looked likely to be no one to challenge him and no one he might promote. But his situation was essentially different from those who left. With the exception of the astute and intelligent

Edwards, the others knew nothing but prize-fighting. Jem Mace, on the other hand, had achieved prominence in popular entertainment. Although boxing was in his blood, he would have much to lose by leaving England. Branded by Scotland Yard as an 'enemy of society', he was still regarded as a hero and even a martyr by many. He faced a tough decision and intended to take his time in making up his mind.

14

A Naked Lady from New Orleans

THE THEATRE AUDIENCE gasped in shock as she came on stage. For the male spectators, that shock was suffused with delight; for the females, it was tinged with both envy and curiosity. Adah Isaacs Menken had just violated the most cherished taboo: that the naked flesh of a woman must not be seen in public. Not an inch of wrist, throat or ankle. Since hands were gloved, or at the least mittened, among polite society, only the face was normally visible. But this was a woman who cared nothing for norms, whether in her native America or in the England which, for the first time, she was visiting. Aged twenty-nine, she had already been married three times, once bigamously, and divorced once. Now, as in New York, she displayed herself, apparently naked, entirely unabashed and concerned only that her performance would be a sellout – which it certainly was.

In the audience that night at Astley's Amphitheatre in Westminster, to see the play *Mazeppa* in October 1864, was Jem Mace. For the next four years, Adah would be the light of his life, and even when they were forever parted by tragic fate, he would never forget her. Astley's, formerly the most famous circus venue in the world, was by now a flourishing playhouse owned by Edward Tyrrell Smith, the proprietor of Cremorne Gardens. Tyrrell Smith had seen to it that Adah's debut was well publicised and throughout the ten-week run it was the talk of London. Her share of the takings amounted to £200 a week, a total of £2,000. Mace, who claimed the Championship of England, was by no means the only famous man in the audience. Others included the Prince of Wales, the writers Dante Gabriel Rossetti and Charles Reade, the poet Algernon Swinburne and England's greatest literary figure, Charles Dickens. Adah, kept fully informed of her admirers, had issued backstage passes to them all, not to mention invitations to her Saturday night supper parties. The Prince of Wales had reluctantly declined, fearing the disapproval of Queen Victoria; the others had accepted. Alongside Jem was his cousin Leopoldius.

After the initial frisson of her stage entrance, it was obvious that Adah was wearing a flesh-coloured body stocking and a pair of cotton briefs, but her bare arms, lower thighs and calves were, in themselves, an affront to the puritanical standards of Victorian England. There were probably two main reasons why she, Tyrrell Smith and her current husband and promoter, fellow American Robert Henry Newell had 'got away with it' – in other words, why the Lord Chamberlain, the official censor of the English theatre, had not ordered the performance to be closed. First, Adah had not walked onstage or danced: she was on horseback but was not riding the horse. Instead she was tied to its back by a rope around her waist. Her head rested on its mane and her heels on its hind quarters. Her legs were kept carefully closed. The horse trotted onstage, cantered up some steps against a papier maché scenic background depicting mountains and cliffs, then dutifully slowed before descending the steps and disappearing at the rear of the stage, amid a backdrop of clouds. All this gave the impression of a helpless heroine, an ideal beloved by the Victorian mind. Secondly, although this one scene in the play had strong sexual undertones, it was sex masquerading as art. *Mazeppa* was based on an epic written half a century earlier by the great poet Lord Byron. It had been adapted for the stage as a melodrama in 1831 by H.M. Milner and subtitled *The Wild Horse of Tartary*.

It told a story of Jan Mazeppa, a Polish nobleman who fell in love with the beautiful Olinska, betrothed against her will to an evil count. Mazeppa challenged the count to a duel with swords and defeated him, winning his right to safe conduct, but the count went back on his word and ordered soldiers to arrest his rival. To ensure both his humiliation and probable death, he was to be stripped naked and tied to an untamed stallion which was then set free. Mazeppa miraculously survived the ride and was taken by the horse back to its native land, where he was liberated, eventually to become Hetman of the Ukraine. Adah was therefore playing a male role which had been debuted at Astley's before she was even born by the famous circus rider Andrew Ducros. So potentially dangerous was it that, for years afterwards, performances in both England and America used a stuffed dummy for this keynote scene – until Adah. The horse she used in London was a carefully trained circus gelding which would be rewarded with sugar cubes as soon as it left the stage.

When Mace was introduced to Adah, he asked how young she had been when she trained as a circus equestrienne. She asked him to guess and he correctly said eight years old. He also told her that he knew her second husband well. This man was none other than John Camel Heenan, whom she had married near New York City in September 1859. Mace remarked that, had it not been for her publicity work with *The Spirit of the Times* newspaper in New York, the match between Heenan and Sayers might never have taken place. But, as Jem knew, she had not come to England with her husband; instead they divorced. He trusted that Heenan had not been cruel to her but if he had, nothing would give him greater pleasure than to go to America and challenge him. In defeating him he would avenge her, but Adah, though flattered, said that Heenan had bored her but never ill-treated her.

Mace discovered that Adah had been born in Louisiana, just outside New Orleans, the city where she had grown up. Her father died when she was only two and her mother enrolled her as a child in the corps de ballet at New Orleans French Opera House. As a teenage dancer she toured with the Montplaisir Troupe, visiting Havana and Mexico City. Like many people in New Orleans she spoke fluent French – her mother Marie was of French descent. But there was one aspect of her heritage which Adah never revealed to anyone. Although Mace made no comment on her unusually dark hair and eyes, other than to compliment her beauty, she was used to fielding such remarks by people who tagged her 'The Naked Lady from New Orleans' simply on account of the horse scene in *Mazeppa*.

Adah claimed that she was of Jewish origin, and her stepfather, a man named Josephs, probably was, but it was only when she married Alexander Isaacs Menken, a Jewish orchestra leader from Cincinnati, that she converted to Judaism. They were married in Texas in 1856 but soon went to live in his hometown. With publication in the *Cincinnati Israelite*, she had begun an alternative career as a poet but, while acclaimed as an actress, dancer and equestrienne, praise for her poetry had been slight. She was outspoken in supporting Jewish causes and, even after her divorce from Menken, had retained his name in support of her identity. In fact Adah was not Jewish at all in the ethnic sense. Her original name was Adah Berthe Theodore and her father was what was known, in the days of black slavery, as a 'free Negro' – a person of mixed European and African ancestry who, in the tradition of Louisiana (a separate nation under French rule until 1803), was not coerced into slavery. In view of pervasive racism in American society, Adah aimed to keep quiet the fact that she was a quarter black. Due to her relatively light skin and her claim of Jewish ancestry, she succeeded.

After causing a sensation in New York with the opening of *Mazeppa* in 1861, she had been acclaimed as the most alluring woman in the world. Highly intelligent and remarkably confident, she was careful not to antagonise other women, and by wearing her hair comfortably short and openly smoking in public, she defied convention while claiming a degree of freedom previously enjoyed only by men. She was an expert in self-promotion and exploited the new medium of photography by having multiple portraits of herself displayed in advance in the shop windows of every American town and city which she played. Her marriages, extra-marital affairs and pregnancies were avidly followed by women, first in America, then Europe. She had an affair with Blondin but was furious when he refused to agree to her suggestion that he carry her across Niagara walking on a tightrope. Suspecting that his refusal might have something to do with her weight, she was mollified when he swiftly declared that he would have been unable to concentrate on the task because he would be dangerously distracted by the proximity of her body to his. Adah had been delighted when she had a baby by the prize-fighter Heenan, but their son died shortly after his birth.

Adah Isaacs Menken was perhaps the first female star of the entertainment world. When her show hit San Francisco, the stage door was besieged by thousands of adoring fans. But she craved the acclaim of Europe even more than that of her native land. This was what had brought her to London in 1864. Suddenly her husband Robert Henry Newell left her and returned to the States. London was rife with gossip that she had had an affair and while one or other of the literati who frequented Astley's was in the frame, this ignored her tendency to cultivate men of letters simply in the hope of furthering her career as a poet. She had not had an affair with any of the American writers who were at her side in San Francisco – Mark Twain, Bret Harte and Joaquin Miller – and among the Englishmen, Dickens's health was failing, while the effeminate Swinburne was actually furious when a photo of him and Menken together was published in a newspaper.

It appeared that her ideal man was one who, like her, would be both athletic and artistic. Menken and Newell failed on the former criterion, while Heenan and Blondin failed on the latter. But Mace, quite apart from his prowess as a pugilist, was a polished violinist; so was there anything between them? Adah made no comment even when the speculation about the identity of her lover widened to include Mace. Her life would be an all too brief one but, in his autobiography, published over forty years later, Mace devoted several pages to her (one of the few examples of material which does not deal with boxing) in a book from which all mention of his wives and children is excluded. There is little doubt about his feelings for Adah. He speaks of her being 'radiant in her youthful beauty' and of 'the peerless beauty of her radiant womanhood'. He makes it clear that it was not just that 'her physical beauty was superb' but that 'her remarkable cleverness and the quickness of her perception' caused him to fall 'under the spell of her witchery'. Comparing her with the many other women he met, he states 'never did I come across one who could hold a candle to this peerless creature'.

These are clearly the outpourings of a man who had been passionately in love and Mace, whenever a girl had attracted his attention on a purely physical level, was quick to turn his desires into fulfilment. All the women who knew him at various stages in his life commented on his looks but even more on his charm and seductive power. Was Adah the only one to resist his advances? Remarkably he seems to suggest, in one passage, that she was. 'For a time I thought she seemed to favour me greatly,' he wrote. 'But I presently discovered that it was really my cousin – Pooley Mace – whom she was after, for which I was not altogether unthankful.' This seems unlikely. Pooley was acknowledged by women as a handsome man and, half-Romany as he was, had the requisite darkness which had attracted Adah to the Jewish Menken and black haired Irish-American Heenan, but they also commented that Pooley's charisma did not begin to match Jem's.

Pooley had a ready sense of humour but lacked his cousin's wit. The second part of the sentence which refers to Pooley is far more significant – that Mace was 'not unthankful' for the linking of Pooley and Adah. 'Life as Adah's acknowledged lover,' he admitted, 'would have been too exciting just then to have been altogether to my liking.'

Mace was adept at using vague language when it suited him and he was also ingeniously economical with the truth. The words 'just then' come in the section which begins, 'It was about this time that I first became acquainted with the famous Adah Isaacs Menken, who was twenty-nine years old.' In other words, it refers to her residency at Astley's Amphitheatre between October 1864 and January 1865. But at that time Mace and Hannah were still in the first year of their marriage. Hannah, like Adah, had begun as a circus equestrienne and at seventeen and only at the beginning of her first pregnancy, she had not yet lost the lissom figure which had first caught her husband's eye. What's more, he was still reliant at the time on the contribution which her father, Ben Boorn, had made to the Boorn and Mace Circus and could not afford to antagonise him. Had Boorn become aware that his new son-in-law was dallying with an American actress, it might indeed have been the case that the consequences would have been 'too exciting for my liking'.

The words 'acknowledged lover' are ambiguous. They don't preclude the possibility of brief encounters in Adah's dressing room – by now her husband was back in America and there was always the ever-loyal Pooley to prevent any of the Saturday night supper guests from being in the wrong place at the wrong time. But what of Adah's feelings for Mace? Without doubt he combined the factors which had drawn her to Menken and Newell with those which had attracted her to Heenan and Blondin, but Mace, in 1864, was not yet as illustrious as he would later become. He had as yet little recognition as a pugilist in America and only a measure of recognition beyond the Prize Ring in England. Adah returned to the States after the ten-week run of *Mazeppa* had ended. She and Newell divorced and she then appeared successfully in several other melodramas before marrying for the fourth time in nine years. Her new husband, James Barkley, was a man of independent means and a wealthy gambler. She left him after scarcely a month but was already pregnant for the second time.

In 1866 she took on continental Europe, once again in *Mazeppa*. She was an enormous hit in Paris, a city which she came to adore and in which her fluency in French gave her a natural advantage, but she suffered a grievous blow when her second son also died in infancy. Adah was consoled in her grief by the French novelist and celebrated author of *The Three Musketeers* and *The Count of Monte Cristo*, Alexandre Dumas. Dumas was, like Adah, a quarter black and, although he was twice her age and looked even older, they began an affair. Throughout her time in Paris, Adah was also harassed by the writer Theophile Gautier, whose desire for her went completely unrequited. To get out of an intolerable situation, she returned to London to reprise *Mazeppa*, this time at Sadler's Wells Theatre. By the autumn of 1867, her fame was on the wane, while Mace was the undisputed Champion of England, living in the splendour of South Chelsea, where his neighbours included those same literary lions who Adah was still seeking to impress with her less than inspired poetry.

Hannah was no longer the vivacious teenager who had filled him with desire. Although still a good-looking young woman, she was busy with their two young daughters and Mace no longer needed to placate Hannah's father. He was a successful man in his own right. In October 1867, his fame turned to notoriety when he was convicted of conspiracy but his new status as an 'enemy of society' only served to make him more desirable to women who deeply resented the sexist constraints which that same society placed on them. Mace's alternative persona as 'Black Jack Davey' would be deeply appealing to a woman such as Adah, who had nothing but scorn for petty bourgeois values, and his tendency to gamble would not have diminished her interest – she had been drawn to James Barkley precisely because he treated life as a roll of the dice.

Dismayed by the stalling of her theatrical career, Adah was desperate to succeed as a poet and that October sent a signed copy of her, as yet unpublished, book of poems to Charles Dickens. Enclosing a portrait of herself, she asked for permission to dedicate the book to him. His brief reply formally gave his permission, but described her portrait coldly as 'a highly remarkable specimen of photography'. He thanked her for the verses enclosed but made no comment whatever on their quality, privately joking that 'she is a sensitive poet who, unfortunately, cannot write'. The implications of Dickens' terse letter were not lost on Adah. While she would not succeed in impressing intellectual men, she would have a home in the heart of men of passion and artistry, whose affection for her was open and unbounded. Men like Dumas, ageing though he was, and Mace, uneducated though he was, but dynamic and, at thirty-six, only four years older than herself.

When Mace came to publish his autobiography forty years later, in 1908, his publishers were still bound by Victorian standards of prudery, even though they operated in the more relaxed climate of the Edwardian Era. Direct references to sexual matters were still taboo. Nevertheless, in speaking of Adah, Mace mentions times when he was travelling alone and by train and refers to 'one of the most delicious and beautiful of my reminiscent daydreams'. And in private conversation with other men in future years, he would speak with relish about roping Adah to her horse, an act with obvious undertones of bondage and which, he asserted, the American actress enjoyed just as much as he did. The pair last saw each other on 30 May 1868, at her farewell performance at Sadler's Wells. She told him that, to further her acting career, she must return to Paris where demand for her appearance was far greater than in London. Before leaving England, Adah sustained internal injuries as a result of a fall from a horse. In Paris, her health worsened but her personal doctor wrongly attributed this to the onset of tuberculosis. Later the theatre management brought in the personal physician of Napoleon III, Emperor of France, who less than three months after her departure from England, diagnosed peritonitis. This could not be cleared up without surgical intervention; since surgery was only in its infancy at the time, Adah was doomed.

Mace knew nothing about any of this until it was too late. Telegrams were sent from Paris begging him to come to her bedside but he was not at home in Milman Row when the first arrived. Hannah must have read it. She had remained unaware of her husband's interest in Adah in 1864, believing the story that Pooley was a great fan, but, four years later, her suspicions could only be confirmed by the thirty-three-year-old American beauty's desperate plea. Another telegram, to the Strawberry Hotel in Liverpool, went unanswered because Mace was not there either. It so happened that he was away at the races and while at Doncaster he was handed a newspaper by a friend who, as he later put it, 'knew of our relations'. He read the devasating news: on 10 August 1868, Adah Isaacs Menken had died in Paris. She was thirty-three years old.

As he boarded a train home, Mace was overcome by sadness. Suddenly his first-class compartment was invaded by a couple of miners. It turned out that both had lost heavily on the horses and they began to curse their luck in a stream of obscenities. Mace, who neither of them recognised, told them to be quiet, explaining that he was distressed as a result of a recent bereavement. One agreed but the other didn't, replying with verbal abuse. Exercising his habitual restraint, Mace left the train at the next stop, waiting for a connection to London, but the more aggressive of the miners followed him onto the station platform and challenged him to a fight. His grief turning rapidly to anger, he dealt the Yorkshireman a swift beating, his would-be assailant's bravado turning to awe-struck admiration as he learned Mace's identity.

When Mace found out that no attempt had been made to alert him to Adah's last request, he became angry with both Hannah and others. Although he maintained to his wife that Adah was merely a friend, a fiction which Pooley backed up, their marriage was under stress for some time afterwards. The strength of Mace's feeling would be made clear in his autobiography. He states about Adah's deathbed plea, 'Of course I would have gone to her had I known.'

He never forgot Adah. Whenever he visited Paris in future years, for business or pleasure, he would visit her tomb, first at Pere Lachaise Cemetery and, later after re-interment, in a specifically Jewish section at Montparnasse Cemetery. To some she was remembered only as the Naked Lady from New Orleans, but for Jem Mace she would remain the epitome of femininity.

15

The Myth of the Queensberry Rules

JOHN SHOLTO DOUGLAS, the Ninth Marquess of Queensberry, was the heir to Lord Drumlanrig, the noble peer who had once argued for Jem Mace to be brought out of his prize-ring banishment. When, shortly afterwards, Drumlanrig had killed himself with a hunting rifle, his teenage son succeeded to the title. He was a hot-tempered and blustering young man of unremarkable intelligence whose peerage name would, however, resonate excessively in the history of boxing. And, on 16 July 1867, while Mace was in training for his doomed bout with O'Baldwin, Queensberry donated three silver cups, worth 25 guineas each, to the winners of a new annual boxing competition at heavyweight, middleweight and lightweight. The competition was held at Beaufort House in London.

This competition was organised by the newly formed Amateur Athletic Club. It was contested by amateur boxers with no money stakes, but what gave it significance were the rules under which it was fought. They were published under the title 'The Marquess of Queensberry's Rules' and they suggested a radically different form of boxing to that under the rules of the London Prize Ring. The Marquess of Queensberry did not devise the rules which bore his name and which would eventually become household words. They were in fact the work of John Graham Chambers, who was often confused in his lifetime with his contemporary Arthur Chambers, an error that would persist. Arthur Chambers, the excellent lightweight, would later travel to America with the Marquess as his effective publicist but he had nothing to do with writing the rules which Queensberry sponsored.

John Graham Chambers, at this time only twenty-four years old, was already in the forefront of amateur sport, having been the prime mover in the foundation of the Amateur Athletic Association in 1866.

Chambers and Queensberry met while at Magdalene College, Cambridge. Queensberry shared Chambers' keen interest in boxing but not in track and field and rowing, two sports in which Chambers excelled. Chambers hailed from Carmarthenshire in Wales and, as an upper-middle-class man, found it advantageous to continue his friendship with a scion of the aristocracy. In advertising their competition, the Amateur Athletic Club published twelve rules, the last of which stated that the contest would in all other respects be governed by the revised rules of the London Prize Ring. The other eleven were what differentiated the Queensberry code from the LPR. A couple of rules were simple refinements, establishing that a man hanging on the ropes in a helpless state or a man on one knee should be considered down. One dealt with footwear, one with resumption after interference had stopped the contest and another with preventing seconds being in the ring during rounds. It was the remaining six rules which outlined something so radically different from the LPR as to herald a new sport.

Rules 1 and 2 outlawed wrestling and defined a bout as a boxing match. Rule 3 established a set time-frame for one round and a set interval between rounds, namely three minutes and one minute. Rule 4 reduced to ten seconds the time allowed for a fallen man to rise unaided and decreed that failure to do so would result in the loss of the contest. Rules 8 and 9 did not mandate the use of gloves in so many words but referred to 'gloves of the best quality, and new', which 'if a glove burst or come off . . . must be replaced to the referee's satisfaction'. What the Queensberry Rules proposed was, in short, boxing alone, no wrestling; the use of gloves; the acceptability of the knockout; and regular timekeeping. Of these key changes, four had been pioneered in practice by Mace between 1861 and 1866. His sparring exhibitions with Fanque's Circus, Ginnett's Circus and his own circus normally had three-minute rounds. In his knockout tour he had insisted on it, and allowed his £5-a-time challengers ten seconds to rise from the floor before being considered 'out'. What's more, from the time when he became boxing instructor at the Myrtle Street Gym in Liverpool, he had firmly advocated the use of gloves. Even the less critical change, the banishment of seconds during a round, had been insisted on when articles were signed for his third bout with Goss. Only in his willingness to countenance wrestling did Mace fail to anticipate the Queensberry Rules.

Mace had good reasons for preferring gloves and emphasising knockouts. Throughout his career, he was concerned that his hands or wrists might be damaged and that, as a result, his career as a musician would be jeopardised. There was always the possibility that he might never be able to play the violin again, even for his own enjoyment. Secondly, he was a particularly hard hitter from whose fiercest punches, if accurately delivered, few men could hope to rise within ten seconds. There had been times when he had effectively knocked out opponents with a single punch. This had happened to Brettle at Foulness Island and Goss at Purfleet, when Goss had begun to slump even before the second punch of a one-two combination had struck him. But the best example had been in the first Goss fight, when Goss was unconscious for nearly five minutes.

The secret of Mace's devastating punching did not lie in power alone, or even hand speed and timing; it resided above all in his knowledge of where to strike and his ability to deliver the shot to that precise point. In future years he would succinctly describe his technique: 'I always used to go for the side of the jaw – not the point of the chin. If you hit them either side of the jaw they can't help their head swinging round with a jerk and you can follow up with anything you like . . . that's if you need to!'

Mace was not consulted by John Chambers when the rules were drawn up, despite the fact that Chambers made it clear that the AAA tournament would be no one-off but rather an annual event. It appeared that Chambers was aiming not merely at amateurs. Rule 7, the one concerning 'unavoidable interference' (i.e. via the police), provided for the resumption of the contest unless 'the backers of both men agree to draw the stakes'. This unmistakably implied that Chambers was attempting to reform the Prize Ring. Rule 11 seemed to indicate just what he had in mind – 'no shoes or boots with sprigs allowed'. If such was to be the decree on footwear, then fighting in the open-air on turf would become out of the question. Without sprigs or spikes, it would be impossible for a boxer to maintain his foothold. Clearly Chambers was looking towards fighting indoors under gaslight. And, in general, he was using the patronage of the Marquess of Queensberry to attract the return of the Corinthians, who had been soured on prize-fighting by the rampant hooliganism of the 1860s. In circumstances such as his rules hinted at, paid admission would become a practical proposition and a rich source of revenue.

Despite Mace's unequalled expertise, there were good reasons – that is from Chambers' point of view – why he would not be consulted. Mace was a former pedestrian who numbered several well-known others among his friends. Pedestrianism was the antithesis of the amateur ethos which Chambers favoured. But, even in the world of amateur athletics, Mace had been associated with Melly and Hulley, the founders of the Liverpool Olympics. Melly and Hulley had been Chambers' rivals for control of the emerging sport of track and field. When Mace read the Queensberry Rules, he could see at once that, as they stood, they were seriously flawed. First, there was no specific mention of the number of rounds. If Chambers was seeking to placate the anti-prize-fight lobby, then this did not address their central concern: not bloodshed per se but the concept of a fight to the finish entailing, at the least, substantial injury to the loser. In fact the new contests, which eventually moved from Beaufort House to Lillie Road, were to last three rounds, with provision for a fourth if no knockout occurred. As Mace realised, the prospect of a bout which would last fifteen minutes at the most would have no appeal to fans of pugilism.

Next, if there was no knockout (which would often be the case) a decision would have to be made by the referee as to who, in his opinion, had fought better. This was subjective in theory and, in practice, in the hardened world of the Prize Ring, with its atmosphere of fevered gambling, would be bound to lead to attacks on the referee by anyone who had lost money as a result of his call. Then there were the points about the weight of the gloves and the size of the ring. Rule 8 simply stated that the gloves must be new and 'fair-sized'. This vagueness did not preclude the use of skintight gloves, which would afford a little protection for the wearer without really diminishing the cutting impact of bare knuckles, which were notorious for producing ugly eye injuries. Rule 1 stated that the size of the ring would be '24 foot' or, with typical vagueness, 'as near that size as possible'. This completely ignored Mace's insistence on a 16ft ring in his third and final match with Goss, which, by common consent, had dramatically increased the tempo of the bout and punished Goss for his previous stalling tactics.

Despite the errors and omissions, Mace could see that the Queensberry Rules provided the basis for a way forward. The showman in him was drawn to the prospect of indoor combat – it would be spectacular, lucrative and far easier to exclude hooligans in such circumstances. The animosity of the magistrates would be drawn to some extent by the use of gloves. However, without at least some specifications about the number of rounds, neither magistrates nor pugilists would be satisfied: the magistrates would imagine the piling up of innumerable 'brutal' rounds, while the pugilists would react with disdain to the restriction of their bravery and stamina to perhaps less than ten minutes of actual fighting – and the spectators would feel deprived of their money's worth.

In the world of the LPR, it was swiftly realised that there would be no point in Mace or anyone else approaching either Chambers and/or Queensberry to persuade them to revise their rules. The leading British heavyweights, men like Wormald and O'Baldwin, were of limited intelligence. Of the lightweights, Arthur Chambers was already currying favour with the Marquess, which left Billy Edwards as the only man sufficiently articulate to join Mace in pointing out the flaws in the rules. The biggest problem of all was, however, Chambers' know-all attitude and the snobbery of the Ninth Marquess. Unlike his late father, John Sholto Douglas did not mix easily with working men. Chambers' university education had fitted him to deal with such matters as the drawing up of rules and regulations and the kind of prose in which they were couched; Mace, by contrast, had been deprived of any education. His writing would remain laborious and clumsy and his spelling, grammar and punctuation primitive, but this did not mean, as Chambers almost certainly supposed, that he was lacking in intelligence. Far from it – Mace's mind was acute, as those who knew him were well aware. The class-ridden nature of Victorian society operated to ensure that Mace did not get the credit he deserved for inspiring the reform of boxing and ultimately led to the propagation of a myth: namely that the future fight game which would sweep the United States and Latin America was indebted to a cantankerous English lord and his old chum from Cambridge.

The result of Mace's arrest and his two years on probation had been to complete the exodus of British fighters to America and it was obviously one option for him to follow suit. At thirty-six, he felt as vigorous as ever, his wellbeing promoted by his regular day's jogging, minimal consumption of alcohol and smoking no more than an occasional cigar. As a man of means he was eating better than ever, with cooks in residence at Milman Row preparing his favourite meals. Then news arrived from America which caused him to change his mind about going there.

American pugilists had enjoyed relative immunity from prosecution because of their role as enforcers for prominent politicians, but as the politicians developed their own party machines, so the need for bareknuckle goons diminished. Suddenly there was a rash of arrests involving men who had previously challenged Mace for the English Championship and, in one case, for the vacant world title. Joe Coburn had retired for several years following his abortive trip to Ireland to meet Mace, but needing money badly, he attempted a comeback. He agreed to give Mike McCoole a second chance at the American Championship. At Cold Springs Station, Indiana, in May 1868, Coburn and McCoole were arrested before they could trade a single blow, charged under state anti-prize-fight legislation and sentenced to forty days in the jailhouse.

Worse was to follow. Amid confusion over who the American titleholder now was, two of the British expatriates, Wormald and O'Baldwin, signed articles to fight at Lynfield, Massachusetts in September 1868. The venue was the village green, but when spectators congregated in the churchyard, where seats on the tombstones provided an ideal view, the parson sent to Boston for the police. Although Wormald succeeded in fleeing to Canada, the hapless Irishman was charged with sacrilege and sentenced to eighteen months in prison. Regardless of his personal attitude towards Coburn, Wormald and O'Baldwin, it seemed obvious to Mace that if he went to America, he would go out of the frying pan into the fire.

Mace was forbidden to fight and, carefully describing himself as 'Retired Champion of England', he decided not to spar. For a time he continued to give exhibitions of his other skills at various venues throughout Britain, which played an important role in the development of the nascent British sporting scene. His influence spread across several other sports. In Edinburgh, he put on a Monstre Fete at the Royal Patent Gymnasium in May 1869. For a sixpenny admission (or two shillings and sixpence in the grandstand), spectators could watch him compete in the mile-and-a-half handicap against Teddy Mills and Robert McKinistry, the Scottish pedestrian champion, among others. In addition, he put up prizes for competition in the 200 yards and high jump. The new sport of velocipedism (cycle racing) was also featured, with prizes for the fastest riders over 400 yards. Typically, in Mace's mind, sport was conjoined with music and dancing. At Edinburgh a 'splendid brass band' would provide the former and the latter would be demonstrated by Champion John McNeill and his troupe of Highland Dancers and Pipers. And, at the Victoria Music Hall, Newcastle, in August, he wrestled with Champion Jamieson and presented the swimming champion, James Renforth, to the audience. While few realised it at the time and fewer still were, in future, prepared to give him credit, Mace's role in presenting sport as spectacle and in stressing the commonality of different sports was of immense importance. It was one which he, as both an outstanding athlete and an audacious showman, was uniquely fitted to fulfil.

For much of the time, Mace was on the road. His father-in-law, Ben Boorn had effectively taken over Mace's Circus and Mace spent several months with him on a tour of Ireland. At other times, he worked as a freelance, giving Grecian Statuary shows with such companies as Barrington's Circus, the Great Allied Circus, the Japanese Circus and Cirque Franconi. Hannah remained at home in London with the children but, in time, the house in Milman Row became too dear to maintain and Mace took a pub in the heart of London, The Old King's Head in the Tottenham Court Road.

In the aftermath of Adah's death, the coolness between the couple persisted and his tendency towards casual relationships began to resurface. One of these affairs was with Isabella Rigby, a thirty-five-year-old cotton weaver from Bamber Bridge in Lancashire. She was unmarried, lived with her parents and had already had two children out of wedlock. Late in 1869, Isabella would give birth to a child by the name of James Rigby and it was widely believed that he was Mace's son. In later years, Mace would speak in an ambiguous but gallant way about Isabella and while he admitted having had sexual relations with her he denied being James' father.

At about this time, a letter bearing a distinctive crest and heavy with red sealing wax was delivered to Mace's home. When he opened the letter, Mace found it was addressed from Wilton Crescent in Belgravia and signed by Henry Cecil Lowther. Lowther was the nephew of the Second Earl of Lonsdale and, since the Earl was a bachelor in his seventies, Henry was expected to inherit the title. A scion of one of England's most aristocratic families, he was heir to an estate which comprised Carlton House Terrace, one of the finest mansions in Belgravia, and three country homes, in Melton Mowbray, Rutland, and the vast baronial estate of Lowther Castle, which extended over 100,000 acres in the Lake District and included the entire coalmining town of Whitehaven. The letter was courteous, brief and to the point. He wished Mace, Champion of England, to act as a full-time tutor in boxing to his troublesome twelve-year-old son, Hugh Cecil Lowther, and was prepared to offer a substantial sum. Hugh had not actually been expelled from Eton, England's most aristocratic public school, but his father had been 'advised to remove him' due to his boisterous behaviour. Mace had no hesitation in accepting the offer. It was only for one term and would fit neatly into his schedule before he decided where his long-term future lay. Although he did not kowtow to toffs, he had learned from his days at the Rum-pum-pas the importance of aristocratic patronage for the Prize Ring and lamented the decline of the LPR when the Corinthians stayed away. Henry Lowther had not been a notable member of the Fancy, preferring foxhunting to bareknuckle combat, but Mace knew the value of links with the upper classes. When he arrived at Wilton Crescent, he was timidly informed by Hugh's mother that her boy was a 'holy terror' who had frightened away his French tutor by playing a dangerous prank on him. She trusted that he would behave himself with Mr Mace. Jem smiled and said he was sure the boy would do just that.

Hugh was a total extrovert who disliked books and had been allowed by his indulgent and obese father to run wild at Melton

Mowbray. He had escaped into the town, mixed with shopkeepers' sons and been taunted into fights, from which he emerged victorious. Hugh was overjoyed by his new tutor's arrival. Such was Mace's charisma that the lad idolised him from the word go. A ring was set up and instruction in the noble art of self-defence with gloves began. Hugh proved an adept learner and was sorry to see his teacher leave at the end of the term's tuition. Mace had not anticipated just how warmly he would be welcomed by the Lowthers. After completing the induction of his young pupil into self-defence, he could scarcely be expected to anticipate the future significance of the Lonsdale name in the history of boxing.

For a time, Mace considered a third option which did not involve staying in England or emigrating to America. Prize-fighting had been established in Australia for fifty years and, while illegal, did not suffer from police disruption. The standard of fighting was high and reports of Australian mills were published regularly in *Bell's Life*. One of the best was the longest fight then on record, between Jim Kelly and Jonathan Smith, at Fiery Creek, Victoria, in 1855. It had lasted six hours, twenty minutes, for a purse of £400. Australia's most notable fighter, Bill Sparkes, had come to England in the 1850s, challenged Nat Langham and, though he lost, had given Langham a good run for his money. It so happened that Mace had relatives in Australia. His elder cousin Hannah had, when he was a boy, married a seafarer from Yarmouth named John Ditcham and emigrated.

By this time the nature of Australian society had changed. The old practice of transportation, of sentencing British and Irish convicts (often men found guilty of minor offences, some of them politically motivated) to be shipped to Australia, had ended. What's more, gold had been discovered in the colony of Victoria, which then began to rival the original colony of New South Wales. Both Sydney and Melbourne were notable cities in their own right and Australians were starting to crave leisure outlets.

Mace considered an exhibition tour, with the Ditchams helping with the arrangements and Pooley as his sparring partner. Going Down Under would be a kind of holiday, an invigorating trip to the opposite end of the world, but he would also be there to test the waters. If Australia seemed open to prize-fighting, not merely sparring, then there might well be a small fortune to be made without the risk of arrest. However, after a sudden change in attitude towards prize-fighting, both *Bell's Life in New South Wales* and *Bell's Life in Victoria* adopted a negative stance similar to their sister periodical in London. Far worse, a public backlash against pugilism followed the tragic events at the bout between two fighters called McLaren and Carstairs. A remote island, accessible only by steamboat, had been selected to avoid the police, but an attempt to land the vessel in dangerous currents was botched and at least a dozen would-be spectators were drowned. With both evangelicals and factory bosses chorusing that prize-fighting was 'illegal, immoral and injurious', prospective matches were put on hold, leaving no room for 'the notorious English bruisers', as one newspaper labelled them.

During this era, Jem visited the photographic studio on several occasions and struck a different and distinctive pose – not only wearing fashionable gloves to cover his contused hands but, when facing the camera, placing his right hand inside the left-hand pocket of his double-breasted jacket. The reference to Napoleon Bonaparte was intended. Mace had always been irritated that Tom Sayers had been referred to by some boxing scribes as the Napoleon of the Ring. Sayers was an instinctively fast-thinking fighter but he did not manoeuvre his opponents as Mace did. Ring generalship was Mace's hallmark. Britain and France had been victorious allies in the Crimean War against Tsarist Russia and so comparison with the reigning Emperor of the French, Napoleon III, was a high compliment to Sayers.

During the 1860s, however, Louis-Napoleon Bonaparte was mistakenly suspected of harbouring intentions to invade England, as his uncle Napoleon I had actually planned to do early in the century. The name Bonaparte once again became a taboo, one which, in the photographic studio, Mace did not hesitate to flout. Though he never had diamonds sewn into the lining of his waistcoat, as the first French emperor did, he was a risk-taker by nature. Throughout his reign as Champion of England, he had bet lavishly on horses but had usually had to divert funds from other sources to cover his losses. Just as he had done when he first threw the dice as a lad in the gypsy camps of Norfolk, he looked on life as a gamble and adventures of all sorts as what raised living above mere existence.

It would not be long before news from the American Prize Ring convinced him that he would follow the other British expatriates into what he hoped would be a productive exile. Tom Allen had, unlike Wormald and O'Baldwin, escaped the clutches of the law. Allen was a far more cunning man than the other two and had a ruthless streak which was fully brought out in the lawless atmosphere of American prize-fighting. During the course of 1869, Allen signed articles five times: once to meet Bill Davis and twice each (with pre-arranged returns) to face Mike McCoole and another Irish-American, Charlie Gallagher. The result of this series was to give Allen the American championship, even though he had not yet completed naturalisation to become a US citizen. An honestly refereed forty-three-round scrap saw him get the better of the genial Davis. That bout, and those which followed, took place on a river island near St Louis, Missouri, which was, at that time, a wide-open town where frontier traditions were strong. Allen was beaten by Gallagher with a flukey early knockout but won the return, when he took only twenty-five minutes to pummel Gallagher into surrender. The referee's verdict of a draw was manifestly absurd and derided as such in the sporting press. As for McCoole, he had shown against Coburn, years before, that he was completely without skill. Allen cut him to ribbons in a mere nine rounds before a mob-threatened referee reversed the verdict for betting purposes. McCoole was nothing if not game but, unsurprisingly, was unable to find backers for the rematch. The series had been fraught but the outcome was undeniable; not only did Allen emerge with a stack of dollars but, Englishman though he temporarily remained, he was acclaimed in the US press as Champion of America.

Mace read about these events with a mixture of amusement, contempt and self-interest. Clearly, if you made sure to fight in the right place and were brave enough to face lawless mobs, as he had already done more than once, there was a fortune waiting in America. What really angered Mace was, however, Allen's extravagant claim to be world champion. This was laughable. First, there never had been such a champion, Heenan and Sayers having fought a draw, King–Coburn having been explicitly designated as not being for the Belt, and Mace–Coburn having fallen through. Secondly, Allen had never even challenged Mace for the English title, let alone won it. Mace felt certain that he could whip Allen with one hand – and decided to go straight to America. First he disposed of his businesses. The circus was sold, as his racehorses had already been, and as the lease on the Strawberry Gardens still had a couple of years to run, Montague lined up a purchaser called Thomas Haig, a prominent Liverpool brewer, for the Strawberry Hotel and Tavern. These deals appeared to mark the end of Montague's role as Mace's factotum, for he had no experience with business in the United States. Mace's business partner on his American adventure would be Fred Abrahams, who he had met through the theatre. Abrahams, who had visited the States, would handle Mace's negotiations with circuses and his first task was to line up a contract for Mace to perform his Grecian statues act. Such an act was, at that time, a hot novelty in America.

Mace told Hannah that he was going to America to see the situation for himself. If it looked as if he might have a successful long-term career in the States, he would send for her and their two children. Matters pugilistic would be left to Pooley, who was confirmed in his role as full-time trainer, and on 15 September 1869, Jem and Pooley, having left Liverpool on the *City of Antwerp*, arrived in New York City. The path into exile had been completed.

PART THREE

CHAMPION OF AMERICA

(1870–77)

16

From Broadway to Bourbon Street

HEADS TURNED AS he strolled down Broadway in the late September sunshine. Coming out of West 23rd Street, where he had his new home in the fashionable Chelsea district, Jem Mace would walk more than twenty blocks on Manhattan's main thoroughfare, passing close to the mansion where ten-year-old Teddy Roosevelt, future President of the United States, was growing up. He crossed Union Square, where many of the city's most stylish houses lay, and skirted the sedate residences of Greenwich Village. At the intersection of 11th Street and Broadway, he strode past the white marble edifice of Grace Church, its stones mined by the convicts at the infamous Sing Sing prison in upstate New York. His journey downtown took him beyond Bleecker Street, where he lengthened his stride as he approached his destination. He was dressed like a dandy, with a dark blue velvet coat, a purple silk vest, a cluster of diamonds in his tie, lavender trousers with a single black stripe and gleaming patent leather boots. As he removed his shining silk top hat, buffed and shining like a mirror, he revealed pomaded black hair, receding more than somewhat with an unruly quiff, and his immaculately trimmed and waxed moustache. His gait was brisk, purposeful and athletic. Seeming less weatherbeaten in comparison with his American contemporaries, he was taken for thirty, although he was in fact nearly ten years older.

Mace was due at Harry Hill's club to meet an old acquaintance – John Carmel Heenan, former Champion of America but now retired, though he was four years younger than Mace. He had welcomed the Englishman's arrival in New York City partly out of comradeship, mainly because it gave him the chance to arrange a lucrative series of sparring exhibitions in the fall of 1869 and winter of 1870. Hill's was, by common consent, the centre of the American fistic universe. Every important bareknuckle match was made there and Harry Hill was invariably the stakeholder and sometimes the referee. Hill was English and had lost none of his Cockney accent, despite living in America for fifteen years. He came from 'travelling horse people' and first arrived with the wealthy racehorse owner Woolsey, of whose stables he was in charge. He had established himself as a racetrack bookmaker at Saratoga, 150 miles to the north, beyond the Catskill Mountains in upstate New York. This was near Troy, Heenan's hometown but, more significantly, also that of John Morrissey, his predecessor as American champion. When Morrissey turned from the ring to the racetrack, he made it clear to Hill that there would be only one boss of the betting industry at Saratoga. Undaunted, Hill had settled in New York City and rapidly became America's answer to Nat Langham. This he was well-equipped to be, knowing the London Prize Ring as he did. A burly man, he was handy with his fists and had once aspired to a career as a prize-fighter.

The *New York Herald* welcomed Mace's arrival in the city with enthusiasm:

> The great attraction at Tammany Hall last night was the 'Grand Assault at Arms' between Jem Mace, the English Champion and his cousin Leopold Mace. The house was crowded in every part with a most pleasant sprinkling of the fair sex who enjoyed not only the preliminary bill of fare . . . but who waited with fresh and unappeased appetite for the choice morsel of the evening. This was the double Mace encounter in which the Champion and his cousin acquitted themselves with great èclat, exciting rapturous applause . . . The general desire prevails to see the most scientific pugilist in the world illustrate the best points of the manly art of self-defence.

After an evening like that, it must have seemed to Mace that he had arrived not in a new country but on a different planet from those bleak beaches and mournful marshes where he had previously plied his trade. In the heart of a great city and at a prestigious venue, before female as well as male spectators, he had convincingly demonstrated that boxing, as practised by him and an accomplished sparring partner, was a compelling and lucrative spectacle.

Soon Mace and Heenan shook hands on a deal. There followed a series of exhibitions in New York, Boston, Philadelphia and Baltimore. On every occasion the fistic fraternity was unanimous: not only that Mace had outclassed Heenan but that America would need to find a very good fighter indeed to stop him. In his opening months in the States, Mace was anxious not to be stereotyped as a prize-fighter. He had never seen himself like this anyway but there were other considerations. First, showbusiness opportunities were opening up fast. Howe and Cushing's Circus was eager for his services and he was soon giving both violin performances and demonstrations of Grecian Statuary – described, to Mace's amusement, by the *New York Herald* as 'more ennobling than his previous calling'. Secondly, he still had to be careful to avoid police harassment. Despite boxing's immense popularity it remained illegal in many states of that same Union which had emerged victorious and intact from the American Civil War only four years earlier. New York was one of these and Mace preferred, as of old, to describe himself as a musician. Soon he had another string to his bow. At Hill's he had been befriended by an Irish-born business-man named Phil Hargrave who ran a saloon in West 23rd Street and was keen to add the lustre of Mace's name to attract custom. Mace and Hargrave became partners, although Mace's general business affairs were dealt with by Abrahams, who had already come over from England. While Mace didn't actively seek a fight, he and his advisers reckoned that it would only be a matter of time before one would come his way.

For four months, Mace lived it up in New York. He was, to all intents and purposes, a single man once again, just as he had been when he first came to London, but even London was staid compared to 'Gotham'. Hill's was the first of a number of what were loosely called 'concert halls' which began to dominate the nightlife in New York City. While the prototypes were in Paris, it was the first recognisable nightclub ever in the English-speaking world. Anglo-Saxon puritanism had long inhibited the development of anything similar but now, in the raucous, cosmopolitan and hedonistic city which emerged in the post-war years, the power of the Church was being challenged. Jem was instantly at home at Harry Hill's, as was Pooley, who always reckoned, accurately enough, that he could secure a good time for himself basking in his cousin's reflected glory. Pooley had been sparring with Jem at various New York City halls since the pair arrived in America.

Hill's was an irregular cluster of two-storey buildings, at Houston and Crosby Street, combined into a theatre and house of entertainment. Admission was twenty-five cents for men, free for women. There was a lengthy lunch counter stocked with the finest foods. Coffee was served piping hot, with tea as an alternative for expatriate Englishmen. Service was by waitresses chosen for their youth and good looks and dressed in tight-fitting outfits. The club theatre showed comedians and blackface minstrel sketches, but the most popular turns were girl vocalists whose legs were adorned only by pink tights and whose breasts were revealed by low-cut bodices. Doors finally closed at 2.30am. Liquor flowed freely, wine and champagne more than beer and spirits. Prices excluded roughs and encouraged young men about town. Hill's began to attract, by means of advertisements, women from uptown New York who wanted to have fun but had jobs as stenographers and were economically independent. What's more, showgirls from the theatres began to attend in large numbers. The personal safety of 'respectable ladies and gentlemen' was assured by Harry Hill himself. At the slightest hint of an imminent quarrel, the burly Cockney, a wrestling enthusiast, would act as his own bouncer: the offender would be seized, frogmarched to the stairs and 'find it to his advantage to descend rapidly to the exit'.

Before long Hill's began to attract VIP customers such as Samuel Tilden, a 'respectable' politician from the state capital in Albany and a future candidate for President. With profits at the club rising sharply, Hill was able to have a country house built for himself at Flushing on Long Island, at the time still a separate township, outside New York City. The establishment on Houston Street immediately became a home from home for Mace. During the day he would be there on boxing business; at night he would go there to relax, as did various other pugilists, notably his fellow expatriate Billy Edwards. While such men could see off troublemakers with the greatest of ease, they preferred not to have to do so while 'off-duty'. Hill could be relied on to take care of that.

Hill also owned furnished apartments at nearby Crosby Street. Mace had always had a liking for the type of young woman who, like himself, rebelled against Victorian morality. He sneered at the ignorance and prejudice of those who labelled any fun-loving theatrical girl or dancer a harlot. Once again a sought-after dancing partner, he was in a position to pick and choose who might accompany him to a Crosby Street apartment in the early hours. Mace's appeal to women went far beyond his growing fame and prospects of a fortune though, and beyond the sharpness of his threads and coolness of his dance-floor moves. Gracious and charming, confident, smiling and humorous, he was believed to typify the English gentleman. No New York girl had the faintest idea that, in his native land, he'd been nicknamed 'The Gypsy' and that his Norfolk accent had been dismissed as a provincial twang. He could have passed for the Marquess of Queensberry himself – but his rules were those of the heart.

Hill's was not Mace's only port of call in those heady months after his arrival. Another was the Bal Mabille on Bleecker Street, once a rowdy saloon that had been renamed by new owner Theodore 'The' Allen to give it a hint of Parisian exoticism. Allen was a ruthless character with a previous conviction for manslaughter – he had kicked a man to death – who had made a fortune from cheap whorehouses and had political protectors. He refurbished the Bal Mabille as an establishment which, though not on a par with Hill's, was still somewhat upscale. A dance orchestra provided 'soirees' where girls were allowed in free, ahead of young men standing in line to pay for admission. Allen's principal innovation in nightclub culture was to have his orchestra play Offenbach's cancan music à la Moulin Rouge, but instead of a chorus line of dancers, the girl customers themselves linked arms and raised their legs in time to the music, revealing limbs clad in pink stockings and suspenders.

Mace also visited 105 Bowery, the location of a club with the almost ludicrously innocent original name of the Old House at Home, popularly rechristened the Bastille on the Bowery. Its owner, Owney Geoeghan, an immigrant from King's County in Ireland, was himself a pugilist, had aspired to the Middleweight Championship of America and claimed to have won it in a controversial pre-war bout with Con Orem at Cheese Creek, New Jersey. With The Allen the ringleader for Orem's bunch of armed thugs, and others brandishing revolvers and cheering for Geoeghan, Hill's call of victory for the Irishman on a foul somehow averted gunfire at ringside. Geoeghan invested his winnings in the Bastille.

Mace was severely disappointed with the Bastille, a much rougher house than Hill's or Allen's. One of its specialities was battles between female pugilists whose combats, due to a loophole in the New York State law on prize-fighting, were exempt from police interference. He was nauseated by this spectacle. As to the women who watched or who came to dance, they were too coarse for his liking. Nevertheless, the Bastille was to impact on his life in other ways. Geoeghan made himself known to Mace and invited him and Pooley to visit Saratoga Springs, which they duly did. Saratoga Springs was an offshoot of John Morrissey's empire on his home turf in upstate New York. Geoeghan knew Morrissey well and the racehorses which the Bastille's owner bought with his club-owning success had appeared on the Saratoga track. By this time, Morrissey had augmented his huge profits from control of pari-mutuel ticket sales and off-track betting. At nearby Saratoga Springs, he opened the greatest gambling parlor of the time. Keen to distance himself from the associates of his rowdy youth in New York City, Morrissey adopted a less abrasive personal manner and began to cultivate socially prominent men, including Cornelius Vanderbilt and Leonard W. Jerome. The latter was the uncle of Jenny Jerome, who would marry Lord Randolph Churchill and become the mother of Winston Churchill.

Jerome and others felt at ease in the tranquil atmosphere of upstate New York and lent their names to the Saratoga Association, of which Morrissey, albeit not named, was the chief stockholder. By association with wealthy, prestigious and influential men, Morrissey's empire at Saratoga Springs enjoyed total protection from the police. Indeed, it became a kind of American Monte Carlo, with V.I.P. gamblers relaxing by the side of Lake Saratoga before turning their attention to the wheel of fortune. Mace was rapidly drawn into the Saratoga Springs scene. His gambling tendencies were released at full blast, and the lure of the tumbling dice became almost irresistible. While he remained a pugilist, he could usually defray his losses by lucrative fights and exhibitions, but he had by now developed an incorrigible habit which would be far harder to sustain once his days in the Prize Ring were done.

Throughout the fall of 1869, negotiations continued for a match between Mace and Allen. These turned out to be protracted because of disagreements as to who should be the challenger. Allen was convinced that, as Champion of America, he was not the one to issue a challenge for a mill on US soil. Mace insisted that, since he had been Champion of England for most of the preceding decade, during which time Allen had never challenged him, it was not up to him to initiate matters; what's more, Mace was determined that the bout should be for the Championship of the World. Ever since the debacle which ended the Heenan–Sayers fight, the global title which they contested without conclusion had remained unclaimed. When Heenan came to England to fight King, that title had not been at stake, though it would have been had the mill between Mace and Coburn gone ahead. And since neither Sayers nor Heenan had responded to Mace's challenge, Mace could and did claim that he was the heir presumptive to the vacant throne.

After a couple of months, Allen seemed to concede his place in the pecking order but muddied the waters in his challenge by insisting that Mace should go to Pittsburgh, where Allen now lived, to sign articles. Mace accepted the challenge but refused to leave New York, not merely out of pride but because of his theatrical commitments on the East Coast – he was in fact rehearsing for his debut as a Shakespearean actor and would shortly be on stage at Niblo's Gardens in the role of Charles the Wrestler in the comedy *As You Like It*. Mace's artistic versatility contrasted sharply with Allen, who was dependent wholly on prize-fighting. Before long, Allen lost his cool and an open letter to Mace was published in his name in the New York sporting periodical *The Clipper*. In the letter, Allen boasted that he would shortly be presented with a belt in honour of his being the American Champion. Then he used the phrase 'put up or shut up', a time-honoured insult in the world of pugilism indicating that a man must either find his stake money or stop bragging. It also carried imputations of cowardice and had not appeared in print before. Mace was onto his opponent as quickly and as severely as if he actually had him in the ring. His open reply was published in *The Clipper* on December 27, dictated verbatim to Abrahams, who contributed only the spelling and punctuation:

I observe your rather debating reply to my acceptance of your challenge and I was somewhat astonished at the tenour [sic] of it . . . You should understand being the challenging party it is your place to put up a deposit as evidence of sincerity and mine to cover it. To show that I mean precisely what I say, however, and do not court notoriety through the Press, I have this day deposited $500 at this office, which I desire you to come forward and cover without any more talk, with which the public do not wish to be bored. My business engagements render it altogether out of the question for me to meet you in Pittsburgh as you propose; but I will meet you at the 'Clipper' office any time you may name (the sooner the better) and will pay one half of your expenses to this city . . . in reference to the belt which you say is shortly to be presented to you, I wish to say that my friends in New York propose to present me with a belt also, which I will put against yours and contest for in addition to the stakes . . . Now, if as you say, you are ready . . . to (meet) me as soon as possible and (sign) articles . . . this is the time to show whether you are in earnest or merely bouncing.

In the course of a few pithy sentences, Mace had first indicated Allen as the challenger and not the other way round, thus putting him completely in his place. Then he hinted, but hinted only, at Allen's insincerity and his attempt to manipulate the media; next, he had trumped Allen's trick by leaving a sizeable sum in cash at the newspaper offices and had stigmatised Allen as a public bore. He had reduced the man, formerly of Birmingham and now of Pennsylvania, to the status of a provincial nobody and had demeaned him by offering him financial assistance. At the same time, Mace had identified himself with New York, home of America's movers and shakers in public opinion. He had gone on to up the ante, in the classic style of a poker player. He had demonstrated his unshakeable confidence by putting his belt up for grabs and, at the same time, implicitly designating it as the insignia of the World Champion. And he had ended by indirectly characterising Allen as a two-bit braggart while using only the non-libellous word 'bouncing' – thus needling his opponent and placing him on the spot.

Never was the power, subtlety, wit, effrontery and remorseless logicality of Mace's mind more tellingly demonstrated. It was the intellectual equivalent of his jabs and feints, his shimmies and thunderous crosses. Mace's open letter swung sporting opinion in his favour and within two weeks Allen had come to heel. Articles were signed in *The Clipper* offices, although Allen was not there in person. Illiterate, he had been offered by Mace the services of his fellow Brummie, Billy Edwards, to read a draft on his behalf and put pen to paper for him. The place of battle was fixed at within fifty miles of New Orleans, the date was set for 10 May 1870 and the stakes were set at $2,500 a side.

Before articles were signed, Mace sent for Hannah to join him in New York. She would travel on the *City of Paris*, sailing out of Liverpool, and have two-year-old Ada with her. But Amelia, two years older, had already started school and it was thought best that she remain there, which was also an indication that her father was unsure whether his long-term future lay in the States. The house in Milman Row had long been sold and it was decided that Amelia should be looked after by Hannah's sister and brother-in-law, Fanny and William Jacey, in Bland Street, Southwark. Fanny and William had no children of their own but had brought up one of his nieces. To their extended family were now added Mace's children by his first marriage. While Adelaide and James were still at school, sixteen-year-old Alfred was a clerk with a firm of linen drapers. Jacey's earnings as a printer and compositor were not enough to keep them unless Alfred paid for his lodgings, and Jem arranged to remit money to take care of James and his two daughters.

Soon Hannah and Ada were installed in Mace's home on West 23rd Street, where Pooley and Hargrave also lived, together with three servants. Despite his casual infidelities during her absence, Mace still had considerable affection for his wife. Although she looked older, she was still only twenty-two and an attractive young woman. The problem in their relationship was – whether Hannah fully realised it or not – that he subconsciously compared her with Adah Isaacs Menken, of course to the latter's advantage. Hannah shed no tears over the actress's death and was aware of her limitations in comparison to sophisticated women such as Adah.

There were good reasons why the Mace–Allen fight should be held in America's Old South. Upstate New York State was out of the

question. For some time New York pugilists had escaped the police
only by re-staging their battles in what was then an undeveloped part
of Canada. Throughout New England, the Puritan tradition ensured a
total ban on pugilism. As for New Jersey, it had already had enough
after Orem–Geoeghan. Allen's Pennsylvania was no more amenable,
although he had fought several battles undisturbed in Missouri. Allen
and his backers had proposed a location near St Louis but Abrahams
wouldn't hear of it. The fight venue should, he argued, be equally
distant from both men's adopted home cities – in New Orleans,
equidistant from New York and Pittsburgh. The point was to ensure
the most expensive train ride possible, to deter the roughs from the
Northern cities from attending. These were the men who would have
been certain to root for Allen, who had declared his intention to
become a US citizen and taken out naturalization papers. Allen was
considered a likely winner because he was nearly ten years younger
than Mace and experienced in American rings, which Mace was not.
The smart money was on him.

The friends to whom Mace referred, in his open letter to Allen,
were as good as their word. They subscribed a belt which was made by
Tiffany of New York, weighed ninety ounces and was mounted on red
velvet. It was embellished by four figures moulded in relief, the
American eagle perched upon a shield and two flags, and a floral
wreath bearing the inscription: 'The New American Belt, presented to
Mr. James Mace as a complimentary testimonial of respect from his
friends in New York City, 11th Feb., 1870.'

* * *

New Orleans was a different world. Its history as the capital of French
Louisiana until 1803, its period under Spanish rule, the fact that
Louisiana had been a Confederate state and the existence of a large
population of 'free men of color' and people of mixed race, combined
to give it a hedonistic and tolerant attitude. In Roman Catholic New
Orleans, there were no fundamentalist zealots to include prize-fighting
as a 'sinful pursuit'. What's more, the old anti-English prejudice in
Louisiana had long since subsided and been replaced by a hostility to
northern Yankees, as a result of the Civil War and Reconstruction.

Since Allen was in the process of exchanging the Union Jack for the Stars and Stripes, it would be Mace, as the proud Englishman, who would evoke more cheers in New Orleans.

While Allen made the mistake of staying as far north as St Louis with his trainer, Mace travelled south two months before the fight, accompanied by Abrahams, Pooley and his American seconds, Jim Cusick and Jerry Donovan, to acclimatise. Even in May, the heat on the tropical Gulf of Mexico coast could be broiling and he needed to get used to this. With his small entourage he stayed at Hyluorn's Hotel at St Charles Street, living in some style, and quickly found himself feted. Mace took an instant liking to New Orleans, wandering around the French Quarter and visiting the Opera House where Adah had first performed in her home city, but soon the party moved out to Mobile, Alabama, to go into strict training. While at the races with Mace in nearby Magnolia, Pooley got talking to an old black man who offered a hut for hire which in the heart of a pine forest, would certainly be desolate. 'Day after day,' recalled Jem, 'we raced, boxed, jumped, wrestled and punched the bag, without a soul being the wiser.' He became thoroughly acclimatised and his skin became toughened and bronzed, while the pines provided a measure of shadow from the full glare of the sun. The site was not far from turpentine logging camps and it was turpentine which Mace used on his fists, finding it more effective than any of the concoctions he'd used in England. The only downside was the mosquitoes, and he was in excellent condition as the date of the fight arrived: he needed to be, for he had been out of the ring for three years and nine months.

On May 10, the Crescent City, its dainty white residences adorned with honeysuckle and bougainvillea, was unusually overcast. At Jackson Railroad Depot, the train bearing Mace, Allen, their entourages and hundreds of perfectly behaved spectators, including city merchants and ex-Confederate officers, made ready to exit New Orleans itself, since byelaws prevented prize-fights within the city limits. The train glided through suburban rows of orange trees, rich with golden fruit, and came to a halt a dozen miles out of the city centre just beyond the town of Kennerville. The party made its way by carriage or on foot to a spot about a mile from a Mississippi riverboat stop named La Salle Landing. Here, at the back of Kenner's sugar house, on the Oakland

Plantation, the ring was pitched and an orderly circle of carriages and horse-drawn buses surrounded it.

* * *

Tom Allen, the first to arrive, was cheered warmly by about 1,000 spectators as he entered the ring. At 5ft 10½in, he was taller than Mace by an inch but seemed overtrained, looking gaunt at 173lb, a full seven pounds below his optimum fighting weight. Mace, at 168lb, was at his ideal weight. He was cheered to the echo by the crowd and the betting had swung four to three in his favour. The referee was Colonel Rufus Hunt, while Heenan stood as umpire for Mace. An ominous note, from Mace's point of view, was the reappearance, in Allen's corner, of none other than Joe Coburn, his would-be foe from six years earlier. Coburn glowered balefully at the English champion, an attitude sharply in contrast to Allen's other second, Sherman Thurston. In his autobiography, Mace recalled the scene in words dictated to young journalists who had not been born at the time of this, the first-ever bout for the Championship of the World:

> To me the sight was as pretty as it was strange. Above our heads, in place of English oak and elm, were orange trees and palms. The grass under our feet was not green but yellow. While all around, instead of waving cornfields or smooth pasture lands, were vast level sugar-cane plantations, varied by cotton-fields and garden-like expanses wherein the tobacco plant flourished luxuriantly.
>
> Nor were the spectators less objects of interest to me than my surroundings. Never in all my experience had I seen or imagined so picturesque and motley an assemblage. Men of all nationalities, seemingly, were there, and of all colours certainly. Creole dandies, glossy-coated and patent-leather booted, jostled bronzed backwoodsmen in homespun. Broad-hatted planters, in suits of white nankeen, were cheek by jowl with smartly-togged sports from New York and St Louis. The Chicago baseball club were there to a man, in their white and crimson playing colours. While the Louisiana Jockey Club, which had its headquarters in New Orleans, had turned out in its full strength, each member clad in correct morning costume – frock coat, light trousers and top hat.

And mingling with these aristocrats of the ringside, were numbers of plantation Negroes, some jet black, some brown to pale yellow, but all attired in the most variegated and brilliant clothing . . .

His account of the 'glittering panorama' bore witness to Mace's utter self-possession as he nervelessly faced up to the supreme moment of his career. Only a man imbued with sublime self-confidence could have detached himself so calmly and totally from the hurly-burly at ringside and could recapture it in simple, direct and vivid prose. He could never have imagined, when he daydreamed as a lad lying alone on the remote beaches of Norfolk, that it would be in such a land, and such a setting, that his career would be consummated, but the belief that he was an exceptional person who, either as a musician or as an athlete, would achieve extraordinary things had always been what drove him on towards his personal summit.

Tom Allen, taller and heavier, stood almost absurdly upright, tilting his head forward in what he supposed was an intimidating manner. In fact, his beady eyes, beaky nose and jaunty movements gave him the aspect of a hungry bird in a forlorn search for prey. Gawky and pallid, his upper lip was a red blotch where he had hastily removed his drooping moustache. But Jem Mace crouched slightly, with his weight perfectly poised and his shoulders relaxed. His black hair was neatly trimmed and his moustache cut to a pencil line. He had seen Allen fight in England and knew his opponent was a brave and rugged man but one completely innocent of science. Allen, who was aware of his own crudity, sought to compensate for it with a sometimes brazen disregard for the rules and a constant attempt to work the mill into the realms of assault and battery. He was an ugly customer, no question – and a better-fed one in the couple of years he had been living in the States. Still, as Mace figured, no amount of prime steak could give Allen the characteristics which he possessed in abundance: Allen could not move, nor could he react, nor could he think beyond the moment. If Mace began the fight even more cautiously than usual it was because of his own ring rustiness, not any perceived threat from his opponent.

For a while Mace was content to circle but, when Allen opened up, he was made to miss repeatedly as Mace sidestepped his punches and began to punish him with jabs. The gap in class was swiftly revealed as Mace ducked under Allen's swings and caught him to the body on the counter. Allen began to rush wildly at Mace. The balding Brummie was boring in, his already sparse brown hair whipped by the breeze into an unruly tangle, his eyeballs popping, his expression furious and flustered. The crowd roared as Mace produced a lightning one-two to the eye and chin. To American onlookers this was a revelation; to those English sports who had travelled 4,000 miles by ship and train, it was the Mace of old. When one of Allen's crude swings landed, it staggered Mace for a moment but, as his opponent lunged in for what he naively supposed might be the kill, Mace adroitly back-heeled him to the turf. Stunned by this impudent manoeuvre, Allen lost the psychological initiative and never regained it.

As Allen resumed his rushes, so Mace stepped calmly aside, and the wilder Allen's charges became, the more Mace danced away, while rarely letting Allen go past without a vexing jab to the brow. Allen had no game-plan and was baffled that his lunges were in vain. He played into Mace's hands, setting a brisk pace which suited the counter-puncher. His timing also let him down. It hadn't mattered against McCoole and Gallagher because they lacked the skill to expose it and went down to his harder punches, but Mace's mastery was such that he could parry punches in mid-air. Allen was being insidiously humiliated and, losing his cool, he tried to body-slam Mace, only to hurtle past him as the English champion moved aside at the last moment. Mace, a master of psychological warfare, grinned at Allen and joked at his expense, maddening him even more.

Mace also showed his expertise at change of pace, sometimes shuffling about the ring and sometimes doing what he, borrowing musical terminology, would call andante. But, just as Allen was lulled into thinking that the older man was running out of steam, he would step up the pace with an allegretto bout of closing and jabbing, striking hard to the eye, nose and mouth. Allen's supporters raised a desultory cheer as he doubled up his opponent with a driving body shot. He soon regretted his insolence. Mace sprang at him with a flurry of lefts and rights and drew first blood. As Allen windmilled wildly, Mace danced back, laughed mockingly and then darted in to pepper

Allen to the body. When an increasingly enraged Allen landed a blow which was an inch below the belt, Mace's seconds protested loudly; the referee hesitated but Mace would have no intervention. For a start, he mistrusted the neutrality of all referees, let alone one who might be biased in favour of the soon-to-be naturalised American. Secondly, it was an opportunity to win over the crowd completely. Raising his hand to wave away the referee, he suggested that Allen's shot had been unintentional. It was nothing of the kind but, taken at face value, would only underscore Allen's inaccuracy. Allen, as naive as he was shifty, uttered an apology which Mace condescended to acknowledge. The crowd lustily cheered his 'sportsmanship' while, in Allen's corner, Coburn bit his lip in fury.

This was the signal for Mace to move in hard. The crowd had already oohed and aahed over his combination punching, a technique far beyond the norms of combat in the Prize Ring; now they gasped as he rattled home his left jab six times in quick succession, the last one so hard that Allen went down. When he rose, his face was shredded with cuts and, from then on, he would fight on courage alone, a quality he had always possessed in abundance. His only hope was a fluke hit and he lashed out wildly in the hope of landing one. In his desperation, Allen seized Mace in an illegal leg-hold. Cusick and Donovan protested loudly but Mace calmly wriggled free as the referee ignored his seconds' shouts.

So contemptuous was Mace now that he deliberately crouched, letting Allen punch downwards and thus hurt his own hands. When Jem straightened up, he shifted his weight and forced Allen to miss so badly that he hit Mace's shoulder, further injuring his own fist. As laughter erupted from sections of the crowd at the challenger's ineptitude, so Mace, with a half-smile, made a gesture to them to refrain from mockery. Most of the spectators, however, praised Allen for his bravery in standing up to this alternating bombardment and humiliation. Mace enthusiastically joined in the applause, working the crowd like a cynical showbusiness veteran.

By this time the bookies had shifted their odds to 4 to 1 on Mace, and as he drew a stream of blood with an uppercut to the nose, it seemed that their assessment was only too accurate. Allen had been outfought and out-thought. To older English observers, the struggle for the American title was becoming reminiscent of the day, nine years earlier, when Mace had reduced the Stalybridge Infant to rubble as he took the English title off the gigantic wrestler. One significant difference between the clashes at Medway and Kennerville was that Mace had, in the closing stages, shown compassion for the helpless, slow-witted but decent and immensely brave Hurst. He showed little sign of this against Allen. He had been exasperated by Allen's cheap bombast prior to signing articles; what's more, he knew from Donovan that while Allen might affect the role of the English gentleman on the fields of the 'Old South', he had shown remorseless brutality when fighting in the frontier atmosphere of Missouri.

The challenger's early speed deserted him and, as he slowed, Mace twice used his wrestling skill to grab a head-lock, battering Allen mercilessly about the face with his free hand. As Allen desperately levered himself free, the crowd gasped to see his right eye fully closed. Mace stalked him and, using the 'pickaxe technique' he first absorbed from Langham, he pounded a tattoo on Allen's left brow. Bent on exposing the myth of American supremacy, he set about blinding Allen. The gospel of the straight left would come before any other consideration, even of Mace's ability to deliver a knockout with his right. As Mace knew, the New Orleans crowd, at first neutral, was potentially on his side; it was, after all, less than five years since the defeat of the Confederacy. While some had heralded the match as a contest between two expatriate Englishmen, Allen's base in the smoky steel town of Pittsburgh, symbol of the industrial muscle which lay at the back of the Union triumph, put a different complexion on matters. For many present, Allen had become a Yankee. It was choice indeed to see his wild slashing and driving being humbled by Old World class and fencing-master panache.

The end came after forty-four minutes and had an element of farce about it. Mace called to Cusick to bring him a drink of water, which he swigged near the scratch as the hapless Allen tottered in front of him. Allen's jaw had dropped open, leaving him at risk of having it broken. Mace effected this with a tremendous right and Allen pitched forward heavily, knocking Mace down with him. As he tried to rise, Allen tripped over Mace, who had curled up like a rider flung from a horse in the Grand National. The challenger hurtled sideways on into a stake-post and screamed in pain. It was obvious that he had dislocated his shoulder and Thurston at once threw in the sponge. Thurston and Coburn carried Allen away, his mangled face and shoulders covered in a horse rug. The victorious Mace was unmarked.

In 1870, no one could know that this was a historic juncture in boxing history. Since Mace had last entered the ring, the Queensberry Rules had been published, but it was Mace's style, not the Rules by themselves, which was the future of boxing. The cream of the London Prize Ring, Mace combined the athleticism and power of Jem Belcher with the guile of Daniel Mendoza, but it was his unprecedented speed of both hand and foot which would pave the way for gloved and time-limited boxing when, in due course, he chose to embrace it. In these opening years of the transition between the LPR and the Queensberry Code, John Chambers' four-rounders held scant attraction for Mace. A decade later, John L Sullivan would seize on them – albeit flouting them when it served his purpose – because a quick knockout suited both his temperament and his gifts. But Mace preferred slowly to punish his opponents and welcomed an open timeframe in which he could demonstrate his superiority to the fullest.

At Kennerville,★ Allen represented the past. He was never more than a bruiser while Mace – dancing, ducking, blocking, and feinting, delivering his switchblade left jabs and cutting off the ring like some fistic jailer – represented the art of violence. Like a fencer, he waited, calm, relaxed and focused, ready to spring forward at an opportune moment and deliver a decisive thrust. His achievement was all the more extraordinary in that he remained a middleweight.

Mace rode back to New Orleans in triumph. He had added the American Championship to that of England and, with Australia as yet unable to produce a challenger of similar class, was almost universally accepted as the first undisputed Champion of the World. Abrahams had arranged for him to give further exhibitions of Grecian statuary in the

---

★ At the place of battle itself, 117 years later, the first decisive contest for the Championship of the World would be memorialised. In what had become the city of Kenner, not far from New Orleans International Airport, the Louisiana sculptor Paul Perret carved a life-size bronze statue of Mace and Allen in fighting attitude – a belated tribute to what was a key moment in the history of sport.

Crescent City, and unknown to him, his business manager had invited women to come onstage and feel the champion's chest and biceps. The admiration he drew, especially from women, was almost too much even for him.

> The fair sex especially showered upon me all sorts of more or less embarrassing attentions, feeling my muscles and openly expressing their admiration for what they were pleased to term my 'fine physique' until – although I am by no means a man of particularly modest disposition naturally – I was fain to take refuge in flight.

Mace did not welcome being a passive object of such blatant female curiosity. Despite the many women he had chosen to embrace in private, such a reversal of gender roles embarrassed him. Nevertheless, he took full advantage of hints dropped by the more attractive ones.

Pooley also enjoyed himself in New Orleans. His Romany appearance led some women of mixed race to suppose that he was what was then called an octoroon – a white person with one black great-grandparent. Pooley did not enlighten them and disappeared into the French Quarter from time to time to pursue amorous adventures. The cousins also took time out to travel upstate some forty miles by the mighty river steamboat to visit the gambling Mecca of Natchez, where Jem's hard-earned stash of dollars disappeared faster than Allen's vain aspirations to pugilistic glory.

In due course, Jem, Pooley and Abrahams returned to New York. Whether Hannah suspected her husband's sexual spree in New Orleans is not clear but she insisted on coming, with Ada, on his next engagement, a tour of the Eastern states organised by Abrahams and featuring sparring exhibitions with Pooley along with his own showbusiness performances. As he had done in Britain, Mace showcased several different sports at the same time. At Brady's Curriculum in Jersey City, he topped the bill sparring with his defeated opponent Allen. Second billing went to the English velocipedist C.A. Booth. Included in the two cents admission were also pedestrianism, club swinging, gymnastics and trapeze. In this way, Mace's kudos as a champion in the Prize Ring paved the way for the acceptance of other sports, notably track and field, as crowd-pulling spectacles.

This was followed by a visit to Canada, again with Hannah and Ada. Canada was in the early years of its effective independence, having achieved Dominion status within the British Empire in 1867. Loyalty to the crown was a strong tradition in English-speaking Canada but prize-fighting was frowned upon and illegal. Ironically, several of the major prize-fights in US ring history had been held on the soil of what was then called Canada West, a thinly inhabited part of the country where communications were still rudimentary and means of enforcing law and order slow. For all his Britishness, though, Mace had to dissociate himself from the prize-fighting ethos. Many of the rural inhabitants of Ontario province were of Scottish or Ulster Presbyterian background and these principled Calvinists found pugilism immoral and deeply shocking. He began his tour in the province of Québec, where the bulk of the population was French-speaking and more open-minded.

Mace was a big hit in both Québec City and Montréal. Here was a man who drank only sparingly and was never intoxicated. He was elegantly dressed, immaculately groomed, and a polished dancer. His only obvious weakness seemed to be a refined one – a taste for the occasional Havana cigar. He wisely chose to include exhibitions of fencing. To the Quebecois this was a sign of European sophistication. After swordplay, he would switch to gloved and time-limited sparring, thus aligning the ancient sport of fencing with what was, although few yet realised it, the nascent sport of boxing. In no time, he found himself lionised by French Canadians. Mace was not the first English fighter to display his boxing skills in Canada. Already Joe Wormald, who had once been Mace's challenger only to cry off at the last minute, had, after fleeing the States, opened a boxing saloon in Montréal. The saloon did quite well and Wormald followed up with another in Québec, where he went to live. Mace and Wormald sparred exhibitions, then Wormald conceived the idea of a fight between them for the American, British and world titles. Mace accepted, not least because of Wormald's inflated idea of his own abilities, but the authorities made it plain that they would prevent it at all costs. Wormald developed a psychotic illness and was confined to an asylum in Québec, where he died the following year. Meanwhile Mace moved on to Toronto with his all-round entertainer show: boxer, fencer, musician and statuarist. His reception in Canada's main English-speaking city was very friendly and for the first time, due to his efforts and persona, Canada slowly began to emerge as a further locus if not of pugilism then of pure boxing. Indeed its lack of a bareknuckle tradition actually helped, in due course, to speed up recognition for gloved combat.

His time in Canada had been a happy one and, when he and his family returned to New York, all seemed set up. His business partner Phil Hargrave had established an upscale saloon on West 23rd Street, complete with a boxing ring, known as The Capitol. Its Roman-style name was intended to signify that its proprietor had class – something which, from Broadway to Bourbon Street, and above all in the little town of Kennerville, Jem Mace had undoubtedly shown.

17

Assassins of the Lower East Side

HE HAD ENJOYED life immensely during his first year in North America. He liked the vibrant atmosphere in mid-town Manhattan and his saloon was thriving. Men and women came just to see the world champion in person. What's more, the circus was eager for his continued services. So rosy did his prospects seem that he considered making New York his permanent home – it would only require Hannah to return to London and come back with Amelia for the family picture to be complete. The next April he would reach his fortieth birthday and he decided to continue his career until that milestone was reached, with the probability that he would then retire from the Prize Ring.

Suddenly the sky darkened. A series of incidents occurred which made it unmistakably clear to Mace that one section of the American community had a fiercely hostile attitude towards him. While he remained simply the expatriate Champion of England, their animosity was contained, but the words 'Jem Mace, Champion of America' stuck in the throats of first-generation Irish-Americans in the cities of the North-East. The bulk of American pugilists were either members of this community or their offspring. Whereas men born in the US of Irish parentage were comparatively tolerant and, in some cases even friendly, most of the immigrants retained an unrelenting hostility towards all things English. There were understandable reasons for their animosity – land exploitation in general, and the Great Famine in particular.

In 1858, the Fenian Association had been formed in the US by Irish-Americans. Its aim was to weaken the resolve of the British Government to maintain its rule in Ireland and to do so by acts of terror carried out on English soil. The Fenians took their name from the Gaelic 'Fianna', the legendary warrior heroes of Ireland, and during the late 1860s their campaign in the UK had reached its height. By the time William Gladstone first became Prime Minister in 1868 that campaign had been wound up, but Gladstone had been obliged to declare his 'mission – to pacify Ireland' – which he chose to do not by repression but by land reform.

Jem Mace had taken little interest in politics, the alternation in power of the two British aristocratic parties, the Whigs and Tories, seeming to him no more than an amusing diversion. However, in New York he was forced to become politically aware. This was the heyday of Tammany Hall, the Democratic party political machine, originally based in a building of that name. By the second half of the century, Irish immigrants were becoming increasingly influential at Tammany Hall. For a dozen years, the leader of Tammany was the notoriously corrupt William Marcy 'Boss' Tweed. When Tweed was ousted, the principal witness against him was none other than John Morrissey: the Irish-born ex-pugilist had a short period as Tammany leader before going on to become first a Congressman and then a New York senator. Between 1870 and his death in 1878, Morrissey was the most influential man in New York City politics.

Morrissey had, during his youth, been investigated on suspicion of involvement in an assassination, but this had no connection with Irish politics. Morrissey preferred to concentrate on events in Gotham rather than the 'Auld Country'. Any appeal to ethnic loyalties from his friends would, however, receive a positive answer, and those friends included Joe Coburn. There had been bad blood between Coburn and Mace since their aborted fight in Ireland six years earlier. Coburn had seconded Allen at Kennerville and he was seething with rage that any 'goddam Britisher' was now Champion of America. It was a situation that Coburn was determined to undo. But as the other potential challengers, such as Gallagher and McCoole, had been worsted by Allen, their chances against Mace seemed slight. Mace would likely dispose of them so emphatically that even a corrupt referee could do no other than confirm the result.

In the circumstances, Coburn began to consider challenging Mace himself. Although he had not fought for a full seven years, he was four years younger and, more significantly, an acknowledged 'scientific' boxer, in contrast to the other American pugilists of his generation –

the 'sluggers', as they were happy to be known. Meanwhile, Coburn determined to make life rough for Mace and he had no shortage of cronies to assist in his endeavour. This hostility was without the slightest justification: Mace was apolitical and had never remotely presented himself as an exemplar of Englishness, still less as some kind of sporting envoy from Britain. He had, by virtue of his gypsy associations, been the victim of ethnic prejudice in his homeland, and while he was polite and well mannered, he was a man of the people who was well accustomed to roughing it when obliged to do so. Not only that but he was enjoying himself in New York and was a highly popular 'mine host' in West 23rd St. None of this made any difference to the gang who were determined that he would be dethroned.

The first incident to show the way the wind was blowing was Fred Abrahams being informed that Mace's safety could no longer be guaranteed if he performed in Boston. The New England port city had an even higher percentage of its population born in Ireland than New York. The second occurred at Hill's, which was normally free from the kind of violent incidents which occurred regularly in the Bowery. Further downtown, less than a mile to the south and east in the heart of the Lower East Side, lay the infamous Five Points district, at that time perhaps the most squalid slum in the Western world. Into the hovels of the Points were crowded thousands of poverty-stricken Irish. Only seven years earlier, the area had been the focus of the bloody Draft Riots when, at the height of the Civil War, the Union authorities introduced conscription. While many in the Five Points worked hard to realise the American dream of rags to riches, others made their fortune by terrorising and shaking down their own kinfolk. Among the worst was the detested gangleader Billy McGlory, who dressed like an undertaker and acted like a butcher. Another was the corrupt ward politician William J. Sharkey, who had committed murder in front of witnesses but remained unconvicted. Both Sharkey and McGlory were well-known to Morrissey and had links to Coburn, whose Grand Street saloon lay in the heart of the Five Points.

The incident at Hill's stemmed from Sharkey's jealousy. He had his eye on one of the sexiest girls to frequent New York's clubland, Maggie Jourdan, who was dating Billy Edwards, Pooley's pal and a brilliantly skilful lightweight pugilist. Edwards was an intelligent man who did his best to avoid trouble outside the ring, but one night Sharkey sent hired thugs into Hill's with orders to stab him to death. Billy and Harry Hill fought back successfully, driving the would-be killers out, but Hill was knifed in the fracas and was scarred for life, nearly losing his sight. No charges were ever brought. Boosted by what he hoped would be a climate of intimidation against English prize-fighters, Coburn and several thuggish buddies made their way into Mace's Capitol saloon one evening early in November 1870 and began to overturn tables and smash glasses. When Mace and Pooley came out to deal with the trouble, both were attacked. Coburn punched Mace in the face, shouting that the Englishman owed him money. This was not true. The police were rapidly on the scene and Coburn then changed his tune, claiming that he had merely come to challenge Mace to a prize-fight and that he only wished 'honour to be satisfied'. Mace verbally accepted the challenge and Coburn and his gang left.

Naturally this was a staged incident, but it was not done with Jem's connivance as some were foolishly to allege. True, Mace was heavily involved in showbusiness but the hostility between him and Coburn was real. Mace certainly did not seek a match with Coburn. He had long regarded him as, at best, a prevaricator, but if the match came off, and if Mace won, then he now feared that he would be in mortal danger. Given that there was no shortage of men in the Lower East Side who, out of political fanaticism or sheer gut hatred of English-men, would have been available for a contract on his life, his fears were well grounded.

While a prize-fight in New York State was always out of the question, Mace now insisted that he would not fight anywhere on American soil, giving as his reason his belief that he would not get fair play against an American fighter. He suggested that the battle must take place on Canadian territory; in this way he could, for starters, level the score, in the sense that Coburn had his own way in selecting Ireland for their aborted encounter in 1864. Secondly, American prize-fighters habitually fought at locations in Canada West, notably Morrissey and Heenan in their duel for the American title at Long Point in 1858. It was a suggestion that Coburn could hardly refuse. Articles were signed for a match for the world championship, scheduled 11 April 1871.

Jem and Pooley chose the training camp on Long Island near the

Union racetrack at Jamaica. Jem found the area far more congenial than Magnolia and there were times, on misty winter days, when he and Pooley were reminded of the landscape of their Norfolk youth.★ Training had to be broken off, however, when a letter arrived from Montague reminding Mace that the lease on the Strawberry Gardens was about to expire. At this stage it was still Mace's intention to settle in America, but his presence in England was required to sign the Deed of Transfer. Mace and Abrahams therefore negotiated a four-week postponement of the bout, to enable Mace to take ship to Liverpool, complete the business, return and resume training for a short period. Back in Liverpool, he signed away the lease of the Gardens to Thomas Haig, the brewer who already had the Hotel and Tavern. While still in England, Mace also learned that his old boss Nat Langham was seriously ill with tuberculosis; he died later that year. On his return to the States, Mace completed his preparations for the upcoming bout with Coburn. Within ten days of the date of battle he was briefly starring at Niblo's Gardens in a repeat performance of *As You Like It*, alongside the outstanding American actor Davenport. He was also rewarded in a Grand Testimonial and Exhibition at the Casino in Houston Street, showcasing Billy Edwards and the Brooklyn fighter Johnny Dwyer.

On the eve of battle, Mace headed north about 300 miles to the town of Erie, Pennsylvania, a small port on the southern shore of Lake Erie. Across the water, some fifty miles away on the Canadian shore, was his destination, Port Ryeson (now Port Dover). The following day, 11 May 1871, his supporters, plus Coburn and his followers, crossed by chartered steamer. Nine hours later, both men would be in the ring. All four seconds were Irish or of Irish descent: Jim Cusick and Jerry Donovan were in Mace's corner and Johnny Dwyer was in Coburn's, along with none other than the notorious Owney Geoeghan, owner of the Bastille on the Bowery. The bantamweight champion Dick Hollywood had been agreed on as referee and the umpires were Alex Mason for Coburn and the English-born Jewish fighter Barney Aaron for Mace. A large crowd of 'sports' was at ringside, its membership

---

★ What was then a secluded beach now reverberates to the noise of international jetliners taking off from JFK airport.

varying from wealthy businessmen to pickpockets. Supporters of both men appeared about equal in number and the action was eagerly anticipated.

What followed was the worst anti-climax imaginable. There ensued one single round which lasted one hour and seventeen minutes without a single blow struck. The antics of the protagonists verged on the absurd. After a few minutes of typical sparring for an opening, Mace led with his left and Coburn not only stepped back from the jab but back-pedalled well out of range. Mace would not follow him. Instead he dropped his fists and retreated to his own corner. Then he began rubbing the palms of his hands against the ropes as if he had nothing better to do. Next, he nonchalantly folded his arms. Opposite, Coburn also lowered his fists and the two began to stare each other out. After a while they moved back to the scratch and resumed going through the motions of feinting for an opening before Coburn retreated to his corner. After fifteen minutes, Mace advanced with his bottle of water in his hand and called out for Coburn to take a drink with him. Coburn accepted the 'invitation', both men using Christian names, but as Mace closed in Coburn backed off, giving vent to a volley of obscenities, including the phrase 'fuckin' coward'.

At this point, the referee, Hollywood, urged both men to begin fighting in earnest and pointed out that many spectators had bet substantial sums on a decisive outcome, but after a few more minutes of desultory shadow-boxing, both retreated. This time Mace retired to a neutral corner and stood with one hand on his hip and the other on the stake post. Coburn followed suit. The baffled but surprisingly patient crowd shouted out for action. Mace and Coburn finally appeared ready to oblige and sparred in classic style for a few minutes while contriving to miss with some ease. Coburn was once again the first to go back to his corner, where Mace refused to follow him. Yet the most vociferous men in the crowd did not yell 'Fix!' – which was a typical cry at matches less inactive than this and which were believed, often with good reason, to be pre-arranged draws. On the contrary, Mace's supporters, a mixture of nativist Americans (with suitably Anglo-Saxon or Dutch names), Canadians and Englishmen, began to behave like late twentieth century soccer hooligans guarding their own goal end. Some chanted, 'Coburn is a coward! Coburn is a coward!' Coburn's supporters, many of whom wore green sashes to indicate Irish ethnicity, replied in kind with the taunt, 'The cleverest man in the world? Ha, ha, ha, ha!' – a sarcastic reference to Mace's reputation for ring generalship.

After about an hour of this ludicrous spectacle, the cry of 'Police!' went up, causing more excitement than anything seen in the ring. Suddenly many of the most aggressive supporters of both men were taking to their heels. For a few minutes, Mace and Coburn returned to the scratch as if preparing to fight rather than stalling. Finally, a force of several hundred militia arrived, headed by Edmund Deeds, the high sheriff of the local county, accompanied by a judge. Deeds made no arrests but he commanded the crowd to disperse, which it did. In the commotion, a pickpocket relieved Deeds of his gold watch and chain, certainly the most skilful piece of work on the day and in keeping with the farcical nature of previous events. After the militia had supervised the removal of the stake posts and the folding up of the ropes, all parties were escorted to the jetty, where the steamer was waiting to return to the US. The following day the principals met the referee at his request. Mason, on behalf of Coburn, had already suggested that they should resume at the desolate site of Long Branch on the Canadian shore, within forty-eight hours, but Hollywood ruled that the match be called a draw and that the two men should begin again at Kansas City, Missouri on June 2. With that, the parties went their separate ways and the whole wretched shambles came to an end.

So what was the explanation for a stand-off which went even beyond the second Mace–Goss meeting into the realms of the ridiculous? At Meopham, at least one participant, Mace himself, had the excuse of an injury to the ankle, but at Port Ryeson both men had been at peak fitness. Decades later, in his autobiography, Mace gave a brief, and false, version of events. He asserted that 'when we stepped into the ring' the police 'appeared from an ambush and completely surrounded us'. Fearing a prison sentence of up to two years, he claimed he and Coburn sparred together for up to an hour 'so as to give the spectators at least a show for their money', before leaving after a warning from the inspector of constabulary. This was obviously untrue. Sheriff Deeds and Wilson, the judge who was with him, had all the evidence they needed to bring charges if they so wished. The fact that Coburn and Mace were not striking a blow in anger made no difference. Deeds could not have known what had happened before he arrived and the mere fact of the two men being within a roped and staked-out square before a crowd was evidence in itself of a criminal offence. In actual fact, the Canadian authorities were more lenient than the American and, even in puritanical Massachusetts, O'Baldwin's eighteen-month sentence was for sacrilege.

What happened in Canada West could have only two explanations. Either there was a prearranged fix, motivated by a desire to sell steamer tickets and share the spoils, or there was an impromptu sham. With regard to the first, the widespread assertions, both then and since, that it was a 'pantomime' are groundless. The hostility between Coburn and Mace was genuine and it was difficult to get them to agree on anything, just as it had been seven years earlier in Ireland. But since Coburn was the one who immediately retreated and would never venture into Mace's half of the ring, why did the champion not set about him? The answer lies partly in another paragraph Mace dictated in his autobiography. In this he says, '. . . to tell the truth I was frightened at what might happen to myself in the event of my winning,' and he goes on to say, 'I did not fear violent knocks, but I did fear a violent death. And that is what a man risked who, being of British nationality, dared to do battle on American soil at that period with a Yankee pugilist.' Undoubtedly, Mace was confident that he could beat Coburn and he could have struck out and forced the issue. Equally, he was convinced that if Coburn was vanquished and wagers lost as a result, assassins would be dispatched from the Lower East Side with orders to kill him – and with the assurance that John Morrissey would turn a blind eye.

Mace's fears were in no way exaggerated. The America he had arrived in was a land of unparalleled opportunity and exuberance but it was also one in which violence was pervasive. Over 600,000 soldiers had lost their lives in the Civil War between 1861 and 1865, which culminated in the assassination of President Abraham Lincoln. The Wars against the Indians were decimating the indigenous community while, in the Deep South, the Ku Klux Klan was under investigation for a reign of terror against not only blacks but Catholics, Jews and 'internationalists'. In the aftermath of the War, Colt revolvers circulated in vast numbers and in the frontier towns gunfire was commonplace. All this was reflected in the world of pugilism – during this era, three prize-fighters had already been murdered in taverns and another was serving a sixteen-year jail term for the attempted murder of a musician. At ringside itself, the violence did not abate, particularly as substantial sums were wagered on the outcome. Incidents of kicking referees, pistol-whipping them and even throwing acid had occurred. Allen had been stabbed after his fight with McCoole, and in Virginia City, Nevada, a spectator was shot dead and four others seriously wounded during a prize-fight. The sporting periodicals of America – *American Fistiana*, *The Spirit of the Times* and the *New Yorker Clipper* – expressed disgust at the degeneration of the American ring and the way in which 'the Manly Art' had become subject to mob rule.

In agreeing to fight Coburn, a man whose hatred of him went back seven years and whose cronies cursed the Englishman nightly in the dives of the Lower East Side, Mace had made a major miscalculation. He had clearly been in two minds whether to accept Coburn's aggressive challenge. Streetwise as he was, he was well aware of what fate might befall him if he revisited the Bowery night or day; but, politically naive as he also had been, he had thought British Canada gave him immunity from intimidation. Mace seemed unaware that Canada West, as yet slackly policed and only 300 miles north of New York City, was not a safe haven. Far from it. American pugilists looked on it as a kind of backyard but Mace only seemed to realise exactly what he might be letting himself in for when he saw Geoeghan in Coburn's corner and watched his former host at the Bastille spit on the turf at the announcement of his name. Even worse were the all too obvious Bowery hoodlums clustered behind Coburn's corner.

The whole scene was vividly described by the young *Chicago Tribune* journalist George Siler, who witnessed it. 'The men had knives and guns in their hands and murder in their eyes,' wrote Siler. 'Joe was there to win if he could but by no means to lose, and, as Mace thought more of his life than he did of the money involved in the battle, he religiously remained on his own side of the ring. Seeing he could not draw Coburn to the scratch and, Coburn seeing he could not induce Mace to come to his territory, they killed time.' Coburn dare not risk defeat in front of his own followers – their loyalty would soon turn to hatred if he lost their money. Mace, for his part, had to keep clear of Geoeghan and the probability that, while the latter was shouting out a claim for payment of an alleged gambling debt, the Bowery thugs would invade the ring and seize him. So it was in the interests of both men to avoid serious combat. However, what Coburn could get away with, Mace could not. As the champion, it was his presence that was requested in theatrical engagements and his image as a heroic figure that was at risk. If he admitted the truth of the events at Port Ryeson, his reputation might be damaged. He therefore glossed over the farce, for good reasons.

Although Mace had every right to fear for his life in the circumstances, the theatre-going public on whom he now depended were naive as to the realities of a prize-fight. To them he had to pretend that the Canadian police had been the villains of the piece. He was stuck with a story he could never reverse so long as he wished to maintain his reputation for exceptional courage. Even at the end of his life, when he dictated his autobiography, he was too proud to admit both that he had miscalculated the situation in Canada West and, above all, that he had participated in a sham.

As the date of the rematch drew nearer, excitement grew in Kansas City. Many made plans to attend and among their number was almost certainly Bartholomew 'Bat' Masterson, the future marshal of Dodge City. Masterson, then aged seventeen and fascinated by prize-fighting, was working on the railroad not far away. Like the others, he was to be disappointed. Mace travelled by rail to Kansas City on June 2 and, in the presence of referee Hollywood, threw his hat into the ring, following the time-honoured ritual of the LPR. But in an inversion of the events at Tipperary in Ireland in 1864, Coburn did not show. Joe argued that Hollywood had exceeded his powers since the time limit originally stipulated in the articles had now expired but Mace claimed the entire purse, a proposal that Hollywood endorsed. As usual, Harry Hill was acting as stakeholder. He and Mace were still good friends but Hill decided that it would be wise if he gave both parties back only the money they had deposited. His decision was not surprising: he had been warned that his life would be in danger if he handed over any of Coburn's money to Mace.

The only way in which the stand-off could be resolved in a

manner acceptable to both parties was by the appointment of a new referee, the drawing-up of fresh articles and a compromise over venue. Mace suggested that the match should take place within 100 miles of New Orleans. This had the advantage, from his point of view, of being in a familiar area and, above all, one about as far removed from New York as possible, making it too expensive a journey for Coburn's crew of roughnecks. At the same time, Mace had been obliged to back down from his earlier insistence on a 'neutral country'. From the point of view of both fighters, switching the bout to the environs of New Orleans would place it in about the only location where law-enforcement officials were virtually certain to allow it to proceed.

On 24 July 1871, Coburn and Mace placed their signatures to articles, with stakes of $2,000 a side and November 30 stipulated as the date of battle. They would compete for the American title and, by implication, the world crown. As the fight would not take place until almost winter, it seemed to Jem that there was no need for acclimatisation, unlike the previous year. Jem and Pooley therefore decided on two training camps. The first would be on the Atlantic seaboard, refreshingly breezy during the hotter months; later they would move well inland where temperatures would, while moderate by Gulf Coast standards, be higher. During a break in training, there were instances of both Mace's continual involvement in sports other than pugilism and, more notably, the willingness of prestigious venues to accommodate gloved sparring matches. At Titusville, Pennsylvania, for example, at the local Opera House, Mace not only sparred with Pooley but also entered the ring with Major James McLoughlin, America's champion wrestler − considered the world's finest. The theatrical aspect was completed by Mace's statuary performance. The prestige which he lent, by virtue of being world champion in an extremely popular, albeit outlaw, sport and of being a performance artist in the wider sense, was highly significant in the history of American sport as spectacle. The second training camp was at Shady Grove, Ohio, not far from Cincinnati. Jem remained here, assisted by Cusick as well as Pooley. He did not move down to New Orleans until a week before the fight. By now Hannah was regularly with Mace but, when she learned that she was pregnant again, she returned to New York.

After arriving in the Crescent City, he was questioned by reporters at Hyluorn's and found himself fielding insinuations that, in view of the Canadian fiasco, there would be no real fight. 'That's absurd,' he rapped, 'I'm as determined to fight as I am to live.' He went on to say that he would have a private fight with Coburn in a small room if need be. Odds were at 100 to 60 in favour of Mace. Although public confidence had been claimed to be shaky, there were some 500 men on the special train which left the city by the Mobile and Chattanooga Railway on the day of the mill. As it happened, the Louisiana authorities in the state capital, Baton Rouge, had refused to allow the fight and police therefore stayed on the train until it crossed the state line into Mississippi. Even they remarked on a notable absence of the 'rough and thieving element', for the spectators included lawyers, bankers and businessmen.

Tom Allen, Mace's defeated opponent from the year before, was now in Jem's corner as deputy second to Cusick. Coburn's seconds were the shifty veteran Tom McAlpine plus Tom Kelly. Coburn's brother Jem stood as umpire for him, while Pooley acted in this capacity for Mace. As at Kennerville, Colonel Rufus Hunt was the appointed referee, even though he was also the stakeholder. The chosen place of battle lay a few miles into Mississippi, close to Montgomery Station and about a mile from the township of Bay St Louis. Shortly after midday, hostilities began under ominously dark skies and within fifteen minutes it began to rain heavily. The turf became churned up, which was to Mace's disadvantage since it nullified his ability to change feet at speed, one of the most distinctive and effective characteristics of his style. He was soon to discover that there was more in store for him than just the vagaries of the elements.

Mace began by an immediate rap to Coburn's ribs to show that he did indeed mean business. Coburn at once went on the retreat and Mace quickly cornered him. Coburn then punched hard and low, striking his opponent's hip. Mace, stunned by the challenger's blatant disregard for the rules, still did not claim a foul. With no reaction from referee Hunt, Mace loudly warned Coburn not to 'do the like of that again!' Coburn's low blow had enabled him to get out of trouble and he now succeeded, after side-stepping, in catching Mace on the nose but took a fierce right to the mouth in return. At long last Coburn was made to stand and fight and he began to implement what was clearly his strategy, punching to the ribs and body. Mace replied with his classic left jab formula but his accuracy was missing and, after a couple of jabs to Coburn's eye and nose, his usual rapier left landed high on Coburn's bald forehead, almost on top of the skull. Mace's seconds noted with alarm that he winced as this blow connected and seemed to have hurt his wrist on impact. It happened in the second round and would be a turning point in the fight.

Coburn sensed a chance and stepped up his body shots. Once again he struck low, landing painfully just below the hip. Mace and his seconds at once protested but Hunt did not even warn Coburn. Boosted by this and taking immediate advantage of the slippery turf, Coburn demonstrated his wrestling skills and threw Mace. In the next round, Coburn struck another low blow. There was an obvious danger of an agonising shot to the crotch, a relic of the worst days of the old London Prize Ring before the rules were amended in 1838. Any blow deliberately inflicted below the waist should have brought about disqualification and Coburn was not so clumsy as to miss the target by such a wide a margin without intent. Still Hunt did not even warn him. Mace decided to punish Coburn and unleashed a fulminating jab to the Irish-American's forehead. It made Coburn stagger but he recovered before Mace could close in on him.

Mace paid for his efforts to force the fight. His left hand was so painful from the impact of the jab he had just thrown that he had to ration the number of lefts he would ordinarily have thrown. The pain made getting a wrestling grip very difficult; Coburn realised this and put his own upper body strength to good use. He was clearly a powerful wrestler and he soon succeeded in throwing Mace again. Jem, well aware that it would be only a matter of time before his left hand swelled up, constantly advanced and, as Coburn sought to back-pedal, he struck hard to the right eye with his jab, following up with a right to the nose. As Mace opened up, so Coburn threw a fierce right to the ribs but, as he lost his balance, Mace threw him. The lack of blood told its own tale: Coburn's jabs were inaccurate and Mace's lacked their usual power. Both decided to fall back on sparring for an opening and did so for about five minutes, the first lull in the proceedings. When Hunt, whose ignorance of the accepted ebb and flow of pugilistic rhythm was all too obvious, bawled out, 'Get fighting!' Mace sarcastically replied, like a soldier obeying his commanding officer, that he would 'do so right away!' This caused laughter among spectators who had been more absorbed than vociferous.

Responding to and even conducting an audience had always been a mark of Mace's mastery. With Coburn's concentration momentarily lulled, he stole in on him and, notwithstanding the pain it caused him, launched his lance-like left at the corner of Coburn's left brow. A stream of blood flowed down the Middletown man's face and onto his chest. As cries of 'first blood' were heard, Mace rapidly fired two darts, one on the open wound and the other on the cheek below. Heedless of the pain in his left fist, he then crashed home a truly thunderous jab closer to the bridge of his opponent's nose. A further stream of blood gushed out. In the crowd, shouts of, 'Four to one on Mace!' were heard, but Coburn, at much closer range, could see that Mace's hand was swelling up like a boxing glove. He knew the Englishman was desperate to blind him before his own left became useless and he pummelled Mace's ribs until Mace decided it was wiser to drop to the ground for a breather.

By this stage, incessant rain had reduced Coburn's corner to a mud-heap and this compelled him to adopt a less defensive posture. He rushed Mace to the ropes but, in an odd moment of levity in this grim and intensely hostile encounter, the two lost their balance simultaneously and fell out of the ring, side by side. Before the next round began, Pooley, who had been scrutinising Coburn's corner with the utmost suspicion, noticed surreptitious movement. As Coburn came out to the scratch, Pooley shouted, 'He's got oakum in his hands!' Hunt ordered Coburn to open his fists and the crowd hushed. There were indeed two pieces of frayed rope in Coburn's dukes, an old dodge of unscrupulous pugilists seeking to add to both their punching power and their cutting capacity.

'As it's nothing more serious, I won't stop the fight,' declared Hunt, to the incredulity of Mace's supporters.

By this time, Mace's left was so swollen that it was useless. He was forced to fight his challenger one-handed, and the pace slowed noticeably. Coburn's battle plan shifted almost entirely to wrestling. Knowing that Mace could get no grip on him, he threw him several times. As

Mace got up, he was caked in mud and began to shake with cold.

At this stage came a significant development outside the ring – an extra passenger train arrived at Montgomery Station and from it descended a further 300 spectators, almost all of them wearing Coburn's colours. From among them, Jim Cusick, a New Yorker himself, recognised several of the worst lowlifes from the Lower East Side. By now Mace had completely changed his stance. With his left hanging useless by his side, he had his right foot forward and was leading with his right hand, in what would later be called southpaw style. Yet Coburn failed to press his advantage. Seeming wary of Mace's good arm, he waited for him to begin to slip on the morass underfoot and then threw him several times more.

By this stage, with the fight duration already some two-and-a-half hours, Mace appeared to give up any hope of winning. His left hand might just as well have been tied behind his back for all the good it was to him and he was badly shaken by the throws. His only hope was to retain his title by a draw. Once he went on the defensive, the match was effectively over. He retreated into his corner, which was still relatively dry, but Coburn refused to follow, seeming to dread what Mace might do even with one hand. The bout continued for over another hour. Hunt ordered the pair back to the scratch four times but each time they complied only to retreat again. This twelfth and last round was effectively a reprise of the Canadian fiasco. Finally, after three hours and thirty-eight minutes, Hunt stepped into the ring and addressed the crowd.

'One is afraid and the other daresn't,' he announced, seeming to think he'd uttered a witticism. He pronounced the match a draw and declared all bets off.

The bout at Bay St Louis had been only the third time in his entire career as a full-time professional that Mace had been extended for more than an hour, excluding the fiascos in Kent and Canada. Only Tom King, at Godstone, and Bob Travers had taken him that far. There would be those who would express suspicion about the fight, but in fact it was an heroic performance by Mace. He had been unlucky in encountering atrocious weather which had deprived him of his customary superiority in speed. He had been unfortunate in injuring his hand early in the bout and eventually losing use of his superb left jab, but he had been very hard done by indeed by Colonel Rufus Hunt. Three times Coburn had struck blatantly low blows and once he had been found with a substance concealed in his fist, yet never once had he been warned, let alone disqualified. There was not even the excuse of intimidation, since the bulk of Coburn's supporters had not yet arrived when Hunt allowed the Irish-American's rule violations to pass unpunished. As for Joe Coburn, he had shown more skill than most of Mace's previous opponents but also demonstrated a distinct lack of fighting heart. He could have carried the fight to an incapacitated Mace with a chance of winning the day but he refused to take the risk.

Mace–Coburn 2 came to be written off as a 'fizzle', to use the language in vogue at the time and Mace's reputation in America was adversely affected as a result of reports relying on secondary sources. Because Mace was obliged, by severe injury, to stall for an hour at the end, some writers falsely segued it to the admitted fiasco in Canada. The other culprit was the referee, Colonel Hunt, whose final comment about fear and daring, pronounced as he called a draw, was a mere tautology. Coburn certainly knew that he'd been in a fight. One eyebrow was badly gashed and his features were swollen by the impact of Mace's punches. As for Mace, he left the ring unmarked on the face but with nasty bruises visible above the top of his breeches. Nevertheless, he had kept his challenger at bay and retained the world title.

Within half an hour, a terrible incident occurred at Montgomery Station, where Jem and Pooley, together with Allen and Cusick, were waiting alone on the platform for the special train to take them back to New Orleans. At ringside, immediately after Hunt had announced his verdict of a draw and Coburn and Mace had stepped out of the ring, one Tom Hart from New York challenged any man present to fight him then and there. His challenge was answered by another man from the North-East, Billy Madden. When the two entered the ring and took off their shirts it was obvious that Hart was far heavier than Madden, who looked like a featherweight. There was no prior notification of the fight and no indication that either man was in fighting trim. Nevertheless, nearly all Coburn's crowd followed his lead in staying to watch the match, which lasted for about three-quarters of an hour. Most of the neutrals stayed on, probably eager for some pugilistic action after the concluding hour of stalemate in the title battle. So did many of Mace's supporters, while others dawdled on their way back to the station. Jem was in no mood to watch the impromptu scrap and hurried away with Pooley and his two seconds. While all four were engaged in conversation on the platform, two masked men dashed out from behind them, having hidden in the cotton fields which surrounded the station. Both brandished Colt revolvers, which they fired: the first shot missed its intended target by the narrowest margin, striking the wall between Jem and Pooley, who were only a foot apart; as the three Englishmen and Cusick hurled themselves to the ground, the second gunman's shot passed well above them. Both assailants ran off and disappeared into the cotton fields as Mace's supporters began to arrive at the platform. As the sound of gunfire was not uncommon in the vicinity of American prize-fights, no one asked any questions. The first of the two chartered trains arrived and Jem and his cousin, the two seconds and many of their supporters boarded it.

It was noted by the supporters that Jem was in a grim mood. Even the normally carefree and jocular Pooley was strangely silent. Assuming their demeanour was due simply to Hunt's biased refereeing, the supporters left the group to themselves. The four journeyed back in the pitch dark and pouring rain through a nightmarish landscape of alligator swamps – in the knowledge that, on the train which followed them, were two men who had attempted to murder Mace. As the bright lights of New Orleans welcomed him back to civilisation, Mace confided his decision and swore his friends to secrecy. There would be no point in reporting what had happened to the New Orleans Police Department: after all it had happened outside their jurisdiction and as prize-fighters they were of course, technically speaking, outlaws. What's more, he did not want Hannah to know.

What happened at Montgomery Station did not appear in a single American newspaper. The only public comment Mace made, on his return to New York, was a statement that he would never again accept a challenge from Coburn. He gave as his reason the fact that, had it not been for Hunt's inefficient refereeing, he would have defeated him. He was therefore the moral victor, whereas Coburn had had two opportunities to take the title and should give way to another challenger, if one came forward.

The shooting incident was no mere murder bid of the kind that occurred all too frequently both in the big north-eastern cities and on the Western Frontier. Mace had been selected for death because he was a public symbol of Englishness to those elements of the Irish-American community who wished to assert their bitter hatred of British misrule in the land of their birth. The campaign of hatred against Mace, and attempt to assassinate him, was an early example of the politicisation of sport.

As to the circumstances of Mace–Coburn 2, the belated arrival of the second train and disgorgement of its raucous occupants destroyed the atmosphere in what had previously been a remarkably well-behaved crowd. The impromptu Hart–Madden scrap had all the hallmarks of a staged diversion and the numerous low-lifes who found the money for an expensive 2,000-mile round trip to the Gulf Coast must have been funded by someone with substantial means at his disposal. There was thus prima facie evidence of conspiracy involving a considerable number of people in addition to Coburn. The attempt on Jem Mace's life had taken place in remote Mississippi but the assassins were undoubtedly from the Lower East Side of New York.

18

Coast to Coast

IN THE NEW Year, Mace began to consider his career options. His left hand had healed perfectly, he had recovered from the shock of the attempted murder, and his public statement that he would never fight Coburn again had led the latter to announce his retirement. While his first instinct was to return to England for his own safety, he did not want to give the crooks the satisfaction of seeing him bolt. Besides, there was much about New York which he loved: he was making a good living and didn't want to subject Hannah to the rigours of an Atlantic crossing in the second half of her pregnancy. Above all, he didn't want to bow out as champion just yet. This would leave the American public with the memory of Coburn's spoiling tactics. He wanted one final battle for the American title, which was by now one and the same as the world title, with a young pugilist who would fight him fair and square. He therefore announced his willingness to meet any other prize-fighter of acknowledged reputation, regardless of nationality.

The trouble was that there were few of them. Heenan wisely decided not to come out of retirement after nine years of inactivity; Gallagher and McCoole had been convincingly beaten by Allen and knew they had little chance against Mace. Among the English, Goss had returned home and Wormald was dead. Allen was in no mood to battle Mace again after his whipping in Kennerville. That left only O'Baldwin, who had completed his eighteen-month jail sentence in Boston and set himself up as a saloonkeeper. He was an associate of Coburn's and had been present in Bay St Louis. Still, Mace was prepared to give the 'Irish Giant' a chance – if only so that it could never be said that he was ducking him. Besides that, police action had deprived O'Baldwin of his shot at Mace's title back in England. For a while the Irishman seemed reluctant to commit himself but it was understood that he was being 'persuaded' by both Coburn and Morrissey. The latter's persuasion would be of a kind difficult to resist. Paradoxically, a fight with O'Baldwin was a temporary guarantee of Mace's personal safety. What Morrissey and Coburn wanted was to see Mace humiliated in the ring and they believed that O'Baldwin, with his height, weight and comparative youth, was the man to do it.

Meanwhile, Mace decided, for the first time in his life, to cultivate politicians. Just as he had benefited from aristocratic patronage in England, it would help to be connected with men of wealth and influence. He got to know Senator Zach Chandler, a Republican from the state of Michigan who had a keen interest in pugilism, married a New York heiress and had a summer residence in the state. Chandler had fallen out with Senator Roscoe Conkling of New York, at that time the acknowledged star of the Senate. He had built a Republican machine, based on the Customs House in New York City, which rivalled Tammany Hall. Conkling's forceful oratory made him one of the most powerful men on Capitol Hill. He was also keenly interested in boxing and, at his lavish apartments in Washington, had a gymnasium built. A tall and powerfully built man of aggressive temperament, he was a very good amateur boxer who liked nothing better than to challenge other young Senators and Congressmen to put the gloves on.

In 1871, the Marquess of Queensberry had visited the US seeking to promote the English lightweight prize-fighter Arthur Chambers. Aged twenty-three and a working-man from Salford in Lancashire, he had no connection with his middle-class namesake John Graham Chambers, the true author of the Queensberry Rules. While those Rules were of no interest whatever to the prize-fighting community, the Marquess's brief presence in America made prominent amateur boxing buffs like Conkling aware of the Queensberry Code. It was at this point that Mace came into the picture. One evening in Washington, Conkling invited a number of businessmen and politicians to a lavish dinner at his apartments, not far from Capitol Hill. Afterwards he challenged anyone to put on the gloves and go four rounds with him in his private gymnasium. Chandler, who was substantially older than Conkling but strongly built, agreed and the guests adjourned to watch the fight. Conkling handed out a shellacking to Chandler, who took his defeat good-naturedly – that is, until he learnt that Conkling had been bragging that he had made the Senator from Michigan look a fool.

Chandler told Mace about the episode and said he wanted to see Conkling put in his place. He would like to give Mace $100 to attend a dinner, already arranged by the Senator from New York, and introduce him as an English businessman who would reluctantly agree to take him on. Conkling, not suspecting the true identity of the 'English businessman', would be in for the shock of his life. Mace accepted at once; it appealed to his sense of humour, the money would come in handy, and it would be an opportunity for him to road-test the Queensberry Rules. He had seen Conkling glad-handing it in New York City and knew that the strapping Senator, who was only a couple of years older than he was, would be able to stand up to his punches without serious injury – that is, the one or two which would be needed to dispose of him. As the star of the Senate was by now publicly bragging that he could, if he had chosen to 'lower himself', have had a career in the Prize Ring and become Champion of America, Mace was more than eager to disillusion him.

Chandler, in his reply to Conkling's second dinner invitation, wrote with regret that he could not attend because, unfortunately, he was being visited by an influential constituent, an English businessman called Mr Howard, who had settled in Detroit. 'Mr Howard' was a stranger in Washington and could scarcely be left on his own without discourtesy. As expected, Conkling replied that he should be brought along. Clearly the overbearing orator was relishing the prospect of giving Chandler another good hiding and the more witnesses there were to this humiliation, the more it would please Conkling. During dinner, Mace assumed the posture of a serious-minded and modest man who was quite content to listen to the conversation of others, particularly the most famous politician on Capitol Hill. Given his undoubted acting ability, his stage experience, and his guile as a poker player, he carried off the role to perfection.

After a lavish supper, one which, as Jem later recalled, was even more delicious than at Langham's aristocratic soirees in the Rum-pum-pas nearly twenty years earlier, Conkling led all his guests to the gymnasium and promptly invited Chandler to a return bout. Chandler demurred but commented that 'Mr Howard' had done some boxing in his time and would probably oblige. Roscoe asked if this was true. 'Howard' replied that he had done a little sparring in his younger days but was out of touch. The rumbustious Republican asserted that he would not hurt him, a remark which caused guffaws among some of those present, for Conkling had a fiery temper and was a natural born bully. Some genuinely feared for 'Howard's' safety, especially as the Senator was a full six inches taller than his opponent. It was agreed that they would box under the time-frame in use at amateur competitions in London: three three-minute rounds, one minute intervals and a fourth round decider if need be.

It was immediately obvious that the wild-eyed Conkling had every intention of hurting his apparently self-effacing opponent. He rushed at him, swinging fiercely, but every time he swung, his adversary ducked and dodged, sidestepped and blocked. This went on for three rounds while onlookers gasped with astonishment at 'Howard's' skill and, in most cases, chortled with delight at Conkling's embarrassment.

In the fourth and final round, Conkling was out of breath as a result of his vain efforts. And at that point he was suddenly struck two body blows which doubled him up. Then came a full tilt left jab to the jaw which sent the dinner host sprawling on the canvas. The rugged Republican was clearly stunned and it was well past the 'ten count', which the spectators gleefully tolled out in unison, before he was able to get to his feet. He muttered that he felt 'as if (he had) been hit by a ton of bricks'. After Conkling recovered, Chandler, tongue in cheek, invited him to give his considered opinion on the skill of 'Mr Howard'. A furious Conkling declined and abruptly cut the soiree short. It was not until the following morning that he learned that his conqueror was none other than the world champion. He did not take the news with good grace. He never forgave Chandler for the trick and strove to keep the incident out of the newspapers, which he succeeded in doing for a couple of years. Conkling swiftly crossed boxing off the list of his hobbies. The shifty Senator then pursued his political career undistracted until, a decade later, he was deselected as a representative of the people in New York following exposure of his record of corruption at the Customs House.

From Mace's point of view, the incident had been an entertaining and rewarding trip to Washington. It had also been, as he would later recall, a very effective demonstration not only of the efficacy of padded gloves in preserving his fists, something which he already knew, but of the ease with which, under the ten seconds rule, a bout could be concluded by someone who possessed fearsome punching power. Given the fact that the fight originated in a joke and was successfully hushed up until it was old news, its significance went unremarked. In fact, it was the first-ever fight under Queensberry Rules in which a professional boxer took part, and Chandler's $100 inducement was effectively the purse for a hilarious but historic episode.

In the spring of 1872, Mace received a challenge which was soon followed by the news, via Abrahams, of a lucrative theatrical invitation. O'Baldwin made up his mind on a mill with Mace and articles were signed. Neither man wished to travel to the South, Mace being particularly keen to avoid Mississippi. He knew better than to suggest Canada but was keen to have the battlefield far away from New York City. As O'Baldwin declined to travel to Missouri, a compromise was reached: they would rendezvous in Baltimore and fight in either Maryland, Virginia or West Virginia. Mace took O'Baldwin very seriously as an opponent and went straight into strict training at what was then the quiet seaside resort of Highlands, New Jersey.

On 1 May 1872, while visiting Mace at his training quarters, Hannah gave birth to a baby boy. He was named Benjamin Franklin Mace – his first name was that of Hannah's father, but the two forenames together were those of one of the most revered figures in American history, the scientist and diplomat Benjamin Franklin. While it was announced that Jem and Hannah hoped that Ben would, in future, be able to 'strike the lightning', the choice of name indicated their continuing allegiance, at this stage, to their adopted homeland.

Mace now heard that he had been invited to California and immediately took up a lucrative offer. The date of the proposed mill with O'Baldwin was 14 August but that didn't affect the issue. The invitation to visit the Golden State came from Jack Wilson, a well-known circus proprietor in San Francisco, but as Wilson wanted Mace, not only for musical and statuary performances but boxing exhibitions, it would be good preparation for his defence of his championship. The bouts would not be simple sparring sessions but combative performances with gloves and some application of the Queensberry Rules. There would be no declared winner.

California had, for many years, seemed to most Easterners half a world away. The former Spanish colony had been part of the United States for less than a quarter of a century following its cession by the defeated Mexicans at the end of the Mexican-American War. This had coincided with the discovery of gold and the Great Gold Rush of 1849. Tens of thousands of men had left their homes in the East or in foreign lands to seek their fortune on the West Coast. In the rugged atmosphere of the mining camps of California and other Western states, prize-fighting had boomed. Several prominent Irish-American fighters travelled to the Pacific Coast in the 1850s to try their luck as pugilists and in other capacities. First, John Morrissey went out. He made a small fortune as a gambling operator, then won a fight after his supporters had threatened the life of his English opponent – who rapidly decided to lose on a foul. Morrissey returned to New York the following year with his pockets bulging with dollars. John Heenan followed as a lad of seventeen, finding employment as a panel-beater at Benicia. The veteran Yankee Sullivan had also gone out there, as had Cusick, future trainer of Heenan and second of Mace. But Heenan and Cusick were forced to leave California in a hurry. Nativist Americans were determined not to allow Tammany Hall-style politics in San Francisco and both these men had found lucrative work as 'shoulder-hitters' for men aspiring to office. Anti-Irish vigilantes formed a kangaroo court which 'sentenced' them. Cusick was illegally deported and Heenan wisely got out before he was thrown out. Sullivan was not so lucky: he was seized, incarcerated and murdered.

This ferocious anti-Irish prejudice, and the utter ruthlessness of the vigilantes, left a stain on the reputation of the newly emergent state, but from a strictly pugilistic point of view, such a background meant that Mace, an Englishman who had seen off the challenge of the Irish-born Coburn, was in great demand. Another big signing already lined up by Jack Wilson's Circus was Billy Edwards, also an expatriate Englishman. The lightweight championship of America had become vacant and Edwards had signed articles to compete for the title against Queensberry's protégé, Arthur Chambers. Billy was not only a skilful boxer but a man who could put on weight, and lose it, in a remarkable way, dependent on the poundage division of his opponent. Despite his long reign as heavyweight champion, Mace remained a middleweight in build and therefore a bout with Edwards, who was unusually tall for his weight, would not be a mismatch. Wilson had also written that he had discovered very useful local fighters who, he believed, would give Mace a run for his money.

Only three years earlier, the idea of a quick trip to California would have been impossible. Travellers from the Eastern states faced a four-month land journey by stagecoach through a forbidding terrain where lawlessness prevailed and wars against the American Indian tribes were still raging. The only viable alternative would involve at least two and a half months by ship via the Isthmus of Panama, where the land crossing put anyone who undertook it at risk of contracting malaria. But in 1869 the massive project for linking the North American continent by railroad was completed when the Central Pacific Railway and the Union Pacific, the former completing track eastwards and the latter westwards, were linked in Utah. Transportation in America was revolutionised. The westward journey on the Intercontinental Railroad now took only six days, with another few days allowed for reaching Omaha, Nebraska (the former terminus of the Eastern Railway network) from New York.

As baby Ben was too young to undertake the trip, Hannah remained in New York with Ada while Jem, Pooley and Abrahams headed for the Golden State. If the journey to Council Bluffs, Iowa, on the old track was less than inspiring, the voyage of discovery for the next 2,000 miles was a wonder in itself. While Abrahams sat indoors writing up expense accounts and suchlike, Jem and Pooley rode on the outside platform absorbing, once the Rockies were reached, the pure mountain air. The exhilarating ride took them into the lawless towns of Cheyenne and Laramie, through the Badlands of Wyoming, across the cusp of the Great Salt Lake beyond the point in Promontory, Utah, where the railroad barons had driven a gold spike at the junction of the tracks which united a continent. From there they travelled across the Nevada Desert, on to Reno and beyond Lake Tahoe, before descending through the magnificent scenery of the Sierra Nevada and on to the end of the line in Sacramento, state capital of California. The assorted cowboys, marshals and silver miners along the route usually stared briefly as the 'Iron Horse' stopped in their neck of the woods. There were, as yet, few towns with newspapers and fewer men who could read them, but when Pooley pointed out his cousin, Champion of America, most raced to shake Jem's hand.

From Sacramento it was only eighty miles to San Francisco. There, in the bustling city centre, people craned their necks for a glimpse of the Englishman who had triumphed on their turf and who would now repose in a palatial hotel in memorable Montgomery Street. Mace felt at home straight away – the city's steep hills, descending dramatically to the magnificent bay crammed with vessels from all over the world, contrasted vividly with the flat plain of his native East Anglia, yet the mist rolling in from the Pacific resembled a North Sea haze. San Francisco, little more than a glorified village a quarter of a century before, had mushroomed into the greatest city in the western United States. The city lived hard and played hard and there were many entertainment outlets. Mace and Pooley visited the American Theatre on Sansome Street, the Metropolitan on Montgomery and Kearney Street and McGuire's Opera House on Washington Street. It was there that an unexpected reference to 'the late, great Miss Adah Isaacs Menken, our dear former star' brought a tear to Mace's eye. The mood had passed by the time he and Pooley went out gambling. In the ethnically mixed Barbary Coast neighbourhood, faro parlors were almost a way of life and Mace joined in with abandon. As usual, he was out of luck when the dice tumbled.

The Barbary Coast was disapproved of by the San Francisco bourgeoisie, not only because of its gambling but other aspects of its hedonistic nightlife. In yet another reversion to bachelor days, Mace, accompanied not only by Pooley but by the even younger Billy Edwards, took off for the Bella Union. This venue on the corner of Washington and Kearney was the favourite haunt both of the young bloods of the town and of seafarers on shore leave. It advertised itself as a 'melodeon' and employed comedians who specialised in ribald humour. But this was not the main attraction for men-only audiences. The Bella Union was known for its nubile showgirls who danced scantily-clad onstage. The proprietor of the Bella Union was the veteran showman Sam Tetlow, who relied on the vain protests of the evangelicals to attract custom to the shows. Complaining letters to the

San Francisco Chronicle about 'dancing of a licentious and profane character' ensured that they were sellouts. Tetlow, although married, enjoyed affairs with his showgirls and, while what he dismissed as the 'average stag' could do no more than fantasise, he welcomed the attendance of like-minded men of fame and fortune and reserved expensive loggias and even more costly individual boxes for them.

Mace's attendance at the Bella Union was a particular highlight from Tetlow's point of view and his girls competed for the opportunity to bring drinks to his private box during intervals, dance for him and leave cards informing him of the whereabouts of their private apartments. One flirtatious filly with a talent for double meaning enquired coquettishly, 'Is it true, Mr Mace, that you like to slowly soften the other person up before delivering the knockout?' He responded with a wink and, later that evening, demonstrated that her assumption was well-founded. Swiftly following Mace's example, Billy and Pooley had their share of young feminine attention in the apartments of the Barbary Coast. Pooley decided not to disillusion Mexican girls who believed he was of similar origin to themselves, albeit, as they supposed, born in America.

Mace had, of course, not come to California merely for sexual adventures or even his musical and statuary performances. Besides boxing in Wilson's Circus, he had to keep himself fully fit in preparation for his return to the East Coast to fight O'Baldwin. He told Pooley candidly that he lacked the pedestrian skills to maintain his stamina and Pooley accepted this good-naturedly and continued to contribute in other aspects of pre-fight preparation. Mace's new co-trainer was Dooney Harris, yet another expatriate English boxer, born in London. Dooney had lost in a fight for the American middleweight championship against Tommy Chandler at Point Isabel, California, five years earlier and had since forged a fine reputation as a trainer. He had Mace pounding the beaches and repeatedly running up and down sand dunes to strengthen his legs.

All four of Mace's exhibition bouts on the West Coast were fought over a few rounds approximating to Queensberry time intervals and, as normal in an exhibition, with no declared winner. Two were entirely unmemorable, one was a fine display of boxing skill and the fourth was a source of controversy. First, Mace took on the burly Martin and utterly outclassed him. Then he fought Sam Collyer, a lightweight whom Billy Edwards had already beaten. Collyer showed skill and pluck but could not cope with Mace's weight of punch. Next, Mace and Edwards squared off. Connoisseurs of 'the noble art' were delighted by the skill and intelligence shown by both men. Here was what some referred to as textbook style, a prescient term in that both men were later to go on to write instruction manuals. Good as Edwards was, he could not match Mace's incomparable skill. The comradeship between Jem and Billy was instantaneous and they were photographed together, along with Pooley, all immaculately dressed in white top hats and dress shirts, with black bow ties and dark double-breasted suits with velvet lapels. They greeted their description in the local press with a mixture of amused approval tinged with resentment. Apparently they were 'men of gentlemanly appearance who no one seeing them on Montgomery Street would dream were professional pugilists'.

The last bout of Mace's Californian tour was against the hitherto unknown Charles E. Bennet on June 25. Bennett was a young drug store clerk from Third Street whose amateur status was underlined by his membership of the Californian Olympic Club. He had a couple of inches height advantage over the champion and was powerful and athletic. They fought six rounds with the gloves and Bennet gave a good account of himself, but the innocent *San Francisco Chronicle* reporter became completely carried away at the novice's instinctive skill and undoubted pluck. Under the laughable subheading 'Jem Mace whipped', he spoke of Bennett's 'superior physical development', his 'consummate skill and grace' and 'left-handed uppercut which sent the dodger sprawling in the sawdust'. The *Chronicle* noted, 'The enthusiasm of the audience became great . . . and Jack Wilson . . . became perfectly wild with delight and rushed into the ring waving his hat and yelling lustily.' It went on to describe Bennett parrying 'nearly all of Mace's blows' and of Mace finding it difficult 'to get anywhere near his "knowledge box" '. At the conclusion, 'Mace seemed quite exhausted while Bennett was . . . as fresh as a daisy.' Of course Bennett would never get the chance for a repeat performance in the Prize Ring because 'he is a gentleman, mixes in good society and, of course, would never think of making use of his talent in a professional way'.

The breathless prose of the *Chronicle* was evidence of its reporter's rampant snobbery and total ignorance not only of boxing realities but, even more naively, of the typical stunts of carnival barkers, such as Wilson was. He never wondered whether Mace was 'carrying' Bennett in order to make the novice look good and to give the crowd something to cheer about. He never asked himself how on earth a man who had never previously entered the ring could possibly cause so much trouble to a veteran of Mace's skill and power. He had no understanding of the wisdom of 'caution' and could not account for Mace remaining unmarked. He seemed to think that 'dodging' was a form of cheating, rather than a skill. Unconscious humour apart, the *Chronicle's* silly account of the exhibition exposed a crucial deficiency in the Queensberry Rules: in the absence of a knockout, there was, as yet, no means whereby an actual referee could give an objective verdict on the outcome. The decision as to the winner depended purely on opinion, even the ignorant opinion of inexperienced scribes eager to sell 'local hero' stories. As the party headed back East, Mace reflected on the inadequacy of the Queensberry Rules as they then stood.

Mace trained throughout July for the forthcoming mill with O'Baldwin. The stakes were $2,000 a side, the match would be in a 20ft ring and the rendezvous would be in Baltimore. With Mace, training in the grounds of the Belmont Hotel at Fordham, was Edwards, who had signed articles to defend his lightweight championship in September against Arthur Chambers. Both men's training was supervised by Dooney Harris. All went smoothly at Mace's training camp but an early sign of trouble ahead between his backers and those of O'Baldwin was the refusal of Harry Hill to carry out his usual role as stakeholder. Evidently he wanted no repeat of the threats made against him by Joe Coburn the year before. O'Baldwin got his own way over Hill's successor, an Irish-American politician from Philadelphia, Alderman McMullen.

By the end of July, Mace, Edwards, Harris and Pooley moved to Jem's old training quarters on the beach at Highlands, New Jersey. O'Baldwin's handlers, Johnny Dwyer of Brooklyn and Tom Kelly, seemed similarly enthusiastic about seaside locations and trained at Atlantic City. Ominously, Dwyer had trained Coburn the year previously and Kelly had seconded him at Bay St Louis. Maryland was a state which had not yet legislated against prize-fighting, but even so, the agreed scheme was to travel by rail from Baltimore, stopping just short of Washington, proceeding up the valley of the Potomac, through Cumberland Gap to the Ohio River at Parkersburg. There, three river steamers would be chartered to go northward into a narrow neck of land, barely five miles wide in some places, where the state lines of Ohio, Pennsylvania and West Virginia almost converged. This was the old trick of choosing places where county or state boundaries met and where precise jurisdiction was therefore unclear. What's more, West Virginia was the newest state in the Union, having seceded from Virginia only a decade earlier in order to support Lincoln against the Confederacy. Its authorities were less assertive than most and a prize-fight had already been successfully staged there. This was in the coalmining district of Colliers Station in a deep ravine where speedy access by the police would be virtually impossible.

By the time Mace and O'Baldwin returned to Baltimore in mid-August, all seemed set for the conclusion of a combat which had been prevented in England five years earlier due to Mace's peremptory arrest by Inspector Silverton. He had trained assiduously but betting was 2 to 1 on O'Baldwin, largely on the grounds of his ten-year age advantage. But, on the eve of battle, history appeared to repeat itself: warrants were issued for the arrest of the two pugilists and an injunction served on the executives of the railway company in Maryland, which prevented them from carrying passengers who were about to commit a breach of the peace. James Mace and Edward O'Baldwin appeared in court at Baltimore and were placed under heavy bonds not to engage in a prize-fight in the state of Maryland. Abrahams soon raised the money to secure Mace's release and a cable from Dwyer to New York provided funds from an unnamed source – which may well have been Morrissey – to release Ned.

Mace's party promptly left by rail for New York while O'Baldwin, Dwyer and Kelly went to Philadelphia, the home of the stakeholder Alderman McMullen, who cabled Abrahams in New York to arrange for the match to go ahead a couple of days later. The idea was for O'Baldwin to wait in Philadelphia for Mace and his party to arrive and then all would proceed via Pittsburgh and on to Steubenville, Ohio. From there, Ohio river steamers would ferry them to within a few miles of Colliers Station. There was nothing wrong with the new route, since it had the obvious advantage of avoiding Maryland, but when Abrahams told him, Mace smelt a rat. In fact, O'Baldwin was already at the proposed rendezvous, something which would never have been heard of in the LPR. What's more, it seemed more than likely that Alderman McMullen would be the referee. Mace refused to accept and the match was called off.

O'Baldwin's disappointment at being denied, for the second time, a shot at the championship was only to be expected, and within hours he began to hurl accusations of cowardice against Mace, who replied in the same vein. In itself, such recrimination was not untypical of the Prize Ring as it had become. But it was not long before far worse was to follow. Hints appeared in the press whose journalists kept in close touch with both camps. The *New York Herald* reported that 'more serious accusations than cowardice are being made by one of the parties against the other but, amid the confusion and the smoke resulting from the bloodless strife, it is difficult to ascertain their true force. Should they be substantiated, however, and that deserving publicity given, prizefighting will have received the worst blow yet in this country.' What had happened was simple yet terrible. The collapse of negotiations meant that Mace's personal safety, guaranteed as long as there was a chance of the Irish Giant giving him a public beating, was now as much at risk as it had been on the platform of Montgomery Station. From the Bowery to the Five Points came numerous death threats. News had reached Jem from reliable sources, not least Harry Hill, that men known to be associates of Joe Coburn had vowed to shoot Mace on sight. If someone from the Grand Street Tavern didn't do it, then the infamous Billy McGlory would, and if not McGlory then William J. Sharkey, who had once put a price on Edwards's head. Whoever succeeded would become a folk hero in the Lower East Side. He would doubtless become far richer as a result and could confidently expect that Morrissey's influence would protect him from prosecution.

Mace had had enough. Even if he carefully avoided visiting Harry Hill's or any other downtown location, there would be nothing to stop his enemies coming to W. 23rd Street as Coburn and others had done a couple of years earlier – this time with revolvers in hand. Besides,

Mace had to consider his wife and two small children. Hannah had heard about the threats and was worried. For a short while Mace considered relocating to San Francisco, where he would be out of harm's way, but New York was the centre of American pugilism, the locale from which everything was organised and publicised. As for his alternative occupation in the circus, San Francisco could not match the money to be made in the many prosperous towns and cities of the North-East. There was only one option: he had to return to England. Before setting sail, Mace intended to keep a promise he'd given to his friend Billy Edwards – to act as umpire for him in the upcoming defence of the lightweight championship against Arthur Chambers.

Mace, Pooley and Edwards headed north and arrived at the place of battle for a clash in which both protagonists were expatriate Englishmen, a remote location in Canada known as Squirrel Island. Tom Allen was Chambers's chief second but Mace had little time for Chambers, the protégé of the Marquess of Queensberry, who had returned home by this time. Chambers, as Mace saw it, was, although powerful, a poor stylist whose abilities had been inflated by Queensberry's ignorant bragging. Edwards, by comparison, was as scientific a boxer on a pound for pound basis as he'd ever seen. What's more, Mace had his doubts about Allen. Yes, Allen had been in his corner at Bay St Louis but Mace had not forgotten Allen's prevarication prior to their own clash for the world title. And he'd heard from American friends that, on Allen's path to the American title before Mace arrived in the country, the Birmingham man had himself been a vicious customer outside the ring. Mace would wait and watch.

For twenty-five rounds, Edwards displayed his mastery of the 125lb division. A flawless display of jabbing, sidestepping and countering punished Chambers remorselessly and the Salford man was only just hanging on. But, as Chambers rushed out wildly for the twenty-sixth round, Jem and Pooley vainly shouted for referee Bill Tracy to stop him before he reached the scratch. Tracy, however, either did not hear them or, more likely, chose not to. Chambers at once clinched and then screamed in apparent agony. He bawled that Edwards had bitten him. Tracy, seeing teeth marks on Chambers' neck, at once stopped the fight and declared Chambers the winner on a foul. Had events been as Tracy claimed, his decision would of course have been the only permissible one – but what Mace and Pooley had seen was that Allen had done the biting in Chambers's corner before the round commenced. Tracy refused to listen to protests by Edwards and the two Maces, and by this obnoxious piece of skulduggery, Arthur Chambers became the lightweight champion of America. On this sour note, Mace's connection with the American Prize Ring ended.

After the party returned to New York, Mace shook hands with Edwards, wishing him all the best. He was still only twenty-seven and had years ahead of him as a fighter. Distraught at the way in which he had been cheated out of his title, he nevertheless wished to remain in America but decided to add another string to his bow by acquiring real estate on Long Island. By this time Fred Abrahams had negotiated the buyout of Mace's own business, namely his half share in the saloon and restaurant at 69 W. 23rd Street. It was bought by his business partner, Phil Hargrave. In view of the haste with which the deal was concluded, the terms favoured Hargrave.

On 19 September 1872 Jem, Hannah, Ada and Benjamin Mace, accompanied by Pooley Mace and Fred Abrahams, left New York bound for Liverpool. Jem, his wife and children would return to London, bringing to an end his three-year stay in the United States. He made no formal announcement of his retirement from the Prize Ring and as he looked back on the disappearing skyline of Manhattan, had mixed feelings. He loved the vibrancy of New York life such as he'd known it in the first year of his stay. He'd been intrigued by historic New Orleans and fascinated with boomtown Frisco. But he had been forced into the role of symbol for the undoubted injustices which Ireland had suffered at the hands of successive British governments. It was an unjust response to a completely apolitical man of humble origin. And whatever his feelings about Morrissey, Coburn and Geoeghan, Mace had made several good Irish-American friends, John C Heenan, Jim Cusick and Jerry Donovan among them.

Nevertheless, the circumstances of his departure had hardened his own sense of Englishness, which many in his homeland, dismissively nicknaming him 'The Gypsy', had once sought to denigrate. Mace had displayed, in the rings of the US, a standard of boxing skill and intelligence which America had never seen before. He was a man among men, and outside a small but still influential coterie in certain districts of New York and Boston, most were sorry to see him leave their shores. For many years afterwards the genuine sportsmen of the United States still considered Jem Mace as Champion of America and one who had been unjustly harried out of the country by gangsters. Mace hoped that the time might come in future years when, with changed circumstances, he could set foot once more at liberty on the streets of New York City.

19

The Music Professor's Wife

NELLIE GORE LEE HAD a secret – one which she was anxious to disclose – but her lifestyle, as a member of a troupe of travelling players whose personnel changed frequently, meant that she had no best friend. She did, however, have her sister Annie, a mature girl though only seventeen. Their age gap had been wide enough to lessen rivalry but near enough, once they reached their teens, to bring them close. Their mother Ellen, a widow, had remarried and, since then, had no longer been as close to her daughters. She would not be told the secret but Annie would listen and understand, of that Nellie felt sure.

As the train steamed out of London and headed north to Liverpool, Nellie began to reflect on her life. Her childhood had been spent in Ireland where she was born twenty-two years earlier, in Dublin. Her father, George Gore, had been a solicitor's articled clerk and her mother a dressmaker. Nellie had been christened Ellen Gore, an event not recorded by the state since civil registration was not introduced into Ireland until 1864, twelve years after her birth. George Gore died when Annie was little more than a baby. His death plunged the family into poverty and so his wife decided to emigrate to England.

Ellen Gore and her two young daughters were living in Liverpool on the edge of the massive Irish ghetto which had Scotland Road as its focal point. Unlike most of her Irish neighbours, Ellen was a Protestant, specifically Church of Ireland. She aspired to move away not out of sectarianism but because escape from Scotland Road, with its grinding poverty, was a key factor in upward social mobility. Ellen worked hard as a self-employed dressmaker, and although she taught both her girls that skill at an early age, was determined they would receive some schooling at a time when state education was not yet compulsory. Before long, Ellen realised that her elder daughter had exceptional talent. Nellie was fascinated by music and begged her mother for piano lessons. What little spare money the family had was spent on these and Nellie became a good pianist and later a fine vocalist.

Soon Ellen began taking her girls to music concerts at St George's Hall and to see plays in one or other of Liverpool's theatres. Nellie read about the famous actresses of the day and aspired to follow in their footsteps. Her mother explained that these were ladies from middle-class homes, whose families could afford to train them for the stage. Still, there was an alternative – the circus – and aged sixteen, attired in the most fetching dress her mother's nimble fingers had created for her, she went for an audition: Fred Ginnett's circus was in town and looking for fresh talent. When he heard Nellie's soprano voice, he took her on straight away even before he listened to her on the piano and harp, another instrument she had mastered. Although Nellie was, at 5ft 1in, a trifle small, her flowing auburn hair, clear blue eyes, trim figure and pale, flawless skin did not escape Ginnett's eye.

Soon other men were looking her way. One of these was Rowland Lee, who styled himself a professor of music. In practice, this meant that Lee was Ginnett's resident bandleader. He was a fine all-round musician, something of a dandy and brimming with confidence bordering on arrogance. Nellie's mother had some reservations about him but Lee spelled money and style and she gave her assent to a marriage. Rowland John Lee, twenty-five, and Ellen 'Nellie' Gore, seventeen, married at All Saints Church in Liverpool in 1869. Lee first decided to settle down in Liverpool, earning his living giving music lessons from his house. By this time Ellen Gore had herself remarried – to Patrick Fortune, also Irish-born, who worked as a shipwright in Cammell Laird's bustling yard in Birkenhead. Their mother's second marriage lessened the bond her daughters felt with her. Patrick Fortune was a devout Roman Catholic and Nellie felt that he disapproved of musicians and circus folk and she was not far wrong. Patrick seemed to think that, once her first child was born, she would abandon her dreams of a return to life on the road. Early in 1870 a son was born, named John, but his father's earnings as a music tutor were not enough to keep up the rent, and by the following year the three

Lees had been obliged to move in with the Fortunes. Young Annie, now aged thirteen, was living there with her mother and stepfather. The Fortunes' suspicions about Lee increased when they discovered that he often referred to himself in official correspondence as Richard, rather than Rowland. A quarrel took place and Lee and Nellie resumed their peripatetic life with Ginnett's Circus while baby John was left in the care of his grandmother and aunt Annie.

Annie had always looked up to her elder sister. She herself had, she hoped, justified her mother's scrimping and saving by becoming literate, which few girls of her age and class were, and by being able to support herself as a dressmaker from the age of fifteen. She became very fond of her nephew and spent more time looking after him than did his grandmother, so when Nellie returned to Liverpool from time to time to see him it was from Annie that she learnt most about his progress. Lee did not return to see his son and it was not long before the elder sister confided to the younger that her husband had little interest in him. What's more, he had a roving eye for other female vocalists, musicians, equestriennes and dancers with Ginnett's and Nellie strongly suspected him of infidelity.

By February 1875, Annie, aged seventeen, was living in Copperas Hill, where her family had a fishmonger's shop, and it was from there that she married twenty-year-old Ted McCall, born in Liverpool. Ted was a coachman and knew the city well; he was very much a man of the world and upwardly mobile. At that time, cabs were chiefly hailed by wealthy men who tipped freely and sometimes revealed details of the lifestyle of the city's many rich and famous citizens. Ted was accustomed to keeping confidences. Nellie had come up for the wedding on her own but had not seemed at ease. Clearly she had no problem with Ted — she took an immediate liking to the intelligent, humorous and easy-going cab driver — but there was definitely something on her mind. It was therefore no surprise when, a few months later, Nellie visited Annie and Ted. She not only wanted to spend time with five-year-old John but to confide with Ted and Annie about a crisis in her life.

★ ★ ★

When Jem Mace abruptly returned to England in September 1872, following the threats on his life made in New York, his lifestyle lost much of its lustre and his assets were diminished. His mansion in Chelsea had been sold, his circus was long gone, his boxing booth defunct and, above all, the Strawberry Grounds were under new management. He rented a modest house for himself and his family at Rolls Road in the humble district of Camberwell, on the south side of the Thames. Most of his children were still dependent on him: Ada and Benjamin came back to England, one as a child of five, the other as a sixteen-month-old baby, and he and Hannah retrieved seven-year-old Amelia from the Jaceys. As to the children of his first marriage, James, fourteen, was not yet working and nor was sixteen-year-old Adelaide. The only young Mace in work was Alfred, still a linen draper's clerk. His financial independence was, from his father's point of view, about the only positive thing which could be said about Alfred.

Mace was stunned to learn that, the previous year, at the age of seventeen, Alfred had experienced a religious conversion. Without the knowledge of the Jaceys he had begun attending gospel hall meetings in London and was soon declaring to all who knew him that 'the Lord had spoken to Him'. Alfred had become a member of the extreme fundamentalist sect the Plymouth Brethren, and it was his burning ambition to set himself up as a preacher of the gospel as soon as he reached the age of adulthood, then twenty-one, in three years' time.

As his father saw it, Alfred's views were preposterous. All his life, Mace had an indifference to religion in general and a loathing of evangelism in particular. He ridiculed Alfred's views but succeeded only in making the lad more stubborn. Alfred denounced his father as a gambler and a womaniser and was sent packing and told where he should stick his Bible. As the years passed, the fierceness of this early exchange abated but father and son were never totally reconciled.

While Hannah shared her husband's hostility towards the young zealot, it would not be long before their own relationship began to sour. Hannah found difficulty in adjusting to the comparative modesty of their English lifestyle after the glamour and luxury of New York. This annoyed Mace; after all, he had put the safety of his wife and their two youngest children foremost in deciding to leave America and was not alone in thinking that Hannah did not like having to look after all her own children by herself, instead of relying on either her sister, Fanny Jacey, or the maid they had employed in New York. As it happened, Hannah was pining for the old life in the circus which she had known since her early childhood, but life on the road was incompatible with educating young children.

For Mace the circus seemed the only option. He had left England because prize-fighting was dead and, three years later, it seemed as good as buried. After a couple of tours with lesser-known troupes, Fred Ginnett offered him a contract. While Mace could no longer ply his trade bare-fisted on remote turf, he could give exhibitions of gloved sparring in a circus – but times had changed and these exhibitions were no longer popular. What did draw the crowds were Mace's performances as a statuarist and his virtuosity on the violin.

From various points of view, Mace was beginning to tire of Hannah. Although she was only in her late twenties, three pregnancies had taken their toll on her figure. His attraction towards her had been strongly physical; emotionally and mentally he had always compared her unfavourably to Adah Isaacs Menken, although he was never cruel enough to do so to her face. One evening, during Ginnett's rehearsals, he heard a beautiful soprano voice coming from a nearby room. Told that it was Nellie Lee, who had recently rejoined the troupe, he strode into the rehearsal room. Normally Mace liked his women dark – Mary, Selina, Hannah and, above all, Adah – but he was captivated by the petite red-blonde with big blue eyes and pale tender skin. When her performance was complete, Mace introduced himself and asked where she was from. They began talking about Liverpool and he enquired about the Strawberry Grounds. To his annoyance, Nellie revealed that it no longer existed. Haig's Brewery had, she told him, retained only the Tavern and the entire Grounds had been sold off, most of it to Ogden's Tobacco Factory. This was a disgrace, Nellie said, and Mace, who never smoked cigarettes, sincerely agreed.

Before long, they were deep in conversation about singing and instrumental playing. At long last, Mace had found a woman who shared his love of music. On an impulse, he played his boyhood composition 'The Cuckoo Song' for her. He was delighted when she responded to his violin's melody by improvising novel harmonies on the piano and asked if she might accompany him in public. That would give her great pleasure, replied Nellie, except for the fact that her husband, temporarily away from the troupe on a trip to his hometown of Chesterfield, would soon be back. Lee was a common surname and Mace had not immediately connected Nellie with the so-called Professor of Music. Although Nellie did not heavily emphasise Lee's probable jealousy over her accompanying another male performer at solo level, she strongly hinted at it.

When Lee returned to Ginnett's, Mace sized him up. While Mace had sometimes been accused of being a love rat, or 'cad', in Lee he beheld a man who actually was one. His possessiveness was in inverse proportion to the lecherous looks Jem spotted him giving to many of the circus girls. As the weeks passed, Jem and Nellie took advantage of times when Lee was rehearsing the band to exchange confidences. She poured her heart out (about her husband's infidelities and other shifty behaviour) and when she asked about Hannah, he revealed that after ten years of marriage, the spark had gone. It was not long before the pair became lovers.

Nellie soon told Annie that she was having an affair with Jem Mace. Lee had already become suspicious and, when challenged, she had told him the truth. No one else knew but, although circus folk were tolerant of all manner of liaisons, gossip was spreading fast. Lee was aware of this and his rage that he had been cuckolded knew no bounds. He quit Ginnett's and disappeared, probably to earn a living as a music tutor. Nellie did not ask for advice; she looked for comfort and support and she received it. Annie asked about Mace, who was twenty years older than his new lover, and smiled as Nellie responded with enthusiasm about his physique, which caused women to flock to his statuary performances. She had, she confessed, winced at the sight of his prematurely gnarled knuckles, an obvious legacy of his days in the Prize Ring, but his fingers were those of a musician, long and slender with immaculately manicured nails. Although he had received no formal musical training, he could, asserted Nellie, knock spots off Professor Rowland Lee.

The consequences of Nellie's marriage break-up had to be faced. Lee had obvious grounds to divorce her but she was sure he would not, simply because the spendthrift bandleader would never have the financial means to proceed. Equally, he would never support his own son. Jem had promised to stand by Nellie, and also make provision for young John. Mace could not marry her though because, quite apart from the wretched Rowland's unwillingness to fork out the legal fees, he had no case for divorcing Hannah – any more than Hannah had, under the one-sided law of the day, for terminating their marriage. Mace was prepared to go through a bigamous ceremony and told Nellie that he had done this when he had married Hannah. He would do so again, if need be; it depended on the reaction of her family, which in view of Nellie's mother and stepfather's imminent return to Ireland, effectively meant Annie and Ted.

When Ted was told the news, he was impressed at the thought of having Jem Mace in the family, in fact if not in name. Ted was a keen sports enthusiast: he played football, he was a regular attender at horse races in the North of England and, as a boy, had stood among the crowd on St George's Plateau waiting for Mace's triumphal return after his final defeat of Joe Goss. Ted knew little about music but enjoyed going to the theatre. Broad-minded and tolerant, he never attended church except for weddings, christenings and funerals. Annie expressed concern that Mace was now chiefly dependent on his circus earnings, which were, in the nature of things, erratic. Why, she wondered, did he not take the licence of a pub, as he had in the past? Ted replied by touching on an issue which, unbeknown to him, had infuriated Mace on his return to England in 1872.

In that year, William Gladstone's Liberal Government had introduced a Licensing Act. Gladstone, a devout Anglican, was very concerned about the high levels of alcohol consumption in the country. He equated alcohol with crime, family breakdown, gambling and debt. In this he had the full support of the large numbers of nonconformist ministers who were increasingly campaigning for the Liberal Party. Although the 1872 Act disappointed these nonconformists because it did not go anywhere near far enough, as they saw it, in restricting pub hours, it caused riots in many English cities. Pubs would now be obliged by law to close at 11pm and could not open at all on Sunday morning. The licensed trade feared that profits would be badly affected and, from then on, gave their full financial backing to the Tory Party. In fact their turnover was not that greatly affected by the Licensing Act, but for many years to come there remained a fear, which was not realised, that a future Liberal government might bring in tougher legislation.

Mace, whose previous interest in British politics had been marginal, now became, like the vast majority of men associated with the licensed trade, a staunch Tory. His anger towards the Liberals was increased by the fact that their core support of nonconformist ministers were the very people who had campaigned for years to wipe out the London Prize Ring. Now, as he saw it, in the 1870s, his ancillary occupation as a publican was also being threatened. In future, like other pub landlords, he would see that the lifestyle of brewers and publicans would be little affected by Gladstone's modest restrictions, but at that moment it seemed to him that he would be wasting his time in becoming, as he had been in the 1850s and 1860s, what was now called a licensed victualler.

Ted McCall also considered the Licensing Act to be the work of fanatics and killjoys and would not, he told Annie, blame Mace for not returning to a trade so obviously under threat. Nellie returned to Ginnett's, uplifted by the support that she had received from the McCalls. She and Annie were now closer than ever and, with no brother herself, she would always in future refer to Ted as her brother rather than her brother-in-law. Mace was pleased too. He was the last man to curry favour with anyone but it made life far simpler if he could establish a better relationship with the McCalls than he had had with the Boorns and Jaceys. By this time, he had told Hannah that their marriage was over – something she had strongly suspected for a couple of years. She knew nothing about Nellie but she did know that her husband would not be without feminine company for long once he was back on the road again. As for their children, Amelia, Ada and Ben would live with her in south London and their father would provide full financial support.

When he and Nellie visited Liverpool together, Mace met Ted and Annie for the first time. They all hit it off. McCall struck the right note from the start. His respect for Mace was obvious but, unlike many others, he showed no sign of deference to celebrity and would laugh and joke. Although Mace's strongest friendships would always be with fellow-pugilists, he was as close to McCall as to any man who did not come from the world of the Prize Ring. They would know one another for over thirty years and, as time passed by, Mace would tell the easy-going but loyal and discreet McCall many details of his life which were known to few others – particularly in connection with his previous liaisons with women.

By this time Pooley Mace, who had been working as a musicians' road manager, dropped out. At thirty-five, he finally decided to end his exuberant bachelor lifestyle, and in January 1874, Leopoldius Mace married Delaiah Smith, aged twenty-nine, in the town of Consett in County Durham. Like Pooley, Delaiah was of gypsy blood. She was the daughter of Ambrose Smith, a well-known Romany showman otherwise known as Jasper Petulengro, and her mother was the noted Romany beauty Sanspi Herne. Pooley's adventurous lifestyle temporarily subsided and for a time Jem saw less of him, although their friendship remained as strong as ever.

For the better part of a year, Mace and Nellie lived together in Liverpool, in her family's fishmonger's shop at Copperas Hill. Mace supported her by giving boxing lessons in nearby premises but it was not long before he hankered to be more actively involved in the fight game. George Langham, the son of his late mentor Nat, invited him to London. George was by now the landlord of one of his father's old pubs, the Cambrian Stores off Leicester Square and it was there that Mace, Nellie and young John went to live. Mace gave boxing lessons at the pub, a better proposition in the heart of the capital than it had been in Liverpool.

Mace's return from America had implicitly signalled his retirement as a prize-fighter. His *de facto* vacation of the American heavyweight title had opened the way for self-proclaimed contenders and it would be a year before a successor was recognised. Three thousand miles away in England, the world of bareknuckle fighting had ceased to exist and the slowly developing and ill-defined amateur boxing scene held no interest for Mace. He waited for news from America. With Coburn seemingly content with retirement once he had got rid of Mace, it was Tom Allen, now a naturalised American, who reclaimed the championship with an easy victory over Mike McCoole in September 1873. A month later, Mace was saddened to learn of the death of John Carmel Heenan. The Benecia Boy, whose name would always stand with that of Tom Sayers in the annals of the Prize Ring, was only thirty-eight when he died at a remote station in Wyoming, heading for California by rail from the East Coast. Ned O'Baldwin's subsequent death confirmed all Mace's fears concerning the safety of pugilists in America. Shortly after issuing a challenge to Allen and desperately needing to raise stake money, the Irish Giant was shot and fatally wounded by his business partner in the saloon they jointly owned.

With Coburn idle and O'Baldwin dead, Allen was running out of credible challengers. He had already disposed of the much-touted Ben Hogan in a mere quarter of an hour. Allen needed fights and the income they provided and he telegraphed a challenge to Mace in London, who declined, stating that the proposed stakes were not high enough. It would have taken a very large sum to alter his determination to keep out of the American Prize Ring. There was, however, one man who was eager to confront Allen: Joe Goss, who had lost to him controversially nine years before. After their protracted draw in Gloucestershire, the pair had arrived in the USA together, with a match in the pipeline. But when it took place, in Cincinnati, Allen was disqualified on a foul after only three minutes for striking the Wolverhampton man while he was down. Yet instead of that result boosting Goss's career and hampering Allen's, Allen had somehow parlayed a reputation for ruthlessness into the series of fights whereby he gained the American championship. A disillusioned Goss had returned to England. For a time, he had been consoled by Mace's demolition of Allen but the old sense of grievance began to smoulder again when Allen re-emerged as American champion.

Back in England, Goss and Mace had become quite friendly. While Jem considered Joe limited as both a pugilist and a person, he found him likeable. At an exhibition bout between them, which drew few spectators, Goss told Mace he was hard-up for cash and would love the chance to return to America and avenge himself against Allen. But Goss had only a brief experience of the United States and virtually no contacts – besides, his modest manner was seen as un-warriorlike in America. On Goss's behalf, Mace got in touch with Howe and Cushing Circus and recommended his friend as a reliable performer and a likely draw. By this time, American circuses were featuring both sparring and wrestling. The English were still considered the best fighters and even an old relic like Sam Hurst had been recruited by a New York circus twelve years after Mace had abruptly terminated his reign as English champion. On receipt of Mace's letter, Howe and Cushing at once made Goss an offer for boxing exhibitions and seemed ready to underwrite a bareknuckle challenge to Allen.

Mace's correspondence with Howe and Cushing had more important consequences: they made him an offer to star with them as both a boxer and a musician and put up money far in excess of what he could expect from Ginnett. Mace thought over the issue. He did not want to be parted from Nellie, all the more so when she told him she was expecting their child, but Howe and Cushing toured throughout the length and breadth of America and had a base in California. If he could tour with them, he would of course have to play New York, with all its dangers, but he could live in San Francisco for much of the year. There would be no pressure on him to return to the Prize Ring which, in any case, he had made clear that he was not prepared to do. He explained the situation to Nellie and she replied without hesitation that she would follow him wherever he chose. Jem would have to return to America on his own but with the birth of their child imminent, Nellie could follow as soon as the infant was old enough to make the ocean crossing.

The birth of Jem and Nellie's child was not registered. There was no penalty on parents for failing to register a birth until 1875, when a £2 fine was introduced. Concealing a birth, usually with a future view to sending a child out to work before the legal age, was not uncommon, especially in the London area, amid the anonymity of the metropolis. Unmarried mothers often left the name of the putative father out and wives who had become pregnant as a result of an extramarital affair frequently gave the names of their husbands. Nellie did not want to do this. By now she loathed Rowland Lee and she would have willingly named Mace as the true father except for the fact of his high public profile. So the matter was left, although their daughter would be known as Ellen Norah Mace.

On 15 April 1876, Mace returned to New York with Goss. He bade Nellie a temporary goodbye in Liverpool where she was staying with Annie and Ted. They agreed to look after John who, at six, needed to be in school. By this time Annie was like a second mother to him and Mace agreed to send money for the duration of his stay in the United States. Nellie waited for over two months more before she felt her daughter was old enough to face the transatlantic crossing. They were greeted by Mace when they disembarked from the *City of Chester* in New York in mid-September. Nellie remained, albeit in name only, the wife of Rowland Lee. Her husband did not rue the break-up of his marriage for long – he joined another circus and took a sixteen-year-old dancer as his mistress, eventually settling down in the Midlands.

As Jem and Nellie were reunited in New York, she reflected that, while she was the nominal wife of an obscure 'music professor', she was the true love of Jem Mace, the most acclaimed sportsman in the world.

20

The Bonanza King

STANDING AT THE window of his sumptuous hillside mansion, John W. Mackay surveyed the townscape below through field glasses. Activity was feverish. Cranes swung and builders swarmed up scaffolding nailing roof tiles into place. The reconstruction of Virginia City was almost complete. Twelve months earlier, the great Comstock Conflagration had burned three-quarters of the town to ashes in a single night. And since John W. Mackay was the richest man in this city of fabulous wealth, he was relieved at the resurrection of the urban sprawl which clung precariously to the steep slopes of Mount Davidson.

The Great Fire of October 1875 had left the source of Mackay's wealth undisturbed, just as it had spared his opulent abode. A former timberman, the Dublin-born immigrant had, with several business partners, been shrewd enough in the previous decade to buy up all the mines and claims of the Comstock Lode. Henry Comstock himself had become rich when the Lode to which he gave his name had been discovered in 1859. Prospectors had cursed the grey-blue dirt that stuck to their hands as they washed out gold in the arid terrain of the Nevada Desert – that is until it was assayed and proved to be silver ore worth over $2,000 a ton. President Abraham Lincoln had been highly enthused by news of the great silver strike and rapidly bent the laws on statehood and population to detach Nevada from Utah Territory. The bullion from the Comstock Lode was to provide the reserves to keep the Union solvent during the Civil War.

In 1873, the partnership which included Mackay hit the main silver vein at 1,200ft below the ground of their Consolidated Virginia properties. What followed was a bonanza. On land they had bought for what had seemed a staggering sum of $75,000, they ran up during the next six years profits of $100 million. Since Mackay had already bought out one of his partners, his wealth alone was estimated at $40 million. Among the Barons of the Bonanza, he was truly the King, and under Mackay, Virginia City was transformed with astonishing speed from a Wild West boomtown replete with faro parlours, one-armed bandits and a red light district into a sophisticated city boasting an array of international-class hotels, up-market restaurants, an opera house and a system of water, electric and gas supply unequalled in the world. The population of 35,000 made it the third biggest urban centre west of the Mississippi, after San Francisco and Denver. True, its location on the forty per cent gradient of Mount Davidson was precarious, and runaway wagons careering down the slopes were an everyday occurrence. As well as this, it was a mile-and-a-half above sea level, its altitude sapping the energy, but gold and silver were a tremendous magnet. Even before the completion of the transcontinental railroad, Mark Twain, then a reporter on the local newspaper, had done much to publicise Virginia City. Once the Transcontinental came, linking with the existing Virginia and Truckee Railway, the future of John Mackay's adopted hometown seemed assured.

The fire of 1875 had destroyed most of the physical fabric but, thanks to heroic efforts the buildings which were the city's nerve centre had been saved. During reconstruction, with miners braving the ninety degree heat in the summer months and living in tents, the cacophony which symbolised the fabulous prosperity of the Comstock Lode went unabated. The clanking metal of the stamp mills echoed day and night in this gouged-out gap in the Sierra Nevada. John Mackay's immense fortune had not been affected by the Great Fire but he was convinced that something was needed to put Virginia City back on the map. He mulled over a list of events which would draw the attention of the nation back to the city rising from the ashes of the old town. After considering and dismissing invitations to opera stars, his mind went back to the city's prize-fights during the 1860s at the Washoe Track. No police would ever intervene because they did the bidding of the silver barons and the barons thought that fights distracted miners from grievances about their conditions. Accordingly, admission charges were fixed at $2.50. On one occasion, a disputed call of 'foul' led to instantly drawn pistols. Five men lay wounded, one of whom, a Mexican labourer, died of his injuries, but in the eyes of

Mackay and his chums, passions inflamed by disputed wagers were far preferable to the prospect of a Miners Union strike. Mackay did not hesitate long. Winter would soon be approaching and sub-zero temperatures could bring Virginia City to a halt, albeit for only a couple of weeks. The Bonanza King wrote a letter containing an invitation and sent it to an Englishman living out of suitcases at a hotel in the East. The envelope was addressed to Jem Mace.

While waiting for Nellie and baby Ellen to arrive, Mace had spent much of his time touring with Howe and Cushing. When they played New York, he was delighted by the sight of the recently opened Central Park, not only because of its beauty but because its construction had been achieved despite the unrelenting opposition of Tammany Hall. The power-brokers of Tammany had formerly had an interest in the illegal distilleries which pockmarked the sleazy expanse of marshland before the site was cleared and drained. Now Frederick Law Olmsted's masterpiece of landscape gardening had provided a breathing-space for the 750,000 residents in the cramped urban space of Manhattan. Most visitors were content to stroll sedately through the park – not Mace. A man born and bred in the country, he was inspired by the expanse of green amid the smokestacks. One morning, he flung off his jacket, rolled up his sleeves and, like the pedestrian he had once been, ran round the entire periphery of the park. In doing so, he became the forerunner of the thousands who happily jog through the park to this day.

A less pleasant interlude occurred when Mace was arrested for the first time in his life on a matter unconnected with prizefighting. The police apprehended him at a circus performance in Jersey City following a complaint by a New York tailor. Edward Underhill, of Fulton Street, had alleged an altercation after he had asked Mace to make good a debt of $175 for two suits. Mace appeared in court and stated that the unpaid bill had nothing to do with him but had been contracted by his employer. The judge ordered Mace to be discharged.

In July 1876, he returned to Canada, where he was always well received and boxed several exhibitions. Mace had agreed to act as second for Goss in his upcoming challenge for the American title against Allen but abruptly changed his mind when he learnt that Joe Coburn's name had also been put forward as another of Goss's seconds.

Only when Coburn was told he was not wanted did Mace revert to his original intention of supporting Goss.

Allen v Goss appeared, at first, to have been well-planned. Goss was appearing in a benefit at the Cincinnati Opera House a few days before the scheduled fight and this drew publicity. A venue had been chosen at Covington, Kentucky, just across the Ohio River from Cincinnati and over the state line. On 7 September 1876, Allen and Goss duly squared off but after half an hour of close combat, the militia arrived and the captain told all concerned that the fight must be stopped at once on pain of arrest. The captain's relative leniency allowed the combatants to move to neighbouring Boone County, where they resumed. Due to this delay, roughneck elements from the big cities discovered the locale. They had bet heavily on Goss and began to shout abuse at Allen and to intimidate the referee. The mill continued for a further hour and a quarter, and the atmosphere at ringside progressively deteriorated. Despite Goss's superior ringcraft, Allen was proving too strong for him and had him down several times. Goss's partisans were now shouting threats to kill Allen. Although Mace, in Goss's corner, was spared the wrath of the mob, he was dismayed by their vicious hooliganism and appalled when guns and knives were brandished.

Allen appeared to have drawn his own conclusions. Nine years earlier, he had shown himself no sportsman when he deliberately fouled Goss for no reason, losing the fight. Now, after knocking Goss down a further time, to a storm of boos and threats, he deliberately smashed Goss in the face as the latter was attempting to rise. Allen was at once disqualified and, in this deplorable manner, the American championship changed hands. Rarely if ever had prize-fighting sunk so low. Although Mace had been a reluctant participant he was quick to distance himself – literally and metaphorically. As the State militia closed in on the disgraceful scenes, he made a run for it and was among those who succeeded in rowing across the river to the safety of the Ohio bank. He later made his disgust known to the sporting press and, as far as the genuine sportsmen of the US were concerned, it was Mace they continued to regard as America's true champion. Allen also succeeded in getting away but Goss was not so lucky: he was arrested and sentenced to a term of imprisonment in Kentucky.

For a couple of months afterwards, while he was continuing to tour with Howe and Cushing, Mace thought over how he could remain a boxer while dissociating himself from the degenerate Prize Ring. It was at this stage that the letter from John W. Mackay arrived. Mackay invited Mace to Virginia City to fight Bill Davis at the National Guard Hall. The fight would last eight rounds and be decided according to Queensberry Rules, except that each round would last four minutes rather than three, with a one-minute interval between rounds. If there was no knockout, the winner would be the man who had scored most 'face-hits' counted by the referee, announced at the end of each round and totalled at the finish. Provided Mace was agreeable to these conditions, neither he nor Davis would need to find a stake. Instead, Mackay put up a purse of $5,000, with three-quarters to go to the winner – and to mark the occasion, Mackay would present a trophy belt made of gold.

Mace jumped at the chance. Although the money was chickenfeed for Mackay, it would be vital for Mace, who had far less ready cash than he was used to and dependants who relied on him. He had some misgivings about the impartiality of the referee but the prospect of fighting what approximated to a Queensberry Rules bout with a fellow professional intrigued him. He was confident of beating Davis, who had lost to Allen seven years earlier in a fight for the American title. Mace believed he might well knock Davis out with the aid of padded gloves. At the least he would outscore him. It was, Mace regretted, rather amateurish for Mackay to exclude body shots but at least this eliminated the possibility of being hit below the belt while the referee looked the other way. And the fight, if there was no knockout, would last twice as long as the four-rounders such as John Chambers supervised with the amateurs at Lillie Road in London. Eight rounds was not really long enough, he felt, but was acceptable. He lost no time in telegraphing his acceptance to Virginia City.

Mace used his advance from Mackay to set up his own troupe of travelling musicians. These would be supporting players to the two stars, namely himself on violin and Nellie on vocals and piano. In addition to the musicians, there would be a nurse to look after baby Ellen. It was with this troupe that he arrived in Nevada. At the Dyer's

Hall in Reno, he combined music and boxing. The second half of the show would comprise a sparring session with a local boxer known only by the odd name of Large Frank. Before that, his troupe gave a full musical performance. One old codger, evidently keen on boxing but bored by matters musical, was seen slumped in his seat snoring loudly, whereupon Nellie shouted out to him, 'Brace up and have some style about you!' The audience responded with shouts of approval for her forthright rebuke and soon Mace appeared at her side, announcing his intention of 'knocking the stuffing out of Davis' and advising the spectators to 'get a bet on me while the going's good'. By this skilful showmanship, Mace drummed up an even larger crowd than were already planning to buy tickets.

On a bitterly cold evening, 16 December 1876, Mace and Davis stayed backstage at the Guard Hall while a crowd of 10,000, women as well as men, waited to see the gaslit contest. Referee Bing Williams, himself an ex-fighter, went through the rules. Although he used the term 'face-hits' to denote the means by which he would score the contest, Mace corrected him with 'points', adroitly using the vocabulary of fencing, a sport at which he was a master. Davis was an amiable man and, as they shook hands, Mace felt sure that his opponent would fight fair and square and hold no grudge against him on account of his nationality. In the arena of the Guard Hall, betting was at fever pitch. Significantly, there were no bets on 'first blood', which seemed no longer relevant. Although few realised that they would be witnessing a turning point in the history of the fight game, there were, on the other hand, those who believed that Mace was still the Champion of the World and that his title was at stake.

As Mace and Davis rose from their chairs and advanced to the centre of a 20ft ring, they touched gloves in a gesture of respect and comradeship which would become ring ritual. Williams, the referee, had used a megaphone to explain the new rules to the crowd, who had listened patiently, but when he introduced the two fighters, the roof was nearly lifted off. Davis, American and by now settled in California, was rapturously welcomed, but the silver miners of Nevada warmly applauded Mace. The scene was a continent away in tone as well as location from the turf on which Mace had been cursed by low-lifes from the hovels of the Lower East Side. The hopes of the crowd for its local hero were raised at the start of the fight. Not only was Mace older, he was out of condition, having had little time to train. Davis, on the other hand, had been training for several weeks in the hope of actually fighting Tom Allen – who had, in the wake of his scandalous fight with Goss, gone back to England. Bill looked trim, whereas, at over thirteen stone, Jem looked what he was: a man who had not fought competitively for a full five years.

In round one, Mace characteristically led with a left jab which landed on Davis's forehead. He moved back at once to avoid the riposte but, at forty-five, he was not as quick as he had been and he took a counter on the nose, greeted with wild cheering. Mace advanced again but Davis blocked his jab. Mace closed and fired home a left-right close combination but Davis's strong counter surprised him and, as he was driven backwards, he slowly lost his footing on the canvas and briefly slipped down before jumping to his feet. There were shouts of 'first knockdown!' but Davis knew that Mace had simply lost his balance. Grinning broadly, he made an obvious signal that he claimed no knockdown. The round ended and Williams announced, 'Mace three, Davis two.'

The tempo picked up in the second round and excitement reached a crescendo as the two men traded blows. It was soon obvious that Mace was by far the better boxer, despite Davis's forceful style and heavy right-hand lunges. Mace jabbed on the retreat and at times his hand speed was such that he landed three to Davis's one. The miners commented that Mace was 'like a goddam leopard'. Suddenly, near the end of the round, a ferocious right from Davis hit Mace but landed on his forehead, not the jaw. Once again, cheers roared out as Mace was, this time, knocked down, but he rose, smiling, before the referee could even begin the count. As the bell sounded, Mace walked confidently back to his corner. Still, he was breathing hard and looked glad to rest his arms on the ropes for a minute as Williams announced, 'Mace eighteen, Davis nine.'

Mace deliberately slowed the pace in the third. He fought entirely on the retreat and Davis unwisely tried to rush him, scoring but leaving himself open to Mace's lightning counters. 'Mace six, Davis four!' Both men seemed to tire in the fourth. Mace was out of condition while Davis had expended unnecessary energy with his raw, rushing style. The pair were also feeling the effects of fighting at an altitude of over 6,000 feet. In the fifth, Mace got in a strong right which shook Davis. The Westerner, in Prize Ring style, dropped to one knee for a breather, misleading many spectators into thinking that the round had ended – as would have been the case in an LPR mill – but after Davis rose, Mace unleashed four stinging jabs in quick succession. Bravely, Davis hurled a strong right cross but Mace's speed of head movement meant that it landed on the mouth, not the chin. To renewed crowd excitement, Davis forced Mace back to the ropes – only for the Englishman to box his way out so cleverly that the crowd gasped in involuntary admiration. The sixth was a complete anti-climax and established a rhythm of ebb and flow which would be a distinctive feature of this new form of combat. Both men were taking it easy and there were some who booed restlessly before Williams intoned, 'Mace two, Davis one.'

The seventh saw the pace pick up but it was still a lull after the storm of the earlier rounds. Mace jabbed frequently, but with his knuckles cushioned by gloves, did not manage to cut Davis about the eyes which, as ever, he was targeting. Davis rushed Mace to the ropes but the Englishman went into a clinch, which annoyed the crowd and baffled the referee. Until then, neither man had seized the other. After all, with wrestling outlawed under Queensberry Rules, there was no point. But there was nothing in those rules to stop one or both boxers taking a rest in this manner.

'Tell 'em to break!' shouted a spectator.

Williams failed to do this but instead his stentorian voice barked out the round score: 'Mace six, Davis five.'

As time was called for the eighth and final round, Mace and Davis sportingly touched gloves and spontaneously invented a second ritual of comradeship. In what would, in the future, prove to be a characteristic pattern, the last round was guaranteed to be a lively one, both for reasons of showmanship and to convince the referee. Mace produced his fastest jabs, aimed at Davis's eyes. Davis was clever enough to dodge the first one but the next rocked his head back. He countered with a brave right but Mace leaped in and caused blood to flow with two rapier thrusts to Davis's eyebrows. Davis was glad to clinch as time was called at the end of the fight, amid thunderous cheering.

Few among the spectators had kept tally of Williams's points score and had little idea that Davis would have to have scored a last-round knockout to win the fight, but despite their partisanship for Davis, it was plain for all to see that Mace, in his cleverly staged grandstand finale, had outclassed Davis.

'The winner,' announced Williams, 'by fifty-two hits to thirty-three . . . Jem Mace!'

He strode over to Mace and raised his right arm. Davis and Mace promptly shook hands and slapped each other on the back. Suddenly gunfire was heard in the crowd and, seeing Mace flinch, Mackay hastened into the ring and was quick to reassure the Englishman that the revolver shots had been fired upwards in a typical expression of exuberance by the Western miners. Then, to great cheers, he formally presented Mace with the gold trophy belt. Mace and Davis left the stage together to tumultuous applause. Only when they were backstage after their forty-minute clash did Jem unlace his gloves and reveal to Bill his obviously dislocated left little finger, sustained during the accidental fall in the first round. Davis had never once seen Mace wince in pain as he punched but must have wondered how effective those stinging left jabs would have been with an intact fist.

The clash was a milestone in the transition from prize-fighting to professional boxing – or from bareknuckle combat in which boxing was only one aspect, to a new sport defined by the use of gloves with rigid adherence to a limited time-frame and from which wrestling had been eliminated. Mace v Davis would not achieve the recognition it merited partly because of confusion over the Queensberry Rules. Mace himself believed that John Chambers' rules were inadequate because they neither stipulated the number of rounds nor how a decision could be effectively arrived at, if there was no knockout, by an unbiased referee. While Mace declared that he would never fight in the Prize Ring again, he did not campaign explicitly for the adoption of the Queensberry Rules by professionals because those rules were, he declared, only a sketch and not the finished picture.

Even the means of reaching the verdict in favour of himself were, Mace argued, inadequate. Privately, he conceded that Davis should have received more points for knocking him down and he stated in public not only that body shots should count but that defensive skills such as blocking and dodging, at which he was a master, should receive points. A truly scientific boxer should, he added, always strive for a knockout but be ready to fight a protracted battle and outpoint his opponent. Davis was not prone to theorise about boxing as Mace did but he also had an eye to business. On the train ride to San Francisco, the pair expressed dissatisfaction over one aspect of the proceedings at Virginia City: a substantial sum of money had been taken by charging for admission but neither of them had seen a red cent of it. Mackay pocketed the lion's share and, having realised his aim in putting Virginia City back on the map after the Great Fire, had no further interest in being a promoter. Mace and Davis decided to promote a return clash between themselves based on Davis's confidence that he could get his wealthy acquaintances in Virginia City to raise a solid purse. Mace needed to find no money. In fact, $600 was subscribed in Nevada and although it was a pittance compared to Mackay's purse, the fact that the winner would take three-quarters made it attractive to Mace.

What heralded the modern era was the agreement that the two fighters would divide the gate money equally. They would meet in San Francisco. Most spectators would be charged a dollar for admission but seats in the grandstand ranged from $5 to $50. Nothing could have been further from the old days of prize-fighters going cap in hand to their backers for a share in the profits from railway special fares. With a return against Davis scheduled for 26 January 1877, Mace went into strict training this time, pausing only on Christmas Day and New Year's Day. As for Nellie, she took a great liking to San Francisco. She had endured the bitter cold of Virginia City but enjoyed the mild California winter. Enclosing a photograph of herself dressed in the latest fashions and taken in a studio, she wrote to her sister and brother-in-law in Liverpool. She believed, at that time, that she might settle in California, returning to England only to bring John to live with her in America.

A sellout crowd saw Mace knock out Davis in the fourth round. The astute and amiable Davis was consoled by his cut of the gate money and returned to Virginia City to buy an upscale saloon. In due course he became mayor of the Bullion City before, with the exhaustion of the Comstock Lode, it declined into a ghost town. Mace had by now become a hero in San Francisco and received many presents and tokens of goodwill – but he announced that, reluctantly, he could not remain in California. He had considered establishing the West Coast as a centre for professional boxing in rivalry to the East Coast's continuing monopoly of the Prize Ring, but the problem was the paucity of top-class opposition for Mace, even if the existing prize-fighters could be persuaded to take the ring under Queensberry Rules or some agreed modification of them. Goss, the official American champion, had by now regained his freedom and settled in Boston, where he ran the Saracen's Head saloon, but Goss knew that Mace had the beating of him and he had no intention of trying conclusions with his fellow countryman.

As for Allen, who had quit the States in fear of his life, he was soon back in England proclaiming himself Champion of Britain and inviting challenges either in the Prize Ring or under Queensberry Rules. But the lack of interest in the 'Old Country' for any form of boxing, ancient or modern, was steadily confirmed. First, the would-be pugilist Jack Knifton, considered quite good, cried off, having been unable to raise the agreed stakes. Next Allen faced an inept nonentity, Tompkin Gilbert, and swiftly disposed of him with gloves on. This was in London in a half-empty house dotted with yawning spectators. Allen tried to make a go of it in England for a couple of years before giving up in despair and sneaking back to St Louis. With both Goss and Allen thus sidelined, all the fighters of Mace's generation were out of the equation. The sole young contender was Johnny Dwyer, from Brooklyn, but Dwyer refused to come to the West. When Mace announced his imminent departure from California, the public was disappointed but understanding. There was simply no competition for him on American soil and therefore no profitable gates to split.

On the West Coast, he was acclaimed both as a man among men and as the supreme boxer-fighter of the age, in contrast to his image fashioned by Tammany Hall as an 'upstart Limey'. These sentiments were combined neatly in a superb present subscribed by collections in the bullion mining camps. The organisers presented Mace with a brick made of solid silver and bearing the following inscription: 'To James

Mace, Champion of the World. Presented by the Miners of California. This is a brick, and you're another.' The West Coast public assumed, naturally enough, that Mace's boxing days were over and that he was returning to England out of homesickness. In fact, his intentions were different and his destination elsewhere – a third country, neither the UK nor the US but one where he believed that he, a sportsman and entertainer supreme, rather than a bullion baron, could become a Bonanza King.

PART FOUR

THE GLOBETROTTER

(1877–83)

21

The Master of Science

BILL DOHERTY WAS in his tenth year. He'd been taunted by another lad in the neighbourhood and had stood up for himself. He got into a fight and came out with a black eye. He trudged homeward dreading that his father would make trouble for the other boy's family and that, at school, he would be branded a telltale and a cry baby. So, as he made his way along the Geelong Road in Footscray, he vowed silently never to disclose the name of his opponent.

On reaching the Rising Sun Hotel, he went in by the back gate, hoping to avoid his father for as long as possible, but his father, William, had been showing off one of his horses to a stranger. Preoccupied, his father didn't notice his arrival. The stranger did. He looked but said nothing. The impression the stranger gave remained in young Bill's mind for the rest of his life and, over fifty years later, he described it in his autobiography:

> Only a glance did I throw at this man, but so powerful and arresting was his personality that a complete picture of him was engraved instantly upon my mind. I saw that he was well dressed, that his tall hat was new and shining, and that his frock-coat fitted well over square, muscular shoulders. But it was the boldness and the resolute set of his hard, strongly chiselled features that impressed me the most; and when he glanced my way there was a challenge in his direct personal gaze that told me he was a fighter . . . (hardly ever) in any other face have I seen such sheer stark courage and fighting strength.

When Bill's father spotted his son and called him over, he asked who had given him a black eye. Bill said that he got it in a fair fight and that he didn't want to get the other boy into trouble. At once, the grim straight lips of the stranger relaxed into a smile.

'That's the breed!' he exclaimed. 'A fair game scrapper. He'll be a man.'

Bill's father appeared to accept this judgment on his son's escapade and Bill was amazed at his father's deferential attitude, as if to a master in high authority. After all, William Doherty was one of Melbourne's – and Australia's – most prominent citizens. As a hotelier, an expert on horses and a sportsman, he was the friend of politicians and entrepreneurs, but his son had never seen him deferring to them as he did to Jem Mace that summer's day in 1877.

What Mace had noticed about the boy was his tolerance of pain and his code of honour. That was the test of his physical and moral courage; his manliness, in short. What young Bill had noticed was Mace's piercing gaze. Mace had a 1,000-yard stare which he had used all his life, alternately to intimidate and charm.

Bill Doherty Senior's reaction was a miniature of the Australian nation's reaction to Mace from the moment he stepped onto Australian soil, disembarking from the mail-steamer *Zealandia* on 3 March 1877. He was followed everywhere by cheering crowds for weeks on end: he had clearly become an icon of a kind that had not existed before. This was the man who was still acknowledged as Champion of the World and he had announced his intention to make Australia his home. But, if Mace's status had changed since his visit to America, so too had Australia's – and, in particular, that of Melbourne. After the richest seams of gold were exhausted, thousands of people flocked in from the goldfields, and the city grew not only as a port but as a manufacturing centre to service the goldfields and inland towns. As Melbourne rapidly overtook Sydney as Australia's largest city, there was an acute shortage of labour; immigration could not keep up with demand. Trade unionism was very powerful in Victoria and the willingness of the unions to take strike action, combined with economic circumstances, pushed up real wages until they were the highest in the world. Victoria was dubbed 'the working man's paradise'. Such extravagant talk held a kernel of truth. Certainly, leisure hours were longer than elsewhere. The eight-hour day had been fought for and won.

By the late 1870s, Melbourne's population had reached a quarter of a million and was the second-largest of any city in the British

Empire. Only London held more but whereas the poorer inhabitants of the metropolis were tightly packed in often squalid conditions, Melbourne's working class lived in clean, detached cottages, often, thanks to the modern train and tram system which served a wide-spread central area, well away from the smoke amidst which they worked. Although Sydney was somewhat overshadowed by Melbourne, it compared favourably to the English provincial cities in terms of quality of life for working-class people, as did the smaller towns of New South Wales. While life in the outback, on the fringe of the Great Central Desert, was harsh, there was little of the lawlessness which was pervasive in the big cities of the U.S. When men quarrelled, they settled their disputes with fists, not guns and knives.

For years the lack of a clear Australian identity had been commented on by visitors to the Southern continent, as had been differences in attitude between the inhabitants of Victoria and the other colonies. Unlike New South Wales and Tasmania, Victoria had not been founded as a convict settlement and many in Melbourne considered themselves as 'freeborn Englishmen'. This had caused resentment, particularly in New South Wales, where at least a third of the population was of Irish descent. In the 1870s, though, a sports boom galvanised the whole of Australia and sport provided the glue which began to bind Australian society together. Aussies began to see themselves as a people who were healthier and more athletic than the British and Americans. Never before had sport played such a role in the history of a country. What's more, sport was, unlike in England, not lauded by the governing classes as a means of gearing the nation's youth for military combat. Geographically remote, Australia was virtu-ally insulated from war and invasion. Australians did not slavishly follow English traditions in team sports. Some games, such as cricket, were easily transplanted but, equally, there was a variant of football, neither soccer nor American, that would be known as Australian Rules. Australia's favourite sport was horse-racing, above all the Melbourne Cup, which was a focus for gambling, a habit entrenched since the days of transportation. In 1876 the whole of Australia rejoiced at the first of Australia's many sporting successes: the victory of Edward Trickett in the rowing championships of the world. This was soon overshadowed by the impending arrival, early the following year, of the All-England touring cricketers, who were scheduled to play Test matches against an eleven chosen from all the Australian colonies that would take the field under the unifying name of 'Australia'. As Mace headed south across the Pacific, interest in sport was touching fever pitch in the great island continent.

With Australia's legal system being essentially the same as in England, prize-fighting remained against the law in every colony. By now the tragedy at the McLaren–Carstairs fight had been largely forgotten, however, and the old enthusiasm for the ring had returned. Half the pubs in Sydney and Melbourne sported portraits of the epic transatlantic clash for the world championship between Sayers and Heenan and at those same taverns matches were made and wagers laid. The police existed to be outwitted and the roll of the dice remained a symbolic act of defiance against the unjust fate which had brought their fathers and their fathers' fathers from the opposite end of the earth.

In California, Mace had met an English-born Australian who was senior physical training instructor at the San Francisco Olympic Club. William Miller was one of the most formidable all-round athletes of his day. Although only 5ft 9in, he had exceptionally powerful neck, shoulder, chest and upper arm muscles. His skill as a gymnast had impressed the Olympians and Mace could see that Miller was also an outstanding fencer and weightlifter, but his forte was wrestling. Mace was a fine wrestler himself and had seconded the American champion James McLoughlin on the latter's recent visit to Britain to take on Richard Snape, the English champion. Jem knew a good wrestler when he saw one and he considered Miller the best he had ever seen. He told him this and encouraged him to become a professional. Although Miller aspired above all to boxing fame, Mace privately considered he was not nimble enough to reach the highest class. But he praised his intelligent approach.

Mace and Miller sparred at the Olympic Club and this provided Miller with the opportunity to pick up Mace's technical advice. They also discussed Mace's clash with Bill Davis in Virginia City and the relatively objective manner in which it had been decided. Mace went on to recommend Miller to Joe Goss as a sparring partner. Listening with interest to Miller's tales of the sports boom in Australia, and the kind of money to be made in Melbourne, Mace posed the obvious question: 'Why did you leave?'

Miller recounted an intriguing tale: boxing in Australia was dominated by one man, Abe Hicken. As Jem was aware, Hicken was an Englishman. Born in Wolverhampton, he had emerged from Bob Brettle's school of hard knocks in Birmingham and at twenty-three had joined the exodus of English prize-fighters to the USA in 1867. He had claimed the lightweight championship of America and remained undefeated for four years before emigrating to Australia. Now, six years later, he had become a middleweight but he was the self-proclaimed 'Champion of Australia'. Hicken was a clever businessman and had gone into partnership with two London-born Jewish brothers, Joe and Jack Thompson (originally Solomon), who ran a thriving bookmaking firm in Melbourne. Hicken had also invested in hotels and thought nothing of writing cheques for £2,000. He made a point of declaring himself to be a boxer and not a prize-fighter. Crowds would pay just to see boxing exhibitions in theatres and the former Staffordshire errand boy was distributing business cards worded in such a way as to imply that he was the world's foremost exponent of the Marquess of Queensberry Rules.

Hicken was, however, distinctly reluctant to put his proclaimed expertise to the test. His favourite opponent was the expatriate black American, Harry Sallers. Whereas an Englishman such as Hicken had de facto Australian nationality, Sallers did not, so while he could not challenge for the championship of Australia, he was content to earn a good living in exhibitions with Hicken at the Princess Theatre in Melbourne. William Miller, a strict amateur who had no income beyond his wages as a railwayman, had challenged the so-called champion at Hicken's Athletic Hall in Little Collins Street, Melbourne, in a thirty-minute glove contest. The referee gave the decision to Hicken, despite Miller's strong showing in the first half of the bout. The referee had pronounced Hicken 'more entitled for science' – but there was only the referee's word for that and no objective test.

The crafty Hicken had succeeded in getting the press on his side. With the disgruntled Miller about to depart for the US, Hicken's crony, Ned Bittan, wrote a piece in the *Port Philip Herald* deriding Miller's inability put up stake money and suggesting that Miller would be looked on in the States, as he allegedly was in Australia, as 'an overgrown dancing booby'. Doing his best to disregard this insult, Miller made his way to California where his abilities as an extraordinary all-round athlete were speedily recognised. In fact the matter of stake money was not an issue. When Hicken's next challenger, John Christie, came forward, it was proposed that they should box at Wilson's Hippodrome and that the proceeds should go to charities. Their bout was described in the press as 'a genuine glove affair' and not a 'disgraceful exhibition of fisticuffs'. But, in deciding 'who is the more scienced man . . . the matter should not be left to outsiders who . . . are apt to be extremely and unnecessarily liberal to seconds, ring-keepers and others on the stage.'

Such was the account of boxing in Australia which Miller gave to Mace. He did not need to spell out the extent of Hicken's hypocrisy. While feigning concern for charities and his disdain for the London Prize Ring, the self-crowned champ intended to keep his cosy little empire going by ensuring that no 'outsider' (i.e. a person who knew the fight game from within) would officiate, leaving all decisions in the hands of a Hicken appointee who could be relied upon to decide in favour of his patron as being 'more entitled for science'.

Mace's appetite was whetted by the prospect of big money in Australia, but he was also filled with contempt for Hicken. So rich were the pickings in Melbourne that, in order to avoid the possibility of losing his title, Hicken could turn down estimated takings of £350 a night for a challenge with the gloves – but only by using referees who were hand-picked. In fact Hicken was hiding behind phrases such as 'the more scienced man' to disguise that very vagueness in the Queensberry Rules to which Mace objected. Without a clear definition of points-scoring such as he'd insisted on at Virginia City, all decisions would be vitiated by subjectivity.

There was one other matter on which Mace closely questioned Miller: had the old English institution of the boxing booth survived in Australia? The lack of a boxing booth tradition in the USA had been a key factor in dissuading him from staying. Miller replied that there were indeed booths doing good business in Australia and no objection from the authorities. This was a key factor in helping Jem decide where his future lay. There was only one master of boxing science and it was certainly not the shifty Staffordshire swaggerer who had dodged out of America before Billy Edwards had the chance of knocking off his lightweight crown. Mace would go to Australia himself, he would find a means of overthrowing the upstart and, with his days of rough combat on the remote turf of two other continents behind him, would reign supreme in the full house theatres of Melbourne. Nellie wrote to the Ditchams and they responded by inviting Jem, Ellen and herself to stay with them in Sydney until Mace was established and they could move to Melbourne.

Just as he had done five years earlier, Mace left America with mixed feelings. He had learned that Joe Coburn had been sentenced to ten years in jail for an unprovoked assault with intent to murder a New York Police patrolman. His worst enemy had therefore been removed. Nevertheless, Mace had committed his future to Australia and any misgivings he might have had were soon dispelled by the cheering crowds which awaited his arrival in Sydney.

Mace went to Australia not merely as an exhibition boxer but in his capacity as an all-round entertainer. He had long dispensed with the services of Abrahams who, he believed, had not looked after his interests well in America, and now his business manager was a man called Saqui. A contract was negotiated for him to combine boxing, music and statuary with Williams Mammoth Circus, the foremost of its kind in Australia. He opened in Sydney within days of his arrival by performing statuesque illustrations and giving an exhibition of fencing with the talented Scottish swordsman Borthwick Reid. The following week he was in a new role, spending two days posing for the painters at the Sydney School of Arts. While he joked with Nellie about his sudden popularity as a male model, Mace kept a straight face during the sessions and pocketed the easiest fee he had ever earned.

Next, he visited Melbourne. The first ever Test match was played at the Melbourne Cricket Ground between 15 and 19 March 1877 and while Mace's interest in cricket was slight, it was a good opportunity to be seen at an event which had gripped the nation. When asked who he supported, he answered diplomatically: he was, he said, an Englishman by birth and upbringing but had chosen to live in Australia because of the bold spirit of its people. The English batsmen were not as able to deal with Australia's bowlers as he had been in evading the question. Australia won by forty-five runs while Mace relaxed, at the end of an Australian summer, which, as he remarked to Nellie, was equalled only by that in California.

* * *

No one welcomed Mace's arrival in Australia more keenly than Larry Foley, a twenty-eight-year-old fighter from Bathurst in New South Wales. At 5ft 8in and weighing no more than 154lb, Foley was a middleweight. His Irish family wanted him to train for the priesthood but he rebelled and went to Sydney, where he worked as a builder's labourer. He encountered sporadic outbursts of sectarian strife within the Irish-Australian community, and when Sandy Ross, a prize-fighter of Ulster stock, made disparaging remarks about 'Fenians', Foley, as a Roman Catholic, was prevailed on to challenge him. Although only seventeen, he agreed and fought for seventy-one bitter rounds at Como in New South Wales in October 1866. Both men were fiercely battered, but Foley was the winner. Over the next ten years, he fought successfully more than a dozen times, mostly prize-fights in the outback of New South Wales but also a couple of street encounters in Sydney, one of them against Ross – whom he again defeated. Foley was disregarded by Abe Hicken though, who derided his technique.

As soon as Mace arrived, Foley sought him out, eager for tuition in 'scientific boxing', a phrase in widespread use. While Foley's family were wary of Mace as an Englishman, that cut no ice with Larry. He would judge as he found and, on meeting Jem, was impressed by his bold, open-minded and friendly attitude. For his part, Jem, while aware of the Foley family's Irish Nationalist views, found Larry the epitome of the 'fair dinkum Aussie sport' of whom Miller had spoken. He decided to test Foley in an exhibition in Sydney before the month was out. There was a good crowd and the combatants were a contrast in every way: Mace, at forty-five, was balding and had put on weight; Foley, seventeen years younger, was lean and trim with a shock of thick wavy hair and mutton chop whiskers. Although Foley's technique was basic, Mace noticed, even as he jabbed, that the young man was learning. Of his bravery there was no doubt. He did not flinch though he was hit harder than ever before.

After the bout, Mace agreed to teach Foley to box scientifically but told him he intended to settle in Melbourne and open a tavern there. Mace agreed to take him on as a barman with boxing lessons in his spare time. Although few would have guessed it at the time, Jem Mace and Larry Foley would become close friends and their partnership would be critically important in the history of the fight game.

During his first full month in Australia, Mace boxed twenty exhibitions for Williams, three-quarters of them in Sydney and the rest in the industrial town of Newcastle in New South Wales. The lucrative contract was enhanced by full houses. Foley boxed one more exhibition but Mace's main opponent was Scots-born John Christie, who had built a reputation as a fine all-round athlete, as an excellent rower and promising glove boxer. Unusually, Christie was a former Melbourne police detective, a colourful character who had resigned from the force after criticism of his unorthodox methods.

Next a ten-bout residency was secured at the Princess Theatre in Melbourne. Christie took the ring with Mace seven times and Harry Sallars once. On the other two occasions he faced Jack Thompson, the younger of the two bookmaker brothers who were in partnership with Hicken. In June, John Christie met Jack Thompson in a prize-fight at Red Bluff in Victoria after the police had unsuccessfully tried to prevent it. Thompson delivered a beating so severe that the referee, Tom Curran, himself seized a sponge from one of Christie's seconds and threw it in, a rare event indeed in the annals of the Prize Ring. Mace was present and he decided that Christie lacked heart and would never be a viable challenger to Hicken.

Mace was, however, determined that Hicken must be pressurised into a prize-fight. Jem had already publicly stated that what held good in England and America must hold good in Australia equally. Namely, the championship must be won on open turf under the rules of the London Prize Ring. If Australia did not follow suit, Mace claimed, she would implicitly be accepting an inferior place in the pecking order of the three countries. Although he was thirteen years older than Hicken, he was still prepared to take on the errant ex-errand boy but believed that it would be better if Hicken was challenged by an Australian rather than another Englishman. In September and early October, Mace and Foley shared a three-bout residency at the Victoria

Theatre in Sydney. Mace, as a man of the stage, was delighted to be starring in theatres but, beyond that, the opportunity to demonstrate scientific boxing on stage was crucial in raising the public profile of this new sport, which could be enjoyed in comfort, in the evening, in gas-lit halls, without fear of police intervention and with women prominent in the audience.

On 8 December 1877, a school of boxing was opened at Mace's Athletic Hall in Melbourne. Mace was using his new-found wealth to copy what Charles Melly and John Hulley had done at Myrtle Street in Liverpool, but this time he would be the instructor and the sole proprietor of the establishment, supervising not only boxing instruction but also running, wrestling and fencing. At the close of a year in which he had earned more than ever before, Mace began to buy racehorses and sent them to be trained by Tom White. Still, fortune refused to smile on him at the track and, as at Saratoga, his inclination for high-stakes gambling resurfaced – even if, in Australia, it was necessarily restricted to betting on the nags. Jem was always happy where horses were and, side by side with Bill Doherty Senior, he led the hunt at the main hare coursing meet.

The Maces moved into family quarters at the Athletic Hall. Jem and Nellie were happy in every way, except that she missed her son John. She wrote to the McCalls in Liverpool and explained the reasons why she believed her future now lay in Melbourne, rather than San Francisco, but whereas Mace had stated publicly that he would remain in Australia, Nellie was privately more cautious. She asked her sister and brother-in-law if they would look after John for a couple of years more and they agreed.

Besides his exhibitions and the fees collected from the many young men eager to enrol at the Athletic Hall, Mace founded a travelling boxing booth with himself, Foley and his second cousins, Bill and Tom Ditcham, the featured boxers. He toured throughout Victoria and New South Wales and his invitation to all comers, 'Who'll take a glove?' became well known in the two major colonies. By the following March, a quarrel erupted between Hicken and the Thompson brothers. All three lost heavily as a result of a streak of unexpected results at the racetrack but while the Thompsons paid out promptly to their punters, Hicken did not. He had shares in Joe Thompson's lavish hotel in Albert Street, the Don Juan House, named after Joe's Melbourne Cup-winning horse, and rather than pay off his creditors from funds set aside by bookies for such eventualities, he withdrew the value of the shares in the Don Juan House from a secret bank account and fled to Sydney. Joe Thompson could not obtain immediate redress against Hicken because New South Wales was a different jurisdiction to Victoria. A burly, hot-tempered man nicknamed 'The Leviathan', he was apoplectic with rage and swore that he would find a means of getting back at the bunking Britisher. Referring to his younger brother Jack as well as himself, he snarled, 'We bloody made Hicken when he came here from America and this is how he repays us. But he'll pay the price for his beastly ingratitude.'

At this stage Mace intervened and offered Jack Thompson an exclusive two-year deal to fight exhibitions with him at Mace's Athletic Hall. Between March 1878 and March 1880, Mace and Thompson took the ring forty-one times. Despite the repetitious nature of the spectacle, very good business was done and by now there was a definite fight public in Melbourne, a hardcore of enthusiasts who did not tire of seeing glove encounters. Behind this facade, Mace had laid a careful plan, one which went down a treat with Joe Thompson when Jack secured his brother's approval. The constant appearance of Jack Thompson in the ring, while the so-called champion Hicken remained inactive, would lead to pressure for a title fight between the two. Hicken would be bound to give in to this pressure sooner or later or lose his status as Australia's foremost 'scientific boxer' and the wealth which he derived from it. But at the end of the day, it would be Foley who would challenge Hicken. Hicken knew Thompson's style inside-out, whereas he scarcely knew Foley's.

For the better part of twelve months, Mace kept Foley under wraps in the privacy of the boxing booth. The aim was twofold: to bluff Hicken and to increase the eventual odds against Foley in preparation for a gambling coup. Mace taught Larry Foley everything he knew and his pupil, an intelligent and patient man, proved an excellent learner. He would closely watch while Mace demonstrated and, when the pair sparred, he had a special motive in adapting to Mace's methods – if he failed to read the older man's intentions, his head would be rocked back by a jolting left jab. Such was the penalty for any lapse in concentration! Mace also taught Foley to fence, for he believed it was vital training for a boxer. 'You have to guard your entire torso in fencing, not just above the waist,' he would point out, adding that a fencer had only one sword arm not the two pistons of a fighter. Learning the more difficult skill of the swordsman made boxing seem easier and increased confidence. What's more, fencing stressed reflexes, agility and timing, as Mace believed true boxing should. Boxing was not, as its opponents believed – and some of its so-called practitioners too – an exercise in brute force typified by wildly flailing fists. The stance was crucially important. 'The eye, the left hand and the left foot should always be in line,' he stressed, as if in response to the cry of 'On guard!'

When training Foley, Mace went through all the main shots he would need for an effective challenge to Hicken under the rules of the LPR. First was the left jab, brought in by Langham but perfected by Mace. It was used to keep an opponent at bay, to find range and to blind the adversary. Another vital punch was the uppercut, which had been invented as early as the beginning of the century by Dutch Sam, a brilliant Jewish boxer from Whitechapel who became the lightweight champion of England. The third was a Mace speciality: the strike to the mark executed with a shift of feet. Then there was the right cross, but, as Mace emphasised, although this was well suited to glove combat, it should be used in the Prize Ring only to finish off a blinded and staggering man. If used prematurely, there was a great danger to the knuckles of naked fists.

In late November 1878, Foley boxed an exhibition with Jem at Mace's Athletic Hall. This was well publicised and Foley made an excellent showing, albeit with Mace contriving to make him look even better than he was. Such was the public interest aroused by the Mace–Foley bout that Foley was empowered to issue Hicken with a challenge. The self-proclaimed Champion of Australia could scarcely ignore it without losing face and jeopardising any future income he might earn by his vaunted boxing skill. Articles were signed and both Hicken and Foley went into training.

By this time, Mace had cemented a new partnership with the Thompson brothers. A splendid hotel was bought between the three of them in Bourke Street, Melbourne, known as the Victoria

Racing Club Hotel, and Mace and his family promptly moved in. The stakes for the Hicken–Foley prize-fight were £1,000 a side, Hicken being his own backer while Joe Thompson funded Foley, who was seconded by Mace. Initially, betting heavily favoured the more experienced Hicken by 3 to 1. The date was set for the bare-knuckle clash which would decide not merely the Championship of Australia. It would also be the means whereby Mace's hidden agenda would be put into effect – namely of dethroning Hicken as the effective kingpin of all forms of boxing Down Under. It would take place on 20 March 1879, and crowds of fight enthusiasts from Sydney and Melbourne would wish to attend, so great care was needed in finding a place where the historic fight could take place without police interference.

On the eve of battle, the principals set off by train from Melbourne and mustered in the small town of Echuca, chosen because it lay on the bank of the Murray River, which separated Victoria and New South Wales. The plan was the time-honoured one of confusing the authorities by convening at a place where at least two jurisdictions met. Rumours were spread among the townsfolk that the mill would come off on the New South Wales side at Goulburn Junction, and a detachment of troopers set off in that direction. In fact, the principals left Echuca at night and travelled along wooded tracks following sundry bends in the river. This made pursuit difficult for the Victoria police, who were in any case caught off guard. Only one officer, Sergeant O'Meara, had succeeded in keeping track when, at dawn on the next day, the ring was pitched on the NSW side of the border between Echuca and Moama known as Murrumbidgee Reef. O'Meara bellowed that he could not permit a breach of the peace. All must desist at once. If not, his evidence would, when matters came to court, secure convictions.

Mace relished the opportunity to humiliate a policeman. He approached O'Meara face-to-face and stared him out. Speaking quietly but menacingly, he told O'Meara that no Victorian police officer had the authority to even issue such a command while on the territory of New South Wales. If matters did indeed come to court, then, Mace bluffed, his lawyers would allege that the sergeant had acted outside his jurisdiction. He then invited the speechless copper to 'sit down and enjoy the show'.

The 'show' lasted an hour and twenty minutes, with the two men adopting different tactics. Hicken struck repeatedly at the body while Foley employed a relentless and highly effective left jab. Despite Hicken's bravery, Foley gradually got the better of him and proceeded, in the classic manner of Langham, to close Hicken's eyes one after the other. He was so badly punished that his seconds threw in the sponge. Over 100 spectators had seen the title change hands and behaved themselves impeccably.

After an excited crowd had seen their train off from Echuca, Foley made several triumphant stops on the way back to Melbourne while the badly disfigured Hicken was closeted with his seconds in a compartment with the blinds drawn. Despite media attempts to portray the fight as an example of rivalry between New South Wales and Victoria, the implications of the Australian-born Foley defeating the Englishman Hicken could not be disguised, as the shouts at several train stops along the line illustrated.

'Good on yer, Larry!'

'You've shown 'em what an Aussie can do!'

'Advance Australia!'

The latter nationalistic slogan was disliked and feared by the British colonial authorities. Among the cries of 'Three cheers for Larry Foley!' were also many calls for 'Three cheers for Jem Mace!' Foley had improved dramatically as a fighter and, as journalists who were in the know correctly wrote, that improvement was due principally to 'the valuable tutorship of such a consummate boxer and perfect master of the ring as Jem Mace'.

Foley, Mace and the Thompson brothers went to the Victoria Racing Club Hotel to celebrate victory, but a few days later warrants were issued for their arrest on charges of conspiracy to bring about a breach of the peace. After receiving a tip-off, Mace and the Thompsons decided to accompany Foley to his home in Sydney, where he lived with his wife Mary. Once back in New South Wales, Laurence Foley was summoned to court on a charge of assaulting Abraham Hicken and causing him actual bodily harm, but the case was dismissed in court due to lack of evidence. Back in Victoria, the public outcry against the police over the warrant for Mace's arrest was so great that all charges were dropped.

A fortnight after the fight, in Sydney, Mace, Foley and Jack Thompson starred in a production of *The Railroad to Ruin* by the French dramatist Dion Boucicault, a play about a retired prize-fighter and adapted to include actual scenes of glove boxing. A largely working-class crowd packed the Victoria Theatre and, to widespread surprise, a police superintendent and two MPs were seen in a box enjoying the evening's performance. Ten days later, Mace and Foley put on an exhibition in the Sydney Guild Hall, a clear sign of official Australia's embrace of boxing in deference to popular opinion. Mace had succeeded in eliminating Hicken as a serious rival to his dominance of all aspects of the sport in Australia. Hicken, apparently chastened by his downfall at Echuca, continued to box exhibitions for many years but was careful to adopt a lower profile. Mace had achieved a status in Australia which matched that which Langham had once enjoyed in England, and was lionised in the newspapers of Sydney and Melbourne.

Even as he approached fifty, Mace was still probably capable of beating any man in the world if he were to choose to accept a challenge, but he had publicly declared that he would not enter the Prize Ring again. He contented himself by implying that Foley, his student, was his effective successor. This was no far-fetched claim. Foley was the proven Champion of Australia. In England, prize-fighting was defunct and boxing a purely amateur sport. In the United States, Goss was still the titleholder but in the two-and-a-half years since taking the title from Allen, he had not entered the Prize Ring. He had, however, boxed for points against his sparring partner. In a bout which closely followed the pattern set by Mace at Virginia City, but at greater length, they boxed thirty gloved rounds at Baltimore in December 1878. The time-frame followed the strict Queensberry pattern but it was agreed that face-hits would be counted to decide the winner. By a total of twenty-two points to nineteen, Goss was defeated by his sparring partner. And who was that sparring partner? None other than 'Professor' (as the Americans now called him) William Miller, the champion wrestler who had learned a great deal in a short space of time in San Francisco – both by sparring with and talking to Jem Mace.

Foley's defeat of Hicken was scarcely mentioned in the American press, whereas the *New York Times* reported the boxing bout between

Goss and Miller. Neither the *Times* nor any other newspaper would later realise that Goss–Miller followed Mace–Davis as an important step in the evolution of boxing from prize-fighting. In Australia, however, Mace was quick to inform the sporting public of the success of their countryman Miller, but he was obliged to add that, with interest in prize-fighting dwindling in America, backers could not be found to put up the stakes for a title fight between Goss and Miller.

As for Foley, he had fulfilled all Mace's expectations and proved his worth under testing conditions. With Mace's blessing, Foley used his winnings to set himself up in a pub in Sydney, the White Horse, where he would give boxing lessons. So separate were the two main cities of Australia that he would be no rival to Mace. If Foley was now a Bachelor of Scientific Boxing in Sydney, Mace remained a Master of Science in Melbourne.

22

A Belt of Virgin Gold

THE BOOTH WAS doing a one-night show in the little bush village and had just finished the last performance when four armed men on horseback rode up. The small crowd looked uneasy but not a word was spoken. Then two men faced each other: the balding forty-eight-year-old English entertainer and the visitor, a twenty-five-year-old Australian bushranger with a bushy black beard, the leader of the gang. The Australian asked for the Englishman by name.

'That's me. How may I help you?'

'We want to see your show and we've ridden forty miles to do so.'

'I regret to say that our regular evening performance is already finished. Both my men and I are tired and are thus not able to give a second show.'

'Oh, stow your gab! I didn't ask for a bloody speech. I asked to see your show. We want to see it and what's more we *mean* to see it. So you get a bloody move on and be quick about it. I'm not a man that's used to being trifled with. How much is the charge?'

'Ten pounds is the price for a private performance, which is what you are asking for.'

'All right. Here's your money. Now get to work!'

After that, Jem Mace's troupe gave their regular show – boxing, wrestling and fencing. The whole time the four grim-faced men sat silently on horseback, watching. Not once did they applaud and only the intensity of their gaze revealed the level of their interest. When it was all over, the leader rode over, thanked the Englishman and shook hands with him.

'You're a celebrity, Mister Mace,' he said, 'and so am I. We ought to be each of us proud to have met the other.'

Then he swung his horse round and, followed by the other three, galloped off in the twilight. Jem Mace had just met the Kelly Gang:

Ned Kelly, their leader, his brother Dan, Joe Byrne and Steve Hart. Ned Kelly was by now rivalling Mace as the most famous man in Australia, wanted with others for the murder of three police officers, bank robberies and hostage-taking. Under the Felons Apprehension Act, his gang had been declared outlaws, with anyone having the right to shoot them on sight. A bounty of £2,000 lay on each of their heads.

Ned Kelly had always been keen on prize-fighting and, at the age of nineteen, had entered the ring to defeat Isaiah Wright in twenty rounds. He had been fascinated by news of the championship clash at Echuca and intended to watch it until he learned of a heavy police presence in the area. Shortly after Echuca, the Kelly Gang began to keep a relatively low profile and it would be another sixteen months before they came into conflict with the law again. Meanwhile, they roamed across an area in northeast Victoria and southeast New South Wales which was about half the size of England. They were either sheltered by sympathisers or they demanded supplies from isolated bush townships, such as the one Mace's boxing booth had been visiting.

Despite Kelly's sullen demeanour, fingering his revolver and using blunt language, Mace had stood up to four armed men on horseback who were initially hostile – and he had done so in a calm manner without the slightest sign of rudeness. Obviously Kelly held the whip hand and insisted on having his own way, but Mace's presence of mind appears to have impressed him. All his life Kelly, the son of Irish parents, his father a transported convict, had been inculcated with the belief that all Englishmen were detestable. He was well-versed in Irish history and knew all about the political implications of the Great Famine of 1845–9. His lengthy publication *The Jerilderie Letter* railed against the treatment of Irish Catholics by the colonial powers and the police of Victoria and New South Wales, many of whom were of Irish Protestant descent and affiliated to the Orange Order. Kelly also knew about the history of the Prize Ring and the alleged injustice to Heenan in his fight with Sayers. Kelly seems to have begun to alter his attitude to Mace after Echuca. Thanks chiefly to Mace's boxing tuition, Larry Foley, an Irish-Australian and the son of pro-Fenian parents, had beaten the Englishman Hicken.

The Mace–Kelly meeting was an example of how Mace's

manly but courteous bearing could defuse the hostility previously borne to him on account of his nationality. Like Kelly, he was an outlaw and, like Kelly, he had been the victim of police persecution. He believed that some of the charges against Kelly were trumped up but dismissed talk of Kelly being a Robin Hood-style friend to the poor. He had seen for himself the intimidating effect that the sudden arrival of Kelly's Gang had on the ordinary inhabitants of a remote township.

When Kelly resurfaced in June of the following year, his three accomplices died and he was arrested during a police siege of an inn where some sixty hostages were being held. For five months these events, plus the inquiry into police conduct, Kelly's trial and conviction, and a subsequent mass petition against the imposition of the death sentence, dominated all other news in Australia. Then, in November 1880, Kelly was executed in Melbourne Gaol.

A couple of months after Echuca, Mace received an unwelcome reminder of his first family in England when his two oldest sons, Alfred and James, arrived in Australia. They were not there to see their father but to preach the gospel according to the Plymouth Brethren. As they saw it, Jem was steeped in sin. As always, he was involved with beastly prize-fighting, with the demon drink and with devilish gambling, and even though it did not seem that he was fornicating, this was probably only a temporary lull in his lust – though the brothers did not publicly condemn their father by name. Their paths would cross from time to time in future years and his reaction to their activities varied from initial anger to subsequent amusement, but mostly indifference.

Of the two, it was James for whom Mace had least time. At least Alfred had made his own way, albeit into what Mace considered an obnoxious sect. Alfred was bold, forthright and outspoken, while James had been converted by his brother and was, felt his father, a meek character. James had just turned twenty-one and was able to commence his mission as Alfred had done four years earlier. By now Alfred was a married man; he had wed a farmer's daughter from Rutland who was eight years his elder and equally devoted to the word of the Lord. Finding Australia less than carried away by his preaching, Alf's evangelical path took him to Huddersfield where his daughter Eliza was born. She was not Mace's first grandchild. His daughter Adelaide had married a commercial clerk in Dulwich and their first daughter, Eleanor, was born in 1880.

Australia saw the high watermark of Mace's wealth. In addition to his ownership of the Victoria Racing Club Hotel, of which he later acquired sole control, there was his acquisition, on the advice of his business managers, of shares in gold-mining companies. Due to his lavish spending and reckless gambling on the horses in the mining town of Ballarat, his wealth fluctuated and it was hard to be accurate about the exact state of his finances. More significant than the actual stake money which he won in the ring were the successful wagers he made on himself to win, the income from his exhibitions and admission to his boxing booth, the contracts offered by circuses and the various and sumptuous belts which were presented to him.

Mace remained careless over money – typified by his laxity over the till at the tavern where, probably, Foley had been the only honest barman – and it was this rather than any secretive tendency which made him vague in his knowledge of his precise wealth. In future years, he would claim that, at the peak of his fame in Melbourne, he could have drawn a cheque for £75,000. Estimates from American sources put his total career winnings at $1,500,000.★

At the end of three years in Australia, having spent a month in Hobart, Tasmania, giving exhibitions, followed by the last two of his contracted appearances with Jack Thompson, Mace did not box in public for a couple of years apart from with his booth. There was one exception: when he was guest of honour at an exhibition given by Australia's lightweight champion Jack King in Melbourne in 1881. After finishing three rounds with King, Mace casually remarked that he'd been 'playing light'.

King replied, 'Thank God I wasn't in the ring with you in the sixties – when you used to play heavy!'

During these years of fistic inactivity in Australia, Mace's energies were absorbed by such pursuits as hunting with hounds and the breeding of bulldogs. He often spoke of his affinity with such animals, and in his early days in Norfolk a bulldog would keep him company on his travels.

★ Approximately $40 million today.

He continued to give instruction in boxing at Mace's Athletic Hall, where he hoped to find a young fighter of outstanding potential whom he could then tutor in his own style. He had no intention of retiring from the world of the ring and, by now fifty years of age, was still remarkably fit and mobile with all his skills and ringcraft intact. His speed was no longer what it had been though, nor his stamina. His aim was to be recognised as the finest teacher and trainer in the world, just as he had been the outstanding fighter, but much would depend on the quality of the raw material with which he had to work.

In Melbourne, the best prospect to come through his doors was Bill Farnan, who was groomed as a boxer rather than a prize-fighter from the start. Although it was some five years after Echuca before the authorities succeeded in suppressing bareknuckle fighting in Australia, Mace kept clear of it. He had used LPR rules to depose Hicken, via his protégé Larry Foley, from the Australian championship. He had no further use for them. In fact it was Mace, together with Joe Thompson, who went so far as successfully to lobby the government of Victoria to enforce boxing on Queensberry Rules only. This was highly significant – the first legalisation of the sport of gloved boxing anywhere in the world.

As for Farnan, he was essentially a middleweight, only 5ft 8in tall. His forte was his powerful punching and he made his name at Mace's Athletic Hall with a series of knockout victories in bouts which were variants on the Queensberry format. With Foley inactive in the ring, it was agreed that a glove match between Farnan and Charlie Richardson would decide his successor as Australian champion – another first for Australia, ahead of both America and England, both still wedded to the ways of the past. In February 1881, Farnan knocked out Richardson in Melbourne, but Mace did not consider Farnan as a model of the correct style in boxing: he relied on body punching and, though tough and brave, did not have the skill to jab, hit and get away. He had not come under Mace's coaching until he was twenty-seven, much later than the optimum age, and he was dependent on his job in Langland's Foundry in Melbourne, so could only train for a week before a bout. This was nowhere near long enough for him to be schooled in the essential skills so that they became automatic. Farnan, strong but limited, was as good a fighter as Mace would work with directly in Melbourne.

In Sydney, Foley was more fortunate. Living conditions were tougher than in Melbourne and young men were soon queuing up at Foley's White Horse in the hope of learning the style which had made its proprietor a champion and which they hoped would lift them out of dire poverty. The style Foley taught was exactly what Mace had imparted to him, the difference being that Foley was an exceptionally patient man, whereas Mace, like many other great sportsmen, sometimes despaired at the slowness of others to see what was second nature to him. Foley, far less gifted, was ideally suited to teach. There was little rivalry between Foley and Mace. If Foley believed he had an outstanding prospect, he would inform Mace and wait for the master to come to Sydney to give his assessment. Then Mace and Foley would spar together and the young hopeful was told to sit and watch, to learn and inwardly to digest.

The first of the new generation was Mick Dooley. Of Irish descent, Dooley had moved to Sydney from Yellow Rock in New South Wales. He was a natural heavyweight, standing 6ft tall and weighing 182lb. From the day of Dooley's arrival at the White Horse, Foley knew he had got an outstanding talent. Dooley was not merely athletic but had an effortless grace, like that of a dancer. He proved an adept pupil and it was not long before he had mastered the left jab which, given the length of his reach, was a particularly effective weapon. He stood bolt upright to maximise his advantage.

Dooley was only eighteen when Mace first saw him. The Sydney lad's skill was obvious but Mace was determined to test his courage. The youngster was ordered into the ring with Mace, who unleashed a series of body blows as hard as he had struck since leaving America. Dooley didn't flinch. The test passed, he was given a full course of tuition in the Mace style of boxing, with Mace remarking to Foley that Mick reminded him of himself when he was young, except that the Australian lad was several inches taller. As Langham had done in his case, Mace kept him under wraps until he was fully schooled. Although Dooley sparred countless rounds at the White Horse, it would be three years before he made his professional debut. He would do so as a glove fighter.

Frank Slavin's background was similar to Dooley's. A blacksmith from Maitland in New South Wales, Francis Patrick Slavin had Irish parents and was known as 'Paddy'. He was 6ft but of very lean build, so much so that his nickname was 'Cornstalk'. Even at nineteen, Slavin had a boldness and confidence which Dooley lacked. With deep-set eyes below a shock of spiky red hair, and a handlebar moustache, Slavin cut an intimidating figure. He moved fast and had a tremendous, raking punch with which he delivered ruthless body shots. There would be no need to test Slavin's courage or keep him under wraps – he was allowed to go north to Queensland where bareknuckle fighting had not yet been suppressed.

If Dooley and Slavin were precisely the sort of lads who could be expected to come knocking on the door of the White Horse, Peter Jackson was as unexpected an arrival at Foley's boxing school as could be imagined. Jackson had been born in the West Indies. The Caribbean island of St Croix lay 9,000 miles from Australia. Situated south and east of Puerto Rico, it was a Danish colony at the time of his birth in 1861, although it would later become part of the U.S. Virgin Islands. Jackson was born in Frederiksted. His father was, unlike millions of black Americans at the time, born a free man. Denmark's policy was well in advance of any other European or former European country and slavery had been abolished at the beginning of the nineteenth century. Jackson's father was a self-employed carpenter who had reason to believe that his Afro-Caribbean ancestors had moved to St Croix from an English-speaking colony. English was exclusively spoken in Peter's home, although at school he was taught in Danish.

At seventeen, Jackson joined the crew of a ship sailing out of New York bound for Sydney. He found work there, labouring in an orchard by day and working as a hotel waiter in the evening. Later he would alternate between being a wharf labourer and a seafarer. He came to the notice of the American shipowner Clay Callahan as a result of his prowess as a swimmer and diver. Callahan was a successful businessman in Sydney and a keen boxing enthusiast. He persuaded Jackson to join in shipboard bouts with other crew members and was so impressed that he took him to the White Horse and introduced him to Foley.

An astonished Foley had never seen any man more naturally suited to boxing than the nineteen-year-old, who sparred with other young hopefuls in the gym. At 6ft 1½in tall and weighing 200lb, Jackson had a sculpted physique with wide shoulders, a deep chest and a narrow waist. His 77½in reach was unusually long and he was remarkably light on his feet for a heavyweight, standing up naturally on his toes with his weight on the back foot without even having to be taught this classic Macean stance. He was also the possessor of a powerful left hand punch.

The next day he arrived with a pair of boxing gloves. Shrewdly, he did not bring the boxing instruction manual he had found in a Sydney bookshop – it had not been written by Foley or Mace. Larry liked the intelligent, polite and attentive student. He asked him about his background but Jackson did not elaborate. He regarded himself as an Australian now, he said, and in what he reckoned was true Aussie fashion, sought to demonstrate this by downing pints of beer and placing bets on the horses.

Mace was asked to come north and give his verdict. He was refreshingly free of racism for a man of his epoch and had fought against, but also got on well with, Bob Travers in England and Harry Sallers in Australia. He owed his first break in showbusiness to Pablo Fanque and his attitude towards black people was positive. Jackson was told to sit down in the gym and watch Mace spar with Foley. Mace noted that, unlike other pupils whose concentration lapsed from time to time, Jackson followed every move with rapt attention and was respectful without being deferential. Clearly such a gifted lad and one so enthralled with boxing was an outstanding prospect. Mace and Foley took Jackson aside and he was shown Foley's belt of virgin gold, presented to him by Cohen's jewellers of Sydney to designate his championship victory over Hicken. Mace told Jackson that he would wear it one day – provided he undertook a full course of tuition at the White Horse. Elated by this compliment from the man he knew to be the world's finest boxer, Peter was ready to do just that. Mace and Foley decided that, as with Dooley, he should be kept under wraps for a couple of years. What's more, Jackson was to be schooled purely as a glove fighter and not as a pugilist.

In the latter half of 1881, Mace was beginning to lose his enthusiasm for his Athletic Hall in Melbourne. Having quarrelled with his first Australian business manager, who, he would later allege, had mismanaged his finances, he took his booth on tour deep into the outback and then beyond Broken Hill to the fringes of the Stuart Desert, where aboriginal Australians watched the show with fascination. He did not begrudge Foley his success at the White Horse. Sydney was a rougher and tougher city than Melbourne and the conditions bred potentially good boxers. Mace was gratified by his success in nurturing Foley, who had now exceeded all expectations as a disciple. At least one of Dooley, Slavin and Jackson would, he felt, emerge as an outstanding boxer but it would be Foley who would be their trainer, not him. With crowds of young hopefuls coming in every day to box in the White Horse, the place became the first true boxing gym for aspiring professionals.★

Looking for new worlds to conquer, Mace began to consider New Zealand. Situated fully 1,000 miles east of Australia, its two English colonies of North Island and South Island now beckoned. Nellie was taken aback when he told her. She saw for the first time how the spirit of adventure ruled his soul. What lay ahead in New Zealand she couldn't be sure. It was an undeveloped land and Jem was a man of both fame and fortune in Australia. She was expecting to make arrangements for her eleven-year-old son John to be placed aboard ship in Liverpool for the voyage which would reunite them; now she was obliged to write to her sister and brother-in-law that New Zealand had replaced Australia as her temporary homeland, just as Australia had replaced California. The McCalls were very understanding. John was no trouble at all to them and Annie was very fond of him. Stifling her doubts, Nellie acquiesced in the Maces' move to New Zealand.

In November 1881, at the Theatre Royal, Melbourne, George Coppin formally presented Mace with a belt of virgin gold subscribed by the miners of Bendigo and Ballarat, in tribute to his work in establishing the sport of boxing on the continent of Australia. Yet his final months in Australia saw him under something of a cloud, due

---

★ The White Horse was the distant ancestor of America's great boxing gyms of the twentieth century, such as Stillman's in New York and the Kronk in Detroit. Foley became the first of the great boxing trainers, a pioneer of the art which would eventually produce such masters as Charlie Goldman, Eddie Futch and Emanuel Steward.

partly to his defiant attitude to legal norms but also to his friendship with John Christie, the renegade ex-policeman and now professional boxer. Mace and Christie had their own methods for dealing with the larrikin gangs who terrorized parts of Melbourne. One night, disguised, they went to Little Bourke Street and pretended to be drunk. Thugs attacked them whereupon the boxers abruptly 'sobered up', handed out good hidings and routed their assailants. As news of this episode became known, the general public applauded but the Melbourne Police did not. Whether the police developed a grudge against Mace for taking the law into his own hands is uncertain but his hotel was later raided. In February 1882 he was heavily fined for allowing illegal gambling on the premises. The hotel remained in his ownership but he was obliged to let it.

On 7 March 1882, Mace set out on the *Roturoa* bound for Auckland. He may well have reflected that, in Mick Dooley, Frank Slavin and Peter Jackson, he and Foley had discovered three brilliant young boxers who, without need of a career in bareknuckle fighting, would soon compete with one another, with the gloves, for the championship of Australia. In a sense, this trio were virgin gold indeed.

23

The Terror and the Strong Boy

THE LAD WHO stepped through the ropes looked as if his body had been sculpted by a drunken Michelangelo. The sledge-hammer shoulders and barrel chest tapered in boxer style to a narrow waist but the imposing upper body sat above two spindle-shanked, knock-kneed, pigeon-toed legs which seemed barely capable of supporting it. The shins were proportionately short compared to the thighbones. His chin receded below a protruding nose and his pallid facial skin was covered in freckles. At nineteen, his cropped ginger hair was already receding, with wisps of fringe plastered to the top of his forehead. He moved flat-footed in a kind of uneasy shuffle. At ringside, in the Theatre Royal at Timaru, came half-suppressed guffaws – but none of them came from those who had already seen him fight.

Bob Fitzsimmons did not rush from his seat when the bell sounded. He shambled towards the centre of the ring and waited for his opponent to come at him. Junior Slade, unlike Bob, was a New Zealander born and bred. He was taller and broader and seemed stronger. As Slade swung wildly, Bob dodged the blow. Then he countered with a left and followed up with a hard right. By the end of the round he was clearly on top. He took his opponent apart in the second, raining left and right hands to the body and driving Slade to the ropes. Fitzsimmons's mouth was set tight, his stare cold. He pummelled Slade who, pinned on the ropes, had nowhere to fall. The referee stepped between them and, while firmly warning off Fitzsimmons from delivering a further blow, raised his arm as the winner. The nineteen-year-old angrily broke free. He wanted to knock out his opponent and hadn't been permitted to do so. A furious row broke out and others leaped into the ring. Fitzsimmons raised his gloves as if to strike the referee. Suddenly the hot-tempered youngster doubled up in pain. The referee – none other than Jem Mace – had shifted his body weight to the right and driven a left into Fitzsimmons' body just below the centre of the ribcage. Fitz was lucky that the punch was not delivered with full force, otherwise he would have been helpless on the canvas. After he had recovered, he apologised to Mace and was duly declared to have beaten Junior Slade – 'the referee having stopped the fight to avoid further punishment'. This was the earliest significant instance in boxing history of a TKO. It also marked the transfer of a historic prize-fighting blow, invented by Jack Broughton in the eighteenth century and perfected by Mace, to the arsenal of a modern gloved boxer. Fitzsimmons would never forget that punch, he would work on it himself and, fourteen years later, astound the fistic world with it.

When Mace arrived in New Zealand, he launched into a full programme of exhibitions which, as in Australia five years earlier, attracted full houses. Between March and December 1882, he fought sixty-eight times, often twice on one day and usually with barely a day or two break. It was not only the theatre in Timaru which spelt out boxing's new-found acceptability under Mace; as a spectacle, it was being assimilated more and more to the world of the theatre and even the municipal hall. He appeared in Auckland, Wellington, Masterton, Greytown, Thames, Christchurch, Dunedin and Oamaru. What's more, he combined his policy of presenting boxing with other sports and with theatrical acts. Among his accompanists were an Irish comedian, a balladeer, a 'lightning sketcher' and 'Nellie Mace, the charming serio-comic singer'.

Jem and Nellie were captivated with the beauty of New Zealand, seen from their private railway compartment as they commuted between the larger cities. Jem was fascinated by the volcanic landscapes in the North Island while Nellie admired the great Alpine mountains in the South. Beginning in the North Island, Mace was accompanied by other boxers and wrestlers, the most notable being an old friend he had invited to join him: William Miller, the Australian he first met in San Francisco and who had put him wise to the potential mint of money that awaited him in Melbourne. Miller, sporting his American monicker of 'Professor', had returned to Australia two years earlier after four years in the States. He was quite some acquisition for Mace's troupe because, in addition to his creditable boxing skills, he had while in the States defeated Theobald Bauer for the Greco-Roman Heavyweight Championship of the World before losing that same title to the Herculean New Yorker William Muldoon. Meanwhile, he had sparred boxing exhibitions with both Joe Goss and Goss's immediate successor as American champion, the virtual novice Paddy Ryan. The American title, as Miller remarked to Mace, had degenerated into a mere bauble, with the press barely interested. A disillusioned and homesick Miller had set himself up in an Athletic Academy in Sydney where he taught wrestling, boxing and fencing.

While Mace was in Australia, at the beginning of the 1880s, the American fight scene had been transformed in the space of a couple of years by two men. The first was a newspaper proprietor named Richard Kyle Fox. An Ulsterman who had worked as a printer and compositor in Belfast, he emigrated to the U.S.A. in his late twenties and, two years later, had bought up a declining New York weekly called the *Police Gazette*. The significance of the title was that it reported almost solely on crime. Fox, the self-styled 'Proprietor', concentrated the format on murder, rape and prostitution. Printed on lurid pink paper and selling for only a nickel, the *Gazette*'s circulation quickly picked up. From *Gazette* HQ on William Street in New York, Fox used a network of agents to turn his mag into a national outlet, available in taverns, saloons and barber shops across the land. Fox was convinced that sport would be an additional incentive to his over-whelmingly male readership and a special issue dealing with Paddy Ryan's victory for the American Championship over Joe Goss in May 1880 had tripled circulation. Fox was effectively the founder of tabloid journalism and his sensationalism brought rich rewards. He was soon a millionaire.

The second man was John Lawrence Sullivan. At the age of seventeen, Sullivan had already weighed a muscular 200lb. He delighted in public feats of strength, such as carrying beer barrels above his head and, on one occasion, taking the lead in righting a derailed Boston streetcar. Drifting from plumbing through tinsmithing to stone masonry, the 'Boston Strong Boy's' restless and combative temperament made him unable to hold a steady job. Intending a career as a professional baseball player, he was diverted into fighting after attending variety shows where members of the audience were invited to come on stage and box one another. Crop-haired, bemoustached and with glowering dark eyes, Sullivan fixed his opponents with a baleful stare and snarled that he 'would soon make mincemeat of (them)'. Completely untrained in boxing technique, he flung caution to the winds at the first bell, hurling himself at his opponent and making full use of his rapid footwork and fast hands. He threw roundhouse shots with both fists and his punching power was phenomenal. Significantly, Sullivan preferred to fight under Queensberry Rules. With his hands protected by gloves, he could launch punches not only to hit a foe's jaw but directly to the skull. Second, Queensberry fights usually lasted barely a quarter of an hour, ideal for a fiercely aggressive fighter with little or no defence, bent on rapid demolition and too lazy to condition himself for protracted LPR combat. Turning professional at the age of twenty-one, he cut a swathe through the ranks of other fighters. Within two years, he knocked out a series of aspirants to the title and, even in exhibitions, had to be restrained from going for the KO.

In the last months of Goss's lacklustre reign, Sullivan took the ring with the Englishman, turning a benefit for the veteran at the Boston Music Hall into a showcase for himself. The 'Highland Boy', as Sullivan was also nicknamed, rained blows on Goss's head. Helped to his feet by the Master of Ceremonies, Goss staggered across the stage as if he was drunk (despite Goss's fondness for the bottle, he never entered the ring other than sober). Realising that Goss was concussed, the M.C. told Sullivan to back off but the Irish-American crowd had gone crazy with delight at Sullivan's savage attack on an English boxer. Sullivan had also fought an exhibition against the bareknuckle middleweight champion of America, Mike Donovan of Chicago. Donovan, the brother of Jerry, was an advocate of scientific boxing and already a skilful instructor but it would take all his know-how just to avoid being knocked out by Sullivan. He managed to make Sullivan miss but, as the last round ended, was taking a battering from the newly risen star. Mike Donovan then hailed Sullivan as the greatest fighter the Prize Ring had ever seen.

Later, in Cincinnati, Sullivan faced the experienced Professor John Donaldson under London Prize Ring Rules in a derelict beer hall.

Eager to finish matters before the police intervened, Sullivan took twenty minutes to crush Donaldson. Charging like a bull at a red rag, Sullivan head-butted and kicked the Professor and almost every round ended with a knockdown until Donaldson was helpless. Sullivan was arrested but, as no one would testify against him, the matter was dropped. He celebrated by having the first of many 'defis' – a French term meaning both 'provocation' and 'challenge' – published, this one in the *Cincinnati Inquirer*. He was, he said, ready 'to fight any man breathing'. Coming to New York, Sullivan took on John Flood, a hoodlum from the Five Points. To avoid the police, the prize-fight was held on a barge moored in the Hudson River near Yonkers. Within a quarter of an hour, Sullivan either hurled or punched Flood to the deck no less than eight times. Flood was carried from the ring senseless, with blood pouring from an ear. Fortunate not to be killed, he never fought again.

Sullivan's manager, Billy Madden, had emigrated to the USA from England, although he was the son of Irish parents. Announcing it as a 'first', Madden promoted a four-month tour taking in all the big cities of the North. Sullivan offered $50 to any man in the audience who could last four Queensberry rounds with him. If no one responded, he would spar either with Madden or with Steve Taylor. Three amateurs and one semi-pro took him up on his offer and Sullivan duly knocked them all out, usually in the first round, disfiguring one for life. The tour was a great commercial success, grossing nearly $7,000. Sullivan's exploits were extensively covered in the *Police Gazette*, as were aspects of his controversial and charismatic personality, notably his boundless self-confidence, extravagant boasting and heavy drinking.

The prospect of a match between John L Sullivan and Paddy Ryan for the American title further boosted circulation of Fox's mag. On 7 March 1882, they met under the rules of the London Prize Ring at Mississippi City, Mississippi. Sullivan's ferocity, even by his own standards, was unprecedented. In nine rounds, lasting only ten minutes, he bludgeoned Ryan into defeat. That Sullivan's punching power was no mere hype was attested by Ryan's post-match remark that he felt 'as if a telegraph pole had been shoved against me endways'. Sullivan returned home to Boston in triumph and proclaimed himself Heavyweight Champion of the World. Next, Madden declared that while Sullivan would fight anywhere, the most appropriate arena for him would be Madison Square Garden in New York City.

Situated at 26th Street and Madison Avenue, and originally named Gilmore's Garden, this was a grim-looking pseudo-Moorish edifice but its circus shows would accommodate 5,000 spectators. The Garden was owned by the railroad baron William Vanderbilt, who enthusiastically signalled his approval for boxing bouts provided they would be time-limited glove clashes. The prospect of Sullivan appearing at the Garden was a sure-fire guarantee of a sellout. By this time, the twenty-three-year-old Sullivan was issuing his own rules of engagement. In his Boston defi of 23 March 1882, he proclaimed: 'I am willing to fight any man in this country – or any man in the Old Country – I to use gloves and he, if he pleases to fight with the bare knuckles as I do not wish to put myself in a position amenable to the law. My money is always ready, so I want these fellows (who say they are desirous of meeting me in the ring) to put up or shut up.'

The Bostonian's natural arrogance had been boosted by endorsements from other prize-fighters. Goss, by now a chum of his who laid down the red carpet for Sullivan at the Saracen's Head, had acclaimed Sullivan as the greatest prize-fighter ever to have lived. There were similar endorsements from Mike Donovan – and Joe Coburn, no less. Coburn had been prematurely released from jail after five years due to 'aiding and promoting prison discipline', a phrase which suggested that the governor was grateful for Coburn's strong-arm assistance in dealing with incipient prison riots. Hero-worshipped as he was by large numbers of Americans, middle-class as well as working-class, native-born as well as immigrants, Sullivan had one very powerful enemy: Richard Kyle Fox, proprietor of the *Police Gazette*. Sullivan and Fox had been introduced by Billy Madden but, in an immediate clash of colossal egos, had fallen out. Fox expected Sullivan to defer to him but Sullivan refused. From Fox's point of view, Sullivan was excellent copy for the *Police Gazette* but, at the same time, he was an impudent braggart who must be dethroned as soon as possible. Already the 'Proprietor' had stated his willingness to bankroll any challenger who might have a chance against the detested Boston Strong Boy. If no American could do this, then England, the cradle of the Prize Ring, would surely provide a man who could lower Sullivan's colours.

Even before he had left Australia, Jem Mace had read about these events. When Miller joined him in New Zealand, he found Mace eager to discuss the rise of Sullivan – and to downplay vehemently the endorsements with which the 'Boston Strong Boy' had been showered. As Mace saw it, Goss was twenty years older than Sullivan and his constitution had been ruined by drunken dissipation. Coburn was a jailbird eager to curry favour with a new generation of Irish-Americans. Ryan had had only one solitary fight prior to gaining the championship. And as for Mike Donovan, Mace liked and respected him for his boxing ability but not for his judgment, which had once included an assertion that Ned O'Baldwin was the greatest living fighter.

Mace did not dispute that Sullivan was the possessor of an exceptional punch but first he would have to land it. He might have swept all before him in his rise to the title but those victories, Mace pointed out, had been achieved against either veterans or novices. It infuriated Mace to think that a completely untutored man like Sullivan could win such acclaim. Anyone who had the guts not to be intimidated by the Highland Boy's eyeballing and who had the technique to dodge or sidestep his rushes could baffle and evade him until he tired himself out. True, four rounds was far too short to be the real test of skill which the Queensberry Rules purported to be, but it was long enough to take the edge off Sullivan's speed and to begin to punish him with the left jab. The Bostonian had not been subjected to counter-attack. How would he, as a bully and a poorly conditioned drunkard, cope with it?

As for Madden's knockout Grand Tour being a 'first', Mace pointed out that it was in fact a re-run, save only for the greater sum on offer, of what he had initiated in England nearly twenty years earlier, when Madden was a mere boy. If Mace was contemptuous of the ballyhoo which surrounded Sullivan, he was very interested indeed by what he learned about Fox's quarrel with the new champion. Here was money for the taking. Jem only wished that he was not fifty-two years of age; at thirty-two he would, he said, have defeated Sullivan with ease; at forty-two he could still have done so, he believed, provided only that he evaded the Bostonian's opening rushes. Alas now his speed of movement had slowed but still, he said, slamming his fist angrily on the table, Sullivan must be beaten. If he remained the title-holder then boxing would be devalued and all that the much-vaunted Queensberry Rules would have done would have been to install a champion noted for his brute force and ignorance.

Before Mace and Miller left North Island for South Island, they had decided to hold tournaments in the South, both for boxing and wrestling, open to all whether amateur or semi-pro. As far as boxing was concerned this would be an historic innovation.

The idea was to find a young New Zealander to challenge Sullivan, and, in view of Fox's largesse, to cash in. Although the Bostonian had stated his unwillingness to fight again under London Prize Ring Rules, his Boston defi if taken literally, was ludicrous. There could, of course, never be a mill between one gloved fighter and one who remained bare knuckled, but if Sullivan were to be beaten in a non-title fight under Queensberry Rules, he would come under great pressure to defend his world championship in the Prize Ring – and therefore any potential opponent for him needed to be both a good boxer and a good wrestler.

Learning that the Theatre Royal in Timaru could be hired more cheaply than any other hall in South Island, Mace and Miller advertised a programme lasting two days, 13–14 June. They would spar together and this would be followed by Miller inviting any man in the audience to wrestle with him; then there would be a lightweight boxing competition. The aspiring wrestler turned out to be Herbert Slade, older brother of Junior. Aged twenty-seven, Slade was of mixed race, the son of an Irish father and a Maori mother, a member of the Ngai Tahu tribe. Brought up on a cattle farm, he became a butcher by trade. At 6ft 2in and weighing 225lb, his physique revealed exceptional muscular development. A splendid all-round athlete, he had excelled as a runner, hurdler, boxer and, above all, wrestler. Slade came on stage and grappled with Professor Miller. He put up an impressive performance, eventually losing on a fall, and was immediately invited to join Mace's troupe. His name was the first to be entered for the Jem Mace heavyweight wrestling competition, the semi-final and final of which were to be held at the Garrison Hall, Dunedin on August 26.

Much as the audience in Timaru enjoyed the Mace–Miller boxing exhibitions, and even more so the competitive wrestling match, the highlight was the Jem Mace lightweight boxing tournament. The spur of competition excited the audience – all the more so as the winner was the local lad Bob Fitzsimmons. Meanwhile, Herbert Slade proceeded as a member of the troupe, losing to Miller in Dunedin on the best-of-five falls and opposing the professor in three exhibitions. On August 26, Slade first won his semi-final in the Jem Mace heavyweight wrestling competition and then won the competition in the final. He was doubly honoured in that Mace invited him to spar three rounds with him in a boxing exhibition.

Mace then advertised for contestants in the Jem Mace middleweight boxing competition, which would take place in Timaru the following month. No sooner had Mace sifted through the postal applications than Fitzsimmons confronted him in the street, eager to be included and ready to put his name forward. Mace tried to dissuade him. Yes, he had put up a fine show to defeat the other lightweights, but this was different.

'It would mean you giving away more than a stone to the lightest of the other lads,' Mace told Fitzsimmons, who weighed less than 140lb. 'I doubt if you can do it.'

But Bob was not to be deterred. Remembering that, in his own younger days, he had spotted at least as much poundage and often more, Mace relented and handed him a pen. Fitzsimmons needed to beat five opponents in two days to become, in effect if not in name, Champion of New Zealand. What's more, Mace had made a significant departure from the usual Queensberry format. While John Chambers' list of rules nowhere stipulated the duration of bouts, four rounds had become the norm. Mace increased this to twelve to provide an approximate three-quarters of an hour time frame, with a decision by him at the end, if need be. Fitzsimmons was not to require that verdict. Against his first opponent, Mace was obliged to stop the fight in the third and Fitzsimmons did not demur; but when Mace halted his bout against Junior Slade in the second, all hell broke loose, leading to the incident in which Fitzsimmons raised his gloved fists at Mace and was punished on the mark as a result. What had angered the red-haired lad was that, unlike his first opponent, Junior Slade was far taller and heavier than himself. In future years Fitzsimmons mistakenly thought that it had been Herbert whom he had whipped, owing to the strong facial resemblance between the two brothers.

Fitzsimmons proceeded to knock out two more opponents before winning the title against his final adversary on an intervention by Mace. Clearly, the gawky lad was head and shoulders above the competition. He was a hero in Timaru and Mace was told all about his background.

In late July news came from America which seemed to confirm Mace's low opinion of John L. Sullivan. Fox, desperate to find a successful challenger, had convinced himself that England might provide the answer. He sought Arthur Chambers' advice and was given the name of Tug Wilson. Wilson, whose real name was Joe Collins, had been a promising young prize-fighter in the late 1860s but had given up following the police crackdown. By now the fierce vigilance of the 1870s was beginning to slacken and prize-fights were sporadically resuming. Wilson therefore had an eleven-year gap in his ring career and, while his age was uncertain, he was believed to be in his late thirties. Squat and jowly, he looked older, but when Fox wrote to him via *Sporting Life*, offering him $1,000 and half the gate money at Madison Square Garden, plus full travel expenses, Wilson was on the next boat to New York.

Before a crowd ranging from Wall Street brokers to ex-convicts from Sing Sing, Wilson used every trick in the book simply to avoid a knockout. He back-pedalled and, if Sullivan closed, went down as soon as he was touched. He managed to duck below a couple of Sullivan's haymakers but never attempted to land himself. By the end of the scheduled four rounds, Wilson had been on the floor twenty-three times, but only a few of these were from Sullivan's blows and these were only glancing shots resulting in flash knockdowns, without ever stunning Wilson. The Englishman's other visits to the canvas either came of his own volition or resulted from throws by an exasperated Sullivan. By the last round, Sullivan, who hadn't bothered to train for the bout, was tiring and Wilson managed to clinch, laughing at Sullivan as the Strong Boy was obliged to hit and hold.

Tug Wilson was declared the winner on the grounds that Sullivan had failed to knock him out. Wilson celebrated in style and in English company, with Chambers at Harry Hill's. He then sailed for Liverpool with the sterling equivalent of $11,000 in his pocket. Promising to come back for a return bout, Wilson in fact stayed at home in Leicester, investing his winnings in a boot and shoe store.

Mace fell about laughing when he read about Wilson's impudence and trickery, of Fox's gullibility and of Sullivan's impotent rage. The chaotic state of the fight game in New York had been thoroughly exposed. The farce at Madison Square Garden had been a ridiculous hodgepodge – a mixture of a Queensberry Rules bout (in that gloves were worn and rounds lasted three minutes with one-minute intervals), an exhibition and an LPR mill (because Sullivan had wrestled Wilson to the floor several times, without being called for a foul, and Wilson had frequently dropped to one knee). As to the sainted Queensbury Rules themselves, they were absurdly ineffective. Wilson had been deemed the winner although he had not struck Sullivan once, whereas 'The Boy' had landed a fair number of punches, albeit mostly off target. What was far from funny, however, was the admission money, the crowd excitement and the demand for a return match. Clearly, Madison Square Garden was a garden of plenty.

★ ★ ★

Bob Fitzsimmons was considered a local lad in Timaru, although he was English-born. At the age of ten he had arrived from Plymouth at Lyttleton, the port of Christchurch, with his parents and elder brother Jarrett, en route to Timaru, which lay the better part of 100 miles further down the east coast of the South Island. Timaru had been settled largely by Cornish people driven, as were Fitzsimmons' parents, by the exhaustion of the tin mines to seek a new life in mining on the opposite side of the world. But neither his father, Jim, nor his brother became miners. Jim, an Irishman who had settled in Helston after serving in the British Army, became a farrier, while Jarrett, one of twelve children, became a blacksmith and employed Bob at his forge.

As a boy, Fitzsimmons was taunted ruthlessly about his odd physical appearance and became the victim of a sadistic bully, a big youth in his late teens who beat him up when he was only eleven. Fitzsimmons, determined on revenge, made boxing gloves from his brother's leather aprons, read up on self-defence and, at eighteen, took a few lessons from Dan Lea, the reputed former bareknuckle champion of

Cornwall. Generally regarded as an easygoing lad, Fitzsimmons was transformed once he entered the ring. There was a cold anger about him, as if he was inwardly determined to cut down taller and heavier opponents, as he had been unable to do with the sadistic bully. He was fearless, no matter how much he was outweighed, and it was almost certainly he who first made the celebrated comment, 'The bigger they come, the harder they fall.'

When Mace and Miller discussed Fitzsimmons, Mace remarked that the young blacksmith – admittedly his own discovery – might have even more potential than the three youthful boxers under Larry Foley's tutelage in Sydney. This judgment was based firstly on Fitz's punching power. He never threw windmill swings but hit immensely hard and with deadly accuracy; in addition, his determination and sheer enthusiasm, combined with a ruthless will to win, marked him out as a true fighter in the making.

Ideally, Mace would have loved to have trained and managed any single boxer from the group comprising Dooley, Slavin, Jackson and Fitzsimmons, and to have taken him to the States to challenge Sullivan. But Dooley was a mere lad, just as Fitzsimmons was, even though his appearance, unlike Fitz's, would not count against him with the image-conscious Fox. Slavin looked the part and was bold and rugged but still something of a wild puncher. Jackson did not yet have the self-belief and, in any case, it was highly unlikely that Sullivan, an outspoken racist, would agree to meet him. Sullivan's bombastic defis always carried the caveat that they 'did not extend to Negroes'.

Mace became increasingly convinced that the towering Slade was the one who should be brought to America. Meanwhile, it would be better for the three Australian youngsters to learn their trade at Foley's gym. As for Fitzsimmons, Mace urged him to turn professional, go to Sydney, look up Foley and hand over the letter of introduction which Mace gave him.

Herbert Slade indeed looked the part. He would be three inches taller than Sullivan and would outweigh him by 30lb. He was older but only by three years. Slade's complexion was that of a Southern Mediterranean man and Sullivan would not draw the colour line against him. Above all, Fox would be impressed with Slade's exotic ethnicity. In terms of showmanship, Slade would be a trump card.

Obviously Slade's boxing skills were limited, but with constant tuition from Mace and the opportunity of facing the master in exhibition bouts where Jem could contrive to make him look good, he would gradually gain confidence and improve, just as Foley had once done. The entire process would probably take about a year. First, Slade had to be signed to a contract conferring exclusive managerial rights on Mace.

On 15 September 1882, the day after Fitzsimmons became Champion of New Zealand, Herbert Slade signed a one-year contract making himself available for boxing exhibitions with Mace, wrestling exhibitions with Miller and for any competitive boxing bouts which Mace might arrange. Shortly after signing Slade, Mace wrote to Fox at the offices of the *Police Gazette*. Given that the letter had to go by mail steamer from Auckland to San Francisco and from there via the Transcontinental Railroad, correspondence was slow. Fox, an admirer of most things English, was delighted to receive a courteously worded letter from the former world champion. Nonetheless, his first reply revealed his ignorance of boxing realities, notwithstanding his business acumen and flair for publicity. Fox hoped that Mace himself could take on Sullivan and Mace had to advise that he was too old for the task. He prudently did not add that he could probably have 'done a Wilson' successfully, but he had no intention of lowering his dignity by resorting to 'floor crawling tactics'. Instead he repeated his recommendation of Slade. This time Fox bit. By late November, Mace had disbanded his troupe and was in Auckland awaiting the fares for himself, his family and Slade – which were being wired by Fox.

Mace's assets in Australia had been disposed of, with the exception of the Victoria Racing Club Hotel and his goldmine shares. As usual, he had been spending lavishly, leaving himself with little ready money. Nellie was obliged to write once again to the McCalls to explain the further change of plan. They understood. After final boxing and wrestling exhibitions, the party was seen off from Auckland by Miller, who returned to Australia to resume his career as an instructor in combat sports, principally wrestling. In due course, Miller would himself go back to the States. He eventually settled in Baltimore and lived to be ninety-one.

There was an inauspicious prelude to the departure. The night before, Slade, who had begun to reveal a quarrelsome streak, got into a fight with a cab driver, coming off worse. Mace, in a pattern of covering up for Slade, dismissed it, claiming that he himself was not suited to street fighting.

While Slade and the Maces travelled by mail steamer across the Pacific, Fox's publicity machine swung into action. Slade was given the nickname 'The Maori'. In ethnic terms, it was only partially correct but it sounded charismatic, which was what concerned Fox. An alternative monicker for Slade was the 'Timaru Terror', a name once jokingly bestowed by Mace on Fitzsimmons but misunderstood by Fox to refer to Herbert Slade. Only time would tell who really lived up to it.

24

Trans-American Tabloid

THE NEW ZEALAND mail steamer's foghorn boomed sonorously as the bow edged into the mist-bound waters of San Francisco Bay. Mace felt elated at the thought that he would soon step off the gangway and set foot once again on American soil, six years after departing Californian shores for a new life. It was the first week in the New Year and the public had been alerted to the return of the man the press was hailing as the world champion's nemesis, at least by proxy and via the fists of his gigantic protégé, Herbert Slade. Whatever his private thoughts, Mace readily adjusted to the new age of tabloid hype, boosting his discovery in no uncertain terms. 'He can outbox, out-wrestle and outjump any man in the world,' he asserted. Pre-empting disagreement, he bluffed, 'He never was in a Prize Ring because there never was a man where he comes from that would dare face him.' His protégé's inexperience did not matter because 'I've had him in training nearly a year and he soon learned all the tricks.' Reverting to the barefaced bluster of the carny barker, he bragged, in a final flourish designed to astound the credulous, 'He's a wonderful wrestler, who threw Professor Miller just as I would a baby.' It seemed that the old champion was determined to raise the ante on the new titleholder's reputation for empty bombast.

Mace lost no time in putting on an exhibition showcasing Herbert Slade, not in a theatre or municipal hall but a church, Kalloch's Metropolitan Temple in San Francisco. Taking full advantage of a clause in the evangelicals' charter which allowed the building to be hired for public speaking, Mace gave a speech – extolling Slade's pugilistic talents. No sooner had he finished than a ring was set up below the pulpit while he and Slade went into the vestry to change. They then performed to a crowd that had paid $2 a head. Gullible reporters noted, without realising that Mace was contriving to make

Slade look good, that 'The Maori' got in more blows than the old master.

Unsurprisingly, the Temple congregants protested vehemently when they found out, firing off letters to newspapers lamenting the 'sacrilegious' turning of their house of worship into 'an arena for . . . a brutal exhibition . . . bringing together the very worst elements of the city . . . unprecedented in the history of Christian churches.'

By this time Mace was in the state capital at Sacramento, where he gave an exhibition for the benefit of the legislators. After addressing them on 'the new scientific boxing', he and Slade sparred. Back in San Francisco, Slade faced a member of the Olympic Club named George Robinson, a bout which Mace, as referee, quickly stopped as Robinson was getting the upper hand. Mace nonchalantly dismissed what was, in effect, a defeat for the New Zealander by cynically declaring that Slade would have had to resort to 'crude slugging' which would, he claimed, have knocked Robinson senseless.

On January 15, the Maces and Slade set off for the East on the Transcontinental Railroad. Fox and the *Police Gazette* reported their progress across America as if describing the regal peregrination of a monarch and his heir apparent. Fox himself, assuming imperial status, informed his tens of thousands of readers that he would travel to Chicago to greet them. Arrangements would be finalised in a clash with John L. Sullivan at $5,000 a side.

The journey from Chicago to New York saw Fox's breathless prose repeated verbatim in many of America's small town newspapers. It revealed, as never before, the power of modern publicity techniques to impress people both high and low on the social ladder, and Mace entered into it with the panache of the circus showman he had been. At Washington, the fighters were greeted by a brass band and a crowd of 3,000. Among them were a senator from Minnesota, the Governor of Wisconsin and an ex-Secretary of the Treasury. These men goggled like schoolboys as Mace produced his English championship belt, John Mackay's Silver Belt and his bullion belts from California and Australia. At Baltimore, the freight cars were alive with people and Mace's party had to be locked in their compartment to avoid the train being forced into an unscheduled stop. At Philadelphia, a crowd of several thousand swelled the concourse seeking the autographs of Mace and Slade.

Much of this adulation came from those who disliked Sullivan and hoped for his downfall. Sullivan had already been arrested after a drunken brawl and been investigated over an incident in which he had been accused of brutally whipping a horse in public view. Women, in particular, detested him as rumours abounded that he had beaten his common-law wife, the rough and ready Annie Bailey. By contrast, as Fox – for once accurately – informed his readers, Nellie Mace was 'a fine-looking woman, elegantly dressed, and a good musician who is skilful on various instruments'.

When the Maces and Slade finally reached New York, Harry Hill played his part. He was quoted as saying that the excitement was the greatest known since the days of Heenan and Sayers. He and his wife accommodated the whole party at their luxury mansion in Flushing. As for Slade, he was described in the *Gazette* in terms which emphasised his exoticism. He was 'the pride of Polynesia' and 'in the South Sea Islands' he was famed for his ability to tackle, bare-handed, ferocious 4ft-high wild hogs with tusks a foot long – and to slaughter them. The sun-loving Slade was, readers were informed, steeling himself to the rigours of the New York winter by wearing three waistcoats, a buffalo-skin overcoat and a kangaroo-skin cap, but soon, Fox crowed, he would be presented at Madison Square Garden not only to spar with Mace but to challenge Sullivan. What's more, the exhibition at the Garden would be treated as a benefit for Mace, who was still strong enough to take on any man in the world – with $1,000 to whoever might last four rounds of Queensberry Rules with him. As for Sullivan, if he dared to take on Mace, $2,500 would be the stake.

Mace was well pleased with all of this except that he had to tell Fox that, on grounds of age, he was not prepared to confront the Boston Strong Boy himself. Much to Jem's rage, Sullivan was circulating a story that Mace had offered money to the new champion if he would allow Mace to last four rounds but that Sullivan had refused with contempt. Mace had made no such offer. If he could no longer risk combat with Sullivan, he would certainly not be party to a demeaning charade. Progress was brusquely interrupted by New York Mayor Franklin Edson, who was alarmed by big-fight fever in the city. He ordered the arrest of Mace and Slade, who were bailed to appear in court a fortnight later. Next, Fox himself was arraigned in the Court of Special Sessions, charged with aiding and abetting a prize-fight. This case fascinated the legal fraternity throughout the U.S.A. How was a 'prize-fight' so defined? According to the prosecution lawyers, it had nothing to do with such pugilistic concepts as the London Prize Ring Rules or the Marquess of Queensberry Rules. No, what defined a prize-fight, they asserted, was the advancement of a monetary prize and nothing other than that.

When Mace was called to the witness stand, he was asked by the chief prosecutor if it were not the case that the ring attracted only the lowest elements in society. He replied that, on the contrary, men of the highest standing were taking boxing lessons and indulging in friendly sparring. 'Name me one!' snapped the counsel, whereupon Mace recounted his own clash with Senator Roscoe Conkling in Washington, later repeating the story to pressmen outside court. The following day, a furious Conkling denied the story and threatened to sue Mace for slander. It was notable that Conkling never made good his threat. The upshot of the proceedings in the Court of Special Sessions was that Fox was convicted and ordered to post a bond of $1,000 to keep the peace for one year.

On February 8, in defiance of their bail, Mace and Slade made their debut at Madison Square Garden. Apart from the affair at the Temple in Frisco and the hushed-up Robinson bout, this was Slade's debut before the American public. Once again Mace did all he could to make Slade look good and succeeded in convincing many of those present. One was a Mr Early, a wealthy Bostonian who presented Mace with a gold-headed cane. 'Thank you very kindly, Mr Early,' he said, pausing for effect before he added, 'How much did this cost?' This caused some startled laughter in the hall. Some took it as an example of audacious humour, others of sheer cynicism, but in fact Mace had all his presents valued. As an inveterate gambler, he liked to know the size of his kitty. There was one notable absentee at the gathering in Madison Square Garden: the Boston Strong Boy himself. Fox slyly attributed his failure to attend to 'his fatigue caused by travels among the saloons'.

The following day, Mace received the most devastating news of his life. It concerned his ten-year-old son Benjamin and came in a telegram dispatched on Hannah's behalf. She had been able to keep track of Mace's movements over the years because of the maintenance money which he had sent for the children of his second marriage. The cable contained the stark fact that Ben was missing, presumed drowned. On a bitterly cold midwinter morning, he had been playing on the south bank of the River Thames, lost his footing and fallen into the icy, swirling waters below. A fast-moving current would have swept him swiftly to his death.

For the first time since she had known him, Nellie saw Jem weep. He hadn't seen Ben for seven years and sometimes wondered if the boy even remembered him. In a few years, Ben would have reached adolescence and it had been his father's intention to invite him to America, the land of his birth, as soon as he was capable of independent judgment. If all went well, the lad would live there with them. Instead, Jem had now lost four sons: two to what he considered a malign fate and the other two, in a metaphorical sense, to evangelical fanaticism. At first, Mace thought of taking the first ship home to England, to find out what had led up to the tragedy. Hannah did not live anywhere near the river and he wondered what Ben had been doing there. He decided, though, that there was nothing he could do and, with the body not recovered, there could be no funeral. The bereavement left him emotionally hurt for a considerable time but, consoled by Nellie, he threw himself into his managerial and promotional activities with even more vigour in an effort to distract himself.

A week later, Judge Donahue, sitting in Supreme Court Chambers, effectively dissented from the verdict in the Court of Special Sessions. In the case of James Mace and Herbert Slade, opined his worship, there was no evidence that they had violated any law and he ordered them to be discharged from arrest. This was the judgment that effectively legalised glove boxing in New York State. Fox hailed it as a triumph for freedom and, ignoring the provisions of his bond, called on Sullivan to sign articles to fight Slade. Sullivan, who was laid up after a prolonged drinking binge, did not respond. Fox assured Mace that he would expose Sullivan if the champion did not come to heel; meanwhile, Mace and Slade should do some exhibitions so that the momentum for the fight would not slacken. Mace and Slade duly sparred at Bridgeport, Connecticut, at Cincinnati and at Pittsburgh, not to mention several return visits to Madison Square Garden. In due course, Slade also sparred twice with – of all people – Joe Coburn. Coburn, recently released from jail, was destitute and eagerly agreed, despite the long history of animosity between himself and Mace. Mace kept his distance but noted that the old antagonism towards Englishmen had greatly slackened. John Morrissey had died five years earlier and this seemed to mark a change of attitude. Indeed, Mace privately told Nellie off for her assertion to a journalist that she 'would never leave his side even if the Fenians put a bounty on his head'. It was not that Jem was not moved by her devotion, but he insisted that it was better to leave political comment alone.

Before long, however, Mace became highly impatient at the lack of progress in signing articles. He had been gambling heavily in Harry Hill's club and, with Sullivan's signature not forthcoming, his exhibitions with Slade were no longer drawing the crowds. Since Sullivan had apparently recovered from his alcoholic excesses, Mace began to suspect that Fox had seen through the carefully shielded Slade and realised that, far from being a fistic phenomenon, as the public had been led to believe, Herbert was in fact a clumsy novice without a single ring victory to his credit. Mace's hunch was partly accurate. Experienced reporters such as George Siler had noted Slade's ponderousness and gauged that Mace was 'carrying' him in their exhibitions, but a far more significant factor was the arrival in America of a young fighter from England who rapidly showed that he was in a different class from Slade. In his U.S. debut in April 1883, he had knocked out the promising Mike Cleary in three rounds. The young Englishman's name was Charlie Mitchell.

Fox had abruptly changed tack after witnessing Mitchell demolish Cleary. The *Gazette* extravagantly proclaimed Mitchell to be 'the greatest fighter seen in this or any other country'. Doubtless this was done to provoke Sullivan – and it succeeded. Articles were signed for Sullivan to meet Mitchell two months hence. It would be a Queensberry Rules four-rounder and, as such, the world title would not be at stake.

Mace was stunned and angered at this turn of events, even though Fox assured him that Slade's turn would come against the winner. Mace countered by demanding a match between Slade and

Mitchell, which, he asserted, would 'eliminate' one of the contestants as a challenger. That match was agreed but persistent harassment by the New York Police Department made it impossible to stage. There even seemed a distinct possibility that Mitchell would not be permitted to face Sullivan. If Mitchell was successful, not merely in staying the distance with Sullivan but in defeating him, this would lead to demands for a bareknuckle scrap under LPR rules, with Sullivan's world title at stake. The last thing that the authorities wanted was a prize-ring encounter, something now regarded with such disdain by the burgesses of every self-regarding city in the United States that it would have to be shunted off to some remote locale in Mississippi.

A compromise was reached whereby Sullivan and Mitchell were allowed to fight, provided it was supervised by Police Captain Alexander Williams of the 29th Precinct, within whose realm lay Madison Square Garden. Williams was usually known by his nickname 'Clubber' due to the enthusiasm with which he used his heavy truncheon. Thus armed, on hand, and in uniform, Clubber would impose restraint even on the ferocious Sullivan. The match between the Bostonian and the Englishman would go ahead on May 14. Jem could not afford to lay in wait any longer. The hiatus occasioned by Sullivan's month-long binge, police interference and Fox's demotion of Slade in the pecking order had led to a rapid decline in press coverage of the New Zealander and fast decreasing attendances at exhibitions. Mace decided to return to England, while waiting for the outcome of Sullivan–Mitchell, and to take Slade with him. He had been away from his homeland for seven years and the advent of Mitchell had exposed how out of touch he was with the sporting scene in England. While there, he would use his old contacts to find out as much as he could about the man who, as he saw it, had usurped Slade's status as number one challenger. Before leaving with Nellie and Ellen, he received news that Ben's body had been discovered. Two months after his disappearance, and some five miles downriver from where he had last been seen alive, a boy's corpse was noticed in shallow water at Rotherhithe. It was recovered and the police notified. The clothing was identical to Ben's, and two days later the Surrey Coroner recorded a verdict of accidental death. While this was harrowing news, the fact that a funeral had finally taken place at least brought Mace some sense of closure.

* * *

Charlie Mitchell had been discovered five months earlier by Sullivan's former manager, Billy Madden. After a quarrel with Sullivan, Madden, with Fox's enthusiastic backing, went to London. There he used the same ploy Mace had exploited six months earlier in New Zealand and which had brought to light Bob Fitzsimmons: he announced a prize-winning tournament, the Billy Madden Heavyweight Championship of England, under Queensberry Rules. The contest, held in London at Chelsea Baths, was won emphatically by Mitchell, who outclassed six competitors in a couple of days. At only 150lb, the 5ft 9½in Charlie was barely a middleweight but his boxing pedigree, both geographically and ethnically, was immaculate. Born in Birmingham of Irish parents, he was a veteran in ring terms at only twenty-one years of age. He had debuted outside his home city at sixteen in a bareknuckle fight at a fiver a side, and his record now was eleven wins, two draws and no defeats. Mitchell had a boyish, almost cherubic, face. Only the arrogant gleam in his eyes denoted his immense self-belief and often truculent demeanour. Inside the ring, he was destructive, with a fierce punch in either fist and a willingness to taunt, humiliate and cut down whoever stood in his way. Outside, he was quick-witted, articulate and impudent.

Mitchell went to London at seventeen and did the rounds of the East End sporting clubs, most of which now had boxing rings on the premises. At the Blue Anchor in Shoreditch, he came under the tutelage of Bill Richardson, Mace's former pal and mentor, now an ageing but still vigorous man. Richardson gave the cocky young Brummie some pointers and then declared him to be the best Englishman since Mace. As the 1870s had been devoid of talent in England, this in itself was an unexceptional accolade, but what he meant was that Mitchell had the hardness of an old-time prize-fighter. Not only did Charlie often fight several opponents in one night in the East End, he took part in sundry provincial bareknuckle fights as well. After more than a decade in which the police had grown complacent over what they, and indeed most people, assumed was the extinction of the Prize Ring, it suddenly revived. The motivation was partly the anti-authoritarian attitude which was pervasive both in the East End and in heavily working-class cities like Birmingham, but above all it was the lack of any legitimate form of the sport which would allow a contest of endurance beyond the meagre four-round Queensberry formula.

No sooner had Charlie absorbed the essentials of Richardson's vast fund of knowledge than he decided to make a living for himself imparting it to others. In the West End, an International Athletic Association had been formed and it advertised for a boxing instructor. The members were astonished when eighteen-year-old Mitchell introduced himself. With boundless self-confidence, he described exactly how he intended to teach his subject, invited a burly member into the ring and demonstrated the art of the left jab, relishing its potent effect with a triumphant smile. From London, Mitchell proceeded to Belgium, the first country outside the English-speaking world to take up boxing. In Antwerp, he challenged the self-styled champion of Flanders, a man who outweighed him by 90lb, and almost battered the living daylights out of him. The following day, he set up an ecole de boxe in the Palais Rubens and was soon barking orders in fractured French and flippant Flemish.

Back in England, Mitchell was not a whit daunted by his arrest on Ascot Heath, together with opponent Jack Burke, at a fight for the welterweight title. He was charged with conspiring to breach the peace by engaging in a prize-fight. He pleaded guilty, was reprimanded by the magistrate for insolence in court and, together with Burke, spent six weeks in the local nick. Mitchell was equally insouciant when asked by immigration officials at Pier Six in New York about the purpose of his visit. He coolly replied, 'I've come to knock out Mister Sullivan.' Such was the man whose chutzpah had drawn the attention of the proprietor of the *Police Gazette*. No greater contrast could be imagined between him and the bulky, inarticulate wrestler from a remote New Zealand farm.

Departing New York in April, albeit temporarily, Mace's position as Slade's manager and promoter was far weaker than when he had landed in San Francisco three months earlier. He had traversed

America on that same transcontinental railroad, through which tens of thousands of copies of the *Police Gazette* were shipped to the biggest cities and the remotest townships in the U.S.A. Mace had participated in an unprecedented outburst of hype, but if he entertained the idea that he was in any sense the master of ceremonies, he had been swiftly disillusioned by the speed with which Fox had dropped Slade for Mitchell. In the era of the Trans-American tabloid, it was the proprietor alone who called the shots.

25

Fiasco at Madison Square Garden

IN THE SPRING of 1883, William Vanderbilt, the owner of Madison Square Garden, was principally concerned with the installation of electric lighting in his already famous arena. The coming of the Electric Age had been saluted in April 1879, when a salvo of artillery boomed out as Monumental Park in Cleveland was suddenly lit up – to gasps of wonderment from a crowd who had no prior conception of electricity as a power source. Two years later, the *Scientific American* ran a cover story on the Brush central electric station in New York at a time when Brush's arc lamps were already the beacons of a new Broadway.

Charles Brush's brilliant career as an inventor had begun as a boy, after his unexpected prowess with his fists had discouraged a gang of bullies who were making his life hell at school. Fired with confidence as a result, he never looked back. At the age of twenty-seven, he assembled the first dynamo and patented it. That led on to the pioneering of a commercially viable system of electric lighting, namely a self-regulating arc lamp which produced a constant illumination in total contrast to the ghostly flickering of gas lamps. Brush's design was perfectly suited to buildings where an intensely bright illumination was required. As Vanderbilt figured, it was perfect for the ring at Madison Square Garden where two men could do battle bathed in light and without fear for the safety of volatile fight fans. Electric arc lighting would thus be the key technological development in the transition to modern boxing.

The Maces had arrived in Liverpool by early May and, with Slade installed in lodgings, Jem, Nellie and Ellen lived temporarily with the McCalls at Ted's house in Hall Lane, Kensington. Nellie was overjoyed to be reunited with John and it was agreed that he would accompany his mother and sister when they returned to the States with Jem. John, now thirteen and regarded by his teachers as an intelligent boy, would complete his education at high school, probably in New York City, where Mace was once again ready to live. Since the two sisters had last seen each other, Annie had given birth to three more daughters. The contrast with Nellie was obvious but, when they discussed it, Nellie stated that she had reason to believe that she was now unable to conceive. Still, she was already the mother of two children and the only thing that upset her was that she was unable to marry Mace. Rowland Lee was, so they had heard, living with his common-law wife and his son in Rowley Regis, Staffordshire, and they knew for certain that Hannah was living in south London.

Jem and Ted talked about Slade's upcoming confrontation with Sullivan. For the first time, Mace revealed his private opinion of the man he had been touting to the American media.

'Don't bet a bloody shilling on him,' he told Ted. 'He'll never be a boxer. He hasn't got the snap.'

This fact had to be hidden from the British public, just as it had from America's because Mace had arranged a twelve-bout series of exhibitions between himself and Slade. They would begin four days after Sullivan–Mitchell and, in a non-competitive atmosphere, with Mace pulling his punches, Slade would look good enough. Fox would be kept aware of Slade and the pressure would be on him finally to arrange a match between the Boston Strong Boy and The Maori. As for the outcome of Sullivan–Mitchell, Mace was obliged, against his personal and boxing instincts, to hope for a Sullivan victory. He disliked the American, contemptuous of his alcoholic excesses and reputation for bullying women and cuffing them when drunk.

Sullivan was also, as Mace was convinced, a crude slugger, albeit an exceptionally powerful one, who had been fortunate never to have been challenged by anyone who had been taught how to box. This situation was about to change now that he had signed articles to fight Mitchell; into the bargain, Sullivan's drinking had been so reckless that he had been unconscious for several hours only a few weeks earlier after coughing up blood. Provided Sullivan prevailed against Mitchell, who he outweighed by 40lb, Fox would leave no stone unturned to bring about a clash between him and Slade, the New Zealander being the only viable challenger. Despite his drinking and reluctance to train,

Sullivan would be highly dangerous over four rounds, but if Mitchell somehow gained a decision, Sullivan would have to put his world title at stake, facing the Englishman under London Prize Ring rules. If this occurred, Mitchell could duck and dive till the Strong Boy was exhausted and then he could jab his way to victory, doubtless using the methods Richardson would have taught him. Mitchell would then be under no obligation to give Slade a shot at the crown – and Fox, who liked Mitchell, would be content to let matters rest. Mace waited with bated breath for news of the encounter in New York.

To Vanderbilt's annoyance, arc lights had still not been installed at the Garden by the time Sullivan and Mitchell faced each other there on May 14. Still, over 8,000 spectators, including many VIPs, stood in line in a rainstorm before the gates opened in the early evening. The referee was Al Smith, a former bareknuckle fighter with a reputation, relatively speaking, for impartiality. However, right from the start, when he ostentatiously examined both men's medium-sized soft gloves, the dominant presence was that of Clubber Williams, who never left the outside apron of the raised platform in the centre of the arena. It was not long before sparks flew. Sullivan rushed Mitchell from the moment time was called, hurling lefts and rights at his head, but Mitchell ducked them all. Then Mitchell counter-punched, not once but twice, three times and once more. As the two men closed, Sullivan unleashed roundhouse shots, poorly targeted but powerful. Mitchell went down four times but promptly got up each time. Sullivan had not expected that and still less what happened afterwards. Mitchell fired a rapid and accurate left to the jaw and sent Sullivan to the canvas. The crowd rocked with excitement. This was the first time in Sullivan's life that anyone had combined guts and skill not only to stand up to him but to knock him down – but he was on his feet within a few seconds. Enraged, he stalked Mitchell, only to find the slim Englishman dancing out of his reach.

In the second, Mitchell resumed the offensive but Sullivan managed to trap him on the ropes before blasting him clean through. Mitchell was hurt more by the desperate scramble to get back on stage within ten seconds than by the punch itself, wrenching his hip in the process. Grimacing in pain, he back-pedalled to see out the end of the round. In the third, Sullivan gained the upper hand and knocked

Mitchell down several times more, but so off-target was his punching that Mitchell was on his feet each time within seconds, unfazed and gloves raised, ready to continue. An exasperated Sullivan barged him into the ropes and forced him to the deck, hurling himself on top of his fallen adversary with every ounce of his 40lb advantage. Mitchell staggered to his feet, badly winded, but resumed a fighting attitude. At this stage, Williams entered the ring and theatrically warned Sullivan not to continue. The Boston Strong Boy graciously consented to comply with Clubber's request, while the captain of the 29th precinct told reporters, as he proudly swung his truncheon, that the match was 'getting to be more than sparring'. Mitchell did not complain, although he might well have done. Satisfied with his loser's cut of forty per cent of the $16,000 gate, he repaired to Harry Hill's. Sore, badly bruised but without serious injury, he quaffed numerous jugs of ale before falling asleep.

Although the crowd had undoubtedly had its money's worth the fight was an absurd fudge of Queensberry and LPR rules. Gloves had been worn and the rounds had been of three minutes' duration with one-minute intervals, but Sullivan had closed the bout with a throw and a fall, which would have been perfectly legitimate in the LPR but should have brought about his instant disqualification under Queensberry Rules. As for Clubber Williams, he had given a whole new meaning to the ancient pugilistic term 'stopped due to police interference'. He had halted the fighting not to arrest Sullivan but, usurping Al Smith's role, to declare him the winner – or rather to declare that Mitchell had not succeeded in lasting the scheduled four rounds of the 'exhibition'. Sullivan had had by far the better of the fighting but that was not the point. The thin man from Birmingham had yet to demonstrate that he was unable to continue and might have seen out time, just as Wilson had done earlier in the year. Such was what passed for boxing in the America of the early 1880s.

The third of the Mace–Slade exhibitions took place in London on May 22 at the prestigious Drury Lane Theatre. It was announced well in advance, and some time before the date a letter was forwarded to Mace which had been left for him at the theatre. It was from his two daughters by his second marriage, Amelia and Ada. They wanted to meet him, told him they had important news and added that their mother would not know of the meeting. He showed the letter to Nellie and she at once decided to go with him to London to meet the two girls.

Jem had not cast eyes on his daughters since they were young children, but Amelia, now seventeen, and Ada, fifteen, warmly embraced him and greeted Nellie with a smile. They gave the impression of being mature girls, with Ada the more articulate but both of them resolute in character. They seemed to Jem preferable to Adelaide Turvill, his other daughter, who, he believed, had been influenced by the religious attitude of her brothers.

The conversation began with them consoling each other on the recent bereavement but what came next was staggering news: Amelia and Ada did not live alone with their mother, as Jem had supposed. Far from it: a year-and-a-half earlier, Hannah had gone through a bigamous marriage ceremony. Assuming that Jem had settled in Australia for good, she had shacked up with a widower named George Harris, a horse-keeper by occupation, and with total cynicism she had married Harris at All Saints Church in Newington on 26 December 1881 – after the reading of banns! Harris was fifteen years older than Hannah but he lived not far above the poverty line. All three Mace children had moved with their mother into Harris's humble tenement home in Darwin Buildings in Barlow Street, Walworth, just off the Old Kent Road. Like Mary before her with Dick Roberts, Hannah had chosen a man as different from Jem as could be imagined. Most of Harris's neighbours had dismissed him as a bore, while some put him down as a skint old skiver. Still, in Hannah's eyes, he had one great attraction: he was devoted to her.

Amelia had left home soon afterwards to work as a housemaid for a well-to-do family in Battersea. Ada had been sent away to a boarding school at Halstead in Essex, over 40 miles away. She would leave soon and expected to become a stenographer. The pattern seemed clear. Hannah had shown little interest in her daughters after meeting Harris, and while some of Mace's remittance money went, as intended, on the maintenance and education of his children, much of it did not. Not only did the usually skint Harris use it for himself, he had an unemployed daughter in her early twenties to provide for and a baby daughter with Hannah who both had to be fed and clothed. The girls stressed that Harris was not a bad man, but he was interested exclusively in his own daughters. Poor young Ben had spent an increasing amount of time away from home. Amelia and Ada blamed their mother more than Harris for the decline of the family. Hannah was not unkind to Ben but he had lacked supervision. When he was last seen alive it had been at Regent Wharf on Battersea Reach, near Gwynne Road, where he and his sisters and mother had lived before her bigamous marriage.

Jem was both stunned and angered. He thanked Amelia and Ada for putting him in the picture, particularly as they had been made unwilling accomplices in their mother's bigamy at a time when they were only adolescents. He shed tears again over Ben's demise. The two girls seemed disappointed to hear that their father intended to settle in the U.S.A. but as he took his leave of his daughters, he reached inside his wallet, split a generous sum between them and, to their pleasure, invited them to visit him in New York later in the year. Nellie spontaneously threw her arms around each girl and was kissed on the cheek by both.

As Mace and Nellie returned on the train to Liverpool, they discussed the turn of events at length alone in a first-class compartment. As far as their own relationship was concerned, Hannah had not known about it, still less did she know about Rowland Lee. She had, under the marriage laws of those times, insufficient grounds to divorce Jem, but while he travelled around the world, she always knew roughly where he was from the money which was wired to her. Had she, once he was in Australia, written to tell him of her wish to marry Harris, and the fact that she was already living with him, he would have had grounds for divorce and would gladly have offered to grant her one. But she had not told him. It seemed to Nellie that Hannah had been motivated by spite. She wished to block a divorce and, in doing so, prevent any woman who loved Jem from becoming his future wife. There and then Mace and Nellie decided to get married. In the eyes of the church that would be sin but they didn't care. What mattered to them was not to make the error of marrying while in England. Soon they would be back in America under an entirely different jurisdiction and they decided to marry as soon as they returned to New York.

In the middle of this personal upheaval, there was a brief and ominous interlude. The precarious revival of the Prize Ring had drawn the attention of young toffs, of the sort who had once patronised Langham's rooms. One such was a naval officer, Lord Charles Beresford, who wrote to Mace, challenging both him and Slade to meet him in a private fight with bare knuckles. It would have to be a clandestine event and Beresford knew a publican in Lambeth who was willing to let a room in his alehouse be used in the early hours, well after the public had gone home. In time news of the event would leak out and be good for business. Mace, who recognised the historic importance of the Corinthians, was quick to agree. The Maori, as he was now universally known, had fought no one other than his manager, with the exception of his hushed-up defeat against Robinson and his impromptu street scrap with the Auckland cabbie, but by this time Mace had been coaching him for nine months solid, striving to impart all the ringcraft that he knew. A fight against Beresford would be a good opportunity for Slade to rough it without any newspaper reporters present to comment on his technique. Mace decided he would 'box dumb' against Beresford. The members of the Fancy would expect Mace to beat his lordship with ease and odds would be laid accordingly, meaning Mace could pocket a tidy sum by backing Beresford as an outsider.

Residents of the notorious Elephant and Castle district were surprised to see young toffs invading their neighbourhood. But the police were not alerted and the first of the two scheduled scraps began. Mace duly offered little resistance to Beresford, a man he could have demolished with ease and, after taking some wild punches, acknowledged the young toff as the 'winner', using a crony who was in the know to clean up from the bookies. However Slade, shocked at what he had seen and kept in the dark by his manager, refused to enter the makeshift ring with Beresford, despite being urged to do so. Mace was angry but stifled his feelings, determined on the big payday at the Garden.

Mace finally received word from Fox that Sullivan had put pen to paper for a bout with Slade and promptly telegraphed an acceptance. The venue would be Madison Square Garden, the date 6 August 1883, and the match would be at the usual four-round time limit under

Queensberry Rules. The gate money would be split, with sixty-five per cent to the winner and the rest to the loser. The Maces and Slade arrived back in New York in mid-July, accompanied by two old friends of Mace's whom he'd looked up while in England: the pedestrian Dick Brighton, who was engaged to help with Slade's training, and Harry Montague. Mace never felt comfortable dealing with business matters himself and he wanted to have a good factotum for his second career in the USA, one he could trust implicitly – as he had never done with Abrahams. The whole of Mace's entourage were invited to stay at Harry Hill's country residence in Flushing, not far from the then undeveloped resort of Coney Island, where Slade was to train.

Physically, Slade was in good shape, a splendid and sober athlete, but from any other perspective his prospects looked bleak against a Sullivan who had forsworn alcohol, at least for the time being. The short bout with Mitchell had shown Sullivan's speed, resilience and unprecedented punching power. If Sullivan had ever been offered boxing tuition – and condescended to accept it – he could have emerged as a truly great champion rather than the super-slugger he remained. Still, Slade was a far bigger man than Mitchell and he seemed to have the physical resources to stand up to Sullivan without being knocked out.

* * *

Wedding arrangements had already been made and, between them, Richard Fox and Harry Hill had ensured that there would be no publicity. On 19 July 1883, Jem and Nellie were joined in marriage in a civil ceremony at the registration station in 112 East 23rd Street. It was accurately recorded that James Mace, a fifty-two-year-old entertainer, had wed Ellen Lee, aged thirty-one, both of Liverpool, England. Mace falsely stated that this was his first marriage and Nellie, with equal disregard for the truth, asserted that she was a widow but gave her true maiden name of Gore. After the ceremony, Mace hailed a cab and they drove down Manhattan to the east end of Chambers Street. Then, in the summer sunshine, they took the walkway across the Brooklyn Bridge, which had been opened less than two months earlier after sixteen years in construction. As they strode together, hand in hand, high above the carriages and the boats, they turned to look back at Manhattan through the artistic wire cable work. Both experienced a feeling of exhilaration. That they were not man and wife in the eyes of the Church mattered not a jot to them: they were now a married couple under the law of New York State where, they assumed, their future lay. The one-mile walk above the East River took them into Brooklyn, then still a separate city, and from there they went by cab to their temporary home on Long Island.

Slade had three weeks to train at Coney Island. Mace concentrated on his physical conditioning, having long since decided that Slade was too clumsy to improve his footwork any further and too stupid to absorb anything more than the most elementary notions of ringcraft. Mace did not believe for one moment that Herbert could defeat Sullivan, despite his public protestations to the contrary, but he hoped that, as Tug Wilson had done, by gallantry rather than cunning, he would survive his quarter of an hour ordeal. To his credit, Slade applied himself unstintingly to a regime of running and hurdling, and shed almost 30lb. During the four intervening months between Sullivan–Mitchell and Sullivan–Slade, Vanderbilt had augmented the gas lamps at Madison Square Garden with a few electric arc lights, making Slade's challenge the first-ever boxing match to be electrically lit.

The day of the fight was swelteringly hot and humid, but by 6pm the temperature was dropping. The entire neighbourhood of the Garden was jam-packed with men and lads jostling for tickets and scalpers doing a roaring trade. Inside the arena, judges and assembly-men, bankers and brokers were in their private boxes, as was Lawrence R. Jerome, great-uncle of the eight-year-old Winston Churchill. A full house of 10,000 filled the hall, many of them standing, while others paid $2 for a seat. Outside several thousand others waited for news. It was 9.20pm before the gladiators entered, still clad in the traditional manner of the prize-fighter except that their shoes were without studs. Mace was in Slade's corner and his old foe Joe Goss was in Sullivan's. The referee was Barney Aaron, Jewish by faith, born in England but settled in New York, and once again, outside the ring but on the platform, was Captain Clubber Williams. In the intense heat, with poor ventilation, the hall stank of gas fumes, tobacco smoke and sweat. In time-honoured Prize Ring style, bets were laid fast and furious with the going rate at the call of time being 10 to 4 on Sullivan.

For a while, Slade's ability as a wrestler kept Sullivan at bay. He went into a clinch on several occasions, an aspect of the LPR style which, in the nature of things, could never be entirely eliminated from any form of boxing, any more than the arm locking which Sullivan used. But the Strong Boy then pummelled Slade about the shoulders and succeeded in loosening his grip. Left at long range for the first time, the bemused New Zealander made a crude rush at Sullivan, who delivered a right-hand chop to the throat which made Slade stagger. Although he quickly recovered his balance, Slade naively backed up against the ropes. Sullivan, smirking with relish, moved in and unleashed a barrage of head shots. To Mace's dismay, Slade made no attempt to dodge, but he withstood them and Sullivan failed to strike to the chin. Suddenly summoning more courage, Slade charged at Sullivan and tried to beat down his guard, only to find the Bostonian getting a headlock on him. Amidst the crowd's roaring came a few shouts of 'Foul!', which it most certainly was if, as was supposed to be the case, the Queensberry Rules were being observed.

Sullivan used his own wrestling strength to throw Slade clear, simultaneously throwing a right to the jaw which staggered Slade again. Sullivan clearly favoured his right and it was this which caused a flash knockdown. On his feet within two seconds, Slade at last showed he had learned something from Mace, launching uppercuts as he rose, but the punches were so telegraphed that Sullivan blocked them with ease. Then Sullivan erupted, driving Slade back to the ropes before blasting him through them with a punch that lifted him off his feet. Whereas Mitchell had scrambled back of his own accord from a similar situation, Slade was pushed back by the unlikely combination of Mace and Clubber Williams – another breach of the Queensberry Rules, but referee Aaron proved as unwilling to intervene as Al Smith had been. Sullivan had bragged that 'the referee is my right fist' and provided that Clubber Williams was satisfied that the public was getting its money's worth, that had proved true. During the interval, Mace muttered something to Slade, who was slumped in his corner and blowing like a blacksmith's bellows. By contrast, Harry

Hill was bawling from his ringside seat. He had bet heavily on the New Zealander – but only to last four rounds.

The beginning of the second round saw the dimmest echo of Mace's style, as the ponderous Antipodean seemed to half-remember some of his many boxing lessons. It was no use. As he attempted the weight-shift and feint, Sullivan punched him on the nose and made blood run. As Slade at long last employed his left jab, Sullivan ducked and clinched. He threw Slade off, then uncorked a ferocious left to the temple which stretched Slade on the platform. Slade managed to beat the count but Sullivan launched a fusillade to head and body, and Slade slumped to the deck again. When he rose, still groggy, the Bostonian drove him against the ropes and felled him once more with a huge right-hand swipe over the ear. Time was called and Slade, bleeding and with head bowed, had to be led back to his chair by Mace.

For a moment it seemed that the New Zealander was reluctant to continue but he did so. Seemingly fired by a wish to avoid total public humiliation, he attacked Sullivan for the first time and landed four crude blows to the head. Sullivan, surprised but not fazed, targeted the face instead of the head. A colossal left closed Herbert's left eye and dropped him to the floor for the sixth time. Blinded and blood-stained, Slade somehow rose. In a daze, he staggered towards his chair, although a minute of the third round remained. Mace moved towards him to prevent Sullivan striking a man with his hands down, and at this point Clubber Williams, who had been so quick to terminate Mitchell's challenge but so willing to let Slade be punished, finally entered the ring and ostentatiously raised a warning finger to a smiling Sullivan. Slade's challenge was over.

Screaming 'Knocked out! Knocked out!' – in disregard for the truth – most of the crowd rushed to the platform. Sullivan stood aloft, his gloves removed, and reached down to shake the hands of those he chose from his flock of adoring followers. From a strictly financial point of view, Sullivan–Slade had been, at least in the short term, a success. Some $4,000 had been netted, as the loser's cut, but Slade's failure to stand up to Sullivan meant that he was a depreciating asset as far as Mace was concerned. What's more, Slade's one-year contract was due to expire in a mere six weeks' time. Mace decided on a challenge under LPR rules. Not to Sullivan, who had forsworn the

Prize Ring in his Boston defi, but to Charlie Mitchell, who was a veteran of such encounters. Charlie had remained in the USA after his clash with Sullivan but had been limited to exhibitions, mostly against his manager Billy Madden. These had not been well attended, so when Mace suggested an LPR mill, Madden and Mitchell eagerly agreed. Given the total hostility of the populous Eastern states to bareknuckle fighting, it was decided to try to bring off the fight in the vicinity of Kansas City, Missouri. The date was fixed for September 11.

Mace and Madden were eager to tap into the enthusiasm for the outlawed and the illicit which, so they believed, still held sway in the frontier towns of America. They were soon to be disillusioned. Missouri State Governor Thomas T Crittenden declared that no prize-fight would take place on his territory and Mace and Slade were hounded out of Missouri on pain of arrest. It was the second victory over 'outlaws' in quick succession for the pious governor. Only the previous year he had put up a bounty on the head of Jesse James. It had been claimed by the traitorous Robert Ford after he killed the defenceless 'enemy of society' by shooting him in the back while he was hanging pictures on the wall of his home.

By this time, Mace's control of Slade was being challenged. A self-styled 'agent for sportsmen', one H.J. Rice, had approached Slade behind Mace's back. He learned that Slade's contract was due to expire and said he could secure far better terms for him, urging him not to renew without considering other opportunities. In the meantime, Rice had no objection to the proposed prize-fight with Mitchell. Indeed, Rice put up $400 of Slade's stake of $2,500, with Mace contributing $1,500 and the rest being found by Al Smith. Rice's next move proved disastrous. With Mace in Chicago giving an entertainment show, Rice took off with the gullible New Zealander for Atcheson, Kansas, one of the most lawless towns in the West but one where locals would certainly be keen to see a prize-fight. Kansas State Governor Glick ordered the Atcheson County prosecuting attorney to intervene. Throughout this time, Mitchell had been working his socks off under Madden's supervision at Independence, Missouri. As soon as they heard of Glick's decision, Madden declared that Mitchell would not go to Atcheson. On August 31, by an exchange of telegrams between Madden and Rice, the match was declared off.

Madden and Mitchell were bitterly disappointed. They were convinced that Mitchell would beat Slade and saw no reason why alternative venues should not have been discussed before cancellation. In particular, there had been an offer from wealthy sportsmen in El Paso, Texas, to host the fight. El Paso lay on the border with Mexico and was ideally suited to foil the authorities. Mace was understandably furious at Rice's interference and the subsequent failure to bring off the mill – all the more so when Montague informed him of the amount of money spent in setting up the abortive encounter, all of which was now down the drain.

Mace summoned Slade to rejoin him in Minneapolis, which he did but with his 'agent and adviser' Rice by his side. There was little time for recriminations. Within three days the deadline fixed for the fight would expire. The stakes had been deposited with Harry Hill in New York and all concerned hastened back there in an attempt to claim forfeit. Madden and Mitchell did likewise, intent on preventing just such an outcome. Hill resolved the matter by returning only each man's individual stake.

The sub-plot to this protracted fizzle was now revealed. Unbeknown to all except Rice, Al Smith, by now Sullivan's manager, had dreamt up a boxing bonanza for the Bostonian. Travelling chiefly via the Transcontinental, Sullivan would crisscross America on a Grand Tour for eight months solid, visiting 136 cities and towns. He would reissue his old challenge to 'any man in the house' to last four Queensberry rounds with him and anyone who took him up on the offer stood to gain $250. Given Sullivan's fearsome reputation, there would be few takers, so he required a so-called 'corps pugilistique' who would fight each other or spar with him. He already had two lightweights, plus Steve Taylor, but he needed one more heavyweight. The ideal choice, as Smith had seen it and as Rice agreed, was a man of considerable bulk but minimal skill: in other words, Herbert Slade. On September 15, Slade's contract with Mace conveniently expired, and three days later, Al Smith announced the Grand Tour, naming Slade as a member of the group.

Almost as soon as he had broken with Mace, Slade began to allege that he had exploited him by paying him only a dollar a week throughout the eight months they had been together in the US. What's more, claimed the New Zealander, he hadn't received a cent of his $4,000 share of the gate from his fight with Sullivan. Soon, however, Rice, acting as Slade's new manager, authorised The Maori to pay Mace $300. This was publicly stated as being compensation for breach of contract but, as the contract drawn up in New Zealand had expired, Slade was now a free agent. Had Slade's allegations been true, Rice would scarcely have let Mace have any money and Slade was careful not to repeat what he had said. The circumstances suggest that Mace and Montague accepted a one-off payment rather than pursuing Rice and Slade through the courts for slander. Mace had paid all the New Zealander's living and accommodation expenses. As for the $300 payment itself, it represented little more than a month's wages for Slade. Rice had negotiated a deal that guaranteed Slade $300 a month for his part in Sullivan's Grand Tour.

Had Slade succeeded in going the distance with Sullivan at the Garden, he would have been a trump card for Mace's shows. Even a defeated Slade would have been a curiosity, but after his transfer to Sullivan and Smith there was no real audience for any exhibitions or shows which Jem might seek to promote – and almost no towns or cities where the locals were not saving up for an announced visit, sometime between the autumn and the spring, by Sullivan. Montague had to take the bull by the horns and tell his pal how the money situation stood. There was only one course of action: to cut his losses and return to England. In October, the Maces, together with Harry Montague and Dick Brighton, boarded the *Oregon* in New York, bound for Liverpool.

As for Herbert Slade, his future ring career was nothing short of pathetic. At the beginning of October, he fought a private match against Mitchell in Harry Hill's mansion in Flushing. Charlie knocked him out in the fourth round. Slade even failed to last out the Grand Tour. After a drunken brawl with Sullivan in San Francisco, he was fired. Slade then attempted a career for himself in the West but never won a single fight. After a lamentable career record of seven losses in seven bouts, five by knockout, he worked as a saloon bouncer in California where, after being involved in several bar room brawls, he was lucky to escape with his life when shot in the chest. The hapless Herbert ended up as a woodchopper in Utah.

Mace's third visit to America had been a disaster. Stalled by Fox's unexpected preference for Charlie Mitchell, tricked by Rice's chicanery, wrongfooted by Slade's desertion and upstaged by Sullivan and Smith, his losses were piling up. He was by no means blameless. Motivated by crass greed, he hadn't hesitated to use the most cynical of showman's tricks to take in a gullible public and to maintain for as long as he could the facade that Slade was a meaningful challenger. This was something which he knew, before he even set foot again in America, was totally without foundation. So patient and calculating in the Prize Ring, Mace was a man who, in ordinary life, could not bide his time. He had rushed in, eager for short-term gain, and paid a price in terms of not only his personal finances but his previously untarnished reputation as a judge of boxing and boxers.

It would take America almost a decade to realise that, far from being a charlatan, Mace had already, in Australia, laid the foundations of the new sport of boxing. But back in the autumn of 1883, his credibility was destroyed. Even those who could see through the hysteria surrounding John L. Sullivan and the travesty of the Queensberry Rules which he purveyed could not avoid linking the name of Mace with that of Slade, one of the biggest stiffs who ever stepped through the ropes of a boxing ring.

PART FIVE

The Boxing Revolutionary

(1884–92)

26

Thwarted Divorce

IN SOME WAYS it was just like old times, in others intriguingly different. There was the familiar muster just before dawn in the heart of London, but instead of meeting at one or other of the capital's railway stations, they had congregated in the cafe of a hotel off Leicester Square. Mace smiled to himself at the assembly of men dressed in tweeds and deerstalkers and sporting fishing rods and shotguns, dressed just as he was, although he was the only one famous enough to require disguise. The Metropolitan Police had been successfully bluffed. These were gentlemen, about to leave for a day in the country to pursue the cherished aristocratic pastime of 'hunting, shooting and fishing' . . . or so it seemed. In the unlikely event of hooligans seeking to gatecrash this toffs' excursion, everyone had to be screened and know the chosen password. All went well and, a few hours later, they were at the village of Linfield, near East Grinstead, chosen because it lay close to the boundaries of Sussex, Surrey and Kent. The London Prize Ring, moribund for nearly two decades, was about to be revived.

When Mace had first heard of the plans, he had been keenly interested. He still hankered after what he regarded as the true test of skill and endurance which the LPR provided and the arrangements seemed admirably suited both to fool the police and keep out the roughs. Since he had returned over two years earlier from America, Mace had been living with his wife and family in Liverpool, a contented existence but one which had lacked the spice he craved. Now it would return, not merely in the defiance of authority but in the promotion of unarmed combat.

The organiser of this new 'Fight for the Championship' was a bookmaker and moneylender John Perceval. Failing to persuade the official champion, the bulky Scots-born Jack Knifton, the so-called '81 Tonner', to discard gloves and defend his crown in a bareknuckle mill,

Perceval chose two young fighters, Jem Smith and Jack Davis, to fight for the succession – and Perceval was eager to secure the support of the last Champion of the London Prize Ring, Jem Mace, to add legitimacy to his promotion by acting as a second to one of the protagonists. This was what had brought about his presence on the morning of 17 December 1885. Davis was reckoned to be a young fighter with some style. The same could not be said for his opponent, yet it was Smith who was regarded as the 'coming man'. Aged twenty-two and born in Shoreditch, he earned his living as a labourer in a timber yard. He had already fought on sixteen occasions and won every time. As a lad he'd won a lightweight competition and, a year later, one at middleweight; by now he weighed all of fifteen stone despite being only 5ft 8in tall. He was as ready to fight with bare knuckles as he was with gloves and had already seen off four opponents in covert scraps – but as Mace had heard from Richardson that Smith had not a clue as to science and neither the wish nor the brains to learn so, he agreed to second Davis.

When Mace first saw the Shoreditch labourer, he was contemptuous both of Smith's physique and his mentality. Built like a weight-lifter, not a boxer, Smith moved as if musclebound and his features were fixed in a vacuous grin. Unfortunately, young Davis lost his nerve and, within ten minutes, Smith was smirking as he thumped and battered his opponent into helplessness. Smith had no time to enjoy his coronation. Somehow the police had got wind of what was taking place and the entire party had to make a run for it. Mace surprised those who didn't know him: at fifty-four, the former pedestrian sprinted like a man at least twenty years younger and made good his getaway.

The clandestine events at East Grinstead were half a world away from the flamboyant scene in America, where John L. Sullivan continued to reign supreme. Only three months earlier, Sullivan had condescended, for the first time, to put his American Championship – and by implication the world title – on the line in a bout which would, it was announced, be fought, as usual, under 'the Marquess of Queensberry's Rules'. On 29 August 1885, at Chester Park in Cincinnati, Sullivan faced the twenty-two-year-old Pittsburgher Dominick McCaffrey, his first serious American challenger. McCaffrey knew how to box and had a victory over Charlie Mitchell to its credit – but he was, at 165lb, only a middleweight. McCaffrey gave a good account of himself but was overpowered by Sullivan. Knocked down several times, he managed to get up and box on, but at the start of round six, a perplexed Sullivan seized McCaffrey, threw him and pinned him to the deck. At once, the referee, Billy Tate, stopped the fight, but instead of disqualifying Sullivan for a blatant foul, he awarded him victory. The Boston Strong Boy was now proclaimed Champion of the World under Queensberry Rules and was richer by $6,000.

When Mace read about Sullivan–McCaffrey, it only confirmed his negative attitude towards the Queensberry Rules. Their intention had been flawed and their effect was simply to provide a bonanza for Sullivan; and while the much-vaunted Rules were inadequate as a measure of boxing skill, Sullivan's version of them was a travesty. It suited him to proclaim his zeal for the Rules because this safeguarded him from arrest but his observance of John Chambers' list of regulations was confined to the wearing of gloves and to boxing three-minute rounds. Against Mitchell, against Slade and now against McCaffrey, the burly Bostonian braggart had not hesitated to flout rule after rule and he had got clean away with it.

Not the least of the inadequacies of Chambers' regulations was the failure to define the role of the referee. As drafted by Chambers, the referee was a marginal figure, mentioned only three times: in Rule 4, the Kayo rule, it was stated only that 'it should be in the power of the referee to give his award in favour of the other man', i.e. the one who remained standing while his opponent was down for at least ten seconds. In Rule 9 it was stated that if a glove burst or came off it must be 'replaced to the referee's satisfaction'. And Rule 7 stated that, in the event of a stoppage by 'unavoidable interference', the referee was 'to name the time and place . . . for finishing the contest'. However, Sullivan's key Queensberry Rules fights depended on 'unavoidable interference' of the kind in which Clubber Williams specialised. Seeing as Rule 6 stated that 'no seconds or any other person to be allowed in the ring during a round', Williams had no right to even step between the ropes, let alone to terminate Mitchell's challenge – or even that of the struggling Slade. The referees in those two bouts, Al Smith and Barney Aaron, might as well have fallen asleep for all they contributed.

Now Billy Tate, in declaring Sullivan the winner after he used an LPR
move against McCaffrey, was both acting beyond his powers and acting
illegally since Rule 2 stated 'no wrestling . . . allowed'. The Queensberry Rules were hopelessly unsuited to bouts between professionals.
While Sullivan's supporters, fuelled by booze and bloodlust, did not
mind, if they even knew, that their hero cared nothing for the Rules
to which he trumpeted his allegiance, boxing scribes, who should have
known better, foolishly hailed Sullivan as an innovator and in doing so
perpetuated a myth.

★ ★ ★

It had seemed, after Mace's abrupt return to England in 1883, that his
days of wandering were over. He had settled with Nellie and their
daughter in Liverpool. It was of course her home city and one which
he had always liked. Mace was by now officially classed as a 'gentleman', meaning that he had independent means and was not obliged to
earn a living. He remained the nominal owner of the Victoria Racing
Club Hotel in Melbourne but, more importantly, he had a source of
income as a result of the shares which he had bought in Australian
goldmines. His bank account was, however, by now substantially
depleted. He took a relatively modest family house at Queens Road in
the Everton district and although it was not far away from the
Strawberry Tavern, he did not often look in at his old abode which, by
now denuded of its grounds, was a pale shadow of what it had been
fifteen years earlier. Anyhow, by now he had a pub project of his own
in hand. One thing he had noted about the rise of Charlie Mitchell
was the role of a new breed of London drum, one which dissociated
itself from the Prize Ring, preferring to host Queenberry Rules
tournaments legally on site. One such was the Blue Anchor, still run
by his old pal Bill Richardson. The East End was, as ever, the greatest
nursery of English fighters and Jem bought an interest in a pub on the
Mile End Road in the heart of Stepney. Adjacent to Whitechapel, it
was an area with many Jewish immigrants – not from the old Sephardi
community, which had produced Daniel Mendoza and Dutch Sam,
but from the Ashkenazy refugees from Tsarist pogroms in Poland and
the Ukraine. Mace believed that young men from ethnic minorities,

gypsies, Jews and those of African descent, had the greatest potential to become boxers and he hoped to find a few and promote them. He visited the pub regularly for that purpose but left someone else in charge of the day-to-day running.

The Mace family included his stepson John Lee, who at thirteen was making fine progress at Liverpool Institute, the most prestigious school in the city. John had inherited his parents' musical aptitude and was soon proficient on the piano, while Jem paid for him to take violin lessons. But it was as a painter rather than as a musician that John excelled. He loved to spend his spare time doing sketches and watercolours of the splendid buildings in Liverpool city centre. St George's Hall was now flanked by the Picton Library and the Walker Art Gallery and he committed these to paper and canvas, hoping to make a living from his work when he was old enough.

Mace got on very well with John and was a good stepfather to him. Anyone with artistic talent would commend himself to Mace, who had painted occasionally as a hobby since he was in his twenties. Realising that John was not athletic, Mace put no pressure on him as far as sports were concerned but taught him the rudiments of self-defence. At the time, notorious gangs of lowlifes, such as the High Rip gang, lurked in Liverpool city centre seeking victims to rob. Knowing that he had the means to protect himself if attacked gave John confidence. The lad liked his stepfather and, bearing in mind that his own father had never shown any interest in him, he preferred to be known as John Mace not John Lee.

Nellie was now living not far from her sister Annie. She and Mace were frequent visitors to the McCall family home in the Kensington district. Annie now had five young children to look after so it was easier if Jem, Nellie, John and Ellen visited her rather than the other way around. Apart from his Australian dividends, Mace supplemented his income by giving boxing exhibitions. Soon after he arrived in Liverpool, Charlie Mitchell was in town, spitting feathers about a decision made by Harry Hill in a fight at the Hill mansion. Mitchell had been awarded a win over William Sheriff, a naturalised German, but, due to gambling pressure, Hill changed his mind and prolonged the contest for another round before declaring a draw. Mitchell promptly took the first boat back to England.

Mace and Mitchell fought an exhibition bout in Liverpool which was well attended. Afterwards, Mace advised his opponent to put his disappointment behind him and return to the States where, as a young fighter, big money was to be made. Mitchell replied that he was doing that anyway and needed no advice. At twenty-two, he knew it all. Relations between him and Mace remained fraught. They would enter the ring together for the purposes of lucrative exhibitions but they really had nothing in common except a shared antipathy to John L. Sullivan. Mitchell's return to America left the British scene almost bereft of talented and still-active boxers. In 1884, Mace undertook a five-bout exhibition series of three-rounders with Jack Smith, considered promising in some quarters. Mostly fought in the Midlands, they were poorly attended and it was obvious that Smith would never get anywhere as a boxer.

By the new year, Jem and Nellie had adjusted to their new life in Liverpool with John and Ellen. Mace commuted to London on business every few weeks and occasionally Nellie went with him, leaving the children with the McCalls to spend a weekend at his pub in the Mile End Road. Before long, they began to consider divorce proceedings against Hannah. In view of what she had done, they supposed that those proceedings would be guaranteed success, which would be one obstacle removed from their new goal of becoming man and wife under English law. What's more, Rowland Lee had let it be known that, provided someone else paid his legal fees, he would not mind divorcing Nellie. A plan of campaign had to be drawn up.

Jem and Nellie went to see Amelia at the house where she was working as a maid. They told her of their plans to use Hannah's bigamous marriage to get a divorce which would leave them free to wed. Amelia was delighted. There was only one thing: Ada was still living in the Harris household, albeit unhappily, and as soon as papers were served on their mother, she would figure out who the 'snitch bitches' – as she would call it – were and Ada's life would be hell. Nellie's heart went out to the girls. 'Why don't you both come and live with us in Liverpool?' she asked. Amelia said she would jump at the chance and Nellie promised to look out a suitable position in the home of a well-to-do family. Amelia agreed to tell Ada that Mace would use his contacts to find a job for her in the commercial sector of Liverpool, which was just beginning to employ female stenographers. Despite their confidence in both girls, Mace and Nellie kept their own bigamous marriage a secret for the time being. Even the McCalls did not yet know about the Manhattan ceremony.

Within a few months, both nineteen-year-old Amelia and seventeen-year-old Ada had joined their father and Nellie at Queens Road. In Ada's case it had been preceded by a bitter row with Hannah. At this stage, the name of Mace was attracting strong newspaper coverage but it was with regard to Alfred, not Jem. In July 1884, Alfred Mace took over Westminster Central Hall for a series of sermons which drew quite large audiences. Alfred was a fine orator and vulnerable souls thrilled to hear him denounce sin in lurid language. His voice grew husky as he fulminated against fornication. But he never descended to airing dirty washing in public – if asked about his father, he merely replied that he wished him well and hoped that he would see the error of his ways. He would be delighted to welcome him into the fold of repentant sinners.

Mace had no intention of seeing the light and waited impatiently for the aggravating Alf to depart on an evangelistic tour of America, the first of many. As it happened, he had inherited his father's combative temperament; he delighted in taking on the other members of his sect in matters of Biblical interpretation and was ruthlessly successful in a struggle for power within the movement. There would be times when Jem had a sneaking sympathy for Alf's bold and direct approach, although not for his beliefs, and he compared him favourably with his brother James. Mace was pleased to see James clear off to the States as his brother's sidekick.

Nellie greeted the departure of Alfred and James with particular relief. She did not share Mace's confidence that his sons would never mention her name in public and this was another reason why the start of divorce proceedings was delayed. When Mace finally consulted a solicitor, he said nothing whatever about his marriage ceremony in New York. He was advised that Hannah's bigamous marriage would be regarded as such a heinous offence that his prior adultery with Nellie would not be regarded as causative. Mace had no intention of making the same mistake as he had done twenty years earlier when his previous affair with Selina Hart had denied him a divorce from his wife Mary. Still, he was careful not to tell his own lawyer about that.

On 4 September 1884, James Mace filed a petition for divorce against Hannah Mace. He cited George Harris as the co-respondent, alleging habitual adultery between her and Harris. There would be no need of evidence in support, other than the apparent clincher: the production of a copy of the Harris-Mace marriage certificate which it was a formality to obtain. Mace looked forward to making a brief and triumphant appearance in the Royal Court of Justice, George Edmund Street's splendid Gothic Revival masterpiece in the Strand. There was a delay of a month due to court procedure, and it was a further month before Hannah and Harris replied, but Hannah's Answer, duplicated by Harris, was devastating to Jem and Nellie's hopes. In boxing terms, Hannah's wily solicitor, Henry Levy, had carried out a classic left-right combination. First, it was argued that the marriage between Hannah and George Harris was in fact lawful. And how could that be? Precisely because her marriage to Mace had been itself a bigamous one, since his wife Mary was still living at the time. Second, she alleged that Mace and 'a woman named Nellie' had been habitually committing adultery. Only the scene of their lustful lapses had varied. Sometimes it had been in London, other times in Liverpool and yet others in 'the City of Brooklyn in New York, America'. Paragraph six was the real knockout blow: 'In or about the year 1880', Mace had 'contracted a marriage with the said "Nellie" at Brooklyn.' Hannah went on to 'pray' that the Court would reject Mace's petition and that it would decree that her alleged marriage with him was null and void and that Hannah was thus free from all bond of marriage with him.

When his own lawyer told him all this, Mace felt he had been struck as hard emotionally as he had ever been physically in all his years in the Prize Ring but he had to compose himself before comforting a tearful Nellie. As for Amelia and Ada, both girls seethed with anger at their mother's public disavowal of her marriage with their father. They had thought that his first wife had died shortly before their parents met. Now the truth was out, they didn't blame their father. It was their mother who was publicly 'making bastards' of each of them. Amelia and Ada vowed never to have anything to do with their mother again and their mutual bond with Nellie was strengthened. All three women saw themselves as victims of Hannah Harris.

At first Mace's solicitor, Henry Sydney, had been apprehensive about disclosing Hannah's answer to Mace. Like some men of his profession, he felt physically uneasy in the presence of a master pugilist, but Mace was unusually subdued. When he asked what options were left to him, Sydney replied tentatively that he could cut his costs by seeking leave to withdraw his petition.

'Write me out a letter and I'll sign it,' said Mace.

Sydney did so and watched Mace perusing it before seizing a pen, dipping it fiercely into an inkwell and producing a signature even uglier than his usual crude scrawl. It was in moments like these that Mace's well of resentment against his long-dead father – the author, as he saw it, of his own illiteracy – caused his hand to tremble with anger when doing the bidding of educated men.

In the following weeks, Mace's fighting instinct resurfaced. He went back to Sydney's office and made points of his own: principally that Hannah had alleged that he had married Nellie four years ago not, as was the case, only last year. How convenient to have a date that preceded her own 'marriage' with Harris by a year! True, sighed Sydney, but 'no court would grant a decree of divorce to a man who was an acknowledged bigamist and not merely once but . . .' His voice tailed off. Mace had to admit defeat and on 2 December 1884 Charles P Butt, the judge who would have heard the case, called all three counsel to his chambers and dismissed Mace's petition, ordering him to pay the costs of both Hannah and Harris, the total being over £20. The judge had been carefully relieved of the need to pass judgment on the validity or otherwise of the marriage between Jem Mace and Hannah Boorn twenty years earlier. Henry Levy had now struck out of Hannah's Answer the sentence where she had asked the court to pronounce that marriage null and void. Hannah doubtless had her motivations and her self-reassurances. She had been unwilling to take the blame for the disintegration of the marriage. She had used Mace's maintenance money to give the clever Ada a good education and had not lived well at his expense – far from it. Before meeting Harris, she had been reduced to taking in laundry. She had been deeply hurt by suggestions, albeit not made in court, that her negligence had contributed in any way to Ben's death and had never put forward the line, which would have been readily believed in certain quarters, that Mace had ever struck her. She had always been relaxed when she had been with him, as had all the women who populated Jem's life and would do so in future.

But how had Hannah found out about Jem and Nellie's bigamous marriage? Amelia and Ada had not been told and neither, at that point, had the McCalls. Only a handful of people knew and, of these, Pooley's loyalty went without saying, as did Montague's. And who could suppose that old Dick Brighton would reveal it? There was Richard Fox, of course, the tabloid tittle-tattler supreme, but he was surely far too busy expanding his personal wealth. There would be no equivalent of Jack Hicks this time around, no betrayal from a man of the Prize Ring. Eventually, although the matter was never proved, suspicion fell on Harry Hill's wife. She was known to hold a grudge against Mace due to the money her husband had lost in betting on Herbert Slade. At the end of the day, the identity of the snitch was scarcely important. Mace and Nellie had been thwarted in their plans to wed in England but Nellie now had two effective step-daughters who would regard her, from then on, as the true mother figure in their lives.

* * *

The mid-1880s were years in which Mace looked at the fight game almost as an outsider. He wound up his interest in the pub in the Mile End Road, having failed to discover any significant boxing talent there. He had been looking in the right place – but at least a generation early. The first half of the twentieth century would see many outstanding Jewish boxers emerge from the East End, notably Ted 'Kid' Lewis (Gershon Mendeloff) and Jack 'Kid' Berg (Judah Bergman). Lewis would be World Welterweight Champion and Berg a later contender for that crown.

With Mitchell remaining in the USA, the quality of active English heavyweights remained mediocre. Officially, the champion was Jack Knifton, and his chief rival was the stocky Midlands middleweight Alf Greenfield. Their principal ambition was to be summoned across the Atlantic by Fox, that great believer in the LPR talent pool, for a lucrative payday against Sullivan. Mitchell had been lined up to fight Sullivan again in June 1884 but the champion showed up drunk at Madison Square Garden and the bout had to be cancelled. It seemed that the Boston Strong Boy had been deceived by news that Mitchell was ill and consequently had gone on a binge. Mitchell's 'illness' was in fact a ruse intended to lull Sullivan into not training but he had not anticipated the outcome.

In November, Alf Greenfield was fed to Sullivan at the Garden, rescued by Clubber Williams as he took punishment, arrested, tried and acquitted, and signed up for a rematch. This was held in Sullivan's hometown and, in Boston, Greenfield now used Tug Wilson-style tactics to evade Sullivan. He lasted the full four rounds. It was less than glorious, but hyped up in the *Police Gazette*, it fascinated the American public. Mace reacted with a mixture of amusement and contempt to news of these antics but, in March 1885, he learned with regret that Goss had died in Boston, aged only forty-seven, a victim of kidney failure brought on by alcoholism. In August 1885, Sullivan's defeat of Dominick McCaffrey established him as World Heavyweight Champion under Queensberry Rules, as well as those of the LPR. Still, no one in England cared. The boxing public remained dormant, unlike in the States where Sullivan's undoubtedly charismatic personality held centre stage.

Few in America, and even fewer in England, paid any attention to the boxing scene in Australia. Mace himself had to rely on occasional letters from Larry Foley to bring him up to date. Bob Fitzsimmons had finally presented himself at the White Horse, having taken two years to break away from family commitments in New Zealand. Peter Jackson had yet to come to terms with body-punching. Expected to overcome the title-holder Bill Farnan, he had indeed given Farnan a boxing lesson until suddenly laid low by three surprise shots to the midriff. A rematch had ended in stalemate. Foley himself had been beaten by William Miller, who claimed the title on the basis of a lineal victory over the last Australian bareknuckle titleholder. Until such confusion was sorted out, the Australian fight scene could not move forward.

For two years Mace boxed a variety of Queensberry exhibitions against such opponents as Jack Smith, Jack Burke, Tug Wilson, Jack Knifton and, above all, Pooley. His cousin was not best off financially and Mace was pleased to help him out, especially as Pooley and Delaiah by now had a young family to support. For several years after their marriage they had tried their luck in Scotland, where Pooley had been a horse trader. His father-in-law Ambrose Smith (Jasper Petulengro) was a prominent figure north of the border and had attracted the attention of Queen Victoria whilst she was in residence at Balmoral. The Queen's fascination with gypsies belied her staid public image and Pooley had been one of a group of Romanies who were presented to her shortly before Petulengro's death. Delaiah and Pooley had four children. Madonna, known as Donna, had been born in Norwich and the other three arrived during their Scottish travels: Herbert (Herbie) at Dundee; Augustus (Gusty) near Stirling and Melbourne (Mel) at Kirkcaldy. Melbourne's name was inspired by news of Jem's triumphs in Australia, which arrived by letter.

Not long after Mace returned to England, Pooley and his family went to live in Essex, where they had a house in Leyton, not far from London. It served as a home from home for Jem but it was not long before he and Pooley were gambling and Jem depleted his capital with spectacular losses on the Grand National at Aintree, only a few miles from his home in Liverpool. It seemed as if he was kicking over the traces at the comparative dullness of his life and his comment to Ted McCall that he was 'in danger of becoming respectable' – something which Ted wisely refrained from repeating to the Gore sisters – told its own tale. It was at this point that he was contacted by John Perceval and asked to participate in the clash between Jem Smith and Jack Davis.

Mace, annoyed by Smith's victory but elated to be back in the thick of things, talked over the prize-fight scene with Perceval and an old friend of his own, former bookie Johnny Gideon, now a well-known sporting journalist, who had been at the mill. Mace remarked that in America, Texan border towns were being used for prize-fights, with the proviso that the participants could always slip across the frontier to lawless Mexico to gain immunity from police interference. Gideon took the point and came up with an idea of his own. At this time France was starting to rival the English-speaking countries in the world of horseracing. Gideon had established many contacts there and knew that, although pugilism was illegal, the French magistrates had power only to detain contestants but not to incarcerate them. What's more, the gendarmerie had no experience of prize-fighting and little inclination to put themselves out to prevent it. It was not long before Smith's first defence of his title was arranged to take place on French soil. His opponent would be Alf Greenfield. The date was set for 16 February 1886 and the mill would be at the equestrian town of Maisons-Laffitte, less than twenty-five kilometres by rail from Paris. To add the lustre of his name to this attempted revival of the London Prize Ring on French soil, Mace was asked to be the referee. He agreed.

On the racetrack at Maisons-Laffitte, constructed on the model of Newmarket and in the shadow of Francois Mansart's splendid 17th-century chateau, Greenfield challenged Smith. Despite the immunity from police interference, matters did not turn out well. After almost an hour of crude brawling, a group of drunken thugs broke into the ring to save their man Greenfield from defeat. They drew knives and threatened to kill Mace, who had no hesitation in abandoning the match, which was called a draw. He was enraged that he had inadvertently presided over a virtual riot and did not linger at the scene, catching a train to Paris where he stayed for a couple of nights. He made his way to the grave of Adah Isaacs Menken and stood silently, remembering happier times with his beautiful lover. Then grief gave way to desire and he made his way to the Folies Bergeres in Montmartre. Mace knew only a handful of words in French but, elegant and confident as ever, he bluffed his way backstage and began chatting to several dancing girls. Asked what was his profession, he replied that he was a well-known musician in England and, finding a violin, proceeded to play. Usually taken for a man in his early forties rather than his mid-fifties, Mace had accentuated the effect by dying his greying hair to its pristine black. Finding a girl who had sufficient grasp of English to hold a conversation with him, he discussed his career as a circus proprietor and statuarist. In the early hours of the morning he accompanied her to her nearby apartment and they made love until daybreak.

★ ★ ★

Not long after the Parisian episode, Nellie took Mace to task for the first time in their life together. The cause was not his night of passion in Montmartre, of which Nellie remained unaware until many years afterwards, but the downturn in his economic fortunes. In 1886 a huge gold strike on the Witwatersrand in the province of Transvaal made South Africa, then under British rule, the centre of world gold production. It was a far larger lode than that in Australia and was skilfully exploited. Shares in De Beers, the extracting company, rocketed and, as a result, Australian holdings began to lose value. Mace did not seem concerned by this setback and failed to moderate his often lavish expenditure. By this time his friend Harry Montague had resigned as his business manager, to be succeeded by George Ware. Montague was doubtless exasperated by Mace's financial recklessness. Though Jem promised Nellie that he would change his ways it was not long before he was again gambling. In the summer, he and Jack Knifton went on an exhibition tour of Britain which, significantly, ended up in Newmarket in high season.

In August came the death of Mace's old pal, Bill Richardson who, while Mace was travelling the world, had remained contentedly as landlord of the Blue Anchor in Bethnal Green. Their friendship had had its ups and downs, often due to political disagreement: Richardson was a lifelong radical who helped with the provision of soup kitchens in the East End. One of the few publicans who was not a staunch Tory, he was equally contemptuous of Conservatives and Liberals. In the boxing world, he had always been wary of the 'so-called Corinthian swells', as he referred to them. In many ways Big Bill had been the heart and soul of the Prize Ring and his death seemed to some to mark the end of an era. Significantly, in the previous year Richardson had formed the Professional Boxers Association and both Jem and Pooley Mace had enrolled. The new terminology indicated how the more progressive ex-prizefighters now regarded themselves.

Richardson's demise coincided with the return from America of Charlie Mitchell, by now disillusioned with Sullivan's failure to grant him a return bout. Richardson, who had known Mitchell since he was a lad, was almost the only man to whom the cocksure Brummie ever seriously listened. He would have been appalled by Mitchell's new-found friends. Mitchell's father-in-law, the inappropriately named George Washington Moore, known to one and all as 'Pony' Moore, introduced him to possibly the most loathsome person ever to haunt the fringes of the Prize Ring: George Baird.

Baird was born in the same year as Mitchell, 1861; but whereas Mitchell had emerged from poverty by dint of his undoubted brilliance as a boxer-puncher, Baird was the profligate heir to an inheritance of £3 million deriving from the accumulated wealth of a family of Scottish iron masters. An orphan at nine, he did much as he liked from then on and was never out of trouble. He fled from Eton to pre-empt expulsion and was sent down from Cambridge. Preferring to be known as 'Squire Abingdon', Baird was, like many adherents of the Prize Ring, a gambler, chain smoker and alcoholic, but he was also a rabid dog-fighting buff and a bar room brawler notorious for kicks to the crotch and for lashing out with broken bottles. As to his relations with women, they chiefly comprised sadistic encounters with whores. Baird revelled in stories of the marathon bloodbaths of the Prize Ring and, contemptuous of any authority seeking to restrain him in the slightest, he sought to revive them. Disdainful of scientific boxing, he gave Mitchell money to fight as dirty as possible.

Mitchell's already large ego was further inflated by the patronage of the Squire, while his reflexes were dulled by the champagne lavished on him. Baird was anathema to Mace. Already soured by what happened at Maisons-Laffitte, it would not be long before the activities of the Brummie brawler and the squalid Scottish pseudo-Squire would lead him to turn his back forever on the remnants of the London Prize Ring. Already Mace made up his mind not to attend any further fights in France.

Towards the end of the year, two bouts for the championship failed to come off. Knifton, who looked on Jem Smith as an upstart, challenged him to a bareknuckle mill. They went first to France but the gendarmerie were alerted and eager to prevent any repetition of the disturbances at Maisons-Laffitte. Five days later they tried again in England but police were on the scene before fighting could begin. They ordered all concerned to disperse. Smith wanted to reconvene in another county but Knifton, believing this the height of folly and considering both of them lucky not to have been arrested and charged, refused. The immediate consequence of these aborted fights was the foundation in London of a club in Soho, located at Gerrard Street and dedicated to both boxing and horseracing. It was known as the Pelican Club.

The official aim of the Pelican Club was to hold boxing bouts on its premises in accordance with the Queensberry Rules. Unofficially, many of its members wished to use it as a kind of super-drum from which prize-fights could be organised safe from police informers. The fights would take place in France and considerable subterfuge would be used in travelling to one or other of the Channel ports without being recognised as would-be participants in an illegal activity. The Pelican Club was founded by William Goldberg, a Jewish journalist on the *Sporting Times*, a periodical which had long taken over from the moribund *Bell's Life*. Devoted mainly to horseracing, the 'Pink 'Un', as it was known from the colour of its pages, was keenly interested in the ring. While Goldberg and his manager Ernest 'Swears' Wells were the owners of the Pelican, it succeeded in its aim of attracting an aristocratic clientele.

Mace's attitude to the Pelican Club was ambivalent. He knew several of its leading lights. He had fought a private match near the Elephant with one – Lord Charles Beresford, with whom he got on quite well – but another member was the Marquess of Queensberry. Much as he had respected Queensberry's father, the former Viscount Drumlanrig, he disliked John Sholto Douglas, the ninth earl. Queensberry had of course been closely associated with John Graham Chambers, the actual author of the Queensberry Rules.

John Chambers had not seen fit to consult Mace about the drafting of these rules, even though he was Champion of England at the time. He was also hostile because of Mace's former association with the Liverpool Olympics. But Chambers had died, aged only forty, in 1883. After his death, the Amateur Boxing Association, which he founded, continued to distance itself from top-class professionals such as Mace. Not one to bear grudges, Jem was nevertheless angered to learn of Queensberry's behaviour at the Pelican Club. Coarse and choleric as ever, he would loudly express his dislike of boxers who attempted 'science'. 'More gore, more gore, more GORE!' bellowed the puce-faced sponsor of the rules supposed to reform boxing. In this blood-thirsty chorus, Queensberry was loudly joined by none other than 'Squire Abingdon', Mitchell's new-found boozing and brawling crony.

As to the actual Boxing Committee of the Pelicans, Mace again held mixed views. The boxing manager was John Fleming, a man in his mid-forties. Fleming was well-known in the sporting pubs of London, many of which had accommodated themselves to the crackdown on prize-fighting by holding competitions for young part-timers under the three-minute, four-round format. When Mace was in London and had visited the sporting pubs, Fleming would approach him and seek his views on possible rule changes. Fleming was known to have been 'in private business' off Worship Lane in Shoreditch before becoming a sporting publican. Mace thought he remembered Fleming as a youngster hawking pornographic photos around Hare Lane market. The Pelicans' manager had an odd manner, brusque, pompous and furtive, but no one doubted his managerial acumen or capacity for innovation. Fleming had, in his youth, frequented the Cambrian Stores while Nat Langham was still alive. Well aware of Langham's connection with the aristocracy at the Rum-pum-pas Club, Fleming dreamt of reviving it under his own aegis even while he was running some of the roughest and toughest pubs in London. But the extent to which Fleming could discriminate between honourable members of the aristocracy and such types as Queensberry and Squire Abingdon was, Mace thought, an open question.

Then there was Arthur F Bettinson, nicknamed 'Peggy', and, at twenty-five, the youngest member of the committee. Bettinson, the scion of an upper middle-class family and raised in leafy Marylebone, had, to his credit, learned the trade of upholstery. Mixing with working men, he became interested in boxing and won the amateur lightweight title in 1882. Bereft of his father figure with John Chambers' demise, Bettinson had attended on every occasion when Mace had subsequently sparred in London. The impressionable Arthur had asked Mace for lessons but seemed reluctant to make the trip to Liverpool to receive them. Still, he was on record as stating in public that it was 'an undeniable maxim that . . . there is only one style in boxing. And that style found its most perfect exponent in the person of Jem Mace.' Clearly a young man of excellent judgment, as Jem joked to Pooley.

But the most encouraging thing about the Pelicans was the identity of the chairman of its Boxing Committee. He was none other than the thirty-year-old Earl of Lonsdale – one and the same as the twelve-year-old Hugh Cecil Lowther for whom Mace had been engaged as a paid boxing tutor. After his father's death and the premature demise of his older brother, Hugh had inherited the peerage at the age of twenty-five. He was as extravagant as Squire Abingdon and a well-known figure at every racetrack and hunt meet in the country.

Lonsdale was nicknamed the 'Yellow Earl' for his flamboyant retinue of coachmen and outriders kitted out in the family colours but, unlike Baird, he despised alcoholic excess, won women by his charm and persuasion and was dignified at all times. Above all, he believed that boxing was at the least a science, at best an art but never an excuse for the coarse brutality which was relished by the likes of Queensberry and Abingdon.

Although cordially invited to attend the Pelican Club by Lord Lonsdale – who always called him 'Jem' whereas he addressed Fleming and Bettinson by their surnames – Mace kept his distance. Meanwhile, in the winter of 1887, he undertook a series of four exhibitions, one with Pooley, one with Greenfield and two with Mitchell. Despite his antipathy towards Mitchell, Mace knew that Charlie was the only English heavyweight of genuine ability. Exhibitions would always be crowd-pullers and by now Mace needed to augment his income.

Before too long a further letter from Foley brought Mace up to date on the Australian scene. Professor Miller himself no longer laid claim to the title; instead, one of his students, Tom Lees, as skilful a boxer as would be expected of a man taught by Miller, had taken on the part-timer Bill Farnan and had beaten him, gaining universal recognition.

Reading Foley's letter, Mace was struck by the straightforwardness and honesty of Australian boxing. It was not conducted in an atmosphere of hype and ballyhoo as in America, nor with the niceties of class distinction as in England, nor with the ever-present probability of police interference in both those countries. Australian title bouts were fought in indoor arenas and under Queensberry Rules but those rules were strictly observed and bouts always scheduled to go beyond a paltry four rounds – the very point which Mace had already made clear to Fleming. Of the White Horse students, it was Peter Jackson and Frank Slavin who were foremost. Jackson's progress was marked by a three-round knockout of Mick Dooley and even though Mick KO'd Bob Fitzsimmons a couple of months later, Fitzsimmons reversed the result not long afterwards. And when it came to Slavin's turn, he dispatched Dooley himself. Although a fine stylist, Dooley had two main weaknesses: when on top he lacked the killer instinct to finish his man; he also had a tendency to lose concentration and allow his normally impeccable defence to be pierced by a sucker punch. Seemingly without any burning ambition to be titleholder, Dooley was at his best as an instructor in the gym. He became Foley's effective lieutenant.

Jackson, Slavin and Fitzsimmons were, by contrast, all determined fighters, although the Cornish New Zealander did not yet have the weight to compete effectively with the other two. Accordingly Foley had chosen Jackson to challenge Tom Lees for the championship. Jackson slowly but surely outboxed Lees before kayoing him in the thirtieth. The plaudits he received for this victory inspired Jackson. Proud to be an adopted Australian, his confidence grew with his public acceptance and he developed into the formidable boxer-puncher which Mace and Foley always believed he might become. The obvious match would be one between Jackson and Slavin for the title. In May 1887, all seemed ready for their clash, but to Foley's bemusement and anger the arrangements collapsed at the last moment. Slavin had come under the influence of Australian racists, a minority but a vociferous one, who objected to Jackson, loudly asserting that a black man had no right to the title.

★ ★ ★

Jake Kilrain was, like John L. Sullivan, a second-generation Irish-American, raised near Boston. Beyond that, the two pugilists had little in common. Kilrain, whose real name was John Joseph Killion, was an abstemious and devoted family man. This commended him greatly to Richard Fox, as tenacious as ever in seeking challengers to the champion he continued to detest – not to mention Kilrain's growing reputation both as a bareknuckle fighter and a glove boxer. In 1887, aged twenty-eight, he remained undefeated in twenty-two fights spanning seven years, including a draw with Charlie Mitchell.

Fox's publicity machine swung into top gear but Sullivan showed no inclination to take up Kilrain's challenge. Fox then awarded the former mechanic the Richard K. Fox Championship Diamond Belt, a somewhat gaudy bauble, and publicly presented this in a ceremony in Kilrain's home town of Baltimore. Sullivan's rejoinder was to dismiss the *Police Gazette* Belt as a 'dog collar'. Soon his admirers in Boston were subscribing an even more extravagant belt with Sullivan's name on it and a description of him as 'Champion of Champions'. It appeared that Fox and Sullivan were deadlocked but, whereas Sullivan claimed the world championship by virtue of his defeats of both Ryan and McCaffrey, Kilrain had defeated no opponent in gaining Fox's version of the title. Fox proposed to put that right and contacted the Pelican Club. It was suggested that Kilrain should come to Britain to fight Jem Smith for the Championship of England under LPR rules. Fox believed that Kilrain would emerge as the winner, but, if not, Smith would be touted as Sullivan's latest challenger and brought over to the United States. John Fleming, by now Smith's effective manager, accepted on behalf of the Pelicans.

Mace knew little of Kilrain, except that he had more science than Sullivan – not in itself a remarkable accomplishment. But whatever he thought of Sullivan, in other ways Mace knew that he was no fool either in the ring or outside and would make mincemeat of the hapless Smith. This would only expose Fox's chicanery in trying to deprive a man of his title outside the ring! His contempt for the proposed Kilrain–Smith encounter alienated him from the Pelicans and his suspicions were strengthened by news that Charlie Mitchell would be acting as Kilrain's manager and adviser. Mitchell and Kilrain were total opposites in terms of their way of life and Mace was convinced that Mitchell's motives were anything but altruistic.

On 6 November 1887, with Kilrain already in England, Sullivan enjoyed a rapturous welcome in Liverpool. Mace did not have to endure it. Two months earlier, hankering after London, he had opened a school of boxing and fencing in Soho. It was in Brewer Street and was known as the Jem Mace School of Arms. He and Nellie went to live at Frith Road in Stratford, East London, not far from Pooley, who was one of his instructors. Mace was, needless to say, not among the thousands who swarmed to the dockside, besieged the Grand Hotel and cheered the champion as his train departed Lime Street Station for London Euston. Twenty years earlier, at that same Liverpool station, Mace had received a hero's welcome after confirming his status as Champion of England – but the crowd who acclaimed him then was predominantly English, whereas Sullivan's constituency was the Liverpool Irish.

Unlike Kilrain, Sullivan was not in England with the intention of fighting. His recent tours in America were no longer the financial successes they had been, partly as a result of him avoiding Kilrain but mostly because of Fox's exposure of Sullivan's drunkenness and wife-beating. These character faults remained largely unknown in England. Within weeks, Sullivan had been admitted as a member of the Pelican Club, where he was feted and showered with gifts. The following day, he was presented to Edward Prince of Wales and he gave an exhibition of sparring with a harmless sidekick at St James Barracks in front of both the heir to the throne and sundry aristocrats, including Lord Randolph Churchill, father of thirteen-year-old Winston. As Mace had suspected, Mitchell was quick to exploit the situation to his own advantage. Well aware that Sullivan was drinking the profits of his tour of England and Ireland and was desperate for cash, Mitchell went to the *Sporting Life* offices and put down a stake of £200, daring Sullivan to take the bait – which he did. Sullivan had long detested Mitchell and was prepared to keep sober for the training period and, after six years away, ready to return to fighting under the rules of the London Prize Ring.

As for Mitchell, he had a ready-made sparring partner in Kilrain and he and his father-in-law, Moore, who still handled his business affairs, seemed set for a double bonanza with Kilrain v Smith as the first helping and Mitchell v Sullivan as the second. With the right results, Mitchell could be fighting Kilrain for Fox's version of the World Heavyweight Championship. John Fleming, boxing manager of the Pelican club, was in cahoots; Lord Lonsdale, chairman of the Pelican Boxing Committee was not. A keen explorer, he was preparing for a trip into the wastelands of Arctic Canada and had no time to argue against what was planned. Mace decided that, under no circumstances, would he attend the upcoming prize-fights, wherever they might eventually be held. Beyond his personal antipathy towards both Sullivan and Mitchell, he would not be party to what he was convinced would be a farce which would put the LPR in terminal jeopardy. With so-called friends such as these, the Prize Ring scarcely needed its many enemies. Above all, in the furore drummed up by the *Police Gazette* and *Sporting Life*, the concept of scientific boxing was being swept aside. The four principals in the two scheduled fights were Sullivan and Mitchell, two braggarts, one of whom had refused to take a boxing lesson in his life and another who had, by drinking, dissipated much of what Bill Richardson had taught him. As for Smith and Kilrain, the former was a brawler and a blockhead and the latter an unschooled dupe.

Six days before Christmas, Kilrain and Smith squared up in France, not far from the Channel port of Dieppe, on a marshy, privately owned island named Isle des Souverains. The spectators numbered only seventy-nine in total; it was virtually the Pelican Club on tour, its boisterous toffs having set up camp in the cathedral city of Rouen. There they toasted one another with lavish doses of champagne, chortling like schoolboys about the various subterfuges they used to avoid apprehension between London and the Channel coast. The match, which would soon be romanticised by stupid Pelicans as a titanic tussle with honours even, was in fact a grotesque farce. A decoy trip consumed so much time that it did not get under way until the early afternoon. It was a one-sided affair. In the first round, Kilrain knocked Smith cold. Revived by his seconds after being carted back to his corner, Smith strode out for the restart. He rushed at Kilrain who promptly smote him senseless to the muddy turf. After his seconds poured cognac down his neck to deaden the pain, Smith carried on — for fifty rounds in fact, twenty of which ended with him being knocked down again, despite Kilrain's mobility being hampered by the slush underfoot as freezing drizzle soaked into an already soggy undersoil. In the fifty-first, Smith's gross viciousness surfaced as he tried to gouge one of Kilrain's eyes. He was only stopped by Mitchell's shouted threat to murder him.

During the next fifty-six rounds, Smith, at the instigation of the Pelicans, began backpedalling and went to ground without being hit time without number — in addition to being struck down fourteen times by Kilrain. Attacking desperately as winter darkness threatened to engulf the scene, the American punched Smith unconscious. But with his umpire Fleming signalling ostentatiously that he could barely read the time off his own watch, the Pelicans, who had bet heavily on Smith not to lose, surrounded the referee, George Atkinson, and pressurised him into calling a draw.

Their leader was the Marquess of Queensberry, who had been bawling himself hoarse throughout the entire 106 rounds, occupying

Mace in his pomp in San Francisco in 1877, shortly before sailing to Australia to become the island continent's boxing supremo. The stern gaze and formal attire belie his sense of humour and relaxed attitude to social mores.

Above: Mace revolutionised the fledgling sport of boxing in Australia. His star pupil was Caribbean-born Peter Jackson, here with manager Parson Davies. Jackson would be acknowledged as the finest heavyweight of his era, but champion John L. Sullivan refused to face him. Another of Mace's Australian disciples was Larry Foley (**below left**), who became the foremost trainer in his country. Next to him is Jack Thompson, Mace's main opponent in the exhibitions which legalised boxing 'Down Under'.

The huge 'Maori', Herbert Slade. Mace's promotion of the towering but inept New Zealander would damage his reputation for years.

The Irish-American Joe Coburn unsuccessfully challenged Mace for the world title. One of their fights was a farcical stand-off, another was declared a draw – and was followed by an attempt to murder the English champion.

In a historic meeting of the masters of scientific boxing in London in 1894, Jim Corbett, the first world titleholder under Queensberry Rules, greets Jem Mace, the first world bareknuckle champion, and hails him as 'the man who elevated our sport'.

The raw appeal of the old prize ring is captured in this rare action photo of a bareknuckle championship bout, between John L. Sullivan and Jake Kilrain, at Richburg, Mississippi, in 1889.

A classic pose captured in New York in 1896, by which time Mace had been acclaimed as the Father of Boxing and praised by such 'modern' champions as Gentleman Jim Corbett, Bob Fitzsimmons and Kid McCoy. The acknowledged master of the ring, he continued to box exhibitions into his mid-seventies.

Two of the many women who gave their hearts to Mace. Nellie Gore Lee (**main picture**) broke with her music professor husband at the age of 22 to live with the fighter. He later deserted her for Alice Stokes (**pictured right with Mace's business manager Bill Bayford**), who at 18 was 40 years his junior when they met.

The ex-champion, pictured at Forest Gate in 1890, proudly displays his array of belts, medals and trophies from three continents.

An old foe and an old pupil: the ageing Mace is joined in the ring by (far left) Brummie braggart Charlie Mitchell and, the great triple champion Bob Fitzsimmons, while the rugged black American Joe Jeanette stands by. Mace holds a lucky horseshoe presented by Fitzsimmons, a former blacksmith. London 1909.

Sam Lang-ford, aged 24, the Canadian-born 'Boston Terror', often ranked one of the greatest boxers of all, meets Jem Mace, aged 76, in London in 1907.

Two of Mace's fourteen children: Adelaide Turvill was a Victorian matriarch and mother of eleven. James Mace junior, pictured here in 1894, was a fencing instructor and sportswriter.

The last portrait. Poverty-stricken but proud, the grand old man of the ring is pictured in Liverpool in 1909. Mace died the following year, aged 79.

two-and-a-half hours. Thus had the alleged great innovator of boxing presided over Smith's flouting of Broughton's Rules (of 1743), let alone the revised rules of the LPR. The East End labourer received no less than £1,000 pounds of Pelican money, as did the Massachusetts machinist.

When Kilrain returned to America, Fox proclaimed him Champion of the World. This was manifestly incorrect since he had not fought Sullivan but (as the *Police Gazette* ringside reporter would have been well aware) had the fight taken place at Madison Square Garden, rather than in a desolate French morass, Kilrain's first-round blows alone would have won him victory by a knockout. If the referee failed in his duty, Clubber Williams would have called the fight off long before even four rounds had expired.

The second Anglo-American bout of the winter, held on 10 March 1888, was not as absurdly one-sided but was a dreary and nasty encounter. Charlie Mitchell challenged John L. Sullivan for the world title at Chantilly in the horseracing stables owned by France's richest man, the international banker Baron Alphonse de Rothschild. Thirty-six hours of incessant rain had churned the turf into a quagmire. This worked to Sullivan's disadvantage. His movement was restricted and he found it hard to get a grip on the much lighter Mitchell and maximise his wrestling prowess. Mitchell, unchecked by the Pelican referee, Bernard John Angle, fouled Sullivan throughout, either by low blows or by kicking his shins bloody with his studded boots. Entirely without support from the wholly English crowd, many of whom had feted him in London, he was subjected to a constant tirade of obscene abuse. In a downpour of ice-cold rain, his alcohol-weakened body shook constantly. Still, after three hours and ten minutes, he was the one going forward, albeit with a swollen mouth spouting blood. Mitchell, by contrast, was dodging back, his breeches torn open at the knees from constantly falling illegally without being hit, and his body a mass of bruises. By this time the parties agreed to a draw, since the amount of viable turf had been reduced by the rainstorm to barely a yard square. After they left the sanctuary of the Rothschild estate, both Sullivan and Mitchell were arrested. Mitchell was released after three days in jail. Sullivan jumped bail and returned to England and then the USA.

As for Jem Mace, his predictions about the likely outcome of these two squalid encounters had proved accurate. A greater contrast with his own epic battles with Tom King and his masterly destruction of Goss could scarcely have been imagined.

While the Police Gazette plied the American public with innumerable column inches about the two fights, it said very little about the fight game in the third continent, Australia. Still, further letters from Foley kept Mace up-to-date. Jackson's victory over Lees had given him immense confidence but he remained restless. No one wished to challenge him for the title other than Slavin, who had been dissuaded by racists. The nearest Jackson and Slavin ever got to a test of their respective abilities was a barroom brawl in January 1888. It was not the first time this kind of thing had happened. Five years earlier, at the White Horse itself, they had tried to slug it out in the gym. At that time the cause of trouble between them had been rivalry for the affections of a girl, Josie Leon, the beautiful niece of a rich Jamaican planter. By now Miss Leon had decided she wanted nothing more to do with either of them and, disheartened by this and angered by Slavin's new-found racism, Jackson had responded to an invitation from a visiting Californian sports writer to relocate to the USA.

Jackson arrived in San Francisco in May 1888, together with two promising fellow Australians, both lightweights. With Jackson gone, Slavin claimed the Australian Heavyweight Championship and, before the end of the year, he had underlined his claim with a first round knockout of Mick Dooley. That fight was a Queensberry Rules clash since, in Australia, the Prize Ring was long dead and buried. Indeed between them Slavin and Jackson had no more than a couple of early fights' experience of bareknuckle combat.

* * *

In quick succession, both Nellie and Jem were widowed. First, in the spring of 1888, Rowland Lee died, in Wolverhampton, aged forty-four. Then, on 3 July Hannah died, aged forty, in the house where she and George Harris lived, in Olmar Street, off the Old Kent Road. She had been suffering from tuberculosis for a year. The deaths of both spouses were significant events in the life of the couple – now there was no reason why they could not legally be married in England. To

Nellie's disappointment, Jem seemed to have no interest in this. She was not motivated by the wish to have a church wedding; nor did the passage, in 1882, of the Married Women's Property Act influence her, since she had never had any property of her own which could have been protected under that law. She simply wished for the status which Hannah had enjoyed and which she did not have. But Jem dismissed the matter, saying that the ceremony which had united them in New York was sufficient. Amelia and Ada, both now adult women, regretted their father's inaction and contrasted it with his eagerness to divorce their mother in the aborted case four years earlier. They were not the only ones to wonder if Mace was beginning to lose interest in what, at over a dozen years duration, was the longest relationship of his life.

Nine months later, Amelia herself got married, at twenty-three, to Andrew McMillin, three years her senior, at Liverpool Register Office. McMillin, who had been born in Ireland, was a joiner by trade. He was a Roman Catholic but was agreeable to any children they might have being brought up as Anglicans. With Amelia now living with her new husband, Nellie and Jem became increasingly aware of an emotional intimacy between her son John Lee and his daughter Ada. Nellie had already glimpsed it and mentioned it to her sister Annie. It represented no problem, since John and Ada were not blood relatives; he was now nineteen and she twenty-one but they had not known each other until both were well into their teens. All family members were happy about the relationship.

Jem's declining financial situation was, however, causing concern. For half a dozen years he had had no source of income within England, other than his regular sparring exhibitions. His capital was substantially depleted, a situation exacerbated by his persistent and unsuccessful gambling on horses, and the family was obliged to move from house to house in Everton, living for a while at Monk Street and later at Queens Road, not to mention his sojourn at Stratford which lasted less than a year and ended when his mismanaged West End boxing school failed. In the late 1880s, Mace took various measures to earn money. First, through his connection with local sportswriters, he became sought-after as an after-dinner speaker. Confident and articulate, he delighted and amused various gatherings of sportsmen in Liverpool, not only reminiscing about the heyday of the Prize Ring but making forthright remarks about both the Pelican Club and the woeful state of the current crop of English heavyweights. He derided the lack of skill shown by Knifton, Smith and Greenfield (even though he had already planned an exhibition tour of England with Alf, scheduled for the end of 1889). As for Mitchell, although Mace was wary of him on a personal level, he acknowledged that the feisty Brummie had genuine ability – when he chose to use it. In spring 1889, Mitchell challenged Jem Smith to a glove contest for the Championship of England, to be held at Sanger's Amphitheatre in London. Mace had agreed to act as Mitchell's second but the bout did not take place. Smith cried off with a convenient foot injury.

Mace's verbal criticisms of the degenerate Prize Ring chimed with those written by the Irish dramatist George Bernard Shaw, who followed pugilism closely, if sceptically. He contrasted the boring crudity of contemporary heavyweights with the class exhibited by the outstanding performers of the 1860s. It was at this time that Tom King's death, aged fifty-three, in London, in October 1888, provoked much nostalgia for the skill with which King, Sayers and Mace had illuminated that bygone era.

Another project of Mace's was the organisation of amateur boxing competitions bearing his name in the North of England and the presentation of small trophies to the winners. London was already well served with such tournaments organised by sporting clubs but these were entered mainly by boxers from the capital or from its perennial rival, Birmingham. Mace's tourneys catered to competitors at the lighter weight divisions, where skill and speed of movement were relatively more important than sheer power. In January 1888, for example, Sam Bird was presented with a sparkling twenty-sided medal as a champion lightweight. It bore the commendation 'for his clever boxing'. Another promising boxer encouraged by Jem was a Liverpool lad in his late teens named Charlie Blackburn. He won the Jem Mace nine-stone champion's belt in a competition at Leeds. These competitions involved considerable expense and Mace showed little profit from them.

A slightly better proposition was his instructional book *On Boxing*, published in 1889. It was edited by a journalist, Henry Sampson, who would have transcribed it from Mace's verbal descriptions. Sampson, who had seen Mace in nearly all his major fights in England and in numerous exhibitions, was unequivocal in his praise for Jem's career in the ring. 'Mace was,' he wrote, 'the very ideal of what a fighter should be. No other man has ever combined such excellences; a wonderful specimen of the ambidextrous boxer who could "change legs" and use either hand with equal rapidity, a most tremendous hitter at half-arm or full length, a judge of time and distance whose superior it would not be possible to find.' Characteristically, On Boxing emphasised the scientific approach. Hardly any of the Pelicans bothered with it but it became the boxing Bible of 'Peggy' Bettinson.

With the passage of time, Mace had become somewhat bored with Liverpool. It was not that he disliked the city, far from it, but Jem was used to the bright lights of London and New York, places where talk was of the theatre, showbusiness and boxing. As the 1880s neared a close he visited the capital more, usually staying in one or other of the West End sporting pubs. He paid the occasional visit to the home of his married daughter, Adelaide Turvill. Adelaide and her husband William, a clerk for a condensed milk company, lived at a series of addresses in the Camberwell area and were a prolific couple. At this time they had eight children: Eleanor, Maud, Edgar, Wilfred, William and Mary; Arthur and Alfred had already died in boyhood. They would eventually have four more: Adelaide junior, Emmie, Lois and Mary, although Edgar and Mary would not survive. Jem was well disposed towards his many grandchildren but found their parents to be suburban, tedious and tinged with religiosity. He made it clear that, if the Turvills had any intention of converting him from his lifestyle, they had another thing coming.

Far more congenial to Mace were his then secret visits to the Covent Garden balls. Opening at midnight and continuing to 4am, the entrance fee was a guinea and many young actresses from the Gaiety and Variety Theatres attended. Mace had always been partial to theatrical girls, showgirls, dancers and hotel barmaids, young women of uninhibited sensuality, and though he was now in his late fifties he remained healthy, athletic and virile. Still a gifted dancer, playful and full of teasing humour, he proved very attractive to these girls, not all of whom were aware of his former fame, some assuming that he was just a musician.

At the end of the decade, Mace, thwarted in divorce and dabbling in extra-marital encounters, was adrift in his personal life. Professionally, he had yet to rid himself of the dinosaurs of the prize ring. But the 1890s would bring dramatic changes both personal and professional.

27

The Boxing Revolution Begins

AT THE TIME Mace's instructional book was published, the number of men who operated as specialist boxing tutors anywhere in the world could almost be counted on the fingers of one hand. In Sydney, Larry Foley and William Miller continued to teach and Foley was producing a steady stream of fine fighters. In London, Bob Habbingham and Nat Donnelly did their best but without end product, while in New York there were Billy Edwards and Mike Donovan. Edwards wrote instructional books when he wasn't too busy with his real estate business on Long Island; Mike Donovan had become the instructor at the New York Athletic Club, appointed on the pragmatic basis that, in 1884, he had defeated Walter Watson, the other applicant, in a bout at the club.

Watson was an English heavyweight who had fought with only modest success but he was skilled in teaching not only what he had personally picked up in the Prize Ring but also in patiently demonstrating the style which he had witnessed and which he believed to be by far the most skilful: that of Jem Mace. Undaunted by being passed over in favour of Donovan, Watson decided to try his luck in California.

In boxing, as in other matters, San Francisco aspired to independence from New York. It contained three sports clubs in all of which gloved boxing held pride of place: the Golden Gate Athletic Club, the California Athletic Club and the Olympic Club. In Frisco, Mace was still held in the highest regard after his earlier sojourn in the city and his brilliant defeat of Davis, witnessed by a large audience in 1877. Unlike in New York, English style was highly appreciated in California. Watson applied for and won the post of boxing instructor at the Olympic Club. It was not long before he had discovered two outstanding teenage prospects. Believing what was then a revolutionary maxim – that sporting prowess, like academic excellence, was best fostered by intensive tuition at an early age – Watson gave both lads extensive tuition in the style of Jem Mace.

The names of his prize students were Jim Corbett and Joe Choynski. Both were excellent athletes and intelligent students. They soon became fierce rivals on the local amateur scene and in September 1887, on Watson's retirement, Corbett, just turned twenty-one, was appointed boxing instructor at the Olympic Club. Of all this Californian activity Mace, at the time, knew nothing. He was not even aware of Peter Jackson's arrival in San Francisco, but in a decision which spoke volumes for the California Athletic Club's boxing judgment and freedom from racial prejudice, Jackson was appointed professor of boxing at the C.A.C. The Club's founder, Jack Seymour, was an Englishman by birth who had gone to Australia and made a name for himself in pedestrianism. He had met Mace and held him in the highest esteem. Soon the C.A.C. became the first American sports club regularly to stage Queensberry glove contests for professionals.

During the next sixteen months, Jackson sped across the American boxing scene like a comet, winning eleven consecutive fights. His victims included George Godfrey, in a fight for the so-called 'coloured heavyweight championship of the world', Joe McAuliffe, the Pacific Coast champion, and Patsy Cardiff, who had once drawn with Sullivan. Knowledgeable boxing followers marvelled at Jackson's thumping left jab, which had the knockout power of many a slugger's fiercest right, not to mention his dancing style, combination punches and ability to slip an opponent's blow by moving his head a few inches. In truth, Jackson was an ebony version of Mace but much taller and heavier. As Jackson went from strength to strength, so Corbett and Choynski fought their first professional fight – against each other. In a titanic battle on a barge in Benecia Harbour, Corbett prevailed by what was effectively a technical knockout. The contest had been marked both by classic boxing and by hitting that was not only fierce but poised and accurate.

The progress of Jackson, Corbett and Choynsky held little interest for Richard Fox, who was still obsessed by the wish to see Sullivan dethroned by Jake Kilrain. On 7 July 1889, Sullivan, under pressure of a denuded bank account, at last faced Kilrain in a fight for the World Heavyweight Championship under LPR rules for $20,000. Their clash differed from those in which each had been separately engaged in France. Instead of the chill and sleet of a miserable Northern European winter, Sullivan and Kilrain squared off in the torrid heat of a Gulf Coast summer. Rather than being watched by a few score furtive spectators, they were viewed by more than 2,000 in a scaffolding-and-bleachers arena in the middle of a pinewood estate. Despite the mobilisation of several state militias, the private estate of the sawmiller Charles Rich at Richburg, Mississippi, served the same function as that of Baron Rothschild. Kilrain, advised by the gun-toting Charlie Mitchell and umpired by the Dodge City gunslinger Bat Masterson, used spoiling tactics. They didn't work. Sullivan, who had been specially trained by wrestler William Muldoon on a high-protein diet, was far fitter than expected. The match turned into a contest of endurance, one in which the pallid and sun-scorched Baltimore man was obliged to concede defeat at the end of two hours and sixteen minutes, comprising seventy-five rounds. Mike Donovan threw in the sponge on behalf of a tottering Kilrain.

For almost a year afterwards both fighters were hounded by various state judiciaries acting in conjunction. Kilrain was actually jailed, while Sullivan lost almost three-quarters of his winner-takes-all stake in legal costs and constant travelling expenses from Boston to the Gulf States to avoid the same fate. Thus ended the series which had been inaugurated by Heenan and Sayers at Farnborough thirty years before and in which Mace had brought the first decisive result, at Kennerville. But for all their undoubted raw courage, Sullivan and Kilrain were beginning to look like dinosaurs with no other source of inspiration than brute force and ignorance.

At the time of their clash, Peter Jackson was in Chicago, halfway through a series of Queensberry Rules contests which took him from coast to coast. By now his retinue included a trainer, a sparring partner, the respected journalist W.W. Naughton and his Irish-born manager Charles 'Parson' Davies – who acquired his nickname from his high collars and sombre mode of dress. Davies had already been in correspondence with John Fleming at the Pelican Club with a view to matching Jackson with Jem Smith. Jackson could legitimately claim to be a citizen of the British Empire and, if he were to beat Smith, would be effectively the Champion of England. As such, Davies reasoned, it would be more difficult for Sullivan to reject the match with Jackson on racial grounds. The problem was that the Pelicans couldn't raise a stake of the kind which was available in the top flight in America.

Lonsdale, however, had seen Jackson box when returning to San Francisco from Alaska. He had been immensely impressed with his boxing skill and, on meeting him, with his intelligence and dignified conduct. Back in England and learning of the financial difficulties which stood in the way of a clash between Jackson and Smith, the Earl put up a purse of £1,000. He made clear to the rest of the Pelicans that the match must be held on club premises, under Queensberry Rules and limited to ten rounds. Then he offered one of his country homes as Jackson's training quarters. Parson Davies promptly accepted and Jackson's party sailed for Liverpool in August. Hugh Cecil Lowther and Peter Jackson had backgrounds which were diametrically different: one was a scion of the English aristocracy, the other was an Afro-Caribbean seafarer. What they had in common was far more significant – they had both been taught to box by Jem Mace.

* * *

When Jem Mace greeted Peter Jackson in Liverpool on 29 August 1889, neither could have anticipated that their meeting was the herald of a boxing revolution which, within three years, would transform the fight game in both America and England. Jackson's party, just arrived by ship from New York, comprised his manager Parson Davies, his Australian trainer Sam Fitzpatrick and his sparring partner Tom Lees. Mace and Jackson shook hands warmly. Mace, remembering a slim lad of nineteen, now saw a man in his prime, aged twenty-eight, over 6ft tall and weighing, as far as he could assess, a muscular fifteen stone. Time for talk was brief. Davies was keen to leave for Nottingham, en route to Lord Lonsdale's country home at Cottesmore in Rutland, but Mace made sure to remind Jackson of the tactics he needed to employ against Jem Smith, and the young Australian joked that he was hearing the voice of Larry Foley all over again.

Jackson spent over a month at Cottesmore, training hard. On learning that Smith was only 5ft 8½in tall, he lowered the punchball in the gym by five inches. Precision was Jackson's watchword. After dinner, he would intrigue Lord Lonsdale and his guests by using his right hand to punch out the flickering candle flames on the dining-room table without touching one of the tall candles. In October, Jackson fought fourteen exhibitions against eight different Englishmen in London. Sometimes, at his own suggestion, he took them on 'right hand barred', so powerful was his left jab alone. A couple of these Cockney scrappers subjected Jackson to racist abuse. He had already encountered it in Sydney, but far more so in America, and had learned not to lose his temper but to turn the tables on the culprits by droll sarcastic humour. As for Lord Lonsdale, it was difficult to know whether his cordiality to Jackson reflected his unconcern for racial difference, his belief that the elegant and modest Jackson confounded negative stereotypes or simply Lonsdale's own wish to shock his fellow aristocrats.

On 11 November 1889, Jackson faced Jem Smith at the Pelican Club in the heart of the West End. Eight hundred club members surrounded the 16ft ring, with a crowd of several thousand massed outside, waiting for news and marshalled by police. Mace had been invited by Lord Lonsdale and sat at ringside, flanked by several lesser pugilists and, not far from Lonsdale, the Marquess of Queensberry and Lord de Clifford Mandeville. Although the fight was for ten rounds under Queensberry Rules, colours were tied to the corner posts after the fashion of the old Prize Ring. Jackson's internationalism was shown by his combining the flag of St George with the Stars and Stripes, together with the letters C.A.C. for the California Athletic Club. But his Australian patriotism was there for all to see with the words 'Advance Australia and without fear or favour' prominently displayed.

Within five minutes of the bell, all that Jem Mace had stood for was publicly vindicated. Jackson, making full use of his superior reach, persistently used the left jab to stun Smith. He cut off the ring in masterly style, outmanoeuvring the Englishman. When Smith swung wildly at his head, he moved quickly out of range. When the English champion pummelled away at his body to cheers from his backers — many of whom absurdly believed that blacks could not take punches in the 'breadbasket' — Jackson blocked them with his elbows. The first round ended with Smith snorting in rage at his own discomfiture.

Jackson opened the second with total confidence, unloading right-handers that sent Smith staggering to the ropes. Sensing imminent defeat, Smith reverted to wrestling tactics, back-heeling Jackson and causing him to trip. Jackson's corner rightfully cried foul and the referee, George Vize, did what various referees had signally failed to do in similar circumstances in Sullivan's fights: he disqualified Smith and awarded the fight to Jackson on a foul. Smith's backers groaned loudly and some of them even booed, but they shut up when Lonsdale rose imperiously from his seat and faced them down with a stare. Then the cry of 'Three cheers for Peter Jackson!' rang out from the more enlightened members of the toffs' sporting club.

Smith tore off his gloves, brandished his fists and had to be restrained by several men from attacking Jackson, who was standing quietly in his corner. He refused to shake hands with the Caribbean-born man until ordered to do so on pain of losing his £200 loser's fee. Jackson, with a cheque for £800 in his wallet, was later driven back to his hotel in triumph, to the cheers of the crowd outside. Mace saw Pelicanism exposed on its own hearth as the anachronism which it was. Smith, its foolish Champion, the very man who had refused lessons from Richardson when debuting at the Blue Anchor, was revealed as a crude mediocrity. And, in hindsight, the Pelicans' boasts that Smith had 'stood more than a hundred rounds with Jake Kilrain' were rendered hollow.

In Jackson, the Corinthians of London had seen the boxing science of Jem Mace resurrected, even more powerful than the original because of Jackson's genuine heavyweight height and build, and not to mention the years of instruction by Foley, exclusively in the Mace style, which had been triumphantly vindicated.

Jackson was not the only Australian boxer in England at this time, for Frank Slavin had arrived in London nearly three weeks earlier. Claiming the Australian championship as a result of Jackson's 'emigration' to the USA, he had beaten twenty men in a row, including Bob Fitzsimmons, the Irishman Jack Burke, who had stood five rounds with Sullivan, and Joe Goddard, the 'Barrier Cyclone', soon to establish himself as one of the most formidable heavyweights in the world. Slavin was helped by Mace to set up fights and Mace was in his corner when he fought a couple of Englishmen, one of them the bulky Bill

'Chesterfield' Goode, whom he KO'd in five, the fifteenth knockout of his career.

Six months younger than Jackson, Slavin also stood 6ft 1½in but weighed under 13 stone. Nicknamed the 'Sydney Cornstalk' on account of his lean and long-shanked build, he was a graduate of the Mace-Foley School and, though not as good with the left jab as Jackson, he used his reach differently, raking his opponent's mid-section with thunderous body punches, aiming for the mark. He moved fast, didn't flinch from punishment and constantly advanced, determined to strike conclusively.

Slavin got his chance to fight for what the Pelicans considered the Championship of England. Parson Davies had dismissed the notion that bare knuckles were a truer test of ability than gloves, but Slavin jumped at the chance, against Mace's advice not to go abroad for the combat. Only six weeks after Smith's humiliation at Gerrard Street, John Fleming arranged a match between Slavin and Smith, not in France but Belgium. The venue was a lawn tennis court in Bruges and it was considered that the Belgian authorities were too disorganised to prevent such an excursion into their territory. A boatload of spectators sailed from Dover to Ostend on 23 December 1889, heading for the home of a retired British Army officer named Atkinson Grimshaw. Lord Lonsdale had washed his hands of the affair but George Baird promptly emerged as Smith's principal backer.

The streets of the ancient, pretty and normally docile Flemish town were empty as residents cowered inside their houses, having spied a collection of the worst lowlifes in England armed with clubs and knives and bawling drunken oaths. At their head was the whisky-guzzling so-called Squire Abingdon, brandishing a revolver. Never, even in the pugilistic annals of America's Wild West had such a scene of lawlessness and intimidation been enacted. The scumbags of the East End and Birmingham, deliberately alerted by Fleming, Baird and, above all, Smith were there for one purpose – to ensure that Smith didn't lose. The extreme Pelicans, badly out of pocket as a result of the Shoreditch brawler's defeat by Jackson at Gerrard Street, were desperate to recoup their gambling losses. As referee they selected the old and easily influenced Joe Vesey. The contrast between Smith and Slavin was marked. Smith's belly bulged with fat, his glaucous eyes still bruised from Jackson's jabs, his incipient jowl and receding hairline making him look more like a man in his early forties than one in his mid-twenties. Slavin, unmistakably Irish with his shock of red wavy hair, deepset eyes and high cheekbones, sported a full but well trimmed moustache.

The bout lasted fourteen rounds, with no reliable record of precise duration. Timekeeping was impossible in conditions which verged on riot throughout. Slavin dominated, slamming Smith about the ring with a welter of punches. Fortunately for the Shoreditcher, the Australian's attack was concentrated on the body and though Smith was doubled up in pain on several occasions, he was rarely grounded, rounds being ended when he went down without being touched. The fight degenerated into chaos with Smith able to kick Slavin's shins and to punch well below the belt without the slightest rebuke from Vesey. The annals of the fight game are replete with stories of exceptional courage but Slavin's bravery was without parallel. True, he was the one who took the fight to his opponent; true, Smith landed few genuine blows; but Slavin, his seconds apart, stood entirely alone. Smith's crowd of gangsters howled abuse at him right from the scratch and far worse was to come. When Slavin was in his corner between rounds he was physically attacked by English thugs. When he resumed, half bricks were thrown at his head. None struck him but he was forced to come to close quarters and thus leave himself open to Smith's wrestling which, thanks to instruction from Professor Miller in Sydney, he withstood. Finally, the Australian, provoked beyond endurance, lashed out at Smith's head. As the English champion staggered, Slavin, regardless of the risk to his own unsheathed knuckles, hooked him so determinedly that it was clear that Smith would soon be rendered senseless – the only way, as was now all too obvious, that Smith's supporters would be unable to prevent Slavin from winning.

At this point the crowd broke the ring, led by George Baird, who, drunk though he was, knew what he was doing. He incited the crowd to murder Slavin, bellowing, 'Come on! Let's do in the Australian bastard!' Slavin, who stood his ground with arms folded, might well have lost his life had he not been protected by Lord Mandeville, who drew a bowie knife. To save the situation, Mandeville loudly called on Vesey to declare the match a draw. Once this was done, the crowd's rage abated as they anticipated their winnings. Even then, Baird's bloodlust was unsatisfied. He drew his revolver but was dissuaded by the roughnecks who did not want to be distracted from claiming their winnings. Baird then ran off, side by side with Smith, panting heavily as he tried to keep pace with his inept and ignominious hero. At the first sign that the mob were about to fight among themselves, the cowardly Fleming, Smith's manager, sought protection in Slavin's corner, pleading for help from English lightweight champion Jem Carney, who had seconded the Australian. Gradually the mob dispersed, unhindered by Belgian police, and made its way back to Ostend.

When the news of this vile episode reached London after Christmas, the newspapers were open in their contempt for Smith. He was variously described as 'a cornered rat', 'a filthy cur' and 'a shabby skunk'. At the Pelican Club, Lonsdale convened a meeting to deal with Fleming and Baird. Fleming was suspended for a year, Baird expelled forthwith. He went to court to contest the decision but his appeal was dismissed. Slavin was acknowledged as Champion of England and awarded the entire purse. When, two months later, he married an English girl, the crowd outside the church cheered him and sang his praises. The debacle of Bruges was the last ever bareknuckle prize-fight. It brought to an end the history of pugilism which had begun 170 years earlier with the opening of James Figg's Academy in London.

* * *

At home in Liverpool, Mace did not lament the passing of the LPR. The series of matches in France and Belgium had, from Maisons-Laffitte onwards, turned him irrevocably against the Prize Ring which he had once graced. Until then, he had ascribed its downfall in the 1860s to the ousting of the aristocrats by a new breed of crooked entrepreneurs and by the hooligan dregs of society. Now he concluded that the biggest blackguard of all was the millionaire iron-master's son with his fake pseudo-aristocratic title. But the Battle of Bruges had also vindicated Mace. Just as Jackson had led at Gerrard Street in strictly regulated circumstances, so Slavin had followed suit on the disfigured lawns of Atkinson Grimshaw. Skill, science and bravery had won the day over brute force and ignorance, and whoever was the true Champion of England, it was one or other of two Australian boxers both trained by Foley and both imbued with the classic style of Jem Mace.

The day after Bruges, Jackson was in Dublin. He fought the Irish champion Peter Maher, who was being considered as a challenger for Sullivan, and beat him inside two rounds. As this news reverberated in America, offers to fund a match between Jackson and the world champion came in from the California Athletic Club, and Davies immediately decided to cut short Jackson's exhibition tour of England and return to the States.

Mace had little time to reflect on Jackson and Slavin's heroic deeds or to ponder their future prospects. Incredibly, at the age of fifty-eight, he was in training himself for a return to the ring. He would fight Charlie Mitchell. He had challenged the younger man because he was short of cash and because £500 would be at stake.

Mace did not believe that he would beat Mitchell, who was no less than thirty years younger than him, except possibly by a first-round knockout blow, but he bet on himself to last the full four rounds, which would be fought for points with six-ounce gloves, at two minutes per round. Unlike Mace, who trained hard for several weeks at Hastings, Mitchell did not bother to train for what he considered would be a swift knockout victory for himself. Indeed, the only fisticuff action he saw was when he beat up George Baird in a London restaurant after they had been on a drinking spree.

The Mace–Mitchell clash took place at the Gaiety Theatre in Glasgow on 7 February 1890. Undaunted by the fact that it was thirteen years since he last fought competitively, Mace tried for a first-round knockout and broke his finger as he threw a hard right to the jaw. This was after Mitchell had stunned him with a surprise punch as 'time' was called. For a while after that, he kept Mitchell at bay with his left jab but his legs were gone and, as he tired, Mitchell moved in and proceeded to punish him. During the fourth round, police entered the ring and ended matters, directing the referee to award the match to Mitchell. Mace was furious: he believed he could stay on his feet and clean up at the bookies. He would always refuse to recognise this as a defeat and insisted for the rest of his life that he had only been beaten twice in his full-time career – once, in his youth, by Bob Brettle and once by Tom King.

The remarkable thing about the Glasgow clash was not that Mitchell was adjudged to have won but that Mace had not been knocked down, much less out, in ten minutes of fierce fighting by a man who was half his age, the very same man who, only two years before, had drawn with the world champion, John L. Sullivan. Mace had retained his pride and gained some much-needed coin.

Jackson had scarcely returned to America when a second boxer based in Australia became the first such to win a world title. New Zealander 'Torpedo' Billy Murphy, a tailor from Auckland, was a featherweight, at that time the lightest of all divisions – or at least all regularly contested divisions. Discovered by Mace and later schooled by Larry Foley, Murphy was pale and narrow-chested with painfully thin arms, but his fierce stare was a better indication of his powerful punching than his deceptively emaciated appearance. In San Francisco, Murphy knocked out the much-touted Irishman Ike Weir in the fourteenth round. But, when the homesick Murphy returned Down Under, American sports writers were quickly into historical revisionism, absurdly declaring that the bout was only for the (non-existent) British Empire title. Two Americans would contest the 'World Championship'. But America would soon learn that the flood tide of Australian boxing could not be dammed up for long.

Just as Jackson and Slavin, despite not meeting in the ring, had been fierce rivals for the Australian heavyweight championship, so another extremely talented duo competed for the island continent's middleweight crown. The first of these was Jim Hall, who unsurprisingly chose not to box under his real name of Montague Furlong. Thoroughly schooled by Foley and Dooley, Hall was a prodigy of boxing skill. His style was like a cool, laidback version of Mace. Rather than dancing, he moved about the ring with effortless ease, seeming hardly to exert himself. He countered, blocked and sidestepped the majority of punches thrown at him, calmly avoiding straight lefts with a minuscule movement of his head. Over 6ft tall, his reach enabled him to score with jabs which may have lacked power but which brushed against opponents' features with annoying regularity. As slick a boxer as Hall seemed to be, he could and did win by knockout, achieved by timing and accuracy rather than sheer force. No man more typified the transition from brute force and ignorance to pure skill

Whereas the careers of Jackson, Slavin and Hall had rapidly taken off, that of Bob Fitzsimmons, Hall's principal rival at middleweight, was slower in unfolding, partly due to his eagerness, while still a middleweight, to take on heavier opponents. In 1889, Fitzsimmons unleashed his punching power, remarkably heavy for a man of such light poundage, on the younger Hall, knocking him out in five rounds. But after 'Fitz', as he was now generally known, had lost the title to Ed 'Starlight' Rollins, Hall regained it. A dozen straight wins brought Hall to the attention of the California Athletic Club and its wealthiest member, John D. Spreckels, owner of the Oceanic Steamship Navigation Company and a frequent visitor to Australia. When Hall knocked out Fitzsimmons in four at Foley's Hall, Spreckels offered to fund Hall's voyage to the States. But Hall suffered a knife wound to the hand in a drunken brawl and Spreckels decided to fund the abstemious Fitzsimmons instead. On arrival in San Francisco, Fitzsimmons was derided by American sports writers, partly because of his freakish physical appearance. When the C.A.C. proposed that Fitzsimmons should challenge the American world middleweight champion, Jack Dempsey, there were hoots of derision. Dempsey was usually known by the moniker 'Nonpareil'. A classy boxer, he was considered well-nigh invincible and Fitzsimmons' chances against him were dismissed out of hand.

Even before Peter Jackson had returned from England to San Francisco, the C.A.C. had also offered to host a match between him and John L. Sullivan. It would be held under Queensberry Rules and be for a purse of $15,000. Astonishingly, the Santa Cruz A.C. at once doubled that, an offer matched by both the Erie County A.C. and the Seattle A.C. This bidding frenzy was an indication of the enormous public interest in such a bout, but Sullivan prevaricated and, when pressed, firmly refused. A lifelong racist, he might well have been tempted by the unprecedented sums on offer but the loser's share was by far the slighter and Sullivan knew that he would have had to face a man who had demolished Smith in two rounds, the same fighter who had stood 106 rounds with Kilrain – who had in turn gone seventy-five with him.

Thwarted and homesick, Jackson returned to Australia to consider his future. He fought Joe Goddard, who had defeated Dooley for the heavyweight championship. Goddard was the significant exception to the rule that all outstanding fighters from the Antipodes fought in the style of Mace. So pervasive was Mace's influence that Goddard differed only because he didn't begin his career until the late age of twenty-six. While others were lining up at the White Horse, Goddard was labouring in the outback ballast pits. The Barrier Cyclone fought neither in the scientific style of Mace nor the ferocious slugging manner of Sullivan. He was a swarmer, a high-energy close-quarters fighter willing to take two shots to get one harder one back. Goddard, one of history's most underrated fighters, was a true 'iron man': durable, rugged and with incredible powers of recovery.

The outlawing of wrestling under the Queensberry Rules paved the way for the emergence of this type of fighter, who could in-fight with impunity safe from the danger of being brutally thrown. Jackson–Goddard proved a memorable encounter. Although Jackson seemed to have the fight won with a knockdown in the third, Goddard got up and fought back. Both men were down in the fifth and a drawn verdict was rendered after the end of the eight scheduled rounds. Unlike the English Championship and the American Championship, the Australian title was now being fought for – and had been for some years – strictly under Queensberry Rules and on a fixed-round format. What was equally significant was that there was no accurate points system in operation which could decide the winner in a closely contested combat. The general opinion was that Jackson had shaded it but such a notion remained anything but satisfactory.

Six weeks earlier, 'Torpedo' Billy Murphy had defended his world featherweight title in Sydney. This was the first time a world title bout had been held on Australian soil, an indication of just how far Aussie and Kiwi boxing had advanced in little more than a decade, chiefly as a result of the influence of Jem Mace. In fact, Murphy lost his title to the twenty-one-year-old Australian Young Griffo.

Never was the contrast between the demeanour of a boxer outside the ring and within it more marked than with Griffo (real name Albert

Griffiths). In ordinary life, the no-necked illiterate newspaper seller from the slums of Sydney was lazy, gross, drunken and perverted. Inside the ring, he was a phenomenon. Spotted by Foley in a gang fight, he was taken to the White Horse and taught how to box but Griffo was stubbornly different in one respect: he scarcely moved his feet. His party trick was to stand motionless on a handkerchief and dodge punches by movement of his head and hips alone. In the ring he proved harder to hit than probably anyone before or since. It was not until 1893 that Griffo went to America, the last of what was a virtual exodus of Australian boxers and one which resembled the similar mass departure of English prize-fighters in the late 1860s. There were good reasons for their collective decision. Australia had become the cradle of world boxing talent but rewards were modest. There was no Australian equivalent, at that time, of Fox or Spreckels. What's more, late in 1890, the hitherto thriving Australian economy began to malfunction. Jackson was advised to return to America and, after only three months back in his adopted homeland, he did so.

It would be a further sixteen months before Frank Slavin joined Jackson, Fitzsimmons, Hall and others of the Australian school in America. Meanwhile, he was involved in a celebrated and highly significant legal case. The opponents of the fight game were not satisfied with the supersedence of the LPR by Queensberry Rules bouts. As far as they were concerned, a prize-fight was defined by competition for a purse: the wearing or otherwise of gloves and the establishment of time limits were immaterial. These people detested all forms of fist fighting, grudgingly tolerating only four-round amateur bouts.

In September 1890, Billy Madden brought Joe McCauliffe to London to fight Frank Slavin at the Ormonde Club in Walworth for £1,000. Fox, unwilling to support Jackson on racist grounds but still seeking a challenger for Sullivan, backed McAuliffe, but made it plain that he would promote whoever was the winner. A few days before the fight was due, both Slavin and McAuliffe were arrested, taken to court and bound over not to commit a breach of the peace. Fox stood bail for McAuliffe but Slavin could not find the money. Mace approached Lord Lonsdale, who unhesitatingly made an intervention which decided the outcome of events. He first put up bail for Slavin and then convened a meeting of all interested parties at his baronial residence, 14 Carlton House Terrace, behind The Mall. With his solicitor at his side, Lonsdale advised the parties to flout the magisterial injunction – as a first step.

The fight went ahead. It was brief. A storm of body punches from Slavin led to McAuliffe being knocked out in the second round. The boxers were immediately rearrested and committed for trial at the Surrey Quarter Sessions. Lonsdale briefed the foremost advocate of the day, Sir Charles Russell, and, after hearing Russell's address, the judge discharged both boxers. Although there would be further legal challenges from time to time, this case, dominated by Lonsdale, whose lifelong love of boxing stemmed from his boyhood tuition by Mace, was decisive in establishing that boxing for a purse (provided it was carried out under Queensberry Rules) was no longer illegal in England. This was not a first, since legalisation in Australia had already been secured, largely thanks to Mace, but at long last the outlaw status of the English fistfighter, first imposed by diktat from 'Butcher Cumberland' a century and a half earlier, was terminated.

With boxing legalised first in Australia and now in England, it remained for America – boxing's new heartland – to follow suit. Given the federal nature of the United States, this could only be decided at the level of the individual state. In March 1890, the New Orleans City Council authorised Queensberry fights with the easily observable proviso of Sunday observance and a ban on liquor sales. The Crescent City's premier athletic club, the Olympic, took the lead in defeating the old Prize Ring statutes for the state of Louisiana. Only the previous year, the dignitaries of the city had hounded out Sullivan and Kilrain; now they were obliged to accept that pugilism had been superseded by a different sport. The judicial and municipal authorities in Louisiana made it possible for a world title fight to be arranged openly and held without fear of police interference under the electric lights of the Olympic Club in its brash new 4,500-seat arena on Royal Street. The middleweight champion, Nonpareil Jack Dempsey, would face the twenty-seven-year-old English-born, New Zealand-raised and Australian-schooled Bob Fitzsimmons.

Fitzsimmons's profile since arriving in California eight months earlier had been raised to a degree which astounded fight followers back in Australia. There he was regarded as a good boxer but no more than that. But Fitzsimmons had assets which had not been fully recognised in his adopted homeland: he was a determined man, amiable outside the ring but ruthless inside it, all the more so as the prize money soared. He was a good boxer but an even better puncher. His blows, delivered with the full force of his blacksmith shoulders, were fearfully powerful for a middleweight and he struck for the 'mark', where as a lad he had been badly winded by a pulled punch from Mace, the man who had started him on his boxing career. In short order, Fitzsimmons knocked out two American middleweights and fellow-Australian Billy McCarthy; then, typically, he took on a heavyweight and stood up to him just as he had done with Slavin years earlier. This time he drew with the highly regarded Joe Choynski.

The Olympic Club of New Orleans then put up $12,000, a full $11,000 of which would go to the winner of Dempsey v Fitzsimmons. This was money which Fitz could only dream about in Australia. Dempsey's title defence began with the American trying to outbox the New Zealander. But 'Ruby Robert', as the American boxing public nicknamed the freckled-faced balding redhead, used his unusually long reach to beat him to the jab. Suddenly Fitz dropped Dempsey to his knees, then uppercut him as he rose. He unleashed a volley of body shots, one of which was close enough to the mark to have stopped Dempsey if he had not been saved by the bell. So unaccustomed were the spectators to legitimate body punching that many of them yelled 'foul!' and, fearing disqualification, the Sydney-trained man switched his attack back to the head. By the thirteenth round, Dempsey had been floored thirteen times. The previously impregnable American had one eye closed and was bleeding profusely from a stream of jabs. Fitz pleaded with the referee to stop the fight, but with Dempsey defiant, he was obliged to deliver the coup de grace. On 14 January 1891, Fitzsimmons became the second boxer from the Antipodes to hold a world title. Had the sullen Sullivan been willing to give Jackson his chance, the probability is that Australia would have held three of the four titles regularly competed for at that time – and this was from a nation whose population was only a tenth of England's and a mere twentieth of America's!

While rough and ready American fight fans spoke about 'an

Australian invasion' and worried themselves with irrational notions such as the alleged superiority of Australian manhood, the thinking sports reporters of the United States were not slow to realise that the new-found Australian strength resulted from the coaching of Dooley and the instruction of Foley but, above all, from the fifty-nine-year-old Englishman, thousands of miles away in Liverpool. With his ruthless determination, his use of the left jab and his relentlessly accurate and often thunderous body shots, Fitzsimmons, although far from being any dancing master, incarnated many of the virtues of Mace.

Three years before the publication of the Queensberry Rules, Mace had been the first to advocate both the use of gloves and the ten-second count, first on his Knockout Tour with his own circus, then at the Myrtle Street Gymnasium in Liverpool. As a showman, he had been quicker than most to realise the need to speed up the vital timeframe to match the tempo of an age increasingly obsessed with speed. As a star violinist, his motivation to campaign for the use of gloves was uniquely personal; at any time, an injury might finish his boxing career and he was desperate to preserve his hands in case he needed to revert to his alternative profession. He had winced too many times at the jarring impact on his wrists as his jabs and crosses struck home and devoutly sought the cushion of leather which would protect his hands and keep them supple enough to coax melodies from his beloved violin.

From the time of his bout with Bill Davis in Virginia City, the first-ever professional fight which approximated to the Queensberry code, through his long series of exhibitions on two continents, beyond his successful call, in Melbourne, for the legalisation of gloved combat in the state of Victoria, and by his renunciation of the London Prize Ring after the hooliganism of the Pelicans in France, it had been Mace who set the pace in the transition from pugilism to boxing. And he had done this while the Marquess of Queensberry, in whose name the Rules had been published, had been bellowing for more blood while comfortably ensconced at the now discredited Pelican Club – and while Sullivan, soon to be touted as the herald of a new sporting age, had bawled his affection for those same Queensberry Rules which he casually flouted whenever it suited his purpose.

Sullivan would survive as world heavyweight champion for

another couple of years but only by playing the race card as his pseudo-justification for ducking the challenge of Peter Jackson, the first exemplar of the school which Mace had founded and which had been nurtured by Foley. But already Nonpareil Jack Dempsey had been dethroned by Mace's own New Zealand discovery, Fitzsimmons.

In California, young Jim Corbett, trained by the expatriate Englishman Walter Watson in the Macean style, had already set his sights on Sullivan's crown. It remained for the Queensberry Rules to be revised, not, needless to say, by the malign Marquess but, among others, by the youthful Earl of Lonsdale who had been imbued with a love of boxing as a boy by Jem Mace. When an appropriate number of rounds – far more than John Chambers' amateurish four – had been decided on, and when criteria for the award of points had been established, the boxing revolution would be complete. The overthrow of Sullivan would do no more than symbolise it.

28

Young Enough to be his Granddaughter

THEY STROLLED HAND in hand in the spring sunshine, exchanging glances, but as he slipped his arm tightly around her slender back, there were mutterings of disapproval from a group of ageing married women who had observed them. 'Young enough to be his daughter,' tutted one old trout, and the others mumbled their miserable accord. Clearly the couple, both elegantly dressed but separated by a generation or more, were openly flouting one of the taboos of Victorian bourgeois society.

In actual fact, she was young enough to be his granddaughter. When they first met, early in 1890, Alice Stokes was eighteen and Jem Mace was approaching sixty. In their world, the world of showbusiness, such liaisons scarcely evoked a lifted eyebrow. What's more, Alice was physically and emotionally mature and could have passed for a young woman in her mid-twenties. Mace was still athletic and vigorous and was taken by those who didn't know his background to be in his late forties, or fifty at the very most.

Alice Caroline Stokes had been born at Icknield Port Road in the Ladywood district of Birmingham on 4 January 1872 and was the daughter of Thomas Stokes, a sheet-iron shearer, and his wife Sarah. By the age of nine, Alice had moved with her parents, two older sisters, two younger brothers and one younger sister to Scotland. Her father continued as an iron worker and they lived near Wishaw in Lanarkshire, fifteen miles from Glasgow, a city where her mother had spent part of her youth. Two further sons and a daughter completed the Stokes family before they moved into Glasgow itself, going to live in the Barony district. Alice had completed her education within the Scottish system but showed no inclination to follow her sisters Lizzie and Polly and become a garment maker. Good-looking and lively, she was keen to join a circus but she was working as a barmaid in Glasgow and it was there that she met Mace, who was staying in the city during his series of exhibitions with Pooley prior to the Mitchell fight. Alice was tall, slim and, like most of Mace's women, dark, with neat features and a pert expression.

Mace had remained without a source of regular income since returning from the USA eight years earlier, living off the declining dividends of his Australian investments and occasional windfalls from boxing exhibitions. Inevitably his capital became severely depleted but, careless as ever in matters of money, he had often spent lavishly when away from home and continued to be an inveterate and unsuccessful gambler on horse races. As the 1890s had opened, his financial situation remained weak, and in comparison with the life he lived in Melbourne, he was impoverished. Nellie, Amelia and Ada all tried to stop him gambling but he never could. He listened politely to what they had to say and went on doing what he had always done. Ostensibly to earn money but, as he admitted to Pooley, to relieve the tedium of life in Liverpool, he rejoined Ginnett's Circus, where Pooley was already working, later touring with Leone's American circus and Bernard's Circus. A return to the road gave him an instant kick. Family life, which he had known for the first time ever in the previous decade, was pleasant but the Circus was in his blood and always would be.

While Mace had indulged in casual liaisons throughout his life, his feelings for Alice, although initially triggered by desire for her willowy young body, went further than that. Just as Mary had once incarnated upward social mobility in his eyes and Hannah the grace and beauty of equestrianism, so Alice symbolised youth. Sadly, Nellie, the woman who had so deeply shared his love of music, had declined physically. Almost forty, she looked fifty and was, of course, twice Alice's age. Jem made no secret of his age to Alice, nor his marital status nor the collapse of his fortune, but it made no difference to her feelings for him. She had never expected to be in love with a man forty years her senior, or to be the girlfriend of one of the most famous men in the land, but soon she was declaring her feelings to Jem. Vulnerable and submissive, she was not likely to irritate him with talk about financial prudence. She was eager for passionate lovemaking and Mace was not the man to hesitate; soon the long-legged Glaswegian girl was putty in his hands. Here was a young woman who would give him a real joie de vivre, such as he had not felt for years, and he was determined to bind her to him. As soon as their relationship was consummated, he knew that he must break with Nellie. He returned briefly to Liverpool and told her that they were finished as a couple. He was deeply sorry, the fault was his and his alone, but he could not help himself. Taking his belongings with him, he returned to life on the road and he and Alice lived together as man and wife.

Nellie was devastated. She was as much in love with him as ever but, well aware of his weakness for very young women, had had some forebodings when he returned to circus life. Nellie needed the full support of her family to get through the emotionally difficult years following his departure. She was sustained by her sister Annie and son John but, above all, by the unswerving loyalty of Mace's own daughters, Amelia McMillin and Ada Mace. They were furious at their father eloping with a girl who was five years younger than Ada. The family felt it would be best for Nellie to move from the rented house in York Villas and it was not long before she was living at Norton Street in Liverpool city centre, where she made a reasonable living taking in lodgers. John and Ada moved in with her. Coping with the emotional storm caused by Mace's abrupt departure matured them and their affection developed into love. In June 1892, John Lee and Ada Mace were married at Liverpool Register Office. The wedding of her beloved son John to a stepdaughter she had come to cherish gladdened Nellie's heart and was the first step in her recovery from emotional trauma. John, who was at the time still trying to make a living from the sale of his paintings and sketches, defied convention by being thenceforth known as Mace rather than Lee.

As 1891 unfolded, Mace was financially ruined. Australia in general and Victoria in particular were plunged into economic recession. Years of wild speculation and unsecured loans culminated in a crash on the Melbourne Stock Exchange and a run on the main Victorian banks. Like many investors, Mace's mining and railway shares were wiped out. Even his hotel, the Old England in Melbourne, was valued at a fraction of its former price. He decided to keep it on even though, as long as he remained in England, it was of no accessible financial benefit to him. His new Australian business manager, Sam Dixon, had failed to warn him of the impending disaster and, ruined himself by the slump, returned to England.

Mace and Alice had to consider establishing a permanent home somewhere. Liverpool was out of the question for obvious reasons and the disapproval of his lover's parents and her older sisters would have made living in Glasgow a daunting prospect. They were shocked by the age gap – Mace was ten years older than Alice's father, Tom Stokes – and they considered Mace to be an old cad who had seduced a vulnerable girl, one who was, in their words, indeed 'young enough to be his granddaughter'. Although Alice regretted that they could not be legally married, her main concern was to assuage her family's disapproval. Mace and Alice therefore concocted a story that they had married in Scotland when Mace was there on boxing business in 1890. Her family clutched at this straw but remained wary.

In spring 1892, Ginnett's ceased touring and took up a summer residency in the booming seaside resort of Brighton, fifty miles from London. An upper-class haven since Regency days, the recent expansion of the railways made it a favourite holiday destination for middle-class and artisan Londoners. It was just the place for a circus residency and Mace and Alice, with him still working as a violinist, went to live at Queens Road, Brighton. Alice was pregnant by now and unable to work. At a stroke their joint income was drastically reduced.

By this time Pooley and Delaiah had decided to emigrate to America with their children. Pooley, fifty-three but still athletic, had always loved the States, where he had shared many action-packed adventures with his famous cousin. When he had first visited, the Romany population had been small and he had often been mistaken for a man of Greek or Italian origin. Ever the joker, he had sometimes played along with this, claiming that he had been brought to America by his parents as a young boy and forgotten his native language. Since then Romanies from the Austro-Hungarian Empire had fled persecution to seek a better life across the Atlantic. Many travelled with circuses while others were horse dealers, doing business in the rural districts in the environs of New York City. This was where Pooley and Delaiah now headed.

Pooley would have loved Jem to have joined him in this move, and

Mace seriously considered returning to America and living the rest of his life there, but Alice had no wish to go – her horizons did not extend beyond the south coast of England. Already, in November 1891, he had been offered the post of boxing instructor at the Olympic Club in San Francisco, in succession to Jim Corbett. He accepted, then changed his mind, doubtless because Alice could not be persuaded. Jem regretted this. Like Pooley, he relished the extra vibrancy of American life. He and Pooley had been closer than most brothers, often inseparable companions over a period of thirty years, and both Delaiah and Alice wept when the cousins shook hands in farewell.

On 2 October 1892, Jem and Alice's first child was born, in Brighton. She was named Alice Lillian Madonna Mace and would be known as Lillian, after one of Alice's younger sisters, to distinguish her from her mother. In contrast to her disapproving parents and older sisters, the younger Stokes found Alice's lifestyle adventurous while the youngest ones simply missed having their big sister around. Ginnett's residency inevitably ended once the summer season was over and the company resumed touring, but Jem did not want to leave Alice on her own, especially with the new baby. Desperate for money, he managed to arrange an exhibition with a little-known boxer, Johnny Stringer, in Leeds. The receipts from this were enough to keep the wolf from the door for the time being but there was no disguising how close Jem and his new family were to the poverty line. Alice had known when she met him that, although he was still famous, he was no longer wealthy. She loved him and he loved her but hard times lay ahead for the founder of boxing and his young mistress.

29

The End of a Revolution

THE PELICAN CLUB never recovered from the Bruges scandal, although it remained open for a couple more years. It was superseded by a club of a very different nature, the National Sporting Club, which, at King Street, Covent Garden, in the heart of London, opened its doors in March 1891. It was founded jointly by John Fleming and A.F. 'Peggy' Bettinson. Fleming had eventually lived down his role in the Bruges scandal and been reinstated at the Pelican Club but he was shrewd enough to see that the Pelicans had been irretrievably tainted, both by its degenerate aristocratic members and by the roughs whom they encouraged when it suited them. The Pelicans were associated with bareknuckle fighting and bareknuckle fighting was a thing of the past. The National Sporting Club would be strictly a boxing venue with a ring constructed in the basement under electric lights, around which were seats for 1,300 spectators.

Fleming set out to establish an atmosphere as different as could be imagined from that of the Pelican Club. His own dour manner intensified into one of extreme solemnity and he forbade all conversation while a round was in progress, intent on establishing an ambience like that of the theatre. He insisted that drinking and betting should take place in other rooms. Dropping Jem Smith like a hot potato, and refusing membership to George Baird, he made public penitence for Bruges by inviting Frank Slavin to open the club's boxing nights with an exhibition. In this way Fleming showed his determination to make the National Sporting Club a home from home for respectable city businessmen and not, as the Pelican had been, a haven for Hooray Henrys.

Bettinson was not yet thirty but seemed much older due to his early baldness and pompous manner. Astute and wealthy, he was the main financial backer of the new club. Bettinson and Fleming secured the services of the two strictest referees in England, Bernard Angle and George Vize, either of whom could operate impartially and without fear of intimidation, unlike their predecessors of the LPR. The triumvirate who ruled the NSC was completed by the Earl of Lonsdale. He responded immediately to Fleming and Bettinson's invitation to become President of the club. Though he was not involved in its day-to-day running, his name conferred the kudos of respectable aristocracy and of total legality.

One of the first questions faced by the NSC was the rules under which boxing should take place on its premises. As Jem Mace had repeatedly pointed out, the Queensberry Rules in the form drafted by John Graham Chambers were suitable only for amateurs. Until they had been augmented, they would serve only as an approximation. Their two principal deficiencies were the failure to stipulate the number of rounds and the lack of any system to determine objectively, in the absence of a knockout, which boxer had won. Without clarification the nascent sport of boxing would remain vulnerable to the legal challenges of the anti-fistic lobby, which could raise all its old objections towards 'a fight to the finish'. What's more, any boxer would be free to claim that he had been robbed of victory on the whim of a referee.

Even before the opening of the NSC, a lot of thought had been given to this matter and when, in 1891, a new set of rules was made public they were known as the Queensberry Rules of Endurance rather than the rules of the NSC. Regrettably, this perpetuated the myth that the cantankerous Marquess was a central figure in the reform of the fight game. In fact, he had done little more than lend his name to Chambers' original version and he certainly had nothing whatsoever to do with its revision.

The original Rules, from a quarter of a century earlier, had sometimes been absolute and precise ('No wrestling allowed' and 'the rounds to be of three minutes duration and one minute time between rounds'), but at others had been vague and slack ('a fair stand-up boxing match', 'a 24 foot ring or as near that size as possible', 'in the power of the referee to give his award', 'the gloves to be fair size . . . of the best quality and new').

The new rules were a masterpiece of logical progression and

unambiguous wording. There were nine in all. The first demarcated the ring – 'not less than 14 foot or more than 20 foot square'. The second eliminated skin-tight gloves, the favourite hand covering of John L. Sullivan, for ever. Gloves were to be 'of a minimum weight of 6 ounces each'. It went on to provide for bandaging and to specify the length of bandages. And, in a remarkably far-sighted move, it insisted on the contestants being medically examined before entering the ring. Rule 3 was a crucial one: the 1867 timeframe was retained but 'no contest shall exceed 15 rounds, except championships which shall be limited to 20 rounds'. The marathon bloodbaths of the past would be replaced by combat which at the most would last an hour of actual fighting or have a total duration of an hour and twenty minutes. Rule 4 banned seconds from the ring during actual boxing, eliminating the possibility of various forms of covert cheating, all well-known to the old LPR seconds. The fifth Rule was also crucial. While reiterating the ten-second knockout as the absolute determinant of victory, it provided a perfect template for the referee if no such knockout were to take place. 'He shall award a maximum number of five marks at the end of each round to the better man, and a proportionate number to the other contestant, or, when equal, the maximum number to each.' Furthermore, 'The referee shall decide all contests in favour of the contestant who obtains the greater number of marks.'

But on what basis were such marks, alternatively referred to as 'points', to be given? 'Marks shall be awarded for "attack" . . . direct, clean hits with the knuckle part of the glove of either hand on any part of the front or side of their head or body above the belt; "defence" . . . guarding, slipping, ducking and getting away.'

Rule 6 empowered the referee to disqualify a contestant 'for hitting below the belt, for using the pivot blow . . . the kidney punch, for hitting with the open glove, the inside or butt of a hand, or with the wrist or elbows, for holding, butting, shouldering, intentionally falling without receiving a blow, wrestling . . . remaining in a clinch unnecessarily, for not trying.' It also initiated the technical knockout, or TKO, by giving the referee the discretion 'to stop the contest if, in his opinion, a contestant is outclassed or accidentally disabled'. Rules 7 and 8 extended disqualification for breach of the rules by a second and to the withholding of prize money from a disqualified boxer. And in case there should be any contingency not envisaged by the rule-makers, Rule 10 empowered the refereed to decide it.

The Queensberry Rules of Endurance were wide-ranging and unequivocal, with the words 'shall' and 'must' constantly used. No one man claimed the credit for them in the way Chambers had done for the original version. Clearly they were drawn up after thorough group discussion, almost certainly involving Fleming, Bettinson and Lonsdale on a regular basis and with occasional contributions from the journalists of the *Sporting Times*. The final drafting, though, was probably Lonsdale's. Neither Fleming nor Bettinson had any gift for the written word, while Lonsdale did. Several of his letters survive and they are written in an unmistakable style – pithy, forceful, intricate and decisive. Had Hugh Cecil Lowther chosen to exercise his intellect in law or politics, as intelligent men of his class normally did, he would have excelled. The fact that he preferred to do so over the three controversial sports which he loved, steeple-chasing, fox-hunting and boxing, does not detract from his mental powers.

What united the triumvirs of the National Sporting Club was their personal contact with, and their professional admiration for, Jem Mace. Lonsdale's life had been partly shaped by the term in which Mace gave him a thorough education in the fistic art. Fleming had picked Mace's brains in various West End drums over the years. Bettinson had watched every exhibition of his in London and, as an excellent public speaker, often lectured on boxing at amateur athletic clubs. Time and again Bettinson reiterated his credo: that there was only one style in boxing and that Jem Mace was it foremost exponent. As to what Mace's style consisted of, it was essentially described within Rule 5 of those issued by the National Sporting Club. 'Points', the term Mace derived from fencing, were to be not only for 'attack' but for 'defence', in other words 'guarding, slipping, ducking and getting away'.

Mace himself, handicapped by the illiteracy of his first thirty years, could not contribute, in a formal sense, to the devising of a system of rules; what's more, during the crucial months in 1890-1 when the rules which would define the new sport of boxing were being worked out, Lonsdale and Bettinson found, to their surprise and puzzlement, that Mace was effectively incommunicado. Shocked by the decimation of his fortune in Australia, and in the throes of a passionate affair with Alice, he had other things on his mind than the niceties of boxing legislation. Nevertheless, it was those very points which he had repeatedly emphasised, over a period of thirty years, which were to provide a framework of the new sport. And it was to be the style which he had demonstrated to perfection both in the LPR and in Queensberry exhibition after exhibition, which was to provide the triumvirs of the NSC with a yardstick by which they would revise and refine the Queensberry Rules and by which all boxers, anywhere in the world, from then on, would be assessed.

California was, as yet, unfamiliar with the new rules that defined boxing, but in San Francisco, on 24 May 1891, the two leading exponents of 'scientific boxing', the code word which distinguished Macean style from brute force, clashed at the California Athletic Club. Peter Jackson, aged twenty-nine and boxing instructor at the C.A.C, fought James J Corbett, aged twenty-four and his counterpart from the city's Olympic Club. Jackson, resident in the city for three incident-filled years, scaled 198lb, sixteen more than the San Francisco-born Corbett, who was the same height. Their bout was eagerly anticipated. By his defeats of Godfrey, McAuliffe, Cardiff and Smith, and the fact that he got the better of a draw with Goddard, Jackson had eliminated most of Sullivan's potential challengers. As to Corbett, he had mastered the brilliant Joe Choynski and easily defeated Sullivan's only significant American victims, Jake Kilrain and Dominick McCaffrey. Except for Frank Slavin, who had only just arrived in the States from England, the two contestants had cleaned up the heavyweight division between them.

Corbett fought in Macean style. While there is no evidence that, as a mere boy of ten, he actually saw the celebrated glove encounter between Mace and Davis in his hometown, he would certainly have been very well aware of it since Mace's scientific mastery was the talk of sporting San Francisco. And when Corbett first put on the gloves himself as a lad at the Olympic Club, his tutor was the Englishman Walter Watson, who was a strict Macean.

Jim Corbett was the son of an Irish-born livery stable owner and was, with the exception of Choynski whose father was a distinguished newspaper editor, the only top American boxer of middle-class origin, having worked as a bank clerk. He had already acquired the moniker 'Gentleman Jim' on account of his polished manners, elegant attire and Pompadour hairstyle. Jackson, whose own high forehead and deep-set eyes surprised some of those who met him, had the manner of a head waiter at an upscale hotel. Like Corbett, he had many female admirers, although he was careful not to be seen in public with white girlfriends, knowing that this would be considered the ultimate provocation to white racists. Peter never imagined that the educated Corbett would be numbered among these, but Corbett had absorbed ethnic bigotry from his parents. In fact his sole reason for agreeing to face Jackson was because he was convinced that a victory over the black Australian would virtually guarantee him a shot at Sullivan's world title.

Unfortunately for boxing connoisseurs, the Jackson–Corbett bout turned out to be an anti-climax. It was undermined from the start by the crass decision to designate it as a fight to the finish. What's more, the gloves were only five ounces and no bandages were worn. The two gladiators showed undue respect for each other's abilities. In terms of style, they almost cancelled each other out, with the significant difference that Corbett, who had begun his career when prize-fighting was virtually dead, was the first man to develop a left hook. This was a punch which Corbett would never have tried had he ever fought with bare knuckles, and he would have run a considerable risk of breaking his hand on an opponent's skull. Otherwise Corbett's incessant feinting with head, hands and feet were straight out of Mace's book.

Jackson was at some disadvantage because he had lost two weeks from his training schedule when he injured an ankle after being thrown from a horse and buggy.

Jackson was able to go no less than forty rounds before his strained ankle began to limit his mobility, but he never risked opening up with a barrage of body shots, as he had been trained to do from his earliest days at the White Horse – probably due to concern that he would leave himself open to Corbett's left hook. This shot was new to him but, equally, Corbett had never before faced a top-class Macean body puncher. Even when Jackson was obliged to slow to a shuffle, Corbett, whose hand speed was exceptional, was unwilling to take risks. In addition, his light gloves frayed almost to the knuckle and so he limited his hooks targeting only the body. From the forty-fourth round on, journalist W.W. Naughton noted spectators leaving the arena, while a few others actually fell asleep. After sixty-one Queensberry rounds, totalling precisely four hours and three minutes, referee Hiriam Cook halted proceedings and called the fight a draw.

Predictably the marathon bout drew derision from the old prize-fight crowd, but the fault lay in the absence of a proper timeframe, a proper points system and in meagre gloves and bandages. Such a fiasco would not have been permitted at the National Sporting Club. Had Jackson known that he needed only to keep going on his jarred ankle for twenty rounds, he might well have been more adventurous; had Corbett known that he would have been rewarded for his wider attacking repertoire, he might have used his left hook to greater effect.

Jackson realised that his failure to beat Corbett removed entirely the slight chance that Sullivan would give him a match for the title, and he went into vaudeville, awaiting a bout between the champion and Corbett. In the early 1890s, Sullivan was showing a distinct disinclination to take on anybody, except in a carefully controlled sparring exhibition. He went on a tour of Australia which was a dismal failure. Hard-up Australians refused to pay to see his theatrical shows and he earned their contempt for the way in which he ducked a challenge from Joe Goddard. On his return to the USA, Sullivan found that his bankers were concerned by his dwindling finances and he was subjected to a barrage of insulting comment from the young aspirants to his throne. Slavin, Corbett and Choynski mocked Sullivan's bulk, his second-rate theatre acting and his three-year period of inactivity since fighting Kilrain.

By March 1892, Sullivan had been needled into issuing another of his famous defis. From St Paul, Minnesota, where he was on tour, he retaliated with a tirade against a 'country – overrun with foreign fighters – seeking notoriety and American dollars'. He did 'hereby challenge any and all of the bluffers who are trying to make capital at my expense' to a fight not later than September at the Olympic Club in New Orleans. But the stakes would be high. There would be a purse of $25,000 and an outside bet of $10,000. The purse would be winner-takes-all and he would 'insist on the bet of $10,000 to show that they meant business'. Sullivan then went on to rank his three leading challengers. First was 'Frank P. Slavin of Australia' who had 'done the greatest amount of bluffing'. Second was 'Charlie Mitchell of England' who was nothing but 'a bombastic sprinter'. Third was 'James J. Corbett of America' who had 'done his share of bluffing'. Sullivan made no reference to Joe Goddard, by now arrived in America, or Joe Choynski but alluded to Peter Jackson, if not by name. Sullivan explicitly stated that he would 'include all fighters . . . who are white'. He would 'not fight a negro. I never have and I never shall.' He concluded by stipulating that 'the Marquess of Queensberry Rules must govern this contest'.

For all the swagger, Sullivan was conceding that the Prize Ring was dead and, by implication, that boxing had been taken over by a new breed of contestant. Of his three nominees, two had been explicitly instructed in Macean style, one by Foley and the other by Walter Watson. As to the third, Charlie Mitchell, it had taken him four rounds to see off the challenge of a man twice his age, fifty-eight-year-old Jem Mace himself. Sullivan's money demands ensured that his likely challenger would be the man with access to the wealthiest backers. At the time, Slavin and Mitchell had palled up and were touring North America together, giving a series of exhibitions. Knowing that the best chance of raising funds lay in England, they returned there. There were only two fight-loving men in England who could afford the kind of money Sullivan was demanding: Lord Lonsdale and George Baird. Baird and Mitchell had been cronies for some years but the 'Squire' thought that Mitchell, who was by this time regularly being arrested after drunken brawls, was past his best – it took one to know one as far as booze was concerned.

Baird seems to have considered backing Slavin, but the Australian would have nothing to do with the man who had urged the mob to attack him at Bruges. He turned to Lonsdale, who was sympathetic but only on condition that Slavin first met Jackson and, if he could, succeeded in beating him. Finally circumstances were obliging Slavin to meet the man he had studiously avoided for so many years.

Frank Slavin and Peter Jackson agreed to fight at the National Sporting Club on 30 May 1892. It was for a purse of £1,000, put up by Lonsdale, and would be a match between the two foremost heavyweight graduates of the White Horse in Sydney. Mace, deciding between these two disciples, hoped and believed that Jackson would be the winner. He regarded Slavin as a fine boxer and a man of immense personal courage, as he had demonstrated at Bruges, but he considered the so-called 'Black Prince' to be an even better boxer and he deplored Slavin's racism. On learning that Mace was living in Brighton, Jackson persuaded Parson Davies to let him train at the seaside resort. In discussing Slavin, Mace insisted that, at all costs, Jackson must keep the man from New South Wales out-fighting, and that he must maintain concentration and make full use of his superior reach to do so. He argued that, as Slavin tired, Jackson could then move in and jab his way to victory. It was highly pertinent advice – for just as Jackson's left was comparable to Mace's, so were Slavin's body punches; the key to the contest was thus to keep the fight at long range.

Mace went up to London to watch a contest which was the talk of the metropolis and, for him, the culmination of the tuition which he had begun with Foley fifteen years earlier. Jackson and Slavin were scheduled to fight twenty rounds for what was billed as 'The Championship of England and of the British Empire'. It fully lived up to expectations. The crowd at the NSC, officially silenced during the rounds by Fleming's diktat, could not help but gasp at the trading of telling punches, and the pandemonium during the one-minute intervals was so great as to disturb the performance at the nearby Opera House in Covent Garden. Slavin sought to force the pace in the opening rounds, determined to get to close quarters. He brushed aside Jackson's jabs in his eagerness to get in body shots. Both men landed effective but not conclusive punches, Jackson demonstrating excellent footwork as he stepped back from Slavin's attack. By the fourth round, Slavin had indeed begun to tire and Jackson pressed his advantage, although still wary of a counter to the body. In the fifth, he opened a deep cut over Slavin's right cheekbone and a rat-tat-tat of jabs closed the Irish-Australian's left eye.

By the close of the sixth, Jackson's relentless jab had caused Slavin's lips to swell grossly. Realising that he was too far behind on points to win by that route, Slavin hurled himself into attack with a ferocity that stunned all who saw it. Leaping off his feet, he drove Jackson against the ropes and immediately slammed a terrible right under the heart. Doubled up in agony and lying on the ropes, Jackson was immensely relieved to hear the bell sound just as referee Angle was preparing to start the count. Within the allotted minute, Jackson was extricated by his seconds and recovered his breath. He danced away from Slavin in the seventh until his momentum had been lost. In the final three rounds, Jackson gave a masterclass in jab and move while Slavin kept in the fight by his sheer strength and courage. With a minute remaining before the final bell, Slavin began to reel, stunned by Jackson at last unleashing his own right-hand and then by a near simultaneous left-right combination. Slavin began to stumble and, barely conscious, dropped his hands. Jackson turned to the referee and requested that he stop the fight.

'No, you must finish it!' barked Angle.

Jackson walked quietly up to Slavin and tapped him exactly on the juncture of upper and lower jaw. He slumped to the floor and was counted out. When he recovered, he heard Lord Lonsdale call for three cheers for the gallant loser and then three more for the winner.

Accompanied by Lonsdale and Bettinson, Jackson visited Slavin in his dressing-room. He offered his hand and Slavin shook it. For the first time in his life he called Jackson by his first name as he congratulated him. The defeat was the beginning of a downward path which would see Slavin, previously undefeated in a ten-year career, decline into drunken obscurity. He was never again in the front rank of heavyweights but, as he reflected over the years not only on Jackson's astonishing skill but also on his humane attitude at the moment of triumph, Slavin publicly repented his earlier racism, and years later saluted him as 'the greatest of all masters and . . . one of the greatest fighters of all the ages'.

News of Jackson's victory, in what was actually the first great fight in the history of heavyweight boxing, was downplayed in the American media. The fact that the victor was black cancelled what otherwise would have been a highly significant triumph as far as the likes of Richard Kyle Fox were concerned. Jim Corbett, who having already sparred an exhibition with Sullivan the previous year had a first-hand knowledge of his style, went to New York to raise the funds to challenge him. Corbett's manager, William Brady, was an impresario and dramatist who had written a play, *Gentleman Jack* (later amended to *Gentleman Jim*) as a vehicle for Corbett. In addition to his many showbusiness connections, Brady knew Mike Donovan, still the instructor at the New York Athletic Club, which was patronised by many wealthy young socialites. The funds were speedily raised. On three successive nights in New Orleans between 5 and 7 September 1892, the Olympic Club staged its Carnival of Champions. Three titles would be competed for: lightweight, featherweight and heavyweight. Middleweights were excluded. Bob Fitzsimmons was the champion and his likely victory over any domestic opponent would have marred the atmosphere of American self-congratulation. Similarly, Young Griffo was still in Sydney and his defeat of Billy Murphy was not recognised. In his stead, George 'Little Chocolate' Dixon won the featherweight crown, most spectators having few problems with a non-white champion in a lower weight division, not realising that the tiny black man was in fact a Canadian. At lightweight, the only division where either the champion or his leading challenger was not Australian, the highly skilful Jack McAuliffe was the victor.

Then Sullivan put his world title on the line, for the first time under an approximation of the Queensberry Rules of Endurance. Aged thirty-three, but greying and looking at least forty, he outweighed twenty-six-year-old Corbett – the taller man by a couple of inches – by 21lb, most of it flab. The fight lasted twenty-six rounds but Sullivan, flailing wildly as usual, was a spent force after five. His bravery kept him in the contest until the twelfth but, from then on, he went from a flat-footed buffer to a shambling wreck. Corbett was characteristically ruthless. He could have ended the fight with one full-blooded blow but he chose to give a one-sided exhibition of all his manifold boxing skills and totally humiliate Sullivan. Finally, he opened up with a two-fisted attack, and with Sullivan glassy-eyed and bleeding profusely, he almost casually knocked him out. The Boston Strong Boy announced his retirement within days. His long and baleful reign was over. As for Corbett, the first world heavyweight champion in the era of true boxing had been schooled in San Francisco, not Sydney, but Jem Mace had always been the yardstick against which he measured his progress – and the effortlessly relaxed manner in which he first evaded, then humbled and finally dispatched Sullivan, was a carbon copy of Mace.

The years 1889-92 had indeed witnessed a sporting revolution.

Pugilism had been transcended by modern boxing fought out not furtively on remote stretches of marsh or beach but in the heart of such great cities as London, New Orleans and San Francisco before fervent but well-behaved crowds. Both men and women sat in comfortable seats enthralled by the dramatic spectacle which unfolded before them in the electrically lit ring. The dinosaurs of the bare-knuckle age had been replaced by skilful, mobile and accurate boxer-punchers such as Corbett, Jackson and Fitzsimmons, and the National Sporting Club had laid down a series of rules which went far beyond the inadequate Queensberry Code.

While Jem Mace had not been proactive in these critical years, the transformation owed more to him than to anybody else: by his legacy in Australia, which led directly to that country's pre-eminence in world boxing; by his discovery of Fitzsimmons; by his association with the triumvirs of the NSC, and, above all, by the fistic style which he personally demonstrated to near-perfection, he was the prime inspiration in the revolution into boxing.

PART SIX
THE LEGACY
(1892–1910)

30

Sons of Jem

GEORGE IV AND Jem Mace had nothing in common except a love of pugilism, but seventy years after its completion, John Nash's Royal Pavilion – a folly built in the style of a Hindu pleasure dome for the former Prince Regent – loomed over the meaner streets of Brighton in which Mace had taken refuge. Lively in summer but bleak and forlorn in winter when the funfairs had gone, Brighton was home to Mace and his family for three years, two of which were spent in a shabby flat on West Street. They were years of near-poverty in which he succeeded, by a narrow margin, in staying solvent. They were also years of love between him and his young mistress, Alice Stokes, who was yet to be reconciled with her disapproving family, far away in Glasgow. At least the Stokes were relieved that Mace did not leave after Lillian's birth, which they feared he might. Far from it, he never left her side in the opening months of his new daughter's life.

As the money from the Stringer exhibition ran out, he had to look for a job, and in November 1892 he opened the Jem Mace School of Arms at the Victoria Hall in Brighton. The following year, electric lighting was installed there, but the School was a failure. In July 1893, he received a conditional offer from an American circus to reprise his statues act on a short tour for $500 a week. He was eager but the offer was withdrawn after Mace had to send over a photo of himself, stripped to the waist. Although a vigorous and virile man, he could not, in his early sixties, be expected to have retained the trim waistline of his younger days. Shortly afterwards Alice learned that she was pregnant again. Desperate for money, Mace sought legal guidance. He was advised to file for bankruptcy and did so.

On 17 April 1894, at Brighton, following an adjudication under the Bankruptcy Acts of 1883 and 1890, he was declared bankrupt and his debts, mostly to bookmakers, were written off on condition that he sold his assets, namely the collection of belts and cups still in his possession. Until this was done he could not apply for discharge or resume any form of business. Reluctant as he was to part with these glittering and hard-earned trophies, Mace realised that he must do so. The trouble was that in remote Brighton there would be little chance of realising their true value, so he retained them for the time being.

On May 6 1894 a son was born to Jem and Alice. He was given the memorable name of James Mace, the third of his sons to receive it. Such a choice of name was an unmistakable indication that he had washed his hands of James Mace Junior, by now in his late thirties. By 1891, James had finished with fundamentalism. He went into partnership with James Waite, son of one of London's boxing 'professors', and they ran The Fenceries, off Regent Street, where James taught both boxing and fencing. James was an intelligent and articulate man and knew how to publicise himself. His photograph appeared in the new sports magazine *The Mirror of Life* and he went on to have a book on boxing technique published. Unfortunately, he tended to refer to himself as 'Jem Mace Junior' and this greatly displeased his father, since he considered that the diminutive form of their shared first name was unique to him.

Around the time of young James's birth, the world heavyweight champion, Jim Corbett, was on a two-month tour in Europe. Like Sullivan before him, he had become a full-time stage actor, boxing only occasional exhibitions. When contacted about the possibility of boxing an exhibition with Mace for the latter's benefit, Corbett agreed but his manager, William Brady, who was well aware that Mace was in need of money, refused to waive a clause in Corbett's contract limiting his exhibitions to France. Despite Brady's intransigence, Corbett and Mace met briefly in London and got on well. Shocked to learn how hard-up Mace actually was, the world champion gave money to the man whose style had inspired his own. Corbett's generosity tided Mace over for some time. On his return to America, Corbett contacted Mike Donovan about the possibility of a match between him and Mace for the 'Veterans Championship of the World'. Donovan was on for it and Mace even more so, but in December 1894 arrangements to fund Mace's voyage to New York fell through and the bout was cancelled.

Early in 1895, Jem's luck changed. His financial situation was desperate and Alice was pregnant once again. When he learned that an obscure boxer named Jack Hall had been left without a fight, due to the unexpected withdrawal of an opponent, he put his name forward. In view of Mace's age, Hall insisted that it should be an exhibition only. The news spread fast that Mace would be in a London ring again – at Canning Town in the East End. 'Peggy' Bettinson regularly visited fight venues other than the NSC, and speaking to Mace after the exhibition with Hall, he was shocked to learn the plight of the man whose praises he was extolling in his many lectures to athletic clubs. He at once offered him the premises of the NSC to auction his trophies before a knowledgeable audience. This sale of assets enabled Mace to clear his debts and have sufficient money left over to move his family from the lodgings they had endured in Brighton to a pleasant house at Favart Road in west London. Although nominally in Fulham, the road overlooked Felbrook Common and lay off the King's Road in Chelsea, a bustling district which Mace knew well and liked. It was here, on 5 May 1895, that Jem and Alice's second daughter, Amy Pauline Mace, was born. She was named after another of Alice's younger sisters, Amy Stokes.

Mace's return to the capital brought him right back into the boxing world from which, for three long years, he had been unhappily separated. He had never failed to keep himself fit and, while in Brighton, he had run for mile after mile along the shore for that express purpose. While Bettinson would never depart from his view that Mace's style was the epitome of boxing skill and guile, he was concerned that the sixty-four-year-old was too old to be an active participant. Not a bit of it, said Jem, and boldly declared his willingness to do exhibitions with even the most prominent young boxers. One was Dick Burge, the English lightweight champion. Soon Mace entered the ring with Burge at Hoxton and gave a good account of himself. Bettinson was amazed and proposed that Mace should fight Burge at the National Sporting Club itself. From Bettinson's point of view, this would be an object lesson in true boxing technique with the man who had perfected it; from Mace's, even though he was sharing the bill, it would be a bumper benefit.

From his reading of the *Sporting Times*, Mace knew the outlines of what had happened to the world middleweight title after Bob

Fitzsimmons crushed Nonpareil Jack Dempsey. Jim Hall had belatedly gone to the States and after a string of KO victories had secured a title fight against Fitzsimmons. Hall was confident he would win on the strength of his better record when both were in Australia. By now, the infant sport of professional boxing was so profitable that the Crescent City Athletic Club in New Orleans was prepared to offer an astounding $40,000 for Fitzsimmons v Hall. Hall, unable to raise the funds, came to England where he effortlessly demolished the English heavyweight champion Ted Pritchard in four rounds at the NSC. Regrettably, Hall was approached by George Baird, still affecting the title of Squire Abingdon. Banned from the NSC, he got to know Hall through Charlie Mitchell and put up the money required by the Crescent City A.C.

Fitzsimmons–Hall, at New Orleans on 8 March 1893 was a brilliant clash between two boxers both trained in Foley's school. The American crowd was treated to a splendid display of guileful boxing as they jabbed, ducked and feinted in what was true Australian – in other words Macean – style. Both appeared to be aiming for a points victory and Hall had built up a lead when Fitzsimmons glimpsed an opening and unleashed a two-fisted combination full on Hall's jaw, knocking the Sydney man senseless. The suddenness of the knockout led to gasps of shock throughout the audience.

After Hall's defeat, Baird, Hall and Mitchell went on a three-day junket through the saloons and whorehouses of New Orleans. The absurd Squire, one of the most villainous men in the history of a sport notorious for the nefarious, was already in poor health. After his fatuous attempts to rival two highly trained professional athletes bent on drunken debauch, he collapsed, and died a few days later.

Hall's successor as challenger to Fitzsimmons was the twenty-five-year-old New Zealander Dan Creedon. Creedon was yet another graduate of the White Horse and, after Hall's departure to the USA, he had defeated Starlight Rollins to take the Australian middleweight title. The clear superiority of Australian boxing was again demonstrated by Creedon's string of knockout victories in America. Then, in September 1894, Fitzsimmons faced Creedon in New Orleans. Another brief but sparkling bout ensued. Creedon cut out a fast pace and jabbed his way into a lead in the first, but once again Fitz's devastating power won the day. A fierce onslaught to the face and body knocked Creedon cold in the second. Hall and Creedon were not poor boxers – they were both very good indeed – their problem was that they faced, in Fitzsimmons, someone who had matured into a truly great performer. With no one left effectively to challenge him for the middleweight crown, Fitzsimmons threw down the gauntlet to Corbett. By now, American sportswriters were thoroughly alarmed by the dominance of Australian boxing. The mood of belligerent nationalism which Sullivan had set, and which chimed with American expansionism in foreign policy, meant they could not bear such a situation. Australian-trained boxers dominated every division, bar heavyweight itself, and one means or another had to be found to deprive them of their due.

Albert Griffiths was the first to experience this. He had finally come to America, where he would fight at lightweight. On four occasions, he was denied the title due to the bringing in of a majority drawn verdict. However obnoxious Griffo might have been outside the ring, this was rank injustice. Worse was to follow. Fitzsimmons was bullied into applying for American citizenship as a precondition for his being allowed to fight Corbett. To emphasise the point, Fitz had already been robbed of victory against Joe Choynski, the only meaningful American contender for the heavyweight crown. A fight between the two of them in Boston was preposterously called a draw after Fitzsimmons had knocked down Choynski five times. Police intervention followed – not to save Choynski from further punishment but to ensure that an American did not lose to an English-born man in the heart of Irish Boston.

When Fitzsimmons stepped up to heavyweight, logic would have suggested a contest between Hall and Creedon for the vacant middleweight title, but logic took second place to the demands of American nationalism – and racism. The leading American middleweight was Frank Craig, but the so-called 'Harlem Coffee Cooler' was *persona non grata* in the rings of his homeland and scarcely recognised as an American. His 'crime' was that his mother was what was then known as a 'Red Indian' and his father a black Cuban, so the path was made easier for Tommy Ryan (Joseph Youngs) – admittedly a classic boxer – to become world middleweight champion.

Craig, who spoke three languages and was a fine harmonica-player, decided to continue his career in England, which led to him facing Dan Creedon on the same bill as the Mace–Burge exhibition at the NSC. Trained at Clark's Academy in Philadelphia, Craig believed he would win with ease, particularly in view of his longer reach, but Creedon's superior footwork led to a points win. On learning that his own bout was to be followed by a Jem Mace exhibition, Craig was at ringside to study every move. It was painfully obvious to him that Foley's school gave better lessons than anything he had ever learned and it was an indication of the keenness with which the more intelligent young American boxers sought to emulate Mace's style.

What followed when Jem Mace faced Dick Burge at the National Sporting Club on 14 October 1895 was exceptional, even in Mace's long and glittering career. Before they entered the ring, Mace stressed to the thirty-year-old in no uncertain terms that he was not to 'go easy'. The bout would last three rounds and Mace was confident that his legs would hold out. While Mace was careful not to carry the fight to a man less than half his age, his incredible evasive skills were there for all to see. He no longer danced as he had in his youth, but with the utmost economy of movement he dodged blow after blow and cut off the ring in masterly style to demonstrate the total superiority of his ringcraft. Burge was anything but a duffer. Indeed, he was, at the time, a contender for the world lightweight championship. At the end of a dozen minutes, the unspoken question in the minds of all who watched Mace's remarkable exhibition was this: if he could perform in such a manner in his mid-sixties, what on earth must he have been like in his prime? Those who witnessed it gave their answer. The members of the National Sporting Club, some of them young enough to be Mace's grandsons, rose as one man and gave him a thunderous standing ovation.

With the proceeds of his benefit exhibition, Mace was able to apply for the discharge of his bankruptcy and once this was granted he would be able to set himself up in business again. The Bankruptcy Court rarely granted any applicant an immediate discharge. The usual practice was to grant it following a period of time, normally two to three years. Mace would have to wait. During his time in Fulham, Mace, in characteristic style, made his way to a well-known and thriving local funfair. To his surprise and delight, he found that the proprietor was a relative of his from Norfolk. William Le Neve had moved to London from Norwich and, with his Scottish-born wife, the former Norah Sullivan, had set up caravans and a showground at Lillie Road. Le Neve was part Romany and, although a generation younger than Mace and Pooley, a distant cousin of theirs. One day at Lillie Road, Le Neve asked Mace if he could still play fiddle in public and he obliged, to cheers all round. Le Neve told Mace to keep in touch because the time might come when they could work together permanently.

The upturn in Mace's fortunes continued when, at the start of the next year, he undertook an exhibition tour of Scotland with Frank Slavin. Slavin had scarcely been active for three years following his defeat by Jackson but by now he had moderated his drinking and was in need of money. Although a shadow of the fighter he'd once been, his name, linked with Mace's, was enough to bring the crowds in. Furthermore, it was the first time that Mace had ever taken the ring publicly against one of his former students. Mace and Slavin had much to talk about. Everywhere the 'Australian style' was triumphing. Only a couple of weeks before, at the NSC, Dan Creedon, while still a middleweight in poundage, had won the English heavyweight title. To the delight of Mace and Slavin, he had knocked out Jem Smith, who had regained the title in a belated post-Bruges comeback. It only took two rounds for Creedon to dispose of the bulky blunderer.

In the States, as Slavin told Mace, Corbett had finally accepted Bob Fitzsimmons' repeated challenge for the title, but the bout, scheduled to take place in Arkansas, had been called off after the State Governor had arrested Fitzsimmons on a breach of the peace charge. Corbett, furious that, by implication, he too was an outlaw and not the showbusiness hero he aspired to be, retired and haughtily nominated the clumsy Peter Maher of Ireland as his successor. Unsurprisingly, Fitzsimmons had refused to accept Corbett's peremptory decision and had insisted on a fight with Maher. It took place in Mexico and Fitzsimmons blitzed Maher to defeat within one round. After this, Fitzsimmons was widely acclaimed as champion. Corbett abruptly cancelled his retirement and arrogantly insisted that he had never intended it to be permanent. What puzzled Mace most was the fact that Corbett had earlier avoided meeting Peter Jackson for the title.

Only the bare details of this had been reported in the English press and Mace was keen to know more. Now Slavin, whose own attitude to Jackson had changed into one of real respect, told him the full story.

In February 1893, Jackson had issued a challenge to Corbett for the title. Corbett said that Mitchell's chance must come first. Not until Corbett crushed Mitchell at the Duval Athletic Club in Jacksonville, Florida, was the way open for Jackson. In the meantime, a year of Jackson's career had already been lost, a vital time frame for a boxer already turned thirty and five years older than the man he was challenging. By the summer of 1894, however, Corbett, Jackson (and their respective managers Brady and Davies) had agreed two things: Corbett would fight Jackson for the title and the purse would be $20,000. The only matter outstanding was the venue. The Olympic Club in New Orleans refused to host the contest, claiming that an interracial clash for the heavyweight title would lead to public disorder. From Jacksonville, Florida, however, the Duval AC signalled their apparent willingness to host it, but Jackson would not agree. He feared that, in a southern state, his life would be at risk from white supremacists, notably the Ku Klux Klan.

The next part of the story was what Mace already knew. While Corbett was on tour in Europe, the National Sporting Club proposed that he should fight Jackson at King Street for a purse of $3,000, bankrolled by Lord Lonsdale. The Club had Jackson's and Davies' prior agreement but Corbett refused. As he saw it, Jackson, an adopted Australian, was considered to be a citizen of the British Empire. In addition, Lonsdale was the patron of the man who had been dubbed 'The Black Prince' by a section of the membership at the NSC. Corbett felt that, unless he was able to knock out Jackson – which he had not been able to do in San Francisco three years earlier – he might go twenty rounds and see the Caribbean-born man given the decision. Slavin took up the story again for Mace's benefit. In New York, in August 1894, Corbett and Jackson had indeed clashed, but in a cramped hotel room not a boxing ring – and with heated words, not clever punches. In what was an eyeball-to-eyeball confrontation, Corbett refused Jackson's offer of an American referee if he fought in England. That refused offer was the only hint of concession from either of them and their rematch would never take place.

When Mace asked Slavin for his opinion on all this, the Australian was reluctant to give it. He had once been known for his hostility to Jackson and, though he changed his opinion of him after their own epic fight, he might still be thought biased. Still, Slavin doubted if race was Corbett's motivating factor. Corbett had publicly rebuked reporters for suggesting that it might be, asserting that 'Peter Jackson is a credit to his profession'. Slavin did reveal that, while most of Jackson's fights outside Frisco had been in the Mid-West or the North-East, he had once ventured into the South. At Louisville in Kentucky, he had knocked out a local hero in the first round and lived to tell the tale. What did Jem think?

Mace liked Peter Jackson and regarded him as the outstanding exponent of what he had himself initiated in Australia and what Larry Foley had nurtured. From all that he had heard and read about Corbett, he concluded that the San Franciscan was a boxer supreme. But when he had met Corbett, their chat was too brief. He could not tell the measure of the man. Wherever the exact responsibility lay in the collapse of negotiations, it was a great shame that the public had been denied the opportunity to watch two well-matched and equally skilful boxers compete for the Heavyweight Championship of the World.

In June 1896, Fitzsimmons returned to England for a tour of music hall engagements. Like Sullivan, Jackson and Corbett before him, Fitz was coining money from the marriage of boxing and theatre which Mace had pioneered at Niblo's Gardens in New York a quarter of a century earlier. Recognised in the land of his birth, but not in the USA, as the world heavyweight champion, he was feted wherever he went. When he met Mace, it was their first chance to talk since Fitz had swept the board at Mace's tournaments in New Zealand fourteen years earlier. Learning that Fitz was off to Epsom to watch the Derby, Mace joined the party of sportsmen. The news that Fitz was backing Persimmon to win purely on name similarity amused Mace who, on a whim, followed suit. It was one of his rare betting coups, the chosen nag romping home at 5 to 1. Afterwards, Mace attended Fitz's slap-up reception dinner at the Palace Cafe in the Strand.

The next day Jem and Fitz, who got on extremely well, talked over what had happened in boxing since Mace first went to New Zealand and sparked off interest in the sport there. Although Fitz was the most rewarded of the fighters from Down Under, the success of the Australian exodus boxers in the U.S.A. was astonishing. The names were reeled off, some of them well familiar to Mace, others less so: Jackson, Slavin, Murphy, Griffo, Hall and Creedon; but also Billy McCarthy, George Dawson and Jim Barnes, with Bill Heffernan preparing to join. Then there was Joe Goddard, who had failed in the States. It was a pity, the pair agreed, that Goddard had taken up the game too late. Immensely powerful and brave though he was, his lack of technique had been exposed. The talk inevitably turned to Fitz's yet-to-be-arranged title shot against Corbett. He was determined to get his chance but somewhat wary of Corbett's peerless left jab. Mace reminded him that body punching was a key part of his arsenal and doubted if Corbett had yet faced an opponent who was so severe to the midriff. Playfully reminding him of his youthful comeuppance at Timaru, Mace mimed the shot. Fitz took mental note.

In the summer of 1896, Mace took part in the first boxing bout to be filmed outside America, Corbett's exhibition with Peter Courtney having been shot at the Edison lab the previous year. Mace was contacted by the American-born photographer Birt Acres, who had been living in England for many years. By 1895 Acres had succeeded in designing a film camera and, during the next few years, he produced a stream of short documentary films in Britain, continental Europe and North America on a variety of subjects. Royalty apart, sport was Acres' favourite theme and he filmed the Epsom Derby. Mace was paid by Acres to box one round with an opponent of his choice and he picked his old acquaintance Jack Burke, who had first come to his attention as a finalist in Mace's Heavyweight Championship Tournament in Manchester in 1883. He had since fought in England, America, Australia and South Africa and faced Mitchell, Kilrain, Sullivan, Slavin and Corbett. Although defeated by them, he had given a good account of himself. The Mace–Burke exhibition was filmed in London and, although entitled 'Prize fight between Jem Mace and Jack Burke', it was a Queensberry bout. Fascinated by the infant medium of the movies, Mace remarked to Birt that he could 'shoot variety turns or even plays'. He couldn't understand Acres' shocked reaction and wondered what a true showman could do with 'a wonderful gadget like this'. Sadly the film of the fight has not survived.

By this time many aspiring American boxers were deciding to box specifically in the Mace-Australian style. The more that this manifested itself, the more America's inevitable superiority due to the size of its population began to be evident. It needed only for young Americans to box in the scientific style (as previously only Corbett and Choynski had done) for America's domination of the fight game to return. Corbett apart, the most brilliant American boxer at this time was a twenty-three-year-old from Indiana. Born Norman Selby, his ring name was Kid McCoy. Already welterweight champion of the world, McCoy was intelligent, unconventional and outspoken. He had insisted that the Australian style was superior and that he intended fully to absorb it before adding variations of his own. To that end, he engaged Mick Dooley as his trainer and travelled to England with a view to watching Mace in action in the exhibition against Burke. McCoy was lean and long-shanked with an unusually lengthy reach, fast footwork and a killer instinct. Where he principally resembled Mace was in his generalship, his capacity to strike unexpected blows and his ability to deal out rapid-fire shots. These lacked knockout force but weakened and demoralised opponents to such an extent that the TKO soon followed. An innovation all of the Kid's own was the so-called corkscrew punch.

McCoy's dismissal of American methods and his open avowal of Mace as the fountainhead of true boxing made the American public sit up and take notice. When he knocked out Tommy Ryan and claimed the middleweight title, McCoy's boxing reputation was made. The once-sceptical boxing scribes in the USA, who had learned that, though Mace might be sixty-five, he was still good for a fine three-round exhibition, became convinced that it would be for the benefit of all aspiring young boxers for the old warrior to be seen in the rings of America once again. In boxing, the world's newest and most popular sport, he was recognised as the father of the finest. These included not only Australians such as Peter Jackson, Frank Slavin, Jim Hall and Young Griffo, New Zealanders such as Bob Fitzsimmons, Billy Murphy and Dan Creedon, but all-American boys such as Kid McCoy and, last and foremost, Gentleman Jim Corbett, his stylistic successor as Champion of the World.

31

The Acclamation of an American Legend

THE FIRST GLIMPSE of the looming, shadowy figure of Liberty brought silence to the decks of the *Etruria*. On this, his fourth visit to America, it seemed that the city of New York had become bolder than ever, reaching out to greet her guests while they were still in the Upper Bay. While the immigrant ships astern made their way to Ellis Island, he stared in fascination at the huge new edifice on what had been Bedloes Island. When he had left the soil of America thirteen years earlier, the statue, then known as Liberty Enlightening the World, was still standing in the studio of Bartholdi, its designer, in Paris awaiting completion, dismantling and shipping across the Atlantic. Gazing at the copper-sheathed figure with the seven-spiked crown brandishing a torch in her upraised right hand, he made up his mind to climb the Statue of Liberty right up to the observation deck. It felt good to be back and, as always, he would sample whatever interesting and new was on offer.

Jem Mace had been invited on a four-month tour and had come accompanied only by his new business manager, Bill Bayford. It was not simply a matter that Alice's mother and older sisters, still unreconciled, could not have been approached to look after the children; Alice herself was reluctant to travel, even if it had been possible. Accustomed as she had been to moving around, she still hankered after either her native Birmingham or her adopted home town of Glasgow. Mace could not help but compare her with Hannah and Nellie and their eagerness to see the world.

Mace had come to the States at the invitation of the Broadway Athletic Club in New York. With the Herbert Slade fiasco long since consigned to oblivion, interest in Mace had been rekindled and his pivotal role in the foundation of boxing was coming to be implicitly recognised in the USA. Although Mace would have been quite prepared to take the ring in an exhibition with a younger boxer, as he had done in London with Burke, the Broadway Club had revived the idea of a 'Veterans Championship of the World'. A veteran was defined as a pugilist of more than fifty years old. At sixty-five, Mace fitted the bill and he would represent England, while Mike Donovan, the NYAC instructor, whose true age was in fact forty-nine, would represent America.

Mike Donovan, brother of Jerry, was an old friend of Jem's. An early pioneer of scientific boxing in the USA, he had a fine record himself, having drawn in a middleweight title fight at the age of forty. At one stage, Donovan had annoyed Mace by his exaggerated praise for John L. Sullivan, but having evidently seen the light, Donovan had seconded Jim Corbett when he won the world title in New Orleans. So great was the interest aroused by seeing Mace, now described as a 'legend', in an American ring, twenty years after he fought Bill Davis in Virginia City, that the six-round bout with Donovan was top of a truly illustrious card. Among the class boxers eager to fight exhibitions on the undercard, despite their own fame and fortune, were Jim Hall, Billy Edwards, Arthur Chambers, George Dixon, and lightweight champion Kid Lavigne. Most important of all was the world heavy-weight champion himself. Mace took particular interest in Corbett's exhibition bout, in which 'Gentleman Jim', in what many believed was a clear attempt to impress Mace, put up a dazzling exhibition of boxing skill, outclassing his hapless opponent, Jim McVey.

Finally, Mace and Donovan took the ring. The date was 14 December 1896. Although Mike was sixteen years younger, he did not look it. White-haired, shiny-bald and wrinkled, his appearance contrasted with that of his opponent. Even though his waistline had expanded and he now weighed 183lb, Mace was described as having 'remarkably clear skin . . . an eye as bright as possible and an elastic step'. Only in one regard did he show that he was, as billed, a veteran. That was in his disfigured hands, briefly visible before he put on the gloves. Unlike the younger boxers, all of them clad in shorts as befitting the greater mobility of modern boxing, Mace and Donovan retained the breeches of their younger days. In the opening two rounds Donovan built up a clear points lead, with Mace surprisingly subdued. The reason for this became clear at the end of the second. His vanity had prevented him from removing his new set of false teeth. This he now did, amid laughter all round. For the next four rounds he gradually outfoxed Donovan, and in the last round was catching him with hard punches. The decision was left to the spectators, most of whom called for a draw. Their verdict was probably prompted by nationalism but almost all the watching professional boxers believed that Mace had won. The only discordant note was struck by Joe Choynski who, despite being a Macean boxer himself, resented Mace's reported praise for Corbett, his bitter rival. Choynski griped that Mace had no left hook; although this was indeed a gap in Mace's repertoire of shots, no man who fought in the bareknuckle era would have attempted a punch so dangerous to unprotected hands. Mace paid little attention to Choynski's belly-aching. After all, he had raked in $4,000 from the bout.

The highlight of the evening was the historic meeting between Jem Mace and Jim Corbett, one man the first world champion of the LPR; the other the first under the Queensberry Rules of Endurance. In a richly symbolic image, they were photographed shaking gloved hands, Corbett, at thirty, towering over the man old enough to be his father. Mace and Corbett had formed a good opinion of each other in their brief London meeting but now they had a chance to discuss boxing at length and Mace noted that Corbett spoke well of Peter Jackson. Donovan took the pair of them into the club instructor's room after Mace had asked to see how Corbett would avoid a jab. Mace had, of course, seen for himself that Corbett had added the left hook to the armoury of the new scientific boxer, but he sensed that Corbett had other strings to his bow which he had not needed to deploy against his clumsy exhibition opponent. Corbett then asked Mace to lead with the left and surprised the old maestro by his use of lateral movement, something virtually unknown even among the best men in the era of pugilism. To the scribes of the press, Mace and Corbett seemed like a mutual admiration society in their praise for one another. Corbett hailed Mace as 'the first pugilist to study out the scientific side of boxing' and remarked that it was 'to (Jem) that we owe the changes that have elevated the sport'. He added that he himself, as an amateur, deliberately assumed the style of Mace but had then adapted it to accommodate the greater flexibility of glove boxing as opposed to bareknuckle combat. For his part, Mace stated that Corbett was the finest boxer he had ever seen. The statements were not made simply for effect or in an atmosphere of conviviality; neither Mace nor Corbett would ever diverge from them in recorded comment.

During Mace's stay in New York, Mike Donovan introduced him to Theodore Roosevelt. Teddy Roosevelt, the future twenty-sixth President of the United States, was at the time Police Commissioner for New York City. Already, at thirty-eight, the bluff and burly Roosevelt was a key figure in Republican party politics. A man of remarkable all-round capabilities, he was highly respected as both a naturalist and a historian. He was also a Wild West rancher, a big game hunter in Africa and an explorer in Brazil. Roosevelt was known as a boxing fan and an enthusiastic amateur boxer. His wealthy father had arranged lessons for him in 'the noble art of self-defence' to galvanise his studious but easily bullied ten-year-old son. Donovan and Roosevelt had been friends for years and Roosevelt had backed the Horton Law which reiterated the legalisation of boxing in New York State.

Recognising Mace's unique significance in the transition from bare knuckles to boxing, Roosevelt congratulated the Englishman and recalled having Mace pointed out to him on Broadway when he was world champion and Roosevelt was a boy of eleven. Mace continued his tour of North America, sparring some exhibitions against both veteran and up-and-coming boxers and others with his arranged tour partner Dan Creedon. Creedon claimed the middleweight championship but it was the 'sitting tenant' of that crown, Tommy Ryan, who Mace faced in Syracuse. In another remarkable performance he succeeded in keeping Ryan at bay.

Meanwhile, Kid McCoy insisted that he was the best middleweight around. He had already KO'd Ryan in a non-title fight and, by the end of 1897, would clinch his claim by defeating Creedon on a TKO after a splendid contest which would see yet another title go to a Macean boxer. Always popular, as an Englishman, in Canada, Mace gave an exhibition in Toronto during the winter. One of those who saw it was a Canadian lad of fifteen, partly of Italian extraction, by the name of Noah Brusso. Three years later Brusso, who had changed his name to the Irish-sounding Tommy Burns, began his professional career and nine years later, Burns, although never more than a natural middleweight, became world heavyweight champion.

While in North America, Mace stayed for a while with Pooley and Delaiah. By this time, Pooley had moved to Ohio, where he traded horses. Gusty and Mel were still in school but their sister Donna had married Gus Middleton, also of gypsy extraction. Born in England, Gus had been taken to the States by his parents as a boy and had met and married Donna there. He was now Pooley's business partner. Mace's reunion with Pooley was a happy interlude during his American tour but he disclosed that Alice would still not consider relocation to the States.

Shortly before he returned to England came the event which transfixed the boxing world and indeed seized the public imagination generally: Corbett defended his world title against Fitzsimmons. The state of Nevada, where Mace had once been a fistic pioneer on the premises of John Mackay, now unconditionally legalised boxing. It had good reason to do so. The Comstock Lode was virtually exhausted. No longer the globally great bullion source it had once been, Nevada politicians hurriedly decided to bank the future viability of their state on boxing, gambling and burlesque. The path which would eventually lead to Las Vegas and Caesars Palace began with competing bids to stage Corbett v Fitzsimmons from such places as Virginia City, Reno and Carson City. What's more, the world of motion pictures, still in its infancy, welcomed a desert location with suitably brilliant sunlight where cameramen could film the open-air bout between 'Gentleman Jim' and 'Ruby Robert' – the latter, albeit due to pressure, now a naturalised American citizen.

When Mace was asked for his prediction, he carefully declared that Corbett was the superior boxer but that Fitzsimmons was the fiercer puncher. He left it at that, declining to elaborate. When Mace had met Corbett and discussed technique, Mace made no mention of Fitzsimmons' body punching. He felt that Corbett rather neglected this aspect of the game and believed it would be fairer on Fitzsimmons if Gentleman Jim was left to figure out for himself a way to counter Fitz's midriff shots.

The bid from Carson City proved successful and it was there, on St Patrick's Day 1897, that the Irish-American champion faced his

English-born challenger. Fitzsimmons was the early aggressor before Corbett showed his class by easily slipping out of danger. His lateral movement caused the New Zealander to miss on several occasions. Swinging loosely to the body and face, he failed to land and Corbett began to jab to the head. As the ring-rusty champion began to find his feet again, his confidence, usually sky-high, returned in full. Fitzsimmons was being taken well beyond the few rounds it normally required him to dispose of opponents, but this was one far superior to any he had previously faced. A masterly ring scientist, expert with both left jab and left hook, Corbett nevertheless had one weakness: he lacked a truly knockout punch. Corbett could build up a big points lead but, absent the terminating blow, would remain vulnerable to a persistent counterpuncher.

By the sixth, Fitzsimmons was battered and bleeding from jabs to his nose and mouth. Then Corbett piled on the pressure, peppering the New Zealander's face with a fast succession of jabs, hooks and uppercuts. Fitzsimmons was knocked down on one knee and, clearheaded, decided to stay there, rising sharply at nine to beat the count. Corbett had failed to put Fitzsimmons away when he had him in trouble and, after that, he kept the fight at long range and seemed to be settling for an eventual points victory. Taking heart, at the beginning of the fourteenth, from the fact that he had gone further than ever before, even against Dempsey, Fitzsimmons assumed the attacking attitude with which he had started the fight. His sudden ascendancy surprised Corbett and soon Fitzsimmons saw an opening. He feinted with a right to the jaw and, as Corbett instinctively raised his left to guard, he shot a right to the heart and unloaded his Sunday punch. It was a left to the mark, delivered within immense force, and connected precisely on its target. Corbett doubled up in agony, ashen-faced and with his legs seemingly paralysed. He tried all he knew but could not revitalise his limbs. Corbett was counted out. Boxing scribes dreamt up the term 'solar plexus' to denote the area in the pit of the stomach just below the rib cage junction where Fitzsimmons' kayo punch had landed, but Fitzsimmons' knockout punch was in fact the old-time blow to the 'mark', a less impressive-sounding term. It was the very shot originally perfected by Mace and first demonstrated to the teenage Fitzsimmons in Timaru fifteen years before.

From Jem Mace's point of view, Fitzsimmons' defeat of Corbett was the summit of his work as the founder of boxing. He did not care about nationality or personality. Neither was a complete boxer-puncher such as himself. Both boxed well, Corbett excellently. Both punched hard, Fitzsimmons especially. But Fitz was Mace's personal discovery, with the old master even more influential in his development than was Foley. If Mace had conquered the world of pugilism himself in Kennerville, then he did that of boxing by proxy in Carson City.

Few throughout America followed these events more avidly than a tiny nine-year-old Jewish boy in New York City. It would be another two years before Nat Fleischer would see his first boxing match but, from the time of Mace's return to Fleischer's home city, the future doyen of boxing writers was enthralled with the fight game. Fleischer would spend a near-incredible seventy-three years at ringside and personally know all the champions, from Jim Corbett to Joe Frazier, but he remained keenly aware of the vital role that Mace played in the transition to boxing. Fleischer would always place Mace in context as a key figure in American sporting history without qualifying adjectives of nationality. Nor would he ever dismiss him as a mere pugilist. He would describe Mace as 'one of the greatest ring men with the gloves that boxing has produced', assert that 'he did more to foster the pure science of boxing than any other man of his era' and conclude that 'great as Mace was when fighting under London Rules, it was as a glove artist that he appeared at his best'.

Unfortunately, Nat was not quite old enough to have seen Mace fight in person but it was Mace's acclamation as 'a legend' on his return to the USA in 1896 that first seized the imagination of the New Yorker who, as the future editor of *The Ring* magazine, was the most influential figure in boxing for half a century until his death in 1972.

32

The Coronation Tournament

ASSOCIATION FOOTBALL HAD never appealed to Jem Mace. His superb all-round athleticism, which stretched to wrestling, running, fencing and horse-riding, did not include team games. Essentially, he was an individualist, eager to stand or fall by his own efforts. He was also a child of his time and, in mid-nineteenth century England, rural lads rode and swam, wrestled and fought each other with fists. But as leisure time expanded and the countryside leaked population into the new industrial cities, so football became a national male obsession. From those who kicked improvised footballs about in the backstreets, the best now aspired to be professional footballers. The Football League had been formed in 1888, and although its founder clubs would be all from the North and Midlands, by the end of the 1890s clubs in and near London were also admitted.

Tens of thousands of spectators regularly watched matches on a Saturday afternoon and the FA Cup Final of 1897, held at Crystal Palace in south London, attracted 66,000 spectators. In the late 1890s, a top-class professional footballer could expect to earn £100 a year. Although this would still be well less than a pro boxer's purse for, say, a couple of fights, it was regular, guaranteed income, not dependent on promoters and the danger of serious injury was far less. On the other hand, there were a series of fatalities at the National Sporting Club at the close of the 1890s. It was still not fully realised how potentially dangerous blows to the head with the new padded gloves really were, so when Mace, at last discharged by the Bankruptcy Court, opened a boxing school in London, there were few takers. Those that came would often explain that most of their mates 'were too busy playing football'. The school was quickly folded up.

Boxing exhibitions were not the source of revenue in England that they were in America. Mike Donovan came to the U.K. to reprise the

Veterans' Championship with Mace. Their six-round draw at Birmingham was quite well attended but it was not long before the novelty of veteran pugilists engaging in glove combat wore off. A three-match series with Bob Travers, two in London, one in Birmingham, made only a small profit, as did a further joust with Dick Burge, still an active young boxer. Such metropolitan venues as the Aquarium Club would never have attracted football-sized crowds even if they'd been large enough to hold them. Mace was able to make only a modest living for himself; he could support his family, but, as ever, was unable to refrain from gambling. The money he had made on the US tour was soon frittered away.

One day in the spring of 1897, Mace was sauntering alone down the Strand, immaculately dressed as ever, upright and loose-limbed despite his years. Suddenly a familiar voice called out his name in the most cordial tones. It was Peter Jackson. Jackson was by this time the proprietor of a boxing school, the Harmony Club, and he suggested to Mace that they go for a drink and refused to let him pay a round. Although Jackson was sober on this particular day, Jem was shocked to notice the deterioration in his appearance from when he had last seen him, at the NSC five years before. Still only thirty-six, he looked like a man in his early fifties. He had not fought for two years, and from his bloodshot eyes and trembling hands it was all too obvious that he had become an alcoholic. His early driving ambition to win the world heavyweight title had been thwarted by Sullivan's intransigence and Corbett's prevarication and he had clearly taken refuge from bitter disappointment by turning to drink.

Jackson did not dwell on his own misfortunes. He wasn't short of money and he had learned from others that Mace had fallen on hard times, which Mace confirmed. Before they went their separate ways, Peter hailed a cab and told the driver to go straight to his bank and to wait there. He emerged with a wad of cash which he pressed Jem to accept before shaking hands and leaving. It was the last Mace would ever see of the man who was probably the greatest of his erstwhile students. Jackson's London boxing school was not a success and he returned to California, where his boxing career was effectively ended in three rounds by the rugged title contender Jim Jeffries, fourteen years his junior. Jackson then made his way to Canada, probably aiming for the Klondike goldfields, but in British Columbia he contracted pneumonia and became seriously ill. He then returned to Australia and died from tuberculosis aged only forty, in 1901.

* * *

On 10 March 1898, Jem and Alice's second son, Albert Edward, was born in their Fulham home. They now had four young children, with the eldest being Lillian, aged five. Mace's first daughter, Adelaide Turvill, expressed interest in meeting them and in bringing over her own younger children from Camberwell. Alice was moved by the gesture and was happy to agree. By this time, Adelaide, aged forty-one, had given birth to eleven children, nine of them surviving. They ranged in age from Lois, a newborn baby, to Eleanor, a single girl of eighteen. Adelaide and Ellen brought the youngest children, Elizabeth, Adelaide junior and Eunice with them. As previously, Mace was kind and affectionate with his grandchildren but large family gatherings would never be his scene.

As for the sons of his first family, he was yet to be reconciled with James, by now based in Manchester, although he worked as a commercial traveller in fancy goods. James's common-law wife, Annie, was nearly twenty years younger but, as yet, they had no children. Alfred had become one of the foremost figures within the Plymouth Brethren. He was frequently on tour preaching in the USA, where fundamentalism was gaining ground. Famed as a dynamic public speaker, his sermons thundered from pulpits from Indianapolis to San Francisco. Mace came to have a sneaking respect for him – not for his views but for his forceful and driving personality. In that, in his physical vigour and his love of travel, he showed at least some characteristics of his father.

As time went by, the older members of the Stokes family came to accept what they believed was Alice's marriage. They did so for several reasons. On a practical level, Mace had been discharged from bankruptcy; on a human one, he had remained by Alice's side and she loved him. Above all, there were four children to consider. Alice hoped for reconciliation with all her family and was delighted when one of her older sisters made contact. Polly had come South with her Scottish husband, Alex McLeish, a commercial traveller, and they were also living in London, at Islington. Polly began to visit Alice regularly. With no children of her own and often alone due to the nature of her husband's job, Polly would frequently babysit while Jem and Alice saw a West End show. Slowly but surely the children came to see Polly as a second mother. In June 1898, Mace was seriously ill with an infection in his home off the Kings Road. He shook it off after a fortnight, with doctors commenting on his robust constitution and mental resilience. Polly's help was invaluable to Alice at such a time.

Tommy Stokes, one of Alice's younger brothers, had also left Glasgow, to return to his native Birmingham. He came to London from time to time and stayed with the Maces. Tommy spoke well of Birmingham, which was now regarded as the grandest of British provincial cities. Its transformation was largely due to its dynamic mayor, the radical politician Joseph Chamberlain, who, beginning in the 1870s, had 'parked, paid, assized, marketed and gas-and-watered' the city. Tommy was a salesman for a wine and spirits company but was hoping to make his way in what was now called 'the licensed trade'. He knew of a vacancy for a pub landlord in Birmingham but, at only twenty-two, the brewery would not consider him. To Alice's delight, Jem decided to apply; he needed a regular source of income and had to accept that boxing would no longer provide him with this. He would have preferred to have stayed in London but the cost of living was higher than elsewhere and he had always liked Birmingham,

The brewery was startled but delighted to receive an application from Jem Mace. The connection between the ring and the alehouse was an historic one and the mere fact that he would be landlord would bring extra custom. In September 1898, Mace was installed as the landlord of the Black Lion at Coleshill Street – or to use the new terminology, forced upon a reluctant brewing trade by Gladstonian liberalism, he was a licensed victualler's manager. The pub was spacious, with rooms for the family and their four children, not to mention Tommy, who became head barman. Takings at the Black Lion, already a thriving pub, went right up and the Licensed Victuallers Association of Great Britain published a photographic portrait of Mace, taken there in May, in its 1899 yearbook. He had not run a liquor establishment since he quit the Victoria Racing Club Hotel in

Melbourne some seventeen years earlier and had not run an English pub since he was at the Old Kings Head thirteen years before that. Much had changed, notably the restrictions on hours, but the old atmosphere was still there and Jem was instantly both in command and at ease. He was doubly suited to be the landlord of the Black Lion as it was a pub which attracted a showbusiness clientele. One regular was a prominent music hall star known as Datas the Memory Man. Datas, whose real name was William Bottle, was a former London stoker blessed with a photographic memory. His stage act consisted of answering impromptu questions from the audience on subjects ranging from current affairs to sport, and he almost always gave the correct answer. After hearing the young performer demonstrate his extensive knowledge of his ring career, Mace, whose own memory for precise dates was not the best, was impressed. He was introduced to Datas and they became firm friends.

★ ★ ★

On 6 June 1899, Bob Fitzsimmons defended the world heavyweight title for the first time. He had settled near New York which, by act of incorporation the previous year, now extended onto Long Island to include the boroughs of Queens and Brooklyn. In the latter, not far from Coney Island, the match took place. The challenger was twenty-four-year-old Jim Jeffries. Besides the obliteration of the ageing Jackson, Jeffries had smashed his way past a dozen other opponents and had never been knocked down. At first glance, he resembled an old-time prize-fighter: 6ft 2½in, weighing nearly 210lb, hirsute and with tree-trunk legs. In fact the Californian boilermaker, who had grown up in the sunshine state on his father's farm, was highly mobile. He could run 100 yards in ten seconds and had cleared a 6ft high jump. His athletic gifts, his immense upper body strength and sheer bravery made him a formidable competitor.

Jeffries had been lucky enough to be taken on by Corbett as a sparring partner. Without really intending to, Corbett passed on a modicum of his boxing skills to the brawny boilermaker; although Jeffries would never become a stylish or clever boxer, he had enough knowledge to be far more than a Sullivan-type slugger. When he was coached by middleweight champion Tommy Ryan, something more was added. Ryan fought out of a crouch, one of the main technical developments – the other being the hook – since Mace's heyday. Jeffries could therefore pose a lot of problems for Fitzsimmons. It would be almost impossible for Fitz to get home with his tremendous body punching against a crouching opponent while, when he himself jabbed, he risked breaking his fist on Jeffries' skull. Jeffries' game plan was clear. As Ryan had taught him, he suddenly straightened up in the second and scored a flash knockdown with a fierce left jab. After that Fitzsimmons did his best to keep the fight at long range and succeeded in cutting Jeffries' brow, but the bloodstained challenger kept boring in. Time and again he sapped Fitz's energy by holding the far slighter Champion in a clinch. As he tired, Jeffries smashed him down for a seven count and then used a right-left combination to knock him out in the eleventh.

In the summer, the new champion came to London for a series of exhibitions. Mace, sceptical but curious, went to take a look and came away less than fully impressed but was friendly to Jeffries when they briefly met. As Mace saw it, there was no denying that Jeffries was an outstanding athlete – had he emerged during the Prize Ring era he would have been even more formidable because his potential as a wrestler was phenomenal. But that did not mask the fact that, in Mace's eyes, the new champion was no scientific boxer. He could see exactly how Fitzsimmons had been dethroned. Not only was the New Zealander at a disadvantage having spotted twelve years in age to the challenger but Fitz had never been the fastest of movers. Deprived, by Jeffries' crouch, of the chance to unleash his body shots, he had been reliant on a jab, which was not precise enough against a crouching target.

Mace remained convinced that, in his own prime, he would have defeated Jeffries by insisting on a 24ft ring, by dancing away from the bear-like Californian, by never letting him close to a clinch and by waiting till the big man tired and could no longer maintain his unnatural posture. When Jeffries finally straightened up, Mace would have begun to close his eyes with pickaxe jabs and then moved in with his own concussive right-hand. Although English boxing opinion, led by Arthur Bettinson, concurred with Mace, the American fight public revered the new title-holder, whose methods were distinctly American rather than Anglo-Australian. Other boxers would adopt his style, notably the sailor Tom Sharkey. Shorter than Jeffries but equally brawny and with a tremendous fighting heart, Sharkey had an ungainly build and didn't move fast. Nevertheless, at Coney Island later that year, in a contest which lasted the full twenty-five rounds, Sharkey went close before the referee's decision was correctly given in favour of Jeffries.

When taken to task by American boxing journalists who felt Mace underrated fighters like Jeffries and Sharkey – variously categorised as 'iron men' and 'swarmers' because of their powers of endurance and preference for infighting – he had one answer. Mace pointed to Jeffries' failure to beat Joe Choynski some eighteen months before he became champion. The drawn verdict in their twenty-round bout in San Francisco was widely recognised as fair, yet Choynski, who could not master either Corbett or Fitzsimmons was, in addition, outweighed by no less than 50lb. Choynski was a Macean boxer with good style, fast movement and, at his best, he threw perfectly timed punches.

On 29 September 1899, Mace's fourth family suffered a loss when Albert, only eighteen months old, contracted a throat infection. His condition rapidly worsened and he died and the doctor diagnosed laryngismus as the cause of death. Devastated as she was, Alice received much comfort and consolation from her family, especially her married sister Polly McLeish, who visited from London frequently.

The following May, Corbett went to Coney Island seeking to regain his crown from Jeffries. The fight was scheduled for twenty-five rounds. In Birmingham, Mace was waiting eagerly for news, hoping and believing that Corbett would win. The bout was an epic of its kind, providing a total contrast in styles. Corbett served up possibly the most dazzling exhibition of boxing skill even he had ever demonstrated. His footwork was as spectacular as ever and he piled up points as his meticulous jabs found their mark on the brow of the crouching target. His confidence growing, Gentleman Jim dealt out punishment with the left hook and Jeffries' face swelled with the impact of repeated blows. Still, in Jeffries he found a man with a seemingly granite jaw and a lion-hearted capacity to take punishment.

In addition, the lean Corbett remained what would soon be called a light-heavyweight, whereas the burly Jeffries was a true heavyweight. Nevertheless, Corbett had established a clear lead up to the end of the twenty-second round but, as he began to tire, the nine-year age difference started to tell – aggravated by Jeffries' persistent clinching, which went unchecked by referee Charlie White. In the twenty-third, Jeffries closed in against a fast-fading Corbett and bludgeoned him with a right, high on the jaw. It did not have the accuracy to knock the ex-champ out cold but he was counted out as he lay stunned on the canvas with his head resting against the lowest rope.

The result was one which Mace could not abide. To those who, as he saw it, welcomed Jeffries' victory as nostalgia for the marathonism of the Prize Ring, he countered that, under National Sporting Club rules, Corbett would have been the winner. Twenty rounds was the maximum at King Street and, what's more, strict referees such as Bernard Angle, George Vize or Eugene Corri would have warned Jeffries for 'laying on' and might even have disqualified him.

Just how much America's more intelligent boxers admired Mace was demonstrated again when, in March 1902, the rising light-heavyweight Philadelphia Jack O'Brien visited England and stayed with Mace and his family at the Black Lion in Birmingham. Jem, aged seventy-two, sparred with the twenty-four-year-old O'Brien and, when he returned to the States, Jack enthused, 'Jem Mace is a wonderfully preserved old man. His muscles are as hard as steel and he is in splendid trim. He exercises daily and his only dissipation is twelve cups of tea a day.' Significantly, O'Brien added, 'Mace was the first man who showed American fighters the advantages of feinting and footwork. You can readily see what a fighter today would amount to without these essentials.'*

* * *

---

* Three years later, O'Brien would demonstrate his proficiency against another of Mace's former pupils. He KO'd Bob Fitzsimmons to take the world light-heavyweight crown.

The advent of the twentieth century coincided with the accession of a new monarch. The octogenarian Victoria died in January 1901 and was succeeded by Edward VII. Mace was one of the minority of British people who remembered, albeit vaguely and from his boyhood, the previous ruler, William IV, who, unlike his brother George IV, had no interest in pugilism. Edward had always had a mild interest but the NSC, ten years into its existence, never needed to depend on royal, or even, Lonsdale apart, aristocratic patronage. But it decided to mark the change at Buckingham Palace by staging a tournament to honour the coronation of Edward VII in 1902. The idea of the Coronation Tournament was to celebrate boxing by inviting its major exponents to London to demonstrate their skills and, even better, defend their titles. Preparations began the previous year and Mace, now seventy, was still well, fit and keen to be involved. He toyed with Bettinson's suggestion that he give an exhibition but decided he would prefer to take part as a second. He would expect demand for his paid services to be high and this would, he believed, rekindle interest in the teaching of boxing. Mace very definitely felt that he still had a part to play in nurturing young talent and making sure it was educated in the right way.

The Coronation Tournament did not attract as many of the world's top boxers as had been hoped. By now, with US fighters using more sophisticated methods than before and with enormous purses on offer, America was well and truly the heartland of the fight game. Even though the Horton Law confirming the legalisation of boxing in New York State had been revoked following an allegedly fixed fight between Corbett and Kid McCoy, California smartly filled the breach. None of the top Californian heavyweights would come to London; neither Jeffries nor Choynski felt the money was good enough and Corbett held a grudge against the NSC for its previous championing of Jackson. One heavyweight who definitely wanted to take part was Bob Fitzsimmons. In fact Fitz had challenged Jeffries to a rematch at the club. Jeffries accepted the challenge but insisted on San Francisco, where he would earn even more. Nevertheless, the remaining two top-class heavies decided to cross the Atlantic. One was Tom Sharkey, the other Gus Ruhlin, a contrastingly technical boxer who, however, had lost to Jeffries in a title fight. By now universally accepted as middleweight champion, the classy Tommy Ryan agreed to participate, as did the black welterweight titleholder Joe Walcott, the 'Barbados Demon'.

Mace was closely involved with tournament preparations from start to finish and was in his element. The opening ceremony was at the Royal Albert Hall in Kensington and there were those, both classical musicians and professional boxers, who thought it odd that fist-fighting should temporarily displace the more usual symphonic activities there. Mace took the opposite view since, to his mind, boxing, at least in the style in which he carried it out, was one of the arts. At any rate, Sharkey, Ruhlin, Ryan and Walcott all sparred within the walls of the red-brick neo-classical rotunda.

The most important aspect of the Coronation Tournament was that it featured not only boxing but several other sports. This was credited to Peggy Bettinson, who, since the death of Fleming five years earlier, was the sole driving force of the NSC. In truth it reflected the breadth of Mace's own athletic interests, of which he had often spoken to Bettinson. The sparring exhibitions were followed by a display of gymnastics by the girl students of the Chelsea Gymnastic Teachers Training College; next came the fencing matches at foil, epee and sabre and finally an exhibition of Greco-Roman wrestling. Mace watched this with the keenest of interest because the NSC had secured the services of the European champion, the great Russian wrestler Georg Hackenschmidt. His display impressed Mace greatly and he declared him the finest wrestler he had ever seen. Mace, himself a very good wrestler, had known the giants of a sport not yet destroyed by crass commercialism – men such as William Muldoon, Donald Dinnie, James McLaughlin and William Miller – but he remained convinced of Hackenschmidt's superiority. After the exhibition, Mace and Hackenschmidt, whose English was excellent, talked and the Russian mentioned that he had been encouraged to begin an alternative career as a boxer; Mace promptly dissuaded him. Georg, also an outstanding weightlifter, was, like most men with exceptional upper body strength, not nimble enough for boxing and Mace did not want to see a man of such eminence in one sport made to look foolish in another.

A deeper significance of the Coronation tournament was missed amid chauvinistic press ravings about the monarchy, Empire and the

English-speaking world. By now the Olympic Games had been revived successfully, once in Athens and once in Paris. In two years' time the United States would stage it in St Louis. Few realised that the spark for this splendid celebration had been ignited at Liverpool four decades earlier; even fewer realised that 'Jem Mace, the pugilist' had been a significant figure among the early Olympic revivalists. He never corrected them. Through the fact of his birth among the rural working-class of remote East Anglia, he would not have the education to argue – but it went beyond that. Mace, for all his unstoppable self-confidence both within the ring and outside it, was never a braggart. Had he wished, he could have pointed out his intimate connection with track athletics, wrestling and fencing and with the ideals which would inspire future pentathletes, but he chose not to. It was not false modesty. Mace was, in many ways, a vain man, and a veritable peacock in his youth, but proud as he was of his astonishing all-round athleticism, he felt it was beneath his dignity to discuss it.

The tournament proper began at the NSC on 21 June 1902. Sadly, Hackenschmidt was injured and could not take part in the Greco-Roman championship – which at least allowed the fifteen other competitors an even chance of winning in a 'sudden death' competition. On the second night, Joe Walcott, the diminutive Barbadian, defended his world welterweight title against the American Tommy West. Although West lasted the fifteen rounds, there could be only one decision: Walcott, an exceptionally powerful man for one who stood little more than 5ft tall, punched with fury and accuracy and two of West's ribs were cracked. Tommy Ryan followed Walcott into the ring. Ryan, born in America of a French father and English mother, disguised his origins by adopting an Irish-sounding ring name, an increasingly common practice. His title was also on the line but not for long; a scientific boxer with a good punch, Tommy kayoed his compatriot Johnny Gorman in the third.

On the final night of the tournament, Mace was in Gus Ruhlin's corner when he faced Tom Sharkey. Billy Madden, the discoverer of Charlie Mitchell, sat next to Mace while Tommy Ryan was in the opposite corner. In a fierce battle, Sharkey swarmed over Ruhlin as he had done over Jeffries in their epic. At times a badly punished Ruhlin spoke of quitting but was talked out of it by Mace. Mace insisted that

Ruhlin ride out the storm and that he must jab and move so as to take full advantage of his longer reach and greater mobility. Eventually, in the eleventh, Sharkey's manager threw in the towel. The Irishman's anger at the surrender knew no bounds and it took several men to restrain him, Mace being one of them. It did not matter to Sharkey how far behind he might be on points. He wanted no one to say he quit. Mace could not help but admire Sharkey's bravery, whatever he thought of his brawling style.

Much as he enjoyed participating in the Coronation Tournament, Mace would have far preferred it if he could have been in Fitzsimmons' corner when the New Zealander tried to regain his title from Jeffries in San Francisco in July 1902. Fitzsimmons varied his tactics from the jabbing style with which he lost the crown to the Californian five years earlier. Fitz had trained with great intensity for this clash and looked far faster than before. He was clearly trying with might and main for an early knockout. Rarely did Fitzsimmons' renowned punching power look more lethal. For obvious reasons he targeted Jeffries' head. After half a dozen rounds his fast two-fisted whiplash shots had broken the champion's nose, cut both cheeks to the bone and, most ominous of all, opened gashes over each eye. It was astonishing bravura from a man of thirty-nine who was conceding almost four stone. Fitzsimmons was well ahead on points but in the eighth round, halfway through the contest, Jeffries turned the tables and threw a heavy smash at the mark. The blow was inaccurate and did not have the paralytic effect which Fitzsimmons' perfect 'solar plexus' shot had on Corbett but Jeffries' power of punch was immense. Fitzsimmons was reduced to half speed before a series of sledgehammer blows drove him to the canvas for the full count.

Afterwards, Fitzsimmons' hands were found to be badly damaged due to the intensity of his hitting. As to Jeffries' severe facial injuries, tabloid scribes soon spread the story that Fitz's seconds had used plaster of Paris on his bandages. These tricks, sometimes used successfully in lower level contests, would have resulted in the loose bandages hardening like surgical plaster as sweat mingled with powdered cement. Due to the obvious problem of proving a negative, Fitzsimmons found it hard to refute such charges and was unfairly branded a cheat in certain quarters. It was a problem Mace had foreseen right from the start of the gloved era. Seconds had been up to all kinds of skullduggery in the days of the LPR and now encased fists made this far easier to do. At the NSC, on Mace's advice, all gloves and bandages were carefully inspected by the referee in the presence of both parties before the start of the contest.

The fact remained that Jeffries was still champion. Corbett would try a second time to regain the crown from him, but this was not a great fight, Jeffries winning in the tenth. During his six years as title-holder, he was almost universally acknowledged as a great champion. But while Mace recognised Jeffries' resilience and courage, he could not reconcile with what he considered the Californian's incorrect style. Swarming out of a crouch had worked wonders for 'Jeff', as he was popularly known, but Mace emphasised that Corbett conceded nine years to him and Fitzsimmons twelve. Both would have beaten Jeffries, Mace believed, when at their peak – just as Ruhlin had triumphed over the swarming Sharkey in the Coronation Tournament.

33

Not a Penny to his Name

SINCE 1899, THE British Army had been fighting the Boer War in South Africa. When Kimberley became the first town to be relieved from siege, celebrations were so lively in Mace's pub that supplies ran low. And when Mafeking was delivered from the Boers, the Black Lion was drunk dry. The news had been relayed by the *Daily Mail*, the first British paper aimed at a working-class readership. During the first four years of its existence, the *Mail* had sold copies by the waggon load based on whipping up popular feeling against the 'insolent' Boers. When these farmers-turned-soldiers, descendants of chiefly Dutch settlers two centuries earlier, actually succeeded in twisting the British Lion's tail, the national sense of hurt pride was immense. But when Lord Roberts's reinforced army turned the tide, the details were reported in the newspaper the length and breadth of England, and the outburst of jingoistic sentiment was enormous. The war in South Africa would, however, last two more years, so adept were the Boers at guerilla warfare. They were eventually crushed by methods so ruthless that the *Mail* and its new rival, the *Daily Express*, did not report them. And when, in May 1902, the Treaty of Vereeniging brought an end to the conflict by re-annexing the rebel colonies of the Transvaal and the Orange Free State, public opinion was tired. After three years of conflict, celebrations at Mace's pub – and anyone else's – were distinctly muted.

It was only the second time during Mace's life that he had known the nation at war. The first, forty-five years earlier, had been the Crimean War, when he was still one of Langham's bodyguards in London. Mace was not a man who reacted with excitement to news of war. An individualist, he found little to enthuse about in news of bloodshed on battlefields in Russia or, as now, in South Africa. To some, this seemed paradoxical. Surely, they figured, a pugilist's sensibilities would be akin to those of a warrior? But they did not realise the outlaw mentality of the boxer. To the extent that South Africa interested Mace, it was as a sports-loving country. He had reason to curse the gold strike on the Rand because it had impacted negatively on his Australian holdings, but he was well aware that, in the aftermath of the strike, boxing had boomed in South Africa. It was always the same in the get-rich-quick atmosphere of goldrush towns, with their isolated, male-dominated communities. What held good for San Francisco, Virginia City, early Melbourne and, later on, the Klondike, was true for Johannesburg.

Johannesburg, the main city in the Transvaal, had experienced a tremendous boxing boom in the 1890s. At the back of it had been the English immigrant and boxing buff Barney Barnato. Barney, whose real name was Barnett Isaacs, had been born in the Jewish ghetto at Whitechapel. After hearing of the discovery of rich diamond fields in South Africa, he headed out, becoming an immensely wealthy diamond magnate while in his thirties. He returned to England regularly on holidays and became well known in the National Sporting Club. With the backing of promoters such as Barnato and Solly Joel, South Africa became a kind of fourth focus for boxing, a sudden rival not only for Australia and England but for America – and in the world of boxing, South Africa meant Johannesburg. It was there that the British boxers Jim Couper and Wolf Bendoff fought for the largest-ever side-stake, £5,000.

South Africa held a particular attraction for Australian boxers. In a climate and with an open-air culture which resembled their own, they could fight for purses which made those at Foley's Hall seem like chicken feed. There was a sudden influx of second-ranked Australians, not good enough to make it in the USA but still fine boxers. Americans also came to fight – a true indication of boxing affluence in South Africa. As early as 1895, boxing was making a beginning in Cape Town. A seaport and the capital of English-speaking Cape Colony, there was an immigrant community from which, as in all countries, boxers tended to come. The English trainer Jimmy Weir was seeking to further boxing in Cape Town and so was the Jewish circus entrepreneur Abe Fillis. Mace had shown an interest in South African boxing as it began to blossom in the early 1890s but at that time the upheaval in his personal life preoccupied him and, even more so, his descent into bankruptcy. He had toyed with the idea of making a fresh start in South Africa, but as hostilities between the Afrikaans-speaking Boers and the people they considered Uitlanders, or foreigners (British, Australians and Americans), deteriorated, he changed his mind. Paul Kruger, President of the Transvaal, had gone so far as to ban boxing, fearing that it would lead to public disorder based on ethnic rivalry.

Now the war was over, with South Africa reunited under British rule and a new century having begun, it seemed obvious to Mace that the boxing boom which had abruptly been curtailed by political interference would re-ignite – and that Cape Town, not Johannesburg, would be the focus. Johannesburg had been ravaged during the war and would need time to recover but Cape Town had remained well outside the war zone. It was essentially British in tone with an affinity for boxing such as there was in America and Australia. The Dutch Reformed Church, which held sway in the Afrikaaner provinces and which denounced all forms of fist-fighting as heinous sin, had relatively little influence in Cape Town. It had been twenty years since Mace had seemed to abandon his old urge to travel the seas in search of adventure, twenty years during which, apart from a stimulating four-month trip to America, he had remained in England. Suddenly his wanderlust revived.

Shortly after the Coronation Tournament, Mace slowly but surely began to feel bored. The chances of discovering a British prospect, someone he could mentor, were slight. English heavyweights were inept and, even at the lighter weights, there were relatively few good performers. The Boer War had shown how physically unfit British working-class lads were, with large numbers of volunteers having to be rejected due to malnutrition and rickets. Jem began to put to Alice the idea that they should move to South Africa. He suggested many good reasons for this: he had money behind him again at last; the climate at the Cape was a truly healthy one; it would be a fine place to bring up the children, all of whom were old enough to make the move, Lillian being ten, James nine and Amy eight. However, Alice would have none of it. Birmingham might be cramped and industrial but it was home. She had struggled to be reconciled with her family but this had now been achieved; she had been to Glasgow to see her parents, taking the children with her to meet their grandparents, and did not want to be parted from her family again. She could not understand Jem's interest in going to South Africa any more than she had understood his nostalgia for America.

Mace made several attempts to talk her round but, as submissive as she was in most aspects of their relationship, she was adamant. Jem could not help but compare her with Hannah and Nellie. He remembered Hannah's youthful excitement over going to the US and Nellie's more mature enthusiasm over making a life in Australia – and he remembered Hannah and Nellie themselves. Alice had never managed to mix in society as his deceased wife and his estranged wife had done. Compared to Nellie, she was a homebody, happy in the world of her children and with little interest in what he considered the finer things in life, music above all.

Jem found his thoughts turning back to Nellie more and more. True she would be fifty, twenty years older than Alice, but Alice had started to let herself go somewhat, preoccupied with domesticity as she had become. He knew Nellie had not remarried and was still living in Liverpool, having become a lodging-house keeper in Norton Street. She'd had the opportunity to be courted by other men but wasn't interested. There would, in her eyes, never be an equal to Jem Mace.

Mace knew how things stood with Nellie because, for some time, he had been back in contact with his brother-in-law Ted McCall. It had been McCall who had had the sad duty of informing him of the death of his daughter by Nellie. Ellen Norah, never a robust child, had been taken ill on a visit to Ireland and died there while still in her teens. McCall's wife Annie, Nellie's younger sister, had died in 1895, and four years later, with his children grown up, he had remarried. Ted had reluctantly deferred to family opinion at the time of Mace's desertion of Nellie but, following Annie's death and his daughters becoming independent, he was more than happy to resume their friendship. Employing McCall as a go-between, Mace let Nellie know to expect him in Liverpool.

Alice had not seen the danger coming. Even after a row in which Mace had cast up Nellie to her, contrasting her willingness to travel anywhere to Alice's stick-in-the-mud attitude, she never believed he would leave her to return to a woman of fifty. She never imagined he would turn away from his three young children. She never supposed that he would quit his post at the Black Lion. She never conjectured that he would leave his gymnasium in Pretoria Street.

Nellie was overjoyed to see Jem back. She had always hoped, but not really believed, that he would return and though it was twelve years since she had last set eyes on him, he still looked athletic. At seventy-two, Mace could easily have passed for sixty – and not only in Nellie's eyes. She gave little thought to Alice's feelings, boosted as she was by the realisation that he had left a woman twenty years younger to return to her, but she was concerned for the three children suddenly left in Birmingham without a father. She insisted that he send maintenance for them and, as Nellie, like Mace's other wives, always dealt with money matters better than he did, she was in a position to see that he carried that out. As for Alice, she was stunned. He didn't just leave but told her in a way as would brook no tearful entreaties for a change of heart. Her sense of betrayal was increased by the fact that she was left with young children, distressed by the sudden departure of their father, to look after and with a busy pub to run.

Suddenly back in the familiar surroundings of central Liverpool, Mace soon became aware of his extended family circle – and of the fact that his return was not universally welcomed. Annie's youngest three daughters, Jenny, Emma and Rose, all reflected what they supposed would have been their mother's attitude had she still been alive, namely that Mace had wronged Nellie badly and that she ought not to take him back. Emma, who was living with Nellie at Norton Street, felt particularly offended by his presence in the house. Their father, Ted McCall, was blithely unconcerned, however. He had shaken hands warmly with Mace and it was not long before Jem told him much of what had happened in the interim – not merely sports chat but conversation about personal matters.

About this time Ted took Mace to see his first professional football match. Ted was a keen supporter of Liverpool FC, founded eleven years earlier and one of the leading clubs in the land. While they were seated side-by-side at Anfield, he had noticed Mace closely following every move of the game. McCall assumed that he must have been enjoying it but, after the match, Mace criticised the players of both teams. He was shocked by what he considered their clumsiness. Using sporting language well ahead of its time, he derided poor ball control and aimless kicking of long upfield balls. McCall could only agree.

Their companion at Anfield was McCall's son-in-law, Tom Much, a publican who followed boxing even more keenly than he did football and had read extensively about the origins of the sport. For him, Mace was history made flesh and Tom, a broadminded man and a music lover, could not have cared less about Mace's bohemian lifestyle. The party returned to Tom's pub and soon Tom's wife Nell was demurring from her younger sister's hostility to the roving old warrior. Having supposed Mace to be a ruthless and inhuman man, she watched with surprise as he sunk to his knees to play with her five-year-old son Harry. 'Punch me as hard as you can, my boy,' said Jem as the lad looked to his father and received a nod of assent. Unblinking at the boy's punch, Mace declared, 'Now you can say you hit the champion of the world right on the chin.'

More significant than this would be the reaction of Mace's own daughters, the surviving offspring of his second marriage having combined with Nellie's family as a result of the marriage of John Lee and Ada Mace. John and Ada lived in the Everton district. Having reluctantly abandoned his dream of making a living as an artist, John, now in his early thirties, was working at Liverpool's Cotton Exchange as a broker's clerk, but he had prospects of becoming a wealthy man in his own right. Jem was welcomed into the home and introduced to the three surviving grandchildren: Ellen, thirteen, Gladys, five, and three-year-old Marion. To Jem's approval, Ellen demonstrated her proficiency on the piano. John welcomed his stepfather warmly. It could not be denied that Mace had deeply distressed his mother in time past but he would always bear comparison with the late and unlamented Rowland Lee. Ada embraced her father. She was glad to see him and her beloved stepmother reunited. Still, there was a note of doubt and scepticism. The reunion seemed to hinge on the proposed move to South Africa. Nellie would leave her home and family behind and who could tell if a sojourn in a new country would be a success?

Amelia and Andrew McMillin lived opposite Newsham Park where Andrew, in his early forties, ran a thriving joinery business. The McMillins had three boys – James, twelve, Tommy, eleven, and Bill, ten

– who were suitably impressed with the famous sportsman who was their grandfather. Amelia fervently hoped that the reunion of Jem and Nellie would be permanent but Andrew had his doubts. Soon he was one of a large family group of Maces, McCalls and McMillins who saw the couple off at Lime Street, whence they took the train for Southampton to embark on the *Avondale Castle*, bound for Cape Town. They arrived at the Cape of Good Hope – a fitting name for the enterprise Mace was undertaking – in December 1903. The voyage had been pleasant, like old times. Jem and Nellie were comfortable together and it seemed like a reprise of the journeys that they had undertaken across the Pacific, twenty and more years previously.

Mace used his money to open a boxing academy in Cape Town. Both he and Nellie revelled in the climate, reminiscent of that of Victoria. It was not in industrial Britain that, in future, the top boxers of the world would be discovered, Mace thought, but in the sunshine cultures of the New World. He had after all planted seeds in California, Canada and above all in Australia and New Zealand. Now the youth of the Cape would benefit, so he supposed, from his unique tuition. Mace was soon to be rudely disillusioned. The wounds of the Boer War were slow to heal. Until he arrived in South Africa, he had, like most British people, been kept in the dark by the new mass media regarding the legacy of hatred which the war had left. It had taken the British two years to break the Afrikaaners' guerilla resistance and, to do so, they had introduced concentration camps where men, women and children were segregated on short rations and several thousand had died of starvation. What's more, casualties in combat on the British side had been high while no one knew, with any degree of accuracy, what the death toll among black Africans was. Jem might be a genial personality in himself; he might try to drum up publicity for his Academy through his reappearance in the ring with an exhibition against the Scots-born middleweight Jack Valentine, but there was scarcely a young man in Cape Colony who wanted to present himself for lessons at Mace's Academy.

To the Cape Dutch, as the Afrikaans-speaking population of the colony were known, Mace was an Englishman and, by implication, an enemy. As for the English-speaking young men, they had volunteered in droves for the war and loss of life among them had been considerable. They made clear that they would prefer to play rugby football than participate in boxing, the sport strongly associated with pre-war Johannesburg. Mace also made it plain that 'persons of colour' would be welcome at his Academy, but they were the ones who had suffered most in the conflict and whose history of oppression could not be instantly contradicted by the tolerant Englishman. After the dismal failure of his second exhibition, against Valentine in mid-January 1904, Mace was forced to conclude that his enterprise had failed after little more than six weeks. He received a pittance for the premises which he had lavishly equipped and he and Nellie decided to leave. Considering their options, they decided that there was but one thing for it: they must return to Australia. The Victoria Racing Club Hotel in Melbourne was his one remaining asset and he would have to sell it to finance a life for them after they returned to England.

At this stage came the first signs of conflict: Nellie wanted to go straight to Victoria, to put the hotel on the market and to return to her relatives in Liverpool, but Mace wanted a voyage to New York, before going by railroad across America, and then by sea from San Francisco to Sydney. He gave as his reason a wish to meet Pooley again and sample New York, always one of his favourite cities. Nellie had no objection to this in itself but she was worried by increased expenses which, she believed, they could only just meet. Nellie and Jem stayed with Delaiah, Pooley and their twenty-three-year-old son Gusty in their home in Brooklyn. Pooley and Gusty were working as horse dealers, also on Long Island but outside the New York city boundary. There was much talk of Pooley's youngest son, Mel. The twenty-two-year-old had gone out West to try his luck in the cattle trade where he had fallen in love with Ida Hathaway, the late-teen daughter of a wealthy Denver rancher. Ida's father had been shocked by his daughter's 'infatuation with a gypsy' but, undaunted, Mel and Ida had eloped to Mexico and secretly married. In due course Hathaway forgave his daughter, met Mel and was impressed by his 'Eastern education'. Pooley remarked that Mel took after Jem and he laughed heartily at news of the episode. It was a brief but happy interlude. Pooley and Jem talked not only about the old days but Pooley's enjoyment of life in New York. This rekindled his cousin's own love of the Big Apple on this, his fifth visit to the U.S.A. There was no press coverage of his presence in the city. He had not come on boxing business and was understandably reluctant for any information to come out about the disaster in South Africa.

One evening, Pooley and Jem went into Manhattan and visited Considine's, one of the newest and hottest nightspots in New York. With a clientele composed of theatre magnates, notably the millionaire Abe Erlanger, top-flight entertainers, men of the turf such as the great American jockey Tod Sloan, the notorious gambler 'Diamond Jim' Brady, giants of the ring and Broadway showgirls, Mace was in his element. He was soon chatting to Bob Fitzsimmons, who had made his home in New York. Others who sought him out included Kid McCoy, Tom Sharkey and Tommy Ryan. Although Mace wished to stand his round as he had always done, the others seemed aware of his precarious financial situation and ensured that he paid nothing for his tipple, which was, as usual, just a few glasses of port.

While at Considine's he met Datas the Memory Man, then on his first theatrical tour to the States. Datas's astonishing feats of memory had been widely covered in the media and he had received $2,000 from a group of American neurologists on condition that, following his death, his brain would be donated for medical research. Datas, still in his twenties, was eager to use the money for a blast in the Big Apple before his imminent return to England. Unfortunately, this bohemian rendezvous was becoming infiltrated by gangsters and it was their intention to waylay Datas, rob him of his $2,000 and shoot him dead. There were rumours that crooked doctors were prepared to pay hitmen up to $20,000 for making the Memory Man's brain instantly available. Mace had picked up hints of these vicious plans and he advised Datas to slip out of Considine's at the earliest opportunity, not to return to his hotel but to go covertly to the ship where his passage had been booked. Datas heeded Mace's advice and escaped with his life. He was followed by a hired gun who, thinking Datas was headed for his hotel, lost the trail. Before he left, Mace said he would see Datas in Australia, where the Memory Man's next engagements were scheduled.

Mace and Nellie travelled by train from New York to San Francisco and then took ship to Australia. Revisiting the country where they had flourished over twenty years earlier was an emotional experience for both of them. Mace was at first tempted to stay on at the Victoria Racing Club Hotel in Melbourne, where the older staff remembered him with affection – it was as if he'd never been away. He met up with Larry Foley in Sydney; by this time, Larry had long ceased to be a boxing instructor; he had built up a prosperous business as a building demolition contractor and was considering a career in politics. The two men who, between them, had transformed the sport of pugilism and discovered and nurtured a golden generation of boxers, reflected on Jackson and Fitzsimmons, Dooley and Slavin, Hall, Griffo and Billy Murphy, but Foley sounded a note of caution: he did not expect Australia to produce such a crop again. Just as young Englishmen now flocked to football, or, as Larry called it, soccer, so young Australians were flocking to Australian Rules football. It was a different story in America, where boxing still held sway over the American version of the football game and even over its closest challenger as a spectator sport, baseball.

Back in Melbourne, Mace met up with Datas one evening after his theatre show. The pair returned to the Old England, where Datas witnessed an incident which testified to Mace's astonishing physical power for a man of seventy-two. In the hotel lounge there were a number of accompanied women, something which Mace had always encouraged in every one of the drinking establishments he had owned or managed. There was also a bunch of young 'diggers', rough and ready Australian working men. Suddenly one of the diggers shouted out foul language. Mace went quietly across to him and politely informed him that he didn't allow such language in the presence of ladies. The digger, a burly young man who had no idea who the ageing host was, merely grinned and asked who he thought he would get to stop him.

'I thought I'd just mention it to you,' replied Mace in a calm, unthreatening voice.

The digger's mates fell silent, anticipating some fun at the old bloke's expense, but Mace added, 'And I shan't get anyone to do it for me, but I shall do it myself.' The big digger roared with laughter and calling on his mates to 'Watch this!' he bellowed a volley of obscenities while all eyes in the by now silent lounge were trained on him. Mace sauntered over, struck the culprit full on the jaw and knocked him to the ground. As the man tried to rise, Mace hauled the groggy digger up and ran him clean out of the premises. There was applause all round while the digger's mates fell silent in awe.

Unfortunately Mace's business acumen had never matched his manifest other skills. When he tried to put the Victoria Racing Club Hotel on the market, he was stunned to discover that a creditor of his from two decades earlier had established a lien on the property. Almost all of the profits had to go to the creditor and the couple, shocked to the core, could only take ship for England. Mace and Nellie had to travel via New Zealand, which increased the fare, and by the time they returned to Liverpool, were virtually penniless. The extent of Mace's poverty was emphasised when specially minted gold sovereigns, liable for duty, were smuggled ashore on the person of McCall's baby granddaughter, Ethel Much, whose mother assumed that Customs officers would not search an infant. While McCall was as cordial to Mace as ever, his youngest daughters Emma and Rose were not. Their aunt had sold her lodging house to go to South Africa with him and they were concerned that he might seek to live at Nellie's expense. This was in fact far from being his intention. He could and did accept one-off handouts but his pride would not allow him to become dependent on anyone else; besides, there was the pub in Birmingham of which he was still the landlord, if only in name, and there was Alice. For all his genuine affection for Nellie, she had not been able to rekindle the desire which he had once had for her – and only 100 miles away lay another woman, little more than thirty. Mace's pulses quickened at the thought of her. He confided in McCall and Ted gave him the train fare to Birmingham. So ended his intended sojourn in South Africa, which had turned into a bizarre voyage around the world and ended with scarcely a penny to his name.

34

Mace and Race

HOWEVER BRIGHT A star he was in the sporting firmament, and even though he was the most famous publican in England, Mace was no more than a bookkeeping entry to the Birmingham brewers' accountants. The wages of James Mace, licensed victualler's manager at the Black Lion, had ceased to be paid as soon as he went absent without leave; indeed, they hoped to install a new manager as soon as possible. It was not so easy any more for breweries to recruit managers, however. Liberal magistrates throughout England, many of them nonconformists or Temperance men, were refusing pub licences. The days of 'a pub on every corner' were receding and the profession of publican was no longer as sought-after as it had been in the nineteenth century. As a result of this, Alice and the children had been allowed to stay on for a while at the Black Lion. She had always been popular with the customers and there was a great fund of sympathy for her after Mace's desertion. But, before long, her sister Polly advised her to come and live with her and her husband Alex McLeish. Polly may well have suspected that Mace would try to return to Alice but assumed he wouldn't know where she was. She was wrong. Not far from the McLeish home in Islington lived Mace's former business manager, Bill Bayford. He put Mace in the picture and Jem travelled on to London. By this time, to provide more space for the children, Alice had moved to Colebrooke Row. There was a vacancy for a landlord at the nearby Old Bluecoat Boy and Bayford put Mace's name forward. Polly McLeish, who had long distrusted Mace, had already persuaded her husband to move into Colebrooke Row, three doors down from Mace's house. It proved a far-sighted decision.

When Mace returned, at the beginning of May 1904, he was passionately greeted by Alice. She had come to blame herself over her reluctance to move to South Africa and, even though her instincts had been proved right in this instance, she forgave him as soon as she set eyes on him. They made love for hours that very night and, as a result, Alice became pregnant. Unlike with Nellie, from whom he had been gone thirteen years, Mace had only been apart from Alice for a matter of months, eventful though those had been. Now that all this 'South African nonsense', as she described it, was out of the way, life together, so Alice believed, could resume its natural course. What's more, Lillian, James and Amy had missed their father and were glad to see him back.

The McLeishes, much as they deplored what Mace had done, were, unlike the younger McCall sisters, also relieved. Alice had been wretchedly unhappy but now she was joyful again – and the children needed their father. For about a year he remained at Colebrooke Row and it was there, on 3 February 1905, that Ellen Norah Mace,* the second of Mace's daughters to bear those names, was born. At the time of her birth, her mother was thirty-three and her father a couple of months short of his seventy-fourth birthday. Mace did not want to be dependent on Alex McLeish. He wanted to set himself up as a boxing instructor. From experience, he knew he must apply to the Bankruptcy Court and he did so. The terms of the adjudication compelled him to sell his precious few remaining assets and imposed the usual additional term before he could be discharged.

His remarkable physical powers, as already witnessed by Datas, would be in evidence once again one evening late in 1904. Despite his straitened circumstances, Mace was never seen in town other that immaculately clad. On this occasion he was strolling down the Strand wearing a long, fawn greatcoat over white flannel trousers; a glittering diamond pin added further to the lustre of his crimson tie and his head was adorned by a glossy silk top hat. Despite his brisk walk, the attention of a young mugger was drawn, perhaps by his white locks and somewhat outdated elegance. Anticipating easy pickings at the expense of an old man, the attacker tried to seize Mace's gold watch. He was immediately struck two fierce and accurate blows and fell unconscious, striking his head on the pavement. A small crowd cheered Mace as a policeman summoned an ambulance. He later learned that the man had remained unconscious for a lengthy period

---

* This child was registered as Ellen but baptised as Ella.

and became worried that, for the first time in his life, he might have struck a fatal blow. Fortunately, his shocked assailant recovered and was convicted of attempted robbery, spending six months in jail.

Mace's appointment as landlord of The Bluecoat Boy did not materialize and he narrowly eked out a living for himself and his family by resuming exhibitions, including a couple against the veteran Tug Wilson. On 13 May 1905, aged seventy-four, Mace fought a much younger opponent at The Horns in Kennington, when he appeared in an exhibition for his own benefit. His opponent was the Jewish middleweight Wolf Bendoff. Seeing that Bendoff was 'going easy' on him, Mace commanded, 'Hit harder, boy, hit harder. I've a hard old nut and a hard old heart.' The spectators were few in number but, on hearing these words, they cheered him long and loud.

Without regular income or assets, Mace and his family faced the workhouse, that relic of nineteenth-century harshness towards the infirm, unemployed and elderly. Introduced in 1834 to 'lift the burden' of those seeking relief on their local parish, these dismal Dickensian institutions were still going strong in the opening decade of the twentieth century. The newly elected Liberal Government, forced to take a radical stance for fear of being outflanked on the left, where fifty-three seats had been gained by the recently formed Labour Party, talked of social security legislation but hesitated to introduce it.

It was then that Alex and Polly McLeish offered shelter to Alice, Jem and the four children in their home at Colebrooke Row. At the age of thirteen, Lillian could already be legally employed and, at eleven, James could follow on before long. This would ease the burden. Alice and the four children moved in and it was expected that Jem would follow – but he failed to do so. Obviously unable to pay the rent on the house where he, Alice and the children had previously lived, he had to get out but took advantage of an offer of a spare bedroom in Bill Bayford's house at Liverpool Road. As the whole Stokes family saw it, Mace's departure from the woman who had been at his side for fifteen years, and from his four surviving children, was an act of betrayal. Mary McLeish, in particular, considered him to be despicable. As Mace viewed it, he was a man of pride and he sensed that the McLeishes looked down on him. He would not become a mere lodger in the same house where his own children lived. With Bill Bayford, it would be different. He was a veteran of the entertainment business and he and his wife Betty were cheery sorts with whom Mace could have a laugh. Alice was devastated. For a while she clung to the hope that he would return but, as his visits to see his children became fewer and finally ended, she was obliged to abandon hope. At least he could not be reproached for lack of maintenance because he had only just enough means to pay Betty Bayford for his food. The Bayfords themselves were hard up; Bill was out of work.

The next four years of Jem Mace's life were marred by poverty. He only had enough money for one meal a day, which invariably consisted of soup, vegetables and two eggs beaten up in a glass of milk. For fifty years he had relied on his wives and mistresses to cook his meals – Mary, Selina, Hannah, Nellie and Alice – and when briefly without female companionship, he had had the means to eat out and to dine well. Now in his late seventies, his restricted diet was difficult to bear. Despite all this, he remained clean, vigorous and healthy. He took a cold bath every day and walked six or seven miles afterwards, even though he no longer ran. Except only in the foulest of weathers, he would be out walking at a sharp pace. His constitution remained basically strong and he never once needed to see a doctor.

Even before he was discharged from bankruptcy, Mace had to face facts: he could not earn an income. Determined at all costs to avoid the workhouse, a fate which befell an old acquaintance Bill Laing, the pedestrian, Mace got by for a while on handouts. He did not solicit these but he did not refuse them either. Among his benefactors while he lived in Islington were Datas and 'Peggy' Bettinson. Bettinson's assistance was especially welcome because it kept Mace close to the world of boxing, which remained his lifeblood. He was therefore able to look in at the National Sporting Club, where not all realised, especially in view of his physical robustness and immaculate attire, just how strapped for cash he was. The NSC also brought him a lifeline. American journalists frequently reported fights at King Street, mailing their dispatches back to the USA where they appeared in syndicated columns. The realisation that Mace was alive and kicking at the NSC drew American newspaper editors' attention. Boxing might have faded in popular appeal in Britain but in America its popularity was immense and the number of column inches devoted to it was phenomenal. Mace was the last survivor of the Prize Ring and his role in transforming pugilism into boxing was now unquestioned in the States. His reminiscences and views on the current generation of fighters were highly sought-after and he gained a much-needed source of income by granting paid interviews to American reporters. 'Mace declared that many American pugilists were too much inclined to use circular swings coupled with the crouching attitude,' said the journalist W.W. Naughton. 'He always maintained that the best early boxers over here were Coburn, [Jack] McAuliffe, [Nonpareil] Dempsey . . . and others who struck out from the shoulder and used straight punches almost exclusively.'

A lifeline then emerged as a result of Mace's reconciliation with his son James, now in his late forties. James himself had to abandon the idea of running boxing schools but he approached his father with the idea that Jem's fighting career should be serialized in the *Sporting Life*. James would act as editor of his reminiscences and the remuneration would be shared between them. By this time, Mace was estranged from his second, third and fourth families and he welcomed the chance to link up again with his first. What's more, the money would be vital. Between December 1905 and June 1906, these fistic memoirs, entitled 'Jem Mace and his Battles', boosted the circulation of the fight magazine.

Mace's interest in the world heavyweight championship had lain dormant for a few years. Despite his stylistic criticism of Jim Jeffries, he did not deny that he was a formidable champion and a worthy successor to Corbett and Fitzsimmons. In 1905, Jeffries retired and announced, like an abdicating monarch, that he would referee a match for the vacant title between two boxers selected by him. The winner of this was Marvin Hart, a moderate boxer, but a year later, the Canadian Tommy Burns took the title, outpointing Hart. Mace, at this time, knew nothing of Burns. He noted that the Vancouver man got good notices in the British sporting press but wondered whether the fact that Burns was a citizen of the British Empire might have influenced this.

In April 1907, he witnessed the English debut of another Canadian boxer at the NSC. Rarely did Mace, usually sparing with praise, enthuse as much about an up-and-coming fighter as he did about Sam Langford. Langford dished out a ferocious beating to an English heavyweight, James 'Tiger' Smith, and six weeks later pulverised another one, Geoff Thorne, in the first round. Langford, a former lumberjack from Nova Scotia, was twenty-four and the descendant of American slaves who won freedom by escaping and fighting on the British side in the War of Independence. Subsequently, they had been evacuated to Canada. At fourteen, he ran away from home and found work in the USA. He began his professional boxing career as a lightweight at nineteen and gradually moved up the weight divisions. Fighting out of his adopted home town, he was dubbed the 'Boston Tar Baby' (a nickname which, for obvious reasons, he detested) and then the 'Boston Terror'. His rise to ring fame was rapid but he was denied championship status. He effectively accounted for the two greatest black boxers at lighter weights, gaining a decision in a non-title fight against the brilliant lightweight champion Joe Gans. The following year he fought for the welterweight championship against Joe Walcott and most spectators considered that the verdict of a draw was grossly unfair on Langford.

What Mace saw from Langford, admittedly against inferior opponents, drew lavish praise from the old maestro. The barrel-chested Sam was no more than 5ft 6in tall but, with arms which stretched almost to his knees, had a phenomenal reach. His shoulders and biceps were exceptionally powerful and he was a fast and nimble mover. Langford was equally adept as an infighter or outfighter. A master of every shot in the book, his jab was fearsome, he could block punches and he could shift his attack from head to body in an instant. His punches were perfectly timed and delivered with immense force. When Smith momentarily trapped him against the ropes, he withstood an ugly bombardment with great bravery before manoeuvring his way out.

In many ways this superb boxer-puncher was a carbon copy of the young Mace and Jem developed a genuine empathy with him. Mace and Langford were photographed sitting side by side at King Street, Langford's modest height leaving him three inches shorter than Mace. Superficially, the contrast between the relaxed, slouching cloth-capped young Bostonian black man and the aged but bolt upright Englishman in his finery could not have been greater – but Jem and Sam were in many ways kindred spirits, Langford being a devil-may-care extrovert.

In discussion with Langford, Mace learnt of his ambition to

become not merely middleweight champion of the world but the heavyweight titleholder. Langford wondered if he was being realistic, in view of his unusual physique, but as Mace saw it, if Fitzsimmons could do it, so could he. Encouraged, Langford broached the race issue. Jim Corbett and Jim Jeffries had refused to fight a black man for the title: Jeffries, although not personally racist, had feared public hostility if he made such a move. What did Jem think about this, particularly in view of his having known Peter Jackson? Mace's reply was unequivocal. He introduced Langford to Lord Lonsdale and Lonsdale, who had also witnessed Langford in action and been highly impressed, asserted that he would do all he could, namely to put up sufficient money for Burns to make a title defence in a bout between the two Canadians at the NSC. It might be clever if it was billed as being for the British Empire title but, if Langford won, it would be hard for anyone to deny his right to be called world titleholder.

The problem was not merely one of racism. The four leading contenders for Burns's title were all black, and competition between them was intense. Both Joe Jeannette and Sam McVey were great fighters but undoubtedly Langford's foremost rival was Jack Johnson, a former Texas stevedore who had won the so-called 'Coloured Heavyweight Championship of the World' four years earlier. There was a link between Johnson and the Macean boxers because, early in his career, Johnson had been knocked out by Joe Choynski in his home state. Boxing was illegal in Texas and both fighters were jailed for a month afterwards. While incarcerated, Choynski passed on to Johnson many of the techniques he had first learnt from Mace disciple Walter Watson in San Francisco. Johnson and Langford had finally met in April 1906. In a fine contest, Langford scored an early knockdown over a man half a head taller and 30lb heavier but then he was knocked down twice by Johnson, once for the nine count. Showing immense bravery, he rode the storm, fought back hard and fully extended the Galvestonian before Johnson's heavy and accurate jabbing took him to a clear points victory. Time seemed to be on Langford's side, however, as he was the younger man by five years. As Lonsdale and Mace saw it, the key to unravelling the situation in Langford's favour was to lure Burns to London.

On being discharged from bankruptcy for a second time, Mace

tried his hand one more time at running a pub. In June 1906, he was appointed manager of the Dick Whittington in Great Barr, Birmingham. The brewery was evidently attracted by the resonance of his name but he did not last long. His desertion of Alice at the Black Lion had got about on the grapevine. Women were unanimously hostile towards him, and though some men laughed this off, many others did not. In the new century, a husband and father who had treated his family so shabbily could not expect to pose as a genial 'mine host'.

Mace then returned to his roots by gathering together a small troupe of young boxers, all fighting at the lighter weights. At this time the NSC monopoly on big-time boxing was being challenged, notably by the theatrical impresario C.B. Cochran. Shows began to be presented at various other metropolitan halls, notably the 'Olympia' in Earls Court. Christmas 1907 brought a hiatus of which Mace took brisk, if brief, advantage. Taking over Olympia during the festive season, he presented his troupe and was at the gate to collect the tuppence and threepence admissions. But he was to be swiftly disillusioned in his notion that this would be the basis for a permanent boxing school. He earmarked some premises in a side street off Leicester Square but the idea never got off the ground.

On 27 January 1908, Alice, who never really recovered emotionally from the shock of Mace leaving her for the second time, died at the home of her sister Polly McLeish in Islington. There had been an abrupt onset of tuberculosis and Alice had scarcely been able to fight it. It seems that Mace did not attend the funeral at Finchley Cemetery, although whether this was a conscious decision or whether Polly had only notified him after the event is not clear. The McLeish-Stokes family paid for a monumental headstone for Alice, the inscription on which began 'Dear Mother' and was phrased as if the sole persons bereaved were her children. Mace could not have afforded such an act. He was certainly greatly distressed to receive the news. Alice was only thirty-six and, at the time, Lillian fifteen, James thirteen, Amy twelve and Ella two. Mace would have no further contact with his four youngest children, for which some strongly reproached him while others deplored the alleged negative influence of Polly. Nevertheless, it was she who gave the children a home and who would bring up Ella. After all, she had seen for herself, at the time of the disastrous South

African episode, how Mace had placed his own love of adventure ahead of his family responsibilities.

There was a certain symmetry in the fate of Mary Ann Barton, Hannah Boorn and Alice Caroline Stokes. All three had caught Mace's eye as beautiful late-teenage girls and all three had been discarded by him, only to be fatally stricken while still young women. However, Alice was the most tragic of the three. Mary and Hannah each found happiness, however briefly, with another man but Alice, heartbroken, did not even seek it.

By this time, Mace had teamed up with his cousins Billy and Norah Le Neve, who toured with a circus, known as Sullivan's Circus after Nora's maiden surname, and they were to be his principal means of support in his later years. Although there would always be a room for him in the Bayfords' house, he preferred to be on the road with the Sullivans. Sometimes he played his cherished violin, on other occasions he would play a dramatic role as a veteran pugilist in such productions as *To Catch A Tartar*. Sullivan's Circus was a modest enterprise. Billy and Norah's profits were variable but they gave Mace the chance to be in the showbusiness world which he loved, and a meagre living. Sometimes he slept in a caravan, just as he had done as a lad in Norfolk, and although he never complained, the cold was arduous for a man of his age.

During 1908, Mace revisited his native county, refereeing an amateur boxing bout at the Theatre Royal in Norwich. It was also in 1908 that his autobiography was published. Entitled *Fifty Years A Fighter*, it was suggested to him by sporting journalists and by his son James and would be an expanded version of what had already appeared in the *Sporting Life* serialisation. His limited capacity for writing meant that he would have to dictate all the material – but unlike the typical ghosted autobiography of later sporting heroes, he did not merely chat about his career and leave others to sort out his thoughts and find adequate words. As the journalists testified, the words were almost entirely his own and reflected his innate intelligence, which had never been refined by formal schooling.

The book gives a vivid and thorough account of his career between his semi-professional pugilistic debut against Farden Smith in 1849 and his first competitive glove fights against Bill Davis in 1876–7, a time of nearly thirty years rather than fifty. Still, in view of his many exhibition bouts, the last of which was in 1905, fifty-six years after he first vaulted the ropes, the title was not altogether inaccurate. Significantly, Mace gave no indication of any nostalgia for the Prize Ring, which some had ascribed to him. 'Prize-fighting in England has been dead . . . for forty years,' he wrote. 'It would be impossible to revive it. And even if it were not impossible . . . it would be eminently undesirable.'

One of the most remarkable aspects of the book is the almost complete absence of reference to his birth family – and the total absence of reference to his four wives (considering Alice as such) and at least fourteen children. Pooley is mentioned in cordial terms on several occasions but Jem is adamant that he himself is not of gypsy blood. He speaks of Adah Isaacs Menken at some length and in terms which leave little doubt as to the fact that she was the love of his life – while narrowly avoiding an explicit statement that she was his mistress. *Fifty Years A Fighter* was poorly marketed and sales were modest. It would have fared much better if it had been sold in America, the heartland of boxing. Ironically, Mace was still a big name there, even as his greatness seemed to be a faded memory in England. In any case, a lifelong weakness of his resurfaced when he frittered much of the book's profits on gambling.

Tommy Burns's six-month tour of Europe occupied the first half of 1908. He proved far too good for the English boxers who he permitted to have a shot at his heavyweight title. Nevertheless he failed to impress Mace, who openly pointed out his technical shortcomings. Mace did not believe that Burns would be able to stand up to Sam Langford. Lord Lonsdale, who relied on Mace's judgment as well as his own, concurred. He said of Langford that 'with a few more inches in height he would have been the greatest boxer ever'. Lonsdale offered a purse for a match for the world title between the two Canadians, to be held at the NSC, but Burns refused. He would not, he said, fight a black man.

With Burns still in England, Jack Johnson arrived from the United States. Johnson and his manager, Sam Fitzpatrick, believed that a Canadian champion taking his title around the world would be far more vulnerable to a challenge than any of the previous white champions had been. Johnson was well equipped to play the part of a title-stalker. An intelligent and articulate man, he brimmed with confidence. An opera-lover who played the bass-viol with skill, Johnson was fascinated with automobiles, at that time ceasing, as Henry Ford adopted mass production techniques, to be merely luxury items for the rich. Johnson's inventive mind led him to develop the first anti-theft device. Fitzpatrick and Johnson claimed priority over Langford by virtue both of Jack being the 'Coloured Heavyweight Champion of the World' and through his points decision over Sam. Mace protested that this was unfair to Langford, who had come to England a year earlier and believed he had an understanding with the NSC concerning a fight for the title.

The last word rested with Peggy Bettinson. In May 1908, the NSC proposed a purse of £2,500 for a title bout between Burns and Johnson at King Street. Fitzpatrick accepted and Johnson appeared delighted to have at last got the chance for a shot at the world crown. But Burns dismissed the offer with contempt. This was not due to racism: Burns had already got wind of the fact that an Australian promoter would offer him £6,000, win, lose or draw, to fight Johnson. Although the land Down Under was no longer producing boxers of the calibre of Mace and Foley's protégés, the sport was still flourishing thanks to the rise of the first big-time promoter of the twentieth century. Hugh D. McIntosh – popularly known as 'Huge Deal' – was years ahead of Foley as a showman. Foley, despite his great skill as an instructor, had always been regarded as stingy by Australian fighters; McIntosh by contrast, a former pie-seller turned bakery chain boss, was a loud-mouthed, raucous extrovert but also an entrepreneur who was prepared to think big and take risks. At Rushcutters Bay in Sydney, a stadium was built capable of holding a massive open-air crowd and guaranteeing the kind of giant purse with which to lure Burns.

Meanwhile, Bettinson, who, unlike Lonsdale and Mace, was not free from racial prejudice, had taken an irrational dislike to Jack Johnson and rather than offering him a bout in London had sent him down to Plymouth to fight the mediocre Ben Taylor. Mace decided that he would see Johnson in action even if Bettinson wouldn't. Johnson could probably have flattened Taylor in the first minute had he so chosen – after all, he was the man who had virtually finished the career of the forty-four-year-old veteran Fitzsimmons, whose nose he had broken while dealing out a second round knockout. In future fights, Johnson would inflict similar injuries on other leading fighters with his ferocious uppercut but he chose to carry Taylor for eight rounds before sending him to the canvas for the count. During that time, he gave a masterly exhibition of defensive boxing skill, feinting, parrying and catching Taylor's crude blows in mid-air. His movements were elegant and economical and he held his guard in a low and relaxed manner, as if to lure in an unwary opponent and set him up for the counterpunch.

Despite these Macean characteristics, Johnson differed in one significant way from what Mace had taught Foley: Johnson's weight was on the front foot and his boots were often wide apart, whereas Mace had fought with the feet together and his weight on the back foot, leaving the front free for stepping in and coming away. What Mace and Johnson shared, though, was an avoidance of the lateral movement which had characterised Corbett. Obviously Taylor was not an opponent who could prove a true test for the American but Mace could see enough to indicate that Johnson was a boxer of the highest class. Nevertheless, he did not like him and had reasons for his antipathy. Throughout the fight Johnson had taunted Taylor and mocked his inadequacies, behaviour which Mace found completely inappropriate.

Back in London, Mace discussed the heavyweight championship with Lonsdale and Bettinson. The unique circumstances of a Canadian champion prepared to take his title round the world rather than defend only in the USA opened up the possibility of the NSC becoming the arbiters of the crown. The Club had always boasted that it conducted business on principle rather than as hucksters concerned only with profit. They could not oblige Burns to defend a title against an opponent if he dug his heels in against it, but if McIntosh made an offer to the Canadian which he would not refuse, things would be different. Mace gave his considered opinion that Burns would not be able to stand up to Johnson, who, in any case, had an advantage of five inches and 30lb over him. Mace was aware, from his recent visit to Australia, that racism was on the rise there. There would be total public apathy towards a match between any two black heavyweights and

McIntosh would not want to risk a substantial financial loss. Still, Mace opined, the NSC was honour bound to give Langford his chance and offer a purse for a fight between the two black heavyweights. The offer should be made now, before Johnson challenged Burns. If Johnson beat Burns, as Mace was convinced he would, then Johnson v Langford would be for the world title. Both Bettinson and Lonsdale accepted his reasoning.

Burns then headed off to Australia in search of rich purses from McIntosh for fighting mediocre Australian boxers and Johnson headed after him, still demanding his right to a shot at Burns's title. Before leaving England, Johnson was sounded out about fighting Langford in London and gave a commitment in writing to the National Sporting Club to do so at King Street in February 1909.

★ ★ ★

In the summer of 1908, the Fourth Olympiad of the Modern Era was celebrated in London, with White City the principal venue. Like all who watched, Mace was caught up in the epic failure of the Italian Dorando Pietri who, having led the marathon for most of its twenty-six-mile, 385-yard course from the stadium to Windsor and back, collapsed only a few hundred yards from the finishing line. As always, Mace followed individual sports with the keenest interest. He was disappointed by Georg Hackenschmidt's loss of his world heavyweight wrestling title to the American Frank Gotch, not because Gotch was anything but a fine wrestler but because, as most reporters concurred, he used unsportsmanlike tactics to rob Hackenschmidt of the crown. It would not be long, although it did not occur during Mace's lifetime, before professional wrestling ceased to be a genuine sport and degenerated into crude showbusiness farce.

It was doubtless such considerations which caused Mace concern about Peddler Palmer, nicknamed the 'Box of Tricks', a gifted White-chapel boxer who, for a short while, had been world bantamweight champion. While conceding the skill and exceptional footwork of Palmer, a product of Ned Donnelly's school, Mace criticised him for 'showboating'. As he saw it, 'playing to the gallery' belonged in the sawdust ring of the circus and should remain there.

One of the few British boxers of the first decade of the century whom Mace admired was Jim Driscoll, a Welsh featherweight of Irish descent and one of the few remaining Macean boxers in the country. Disdaining the showmanship associated with Palmer, he was widely recognised as the most scientific boxer that Britain had ever produced among the lighter divisions. He attracted the adjective 'Peerless' and thoroughly deserved it, a classical boxer if ever there was one. Driscoll should have won the world championship, but when he went to America to fight the titleholder, Abe Attell, he was double-crossed. Under New York's 'no decision' law, when newspaper reporters decided the verdict rather than a referee who was open to influence, Driscoll was recognised as the victor. But Attell disavowed his earlier agreement that the title would stay or go with the newspaper decision. Back in Britain, matters were different. Titles were won and lost in the ring, normally on the premises of the NSC at King Street in London. Successful boxers were presented with special belts, known as Lonsdale Belts, to denote their championship status.

As Mace collected the meagre admissions to view his troupe in Olympia at Christmas 1908, he was frequently asked 'How many rounds do you think it will take him?' His reply to puzzled enquirers was invariably, 'As many as he chooses.' Jack Johnson had followed Tommy Burns on his world tour through Britain, Ireland and France. Now, in Australia, Hugh D. McIntosh had put up the £6,000 which the champion required in order to defend his world title against Johnson. For Burns, race remained a significant issue but less so than money. An astute businessman who was his own manager, Burns stood to receive the largest amount ever earned by a boxer for a single fight. Burns was a betting favourite, largely due to the general public's lack of awareness that, since Jeffries retired, all the top heavyweights were in fact black. That, plus out and out racism. Mace's answer implied that Johnson was the certain winner but would probably 'carry' Burns for as long as he chose while publicly humiliating him.

From the amphitheatre at Rushcutters Bay in Sydney, on 26 December 1908, Johnson's victory reverberated beyond the world of boxing. Although three years older than Burns, Johnson had great advantages in terms of height, weight and reach – but his biggest advantage was his far superior skill. As Mace had predicted, Johnson toyed with his opponent, sneering at him, taunting him and mocking him at every turn. Only Burns's pride and courage kept the battle going as long as the fourteenth round, by which time the police, fearing a riot, told McIntosh, the referee as well as the promoter, to stop it. He did so, awarding the bout and therefore the world title, to the thirty-year-old black man from Galveston.

Early in the New Year, a letter was sent from King Street to Fitzpatrick and Johnson, reminding the new champion of his written commitment to meet Sam Langford at the National Sporting Club on 22 February 1909. Johnson's written reply came as a shock: he had, he implied, agreed to fight Langford at a time before he had won the world title. Circumstances had changed and he now required £6,000, the precise sum McIntosh had paid to Burns, before he would fight Langford.

The Committee of the NSC were appalled by Johnson's duplicity and arrogance. They would not, they said, be held to ransom. Mace argued for a change of mind. He knew that, only the previous year, Johnson had been understandably furious when deliberately kept waiting in the hall at King Street while Bettinson talked business with his manager, Fitzpatrick. There was more at stake for the new champion than money alone. Mace also knew that Lonsdale could easily have afforded to put up the purse and believed that the Club should, at the least, open negotiations with Johnson. Bettinson refused to listen to Mace, while Lonsdale kept his distance. Until then, Mace had not felt that his status as the foremost judge of boxing and boxers had been jeopardised by his impoverished status. If, as he now sensed, the prosperous Bettinson and Lonsdale, one of the richest men in the world, preferred to keep him at arm's length, he was too proud to let that trouble him. The loser, sadly, was Langford, of whose thwarted ambitions the NSC appeared to have lost sight.

Johnson's victory at Rushcutters Bay would also provoke the search for a so-called 'Great White Hope' who could 'return the title to the Caucasian race'. Mace was one of the few who believed that boxing ability rather than ethnicity should determine who held the championship – and who had believed until then that Langford would get his chance in the ring.

35

Old Man from Fun City

THE PIMPLY-FACED, PREMATURELY bald, bespectacled young clerk stubbed out his cigarette. He motioned the white-haired old man who stood before him to take a seat, asked for his full name in its formal version and, when told, clearly did not recognise it. When the address was asked for, the old man replied, 'Fun City — at present that is.' Assuming an attempt at facetiousness, the clerk became vexed. However, he wrote 'peripatetic entertainer' on his notepad, accompanied by 'no fixed address, last was in Islington'. He began asking the old man searching questions about his sources of income and wrote down the answers punctiliously. Before the interview was over, an older colleague of the clerk came into the room and gave a startled glance in the old man's direction.

'Are you . . . er . . . Jem Mace?' he enquired tentatively.

The answer was in the affirmative and the young clerk asked the older one what he should write down under the subheading: last known full-time occupation. 'Champion pugilist!' retorted Mace and, with that, he ended the interview.

The previous year's Budget, that of 1908, had seen a highly significant initial step towards the eventual creation of the welfare state in Britain. The Chancellor of the Exchequer in the Liberal Government, swept into office with a landslide majority, was the Welsh radical David Lloyd George. He introduced a scheme of non-contributory old age pensions. The pension began at the age of seventy and a single pensioner was entitled to claim five shillings a week from the state — but if such a person had an income of ten shillings a week, then he or she would be disqualified. Accordingly, pensions administration boards were set up throughout the country and applicants were obliged to undergo a means test before their eligibility could be confirmed. The scheme was scheduled to start on 1 January 1909.

Mace applied. He obtained a copy of his baptismal record from Beeston confirming that he was seventy-seven but his record in the ring puzzled the board officials. Here was a man who would have won vast sums as a prize-fighter. Clearly, there was no sign of alcoholic 'dissipation'. Where had the money gone – if indeed it had gone and the old rogue was not trying to pull a fast one. His connection with the circus did not help matters. Sometimes he would not be available for a follow-up interview and suspicions grew, albeit unfounded, that he was attempting to obtain a pension by dishonest means. While the average poor old soul who turned up, shabbily clad, at his local pension board office would soon enough get approval for his meagre stipend, Mace's nomadic way of life told against him. Urged by those who knew him to attend an interview in old clothes, his vanity would not permit this. He was always immaculately dressed and looked like a dandy some twenty or thirty years out of time. For months his pension application gathered dust.

By now he had accepted that he would no longer be able to influence the destination of the world heavyweight championship. That title, of which he was the inaugural holder and for which, either by discovery, proxy tuition or, at the least, stylistic inspiration he had provided champions and contenders such as Corbett, Jackson and Fitzsimmons, was now subject only to the bids of promoters and the whims of the successive title-holders. In the spring of 1909, Sam Langford returned to England to contest the British Empire title with the current English champion Iron Hague, a ponderous Yorkshire coalminer. A few weeks before the contest, Peggy Bettinson visited Hague at his supposed training quarters in Mexborough in Yorkshire and found him having a boozy nap. Shocked, Bettinson paid for Jem to go to Mexborough to impart some of his knowledge to prevent patriotic embarrassment on the night of the fight. Mace accepted simply because he would get a short paid holiday, not because he thought Hague had a chance. Bob Fitzsimmons, then on a variety tour of England, had also been asked to go to Mexborough to try to buck up the beefy boozer. By this time Hague was making some effort to get in shape in the ring but he was so pathetic that Mace and Fitzsimmons turned their backs to the roped square and spent their time reminiscing together. Langford subsequently knocked Hague senseless in four rounds.

In conversation after the fight, Mace was relieved to learn that Langford's betrayal by Johnson had not left him embittered. As in their previous meeting two years earlier, the two got on famously. They shook hands and Mace urged him to campaign for the middleweight title. It had already become obvious that Johnson had no intention of allowing fellow blacks to challenge for his title. For starters, they would be in with the chance of beating him; second, there was no money to be had from a black-on-black contest. Mace reacted with total derision when Hague was taken up as a possible White Hope. An American syndicate proposed to back him, take him to the USA and provide him with full training facilities. In fact, Hague couldn't be bothered to accept but the incident, as Mace saw it, pointed out the ignorance of many British pundits and confirmed what he saw as America's foolish obsession with race.

One of the feeblest of the White Hopes was another Englishman, Billy Wells. Boxing had become a much encouraged sport in the army and Wells first made his name while serving in the Royal Artillery in India. His army rank of Bombardier was made part of his ring moniker and, in 1910, he was taken up by Hugh D. McIntosh, who thought Wells was a good commercial prospect – his military career made him a potential hero at a time of intense national rearmament, and McIntosh wanted to tap the market for female spectators in rival venues to the all-male NSC, such as the Kings Hall. The handsome Wells fit the bill. Soon, McIntosh's publicity machine was touting him as a future world champion. In fact, Wells had a fair left jab but, as Mace was quick to point out, he lacked the fortitude to stand up to body punches. Mace's low opinion of Wells would be vindicated in future years.

During this time, Mace had no settled address. Sometimes he was on tour with the Sullivans, at others he lodged with Bill and Betty Bayford in Islington. By this time, Bayford was not much better off than Mace. Approaching seventy, he was awaiting the day when he and his wife, who was a year older, would be eligible for the married couple's state pension. Now Mace's principal benefactor was a Church of England clergyman named George Hall. The Reverend George, aged forty-five, was one of a small group of academics who had formed the Gypsy Lore Society. Like George Borrow before him, he was fascinated by gypsy life and culture and had learned the Romany language. He did genealogical research on Ambrose Smith and had got to know Pooley, who had spoken to him freely about his family tree. George was eventually introduced to Mace and was impressed. He saw him as a remarkably gifted man, especially in view of his lack of education. Mace disclosed to him that he would've preferred a career in music to the one he had had in the Prize Ring but that he had been held back by his inability to read formal notation. Still, he had been flattered by the nickname 'the Pugilistic Paganini' which had been bestowed on him in America.

Hall had a gramophone which he loaned to Mace and he once arrived at the Bayfords' house and heard classical violin music emanating from the gramophone in Mace's bedroom. Hall commented, 'When he came out of his room, he was not Mace the fighting man but one who had emerged from quite another sphere.'

Hall was rarely in London, having to tend to his parish duties as Rector of St Olave's Church at Ruckland, Lincolnshire, but he sent cheques from time to time to tide him over. As a clergyman, Hall felt bound to speak to Mace about matters of religion and Mace heard him out but remained unconvinced. When George wrote via Bayford to enquire about the number of his children and their names and dates of birth, Mace became vexed. Bayford, who knew full well what Mace's reasons were for being cagey, wrote back, stating disingenuously that 'Jem has asked me to say he does not know how many children he has.'

Another man who helped Mace out in these difficult times was the editor of the illustrated *Mirror of Life*, Frank Bradley, who had been taught to box by Mace and, over the years, had got to know him well. Bradley had contacts at the Gaumont Cinematographic Company and, in February 1908, it was arranged for Mace and Bradley to be filmed performing a humorous sketch about two veteran boxers. This took place at Chrono House, Piccadilly Circus and included actual sparring (regrettably the film has been lost). Mace continued to give occasional exhibitions till the penultimate year of his life. His last appearance was in October 1909 when, aged seventy-eight, he took the ring with Bill Bayford at Bluetown in the Isle of Sheppey. Only when he showed signs of lameness did the old warrior finally consent to hang up his gloves.

Another place where Mace could be found was a gypsy camp in Lancashire. White House Farm, formerly the property of the wealthy farmer William Akrigg, had been settled by Romanies and stood in the village of Grassendale. Ironically, Grassendale lay only seven miles south-east of the city centre of Liverpool but Mace did not venture into the area where many of his relatives and in-laws lived. His reasons for being at Grassendale were linked to his boxing booth, which was based there and which was in use whether he was there or not. The booth went on the road in Lancashire, Cheshire and North Wales and Mace still lived in hope, a vain one as it happened, of discovering an outstanding young prospect just as Langham had discovered him over half a century earlier.

By this time Mace's name had disappeared from the columns of the British press and few people would have recognised the weather-beaten old fellow who looked a shell of the man whose image had dominated the sporting media of the previous century. And yet, across the Atlantic in America, his name was still revered as 'the Father of Boxing'. Mace was acutely aware of this disparity. He had emblazoned his own caravan with a large painted Stars and Stripes. Travelling with the booth took its toll on him. At Grassendale the biting wind from the nearby River Mersey chilled him to the bone. Uncomplaining about the conditions, he was always smartly dressed; though unable to afford a new jacket, let alone a new suit, his out-of-date but expensive garments were always well pressed and his shirts crisply starched. When Mace was away with the Sullivans, he was sometimes impersonated by a couple of elderly gypsy men deriving amusement from bluffing impressionable local youngsters that one or the other was 'the great Jem Mace'. This deepened the myth of Mace as someone who spoke broken Romany – when he wasn't yarning in broad Norfolk dialect. In fact, while Mace retained his Norfolk accent to the end of his days, and his speech was ungrammatical, his command of spoken English was fluent, vivid and impressive and he insisted, not least to Hall, that, much as he enjoyed the company of Romanies, he was ethnically English.

With nothing in writing from the pension board, Jem presented himself for interview once again – and for the second time faced a barrage of questions about his means. The fact that he had had, however briefly, the Fun City franchise – the name given to various Yuletide amusement shows at The Olympia in Earls Court – and that he secured sporadic employment with a circus made him suspect in the eyes of the board. Had he been prepared to reside in one place permanently things might have been different but staying put was, as ever, foreign to his nature. The interview ended in a row and Mace told the officials, who to him were 'pen pushers of the worst kind', exactly where they could stick their pension. The consequences of this were that Mace threw in his lot with Sullivan's Circus, with whom he had already been working intermittently. Sullivan's, as ever, was a modest outfit but Mace was useful to the extent that his name was put up on a board at the front of the show, together with paintings of his famous fights. Sometimes he entertained with his violin, but as Sullivan's made the circuit of fairs and marketplaces, the usual drill was to advertise a boxing competition for boys under thirteen with a prize of a 'Jem Mace' cup. The cup-winning boys got the chance to spar a couple of rounds with him.

His travels took him back to Islington, where Sullivan's took over the Grand Theatre and Mace was warmly welcomed by the customers when he revisited the Blue Coat Boy. More usually, however, the Sullivans were in the North of England – among their favourite stops were Hull, Manchester, Liverpool and, in particular, Newcastle. At this late stage in his life, Mace saw something of his first family. He had had intermittent contact with Adelaide for some years and knew his grandchildren and, by now, great-grandchildren. He now agreed to meet Alfred but on one condition: no attempt must be made to get him to accept any form of worship.

Mace had no fear of death. He had enjoyed his life, had few regrets and, as the conclusion of his autobiography had made clear, intended to accept the inevitable without cringing or making the slightest reference of a religious nature. Speaking of 'being challenged to fight my last battle' against an invincible enemy, he concluded, 'Well, I trust I shall be given strength and courage to toe the scratch without flinching and to face him with a bold front. I know I shall try to. For what use is it to show the white feather even to Death. After all, he can but knock me out.'

Mace's last visit to Liverpool took place in 1909, at a time when the city's future symbols, the Three Graces buildings at the Pier Head, were nearing completion. While in the city, the last portrait of him was taken. Jem, aged but smiling broadly, is sporting an unwaxed white moustache and wearing a starched collar and silk tie. He got in touch with Ted McCall, who was living on the outskirts of the city with his second wife, a woman of some means. McCall was shocked by the change in Mace's appearance: in five years he had aged at least twenty. The meagreness of his diet and the privations of life on the road had taken their toll and at seventy-eight, he looked like a man in his mid to late eighties. Ted invited Mace to live with him and his wife but he declined with thanks. Their conversation was as cordial as ever and he disclosed most of what had happened in his life since they last met. McCall told him that, with the passage of time and the departure to North America of his youngest daughters who had emigrated with their husbands, family hostility towards him had abated. McCall knew that Mace had no designs on Nellie's income from the temperance hotel in Norton Street, which she had set up after returning from Australia. The two men agreed that it might be less distressing for both Mace and Nellie if they did not meet but both John and Ada Mace and Andrew and Amelia McMillin and their children met him at McCall's house. Ada and Amelia were fully reconciled with their father but Amelia was the closer. It was Amelia who made herself known to Norah Le Neve, disclosing her address and asking to be kept informed if the worst came to the worst. Norah promised to do this.

In February 1910, Mace was once again at Fun City when a photograph of him was taken. It features his latest innovation, a troupe of female athletes headed by Norah Sullivan Le Neve. He sits clad in topper and sporting a silver cane; standing behind him, Billy Le Neve, dapper, bemoustached and, at thirty-nine, exactly half his age, looks puny in comparison. The five women comprise one petite and relatively scantily clad damsel and four Amazons, notably Norah herself. Aged forty-two and from Galashiels in Scotland, the hefty Norah aspired to success as a female boxer. The carefully posed but out-of-date photographs hid an impoverished reality. More than anyone, the Le Neves had saved Mace from the workhouse but what he got from them sufficed only for his keep and he was reduced to 'selling his handshake' for a few coppers a time.

In May, Edward VII died and was succeeded by his son George V as King of England. As ever, Mace had little interest in monarchy. His thoughts were focused on the lineal world heavyweight championship and he read the *Sporting Life* eagerly to keep up with events. In the spring of 1910, Jim Jeffries came out of retirement and signed articles to challenge Jack Johnson for the title on Independence Day, July 4. The match resulted from a flow of white supremacist propaganda led by the novelist Jack London, who had written, 'Jim, it's up to you!' Shortly afterwards, Mace received an invitation to appear on the Johnson–Jeffries undercard. The idea was that he should fight his old trainer Billy Clark who, at eighty-two, was three years older than him. The promoter was the Westerner George 'Tex' Rickard, ex-cowboy, ex-gold prospector and gambling saloon operator. Rickard succeeded in outbidding Hugh D. McIntosh, among others, and he put up a purse of $101,000 for a fight, which would take place in a specially constructed open-air stadium at Reno, Nevada, not far from Mace's old stomping ground at Virginia City.

By this time, Mace's health was at last giving way, as a result of his meagre diet and exposure to the elements. Still he maintained his charisma. A reporter from the *Sunday Chronicle* found him in April 1910 and wrote:

> And in a small overcrowded and overheated boxing booth, smelling of damp sawdust and burning naphtha . . . in a corner of the ring, seated on a chair, is a very old man. At the end of each round everybody stares at this old man – half in reverence, half in curiosity.
>
> Jem Mace is well worth staring at. He is nearly eighty years old but his face is the strongest and most striking in the crowd. It is the face of a man who in his day has been given power over his fellows. There is power in the deep-set eyes, which suggest hidden fires; power in the strong jaw and the square chin; power in the big gaunt frame; power in the twisted and knotted hands. There is power and there is pathos; for these indications of power are like surviving signposts pointing to a crumbling city. The signs are there but the power has gone and a frail old man stands where once a god among men proudly hurled his challenges to the world.

The old warhorse toyed with the idea of another visit to the States. It would give him the chance to link up with Pooley in New York but the ocean crossing, followed by the transcontinental railroad journey, seemed daunting. What's more, although Clark had never been anywhere near Mace's class, he was living off the fat of the land in St Louis and was more robust. Above all, Mace had no wish to see himself presented as part of a freak show. He sent a cable, declining. Besides anything else, Mace regarded the upcoming Johnson–Jeffries bout with the utmost scepticism. Although Jeffries was only three years older than Johnson, he had been out of the ring for six years, surely an insuperable handicap against a boxer of Johnson's stature. The whole thing stank of both racism and Rickard's desire to exploit the ballyhoo which surrounded Johnson for commercial purposes. True, Johnson's arrogant demeanour had antagonised the public, but the media hostility towards him would still have been there even if his lifestyle had been more modest. The fact was that this criticism was fuelled by racism of the grossest nature.

Throughout his life Mace had nothing to do with racism. He had known, liked and fought against such black boxers as Bob Travers and Harry Sallars. He had been not only Peter Jackson's mentor but a personal friend. And he had championed the ambitions of Sam Langford. Although Jem personally disliked Jack Johnson, he recognised him as a great boxer whose counter-attacking style and elegant movements were far closer to Macean methods than the crouching Jeffries with his swarming, abrasive approach. It was more important to Mace that the world title was in the hands of a classical boxer than that it should be held by a white man. Rather than fostering the White Hope craze, the boxing press should, he thought, have pressurised Johnson to put his title on the line against one or other of the men who could make a serious challenge for it – Jeannette, McVey and, above all, Langford. As for Jeffries, whatever his stylistic failings, he had been a worthy champion in his time and Mace had no wish to see him humiliated. In the event, Jeffries had nothing to offer but courage, and received a merciless beating from the sneering Johnson until, in the fifteenth round, 'Lil Arthur' finally relented and dispatched the ex-champion with a knockout. Jeffries was a pale shadow of the fighter he had once been but his defeat only intensified the frantic search for a White Hope.

In November 1910, Sullivan's Circus visited the North-East of England. At St James Hall in Newcastle, in what was his effective swansong, he played to a packed house. This was greatly to the chagrin of campaigning local politicians. The Prime Minister, Herbert Asquith, had called a general election and the result was expected to be close between the reforming Liberal government and the Tories, who were adamant that Ireland should not be granted home rule. Nevertheless, a reporter for the recently founded showman's journal *World's Fair* wrote as follows:

> Jem Mace was appearing with his troupe of lady athletes and gentleman boxers. It was here that the crowds were flocking, irrespective of party politics. They did not want to be bothered with political speeches, all they wanted was to see and hear the unconquered champion of the world. Their sole ambition was to gaze upon the veteran of the pugilistic ring, so that every day and every performance throughout the week the standing order in this world-famous establishment was either standing room only or house full. The reporter noted the ringing choruses that used to greet a visibly moved Mace as he took the stage.
>
> Good old Jimmy, Brave old James
> Take a list and run down all the pugilistic names
> Search in Fistiana and see if you can trace
> A man with such a record as old Jem Mace.

Sullivan's tour culminated at Jarrow Fair. One site they used was a disused pit heap where they gave shows to the people of Jarrow, one of Britain's poorest towns. The site had originally been used by Ginnett's but they had been bought out by the bustling Newcastle showman Tom Barrasford, who transformed it into an open-air theatre which he named the Jarrow Palace of Varieties. In the winter months, Barrasford leased it to the Le Neves, who lived on site in caravans and gave a performance consisting of a Punch and Judy show, a couple of clowns and a few acrobats. Mace's role was to play his beloved violin, by now his sole remaining possession apart from his cherished bust of Tom Sayers, which he refused to sell. The takings were slight and his share more meagre than ever, so during the residency he went busking in the street outside pubs, much as he had done in Great Yarmouth as a lad.

In late November, Mace caught a heavy chill and, back at the pit heap, he collapsed. Norah got four men to carry him semi-conscious about a quarter of a mile to a pub known as the Victoria. There, at Princess Street, he could at least sleep in a warm bed. She stayed with him and on the twenty-eighth he rallied and seemed much better, but his condition worsened next day and he had great difficulty breathing normally. Even the old ruse of setting a kettle near the bedside and allowing the steam to pass over the patient's breathstream failed to do the trick. At this time, all doctors required payment for attendance on a patient. Norah quickly found the necessary and took it to a local doctor named Jennings, who agreed to go to Princess Street.

On 30 November 1910, during the early hours, with Norah at his bedside, Mace passed away. He was seventy-nine.

Dr Jennings arrived, and instead of giving a detailed description of the cause of death, which might well have been pneumonia, he simply wrote down 'senile decay'. This was a form of words characteristically used on a death certificate in reference to old people of no fixed address. When Norah registered the death, her address was recorded by the clerk as 'Jarrow Pit Heap'. This was only a partial truth and smacked of typical prejudice against Romanies, the community with which Mace spent his last days. Norah Le Neve contacted Amelia McMillin as agreed and arranged for the press to be informed by telegram to the offices of the major national newspapers. The cable read simply, 'Jarrow–November 30–after short illness–Jem Mace died today.'

Epilogue

RESPONDING TO THE driver's shout of 'Whoa!' the horses
stopped beside St George's Plateau. There, where 10,000 had greeted
him nearly half a century before on his triumphal return to Liverpool,
hundreds stood in silence, heads bowed, to pay their last respects. The
hearse moved on and turned up London Road. At Norton Street, a
limousine began to follow. Inside were Nellie, veiled and weeping, and,
comforting her, his daughter Ada and her husband John, Nellie's son.
It ascended the steep hill leading away from Liverpool's city centre and
passed a tiny shuttered remnant of what had once been the glory of
the Strawberry Gardens, his sadly neglected creation. At 20 Walton
Park, on the road to Aintree Racecourse, the cortege began. Amelia,
the effective mistress of ceremonies, led it with her husband Andrew
and her surviving sons, Tom and Bill, Mace's grandsons, nearing twenty
years of age. The horses were then turned back toward the city and, a
mile further on, the carriage came to rest outside the huge municipal
burial ground on Walton Lane. Here hundreds had gathered, many of
them up from London, including pugilists young and old – but there
was no sign of A.F. Bettinson nor of Lord Lonsdale. The NSC
contented itself with a wreath.

In the Church of England section of Anfield Cemetery, the
ceremony was conducted by Alfred Mace. Tall and sombre, Alfred
remained of a different religious persuasion to all others there, including his younger brother James. Their sister Adelaide was unwell but her
husband William Turvill was present, as was Alfred's daughter Eliza,
wife of the art critic Thomas Shepherd, the oldest of a score of grandchildren, together with her younger brothers, the debonair dentist
Alfred Henry, future Wimpole Street practitioner, and John Farnham
Mace. Mace's first family blended with the already intertwined second
and third families, which included his brother-in-law Ted McCall.

Sadly but predictably there was no one from his fourth family, although Lillian, at eighteen, James, sixteen, and Amy, fifteen, could easily have made the journey. Pooley could not be there – it would have proved impossible to delay the funeral to give him time to make the Atlantic crossing – but Mace's lifelong connection with the Roma was reflected by the presence of his employers Billy and Norah Le Neve, who had accompanied the coffin on its journey by rail from Newcastle. Mace's close ties with Australia were indicated by the presence of his former business manager there, Sam Dixon. Alfred's sermon, by agreement, contained no fundamentalist rhetoric. It was brief, to the point and entirely fitting.

The local newspapers stated that it was appropriate that Mace should be laid to rest in Liverpool, and it was, but he could just as easily have been buried in Norwich*, London, Birmingham, New York, San Francisco or Melbourne. Jem Mace was truly an international man. Equally, given the poverty of his last days, his corpse could just as readily have been interred in a pauper's grave in Newcastle. There were those who expressed shock at the absence of a headstone and all but the most perfunctory numerical marker. They did not understand. Mace had never made a will and was penniless when he died. It was to Amelia's credit that she brought her father to her own family plot which she had bought nearly fifteen years before, and which already contained the remains of her infant children, Amelia Junior and Richard, who had died within months of each other in 1896, and her thirteen-year-old son James, who had died in 1904.

John Lee Mace and Andrew McMillin were both men of some means but they should not be criticised because of their pragmatic attitude towards a headstone. In the last twenty years of his life, Mace had spent barely a year with the woman who was John's mother and Andrew's mother-in-law. And, after all, a lavish memorial could have been commissioned from Lord Lonsdale's small change had the noble Earl been so inclined.

---

* Admirers in Norwich did subscribe a monumental stone in his memory. It was intended to place it permanently in Norwich Cemetery but eventually the white memorial cross was donated to the parish of Beeston, where it was ceremonially unveiled in 1976. It bears the inscription, 'Jem Mace Champion of the World'.

In the early days of December 1910, the obituaries poured out in the columns of the great newspapers of Britain and America: *The Times*, *The Manchester Guardian*, *The Washington Post* and the *New York Times* as well as in countless other titles throughout the English-speaking world. Some were more acute than others but none fully realised the significance of Mace's life.

Frank Bradley, editor of *Mirror of Life* and a man who had known Mace for thirty-five years limited his remarks to bareknuckle fighting but said this:

> In the history of the Prize Ring, the names which stand out are Broughton, Mendoza, Belcher, Gully, Cribb, Spring, Jem Ward, Sayers and King. In point of science I do not think that any one of these was a better man than Mace. It was his misfortune to appear in the ring when the patronage of pugilists had fallen from noblemen and gentlemen into the hands of flash publicans, night-house keepers and gangs of robbers, whose sole object was to fleece the fast and foolish toffs. It is greatly to Mace's credit that he kept as straight as he did . . . I say that Jem Mace is worthy to be ranked with such champions as Jem Belcher and Jem Ward and when I say that I mean very high praise indeed. I do not consider Sayers to have possessed anything like the science of Mace. Tom was a grand fighter but no one will presume to place him on the same pedestal with Mace as an artist.

England was then preoccupied by the sporting deeds of C.B. Fry, captain of England at cricket, footballer in the FA Cup Final, out-standing long jumper and excellent rugby player. Thirty-eight-year-old Fry was hailed as a true Renaissance man whose athletic prowess was complemented by his flair as a journalist, his political activism and his penchant for poetry. Fry was, of course, a scion of the upper-middle class, educated at Repton and Oxford and heir to the cultural traditions of nineteenth century England.

By contrast, Jem Mace, born in an obscure Norfolk village, the son of a roving rural working man, was, like the vast majority of boys in his class in the first half of that century, deprived of all education. He was, for the first thirty years of his life, illiterate. Stigmatised, albeit inaccurately, as a gypsy, he guarded his treasured second violin and kept it with him to the very end, testament to the career in music to which he originally aspired. When his first instrument was so cruelly trashed in Great Yarmouth, he had cleaved to a different path. His dexterous dancing, lightning reflexes, ice-cold nerve and murderously accurate punching had enabled him to rise, within a few short years, to the Championship of England – and, when harried out of the land by punctilious policemen directed by evangelistic fanatics, he had gone to America and become the first Champion of the World.

There was no one, absolutely no one, whose role could be compared to that of Jem Mace in transforming the primitive practice of pugilism into what was, at least when performed by him and those he taught or inspired, the elegant sport of glove boxing. As the first real boxer, he became a legend not merely in the lands of the British Empire but throughout the United States of America, boxing's true homeland. Not only was Mace a boxer supreme, he was an influential wrestler, as fine a fencer as could be found outside the Latin countries and a splendid runner. Given his role in the Liverpool Olympics, he was a true precursor of the revival of the Olympic Games. It was Mace also who was the first to present shows combining all these sports and also including gymnastics and cycling. As such, he was an unrecognized but significant pioneer in the transformation of the notion of sport which had prevailed in pre-industrial England into the modern international concept of sport as mass spectacle. It was a role for which, by virtue of his charismatic personality, his roots in circus shows and his journeys across the globe, he was uniquely fitted to fulfil. But, living in the moment as he did, he had scant idea of his true influence and no regard whatever for his legacy.

Throughout the nineteenth century he remained a kind of anti-hero whose values defied those of Victorian England. A circus showman, flamboyant to his fingertips, he rode roughshod over convention. A hedonist and a lover of women, Mace, in his affirmation of his polygamous nature, never promised a fidelity to which he could not adhere. In a day when few people of humble origins proceeded further than a few miles from their birthplace, unless it was to disappear for ever into an industrial city, he roamed the globe in search of risk and adventure. By his eye for a business opportunity, he made a fortune, but by his recklessness with money and incorrigible love of gambling, he lost every penny of it. The dice he rolled glittered brilliantly under the bright lights of New Orleans but came to a dusty rest in the mean streets of Jarrow. Nevertheless, vain as a peacock to the end of his years, he was immaculate even in the days of his penury.

As the ceremony ended on 6 December 1910, a biting winter wind began to scatter the floral tributes which had been sent from far and wide. One was retrieved and its words duly noted. Almost a century later, in 2002, as a result of subscriptions organised by the Merseyside Ex-Boxers' Association, a gleaming new black granite headstone was dedicated in Anfield Cemetery, Liverpool. Engraved in white, below a ring depicting two gloved combatants is the inscription:

JAMES (JEM) MACE April 8th 1831–November 30th 1910

Where Hardy Heroes Nature's Weapons Wield
He Stood Unconquered Champion Of The Field
Time Counts Him Out But Memory Will Remain
We Ne'er Shall Look On His Like Again.

Acknowledgments

I should like to thank the following: Harold Alderman, for supplying detailed notes on Mace's fighting record; Jim Jenkinson and Terry Kavanagh of the Merseyside Ex-Boxers Association for discussion on their provision of a headstone for Mace's previously unmarked grave; Eric Mace and Chris Shaw for correspondence on Mace genealogy; my son Oliver and my cousin Brian Street for encouragement of the project; Paul C., Denis Farnham Mace, Martin Farnham Mace, Clive Mannering, Diana Pursall and Chris Shaw for photographs, Erik de Jonge and Robins Jans of Active8 for the design of my website www.jemmace.net and my publisher Peter Walsh for his appreciation of Mace's place in sporting history.

APPENDIX

Jem Mace's Fight Record

As well as his competitive fights, Mace boxed numerous exhibitions and non-competitive demonstrations. Only the more significant of these latter have been mentioned below. For Mace's early record (1849–55), I have relied on his own account in his autobiography and in interviews. For his later record in Britain (1855–1909), my thanks are due to boxing historian Harold Alderman, a member of International Boxing Research Organisation and voting member of the Boxing Hall of Fame. I compiled the list from extensive notes kindly supplied by Harold. Any inaccuracies are mine, not his. For Mace's record in the USA, Canada, Australia, New Zealand and South Africa, I have relied principally on the Cyberboxingzone website and on archive American newspapers.

1849–50

Sydney Smith	Wisbech, Cambs	W (two hours)
Charlie Pinfold	Norwich Hill	W4
Farden Smith	Norwich Hill	5 disrupted by police.

Smith conceded defeat at Mousewell Hill next day

Tom Brewer	Horncastle, Lincs	W (one hour 50 minutes)

1850

Apr 17	John Pratt	Drayton, Norfolk	L50 (two hours ten minutes)

1851

Jan 14	John Pratt	Drayton, Norfolk	W10 (30 minutes)

1851-5
Proprietor of a travelling boxing booth, taking on all-comers with the gloves.

1852

Nov 12	Tom Harvey	Harlaston, Staffs	W31	(one hour)

1855

Oct 2	Bob Slack	Mildenhall, Suffolk	W9	(19 minutes)

1856
Beats Lord Drumlanrig, Johnnie Walker, Mo Betson and an unnamed fighter all in one evening with the gloves at Nat Langham's club in London.

1857

Feb 17	Bill Thorpe	Canvey Island, Essex	W18	(27 minutes)

Oct 20   Mike Madden. Unknown location. Both men were in the ring but Mace objected to the referee because he had allegedly bet on Madden, and refused to fight. *Bell's Life* ruled that Mace had forfeited.

1858

May 10   Failed to show for fight with Mike Madden. Indicted for cowardice in columns of *Bell's Life*.

Sept 21	Bob Brettle	Medway Bank, Kent	L2	(three minutes)

Middleweight Championship of England

1859

Jan 25	Posh Price	Hants-Surrey border	W11	(70 minutes)

1860

Feb 20	Bob Travers	Kent Marshes	6	(21 minutes) disrupted by police

Feb 21	Bob Travers	Kent Marshes	W57	(one hour 31 minutes)

Sept 19	Bob Brettle	Wallingford, Oxon	6	(12 minutes) disrupted by police

Middleweight Championship of England

Sept 20	Bob Brettle	Foulness Island, Essex	W5	(seven minutes)

Middleweight Championship of England

1861

June 18   Sam Hurst   Medway Island, Kent   W8   (50 minutes)
            Heavyweight Championship of England

1862

Jan 28   Tom King   Godstone, Surrey   W43   (one hour eight
                                                   minutes)
            Heavyweight Championship of England

Nov 26   Tom King   Thameshaven, Essex   L21   (38 minutes)
            Heavyweight Championship of England

Mace challenged King to a rematch but on December 7 King announced his retirement and returned the Championship Belt to the offices of *Bell's Life*, which declared that the title was in abeyance until Mace fought for it with a new challenger.

1863

Sept 1   Joe Goss   Wootton Bassett, Wilts   1   (four minutes)
                                                   disrupted by police
                  Middleweight Championship of England

Sept 1   Joe Goss   Plumstead, Kent   W19   (one hour
                                                  55 minutes)
                  Middleweight Championship of England

1864

Joe Coburn (Champion of America) challenged Mace (no longer recognised as Champion of England). Both men agreed to fight in Ireland. But Mace, objecting to Coburn's nominated referee, refused to proceed beyond Dublin.

1865

Jan 4   Joe Wormald recognised by the Pugilistic Benevolent Association as new Champion of England after defeating Andrew Marsden.

May 15   Signed articles to meet Joe Wormald on September 26 for the Championship of England.

Sept 21   Wormald cried off with injury. Wormald told to pay Mace forfeit but the P.B.A. refused to recognise Mace as champion until he regained the title in the ring.

1866

May 24 Joe Goss   Meopham, Kent   D1   (one hour and
                                                                40 minutes)

Both fighters inactive throughout.

Heavyweight Championship of England

P.B.A. resolved that neither Mace nor Goss could contend for the title again
but after Mace successfully argued that he had attempted to fight despite an
ankle injury and had returned all stake money to his backers, Mace and Goss
were allowed to fight again for the title.

Aug 6   Joe Goss   Purfleet, Essex   W21   (31 minutes)

Heavyweight Championship of England

1867

Oct 15 Scheduled to meet Ned O'Baldwin for Heavyweight Championship
        of England but Mace arrested the night before and bound over not
        to fight again.

1868

Inactive

1869

Sept 15 Arrived in New York City accompanied by his cousin Pooley Mace.
         Subsequently toured the U.S. with John C. Heenan giving sparring
         exhibitions.

1870

May 10 Tom Allen   Kennerville, La.   W10   (44 minutes)

World Heavyweight Championship

1871

May 11 Joe Coburn   Port Ryeson, Canada   D1   (one hour
                                                                17 minutes)

World Heavyweight Championship

*Not a blow was struck. After the arrival of police, the bout was abandoned, called a draw
and re-scheduled for June 2.*

June 2   Kansas City, Mo. Mace was present but Coburn did not show.

Nov 30 Joe Coburn   Bay St. Louis, Miss.   D12   (three hours
                                                                38 minutes)

Heavyweight Championship of the World

1872

Mace conducted an exhibition tour of California with Billy Edwards and Pooley.

Aug 13 Scheduled to fight Ned O'Baldwin for Heavyweight Championship of the World but both arrested in Baltimore and placed under heavy bonds not to fight in the state of Maryland.

Aug 15 After release, O'Baldwin went to West Virginia where the fight was originally scheduled to take place but Mace, having objected to the nominated referee, refused to proceed.

1873 and **1874**

Inactive.

1875

Boxed exhibitions against Joe Goss in London.

1876

Apr 15 Arrived in New York accompanied by Joe Goss. Boxed exhibitions there and in Toronto, Canada.

Dec 16 Bill Davis   Virginia City, Nv.   W8

This was a historic early contest between two professionals under Marquess of Queensberry rules. The referee awarded the bout to Mace by 52 hits to 33.

1877

Jan 26 Bill Davis   San Francisco   WKO4
(Queensberry Rules)

Mar 3   Mace arrived in Sydney, Australia. Over the next five years he would box numerous exhibitions in Sydney, Melbourne and Hobart, Tasmania, often against Larry Foley, John M. Christie or Jack Thompson.

1882

March 7 Mace arrived in Auckland, New Zealand, and went on to box numerous exhibitons all over the country, most often against William Miller, Fred Edmonds and Herbert Slade (who he signed to a managerial contract).

1883

Jan 6   Arrived in San Francisco accompanied by Herbert Slade. Boxed
           exhibitions with Slade in California, New York, Connecticut,
           Ohio and Pennsylvania.

May 9   Mace and Herbert Slade arrived in Liverpool. They box exhibitions
           in Sheffield, London, Manchester, Birmingham, Chester, Leicester
           and Newcastle.

1884–90
Mace boxed numerous exhibitions throughout the UK, often against his
cousin Pooley Mace, Jack Smith and Wolf Bendoff.

1890

Feb 7   Charlie Mitchell   Glasgow   No valid
                                                   decision 4
This bout has wrongly been described as being for the championship of
England under Queensberry Rules. Although judges were appointed, Mace
was led to believe it was a sparring exhibition. When Mitchell broke that
agreement, Mace fought back. As the fight was ending, police intervened and,
amid confusion, Mitchell prompted the judges to announce a points decision
in his favour.

1890–95
Various exhibitions, including one against Dick Burge on 15 October 1995 at
the National Sporting Club, Covent Garden, London, for which he received a
standing ovation from the members.

1896

Dec 14   Mike Donovan   New York   D6
                         Veterans Championship of the World

1897

Sept 3   Mike Donovan   Birmingham   D6
                         Veterans Championship of the World

1898–1900
Inactive

1901–1909
For the rest of his life, Mace would box occasional exhibitions, all in the UK
apart from a brief sojourn in South Africa. His final known appearance was on

2 October 1909, against Bill Bayford, at Bluetown in the Isle of Sheppey, Kent.

Mace's traceable record in competitive fights is:

London Prize Ring Rules	W15	D3	L3	
Early Glove Contests	W5	D0	L0	
Queensberry Rules	W2	D2	L0	ND 1

Children of Jem Mace

JAMES 'JEM' MACE (1831-1910)

=1	Mary Barton	(1834-67)
		James I (1852-7)
		Alfred b.1854
		Adelaide b.1856 = William Turvill
		James II b. 1858

| =2 | Selina Hart | (1842-?) |
| | | Frances 'Fanny' b.1860 |

=3	Hannah Boorn	(1847-88)
		Amelia b. 1865 = Andrew McMillin
		Ada b.1867 = John Lee
		Benjamin (1871-83)

| =4 | Ellen 'Nellie' Gore Lee b.1852 |
| | | Ellen I (1876-95) |

=5	Alice Stokes	(1872-1908)
		Lillian b.1892
		James III b.1894
		Amy b.1895
		Albert (1898-9)
		Ellen II 'Ella' b.1905

Note: All women of whose children he acknowledged paternity are included, irrespective of status of/absence of marriage. Dates of death for other persons only included if event occurred during his lifetime.

Sources

Books

Bottle, William J.M., *Datas The Memory Man*, Wright and Brown

Brailsford, Dennis, *Bare Knuckles: A Social History of Prize-Fighting*, Lutterworth Press

Deghy, Guy, *Noble and Manly: the History of the National Sporting Club*, Hutchinson

Doherty, W.J., *In the Days of the Giants*, George G. Harrap

Fleischer, Nat, and Andre, Sam, *An Illustrated History of Boxing*, Citadel Press

Gee, Tony, 'Jem Mace (1831-1910)' in *Oxford Dictionary of National Biography*

Gorman, Bartley and Walsh, Peter, *King of the Gypsies*, Milo Books

Gorn, Elliott J., *The Manly Art: A History of Bare-Knuckle Fighting in America*, Cornell University

Henning, Fred, *Fights for the Championship: The Men and their Times*, Licensed Victuallers Gazette

Isenberg, Michael T., *John L. Sullivan and his America*, University of Illinois Press

Jackson, Lee, *Victorian London*, New Holland

Lahey, John, *Damn You, John Christie: The Public Life of Australia's Sherlock Holmes*, State Library of Victoria

Mace, Jem, *Fifty Years A Fighter*, Sporting Life

McCall, Ted, *Recollections about Jem Mace*, unpublished.

Miles, Henry Downton, *Pugilistica*, The Author

Montague, C.W., *Recollections of an Equestrian Director*, Chambers

Myler, Patrick, *Gentleman Jim Corbett: The Truth Behind a Boxing Legend*, Robson Books

O'Connor, Freddie, *A Pub on Every Corner*, Bluecoat Press

Odd, Gilbert, *The Fighting Blacksmith: A Biography of Bob Fitzsimmons*, Pelham

Sutherland, Douglas, *The Yellow Earl: The Life of Hugh Lowther, Fifth Earl of Lonsdale 1857-1944*, Cassell

Van Every, Edward, *Sins of New York City*, Richard K. Fox Gazette

Ward, Geoffrey C., *Unforgivable Blackness: The Rise and Fall of Jack Johnson*, Knopf

Articles

Austin, Professor A., 'A Bout with Gloves', *Journal of Manly Arts*

Parker, Christine, 'An Investigation into the Australian Passion for Sport' in *Australian Studies*, November 1996

Phillips, Bob, 'The Liverpool "Olympic Festivals" of the 1860s', www.noeaa-athletics.org.uk

Stoddard, Charles, 'La Belle Menken', *The National Magazine*

Wiggins, David K., 'Peter Jackson and the Elusive Heavyweight Championship', *The Journal of Sporting History*

Boxing websites

www.antekprizering.com
www.aussiebox.com
www.boxrec.com
www.cyberboxingzone.com
www.coxscorner.tripod.com
www.eastsideboxing.com
www.geocities.com/kiwiboxing
www.iabpff/regions/site/samlangford
www.ibhof.com

Newspapers

Atchison Globe, Atlanta Constitution, Arizona Republican, Brooklyn Eagle, Butte Daily News, Chester Chronicle, Delphos Herald, Edinburgh Courant, Edwardsville Intelligencer, Fort Wayne Gazette, Fresno Republican, Hagerston Herald and Torch Light, Liverpool Citizen, Liverpool Daily Courant, Liverpool Daily Post and Echo, Liverpool Mercury, Lowell Daily Sun, Manchester Guardian, Marion Daily Star, Nebraska State Journal, Newark Daily Advocate, New Orleans Times-Picayune, New York Illustrated News, New York Times, Oakland Tribune, Ohio Democrat, Port Philip Herald, Reno Evening Gazette, San Francisco Chronicle, Sedalia Daily Democrat, Staffordshire Sentinel, Steubenville Herald, Sunday Chronicle, Syracuse Post Telegraph, The Sportsman, The Times, Timaru Herald, Titusville Morning Herald, Trenton Times, Washington Post.

Periodicals
Bell's Life in London, Mirror of Life, National Police Gazette, Richard J. Fox Gazette, Sporting Life, The Era, World's Fair

The Circus
www.100greatblackbritons.com/pablo fanque
www.peopleplay.org.uk
www.thegalloper.com
www.fairground-heritage.org.uk

Fencing
www.fencing101.com
www.fencing.net

Victorian London
www.victorianlondon.org

California and Nevada in the Nineteenth Century
www.sfmuseum.org
www.sfgenealogy.com
www.raken.com/american wealth

Colonial Australia
Dictionary of Australian National Biography
www.bailup.com/ned kelly

Romanies
Journal of the Gypsy Lore Society Scott Macfie Collection Liverpool University
www.patrin-web.com (Journal of Romany History and Lore)

Adah Isaacs Menken
Adah Isaacs Menken by Seymour Brody at Florida State University Library
Adah Isaacs Menken by Samuel Dickson at Museum of San Francisco

Judicial
Mace vs Mace and Roberts 1863–4, National Archives, Kew
Mace vs Mace and Harris 1884, National Archives, Kew

Genealogy

Parish Register of Beeston-next-Mileham, Norfolk

Marriage Register of Great Fransham, Norfolk

General Register Office, Southport (various certificates of birth, marriage and death)

City of New York Department of Records Register of Marriages (Mace-Lee marriage certificate)

Census Records of England and Wales 1841–1901, National Archives, Kew

Census Records of Scotland. General Register Office for Scotland, Edinburgh

U.S. Federal Census 1870 and 1900, Bureau of the Census. Washington D.C.

Miscellaneous

www.senate.gov/senators/conkling

www.gmrs.com. Geppi's Memorabilia Road Show Timonium. Md.

www.lafavre.us/brush

British Film Institute Archives

Gore's Street Directories of Liverpool

National Museum of Photography, Film and Television

New York Passenger Lists Port of New York 1851–1901

Philp, A.J., *Papers of the Swedenborgian Society*, Stoke Newington

Register of Alehouse Licences, City of Liverpool

Index

Aaron, Barney, 227, 341, 342, 353
Abrahams, Fred, 45, 199, 205, 209, 211,
    219, 220, 225, 227, 245, 247, 252,
    255, 340
Acres, Birt, 426
Akrigg, William, 478
Albert, Prince Consort, 127
Albison, Siah, 45, 118
Alexander II, Tsar, 116
Ali, Muhammad, ix
Allen Theodore, 207
Allen, Tom, 167, 170, 198, 209, 210, 213,
    214, 219n, 231, 234, 239, 241, 254,
    255, 266, 274, 279; background, 169;
    emigrates to U.S., 170; character, 198;
    becomes American citizen, 198;
    challenges Mace for world title,
    209–210; fight with Mace for world
    title at Kennerville, 215–19; regains
    American championship, 265; fight
    with Goss in Kentucky, 272
Angle, Bernard John, 373, 403, 411, 442
Asquith, Herbert, 483
Astley, Philip, 61
Atkinson, George, 372
Attell, Abe, 472

Bailey, Annie, 325
Baird, George (Squire Abingdon), 364–5,
    366, 385, 386, 387, 388, 409, 420
Baker, Lurena (Lurena Mace), 4, 10
Barclay, Captain, 33
Barkley, James, 184, 185
Barnato, Barney, 449
Barnes, Jim, 426
Barrasford, Tom, 483
Bartholdi, 428
Barton, Martha, 65, 78, 111, 112, 121, 144
Barton, Mary Ann (Mary Ann Mace), 20,
    25, 31, 32, 77, 78, 112, 462, 487;

background, 17; marries Mace, 17;
children by Mace, 20, 31, 32, 33; at
White Swan, Norwich, 33, 35; head
for business, 54; at Old King John,
Shoreditch, 62, 65; and Mace's
adultery with Selina Hart, 112, 113;
Mace never violent to, 114; Deed of
Separation, 114–5; association with
Dick Roberts, 113, 121, 122; unaware
of Mace's relationship with Hannah
Boorn, 124; Mace v Mace and
Roberts, 124–127; incarnated upward
social mobility for Mace, 398; death
of, 164
Batty, William, 59
Bauer, Theobald, 311
Bayford, Betty, 461, 476
Bayford, Bill, 428, 459, 461, 476, 477
Beatles, The, 60n
Beesley, Mr, 125
Belcher, Jem, 73, 219, 487
Bendoff, Wolf, 449, 461
Bennett, Charles E., 250, 251
Beresford, Lord Charles, 339, 366
Berg, Kid, 360
Bettinson A. F. 'Peggy' 367, 377, 402,
    403, 405, 419, 440, 443, 444, 462,
    469, 470–1, 473, 475, 485
Bird, Sam, 376
Bishop, James, 149
Bittan, Ned, 287
Blackburn, Charlie, 370
Blondin, 67, 96, 97, 182
Blythe, Bunny, 12, 18, 28–9, 61
Boorn, Alfred, 115
Boorn, Ben, 115, 116, 117, 194
Boorn, Fanny see Fanny Jacey
Boorn, Hannah (Hannah Mace Hannah
    Harris), 153, 155, 194, 199, 220, 221,
    223, 248, 254, 260, 327, 334, 360,

428, 451, 462, 467; background,
115–6; meets Mace, 116; falls in love
with Mace, 117; Mace's business
relationship with her father, 117;
complicit with Mace in bigamous
marriage, 123; children with Mace,
144, 165, 245; and Mace's children by
Mary Ann Barton, 165; friction with
Mace over his relationship with Adah
Isaacs Menken 186, 194; rejoins Mace
in New York, 211; household at W.
23rd St., 211; returns to England with
Mace, 255; told by Mace their
marriages is over, 264; bigamous
marriage with George Harris, 337;
quarrel with her daughter Ada, 357;
complete break with both her
daughters, 358; Mace v Mace and
Harris, 358–60; incarnated grace and
beauty of equestrianism for Mace,
398; death, 374
Booth, C. F., 220
Borrow, George, 5, 476
Boucicault, Dion, 297
Bowler, James, 132
Brabach, 45
Bradford, Superintendent, 119
Bradley, Frank, 477, 487
Brady, Diamond Jim, 455
Brady, William, 411, 418, 424
Brettle, Bob, ix, 38, 40–1, 43, 56, 57, 70,
89, 168–9, 177, 267, 389
Broome, Johnny, 46, 47
Broughton, Jack, 21, 310, 373, 487
Brown, George, 39
Brunton, Harry, 68, 131, 132
Brush, Charles, 333
Burge, Dick, 419, 422
Burke, Jack, 361, 384, 426, 427, 429
Burnand, Sir Frank, 157
Burns, Tommy, 431, 432, 463, 465, 468,
469, 470
Bush, Charlie, 119
Butt, Charles P., 359
Byrne, Joe, 300
Byron, Lord George, 180

Callaghan, Clay, 305
Cardiff, Patsy, 380, 406
Carlyle, Thomas, 164
Carney, Jem, 387

Carstairs, 196, 286
Caunt, Ben, 24
Chamberlain, Joseph, 438
Chambers, Arthur, 177, 188, 192, 242,
246, 251, 254, 255, 318, 429
Chambers, John Graham, 188, 189, 190,
191, 192, 219, 273, 277, 353, 366,
367, 396, 403
Chandler, Tommy, 249
Chandler, Senator Zach, 242, 243, 245
Choynsky, Joe, 380, 394, 406, 408, 421,
427, 430, 441, 443, 465
Christie, John M., 288, 291, 308
Churchill, Lord Randolph, 208, 371
Churchill, Winston, 208, 341, 371
Clark, Billy, 30, 34, 35, 61, 104, 481, 482
Coburn, Jem, 234
Coburn, Joe, 130, 132, 133, 214, 217,
238, 272, 314, 315, 328, 463;
background, 128; challenges Mace,
130; proclaims himself world
champion, 133; reclaims American
championship, 193; bad blood
between him and Mace, 224–5;
incident at Mace's saloon, 226; fiasco
of first fight with Mace, 228–9; no-
show at Kansas City, 232; fight with
Mace for world title at Bay St. Louis,
234–7; possible role in conspiracy to
murder Mace, 240; sentenced to ten
years jail for assault, 289
Cochran, C. B., 466
Collins, Wilkie, 97
Collyer, Sam, 249
Comstock, Henry, 269
Coney, Jack, 173, 175, 177
Conkling, Senator Roscoe, 242, 243,
244, 326
Conn, Billy, ix
Cook, Hiriam, 408
Coppin, George, 307
Corbett, Jim, viii, 380, 406, 407, 408, 409,
411, 418, 423, 426, 427, 429, 430,
432, 439, 443, 447, 463, 465, 474;
taught by Watson in Macean style,
380, 396; background and personality
406–7; beats Sullivan to become first
gloved world heavyweight champion,
412; first meeting with Mace, 418;
refuses to fight Jackson, 424; Mace's
stylistic successor, 427; meets Mace in

New York, 430; states he absorbed
Mace's style and adapted it, 430–1;
praised by Mace as finest boxer he
ever saw, 431; fight with
Fitzsimmons, 432–3; KO'd by solar
plexus punch, 433; fights with
Jeffries, 441–2, 447
Corri, Eugene, 442
Coubertin, Baron Pierre de, 140
Couper, Jim, 449
Courthorpe, George, 120, 121
Courtney, Peter, 426
Craig, Frank, 421, 422
Creedon, Dan, 420, 421, 422, 423, 426,
427
Cremorne, Lord, 148
Cribb, Tom, 487
Crittenden, Governor Thomas T., 344
Cromwell, Canon John, 156
Cubitt, Thomas, 26
Cumberland, Duke of, 21, 393
Curran, Tom, 291
Cusick, Jim, 213, 217, 227, 233, 237, 238,
246, 255

Darby John, 59
Datas (William Bottle), 439, 456, 457,
460, 462
Davenpor the actor, 227
Davies Charles 'Parson', 381, 382, 385,
388, 410, 424
Davis, Bill, 198, 273, 274, 275, 276, 277,
278, 286, 395, 379, 406, 429
Davies, Jack, 351, 362
Dawson, George, 426
Deeds, Edmund, 229, 230
Deerfoot, 80
Dempsey, Jack, ix, 463
Dempsey, Nonpareil Jack, 390, 393, 394,
395, 420
Derby, 14th Earl of, 146
Derby, 15th Earl of, 146
Dickens Charles, 52, 96–7, 164, 166, 179,
185, 186
Dinnie, Donald, 444
Dismore, Dan, 35, 46
Ditcham, Bill, 292
Ditcham, Hannah, 196
Ditcham, John, 196
Ditcham, Tom, 292
Dixon, George, 49

Dixon, Sam, 399–400, 412, 485
Doherty, Bill, 283
Doherty, William, 283, 284, 292
Donaghue, Judge, 327
Donaldson, John, 312–3
Donnelly, Ned, 379, 471
Donovan, Jerry, 213, 217, 227, 255, 314,
429
Donovan, Mike, 312, 315, 379, 381, 412,
418, 419, 430, 431, 435
Dooley, Mick, 304, 308, 320, 368, 389,
391, 395, 427
Dowling, Frank, 93, 119, 135; influence
as editor of *Bell's Life*, 31; character
31; initial praise of Mace, 32; indicts
Mace for cowardice after Madden
fiasco, 35; insults Mace before first
fight with Brettle, 40; advises Mace to
stick to teaching boxing, 41; describes
Mace as chicken-hearted, 43; revises
his opinion of Mace, 56; rescinds his
criticism of Mace, 67; presents Mace
in *Bell's Life* printing room, 93–4
Dowling, Vincent George, 31
Driscoll, Jim, 472
Drumlanrig, Lord (Archibald Henry
Douglas, eighth Marquess of
Queensberry), 28, 39, 188, 194; and
the Douglas curse, 38; helps to save
Mace's career, 38; found shot dead, 38
Ducros, Andrew, 180
Dumas, Alexandre, 185, 186
Dutch Sam, 294, 354
Dwyer, Johnny, 227, 251, 252, 279
Dylan, Bob, 15n

Early, Mr, 326
Edson, Franklin, 32
Edward VII (Edward, Prince of Wales),
127, 179, 371, 443, 481
Edwards, Billy, 177, 178, 192, 206, 211,
225, 226, 227, 246, 247, 249, 250,
251, 253, 254, 255, 289, 379, 429
Elmes, H. L., 162
Erlanger, Abe, 453

Fanque, Pablo (William Darby), 60, 65,
88; background, 59; sets up Circus
Royal, 59–60; invites Mace to tour
North of England, 60–1; and Mace's
second tour, 80; death, 86

Farnan, Bill, 303, 361, 368

Figg, James, 387

Fillis, Abe, 449

Fitzpatrick, Sam, 382, 468, 469, 473

Fitzsimmons, Bob, 317, 318, 320, 394, 410, 412, 423, 432, 439, 446, 447, 456, 457, 463, 465, 470, 474; discovered by Mace, 309; learns shot to the mark from Mace, 310; English background, 319; tremendous punching power, 320, 394; goes for tuition at White Horse, 361; fights with Hall, 390; bankrolled to go to America, 390; derided by American sportswriters, 390; wins world middleweight title, 394; a Macean body puncher, 395; defends title against Hall and Creedon, 420–1; bullied into applying for US citizenship, 421; friendly relations with Mace, 425; reminded by Mace of shot to the mark, 426, 427; fight with Corbett for world heavyweight title, 432–3; fights with Jeffries 440, 446–7

Fitzsimmons, Jarrett, 319

Fitzsimmons, Jim, 319

Fleming, John, 366–7, 370, 371, 372, 381, 385, 387, 402, 403, 405, 410, 444

Flood, John, 313

Foley, Larry, ix, 290, 291, 296, 297, 300, 457; background and early career, 290; seeks out Mace out, 290; Mace teaches him, 293–4; challenges Hicken for championship of Australia, 294–6; sets up as boxing trainer at White Horse in Sydney, 298; teaches Macean style at the White Horse, 304; discovers Peter Jackson, 306; White Horse first of the world's great boxing gyms, 307; updates Mace on Australian boxing, 361, 368, 374; schools Murphy and Hall, 389; spots Griffo in a gang fight, 392; Jackson-Slavin vindication of his tuition, 410; Fitzsimmons-Hall a tribute to his tuition, 420; regarded as stingy by Australian fighters, 409; retires, becomes demolition contactor, 457

Ford, Henry, 469

Ford, Robert, 344

Fonda, Jane, 95

Foreman, George, ix

Fortune, Patrick, 258

Fox the cabinet maker, 9

Fox, Richard Kyle, 325, 326, 328, 334, 339, 347, 350, 392, 411; background, 311; influence as proprietor of *Police Gazette*, 311; pioneer of tabloid journalism, 311; clash of personalities with Sullivan, 314; hopes Mace himself will challenge Sullivan, 321; hypes Slade, 325; promotes Mitchell, 328; awards Diamond Belt to Kilrain, 369; proclaims Kilrain champion of the world, 373; preoccupied with Kilrain rather than scientific boxers, 392

Franklin, Benjamin, 245

Frazier, Joe, 434

Fry, C. B., viii, 487

Fuller, Bob, 45, 47

Fullmer, Gene, ix

Futch, Eddie, ix, 307n

Gallagher, Charlie, 198, 241

Gans, Joe, 464

Gautier, Theophile, 185

Geoeghan, Ownie, 207, 208, 231, 232

George III, 22

George IV, 22, 417, 443

George V, 481

Gideon, Johnny, 92, 362

Gilbert, Tompkin, 279

Ginnett, Frederick, background of, 86; rivalry with Fanque, 86; offers Mace tour, 87; offers Mace another contract, 261

Gladstone, William, 224, 263, 264

Glick, Governor, 344

Goddard, Joe, 384, 391, 406, 408, 409, 426

Goldberg, William, 366

Goldman, Charlie, ix, 307n

Goode, Bill 'Chesterfield', 385

Gore, Ellen, 257

Gore, George, 257, 258

Gore, Nellie (Nellie Mace), see Nellie Lee

Gorman, Bartley I, 134, 135, 136

Gorman, Bartley V, 135

Gorman, Johnny, 445

Goss, Joe 104, 107, 157, 158, 160, 169,
170, 266, 279, 286, 297, 374;
background and personality, 103–4;
challenges Mace for middleweight
title, 103; first fight with Mace,
108–110; challenges Mace at
heavyweight, 156; fiasco of second
Mace fight, 156–8; summoned by
Mace to Liverpool, 159; overruled in
arrangements for third fight, 159;
arrested with Mace at Croxall, 159;
third fight with Mace, 161–2; joins
exodus to USA, 170; returns to
England, 241; returns to US with
Mace, 267; fight with Allen, 272; loses
American title to Ryan, 311; endorses
Sullivan, 314; alcoholism, 315; death
361
Gotch, Frank, 471
Greenfield, Alf, 360, 361, 363, 368, 376
Griffo, Young, 391–2, 412, 421, 426, 427,
457
Grimshaw, Atkinson, 385, 388
Gully, John, 487

Habbingham, Bob, 379
Hackenschmidt, George, 444, 445, 471,
475, 476
Hague, Iron, 475, 476
Haig, Thomas, 199, 227
Hall, Jack, 419
Hall, Jim, ix, 389–90, 392, 420, 421, 426,
427, 429
Hall, Rev. George, 476, 477, 478
Hargrave, Phil, 205, 222, 255
Harris, Dooney, 249
Harris, George, 337, 338, 358, 359, 374
Hart, Frances, 49
Hart, Frances 'Fanny' (Mace's daughter),
49
Hart, Marvin, 463
Hart, Selina, 123, 357, 462; background,
49; meets Mace, 50; visits West End
clubs, 50–1; pregnant by Mace, 53;
jilted, 55; birth of her daughter by
Mace, 55
Hart, Steve, 300
Hart, Tom, 238, 240
Harte, Bret, 183
Hathaway, Ida, 455
Heenan, John C., 119, 130, 183, 241, 381;
background 203, 246; fights with
Sayers for world title, 51–3; returns to
England but refuses to challenge
Mace, 102; fights King at Wadhurst,
120; bound over and returns to
States, 120; comparison with Mace
and Sayers, 133; marriage to Adah
Isaacs Menken, 181–2; welcomes
Mace to New York for series of
exhibitions, 203; outclassed as boxer
by Mace, 205; becomes good friend
of Mace, 255; death of, 265–6
Heffernan, Bill, 426
Hengler, Charles, 60, 115
Henry, Sir Thomas, 176
Herne, Sanspi, 265
Hicken, Abe, 287, 288, 290, 291, 292,
293, 294, 295, 296, 297
Hicks, Jack, 47, 55, 82, 84, 112, 125–6,
172, 360
Hill, Harry, 205, 206, 208, 325, 328, 336,
343, 355, 360; background, 203; club
in New York, 203; knifed in fracas,
226; in danger of his life, 232; refuses
to hold stake for Mace-O'Baldwin,
251; learns of threats to Mace's life,
252; accommodates Mace's party at
his Flushing mansion, 325;
stakeholder for abortive Mitchell-
Slade fight, 343–5
Hodgkiss, Jem, 70, 71
Holden, George, 159, 169
Hollywood, Dick, 227, 229, 232, 266
Horne Payne, Mr, 125
Hoyles, Joe, 54
Hulley, John, 141, 142, 146, 155, 191, 292
Humphreys, Richard, 73
Hunt, Colonel Rufus, 214, 234, 235,
236, 237, 238, 239
Hurst, Sam, 71, 72, 73, 154, 267; becomes
Champion of England, 64; minimal
skill, 64; a champion wrestler, 65; low
intelligence of, 65; Mace's pen
portrait of, 69; fight with Mace for
the championship, 69–71
Hutton, Tommy, 65, 89

Jacey, Fanny (Fanny Boorn), 211, 261
Jacey, William, 115, 211
Jackman the publican, 11
Jackson, Peter, ix, 306, 320, 361, 368,

382, 384, 385, 387, 388, 389, 390,
391, 392, 408, 409, 410, 411, 413,
423, 424, 426, 427, 436, 457, 465,
474, 482; Afro-Caribbean
background, 305, 382; learns to box
in Australia, 305; told by Mace he
would be champion of Australia, 306;
wins Australian title, 369; Slavin's
animosity towards, 369, 374; relocates
to California, 374, 380; appointed
professor of boxing at California A.
C., 380; impresses Lord Lonsdale,
382; crushes Jem Smith at Pelican
Club, 383–4; resurrects Mace's boxing
science, 384; Sullivan refuses to fight
on grounds of race, 390–1; fight with
Corbett in San Francisco, 406, 407–8;
fight with Slavin, 410–11; Jackson-
Slavin first fight in modern
heavyweight boxing history, 411;
helps out Mace out with cash gift,
436; challenges Corbett for title in
vain, 424; regarded by Mace as finest
exponent of his school, 395;
alcoholism, 436; death of, 437
James, Edwin, 132
James, Jesse, 344
Jamieson, Champion, 194
Jeanette, Joe, 465, 482
Jeffries, Jim, 436, 439, 440, 443, 445, 446,
447, 463, 465, 481, 482
Jennings, Dr., 484
Jerome, Jenny, 208
Jerome, Leonard W., 208, 341
Joel, Solly, 449
Johnson, Jack, 465, 468, 469, 470, 4 71,
472–3, 476, 481, 482
Jones, Jack
Jourdan, Maggie, 225

Keene, Alex, 46
Kelly, Dan, 300
Kelly, Ned, x, 299–301
Kelly, Tom, 234, 251
Kilrain, Jake, 369, 370, 371, 372, 373,
380, 381, 384, 406, 426
King, Jack, 302
King, Tom, 81, 99, 129, 374, 389, 487;
background, 79, 92; character and
personality, 79; challenges Mace at
Medway Island, 79; meteoric rise, 18;

hero of Stepney, 82; first fight with
Mace, 82–5; tours with Mace for
Ginnett, 87; gentleman's agreement
with Mace for a rematch, 80; friendly
with Mace despite contrast in
temperament, 88; wins
Championship of England from
Mace at Thames Haven, 92; friendly
with Mace and Sayers, 98; shock
retirement of, 99–100, street fight
with Mace outside Tattersalls,
100–101; defeats Heenan at
Wadhurst, 120; bound over at Lewes,
120; comparative merits of King,
Mace, Sayers and Heenan, 133;
retirement, 101; death of, 376
Knifton, Jack, 279, 39, 351, 360, 361,
364, 365, 376
Kruger, Paul, 450

Lang, Bill, 45, 118, 462
Langford, Sam, 464, 465, 469, 475–6;
debut at National Sporting Club 463;
background and character, 464;
introduced by Mace to Lonsdale, 465;
fight with Johnson, 465; Lonsdale's
praise of, 468; Johnson turns him
down for title shot, 473; urged by
Mace to campaign for middleweight
title, 482
Langham, George, 265
Langham, Nat, 27, 160, 196, 367, 448,
479; background, 39; discovers Mace
at Lincoln Fair, 18; angered by Mace's
loss to Pratt, 19; 'pickaxe' left jab, 21;
wants to keep Mace out of limelight,
26, 29; summons Mace to London,
26; runs Cambrian Stores, 27;
proprietor of Rum-pum-pas Club,
28; involvement with Mace's abortive
fight with Madden, 33; bans Mace
from Rum-pum-pas, 37; persuaded
by Drumlanrig to rehabilitate Mace,
39; backs King at Godstone, 88; drops
King, 89; detested in the East End,
98; promotes Mace-Goss, 2, 156;
Mace distances himself from, 173;
death of, 227
Large Frank, 273
Lavigne, Kid, 429
Lea, Dan, 319

Lee, John (John Lee Mace), 258, 263,
265, 267, 278, 292, 333, 355, 356,
375, 399, 453, 480, 485, 416
Lee, Nellie (Nellie Gore) (Nellie Mace),
258, 259, 271, 278, 289, 290, 292,
307, 310, 314, 325, 327, 328, 356,
358, 364, 375, 399, 429, 451, 455,
480; background, 257; ability as
pianist and vocalist, 258; joins
Ginnett, 258; marriage and
motherhood, 258; meets Mace, 261;
she and Mace become lovers, 262;
birth of daughter to Mace, 267;
rejoins Mace in America, 268;
musical accompanist of Mace on
world tour, 223, 310; unable to
conceive again, 334; bonds with
Mace's daughters from previous
marriage, 337, 356, 358, 360;
bigamous marriage with Mace, 340;
returns to England with Mace, 354;
unable to stop Mace gambling, 364;
happy about relationship between her
son and Mace's daughter, 375; Mace
leaves her for Alice, 399; gladdened
by marriage of John Lee and Ada
Mace, 399; death of her daughter,
451; overjoyed by Mace's return to
her from Alice, 452; goes to South
Africa with Mace, 454; Mace leaves
her for Alice for second time, 458; at
Mace's funeral 485
Lee, Rowland, 258, 259, 262, 263, 267,
268, 334, 338, 356, 374, 453
Lees, Tom, 368, 369, 382
Le Neve, Billy, 423, 480, 485
Le Neve, Norah (Norah Sullivan), 423,
480, 484, 485
Lennon, John, 60n
Leon, Josie, 374
Leotard, Jules, 95, 96, 97
Levy, Henry, 358
Lewis, Mr, 175, 176
Lewis, Ted Kid, 360
Leybourne, George, 95, 96
Lincoln, Abraham, 86, 230, 269
Lind, Jenny, 25
Lipman the publican, 47
Lloyd George, David, 474
London, Jack, 480
Lonsdale, fifth Earl of (Hugh Cecil

Lowther), viii, 196, 385, 387, 405,
409, 424, 485, 486; background and
character, 367–8, 371, 382;
misbehaviour at Eton, 195; Mace
becomes his boxing tutor, 195;
idolises Maces in boyhood, 196;
attitude toward Peter Jackson, 382–3;
expels Baird forthwith from Pelican
Club, 387; establishes legality of
Queensberry Rules boxing, 392–3;
imbued with a lifelong love of
boxing by Mace, 396; becomes
President of National Sporting Club,
403; role in drafting National
Sporting Club Rules, 405; discusses
boxers with Mace, 470–1; establishes
Lonsdale belts, 472; keeps his distance
from Mace over Langford 473
Louis, Joe, ix
Lowther, Henry Cecil (third Earl of
Lonsdale), 195

McAlpine, Tom, 234
McAuliffe, Jack, 412, 463
McAuliffe, Joe, 380, 392, 406,
McCaffrey, Dominick, 352–3, 361, 370,
406
McCall, Annie (Annie Gore), 257, 259,
262, 264, 267, 292, 307, 321, 334,
355, 356 360, 451
McCall, Emma, 452, 458
McCall, Jenny, 452
McCall, Rose, 452, 458
McCall, Ted, 259, 263, 264–5, 267, 292,
307, 321, 333, 334, 356, 360, 362,
451, 452, 453, 458, 480, 485
McCarthy, Billy, 394, 426
McCoole, Mike, 129, 193, 198, 241, 265
McCoy, Kid, ix, 427, 431, 443, 456
Macdonald, Jack, 47, 130
McGlory, Billy, 225, 253
McIntosh, Hugh D., 469, 471, 472, 473,
478, 481
McKinistry, Robert, 194
Mackay, John D., 269, 27n, 273, 277, 329,
432
McLaren, 196, 286
McLeish, Alex, 438, 459, 460, 461
McLeish, Polly, (Polly Stokes), 397,
437–8, 459, 461, 466, 466–7

McLoughlin, James, 233, 286, 444

Mc Millin, Amelia, see Amelia Mace

McMillin, Andrew, 375, 453, 459, 485, 486

McMillin, Bill, 453, 485

McMillin, James, 453, 486

McMillin, Richard, 486

McMillin, Tommy, 453, 485

McMullan, Alderman, 251, 252

McNeill, Champion John, 194

McVey, Jim, 429

McVey Sam, 465, 482

Mace, Ada, 165, 211, 220, 221, 255, 260, 336, 337, 338, 356–7, 375, 398, 399, 453, 485

Mace, Adelaide (Adelaide Turvill), 62, 65–6, 111–2, 122, 165, 211, 337, 377, 437, 479, 480, 485

Mace, Albert Edward, 437, 441

Mace, Alfred, 35, 62, 112, 165, 211; birth, 20; taught to box by Jem, 165; converts to Plymouth Brethren and quarrels with Jem, 260; goes to Australia to preach, 301; oratory at Westminster Central Hall, 357; hopes Jem will repent, 357; begins series of evangelistic tours in America, 357; struggle for power in Plymouth Brethren, 357, 437; resembles Jem in some ways, 437; Jem reconciles with, 479; leads service at Jem's funeral, 485, 486

Mace, Alfred Henry, 485

Mace, Amelia (Jem's sister), 5, 9, 65, 93, 111, 121, 124, 144

Mace Amelia (Jem's daughter) (Amelia McMillin), 144, 153, 155, 211, 260, 336, 337, 338, 356–7, 374, 398, 399, 453, 454, 480, 484, 485, 486

Mace, Amelia (Jem's granddaughter), 486

Mace, Amy, 419, 450, 460, 466, 485

Mace, Ann (Ann Rudd, Jem's mother), 3, 48n

Mace, Augustus 'Gus', 10, 61, 172, 173, 174, 175

Mace, Augustus, 'Gusty', 362, 432, 455

Mace, Barney, 4, 5, 10

Mace, Billy (William Mace Rudd), 5, 6, 8, 48n, 4–9

Mace, Ben, 245, 255, 260, 326–7, 329, 338

Mace, Bosevannah, 61

Mace, Donna, 362, 432

Mace, Eliza (Jem's sister), 5

Mace, Eliza (Jem's granddaughter), 301, 485

Mace, Ella, 460, 460n, 466

Mace, Ellen Norah, 333, 355, 356, 451

Mace, Ellen (Jem's granddaughter), 453

Mace, Gladys, 453

Mace, Hannah, 5

Mace, Herbie, 362

Mace, James (Jem's uncle), 4

Mace, James (Jem's brother, dead in infancy), 3

Mace, James Junior I, 20, 32

Mace, James Junior II, 62, 66, 112, 122, 165, 211, 301, 418, 437; birth, 33; taught to box and fence by Jem; 165; Jem's early disapproval of, 301, 357; boxing and fencing instructor, 418; publicises himself in *Mirror of Life*, 418; edited Jem's reminiscences in Sporting Life, 463; suggests Jem's autobiography, 467

Mace, James Junior III, 418, 450, 460, 461, 466, 485

Mace, Jem, general:

actor, 227, 279, 467; arrests 135, 159, 173–5, 252, 271, 325; attempted arrests, escape from, 272, 352; author, 376, 467–8; belts, 57, 73, 73n, 101, 164, 212, 279, 307, 324; birth, 3; bodyguard, 28,29; bouncer, 41, 457–8; bulldogs, 21, 302, 362; cigars, liking for Havana, 21

circuses, involvement with: x, 66, 74, 114; Bernard's, 398; Bunny Blythe, 82; Ginnett's, 87–8, 137, 261, 398, 400; Howes and Cushing, 80, 205, 261, 267; Jem Mace Circus, 97, 98, 102, 194; Leone's American, 398; Pablo Fanque, 65, 66; Sullivan's, 467, 479; Williams Mammoth, 289; Wilson's, 245, 246, 249

class, views on, 42, 43, 53, 145–6,147,171, 387; conviviality, 58; court appearances, 121,125–6,169,175–7, 252, 271, 308, 326; cowardice, early accusations of, 35, 41,139; crowds, cheered by large, 101,162, 284, 324; dancing skill, 15,17, 29, 207, 221; death and funeral, 484–6; disguises, 160, 308; drank only in moderation, 17, 32, 35, 63; education, total lack of, 82, 97, 203, 471, 475; elegant clothes, love of, 82, 97, 203, 471, 475; fists, concoctions for pickling, 19, 30–1, 213

fluctuating wealth: bankruptcies, 417–8, 465; bored by book-keeping, 63; benefactors, 436, 462, 476, 477; career winnings estimate, 302; carelessness at the till, 63; entrepreneurial flair, xi, 149, 152–4; mismanagement of boxing schools, 375, 417, 485; old-age pension, attempts to get, 475, 479; penniless, 458

gambling: 197, 209, 28, 292, 302, 307, 318, 326, 364, 375, 468, 488–9; at Aintree, 88; Ballarat, 302; Barbary Coast, 248; Doncaster, 88; Liverpool Olympics, 141; Natchez, 220; Newmarket, 17, 88; Saratoga Springs, 208

Grecian statues performances, 29, 205, 219–20, 233, 262, 417; gnarled knuckles, 262; grave, viii, 486, 486n, 489

gypsy controversy: widespread belief that he was of gypsy blood, viii, xi, 5, 6, 487; denial of Romany origin, xi, 5, 81, 471; fondness for gypsy company, xi, 478

hairstyle and moustache, 82, 97, 303; horses, affinity for, 6, 10, 292

hotelkeeper: in Liverpool, 153, 154, 155; in Melbourne, 294–5, 296, 302, 321, 354, 399, 438, 455

ill, seriously aged sixty-seven but shook it off, 431; intelligence, 68, 90–1, 192, 210

machismo, dislike of petty, 167; male model, 289; monarchy, lack of interest in, 481

murder: attempt on his life at Montgomery Station, 238–40; threats to kill him at Maisons-Laffitte, 363

music: originally aspired to career in, x, 477; talent for composition, 9, 261; violinist 6, 9, 10, 11, 15, 17, 21, 28, 191, 261, 395, 423, 467, 477, 483

Olympics, vii, 140, 141, 142, 146, 155, 471, 488; poker player, 108; politics, views on, 224, 225, 242, 263, 264, 328; prison sentence, 169

publican: in Norwich, 33, 35–6; in London, 58, 62, 63, 65, 72, 89, 92, 98, 194; in Manchester, 118; in Leeds, 142; in Birmingham, 438, 439, 452, 461

quoted, 7, 8, 14, 16, 69, 70, 71, 91, 106, 135, 144, 171, 183, 184, 186, 190, 210

race: without racial prejudice, 306, 469; positive attitude towards black persons, ix, 306, 402, 465, 482; contempt for 'White Hope' campaign, 473, 476, 482

religion, negative attitude towards, 7, 63–4, 117, 147, 150, 324, 357, 477; saloon-keeper in New York, 205, 222; semi-literacy, 45,192, 487

shows: combining boxing, wrestling, running, cycling and gymnastics, x, 194, 22–l, 233, 488; combining sport with music, 194, 273, 310

sport as spectacle, concept of, 74, 233, 480; sporting kudos as world champion leading to acceptance of other sports, 220

sportsman, excellent all-round: as a fencer, 154–5; as a pedestrian (runner), ix, 6, 23, 45, 50, 104, 118; as a wrestler, ix, 6; swearing, never resorted to repetitive, 63; thousand-yard stare, 284; vivid command of the spoken word, 46, 71,135, 215, 471

women: see Mary Ann Barton, Hannah Boorn, Selina Hart, Nellie Gore Lee, Ada Isaacs Menken and Alice Caroline Stokes; appeal for, xi, 97–8, 207; empathy for, xi, 63; abhorrence of violence to, 114, 360; casual sexual encounters, 78, 207, 220, 249, 363, 377; dislike of

reversal of gender roles, 220; fondness
for actresses, dancers, showgirls, 99,
207, 377; attracted to dark women,
261; loathing of swearing and
innuendo in front of 63
Mace, Jem, boxing:
ability to respond to and influence
mood of crowd, 116, 236;
ambidextrous, 21
books: *On Boxing*, 376; *Fifty Years a
Fighter*, 467–8
booths: in Norwich, 11; Langham's,
11; Young Mace's, 21; lack of
boxing booth tradition in
America, 292; Mace's Australian,
292; Old Mace's, 478
drums, frequented the great London,
46; electric lighting for boxing,
early interest in, 341; English
heavyweights of the 1880s,
derided, 378; exhibition, last
recorded, 478; eyes targeted, 218,
276; fencing, sees close parallel
between boxing and, 155, 219
films: of fight with Burke (film lost),
426; of fight with Bradley (film
lost), 477
first to bring in grandstanding for last
round, 276; first to bring in
touching gloves ritual, 274, 276;
first to demonstrate concept of
boxer as all-round athlete, 81; first
world champion, ix
gloves: publicly advocates use of, 155;
reasons for preferring, 190; role in
securing legalisation of glove
boxing in Victoria, 303; heralded
classic boxers of the 20th century,
ix; Hollywood chose to ignore
him, viii; impatient with less
gifted pupils, 304
knockout: set template for great kayos
of boxing history, ix, 139; aimed
for junction of upper and lower
jaw, 139, 190; effective knockout
of Brettle at Foulness Island, 139;
effective knockout of Goss at
Plumstead Marshes, 110, 139;
historic significance of circus
knockout tour, 136–9; birth of
the, 139

London Prize Ring (LPR): debut in,
30; distances himself from, 144;
hankers after, 351; turns his back
on forever, 365; does not lament,
387; knowledge of history of, 22;
making the weight, struggle
before Mace-Goss, 104–5; mark,
shot to (solar plexus punch), 137,
310; middleweight his natural
weight, 219; music, borrows terms
from to describe change of pace
in boxing, 216
National Sporting Club: points
system of essentially his style, 405;
his influence on triumvirs of 406
Note-taking at King-Broome, 81;
Olympic Club, San Francisco,
reluctantly declines appointment
at, 401; Professional Boxers
Association, joins, 304
Queensberry rules: anticipation of,
189; not consulted by J. G.
Chambers over, 119; notes flaws
in, 192; will not campaign
explicitly for, 277–8; considers as
bonanza for Sullivan, 353
referee, at Maisons-Laffitte, 367;
ringcraft, master of, 197; seconds,
acquaintanceship with leading, 46;
science, considers boxing as, 74;
sixteen-foot ring, 159; style,
description of his, 20–1, 56;
theatres in New Zealand, raises
boxing profile at, 310; training
regime, 30, 31, 62, 81, 104, 160,
249
transition to gloves: unparalleled role
in, 445; significance of Mace-
Davis in, 277; sets the pace in, 395
Mace, Jem, fights in the ring:
Sydney Smith, 16; Pinfold, 16; Farden
Smith, 15, 16; Brewer, 18; Pratt,
18, 19; Slack, 26; Brettle 1, 40–1;
Price, 41, 42; Travis, 51; Brettle 2,
56; Hurst (for Championship of
England), 68–71; King 1, 82–5;
King 2, 292; Goss 1; 108–110;
Goss 2; 156–7,158–9; Mace-Goss
3, 161–2; Allen (for world title),
215–19; Coburn 1, 228–30;
Coburn 2, 234–7; Bill Davis,

274–7; Mitchell, 389; Mike Donovan for veterans championship, 429–30, 436

aborted fight with Madden, 33; Madden fiasco (Mace's no-show), 34; aborted fight with Coburn in Ireland, 132–3; aborted fight with O'Baldwin in England, 171–3; aborted fight with O'Baldwin in America, 252–3; exhibition with Bennett, 250–1; exhibition with Burge at the NSC, 422; private fight with Senator Roscoe Conkling, 244–5; private fight with Lord Charles Beresford, 339; circus tour fight with foundryman at Bolton, 135

street fights: with drunken fishermen in Great Yarmouth, 11; with Tom King outside Tattersall's 100–1; with Bartley Gorman, 133; with Yorkshire miner, 187; with would-be mugger in the Strand when aged 73, 460

Mace, John Farnham, 485
Mace, Leonora, 61
Mace, Lillian, 401, 437, 450, 460, 461, 466, 485
Mace, Madonna, 61
Mace, Marian, 453
Mace, Melbourne, 362, 432, 455
Mace, Montrosser, 61
Mace, Pooley (Leopoldius Mace), 61, 65, 87, 90, 101, 108, 160, 205, 167, 171, 208, 220, 248, 249, 250, 361, 368, 370, 398, 432, 455, 477, 482; birth of, 4; partial Romany background, 5, 61; debut in the prize ring, 61; insulted in West End, 167; becomes Jem's chief trainer, 172; humour at Herne Hill, 174; charged with conspiracy, 175; speculation concerning relationship with Adah Menken, 183–4; loyalty to Jem, 36, 184, 187, 360; sails to America with Jem, 199; spars with Jem at Tammany Hall, 204; trains Jem in Alabama pine forest, 213; trains Jem on Long Island, 226–7; trains Jem in Ohio, 233; umpire at Bay St. Louis, 234; calls Coburn for having oakum in his

hands, 236; narrowly escapes murder bid on Jem, 239; goes with Jem by rail to California, 247–8; trains Jem at Highlands, N. J., 245; calls Allen for biting Chambers, 255; returns to England with Jem, 255; marries Delaiah Smith, 265; lives in Scotland, 361; meets Queen Victoria, 362; his house in Leyton a home from home for Jem, 362; emigrates to America, 400; described in Jem's autobiography, 468; unable to attend Jem's funeral, 485

Mace, Robina, 61
Mace, Thomas, 4
Mace, Tiras 'Tirey', 61
Mace, Trafalgar, 61
Mace, Walter, 61
Mace, William (Bill), Jem's father, 3, 5, 8, 48
Mace, Zubliria, 61
Madden, Billy, 238, 240, 313, 314, 315, 330, 344, 392, 405
Madden, Mike ,33
Maher, Peter, 368, 423
Mandeville, Lord, 386
Mansart, François, 363
Marciano, Rocky, ix
Marsden, Andrew, 144, 169
Marshall, Mary, 122
Martin, George, 118
Martin, American prizefighter, 248–9
Mason, Alex, 227, 229
Masterson, Bat, 232, 381
Mazeppa, Jan, 180
Melly, Charles, background, 140–1; founds Liverpool Athletic Club, 140; Liverpool Olympic Festival, 140; interest in boxing, 141; meets Mace, 141; Grand Olympic Festival, 142; sets up Myrtle Street Gymnasium, 155, 191, 292
Mendoza, Daniel, 73, 219, 354, 487
Menken, Adah Isaacs, 183, 363; debut at Astley's Theatre in Mazeppa,179; introduced to Mace, 180; background, character and personality, 179–182; speculation over identity of her London lover,183; Mace quoted on her, 183; reasons for Mace's ambiguity concerning an affair with,

184; career and travels, 184–6; sustains
serious injuries, 186; telegrams to
Mace, 186; death of, 187; Mace's
inability to forget her, 187, 468
Menken, Alexander Isaacs, 181, 182
Middleton, Gus, 432
Miles, Henry Downton, 72, 73, 85, 93
Miller, James, 62, 81, 104, 131, 133
Miller, Joaquin, 183
Miller, William, 286, 287, 288, 290, 297,
298, 310, 311, 314, 315, 316, 320,
321, 323, 361, 368, 379, 386, 449
Mills, Teddy, 118, 194
Milner, Alf, 45
Milner, H. D., 180
Mitchell, Charlie, 308, 329, 331, 334, 335,
336, 344, 345, 352, 354, 355, 356,
364, 368, 369, 370, 409, 420; background and personality, 330; early
career, 330–1; first fight with Sullivan,
335–6; aborted prizefight with Slade,
344–5; antipathy to Sullivan, 356;
brilliant boxer-puncher, 364; given
money by Baird to fight as dirty as
possible, 365; starts drinking heavily,
365; second fight with Sullivan
(Chantilly), 373; fight with Mace in
Glasgow, 388–9; regularly arrested
after drunken brawls, 409; debauchery
in New Orleans, 420; crushed by
Corbett in Jacksonville, 426
Montagu, C. W. 'Harry', meets Mace
when equestrian director for Ginnett,
137; sets up Mace's tour in France,
102; Mace's factotum and close
friend,137; negotiates lease of
Strawberry Gardens, 152; advises
Mace to rein in his spending, 176;
lines up purchase of Strawberry
Gardens, 199; becomes Mace's
business manager again in US, 314;
informs Mace of desperate money
situation in America, 345; returns to
England, 346; resigns as Mace's
business manager, 364
Moore, Archie, ix
Moore, George Washington 'Pony', 364,
371
Morris, Peter, 159, 169
Morrissey, John, 51, 52, 129, 203, 224,
230, 292, 246, 252, 253, 328

Much, Ethel, 458
Much, Harry, 453
Much, Nell, 453
Much, Tom, 453
Muldoon, William, 311, 381, 444
Murphy, Torpedo Billy prologue, 389,
391, 412, 426, 427, 457

Napoleon I (Napoleon Bonaparte), 197
Napoleon III (Louis-Napoleon
Bonaparte), 186, 197
Nash, John, 417
National Sporting Club, 402, 442
National Sporting Club Rules, 403–5
Naughton, W. W., 381, 408, 463
Newell, Robert Henry, 180, 182, 183
Noon, Jerry, 70, 71, 120, 130, 159

O'Baldwin, Ned, 167, 169, 170, 172,
193, 251; background of, 171; limited
intelligence, 192; challenges Mace for
championship of England, 172;
escapes after Mace's arrest, 175;
threatens to bludgeon stakeholder,
177; emigrates, 177; in jail in
America, 193; persuaded to challenge
Mace again, 242; arrested at
Baltimore, 252; mutual accusations of
cowardice between Mace and, 252;
shot dead, 266
O'Brien, Philadelphia Jack, ix, 442, 442n
O'Meara, Sergeant, 295
Olmsted, Frederick Law, 271
Orem, Con, 207

Paddock, Tom, 64
Palmer, Peddler, 471
Palmerston, Lord, 52, 86
Pep, Willie, ix
Perceval, John, 351, 362
Pereira, Madame, 150
Perowne, George, 19
Perret, Paul, 219n
Perry, Charlie, 66
Phillips, Julia, 49, 55
Phillips, Simon, 49, 55
Pietri, Dorando, 471
Pinfold, Charles, 16
Pratt, Jack, 18, 19
Price, Posh, 41, 42, 104
Pritchard, Ted, 420

Queensberry, ninth Marquess of (John Sholto Douglas) viii, 188, 189, 192, 242, 254, 287, 366, 372, 395, 396, 403
Queensberry Rules (1867), 189–191; Mace's criticism of, 191–2; Sullivan's version, 353; vagueness of, 403
Queensberry Rules of Endurance, see National Sporting Club Rules

Reade, Charles, 179
Reid, Alex, 46
Reid, Borthwick, 289
Renforth, James 194
Rice, H. J., 344, 345, 346, 347
Rich, Charles, 381
Richards, Bill, 118
Richardson, Bill, 48, 55, 64, 68, 120, 173, 372, 384; landlord of the Blue Anchor, 47; phenomenal strength, 47; becomes Mace's backer, 48, 51; sets up Mace in sporting drum, 54; perceives Mace stepping beyond the bounds of pugilism, 56; helps plan arrangements for Mace-Hurst, 68; backs Mace for King fight, 82; role in reviving Mace's career, 89; blazing row with Mace, 89; disperses rioters at Fenchurch Street, 91; buys Mace out of Old King John, 98; routs blackguards at Paddington Station 106–7; back on Mace's side for Goss fight, 161-2; instructs Mitchell, 330; adjusts to gloved boxing, 354; forms Professional Boxers Association, 364; death, 364
Richardson, Charlie, 303
Rickard, Tex, 481, 482
Rigby, Isabella, 194-5
Rigby, James, 195
Roberts, John Richard (Dick Roberts), 112, 113, 121, 122, 165, 337
Roberts, Lord, 448
Robinson, George, 324
Robinson, Sugar Ray, ix
Rooke, Jack, 168
Rollins, Ed 'Starlight', 420
Roosevelt, Theodore, 203, 431
Ross, Sandy, 290
Rossetti, Dante Gabriel, 164
Rothschild, Baron Alphonse de, 373
Ruhlin, Gus, 443, 444, 445, 446, 447

Russell, Sir Charles, 393
Ryan, Paddy, 311, 313, 370
Ryan, Tommy, 421, 427, 431, 440, 444, 445, 456

Sallers, Harry, 287, 291, 366, 482
Sampson, Henry, 40, 76
Sanger, 'Lord' George, 97–8, 150
Sayers, Tom, 57, 99, 102, 121, 130, 144, 168, 376, 381, 383, 487; background, 25; becomes Champion of England, 24; versus Heenan, 51–3; retirement, 55, 64; fails to take up Mace's challenge, 64; lack of intelligence, 98; accepts Mace's challenge but is dissuaded by his minders, 103; seconds Heenan at Wadhurst, 120; bound over at Lewes Crown Court, 120–1; becomes an alcoholic, 143; vents drunken abuse at Mace, 143; death, 145; riotous scenes at funeral of, 145
Seymour, Jack, 380
Sharkey, Tom, 441, 443, 444, 445, 446, 447, 456
Sharkey, William J., 225, 226, 253
Shaw, George Bernard, 376
Shepherd, Eliza, 485
Shepherd, Thomas, 485
Sherriff, William, 359
Siler, George, 231, 321
Silverton, Inspector George, 167, 168, 169, 170, 171, 172, 173, 174, 175
Slack, Slasher, 26, 62
Slade, Herbert, 321, 322, 323, 325, 326, 327, 328, 333, 334, 336, 338, 347, 353, 404, 420; background and wrestling skill, 316; signs managerial contract with, Mace 320–1; hyped by Mace and Fox, 324; goes to England with Mace, 324; returns to New York, 340; fight with Sullivan, 342-3; approached by sportsman's agent, 344; leaves Mace and joins Sullivan's Grand Tour, 345; claims Mace exploited him, 345–6; fired by Sullivan, 346; ineptitude and career failure, 347
Slade, Junior, 309, 316
Slavin, Frank, 368, 374, 387, 388, 389, 390, 408, 423, 424, 425, 426, 427, 457; background, 305, 386;

personality, 309; gym fight and
barroom brawl with Jackson, 374;
arrives in London unbeaten, 384;
fierce Mace-style body puncher, 385;
fight with Jem Smith at Bruges,
385–6, importance of Slavin-
McAuliffe legal case, 392; arrest and
discharge, 392–4; goes to America,
406; ranked number one challenger
by Sullivan, 409; fight with Jackson,
410–11; repents racism and salutes
Jackson's greatness, 411
Sloan, Tod, 455
Smith, Al, 335, 336, 342, 344, 345, 347, 353
Smith, Ambrose (Jasper Petulengro), 265,
362, 477
Smith, Delaiah (Delaiah Mace), 265, 361,
400, 401, 432, 455
Smith, Edward Tyrrell, 148, 150, 151,
179, 180
Smith, Farden, 14, 16, 467
Smith, Jack, 356, 361
Smith, James 'Tiger', 463
Smith, Jem, 352, 362, 363, 365, 370, 372,
373, 376, 381, 382, 383, 384, 385,
386, 406, 423
Smith, Jonathan, 196
Smith, Sydney, 16
Smith, Warren, 14n
Smith (*Bell's Life* reporter), 133
Smithdale, Emma, 66
Snape, Richard, 286
Sparkes, Bill, 196
Spreckels, John D., 390, 392
Spring, Tom, 487
Stamps, Mary, 59
Steward, Emanuel, ix, 307n
Stokes, Alice Caroline, 407, 417, 451,
458, 461, 468; meets Mace, 397;
background and personality, 397–8;
falls in love with Mace, 398; false
claim of marriage with Mace, 400;
can't be persuaded to emigrate to
America, 401, 432; and her children
to Mace, 401, 418, 419, 437, 441,
460; influenced by her sister Polly
McLeish, 438; reluctance to travel
overseas, 450; Mace returns to Nellie
from her, 452; greets Mace's return
from Nellie, 459; devastated by
Mace's refusal to live in McLeish

household, 462; death, 466; symmetry
of her fate with that of Mary Ann
Barton and Hannah Boorn, 467
Stokes, Amy, 419
Stokes, Lillian, 401
Stokes, Lizzie, 397
Stokes, Polly, see Polly McLeish
Stokes, Sarah, 397
Stokes, Thomas, 397, 400
Stokes, Tommy, 438
Sullivan, John L. viii, 219, 314, 375, 361,
369, 370, 371, 372, 375, 380, 382,
384, 388, 389, 391, 393, 394, 395,
396, 406, 408, 418, 421, 425, 426,
429, 436; background, character and
personality, 311–2, 325; cuts swathe
through ranks of heavyweight boxers,
312–3; first KO tour, 313; batters
Ryan to defeat to become world
heavyweight champion, 313; clash of
personalities with Fox, 314; flouts
Queensberry Rules, 319, 347, 353–4;
Mace's view of, 315, 319, 334, 370;
drunkenness of, 326, 334, 360; first
fight with Mitchell, 335–6; fight with
Slade, 342–3; second fight with
Mitchell, 373; fight with Kilrain,
380–1; refusal to fight Jackson, 390–1;
defeated by Corbett and loses title,
412; announced his retirement, 412
Sullivan, Yankee, 129, 246,
Swift, Owen, 46, 102
Swinburne, Algernon, 164, 179, 183
Sydney, Henry, 359

Talgutt, C. F., 165–6
Tate, Billy, 353, 359
Taylor, Ben, 469, 470
Taylor, Steve, 313, 345
Tetlow, Sam, 248, 249
Thackeray, William, 52
Thomas, Joe, 158
Thompson, Jack, 287, 293, 294, 296, 297,
302
Thompson, Joe, 287, 291, 292, 293, 294,
295, 296, 303
Thorne, Geoff, 463
Thorpe, Bill, 30, 31
Thurston, Sherman, 214, 219
Tilden, Samuel, 206
Tipton Slasher, 24, 154

Tracy, Bill, 254, 255
Travers Bob, 51, 56, 91, 306, 436, 482
Trickett, Edward, 285
Truckle, Tom, 80
Turvill, Adelaide see Adelaide Mace
Turvill, Adelaide junior, 377, 437
Turvill, Alfred, 379
Turvill, Arthur, 377
Turvill, Edgar, 377
Turvill, Eleanor, 307, 377,437
Turvill, Elizabeth, 47
Turvill, Eunice, 377, 437
Turvill, Lois, 377, 437
Turvill, Mary, 377
Turvill, Maud, 377
Turvill, Wilfred, 377
Turvill, William, 377, 465
Turvill, William junior, 377
Twain, Mark 183, 270
Tweed, Boss, 224
Tyler, Bos, 47, 69, 108, 120, 173, 174
Tyson, Mike, ix.

Underhill, Edward, 271

Valentine, Jack, 454, 455
Vanderbilt, Cornelius, 208
Vanderbilt, William, 313, 333, 335, 341
Vere, Pauline de, 97, 98
Vesey, Joe, 385, 386
Victoria, Queen, 53, 127, 148, 180, 362, 443
Vize, George, 384, 403, 442

Waite, James, 418
Walcott, Jersey Joe ix

Walcott, Joe, 444, 445,464
Ward, Jem, 47, 80, 82, 89, 487
Watkins the publican, 46
Ware, George, 364
Watson, Walter, 379, 395, 409, 465
Weir, Ike, 389
Weir, Jimmy, 449
Wells, Bombardier Billy, 476
Wells, Ernest 'Swears', 366
Welsh, Jemmy, 47
West, Tommy, 445
Weston, Stanley, 73n
White, Charlie, 442
White, Jack, 80
White, Tom, 292
White Stripes, The, 15n
Wilde, Sir James Plaisted, 125
William IV, 4, 443
Williams, Bing, 274, 275, 276, 277
Williams, Clubber, 329, 335, 336, 341, 342, 343, 353, 361, 373
Wilson, Jack, 245, 250, 251
Wilson, Judge, 229
Wilson, Tug , 318–9, 361, 461
Winburne, Old Ma, 79, 87, 99
Windham,Lord William Frederick, 81, 101
Woodey, George, 69, 77, 78
Woolsey the horse dealer, 204
Wormald, Joe, 144, 170, 177, 192, 193, 198, 221
Wright, Isaiah, 300

Young, John, 77
Young, Selina (Madame Geneviève), 149